CANADA

Ontario Tourism Marketing Partnership Corp.

Editorial Director	Cynthia Clayton Ochterbeck

THE GREEN GUIDE TO CANADA

Editor	Gwen Cannon
Contributing Writers	Eric Fletcher, Margaret Lemay
Production Coordinator	Natasha G. George
Cartography	GeoNova Publishing, Inc., Peter Wrenn
Photo Editor	Lydia Strong
Proofreader	Jonathan P. Gilbert
Layout and Design	Tim Schulz and Nicole D. Jordan, Natasha G. George
Cover Design	Laurent Muller and Ute Weber

Contact Us:

The Green Guide
Michelin Maps and Guides
One Parkway South
Greenville, SC 29615
USA
☎ 1-800-432-6277
www.michelintravel.com
michelin.guides@us.michelin.com

Michelin Maps and Guides
Hannay House
39 Clarendon Road
Watford, Herts WD17 1JA
UK
☎ (01923) 205 240
www.ViaMichelin.com
travelpubsales@uk.michelin.com

Special Sales:

For information regarding bulk sales,
customized editions and premium sales,
please contact our Customer Service
Departments:
USA   1-800-432-6277
UK   (01923) 205 240
Canada 1-800-361-8236

Note to the Reader

One Team ...
A Commitment to Quality

There's just one reason our team is dedicated to producing quality travel publications—you, our reader.

Throughout our guides we offer **practical information**, **touring tips** and **suggestions** for finding the best places for a break.

Michelin driving tours help you hit the highlights and quickly absorb the best of the region. Our descriptive **walking tours** make you your own guide, armed with directions, maps and expert information.

We scout out the attractions, classify them with **star ratings**, and describe in detail what you will find when you visit them.

Michelin maps featured throughout the guide offer vibrant, detailed and easy-to-follow outlines of everything from close-up museum plans to international maps.

Places to stay and eat are always a big part of travel, so we research **hotels and restaurants** that we think convey the essence of the destination, and arrange them by geographic area and price. We walk you through the best shopping districts and point you towards the host of entertainment and recreation possibilities available.

We **test, retest, check and recheck** to make sure that our guidebooks are truly just that: a personalized guide to help you make the most of your visit. And if you still want a speaking guide, we list local tour guides who will lead you on all the boat, bus, guided, historical, culinary, and other tours you shouldn't miss.

In short, we remove the guesswork involved with travel. After all, we want you to enjoy traveling with Michelin as much as we do.

The Michelin Green Guide Team

PLANNING YOUR TRIP

MICHELIN DRIVING TOURS   10

WHEN AND WHERE TO GO   17
When to Go 17
Themed Tours 17

KNOW BEFORE YOU GO   18
Useful Websites 18
Tourist Offices 18
International Visitors 18
Accessibility 19

GETTING THERE AND GETTING AROUND   20
By Plane 20
By Ship 21
By Train 21
By Coach/Bus 21
By Car 22

WHERE TO STAY AND EAT   24
Where to Stay 24
Where to Eat 28

WHAT TO SEE AND DO   29
Outdoor Fun 29
Spas 30
Activities for Children 30
Calendar of Events 30
Shopping 30
Sightseeing 32
Books 33
Films 34
Useful French Words 34

BASIC INFORMATION   35

INTRODUCTION TO CANADA

NATURE   40
Geologic Past 40
Major Natural Regions 40
Geographical Features 42

HISTORY   45
Prehistory to Present 45
Time Line 49

ART AND CULTURE   52
Art 52
Literature and Language 57
Music and Dance 59
Cinema 61

THE COUNTRY TODAY   62
The Economy 62
Government 65
Population 66
Food and Drink 67

SYMBOLS

🛈	**Tourist Information**
🕐	**Hours of Operation**
🕐	**Periods of Closure**
😊	**A Bit of Advice**
😐	**Details to Consider**
☜	**Entry Fees**
Kids	**Especially for Children**
☞	**Tours**
♿	**Wheelchair Accessible**

CONTENTS

DISCOVERING CANADA

British Columbia, Rockies, Yukon **70**
Alaska Highway 77
The Cariboo 81
Dawson City 84
Fort St. James 88
Fraser Canyon Country 89
Inside Passage 92
The Kootenays 93
Monashees and Selkirks 95
Okanagan Valley 98
Queen Charlotte Islands 102
Rocky Mountain Parks 105
Skeena Valley 123
Vancouver 126
Vancouver Island 144
Victoria 149
Waterton Lakes National Park 156
Whitehorse 157
Yukon Circuit 162
Prairie Provinces **166**
Alberta Badlands 171
Austin 174
The Battlefords 174
Calgary 176
Cardston 182
Churchill 183
Cypress Hills 185
Edmonton 187
Fort Macleod 192
Lethbridge 194
Moose Jaw 195
Prince Albert National Park . . . 196
Regina 197
Riding Mountain National Park 200
Saskatoon 201
Winnipeg 205
Yorkton 213
Ontario **214**
Brantford 221
Dresden 222
Georgian Bay 223
Goderich 226

Gravenhurst 228
Hamilton 229
Kingston and the
    Thousand Islands 232
Kitchener–Waterloo 236
London 238
Niagara Falls 240
North Bay 245
Orillia 246
Oshawa 246
Ottawa 247
Peterborough 260
Point Pelee National Park 261
Prescott 262
Sault Ste. Marie 263
Stratford 265
Sudbury 266
Thunder Bay 268
Toronto 271
Upper Canada Village 297
Windsor 299
Quebec **300**
Île d'Anticosti 304
Bas-Saint-Laurent 305
Côte de Charlevoix 308
Côte-Nord 309
Cantons de l'Est 310
Gaspésie 312
Gatineau 316
Laurentides 318
Îles de la Madeleine 320
Montreal 322
Nunavik 337
Québec 338
Vallée du Richelieu 349
Fjord du Saguenay 351
Trois-Rivières 354
Atlantic Provinces **356**
New Brunswick 362
Nova Scotia 379
Prince Edward Island 409
Newfoundland and Labrador . 418
Northwest Territories **438**
Nunavut **452**

Index 466
Maps and Plans 477
Legend 479

HOW TO USE THIS GUIDE

Orientation

To help you grasp the "lay of the land" quickly and easily, so you'll feel confident and comfortable finding your way around the region, we offer the following tools in this guide:

- Detailed table of contents for an overview of what you'll find in the guide, and how it is organized.
- Map of Canada on the inside covers of the guide, with the principal sights highlighted for easy reference.
- Detailed maps for major cities and villages, including driving tour maps and larger-scale maps for walking tours.
- Maps of Regional Driving Tours, each one numbered and colour coded.
- Thematic maps for historical reference.

Practicalities

At the front of the guide, you'll see a section called "Planning Your Trip" that contains information about planning your trip, the best time to go, different ways of getting to the country and getting around, basic facts and tips for making the most of your visit. You'll find driving and themed tours, and suggestions for outdoor fun. There's also a listing of principal festivals within the provinces. Information on shopping, sightseeing, kids' activities and sports and recreational opportunities is also included.

WHERE TO STAY

We've made a selection of lodgings, arranged them within the provinces by city, and categorized them by price to fit all budgets *(see the Legend on the cover flap for an explanation of the price categories)*. For the most part, we selected accommodations based on their unique regional quality. So, unless the individual hotel embodies local ambience, it's rare that we include chain properties, which typically have their own imprint. We've included a description of nontraditional lodgings as well, such as houseboats, lighthouses, teepees, igloos and even an ice hotel *(see Off-Beat Stays in Planning Your Trip)*.

WHERE TO EAT

We thought you'd like to know some of the popular or unusual eating spots in the country. So we selected restaurants that capture the Canadian experience—those that are well-frequented and give you the flavor of the region or area. We're not rating the quality of the food per se. As we did with the lodgings, we organized the restaurants within the provinces by city and categorized them by price to appeal to all wallets *(see the Legend on the cover flap for an explanation of the price categories)*.

Attractions

The attractions are arranged alphabetically within each province, territory or entity, such as the Rockies. They are divided into local Sights or Walking Tours, nearby Excursions outside the town, or detailed Driving Tours—suggested itineraries for seeing several attractions around a major town. Contact information, admission charges and hours of operation are given for the majority of attractions. Unless otherwise noted, admission prices shown are for a single adult only. Discounts for seniors, students, teachers, etc. may be available; be sure to ask. If no admission charge is shown, entrance to the attraction is free.

If you're pressed for time, we recommend you visit the three- and two-star sights first: the stars are your guide.

STAR RATINGS

Michelin has used stars as a rating tool for more than 100 years:

★★★	Highly recommended
★★	Recommended
★	Interesting

SYMBOLS IN THE TEXT

Besides the stars, other symbols in the text indicate: sights that are closed to the public ⊶; on-site eating facilities ✕; also see ⊙; breakfast included in the nightly rate ☕; on-site parking 🅿; spa facilities Spa; camping facilities △; swimming pool ☂; and beaches ⌒.

See the box appearing on the Contents page and the Legend on the cover flap for other symbols used in the text.

See the Maps explanation below for symbols appearing on the maps.

Throughout the guide you will find peach-coloured text boxes or sidebars containing anecdotal or background information. Green-coloured boxes contain information to help you save time or money.

Maps

All maps in this guide are oriented north, unless otherwise indicated by a directional arrow. The term "Local Map" refers to a map within the chapter or Tourism Region. See the map Legend at the back of the guide for an explanation of other map symbols. A complete list of the maps found in the guide appears at the back of this book.

Addresses, phone numbers, opening hours and prices published in this guide are accurate at press time. We welcome corrections and suggestions that may assist us in preparing the next edition. Please send your comments to:

Michelin Maps and Guides
Hannay House
39 Clarendon Road
Watford, Herts WD17 1JA
UK
travelpubsales@uk.michelin.com
www.michelin.co.uk

Michelin Maps and Guides
Editorial Department
P.O. Box 19001
Greenville, SC 29602-9001
USA
michelin.guides@us.michelin.com
www.michelintravel.com

Hot Air Balloon Festival, Quebec
©iStockphoto.com/Hamiza Bakirci

MICHELIN DRIVING TOURS

Driving allows travellers to appreciate the vastness of this country, where distances between cities and towns can be great.

The following fast-paced tours, two- to three-weeks in duration, are intended as planning tools, not as fixed routes.

1 British Columbia and the Rockies

Round-trip of 3,309km/2,056mi (not including ferries) from Vancouver. Time: 18 days. This tour combines the beauty of British Columbia's coast with its mountainous interior culminating in the Rockies. The cities of Vancouver and Victoria are highlights as is the Skeena Valley with its native villages.

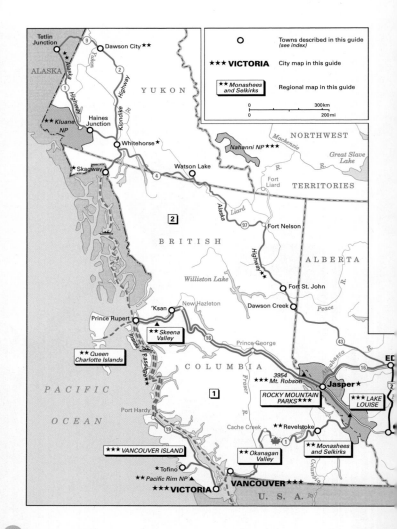

DAYS/ ITINERARY/ SIGHTS

1–3 **Vancouver**★★★
4 **Vancouver – Cache Creek**
(335km/208mi); Fraser Canyon★★
via Hope and Lytton
5 **Cache Creek – Revelstoke**
(286km/178mi); Thompson
Canyon★ via Shuswap Lake,
Monashees and Selkirks★★, Eagle
Pass★, Revelstoke★★
6 **Revelstoke – Lake Louise**
(228km/142mi); Rogers Pass★★,
Rocky Mountain Parks★★★,
Emerald Lake★★★, Yoho Valley★★,
Kicking Horse Pass
7 **Lake Louise excursions**
(81km/50mi); Lake Louise★★★, Mt.
Whitehorn★, Moraine Lake★★★
8 **Lake Louise – Jasper**
(233km/145mi); Rocky Mountain
Parks★★★, Icefields Parkway★★★
9 **Jasper excursions**
(167km/104mi); Jasper National
Park★★★, Mt. Edith Cavell★★,
Maligne Valley★★★
10 **Jasper – Prince George**
(376km/234mi); Yellowhead
Highway★★, Mt. Robson Provincial
Park★★, Mt. Robson★★★
11 **Prince George – New Hazelton**
(446km/277mi); 'Ksan
12 **New Hazelton – Prince Rupert**
(295km/183mi, *described in opposite direction*); Skeena Valley★★
13 **Prince Rupert – Port Hardy** by
ferry; Inside Passage★★
14 **Port Hardy – Tofino** (from
542km/337mi);
Vancouver Island★★★,
Parksville to Pacific Rim★

15 **Tofino – Victoria** (320km/198mi);
Pacific Rim National Park
Reserve★★★
16–17 **Victoria**★★★
18 **Victoria – Vancouver** by ferry;
Butchart Gardens★★★

2 Northern British Columbia and the Yukon

Round-trip of 5,185km/ 3,222mi (not
including ferry) from Edmonton. Time:
17 days. This tour combines the wild
beauty of the Yukon with the adventure of driving the Alaska Highway,
and the misty and romantic Inside
Passage cruise down the West Coast.

DAYS/ ITINERARY/ SIGHTS

1–2 Edmonton★★
3 **Edmonton – Fort St. John**
(665km/413mi);
Alaska Highway★★
4 **Fort St. John – Fort Nelson**
(416km/258mi);
Alaska Highway★★

From Fort Nelson, travellers can
make an optional 1-day excursion to
Nahanni National Park★★★.

5 **Fort Nelson – Watson Lake**
(546km/339mi);
Alaska Highway★★
6 **Watson Lake – Whitehorse**
(455km/283mi);
Alaska Highway★★

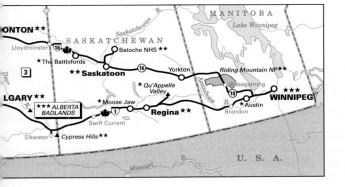

Distances between major cities

Seattle to **Vancouver**
270 km/168 mi

Vancouver to **Calgary**
953 km/591 mi

Calgary to **Edmonton**
304 km/188 mi

Calgary to **Regina**
744 km/461 mi

Saskatoon to **Regina**
251 km/156 mi

Regina to **Winnipeg**
573 km/355 mi

Winnipeg to **Sault Ste. Marie**
1395 km/865 mi

Sault Ste. Marie to **Toronto**
715 km/443 mi

Toronto to **Ottawa**
398 km/247 mi

Toronto to **Detroit**
378 km/234 mi

Ottawa to **Montreal**
185 km/115 mi

Montreal to **Quebec**
262 km/162 mi

Montreal to **New York**
631 km/391 mi

Quebec to **Fredericton**
521 km/323 mi

Fredericton to **Halifax**
480 km/298 mi

7   **Whitehorse**★
8   **Whitehorse – Dawson City**
(540km/336mi); Yukon Circuit★★,
Klondike Highway
9   **Dawson City**★★
10 **Dawson City – Haines Junction**
(744km/462mi); Yukon Circuit★★,
Top of the World Highway★★,
Alaska Highway★★,
Kluane Lake★★
11 **Haines Junction – Whitehorse**
(161km/100mi);
Kluane National Park★★
12–13 **Whitehorse – Prince Rupert**
(180km/112mi and ferry); Klondike
Highway to Skagway★★, Skag-
way★, Inside Passage (US)

From Prince Rupert, travellers can
take the ferry through the **Inside Passage**★★ to Seattle, arriving Day 15, or
optional 3-day excursion to **Queen
Charlotte Islands**★★.

14–16 **Prince Rupert – Jasper**
(◉see Days 12, 11, 10 of Tour 1)
17 **Jasper – Edmonton**
(361km/224mi)

③ Prairies

Round-trip of 3,371km/2,095mi from
Winnipeg. Time: 17 days. This tour
enables visitors to discover some of
the fascination of the Prairies—grand
vistas, wheat fields, ranches and cowboys. The oil-rich Alberta cities of Calgary and Edmonton are visited as well
as the interesting city of Winnipeg.

DAYS/ ITINERARY/ SIGHTS

1–2 **Winnipeg**★★★
3   **Winnipeg – Wasagaming**
(265km/165mi); Riding Mountain
National Park★★
4   **Wasagaming – Yorkton**
(230km/143mi); Yorkton
5   **Yorkton – Saskatoon**
(331km/205mi); Saskatoon★
6   176km/109mi;
Excursion to Batoche★★
7   **Saskatoon – Lloydminster**
(276km/171mi); The Battlefords★
8–9 **Lloydminster – Edmonton**
(248km/154mi); Edmonton★★

Optional 5-day excursion, 1,034km/642mi, can be made to the Rockies: Edmonton–Jasper 339km/210mi; Jasper–Lake Louise ⓒ *see Days 9, 8, 7 of Tour 1*; Lake Louise–Calgary 214km/133mi.

10–11 **Edmonton – Calgary**
(297km/185mi); Calgary★★
12 **Calgary – Elkwater**
(432km/268mi); Alberta
Badlands★★★
13 **Elkwater – Swift Current**
(227km/141mi); Cypress Hills★★
14 **Swift Current – Regina**
(243km/151mi); Moose Jaw★
15 **Regina**★★
16 **Regina – Brandon**
(423km/263mi);
Qu' Appelle Valley★
17 **Brandon – Winnipeg**
(211km/131mi); Austin★

④Northern Ontario

Trip of 2,271km/1,411mi from Ottawa to Winnipeg. Time: 10 days. On this tour visitors can experience the wild, untouched beauty of the Canadian Shield country with its rocks, trees and lovely lakes. The drive around Lake Superior is particularly attractive.

DAYS/ ITINERARY/ SIGHTS

1–2 **Ottawa**★★★
3 **Ottawa – North Bay**
(363km/226mi); North Bay★
4 **North Bay – Sault Ste Marie**
(427km/265mi); Sudbury★★
5 Sault Ste. Marie★★
6 **Sault Ste Marie – Thunder Bay**
(705km/438mi); Lake Superior
Drive★★, North Shore Lake
Superior★★, (described in
other direction)
7 **Thunder Bay**★★
8 **Thunder Bay – Kenora**
(569km/353mi); Kakabeka Falls★★
9–10 **Kenora – Winnipeg**
(207km/129mi); Winnipeg★★★

5 Southern Ontario

Round-trip of 1,737km/1,079mi from Niagara Falls. Time: 18 days. This tour combines the vibrant city of Toronto with the magnificent falls on the Niagara River, the highly cultivated southern Ontario, some Canadian Shield country and the nation's capital of Ottawa.

DAYS/ITINERARY/SIGHTS

1–2 60km/37mi; **Niagara Falls**★★★, Niagara Parkway (North)★★
3 **Niagara Falls – Toronto** (147km/91mi); Hamilton★
4–7 **Toronto**★★★
8 **Toronto – Kingston** (269km/167mi); Oshawa★★
9 **Kingston and the Thousand Islands**★★
10 **Kingston – Ottawa** (201km/125mi); Upper Canada Village★★★
11–12 **Ottawa**★★★
13 **Ottawa – Gravenhurst** (406km/252mi); Gravenhurst★
14 **Gravenhurst – Midland** (56km/35mi); Orillia★, Ste.-Marie among the Hurons★★, Midland★
15 **Penetanguishene**★, Georgian Bay★★
16 **Midland – Goderich** (249km/155mi); Wasaga Beach★, Blue Mountains, Goderich★
17 **Goderich – London** (140km/87mi); Stratford★, London★

Optional 2-day excursion, 482km/300mi, can be made to **Windsor**★ and **Point Pelee National Park**★★; overnight stop at Leamington.
18 **London – Niagara Falls** (209km/130mi); Brantford★

6 Quebec

Round-trip of 2,359km/1,466ml (not including ferries) from Montreal. Time: 17 days. This tour combines the charm of Quebec city, the ancient capital, with the impressive fiord on the Saguenay; the beautiful Gaspésie (Gaspé peninsula) culminating in the scenic wonder of Percé; and the vibrant city of Montreal.

DAYS/ITINERARY/SIGHTS

1–3 **Montreal**★★★
4 **Montreal – Quebec City** (277km/172mi); Trois-Rivières★★
5–6 **Quebec City**★★★
7 **Quebec City – Île aux Coudres** (107km/67mi and ferry); Côte de Beaupré★★, Côte de Charlevoix-★★★, Île aux Coudres★★
8 **Île aux Coudres – Tadoussac** (104km/65mi and ferry); Cote de Charlevoix★★★, Tadoussac★★
9 Whale-Watching Cruise★★ or Cruise on fjord du Saguenay★★★
10 **Tadoussac – Matane** (204km/127mi, ferry Les Escoumins – Trois-Pistoles);

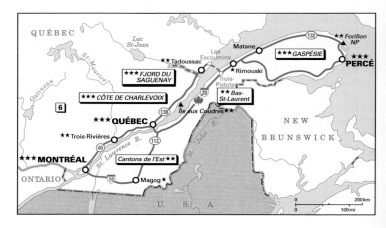

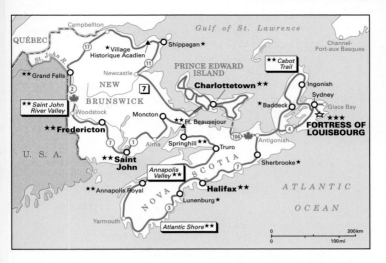

Gaspésie★★★, Jardins (gardens) de Métis★★, Matane
11 **Matane – Percé** (404km/251mi); Parc national Forillon★★, Gaspé★
12–13 Percé★★★
14 **Percé – Rimouski** (466km/290mi); Gaspésie★★★, Côte Sud (South Coast), Rimouskia
15 **Rimouski – Quebec City** (312km/194mi); Bas-Saint-Laurent★★, (described in opposite direction)
16 **Quebec City – Magog** (275km/171mi); Cantons de l'Est★★, Magog★
17 **Magog – Montreal** (210km/130mi); Vallée du Richelieu★★

⑦ Maritime Provinces

Round-trip of 4,235km/2,632mi (not including ferries) from Halifax. Time: 22 days. This tour of the three Maritime provinces is an interesting blend of seascapes, rocky headlands, sandy beaches and the high tides of the Bay of Fundy with historical high-lights such as the French fortress of Louisbourg, Halifax and its citadel, the Acadian country and the important port of Saint John.

DAYS/ ITINERARY/ SIGHTS

1–2 Halifax★★
3 **Halifax – Antigonish** (261km/162mi); Sherbrooke★
4 **Antigonish – Sydney** (212km/132mi); Louisbourg Fortress★★★
5 **Sydney – Ingonish** (127km/79mi); Glace Bay (Miners' Museum★★), Cabot Trail★★ (described in opposite direction), Ingonish
6 **Ingonish – Baddeck** (233km/145mi); Cabot Trail★★, Cape Breton Highlands National Park★★, Chéticamp, Baddeck★
7 **Baddeck – Charlottetown** (263km/163mi and ferry); Prince Edward Island, Charlottetown★★
8–9–10 800km/500mi (maximum) Prince Edward Island Scenic Drives
11 **Charlottetown – Newcastle** (259km/161mi and ferry)
12 **Newcastle – Campbellton** (301km/187mi); Shippagan★, Village Historique Acadien★
13 **Campbellton – Woodstock** (311km/193mi); Saint John River Valley★★ (described in opposite direction), Grand Falls★★, Hartland★
14 **Woodstock – Fredericton** (101km/63mi); Kings Landing★★
15 **Fredericton – Saint John** (109km/68mi); Fredericton★★
16 Saint John★★

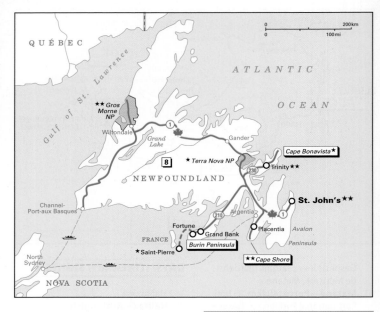

17 **Saint John – Alma** (143km/89mi);
Fundy National Park★★

18 **Alma – Truro** (254km/158mi);
Hopewell Cape★★, Moncton, Fort
Beausejour★★, Springhill★★

19 **Truro – Annapolis Royal**
(243km/151mi); Truro, Annapolis
Valley★★ (described in other
direction)

20 **Annapolis Royal – Yarmouth**
(131km/81mi); Annapolis Royal★★,
Port Royal Habitation★★

21 **Yarmouth – Lunenburg**
(311km/193mi); Atlantic Shore★★
(described in opposite direction),
Liverpool, Ovens Natural Park★,
Lunenburg★

22 **Lunenburg – Halifax**
(176km/109mi); Atlantic Shore★★,
Peggy's Cove★★

8 Newfoundland

Round-trip of 2,073km/1,288mi (not
including ferries) from North Sydney,
Nova Scotia. Time: 12 days. This tour
of Canada's most easterly province
enables visitors to discover the scenic
wonders of Gros Morne, the French
island of St.-Pierre and the old port
city of St. John's.

DAYS/ ITINERARY/ SIGHTS

1 **North Sydney – Port aux
Basques by ferry**
(🛳 it is advisable to spend the
previous night in Sydney)

2 **Port aux Basques – Wiltondale**
(305km/190mi)

3 191km/119mi; Gros Morne
National Park★★

4 **Wiltondale – Gander**
(356km/221mi)

5–6 **Gander – Trinity** (182km/113mi);
Terra Nova National Park★, Cape
Bonavist★★, Trinity★★

7 **Trinity – Grand Bank**
(333km/206mi); Burin Peninsula,
Grand Bank

8 **Grand Bank – St.-Pierre**
(by ferry from Fortune); St.-Pierre★

9–10 **St.-Pierre – St. John's**
(362km/224mi); St. John's★★

11 **St. John's – Cape Shore**
(175km/109mi); Placentia (Castle
Hill★), Cape St. Mary's★

12 **Cape Shore – North Sydney**
(by ferry from Argentia)

WHEN AND WHERE TO GO

When to Go

CLIMATE

Climatic conditions vary greatly throughout Canada (for climate information see regional introductions). Daily weather reports by Environment Canada are available through television, radio and newspapers. For weather for specific cities covered in this guide, visit the websites, if available, listed within the Principal Sights in the *Discovering Canada* section.

SEASONS

Canada's main **tourist season** extends from the last weekend in May (Victoria Day) to the first weekend in September (Labour Day). Many attractions lengthen the season to the Thanksgiving weekend (second Monday in October). In mid-size to large cities, sights are usually open year-round.

From mid-March to mid-May, visitors can enjoy comfortable daytime temperatures but chilly nights in **spring**; in some areas, spring skiing is still possible. Ontario, Quebec and New Brunswick celebrate the harvest of maple syrup with sugaring-off parties. Most visitors go to Canada during the **summer** season, extending from the last weekend in May to early September. July and August are considered peak season and are ideal for outdoor activities such as sailing, kayaking, canoeing or hiking. Hot and often humid days with temperatures ranging from 22°-35°C/70°-95°F can be enjoyed in most provinces. May and September are pleasant months with warm days but cool evenings. However, many attractions have curtailed visiting hours, so phone ahead. The southern regions along the Canada/US border offer spectacular displays of **fall** colours from mid-September until early October.

For the sports enthusiast, the Canadian winter, generally from mid-November to mid-March, offers excellent opportunities to enjoy numerous **winter** activities such as downhill skiing, cross-country skiing and snowmobiling. Most provinces experience heavy snowfall. Main highways are snowploughed, but vehicles should be winterized and snow tires are recommended.

Note:

The extreme northern regions of Canada are most accessible during July and August since the temperature rises above 0°C/32°F for only a few months each year.

WHAT TO PACK

Year-round, it is advisable to have a raincoat or hooded coat, and umbrella, in view of the range of weather across this vast country. Warmer wear, including a hat, neck scarf and gloves, is necessary in early spring, late autumn and, of course, winter, when heavy top coats and layers of clothing are essential. In summer it can be cool in the evenings in many places, so taking some warmer clothes is recommended. As there will be numerous times when walking is the ideal means of transport in both the cities and the countryside, comfortable footwear is essential, especially for sightseeing. If you are an outdoor enthusiast, pack your hiking boots as well.

It's a good idea to take along an extra tote bag for shopping at outdoor markets, carrying a picnic, and for bringing your purchases home.

Themed Tours

⬧*see Special Excursions in the Practical Information section within each province.*

KNOW BEFORE YOU GO

Useful Websites

Canadian Tourism
www.canada.travel/select
Country.html
(The official site of the Canadian
Tourism Commission)

Government of Canada:
www.canada.gc.ca
(links to all government
departments)

Canadian Government Publishing:
http://publications.gc.ca

The Canadian Encyclopedia online:
www.thecanadianencyclopedia.com

Current information:
www.canoe.ca
www.canada.com
www.cbc.ca

Tourist Offices

*Also see Visitor Information in the
Practical Information section within
each province.*

Official government tourist offices
operated by provincial, municipal
and regional agencies distribute road
maps and brochures that provide
information on points of interest,
seasonal events, accommodations
and recreational activities. All publications are available free of charge
(*see regional introductions*). Local
tourist offices (telephone numbers
and websites listed under each blue
entry heading in this guide) provide
additional information about accommodations, shopping, entertainment,
festivals and recreation. On the maps
in this guide, information centres are
indicated by the symbol ▣. A Website
that may be useful in planning your
trip is *www.travelcanada.ca.*

International Visitors

In addition to tourism offices, visitors
from outside Canada may obtain information from the nearest Canadian
embassy or consulate in their country
of residence. Embassies of other countries are located in Canada's capital,
Ottawa. Most foreign countries maintain consulates in Canada's provincial
capitals. For further information on
all Canadian embassies and consulates abroad, contact the website of
**Foreign Affairs and
International Trade Canada**:
www.international.gc.ca/.

SELECTED CANADIAN
CONSULATES AND EMBASSIES

US
1175 Peachtree St. NE, 100 Colony
Square, Suite 1700, Atlanta,
GA 30361-6205, ☎ 404-532-2000
1251 Avenue of the Americas,
New York, NY 10020-1175,
☎ 212-596-1628
550 South Hope St., Los Angeles,
CA 90071-2627, ☎ 213-346-2700

Australia
Quay West Bldg., 111 Harrington St.,
Sydney, NSW 2000, ☎ 9-364-3000

Germany
Leipziger Platz 17, 10117 Berlin,
☎ 30-203120

United Kingdom
38 Grosvenor St., Macdonald House,
London W1K 4AA,
☎ 020 7258 6506

ENTRY REQUIREMENTS

As of January 2007, citizens of the US
need a valid passport or Air NEXUS
card to visit Canada and return by
air. A driver's license and a birth
certificate together are currently
accepted to enter Canada by land or
sea. Parents bringing children into

Canada are strongly advised to carry birth certificates. As of 2008, only a passport or secure passport card will be accepted to return to the US. All other visitors to Canada must have a valid **passport** and, in some cases, a visa *(see list of countries at www.cic. gc.ca/english/visit/visas.asp)*. No vaccinations are necessary. For entry into Canada via the US, all persons other than US citizens or legal residents are required to present a valid passport. Check with the Canadian embassy or consulate in your home country about entry regulations and proper travel documents.

CUSTOMS REGULATIONS

Non-residents may import personal baggage temporarily without payment of duties. Persons of legal age as prescribed by the province or territory (see regional introductions) may bring into Canada duty-free 200 cigarettes, 50 cigars and some other forms of **tobacco. Alcohol** is limited to 1.14 litres (40 imperial ounces) of wine or spirits, or 24 bottles (355ml or 12 ounces) of beer or ale. All **prescription drugs** should be clearly labelled and for personal use only; it is recommended that visitors carry a copy of the prescription. For more information, call **Border Information Service** ☎ 800 461-9999 (within Canada) or ☎ 204-983-3500; or visit **Canada Border Services Agency**: *www.cbsa-asfc.gc.ca.*
Canada has stringent legislation on firearms. A firearm cannot be brought into the country for personal protection while travelling. Only long guns may be imported by visitors 18 years or older for hunting or sporting purposes. Certain **firearms** are prohibited entry; restricted firearms, which include handguns, may only be imported with a permit by a person attending an approved shooting competition. For further information on entry of firearms, contact the **Canadian Centre for Firearms** *(284 Wellington St., Ottawa, ON K1A 1M6; ☎ 800-731-4000; www.cfc-cafc.gc.ca).*

Most animals, except domesticated dogs and cats, must be issued a Canadian import permit prior to entry into Canada. **Pets** must be accompanied by an official certificate of vaccination against rabies from the country of origin. Payment of an inspection fee may be necessary. For details, contact **Canadian Food Inspection Agency**, *(59 Camelot Dr., Ottawa, ON K1A 0Y9; ☎ 613-225-2342; www.inspection.gc.ca).*

CURRENCY EXCHANGE

⌖*See Money in Basic Information.*

HEALTH

Before travelling, visitors should check with their health care insurance to determine if doctor's visits, medication and hospitalization in Canada are covered; otherwise supplementary insurance may be necessary. Manulife Financial offers reimbursement for expenses as a result of emergencies under their Visitors to Canada Plan. The plan must be purchased before arrival, or within five days of arrival, in Canada. For details contact **Manulife Financial** *(2 Queen St. East, Toronto, ON, M5W 4Z2; ☎800-268-3763; www.coverme.com).*

Accessibility

Full wheelchair access to sights described in this guide is indicated in admission information by the symbol ⌖. Most public buildings and many attractions, restaurants and hotels provide wheelchair access. Disabled parking is provided and the law is strictly enforced. For details contact the provincial tourist office *(⌖see regional introductions).*
Many national and provincial parks have restrooms and other facilities for the disabled (such as wheelchair-accessible nature trails or tour buses). For details about a specific park, call ☎ 888-773-8888 or visit *www.pc.gc.ca.* Additional information is available from **Easter Seals Canada**, *(90 Eglinton Ave.*

East, Suite 208, Toronto, ON M4P 2Y3;
☎*416-932-8382; www.easterseals.ca).*
Passengers who need assistance
should give 24-48hrs advance notice;
also contact the following transportation providers to request their
informative literature for riders with
disabilities:

Via Rail
☎888-842-7245
Special Needs Services:
☎800-268-9503 (TDD)
www.viarail.ca

Greyhound Canada
☎800-661-8747 (Canada)
☎800-397-7870 (TDD)
www.greyhound.ca
Reservations for hand-controlled cars
at rental companies should be made
well in advance.

👌*Also see the Practical Information
section for each province.*

GETTING THERE AND GETTING AROUND

By Plane

👌*See also the Practical Information
section for each province.*
American carriers offer **air** service to
Canada's major airports. Air Canada
(☎*888-247-2262 Canada/US; www.
aircanada.com) flies from larger US
cities. Amtrak offers daily **rail** service
to Montreal from Washington DC and
New York City, as well as from New
York City to Toronto. Aside from these
direct routes, connections are offered
from many major US cities. For schedules in the US ☎*800-872-7245* or *www.
amtrak.com*. **Bus** travel from the US is
offered by Greyhound. For information and schedules *www.greyhound.
ca* or call the local US bus terminal. It
is advisable to book well in advance
when travelling during peak season.
Air Canada offers service to and from
all major European cities, the
Caribbean, Asia and the Pacific.
Vancouver is the western gateway city,
offering connections to Australia, New
Zealand and the Far East.
Domestic air service is offered by
Canada's national airline Air Canada
(☎*888-247-2262 or 800-361-8071 TDD)*
as well as its affiliated regional airlines
and by Calgary-based WestJet (☎*800-
538-5696 or 877-952-0100 TDD)*. Air

service to remote areas is provided by
many charter companies. For specifics,
contact the provincial tourist office
(👌*see regional introductions).*

Major airports in Canada serviced by
international airlines are:

Vancouver, BC
Vancouver International Airport
(airport fee applied)
14km/9mi south of downtown
☎604-207-7077
www.yvr.ca

Calgary, AB
Calgary International Airport
17km/11mi northeast of downtown
☎403-735-1200
www.calgaryairport.com

Edmonton, AB
Edmonton International Airport
(airport fee applied)
20km/14mi south of downtown
☎780-890-8382
www.edmontonairports.com

Winnipeg, AB
Winnipeg International Airport
8km/5mi west of downtown
☎204-987-9400
www.waa.ca

Toronto, ON

Lester B. Pearson International Airport
27km/17mi northwest of downtown
☎416-247-7678
www.gtaa.com

Montreal, QC

Pierre Elliott Trudeau International
Airport *(airport fee applied)*
22km/14mi west of downtown
☎514-394-7377
www.admtl.com

Ottawa, ON

Ottawa International Airport
18km/11mi south of downtown
☎613-248-2125
www.ottawa-airport.ca

St. John's, NF

St. John's International Airport
10km/6mi northwest of downtown
☎709-758-8500
www.stjohnsairport.com

Note: Upon departure from some
Canadian cities, travellers should
be prepared to pay a $10 or higher
Airport Improvement Fee before
boarding the aircraft.

Many smaller regional airlines serve
the provinces and territories. Air
service to remote areas is provided by
several charter companies. Check with
the regional tourist offices regarding
your specific destination.

By Ship

Canada maintains an extensive
ferry-boat system. Contact the
regional tourist offices for information and schedules *(see regional
introductions for details; for Vancouver
Island, see Entry Heading).*

By Train

VIA Rail, Canada's national passenger
rail network, traverses the country
with 18 major routes from coast to
coast. First-class, coach and sleeping accommodations are available
on transcontinental, regional and
intercity trains. Amenities offered are
dome cars, dining cars and lounges,
baggage handling (including bicycles),
reservation of medical equipment,
wheelchairs and preboarding aid
with 24hr minimum notice. Unlimited train travel for 12 days within a
30-day period is available systemwide
through **CANRAILPASS** *(Jun to mid-
Oct, 12 days $837, 3 day extension at
$71/day; off-season $523).* Special rates
are offered for students with an ISIC
card, youth and senior citizens.
Reservations should be made well in
advance, especially during summer
months and on popular routes like
Edmonton to Vancouver. Canada's
legendary cross-country train,
The Canadian, travels the almost
4,424km/2,700mi from Toronto to
Vancouver in four days *(one-way from
$597, advance purchase, plus sleep-
ing accommodation surcharge).* For
information and schedules in Canada
contact the nearest VIA Rail office or
call ☎888-842-7245 (US & Canada);
www.viarail.ca. The Travel Planner
section of the Via Rail website lists
overseas sales agents.

By Coach/Bus

Long-distance buses reach almost
every corner of Canada. **Greyhound**
Canada Transportation Corp., *(877
Greyhound Way SW, Calgary, AB T3C
3V8)* operates the only trans-Canadian service and offers Canada Travel
Passes, which are sold internationally.
Unlimited travel from 7 days up to
60 days is available. Peak season rates
range from $329 to $750 *(reduced rates
available in off-season and for senior
citizens).* For fares and schedules, call
Greyhound: ☎800-661-8747 (Canada),
☎800-231-2222 (US); www.greyhound.
ca. A 14-day **Rout-Pass** for travel from
May–Oct ($263) is available for most of
Quebec and Ontario *(☎416-393-7911;
www.routpass.com).*
Other regional companies supple-
ment Canada's extensive motorcoach
service *(see the yellow pages of local
telephone directories).*

By Car

See also the Practical Information section for each province.

Given Canada's enormous size, it is impossible to cover all of the country during one visit. *See Driving Tours for suggested two- to three-week itineraries.*
Canada has an extensive system of well-maintained major roads. In the northern regions and off main arteries, however, many roads are gravel or even dirt. Extreme caution should be taken when travelling these roads.

DOCUMENTS

Foreign **driver's licenses** are valid for varying time periods depending on the province. Drivers must carry vehicle **registration** information and/or rental contract at all times. Vehicle **insurance** is compulsory in all provinces (minimum liability is $200,000, except $50,000 in Quebec). US visitors should obtain a Canadian Non-Resident Inter-Province Motor Vehicle Insurance Liability Card **(yellow card)**, available from US insurance companies. For additional information contact the Insurance Bureau of Canada, *(777 Bay St., Suite 2400, Toronto, ON M5G 2C8; ☎416-362-2031; www.ibc.ca).*

GASOLINE

Gasoline is sold by the litre (1 gallon = 3.78 litres); prices vary from province to province. All distances and speed limits are posted in kilometres (1 mile = 1.6 kilometres). During winter it is advisable to check road conditions before setting out. **Snow tires** and an **emergency kit** are imperative. Studded tires are allowed in winter in some provinces; for seasonal limitations, contact the regional Ministry of Transportation *(check the blue pages in the local telephone directories).*

ROAD REGULATIONS

Unless otherwise posted, the speed limit on rural highways is 80km/h (50mph) and in urban areas 50km/h (30mph). Service stations that are open 24 hours can be found in large cities and along major highways. The use of **seat belts** is mandatory for all drivers and passengers. Most provinces prohibit **radar detection devices** in vehicles. Traffic in both directions must stop (except on divided roads) for a yellow school bus when signals are flashing. In all provinces *except* some cities in Quebec, **right turns on red** are allowed after coming to a complete stop. Information on highway conditions in each province can be obtained by contacting the regional Ministry of Transportation *(check the blue pages in the local telephone directories).*

IN CASE OF ACCIDENT

If you are involved in an accident resulting in property damage and/or personal injury, you must notify the local police and remain at the scene until dismissed by investigating officers. For assistance contact the local Government Insurance Corporation. First-aid stations are clearly designated along highways.

CANADIAN AUTOMOBILE ASSOCIATION (CAA)

This national member-based organization *(1145 Hunt Club Rd., Ottawa, ON K1V 0Y3 ☎613-247-0117, www.caa. ca)* offers, through its offices across Canada, services such as travel information, maps and tour books, accommodation reservations, insurance, technical and legal advice, and emergency roadside assistance. These benefits are extended to members of other internationsl affiliated clubs (proof of membership is required). The CAA maintains for its members a **24hr emergency road service ☎800-222-HELP** (*see regional introductions for CAA listings).*

Prince Edward County, Eastern Ontario

CAR RENTAL

Most major rental car agencies have offices at airports and in large cities in Canada. Minimum age for rental is usually 25. To avoid a large cash deposit, payment by credit card is recommended. More favourable rates can sometimes be obtained by making a reservation before arriving in Canada, but be aware of drop-off charges.

- **Avis:** ☎800-331-1212
- **Hertz:** ☎800-654-3131
- **Budget:** ☎800-268-8900
- **National/Tilden:** ☎800-227-7368

WHERE TO STAY AND EAT

Hotel & Restaurant listings fall within the Address Books of each province. For prices, ⓖ see the Legend on the cover flap.

Where to Stay

*ⓖ For a selection of accommodations, see the green boxes titled **Address Books** within the major cities and areas described in the guide. Lodgings in this guide can also be found in the Index under the heading **Where to Stay**.*
Canada offers accommodations suited to every taste and pocketbook. Luxury **hotels** generally are found in major cities, while **motels** normally are clustered on the outskirts of towns. **Bed-and-breakfast inns** (B&Bs) are found in residential areas of cities and towns, as well as in more secluded natural areas. Many properties offer special packages and weekend rates that may not be extended during peak summer months *(late May–late Aug)* and during winter holiday seasons, especially near ski resorts. Most resort properties include outdoor recreational facilities such as golf courses, tennis courts, swimming pools and fitness centres. Activities—hiking, mountain biking and horseback riding—often can be arranged by contacting the hotel staff. Many cities and communities levy a **hotel occupancy tax** that is not reflected in hotel rates. Provincial and regional tourist offices offer free publications listing accommodations by location and type *(ⓖ see regional introductions for addresses)*. Government tourist offices supply listings *(free)* that give locations, phone numbers, types of service, amenities, prices and other details *(ⓖ see regional introductions for addresses)*. Canada is a vast country, and in less populated regions it may be difficult to find accommodations at the end of a long day's drive. Advance reservations are recommended, especially during the tourist season *(Victoria Day to Labour Day)*.
During the off-season, establishments outside urban centers may be closed; it is therefore advisable to telephone ahead. Guaranteeing reservations with a credit card is recommended.

HOTELS

Rates for hotels vary greatly depending on season and location. Expect to pay higher rates during holiday and peak seasons. For deluxe hotels, plan to pay at least $300-$500/night per standard room, based on double occupancy in peak season. Moderate hotels usually will charge $90-$200/night. When making a reservation, ask about packages including meals, passes to local attractions, etc.. Typical amenities at hotels include televisions, alarm clocks, in-room phones, smoking/non-smoking rooms, restaurants and swimming pools. Suites and in-room efficiency kitchens are available at some hotels. Always advise the reservations clerk of late arrival; unless confirmed with a credit card, rooms may not be held after 6pm.

MOTELS

Along major highways or close to urban areas motels such as Comfort Inn, Quality Inn and Choice Hotels ☎800-221-2222, Travelodge ☎800-667-3529 and Days Inn ☎800-325-2525 offer accommodations at moderate prices ($50–$115), depending upon the location. Amenities include in-room television, alarm clock and telephone. Smoking and non-smoking rooms, restaurants and swimming pools are often available on-site. Some in-room efficiency kitchens may be available. Family-owned establishments and small, independent guest houses that offer basic comfort can be found all across Canada.

BED AND BREAKFASTS AND COUNTRY INNS

Most B&Bs and country inns are privately owned; some are located in historic structures in residential sections of cities or small towns. In rural areas lodgings can be a rustic cabin or a farmhouse. At B&Bs the room rate includes complimentary breakfast ranging from continental fare to a gourmet repast; some offer afternoon tea and evening sherry or light snacks. Guests are invited to use the sitting room and garden spots. Country inns are larger establishments, usually with more than 15 rooms and with full-service dining facilities. Private baths are not always available, and often there is no phone in individual rooms. Smoking indoors may not be permitted. Reservations should be made well in advance, especially during peak seasons and holidays. Ask about minimum stay requirements, and cancellation and refund policies. Most establishments accept major credit cards, but some B&Bs may not. Rates vary seasonally ($75–$200) for a double room per night. Rates may be higher when amenities such as hot tubs, private entrances and scenic views are offered.

RESERVATIONS SERVICES

Numerous organizations offer reservation services for B&Bs and country inns. Many services tend to be regional, such as **Town & Country Reservation Service** (*☎604-731-5942, Vancouver*), but the **Professional Association of Innkeepers International** (*☎856-310-1102; www. paii.org*) and **Wakeman & Costine's North American Bed & Breakfast Directory** (*☎828-387-3697; www. bbdirectory.com*) include properties for Canada as a whole. The **Independent Innkeepers' Assn.** publishes an annual register that includes Canadian B&Bs and country inns; *☎269-789-0393 or 800-344-5244* or book online: www.selectregistry.com. For a complete listing, search the Internet using the keyword "bed and breakfast" or ask your travel agent.

Auberge St-Pierre, Quebec City

HOSTELS

Hostelling International Canada, affiliated with the International Youth Hostel Federation, offers a network of budget accommodations from coast to coast. A simple, no-frills alternative to hotels and inns, hostels are inexpensive dormitory-style accommodations (blankets and pillows are provided) with separate quarters for males and females. Many have private family/couples rooms that may be reserved in advance. Amenities include fully equipped self-service kitchens, dining areas, common rooms and laundry facilities. Rates average $15–$25 per night for members (higher for non-members). Hostels often organize special programs and activities for guests. Advance booking is advisable during peak travel times, but walk-ins are welcome. Membership is $25/year, but non-members are also admitted. When booking, ask for available discounts at area attractions, rental car companies and restaurants. For information and a free directory, contact **Hostelling International Canada** (*400-205 Catherine St., Ottawa, ON K2P 1C3; ☎613-237-7884 or 800-663-5777; www.hihostels.ca*).

UNIVERSITIES AND COLLEGES

Most universities make their dormitory space available to travellers during summer vacation (*May–Aug*). Rooms are sparse; linens are provided. Bathrooms are communal and there are no in-room telephones. Rates average $20–$35/day per person. Reservations are accepted. When booking, ask about on-campus parking and food service. For more information contact the local tourist office or the university directly.

FARM AND RANCH VACATIONS

Farm and ranch lodgings are rustic and especially suited for families with children. Visitors are paying guests on a working grain or livestock farm or a cattle/horse ranch, and participation in daily chores depends on the host's preference. Guests might be asked to gather eggs, feed animals or perhaps milk a cow. Wagon and sleigh rides, hiking through pasture, canoeing or fishing at an on-site pond, even berry picking, may be available activities. Breakfast is included. Other meals can often be requested and may be taken with the host family. Rates begin at $40-$60 for double occupancy. Inquire about deposit and refund policies and minimum stay requirements. Credit cards may not always be accepted.

GUEST RANCHES

Primarily located in the mountain regions of British Columbia or the rolling hills of the Prairie provinces, guest ranches offer a vacation that can be enjoyed by singles, couples or families. Comfortable accommodations may be a room in a main lodge or in a cabin. Home-cooked meals are usually served family-style; in addition, scenic trail rides, overnight camp-outs, hiking, guided fishing trips, swimming, rafting, country dancing and campfire gatherings are often available. All equipment is provided and some ranches offer supervised youth programs. Many are working cattle and horse ranches and guests are encouraged to pitch in. Rates average $670–$1,750/week per person; some ranches may require a minimum stay. Ask about deposit and refund policies when booking a reservation.
For a selection of BC guest ranches, see Entry Heading Cariboo. For more

information on ranch vacations in British Columbia, contact the **Dude Ranchers' Assn**. (*866-399-2339; www.duderanch.org*) or the **BC Guest Ranchers' Assn**. (*877-278-2922; www.bcguestranches.com*).

CAMPING AND RV PARKS

Canada has excellent campgrounds that are operated privately or by the federal and provincial governments. Government sites are located in the many national and provincial parks. Fees are nominal. These campgrounds are well equipped and fill up quickly. Most park **campgrounds** are open mid-May through Labour Day, and usually operate on a first-come, first-served basis. Dates are subject to change: visitors should check with park visitor centres for rates and maximum length of stay. Some parks offer reservation services; some offer winter camping. Campsites often include a level tent pad, picnic table, fireplace or fire grill with firewood, and parking space near a potable water source. Most have toilet buildings and kitchen shelters. Some campgrounds are for tents only; others allow recreational vehicles; most do not have trailer hook-ups – although many have sewage disposal stations. Many accommodate persons with disabilities. Rustic campgrounds, located near hiking trails in the backcountry, can be reached only on foot. Some parks offer hut-to-hut cross-country skiing with rustic overnight accommodations or winter tent sites.

For a list of campgrounds contact the provincial tourist office (*see regional introductions for addresses*). Advance reservations are recommended, especially during summer and holidays. In most parks and forests, campgrounds are available on a first-come, first-served basis.

NATIONAL AND PROVINCIAL PARKS

Campgrounds are relatively inexpensive but fill rapidly, especially during school holidays. Facilities range from

King Pacific Lodge, Princess Royal Island, BC

simple tent sites to full RV hook-ups *(reserve 60 days in advance)* or rustic cabins *(reserve one year in advance).* Fees vary according to season and available facilities (picnic tables, water/electric hook-ups, used-water disposal, recreational equipment, showers, restrooms): camping & RV sites $8–$21/day; cabins $20–$110/day. For all Canadian national park reservations, contact the park you are visiting or **Parks Canada** *(888-773-8888; www.pc.gc.ca).* For **provincial parks**, contact the provincial or local tourism office for information *(see Provincial Parks in the index).*

As well as national parks, there are some 1,000 **provincial parks**, more than 750 **national historic sites**, and 14 **UNESCO World Heritage Sites**. Designed for daytime visits, most sites are open from Victoria Day to Labour Day, with reduced hours in the early spring and fall. Most charge a nominal admission fee and at many, interpretation centres and costumed guides provide insight into Canada's history and cultural heritage.

For more information, contact Parks Canada (above).

PRIVATE CAMPGROUNDS

Commercial campgrounds offer facilities ranging from simple tent sites to full RV hook-ups. They are slightly more expensive *($10–$60/day for tent sites, $20–$25/day for RVs)* but offer amenities such as hot showers, laundry facilities, convenience stores, children's playgrounds, pools, air-conditioned cabins and outdoor recreational facilities. Most accept daily, weekly or monthly occupancy. During the winter months *(Nov–Apr),* campgrounds in northern regions may be closed. Reservations are recommended, especially for longer stays and in popular resort areas.

FISHING CAMPS, FLY-IN LODGES AND WILDERNESS CAMPS

Individual lodges are described in coloured boxes throughout the BC/Rockies/Yukon section of this guide.

Canada offers the experienced angler or the outdoor enthusiast a variety of fishing lodges and camps, some of which are so remote they can only be reached on foot or by private boat or float plane. Cabins, backcountry huts, main lodge and dormitory-style buildings are typical accommodations. Summer tent camping may also be offered. Outfitters offer packages that include transportation, accommodations, meals, supplies, equipment and expeditions led by experienced guides. Activities can include trail riding, lake and stream fishing, boating and climbing. Some camps have hot tubs or saunas.

Wilderness camps located in Canada's northern regions offer all-inclusive hunting packages. Non-residents must be accompanied by licensed guides.

Off-Beat Stays

In British Columbia's Fraser Canyon, the **houseboat** industry thrives in summertime. Many vacationers rent houseboats in the town of Sicamous to drift along on Shuswap Lake. The Saint John River in New Brunswick is also a popular houseboating spot. Near Yoho National Park in the Rockies, patrons of Beaverfoot Lodge can choose to sleep in **wagon train** bunks (☎ 250-984-1583; www.beaverfootlodge. ca). Along the BC coast, travellers often book a berth on a cruise ship, or even on a ferry: on the Alaska Marine Highway route, passengers are permitted to camp overnight outside on the deck. Farther west, in the Prairies, campers can gaze at the stars before bedding down in a **teepee** (or tipi) at the foot of remote Head-Smashed-In Buffalo Jump; Quaaout Lodge in Salmon Arm, BC, also offers teepee stays. Near Churchill, Manitoba, polar bear-watching patrons find haven in a **tundra buggy** train, while overnight guests in that province's town of Souris can slumber in a converted **grain elevator** (Rustic Retreat B&B ☎204-483-2834). On Cape Breton Island in Nova Scotia, a whisky **distillery** beckons tired travellers to its adjoining inn (Glenora Inn & Distillery, Rte. 19 near Inverness ☎800-839-0491; www.glenoradistillery.com). Also in Nova Scotia, an inn within a former train station puts guests up in **cabooses** (Train Station Inn ☎888-724-5233; www.trainstation.ca). On Prince Edward Island, folks can book a room in a working **lighthouse,** complete with ocean views. And way up north in Nunavut, visitors can stay overnight in an **igloo,** while in Quebec City, accommodations are possible in an **ice hotel,** appointed with standard amenities. For details on the above accommodations, contact provincial tourist offices (👆see regional introductions).

Permits can be obtained through the outfitter, who can also assist with game registration (👆required by law). These packages are costly and the number of spaces is usually limited. It is advisable to make reservations well in advance. For information on fishing and hunting regulations and license fees, as well as listings of outfitters, contact the provincial tourist office (👆see regional introductions).

Where to Eat

👆For a selection of restaurants, see the green boxes titled **Address Books** within the major cities as well as other areas described in the guide. Restaurants in this guide can also be found in the Index under the heading **Where to Eat**, where they are arranged by province or territory and city.

From Quebec's tortière (meat pie) to Calgary's 1969 invention of the Bloody Caesar beverage (tomato-and clam-juice with vodka), Canada's regional cuisines encompass traditional comfort foods as well as novel creations. Originally, foods that were hunted and gathered (moose, salmon, goose, whale blubber, berries, and wild rice, for example) formed aboriginal and early Europeans' diets. Since then, Canada's traditional dishes, supplemented by those of its diverse ethnic population, have resulted in a richly varied cuisine. In-season and not-to-be-missed culinary experiences include Quebec's sugaring-off season, where sugar shacks serve freshly made maple syrup with pancakes, beans and sausages; or Atlantic Canada's choice seafood (lobster, scallops, mussels, oysters). Quebec's artisinal cheeses are renowned, with excellent selections found in Montreal's Atwater Market. Today, Canadian wines, icewines and ice-apple ciders win international awards.

©iStockphoto.com/Nick Free

Fresh Lobster

WHAT TO SEE AND DO

Outdoor Fun

See Recreation in the Practical Information section of each province.

CANOEING AND KAYAKING

From circuit canoe trips (Bowron Lakes, BC; Killarney and Quetico parks, Ontario), sea kayaking (Broken Islands, BC; Malpeque Bay, PEI), white-water rafting (Ottawa River, Ontario), numerous accessible routes in Ontario's Algonquin Park, to lodge-based paddles of tranquil lakes (Kenauk, Quebec), Canada is a paddler's heaven. Lifejackets are mandatory in Canada and it's illegal to drink and boat. For trip planning and information about the sports in Canada, visit www.paddlingcanada.com, www.canoekayak-canada.ca – and for leaving no trace travel, go to http://lnt.org/.

FISHING

Licences are required for **fishing** and can be obtained from national and provincial park offices, designated sporting goods stores or other retail businesses. Some parks offer boat and canoe rentals. Hunting is not permitted within the national parks.

HIKING

Hiking in Canada is primarily enjoyed in national and provincial parks. Hikers should ask park officials about trail conditions, weather forecasts and safety precautions. Overnight **hikers** in backcountry areas are required to register at the park office before setting out and to deregister upon completion of the trip. Trail distances are given from trailhead to destination, not round-trip, unless otherwise posted. Topographic maps and a compass are indispensable for backcountry hiking; Gem Trek Publishing (☎250-380-0100 or 877-921-6277; www.gemtrek.com) and Federal Maps, Inc. (☎416-607-6250 or 888-545-8111; www.fedmaps.com) are two sources for obtaining detailed topographic maps.

RIDING

Horseback riding opportunities in Canada range from hour-long trail rides to week-or-more expeditions, dude ranch experiences where you can round up cattle, and workshops where you learn from experts – with or without your own animal. Also check the Royal Canadian Mounted Police Musical Ride for summer demonstrations else visit their stable in Ottawa, Ontario. For Canadian equestrian events, contact Equine Canada (☎866-282-8395; www.canadaequine.com).

SKIING AND BOARDING

Canadian skiing and snow boarding opportunities are as varied as the country is vast. Enjoy spectacular mountain conditions for alpine as well as nordik (cross-country) skiing and boarding (British Columbia, Alberta, Quebec) and nordik skiing with some alpine in other provinces and territories. Check www.skicanada.org for packages, resorts, ski and snowboard organizations across Canada; for snowboarding: www.out-there.com.

Precautions

Although Canada experiences severe winters, many regions are afflicted by hordes of biting insects in the summer. Late May to June is black-fly season, and in July the mosquitoes arrive. For outdoor activities, insect repellent is a must.

Sturdy footwear with nonslip soles is recommended for hiking.

To protect against surprise storms or cool mountain evenings, carry raingear and warm clothing.

WILDLIFE WATCHING

Canada is renowned for its wildlife, whether it's viewing grizzly or polar bears, gazing at beluga whales, or observing birds such as bald eagles and warblers. For information about Canadian wildlife, visit the Canadian Wildlife Federation's website: www. hww.ca. Wildlife is best observed in Canada's provincial and national park systems, which include marine parks such as Saguenay-St. Lawrence Marine Park for whale observation. When watching or photographing wildlife, respectful distance is crucial. Stiff fines are given in parks for feeding and otherwise habituating wildlife – so never feed, pet or disturb wild creatures of any kind.

Spas ⚕

Wellness and spas go hand in hand, particularly when married to idyllic, spectacular nature. In Canada, you can be pampered with a massage beside the Pacific Ocean, soak in a hot tub overlooking the Rocky Mountains, or enjoy treatments at a heritage estate. Day spas, destination spas (which serve spa cuisine and offer lifestyle improvement), resort spas, mineral and medical spas are thriving. Browse *www.leadingspasofcanada.com* to see what Canada has to offer.

Activities for Children `Kids`

In this guide, sights of particular interest to children are indicated with a `Kids` symbol. Many of these attractions offer discounted admission to visitors under 12 years of age as well as special children's programs designed for all ages. Canada's national parks usually offer discount fees for children. In addition, many hotels and resorts feature special family discount packages, and most restaurants offer children's menus.

Calendar of Events

Canada has a wide variety of fairs, festivals and celebrations throughout the country, many based on historic events. *See Principal Festivals in the Practical Information section of each province.*

Shopping

BUSINESS HOURS

Business hours in Canada are, for the most part, Monday to Friday 9am-5pm. In general, retail stores are open Monday to Friday 9am-6pm (until 9pm Thursday and Friday), Saturday 9am-5pm. In most cities, shops are usually open on Sunday afternoon; many small convenience stores in gas stations may be open much longer hours. *For banking hours, see Money in the Basic Information chapter.*

GENERAL MERCHANDISE

Downtown areas provide opportunities for shopping at department stores, national chains, specialty stores, art galleries and antique shops. Major department stores in Canada include Hudson's Bay Co. (known locally as "The Bay") and Eaton's, which was recently purchased by Sears. Revitalized historic districts, such as the Old Port in Montreal or the Exchange District in Winnipeg, house boutiques, art galleries, cinemas and restaurants. Large **shopping malls**—or mammoth ones like West Edmonton Mall on the outskirts of Edmonton—are generally located outside downtown areas. Bargain hunters will want to look for **outlet malls** that offer savings of up to 70% at brand-name factory stores. Recreational **outerwear** companies, such as Mountain Equipment Co-op enable visitors to equip themselves from head to toe before setting out on hiking, hunting or fishing trips. As for fashionable, but probably pricey, **ski clothes**, try Whistler, Banff, Calgary and even Vancouver. Searching for a cowboy hat or colourful neckerchief? The latest in **Western gear** is available at stores in Calgary and Whitehorse. How about a full-length silver fox coat with matching hat? **Furriers** are plentiful, particularly in Ottawa, Toronto and Winnipeg, the latter being the site of the Fur Exchange, with its vast selection.

ARTS AND CRAFTS

Hooked rugs, mats and other **Acadian crafts** can be found at the gift shops at the Acadian Museum in Cabot Trail's Chéticamp and at Grand-Pré National Historic Site east of Wolfville. Tartans, kilts and other **Scottish attire** are for sale in Nova Scotia, particularly along the Cabot Trail. Bordering the Chaudière River, the Beauce region of Quebec is famed for its **maple products** like taffy, maple syrup and liqueurs. In the outports of Newfoundland, handknit items such as mittens, scarves and hats can be purchased at local historical museums. In many parts of the country, native arts and crafts are plentiful; museums, and cultural centres on tribal lands, exhibit and sell baskets, carvings, jewellery and other handiwork. To visit Haida artists' on Queen Charlotte Islands, inquire at the local band office. The museum shops at Victoria's Royal British Columbia Museum and Vancouver's UBC Museum of Anthropology are filled with First Nations art, as are the gift shops at Wanuskewin in Saskatoon, and Head-Smashed-In Buffalo Jump near Fort Macleod in Alberta. The Alcheringa Gallery in Victoria has a fine selection of native art, with emphasis on the Northwest Coast region. Inuit arts, especially stone sculpture, are highly prized works among collectors and connoisseurs. A number of sales outlets, including artists' studios, are located in Nunavut, particularly on Baffin Island.

FARMERS' MARKETS

Prince Edward Island is known for its potato harvests, and Quebec's southern regions, especially the Montreal, St. Lawrence Valley and Lac Saint-Jean areas produce fruit and vegetables, beef and daily products. Alberta beef is world renowned and the Maritimes are famed for oysters, mussels, clams, and other fruits of the sea. A number of towns and cities across Canada hold seasonal and year-round markets. In Ontario, **Kitchener's** indoor market is held throughout the year, as is neighbouring **St. Jacob's,** a popular tourist attraction. St. Lawrence Market (open year-round) in **Toronto** sells fresh produce, seafood, baked goods, flowers, souvenirs and crafts. Nearby Hamilton boasts one of Ontario's largest indoor markets, open throughout the year. A festival atmosphere prevails at **Ottawa's** year-round ByWard Market, stretching over several blocks (indoors in winter). Charlottetown's lively farmers' market gives islander craft and food vendors a place to display their wares.

During harvest time, many farmers sell produce at roadside stands as well as at farmers' markets. Visitors can pick their own fruits and vegetables (for a small fee) at farms that are open to the public. **Annapolis Valley** in Nova Scotia is a large apple-growing area; many fruit stands can be seen here along the roads in autumn. Producers invite visitors to try the many varieties that grow in the **Niagara Peninsula**, one of Canada's chief fruit-growing regions. In British Columbia, the **Okanagan Valley's** climate fosters a variety of crops that include apples, peaches and apricots.

WINERIES

A wine-making industry thrives in the **Niagara Peninsula** on the shores of Lake Ontario. The **Okanagan Valley** in British Columbia produces some of the finest pinot noir, chardonnay and riesling wines, and Okanagan's pricey icewines are growing in popularity as dessert drinks. Most wineries welcome visitors with guided tours that include free wine tastings. Many wineries will sell their vintages to the public. During the fall harvest season, check with area visitor centres to find out about festivals and special events. ✆*For a list of specific wineries see OKANAGAN VALLEY.*

Sightseeing

NATIONAL PARKS AND RESERVES

Since the creation of the first national park in Banff in 1885, the amount of protected land managed by Parks Canada has grown to 244,540sq km/ 94,392sq mi. Canada's 41 national parks and national preserves (including two marine parks) offer the visitor spectacular scenery, a wealth of wildlife and fauna, as well as unlimited recreational opportunities. Some 14 million people visit the parks each year.

General Information

Most points of interest are in the southern national parks, accessible by car. Well-marked hiking trails permit outdoor enthusiasts and novices alike to enjoy the backcountry. Parks are open year-round; however, some roads may be closed during the winter. Daily entry or use fees range from $2.50 to $6 per adult. Discounts are offered at some parks to senior citizens (25%) and children (50%). Additional fees are charged for camping, fishing and guided programs.

Visitor centres (🕐 *open daily late May–Labour Day; reduced hours the rest of the year*) are usually located at park entrances. Staff are available to help visitors plan activities. Trail maps and literature on park facilities, hiking trails, nature programs, camping and in-park accommodations are available on-site free of charge. Interpretation programs, guided hikes, exhibits and self-guided trails introduce the visitor to each park's history, geology and habitats. ✆ *For a listing of in-park activities, see the description of specific parks within each province.*

😊 A Word of Caution 😊

Bears and other large animals are present in many of Canada's national parks. Human encounters with them may result in serious injury. Visitors are asked to respect wildlife and observe park rules: don't hike alone; do not take along a dog; stay in open areas wherever possible; never go near a bear or bear cub; keep campsites clean; and store food away from tent or in the trunk of your car. Visitors should keep a safe distance from bears, moose, elk and other large animals and practice safe camping rules. Consult local authorities for current warnings. Detailed information is available at all visitor centres and park offices. Avoid hypothermia. Beware of wind, dampness and exhaustion in regions where weather changes rapidly; carry weatherproof clothing, plastic sheeting and nylon twine for emergency shelter; and eat high-calorie foods.

©iStockphoto.com/Matt Naylor

Banff National Park

A good reference for planning a visit to Canada's national parks is Roberta Bondar's **Passionate Vision: Discovering Canada's National Parks** *(Douglas & McIntyre, Ltd., 2000).*

DISCOUNTS

For Students and Youths

Student discounts are frequently available for travel, entertainment and admissions. Age eligibility varies: child rates usually apply for up to 12 years old; youth rates from 12–17. With a valid student card, any student 12 years and older can obtain an International Student Identity Card for discounts on rail travel and more. (Available at many ViaRail stations, or online from www.isic.org.)

For Senior Citizens

Many attractions, hotels, restaurants, entertainment venues and public transportation systems offer discounts to visitors age 62 or older (proof of age may be required). Canada's national parks usually offer discount fees for seniors. Although Canada has no national organization for retirees or older citizens, visiting seniors should feel free to ask specific businesses if such a discount is available.

Books

The Group of Seven and Tom Thomson. David P. Silcox. (2006)
Nearly 400 colour reproductions illustrate how Canada's best known artists interpreted their deeply personal views of their surroundings, and how they were influenced by one another's styles.

Canada's Century: An Illustrated History of the People and Events that Shaped Our Identity. Carl Mollins. (2001).
Selected articles from 2,500 issues published by *Maclean's* magazine since its inception in 1905 provide an interesting historical perspective through well-organized tidbits of news and commentary.

Canadians are Not Americans: Myths and Literary Traditions. Katherine L. Morrison. (2003)
Examines both country's national views of history, home, humour, law, religion, race and class to provide insights as to why Canadians differ from Americans.

Canadians: A portrait of a country and its people. Roy MacGregor. (2007).
Entertaining insight into what makes a Canadian: anecdotes and reflective writing about recent historical topics from the perspective of an accomplished journalist.

Notes from the Century Before: A Journal from British Columbia. Edward Hoagland. (2002)
The author's three-month exploration of northwestern BC blends his observations of the land and people with those of the current inhabitants.

Plant Technology of the First Peoples of British Columbia. Nancy Turner. (2001).
Explains how First Peoples used plant materials for the necessities of life—clothing, transportation, heat, shelter, nets, ropes, and containers—as well as for insect repellents, cleansing agents, scents and recreational activities.

Nitsitapiisinni: The Story of the Blackfoot People. Glenbow Museum (2001).
Produced by The Blackfoot Gallery Committee of Calgary's Glenbow Museum, this book chronicles all the important aspects of Blackfoot life and history.

Roughing It in the Bush. Susanna Moodie. (1852, 1997).
Land agents eager to attract immigrants painted Canada as a promised land; this still very readable account by the wife of a military officer describing the harsh reality of daily pioneer life caused a sensation when it was first published in 1852.

Films

Titles listed below represent recent filmmaking highlights.

The Sweet Hereafter (1997)
A small community is torn apart by tragedy that takes the lives of most of the town's children.

The Red Violin (1998)
Epic tells of lives touched by a mysterious violin over three centuries.

Last Night (1998)
Residents in a Canadian city come to terms with news that the world will come to an end at midnight.

Le Cœur au Poing (1999; French)
A young woman tries to break free from her social isolation by devising provocative means of sharing experiences with strangers.

Stardom (2000)
Young female hockey player evolves to celebrity status and scandal as a successful fashion model.

Possible Worlds (2000)
Portrays the permutations of George Barber's life in parallel universes.

Atanarjuat (The Fast Runner) (2001)
Canada's first feature-length film in an aboriginal language (English and French subtitles) depicts the disruptive impact of long-standing hatred between two Inuit families in Nunavut.

Waydowntown (2002)
Four young office workers each bet a month's salary to see who can go the longest without leaving their downtown apartment-office-shopping complex.

Man with Brooms (2002)
Antics of four old curling buddies who reunite to realize their late coach's dream of winning a big trophy.

The Corporation (2003)
Documentary examines the impact of how a corporation, legally defined as a person, can operate without the moral responsibility expected of individuals.

Useful French Words

anse	cove, bay
autoroute	highway
baie	bay
belvédère	viewpoint
cap	cape
centre d'accueil	welcome centre
centre d'interprétation	interpretation centre
chute	waterfall
côte	shore, coast
croisière	cruise, boat trip
Est	East
église	church
gare	train station
hôtel de ville	city hall
île	island
jardin	garden
lac	lake
maison	house
manoir	manor
métro	subway
monastère	monastery
mont	mount
montagne	mountain
moulin	mill
musée	museum
Nord	North
Ouest	West
palais de justice	courthouse
parc	park
phare	lighthouse
place	square
plage	beach
pont	bridge
rapides	rapids
réserve faunique	wildlife conservation area
rivière	river
rocher	rock
rue	street
stationnement	parking
Sud	South
téléphérique	gondola
traversier	ferry boat
vallée	valley
ville	city, town

BASIC INFORMATION

Electricity

120 volts, 60 cycles. Most small American appliances can be used. European appliances require an electrical transformer, available at electric supply stores.

Emergencies

Most Canadian cities and many rural areas have 911 telephone service for emergency response. When 911 is dialled from any telephone in a served area, a central dispatch office sees the dialling location and can redirect the call to the appropriate emergency response agency—fire department, police or ambulance. Much of rural Canada is not within range of cellular telephone service, and although coverage extends along most major highways, service can be unreliable in mountainous regions.

Public Safety Canada maintains extensive links to information and services on public safety: www.safecanada.ca.

Mail/Post

Post offices across Canada are generally open Monday to Friday 8am–5:30pm; extended hours are available in some locations. Sample rates for first-class mail (letter or postcard; up to 30 grams): within Canada, 52 cents; to the US, 93 cents; international mail, $1.55. Mail service for all but local deliveries is by air. Visitors can receive mail c/o "General Delivery" addressed to Main Post Office, City, Province and Postal Code. Mail will be held for 15 days and has to be picked up by the addressee. Some post offices have fax services, and all post offices offer international courier service. Postal facilities are located at selected Canadian retailers throughout the country. For information regarding postal codes or locations of facilities call ☎866-607-6301; www.canadapost.ca.

Money

Canadian currency is based on the decimal system (100 cents to the dollar). Bills are issued in $5, $10, $20, $50, $100, $500 and $1,000 denominations; coins are minted in 1 cent, 5 cents, 10 cents, 25 cents, $1 and $2. Exchange money at banking institutions for the most favourable exchange rate.

You don't need to carry much cash while visiting Canada: ATM machines are widely available, and most merchants accept debit or credit cards. Self-serve gas, parking lots and even store check-outs are common. Do carry a few "loonies" or "toonies" – the $1 and $2 coins – for parking meters, tips and snacks. Most public telephones accept calling cards at no charge, but local calls cost 25–50¢ (one or two quarters). Most ATMs dispense cash in increments of $20.

BANKS

Banking institutions are generally open Monday to Friday 9am–5pm. Some banks are open on Saturday morning. Banks at large airports have foreign exchange counters and extended hours. Some institutions may charge a small fee for cashing traveller's cheques. Most principal bank cards are honoured at affiliated Canadian banks.

🖰Use bank branded ATM machines to avoid the higher fees charged by private operators.

CREDIT CARDS AND TRAVELLER'S CHEQUES

The following major credit cards are accepted in Canada: American Express, Carte Blanche, Discover, Diners Club, MasterCard/Eurocard and Visa. Most banks will cash traveller's cheques and process cash advances on major credit cards with proper personal identification.

CURRENCY EXCHANGE

The most favourable exchange rate can usually be obtained at branch offices of a national bank. Some banks charge a small fee for this transaction. Private exchange companies generally charge higher fees. Airports and visitor centres in large cities may have exchange outlets as do some hotels. The Canadian dollar fluctuates with the international money market. Exchange facilities tend to be limited in rural and remote areas. If arriving in Canada late in the day or on a weekend, visitors may wish to exchange some funds prior to arrival (a few banks are open on Saturday mornings in major cities, however).

😊You can use ATMs to withdraw Canadian currency from your home account, but check with your bank first to see if it has reciprocal arrangements with a Canadian bank for a lower fee.

TAXES

Canada levies a 5% Goods and Services Tax (GST) on most goods and services. Provinces (except Alberta) levy additional taxes ranging from 6–8% on some goods and services.

Public Holidays

For provincial holidays see regional introductions. The following holidays are observed throughout Canada. Most banks, government offices and schools are closed:

New Year's Day:
    January 1
Good Friday:
    Friday before Easter Sunday
Easter Monday:
    Monday after Easter Sunday
Victoria Day:
    Closest Monday to May 24

Canada Day: July 1
Labour Day:
    1st Monday in September
Thanksgiving:
    2nd Monday in October
Remembrance Day:
    2nd Wednesday in November
Christmas Day:
    December 25
Boxing Day:
    December 26

Smoking

All Canadian provinces and territories have enacted comprehensive smoke-free legislation, and municipal bylaws are commonplace. Smoking has been banned from aircraft, buses, trains and most offices for some time, but restrictions for other public spaces vary: for example, Quebec's 2006 legislation banned smoking in bars, restaurants, taverns, casinos, on school grounds and within nine metres of any exterior door of a health, social services or educational institution—yet smoking is still allowed on outdoor patios. Smoking in public places is increasingly unacceptable; if you want to smoke, ask before you light up.

Telephones

To call long distance within Canada and to the US, dial 1+ area code + number. For overseas calls, refer to the country codes in most telephone directories, or dial "0" for operator assistance. All operators speak English and French. Collect calls and credit card calls can be made from public pay phones. For local directory assistance, check the white pages of the phone directory or dial 411; outside the local area code dial 1+ area code + 555-1212. Telephone numbers that start with **800, 866, 877** or **888** are toll-free *(no charge)*. A local call costs 25 to 50 cents. Be aware that many hotels place a surcharge on all calls.

Emergency Numbers

911 service is operative in major cities; otherwise dial "0" for the operator and ask for the police. In most provinces a Tourist Alert Program is operated by the Royal Canadian Mounted Police from June until September. If you see your name in the newspaper or hear it on the radio, contact the nearest RCMP office immediately.

Time

Canada spans six time zones, but the coast-to-coast time difference is only 4hrs 30min because Newfoundland time is 30min in advance of the Maritime provinces, which are on Atlantic Time. Daylight Saving Time (clocks are advanced 1 hour) is in effect from the second Sunday in March to the first Sunday in November (*see regional introductions for details*).

Tips

Tips or service charges are not normally added to a bill in Canada. However, it is customary in Canada to a tip (a small gift of money) for services received from food servers, porters, hotel mails and taxi drivers. In restaurants and for taxi drivers, it is customary to tip 10-15% of the total amount of the bill. At hotels, porters should be tipped $1 per bag, and maids $1 per night.

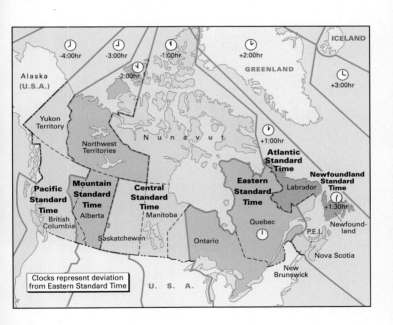

Clocks represent deviation from Eastern Standard Time

Two Jack Lake, Banff National Park
Tourism Alberta

NATURE

Covering nearly 10 million sq km/3.9 million sq mi, Canada is the second largest country in the world in terms of physical size. It is exceeded only by Russia, whose landmass totals some 17 million sq km/6.6 million sq mi. Having shores on three oceans (Atlantic, Pacific and Arctic), Canada occupies most of the northern part of the North American continent. Yet its inhabitants, largely concentrated along the Canadian/US border, number only about 32 million. The country is divided into 10 provinces and three territories.

Spanning six time zones, the country stretches from latitude 41°47'N at **Pelee Island** in Lake Erie (the same latitude as Rome, Italy) to 83°07'N at **Cape Columbia** on Ellesmere Island, a mere 800km/500mi from the North Pole. This north-south extension of about 4,600km/2,900mi is countered only by its width. Canada covers more than 5,500km/3,400mi from **Cape Spear** in Newfoundland (longitude 52°37'W) to the **Yukon/Alaska** border (141°W). One of the most remarkable features is the immense bite cut out of the coastline by **Hudson Bay,** named for famed British explorer Henry Hudson. This enormous gulf or inland sea (637,000sq km/245,946sq mi) could be considered part of either the Atlantic Ocean or the Arctic Ocean. In common with the US, Canada shares another noteworthy feature—the **Great Lakes,** which together form the largest body of fresh water in the world. Finally, the country is characterized by its extremely mountainous western rim.

See also the introduction for each province or territory.

Geologic Past

THE GREAT ICE AGES

The physiographic regions described below have been extensively modified in more recent geological times by the advance and retreat of glacial ice. Four times during the past million years, the North American climate has become progressively colder. Snowfall became increasingly heavy in the north and was gradually compressed into ice. This ice began to flow south, reaching as far as the Ohio and Missouri river valleys in the US before retreating. At peak coverage, 97 percent of Canada was submerged under ice up to 3km/2mi deep at the centre and 1.6km/1mi deep at the edges. Only the Cypress Hills and the Klondike region of the Yukon escaped this cover. The last Ice Age receded more than 10,000 years ago.

A sheet of ice of such thickness exerts a great deal of pressure on the earth below. As the ice from each glacial advance retreated, hollows were scoured out of the land and filled with water, and mountain ranges were worn away and sculptured. Today about 2 percent of Canada is covered by glacial ice, mainly in the Arctic islands, but glaciers are found in the western mountains (Columbia Icefield and St. Elias Mountains).

Major Natural Regions

Physiographically, Canada has at its centre a massive upland known as the Canadian Shield, which forms the geological platform for the whole country. This upland is partially surrounded by areas of lowland that in turn are rimmed by mountain ranges on three of Canada's four sides; to the south the country lies open to the US. Only in parts of the north do these mountain rims flatten out to form a coastal plain. Seven major physiographic regions can be distinguished.

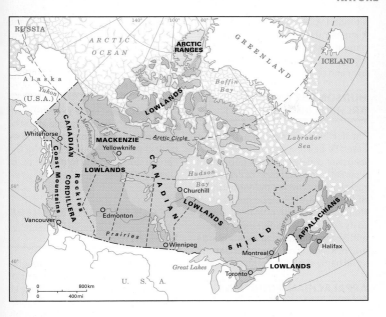

THE CANADIAN SHIELD

This massive horseshoe-shaped region surrounding Hudson Bay encompasses nearly half of Canada's area. The terrain is formed of ancient, hard rocks of the **Precambrian** era (over 500 million years old) known for their great rigidity and strength. This strength and the region's shape are the origin of the name "Shield." The region is characterized by its innumerable lakes and rivers (Canada possesses as much as a quarter of the world's total supply of fresh water, largely concentrated in the Shield), by its rugged nature (a combination of rock and bog that makes much of the area inaccessible) and by its lack of agricultural soil. However, the region is also the source of much of the country's extensive mineral, forest and hydroelectric wealth.

GREAT LAKES/ ST. LAWRENCE LOWLANDS

Despite their comparatively small size, these lowlands, which extend south into one of the great industrial and agricultural belts of the continent, are home to over 50 percent of the country's inhabitants. They were created in **Palaeozoic** times (200 million–500 million years ago) when great stretches of the region were flooded by the sea for long periods. During this flooding thousands of feet of sedimentary rock accumulated on top of the Canadian Shield, providing fertile soil that has made the region important for agriculture today. This factor, combined with a favourable climate and proximity to the US, has made these lowlands Canada's richest and most industrialized area as well as its most populous.

PRAIRIES AND MACKENZIE LOWLANDS

The geologic history of these lowlands is similar to those of the Great Lakes/St. Lawrence region. Material eroded from the Shield and the marginal mountains (in particular, the Rockies) was first deposited in shallow seas. Subsequently swept by glaciers, the flat plains in the south consist of fertile soils ideal for wheat and general farming. The Mackenzie Lowlands begin north of a low divide between the Saskatchewan and Athabasca rivers, and support little agriculture because of their northerly latitude. In places where the Mackenzie Plain joins the Shield, a series of large natural basins form great lakes—Winnipeg, Athabasca, Great Slave, Great Bear and others.

HUDSON BAY AND ARCTIC ARCHIPELAGO LOWLANDS

The northern counterpart of the Great Lakes/St. Lawrence region, these lowlands are widely scattered portions of a partially drowned plain of Palaeozoic rock that once covered the northern part of the Shield. They slope gently away from the Shield with little relief. Owing to its northerly latitude, severe climate and frozen soil, this area supports little except a vegetation of moss, lichens and small hardy shrubs in sheltered areas.

APPALACHIAN MOUNTAINS

About 200 million years ago, these mountains, which stretch from Alabama in the US to Newfoundland, were the first to be folded on the edges of the continent. Since then, extensive erosion by ice, rivers and sea has reduced them to mere stumps of their former heights. Today the region is a series of generally flat to rounded uplands, with few sharp peaks rising to no more than 1,280m/4,200ft. Prince Edward Island, and the Annapolis, Ristigouche and Saint John River valleys are notable areas of plains where ancient glacial lakes have left fertile soil.

CANADIAN CORDILLERA

The Canadian Cordillera consists of five major parts (from east to west): the Rocky Mountains, the interior basins and plateaus, the Coast Mountains, the Inside Passage along the coast and, finally, the outer system of islands. Covering the western quarter of the country, this great sweep of mountains is part of North America's long mountain system known as the **Western Cordillera.**

The Canadian Cordillera is a relatively recent geological development. About 70 million years ago, enormous earth forces thrust these mountains up with a great deal of faulting, folding and vol-

canic activity. Since then, erosion and uplifting by glaciers, and partial drowning by sea have produced a deeply indented coast.

ARCTIC RANGES

These mountains in the extreme north of the country probably rose after the Appalachians. They consist of two fairly distinct parts: the rounded hills of the Parry Islands and the folded peaks of Ellesmere Island.

Geographical Features

VEGETATION

The flora of Canada consists of roughly 4,200 species, about 30 percent of which have been introduced. The tree line crosses Canada in a rough diagonal from the Mackenzie Delta to Hudson Bay and the Atlantic. The **tundra** lies north of this line, a land of lichens, sedges and stunted shrubs. Because the growing season is too short to allow vegetation to germinate and produce seed, most flowering plants are small perennials, sprouting large flowers to attract insect pollinators. Farther north, ice and bare rock dominate, yet some hardy species flourish here, growing as dense mats wherever moisture, heat and nutrients create favourable microhabitats.

South of the tree line, the **boreal forest** of spruce, tamarack and other conifers gradually begins, interspersed with innumerable bogs, marshes and other wetlands. Farther south, broadleaf trees such as birch, aspen and poplar appear, and some wetlands support commercial cranberry and blueberry farms. More deciduous trees are found until **mixed forest** predominates.

In the east, forestry, agriculture and urbanization have left only isolated pockets of old-growth forest. Hardwoods such as maple, birch and beech compete for well-drained soils with commercial stands of conifers like spruce and pine, while stands of cedar and alder occupy wetter areas. Only in Southern Ontario are the conifers of the north completely left behind and a true **deciduous forest**

Canadian Burnet

Mountain goat

exists. The remaining wetlands support cattails, water lilies, sedges and ferns, as well as successful alien species like purple loosestrife, which came from Europe some 200 years ago as seeds in cattle fodder.

In the west, conifers give way to vast groves of aspen and poplar as one travels south from the tree line, until trees almost completely disappear once again, replaced by rolling prairie **grasslands.** The region is now highly cultivated, producing much of Canada's grain crops, so that only scattered remnants of the natural grasses remain in their native state. The mountain region of the West also has its own vegetation pattern, the trees thinning out as they approach the alpine tree line in the same way as they do in the North. Along the Pacific Coast, temperate rain forests with the highest biomass per hectare on earth flourish due to a combination of year-round mild temperatures and very heavy rainfall. As clouds move eastward, they deposit most of their moisture on western slopes, leaving pockets of the interior mountain region dry and dominated by sparse grasses, sagebrush and cactus.

WILDLIFE

Canada's varied landscape hosts several species of animals typical of

regional fauna. Vast forests provide habitat for **white-tailed deer, black-tailed deer** and **mule deer,** while **wapiti,** also known as the American elk, populate mountainous terrain and prairieland. Largest of the deer family is a distinctively Canadian animal, the **moose,** which inhabits the forests of Newfoundland west to British Columbia, as do **woodland caribou,** another member of the deer family. Also distinct is the Canada **lynx,** previously located throughout the country but now surviving in the northern mainland and in Newfoundland. Rare in Canada is the **wolverine** (of the weasel family), found in sparse populations in the western and northern part of the country. The **grizzly bear** and particularly the **black bear** are common denizens of Canada's coniferous and deciduous forests. Trapped nearly to extinction, **beavers** once again thrive across Canada, occupying the streams and ponds of forested regions. Once common to forest, prairies and tundra, **wolves** reside primarily in the northern wilderness.

Populating Arctic coasts and islands are **polar bears** that feed on Canada's varied **seal** population, such as the grey, harp and hooded seals. Over 30 species of **whales** ply Canada's coastal waters, including the humpback and fin (off Newfoundland); the orca and the grey (off British Columbia); and the beluga, blue, fin and minke (St. Lawrence estuary). The Arctic tundra supports **musk-oxen,** lemmings, foxes and wolves as well as barren-ground caribou.

Wildlife of the prairies includes the **gopher, jackrabbit** and **grouse** in addition to **pronghorns** and **bison** (cattle family), known more commonly in North America as buffalo. Once numbering in the millions, bison were nearly extinct by 1885, hunted for their hides and meat. Wood Buffalo National Park protects a large population today.

Roaming the mountains of western Canada are **mountain goats** and mountain sheep. Thinhorn or **Dall sheep** are found along Canada's Alaska Highway, while **bighorn sheep** frequent British Columbia's south-central ranges and the Canadian Rocky Mountains.

Canada's bird population ranges from waterfowl such as the Canada goose, Atlantic puffin and piping plover to the interior's peregrine falcon and rare whooping crane. The **bald eagle** breeds in parts of northern and eastern Canada, but is most commonly seen along the British Columbia coast. Although most species are migratory, over 400 species of birds have been documented as breeding in Canada.

CLIMATE

Canada's climate is as varied and extreme as its geography. In a large area of the country, winter lasts longer than summer, yet the latter, when it comes, can be very hot. In the north, long hours of daylight in the summer cause prolific plant growth. The central provinces of Canada receive the most snow, far more than the Arctic, which in fact receives the least precipitation of any region.

One major factor influencing climate is proximity to large bodies of water: chiefly, the Pacific and Atlantic oceans, Hudson Bay and the Great Lakes. Such expanses tend to make winters warmer and summers cooler. Regions distant to them are inclined, therefore, to have much colder winters and hotter summers. But terrain is also a factor. In the West the high Coast Mountains shield the interior of British Columbia and the Yukon from the mild and moist Pacific air, making their climate more extreme than their location would indicate. The Rockies intensify this trend, leaving the prairies vulnerable to both Arctic winds and hot southern breezes.

Each regional introduction has a summary of climatic conditions with average summer temperatures and precipitation.

Floral Emblems of the Canadian Provinces and Territories

Traditionally, the flora selected to represent a territory or province in Canada must be fairly prevalent within that province or territory. Tree branches or leaves, as well as flowers, may serve as emblems. Floral emblems typically appear on provincial or territorial flags, coats of arms or other official seals.

Canada	sugar maple
Alberta	wild (or prickly) rose
British Columbia	Pacific dogwood
Manitoba	prairie crocus (or crocus anemone)
New Brunswick	purple violet
Newfoundland	pitcher plant
Northwest Territories	mountain avens
Nova Scotia	mayflower
Nunavut	arctic poppy
Ontario	white trillium
Prince Edward Island	pink lady's slipper
Quebec	Madonna lily
Saskatchewan	western red (or prairie) lily
Yukon	fireweed

HISTORY

Immigration and exploration have shaped Canada's history, with archaeological evidence of people in the northwest some 26,000 years ago. Vikings settled briefly in Newfoundland 1,000 years ago, and Europeans established temporary settlements as they fished the rich Gulf of Saint Lawrence some 500 years ago. Reports of abundant natural resources from French and English explorers led to colonization and brought European conflicts to the New World, with alliances on either side with various aboriginal peoples. The fur trade pushed exploration westward, and by the late 1800s, completion of a transcontinental railroad enabled the Dominion of Canada to extend to the Pacific Ocean.

See also the introduction for each province or territory.

Prehistory to Present

PREHISTORIC AND NATIVE PEOPLES

Man is not indigenous to North America. According to recent archaeological findings, prehistoric tribes from the mountains of Mongolia and the steppes of Siberia came to the continent some 15,000 to 26,000 years ago by a land bridge that once existed over the **Bering Strait**. They gradually moved south across the whole continent and into South America. Their descendants are the native Indian and Inuit peoples of Canada today, and they can be divided into six groups.

The **Northwest Coast tribes** constituted a highly developed civilization, well known for its totem poles and other carved objects. Principal tribal groups are the Bella Coola, Coast Salish, Haida, Kwakiutl, Nootka (along the West Coast), Tlingit and Tsimshian (including the Gitxsan). Also known as the Plateau culture (named after the Columbian Plateau region), the **Cordillera Indians** eked out an existence in the British Columbia interior as hunters and fishermen. The Athapaskan, Salishan and Kutenai language families are indigenous to this native culture. The **Plains Indians**—the Assiniboine, Stoney, Blackfoot, Plains Cree, Plains Ojibwa and Sarcee tribes—were nomadic buffalo hunters who lived in teepees and wore decorative clothing made of animal skins.

The Beothuk, Cree, Dene, Montagnais and other **subarctic Indians** lived a nomadic existence hunting caribou and other animals. The Algonquin and the Iroquoian peoples formed the **Eastern Woodlands** culture of bellicose farmers who lived in fortified villages, growing corn and squash. Nomadic inhabitants of the most northerly regions, the **Inuit** traditionally lived in ice houses in winter, and in tents and sod houses during the summer. Using their highly developed navigational skills, they hunted seals and whales off the coast, and caribou and waterfowl in the interior.

FIRST CONTACT

Long after the migrations of Asiatic peoples from the west, Europeans arrived on the shores of present-day Canada and proceeded to conquer the land and impose their own civilization. The Norse explored the coast of Labrador in the 10C and are believed to have founded the earliest known European settlement in North America around AD 1000. Basque and English fishermen knew of the rich resources of the Grand Banks as early as the 15C.

However, the first permanent settlements began in the 17C. Within seven years of each other (1603-10), Frenchman **Samuel de Champlain** and Englishmen Henry Hudson (who, in 1610, discovered the huge waterway that bears his name) and John Guy claimed the riches of the continent for their respective kings. Their claims led to nearly two centuries of war among the empires of France and England and the indigenous peoples for hegemony. The rivalry in North America

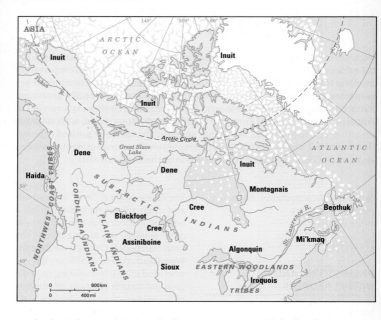

revolved mainly around the lucrative fur trade. In 1713 the **Treaty of Utrecht** secured a temporary peace that lasted until the **Seven Years' War** (1756-63), in which France, Spain, Austria and Russia opposed Britain and Prussia. Before their final defeat by the British on the **Plains of Abraham** in 1759, the French not only established enduring settlements in the St. Lawrence Valley, but also explored half the continent, founding an empire known as **New France**, which, at its greatest extent, stretched from Hudson Bay to New Orleans (Louisiana) and from Newfoundland nearly to the Rockies. This empire thrived on the

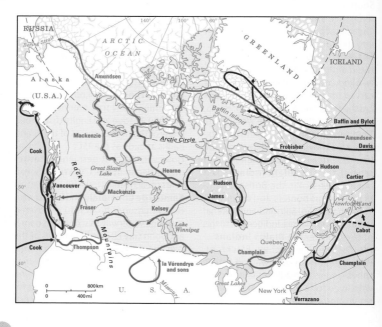

fur trade. However, England's **Hudson's Bay Company (HBC),** founded in 1670, gained control of all the lands draining into the great bay and exercised a monopoly over that area, challenged only by Scottish merchants who established themselves in Montreal after the British conquest of France and formed the **North West Company** in 1783.

TOWARD CONFEDERATION

In 1763, when the fall of New France was confirmed by the **Treaty of Paris**, the population of the future confederation of Canada was overwhelmingly French. A few settlements in Newfoundland and Halifax in Nova Scotia were the only English-speaking exceptions. This imbalance was not to endure. The aftermath of the American Revolution brought thousands of **Loyalists** to the remaining British colonies (Nova Scotia, Prince Edward Island and Lower Canada, later named Quebec) and led to the creation of two more colonies—New Brunswick and Upper Canada (later Ontario).

Lower Canada and Upper Canada were reunited by the British Parliament's **Act of Union** in 1841. This law was prompted by a report by then-governor general Lord Durham, based upon his investigation of the 1837 rebellions in which Americans had participated. In addition to recommending union, the report proposed **responsible government,** a system of majority-party rule in the assembly (the British government did not formally implement this system until 1847), partly in the hope of reducing American influence.

Threats and incursions by Americans during the War of 1812, the Rebellions of 1837, the American Civil War and the Fenian Raids of 1866-70 convinced the British government that more settlers were needed if their colonies were to survive. The policy of offering free land to potential settlers played a significant role in the development of Canada during the 19C and early 20C.

Fear of American takeover encouraged the small groups of British colonists to unite for common defence. Their actions helped to propel the British Parliament into ratifying the **British North America Act** of 1867, which provided for **Canadian Confederation**. The resulting new political entity, initially composed of four founding provinces—**Ontario, Quebec, New Brunswick** and **Nova Scotia**—adopted a parliamentary system of government and separation of federal and provincial powers. Even as confederation was negotiated, chief proponents John A. Macdonald and George-Étienne Cartier envisaged a dominion stretching from coast to coast. Between the eastern provinces and the small colony of British Columbia on the West Coast lay the immense, empty domain of the Hudson's Bay Company. Pressured by the British government, the company finally agreed to relinquish its lands to the new Confederation for a cash settlement and rights to its posts and some land. As the new Dominion of Canada took possession, the Métis rebellion in the Red River Valley led to the creation of the fifth province, **Manitoba,** in 1870. Meanwhile, **British Columbia** began negotiations to become the sixth province, prompted by fear of an American takeover, and **Prince Edward Island** joined its sister Maritime provinces in Confederation in 1873. The Yukon Territory was created in 1898 and entered Confederation in the same year.

"Canada has been created because there has existed within the hearts of its people a determination to build for themselves an enduring home."

A.R.M. Lower, *Colony to Nation,* 1946

THE TRANSCONTINENTAL RAILWAY

To encourage British Columbia to join Confederation in 1871, the province was promised a transcontinental rail link. After a few false starts, construction of the **Canadian Pacific Railway** finally got under way in 1881. It was an immense and difficult project, the western mountain ranges alone posing a formidable barrier. Building the line over the steep grades of **Kicking Horse Pass,** for example, was one of the great achievements of railroad engineering.

Rogers Pass and **Fraser Canyon** were only slightly lesser obstacles.

Serious problems beset the laying of track in the Canadian Shield country north of Lake Superior, where, at one moment, tonnes of granite had to be blasted out and, at the next, track lines would sink into the muskeg. In the Prairies, however, all records for tracklaying were broken: in one day, a total of 10km/6mi were laid, a record never surpassed by manual labour. This progress was achieved under the dynamic management of American-born **William Van Horne,** who later became president of the Canadian Pacific Railway Co. In only four years, the line was completed.

THE 20TH CENTURY

Canada's purchase of land controlled by the HBC opened the way for settlement of the West; the building of the transcontinental rail line provided the means. Thousands of immigrants poured into the region, necessitating the creation of two new provinces in 1905: **Saskatchewan** and **Alberta.** By 1912 the remaining parts of the Northwest Territories south of the 60th parallel had been redistributed to Manitoba, Ontario and Quebec.

Canada played a substantial role in both world wars, and finally achieved complete control of its external affairs in 1931 by the **Statute of Westminster,** a British law that clarified Canada's parliamentary powers. After World War II Canada's tenth province was added when the citizens of **Newfoundland** voted to join Confederation in 1949. In the postwar years Canada found itself becoming a major industrial country, with an influx of immigrants who provided the skills and labour vital to economic growth.

The 1960s saw the beginnings of Quebec's **separatist movement,** resulting from cumulative grievances of French Canadians. The federal government accelerated efforts to accommodate Quebeckers' demands, including broader educational funding and official recognition of the French language. In 1969 institutional bilingualism was established at the federal level by the Official Languages Act. Separatists were defeated at the provincial polls in 1973, but were victorious in 1976. In 1980 the Quebec electorate rejected a move toward independence, but the controversy continued.

In 1982 the British North American Act (1867) was renamed the Constitution Act, which repatriated the constitution from London. Quebec refused to sign the constitution, mainly because the agreement did not provide for transfer of legislative powers between federal and provincial governments. In 1987 the **Meech Lake Accord** called for special status for Quebec. Federal and provincial ratification was not forthcoming by 1990, however. In 1992 a national referendum that would have granted special constitutional status to Quebec was defeated, but the movement toward independence gained support within Quebec. Secession from Canada was narrowly defeated in the fall of 1995 by voters in the province by a margin of just over 1 percent. In 1998 Canada's Supreme Court declared that, under constitutional law, Quebec has no legal right of unilateral secession.

Canada's native population continues to press for autonomy and land settlements. A goal of the **Assembly of First Nations** (AFN), representing some 500,000 of the country's nearly one-million-strong native population, is constitutionally guaranteed rights of self-government. The defeated 1992 referendum included a provision for self-governing powers for natives. In a plebiscite earlier that year, however, Northwest Territories voters approved proposed boundaries of a new territory to be formed in the eastern part of the region. A large majority (84.7 percent) of the region's voters ratified terms of the Land Claim Agreement in November as the final step in dividing the Northwest Territories. After a seven-year transitional period, the self-administered Inuit homeland called Nunavut became Canada's third territory, in April 1999.

THE NEW MILLENNIUM

Many of the same issues of the past century face Canadians as the new millennium begins. The **Nisga'a Treaty** signed in April 2000 is considered by some Canadians to be a contentious model for self-governance for other native peoples. In addition to providing law-making powers for British Columbia's Nisga'a over their lands, assets, language and culture, the treaty includes cash payments and control over natural resources. Critics fear that overall costs of treaties based on this model will be too high and that clear definitions of territory claimed by other First Nations groups will be difficult to achieve.

In June 2000 Canada's political landscape changed with the emergence of the Canadian Alliance Party. An initiative of the western-based Reform Party, this new entity challenged the domain of the Progressive Conservatives, one of the country's two founding political parties. The parties agreed to merge in 2003, forming the new Conservative Party of Canada. Despite their hopes this move would unite the right, the new party was unable to unseat the governing Liberals in the 2004 general election. However, political scandals and party discord weakened the Liberals, and the January 2006 election resulted in a minority Conservative government.

Sovereignist politicians in Quebec have vowed to try yet again for a mandate to separate the province from Canada. The issue shows no sign of disappearing. Multiculturalism is nothing new to Canada, a nation of great ethnic and racial diversity. It remains to be seen, however, if the current socio-political upheaval and continuing introspection will fracture national unity or restore it.

Time Line

PRE-COLONIAL PERIOD

20,000-15,000BC — Estimated earliest human crossings of the land bridge across the Bering Strait from Mongolia to present-day Alaska.

c. AD 1000 — Norse reach Newfoundland.

1492 — Christopher Columbus lands on San Salvador.

1497 — **John Cabot** explores east coast of Canada.

NEW FRANCE

1534 — **Jacques Cartier** claims Canada for France.

1565 — St. Augustine, Florida, the oldest city in the US, is founded by Spaniards.

1583 — Sir Humphrey Gilbert claims Newfoundland for England.

1605 — Samuel de **Champlain** establishes **Port Royal.**

1610 — **Henry Hudson** enters Hudson Bay.

1620 — Pilgrims found Plymouth, Massachusetts.

1670 — **Hudson's Bay Company** is formed.

1713 — Treaty of Utrecht is signed. France cedes Acadia to Britain.

1722 — **Six Nations Iroquois Confederacy** is formed.

1730s-40s — La Vérendrye family explores Canadian West.

1755 — Acadian Deportation from Nova Scotia begins.

1756-63 — Seven Years' War.

1759 — British defeat the French in Quebec City.

1763 — **Treaty of Paris** is signed. France cedes New France to Britain.

BRITISH REGIME

1775 — War of Independence begins in American colonies.

1778 — James Cook explores coast of British Columbia.

1783 — American colonies gain independence from Britain. Loyalists migrate to Canada.

1791 — **Constitutional Act** creates Upper Canada (Ontario) and Lower Canada (Quebec).

1793 — Alexander Mackenzie crosses British Columbia to the West Coast.

1812-14 — War of 1812.

1837 — Rebellions in Upper and Lower Canada.

1841 — **Act of Union** creates the United Province of Canada.

Historic Urban Plans

Montreal Map 1768

1847 — **Responsible government** system is implemented in Canada.

1848 — California Gold Rush begins.

1858-61 — British Columbia's gold rushes.

1861-65 — American Civil War.

CANADIAN CONFEDERATION

1867 — British North America Act establishes Canadian Confederation.

1869-70 — Riel Rebellion occurs in Red River Valley.

1870 — Canadian Confederation buys Hudson's Bay Company land; Manitoba is created.

1872 — **Dominion Lands Act** is passed.

1873 — North West Mounted Police established.

1881-85 — Canadian Pacific Railway is constructed.

1885 — Northwest Rebellion occurs. Canada's **first national park** is created.

1896 — Gold is discovered in the Klondike.

1914-18 — World War I.

1931 — **Statute of Westminster** grants Canada control of external affairs.

1939-45 — World War II. Canada receives large numbers of European immigrants.

1942 — Alaska Highway is completed.

CONTEMPORARY CANADA

1959 — **St. Lawrence Seaway** is opened.

1962 — Trans-Canada Highway is completed.

1968 — Québécois Party is founded.

1982 — **Constitution Act** is passed. Quebec refuses to sign the new constitution.

1987 — **Meech Lake Accord** calls for special status for Quebec.

1990 — Manitoba and Newfoundland refuse to sign Meech Lake Accord. Quebec refuses to sign 1982 constitution. **Oka**, Quebec, is site of armed conflict between Mohawks and Canadian government over native land claims.

1992 — A national referendum to grant Quebec special status is defeated. Voters in Northwest Territories ratify land claim agreements, a key step to Nunavut's establishment.

1993 — Negotiation of **North American Free Trade Agreement** (NAFTA) among Canada, Mexico and the US.

1994 — Approved by Canada, Mexico and the US, NAFTA takes effect Jan 1.

Courtesy Royal Canadian Mounted Police

Royal Canadian Mounted Police

1995 — Quebecers vote by a narrow margin (50.6 percent to 49.4 percent) not to grant the provincial government the mandate to negotiate secession from the rest of Canada.

1996 — Canada's last census of the century is conducted in May. The country's population stands at 28.8 million.

1998 — Canada experiences its worst ice storm in the country's history. Some 3.5 million people in Quebec, Ontario and New Brunswick are without power.

1999 — Self-administration for the new territory of **Nunavut** officially begins. In business for 130 years, Eaton's (a department store chain) files for bankruptcy.

THE NEW MILLENNIUM

2000 — Newfoundland commemorates Norse landing 1,000 years earlier. Landmark federal treaty with British Columbia's **Nisga'a** native people becomes law, granting them a form of self-governance.

2001 — A nationwide **census** confirms a population of 29.5 million in Canada. Federal and Quebec elections renew debate about Quebec sovereignty.

2002 — Canadian troops join international peacekeeping mission in Afghanistan.

2003 — Months of negotiations result in the merger of the Canadian Alliance and Progressive Conservative Party, uniting Canada's right under the banner of the Conservative Party of Canada.

2004 — After a tightly-fought election, the Liberal party forms the first minority government in 25 years.

2005 — Haitian-born broadcaster **Michaëlle Jean** becomes 27th Governor General.

2006 — A January election results in another minority government, this time formed by the new Conservative Party. The national **census** gathers information about 31.6 million Canadians—and reveals that more than 80 per cent live in urban areas.

2007 — In September, the Canadian dollar closed slightly above parity with the US dollar for the first time in 31 years.

2008 — Denmark to host Canada, Russia, the US and Norway to discuss their separate claims to the Arctic and its riches.

ART AND CULTURE

Canadian culture is rooted in a blend of British, French, and Aboriginal traditions, and influenced by successive waves of emigration. American media and entertainment dominate, but various federal government programs and laws attempt to support Canadian cultural initiatives. The federally funded Canadian Broadcasting Corporation (CBC) provides country-wide television and radio coverage; the National Film Board provides funding and distribution support for film; and other federally funded programs support art, music and dance.

Art

NATIVE EXPRESSIONS

Over centuries, Canada's indigenous peoples have developed diverse modes of artistic expression that bear witness to their distinctive lifestyles and beliefs. Since the aboriginal peoples were generally nomadic, little remains of their prehistoric art. However, petroglyphs, or carvings on rock, found in various sites in British Columbia and Ontario are as much as 5,000 years old. The remains of totem poles and stone and bone carvings discovered in sites along the West Coast date back to 500BC. Decorated with representations of animals and geometric designs, Iroquoian pottery dating from 900-1600AD has been unearthed in Ontario and Quebec.

A Totem Pole

©iStockphoto.com/Miranda Gillespie

Traditional Art

Most Algonquian-speaking aboriginals (notably Abenaki, Algonquin, Cree, Mi'kmaq, Montagnais and Naskapi) are descended from nomadic peoples, who excelled in the art of beadwork (shell, bone, rock or seed) and embroideries (porcupine quills and moose or caribou hair). Caribou-hide vests and moccasins and various birchbark objects were often adorned with geometric incisions and drawings. Elaborate belts of **wampum** (beads made from shells) feature motifs illustrating significant events in native history. Wampum was exchanged at peace ceremonies and during the signing of treaties. The smaller, quasi-sedentary, Iroquoian-speaking groups included Hurons, Mohawks, Onondagas and Senecas. As agricultural societies, they formed semipermanent villages and constructed multifamily dwellings known as longhouses; out of their sedentary lifestyle evolved an artistic repertoire free from the constraints of nomadism. Among their most beautiful works are exquisite moosehair embroideries that gradually began incorporating floral motifs under European influence. Wooden masks known as **false faces** represented mythological figures associated with traditional healing practices. The native peoples of the Plains, such as the Assiniboine, Blackfoot and Cree, painted their teepees, robes of bison and rawhide containers with everyday motifs; the horse quickly became an important icon in their decoration.

The art of the Northwest Coast cultures is unlike any other in North America. Having leisure time, they developed a creative expression unequalled on the continent north of Mexico. Tall tree trunks were chiselled with designs of birds, animals, humans and mythological creatures and raised as **totem poles**. Their purpose varied: sometimes they were functional, serving as house corner posts; sometimes decorative, serving as the entrance to a house (a hole was made at the bottom of the pole); other times they were memorials to deceased relatives. The golden age of carving was 1850 to 1900, after the introduction of metal tools by Europeans. Haida carvers often worked in **argillite,** a shiny, black slatelike rock, creating miniature figures of animals and humans, totem poles and pipes.

Contemporary Works

Native art has undergone a profound transformation in recent years. Whereas artists traditionally relied on the use of natural materials such as hide and bark, today they are experimenting with canvas, acrylics, charcoal and other new media; consequently, innovative techniques have emerged, although inspiration is still drawn from social and cultural traditions. The result is a fresh, contemporary vision of aboriginal art that keeps alive the memory of the past.

Three major schools prevail in contemporary native art: Woodlands, West Coast and Inuit. Woodland artists in eastern Canada have been influenced by the iconographic style of Ojibwa **Norval Morrisseau** in the 1970s, in particular his renderings of mythological creatures. His contemporaries Odawa artist **Daphne Odjig** and Cree artist **Carl Ray** (1943-78) further evolved Morrisseau's style through personal interpretation. Hailed as the country's first native modernist, **Alex Janvier,** also a Morrisseau contemporary, forged a unique style. The elegant but spare representations of birds and animals by Benjamin Chee Chee (1944-77) are widely imitated. On the West Coast, a resurgence of Haida art was begun in the late 1950s under the leadership of famed artist **Bill Reid** (1920-98). Reid achieved worldwide recognition as the popularizer of his ancestral Haida artistic style, to which he brought modern design sensibilities and savvy. *Raven and the First Men,* a large carving in yellow cedar, is considered his masterpiece. The Haida style has been continued in the works of master carver **Robert Davidson** and his brother **Reg Davidson**.

INUIT ART

Art forms developed over centuries have brought no small renown to the inhabitants of North America's Arctic regions.

Origins

The earliest known artifacts produced by the Inuit are small stone projectile points attributed to the Pre-Dorset and Dorset cultures in the first millennium BC. Petroglyphs attributed to these cultures have been found in the steatite (soapstone) hills of Kangiqsujuaq in Nunavik. The Thule people, generally considered to be the ancestors of the present-day Inuit, crafted small objects including combs and figurines; these early artifacts were generally associated with religious beliefs.

Beginning in the 19C, many miniature sculptures made of stone, ivory (walrus tusks) and whalebone were traded for staples such as salt and firearms, provided by Europeans. With the decline of traditional lifestyles resulting from increased contact with nonindigenous peoples, sculpture and other forms of arts and crafts gradually lost their magic or religious significance and provided

Bill McLennan/UBC Museum of Anthropology

The Raven and the First Men,
Bill Reid (1980)

a new source of income to the Inuit population.

Inuit Art Today

The term "Inuit art" evokes images of **stone carvings.** Abundant in the northern regions, soapstone is a soft rock ranging from greyish green to brown. Other harder rocks commonly used include green serpentine, argillite, dolomite and quartz. Modern Inuit sculptures, which can reach impressive dimensions, represent local fauna, life in the great northern regions and other arctic themes. Printmaking, sculpted caribou antlers, rock engravings and tapestries are other common art forms in the Arctic.

The most renowned centres for Inuit sculpture are the villages of Povungnituk, Inukjuak, Salluit and Ivujivik in the Nunavik region of Quebec, and **Cape Dorset,** Iqaluit and Pangnirtung in the territory of Nunavut. Three artists who had a profound effect on the development of Inuit sculpture are Nunavik's **Joe Talirunili** (1893-1976), **Davidialuk** (1910-76) and **Charlie Sivuarapik** (1911-68). Among the foremost sculptors of the current generation are Joanassie and Peter Ittukalak from Povungnituk, and Eli Elijassiapik, Lukassie Echaluk and Abraham Pov of Inukjuak. Nunavut's best-known carvers include **Osoetuk Ipeelie,** Kiawak Ashoona and **Pauta Saila,** all from Cape Dorset.

Inuit prints, in general, illustrate the animals, legends and traditions of the North in a highly decorative, two-dimensional style. Cape Dorset artists **Kenojuak Ashevak** and Lucy Qinnuayuak are well known, especially for their depiction of birds. Printmakers from Baker Lake exhibit highly individualistic styles and include artists William Noah and Simon Toookoome.

PAINTING AND SCULPTURE

17C-18C

The arrival of French and British colonists in the early 17C introduced European aesthetics and forms to the artistic landscape. Religion dominated life in what was then New France; thus, church decoration was the focus of early Canadian art. Paintings and statuary were first imported from France, but craftsmen were soon trained locally. Decorative arts for use in the liturgy flourished; prominent sculptors of the time included brothers **Noël Levasseur** and **Pierre-Noël Levasseur,** who were commissioned to decorate ships of the French navy, as well as churches. In Quebec three generations of the **Baillairgé family** were widely recognized for their exquisite wood sculptures and church decoration in general. After the British victory on the Plains of Abraham (1759), religious art declined and nonreligious painting gained prominence. Artists, primarily European-trained, began producing works that focused on such popular subjects as **landscapes** and, above all, **portraits,** commissioned by an emerging and wealthy bourgeoisie. The best known among these artists is **Antoine Plamondon** (1802-1895), who also painted religious themes (*Portrait of Sister Saint-Alphonse,* 1841).

Art was the means of depicting topography. British army officers were sent to Quebec to paint topographic views of the colony for military purposes. Some of these works, inspired by the romantic ideals of late 18C England, are best exemplified by the carefully executed watercolours of officer Thomas Davies (1737-1812).

19C

Secular art blossomed in the early 19C with such works as **William Berczy's** (1744-1813) Neoclassical painting *The Woolsey Family* and his portrait of Mohawk chief Joseph Brant. The expanding middle class wanted portraits of themselves. their pets and horses—as well as their pastimes and business ventures. Robert Clow Todd (1809-1866) was commissioned by the Gilmour family to paint its shipyards (*Wolfe's Cove, Québec,* 1840), for example.

Throughout the 19C, the arrival of European artists had a decisive impact on Canadian painting. **Paul Kane** (1810-71), born in Ireland, came to Canada as a child. He travelled the country extensively; his detailed portraits of native peoples (*The Death of Omoxesisixany* c.1856) are of significant historical interest today. Dutch-born **Cornelius Kreighoff** (1815-72) captured colourful French Canadian rural life in unprecedented detail in *The Habitant Farm* (1856) and other paintings. He is known for his superb landscapes and scenes of daily life in the Montreal region.

By the mid-19C Montreal had evolved into a sophisticated city, prosperous and interested in the arts. The oldest art gallery in Quebec, the **Art Association of Montreal,** was founded in 1860, the forerunner of Montreal's Museum of Fine Arts. In Ottawa, governor general the Marquess of Lorne created the **Royal Canadian Academy of Arts** in 1880, which eventually became the National Gallery of Canada. At this time, however, most artists trained in Paris (then the art capital of the world). though the subject matter of both their paintings and sculpted works was largely Canadian.

Early 20C

At the onset of the 20C, the influence of the so-called Paris school was visible in Canadian art, particularly in the works of Quebec artist Wyatt Eaton (1849-1896) and Montreal art professor **William Brymner** (1855-1925), one of the first Canadians to study abroad; his painting *A Wreath of Flowers* (1884) is an embodiment of French techniques. Their followers include Impressionist-style painters **Marc-Aurèle de Foy Suzor-Côté** (1869-1937), **Clarence Gagnon** (1881-1942) and **James Wilson Morrice** (1865-1924). **Robert Harris** (1849-1919) left Prince Edward Island to train in Paris, but returned to execute perhaps the most prestigious commission in Canada, *The Fathers of Confederation* (1883); thereafter, Harris became one of Canada's eminent portraitists. Hailing from London, Ontario, **Paul Peel** (1860-92) studied and lived abroad, though he exhibited in Canada. His works, several of which were controversial (*A Venetian Bather* and *After the Bath*), gained him international attention.

Sculpture

The turn of the 20C was the era of great commemorative monuments. Among the most notable sculptors in Quebec were artist-architect Napoléon Bour-

assa (1827-1916) and the celebrated **Louis-Philippe Hébert** (1850-1917). **Alfred Laliberté** (1878-1953) fashioned sculptures along the fluid lines of the Art-Nouveau style while maintaining an academic approach. Suzor-Côté, a close friend of Laliberté, used the same Art-Nouveau techniques to create a series of bronze works. In the 1930s the Art-Deco style influenced several Canadian sculptors, including Torontonian **Elizabeth Wyn Wood** (*Passing Rain*).

Cubism, constructivism and other European styles did not surface in Canadian sculpture until the early 1950s, when they were evident in the works of **Anne Kahane** and **Louis Archambault.** Following World War II, Canadian sculpture was invigorated by the availability of many new materials, which fostered experimentation in techniques and shapes. A movement known as structurism developed in the 1950s, particularly in the Prairie provinces, under the guidance of Eli Bornstein. In the 1960s talented painters **Michael Snow** and Les Levine established reputations based largely on their sculpted works: Snow's stainless steel forms and Levine's plastic modules. Yves Trudeau and Gerald Gladstone experimented with welded-steel constructions. Otto Rogers in Saskatoon and John Nugent in Regina also worked with steel. **Sorel Etrog** is recognized for his signature knotted-bronze works, which suggest the influence of cubism, and **Robert Murray** is internationally known for his large, colourful metal structures. Ed Aelenak and Walter Redinger turned to fibreglass for their constructions, while Michael Hayden created his kinetic works from neon tubing.

Budding Nationalism

World War I profoundly affected artists who regarded Canada as a proud young nation to be accepted on its own terms: why look to Europe, they felt. Trained in commercial design, **Tom Thomson** (1877-1917), an expert outdoorsman, painted Algonquin Park and other parts of Ontario in a bold new way. Thomson's vibrant colors and intense brushwork infused his paintings of the rugged terrain with a vitality that leaps from the canvas. *The West Wind* and *The Jack Pine* are among his best-known works. Like-minded artist-friends based in Toronto formed the **Group of Seven** in 1920, the first truly Canadian school, which included Lawren Harris (1885-1970), J.E.H. MacDonald (1873-1932) and A.Y. Jackson (1892-1974). Harris' austere depictions of the Canadian landscape, in particular *North Shore, Lake Superior* (1926), inspired the country's new modernists. Influenced by members of the Group of Seven, Carl Schaefer, painting in the 1930s, imbued psychological and sociological symbolism into his renderings of the Canadian landscape (*Ontario Farmhouse*, 1934). Another painter profoundly attached to the Canadian landscape, particularly that of British Columbia, was Victoria-born **Emily Carr** (1871-1945), Canada's first prominent female artist; her reverence for native art and culture, as well as nature, manifested itself in her unique style. Ontario-born **David Milne** (1882-1953) emphasized form and brush technique over subject matter; his paintings exhibited a wide variety of subjects, from cityscapes and rural scenes to still life (*Water Lilies and the Sunday Paper,* 1929).

In the 1930s Montreal artists began to rebel against the "wild landscape nationalism" of the Group of Seven. A staunch critic of the group, **John Lyman** (1886-1967) attempted to redirect Canadian art according to the precepts of the Paris school of thought. In 1939 he created the Contemporary Arts Society and organized a group known as the Modernists. Its members included **Marc-Aurèle Fortin** (1888-1970), Goodridge Roberts (1904-74), and Paul-Émile Borduas (1905-60).

THE POST-WAR ERA

World War II marked a turning point in the evolution of Canadian art. In 1940 **Alfred Pellan** (1906-88) returned to Quebec from France to exhibit paintings influenced by Picasso and other proponents of Cubism. **Paul-Émile Borduas** and several fellow artists, including **Jean-Paul Riopelle** (1923-2002), founded the **Automatist** group, whose paintings reflected Surrealism's goal of transferring the creative impulses of the psyche to the canvas. As a response to the spontaneity of the Automatists, **Guido Molinari** and **Claude Tousignant** founded the **Plasticist** group (1955) with the intent of freeing painting from the Surrealist idiom through the use of an abstract geometric vocabulary; form and color were key elements of their work.

After World War II, however, no single school of thought prevailed over the inspirational and creative effervescence of contemporary art, although several Montreal painters, such as **Yves Gaucher** and Ulysse Comtois, and sculptors Armand Vaillancourt, Charles Daudelin and Robert Roussil, exhibited intensely individual modes of expression. Throughout Canada, artists strove to develop their own highly personal styles, like the representational art (*To Prince Edward Island,* 1965) of Atlantic artist **Alex Colville** (b.1920) or William Kurulek's (1927-77) personal reminiscences of Ukrainian prairie life.

THE CONTEMPORARY SCENE

In recent years, Canadian art has evolved alongside major international currents; it has distanced itself from traditional painting while emphasizing more diversified forms and techniques, including "installation," a primarily sculptural idiom that also includes other art forms, such as painting and photography. Among its proponents are **Betty Goodwin,** Barbara Steinman, Geneviève Cadieux, Jocelyne Alloucherie and Dominique Blain. Art becomes "performance," having little intrinsic worth, in the mixed-media installations of such artists as Toronto-based A.A. Bronson, Felix Partz and Jorge Zontal. As new technologies emerge (lasers, computers, holograms), Canadian artists continue to express themselves in different genres and contexts. Contemporary movements aside, the precise realism of the paintings by **Robert Bateman,** who depicts animals in their natural habitats, remains popular with an international as well as a domestic buying public.

Literature and Language

LITERATURE

In large measure, Canadian literature resonates with a rich sense of place. Whether in the explorers' journals of the early 17-18C, the diaries and novels of 19C immigrant settlers, or the poems and literary works of the 20C and 21C, writers grapple with what it means to be Canadian.

Early Works

Throughout the era of exploration and colonization, the literature of New France was limited to travel memoirs (Cartier, Champlain), stories, descriptive writings (Sagard, Charlevoix) and the famous historical missives known as the **Relations,** written by Jesuit missionaries, who recorded their lives and work in the New World. In 1837 Philippe Aubert de Gaspé published the first French-Canadian novel *L'influence d'un livre,* based primarily on legends. The first fiction novels were influenced mainly by rural traditions, as evidenced in *The Canadians of Old (Les Anciens Canadiens)*, written in 1863 by **Philippe Aubert de Gaspé** senior. Historical novels, inspired by **François-Xavier Garneau's** *History of Canada (Histoire du Canada)* published in the 1840s, became very popular in the mid-1800s, as did the romantic poetry of Octave Crémazie (1827-79) and Louis-Honoré Fréchette (1839-1908). English settlers, such as **Susanna Moodie,** described the challenges of making a home in the Canadian wilderness (*Roughing It in the Bush,* 1852).

The Emergence of Canadian Literature

Canadian Confederation, in 1867, engendered confidence: Canada became a nation and its writers found their voice. "Confederation Poets" **Duncan Campbell Scott** and **Archibald Lampman** celebrated the realities of the Canadian landscape; Scott particularly admired Québécois and native culture. Meanwhile, anthropomorphization of wild animals, à la Beatrix Potter, characterized books by **Charles G.D. Roberts,** while his contemporary Ernest Thompson Seton wrote from a more scientific point of view. Children's literature blossomed at the end of the 19C with Margaret Marshall Saunders' *Beautiful Joe* and, in 1908, when **Lucy Maud Montgomery** began her enduring *Anne of Green Gables* series. The early 20C brought the humorous poems of **Robert Service,** the poet of the Yukon, who has also been dubbed "Canada's Kipling."

Quebec's early-20C writing was dominated by the nationalist works of writer and historian **Lionel Groulx** (1878-1967), leader of the "Action française," and by the poet Émile Nelligan (1879-1941). In 1916 French-born **Louis Hémon's** novel *Maria Chapdelaine,* depicting life in rural Quebec, was published posthumously, and is now translated into eight languages. In 1933 **Claude-Henri Grignon** wrote his celebrated novel *The Woman and the Miser (Un homme et son péché).* The story of survival, this time in the parched prairies, resurfaced in the first novel of Sinclair Ross, *As for Me and My House* (1941); and later, Northern Manitoba's wilderness was the setting for Gabrielle Roy's *Where Nests the Water Hen* (1951).

Post-War Perplexities

Urbanization and the trauma of World War II resulted in greater introspection among Canadian writers as they questioned the established order. Novelist Robert Charbonneau abandoned his tales of rural life for psychological novels. The McGill Group of poets (F.R. Scott and A.J.M. Smith, among others) paralleled the Group of Seven's avant-garde approach to painting. Meanwhile, feminist authors **Madge Macbeth** and others examined how urbanization and post-war reality affected women in society. Other writers grappled with racism, immigration and social upheaval. **Frederick Philip Grove,** who described Swedish immigrants taming the prairies in his novel *Settlers of the Marsh,* is credited with introducing realism into Canadian literature. Mazo de la Roche penned the *Jalna* series, chronicling how generations of a Southern Ontario family adapted to life there between the years 1927-60. Farther west, in Victoria, BC, artist Emily Carr's autobiographies introduced the world to West Coast native art and sensibilities.

In the 1950s Montreal modernists **Irving Layton,** Milton Acorn and Al Purdy changed the face of Canadian poetry; they influenced future generations of poets, including Gwendolyn MacEwen (*The Shadow-Maker,* 1969), with an earthy, streetwise style, freed from the taboos of subject matter and language. Poets **Gaston Miron** (1928-96), Gatien Lapointe and Fernand Ouellette instilled energy into Quebec literature during the Quiet Revolution of the 1960s. New novelists rose to prominence, and already well-known writers became associated with the finest of Quebec letters, among them **Anne Hébert** (*Kamouraska,* 1973) and Yves Thériault *(Agaguk).* Nova Scotia-born novelist **Hugh MacLennan** (1907-90), a professor at Montreal's McGill University, focused on contemporary life, and became the first major English-speaking writer to forge a national character for the country. His best-selling novel *Two Solitudes* (1945) confronted the issue of Quebec's relationship to the rest of Canada. Well-known Anglophone Quebec novelist **Mordecai Richler** (1931–2001) *(The Apprenticeship of Duddy Kravitz)* has won numerous literary prizes, including the prestigious Prix du Gouverneur Général. In the 1960s and 70s, poet-singer-novelist **Leonard Cohen** wrote of the sexual revolution and resistance to the Vietnam War. The times were characterized by a broad diversity of styles, most notably the psychological novel. Prominent authors from this extremely prolific period of literature include Louis Hamelin *(La rage)* and Monique Larue *(True Copies/Copies conformes).* In chronicling the building of Canada's transcontinental railroad *(The National Dream: The Great Railway 1871-1881),* Pierre Berton infused Canadian historical writing with a compelling new style and gained immediate commercial success. Best-selling author **Farley Mowat** *(Never Cry Wolf, Sea of Slaughter)* remains Canada's champion of the environment with his compelling recountings of humanity's destructive impact.

Contemporary Currents

Beginning with the late 1960s and continuing into the 21C, the fertile years of Canadian writing have produced a harvest of talented authors who probe the Canadian consciousness and explore the nation's cultural mosaic: **Margaret Atwood** *(The Handmaid's Tale),* Margaret Laurence *(The Stone Angel, The Diviners),* Timothy Findley *(The Wars),* **Robertson Davies** *(The Deptford Trilogy),* Joy Kogawa *(Obasan)* and Rudy Wiebe *(The Temptations of Big Bear),* among others. Atwood's book *Survival* elevated the internationally acclaimed author to guru status, to the point where her questioning of Canadianness became a yardstick of Canadian culture. It is fitting that, in the year 2000, Atwood should win Britain's most coveted literary prize, The Booker. Along with other world writers working in a multitude of genres, Canadian authors, such as **Michael Ondaatje** *(The English Patient, Anil's Ghost),* Alice Munro *(Lives of Girls and Women, Runaway)* and New Brunswick's Antonine Maillet have won international honours.

LANGUAGE

Canada is a land of immigrants. A population of 5 million in 1900 grew to 12 million by the end of World War II and to more than 32 million in 2006, thanks largely to immigration. Considered to be the **"founding" nations,** the British and the French are the largest populations (37 and 32 percent respectively). To reflect this composition, Canada is officially bilingual. The largest concentration of French-speaking people is in Quebec, but Francophones are found in every province. The federal government tries to provide services in both languages nationwide. There are significant numbers of Germans, Italians, Ukrainians, Dutch and Poles, especially in the Prairie provinces, and of aboriginal peoples, resulting in an interesting mosaic of cultures across the country.

"Canada could have enjoyed: English government, French culture, and American know-how. Instead it ended up with:

English know-how, French government, and American culture."

John Robert Colombo,
Oh Canada, 1965

Canada practises institutional bilingualism: English and French are the official languages for all federal and judicial bodies, federally mandated administrative agencies and Crown corporations. The practice has spread to provincial governments and some parts of the private sector. However, in the province of Quebec, the official language is French. In Nunavut, official languages are Inukitut and English; since the territory is part of Canada, all federal communications are also in French.

Music and Dance

CANADA'S MUSIC

From throat singing to classical music and rock, Canada's multifarious musical genres hum with creativity. Every region boasts its form of **traditional music,** whether the Celtic rhythms of Cape Breton Island; the Irish, Scottish and French fiddle music found in Quebec and Eastern Ontario; or the Inuit throat singing heard in Nunavut. Today, singers **Susan Aglukark** and the duo named Tudjaat continue to popularize Inuit songs. Montreal is known for its international **jazz** festival and great jazz musician **Oscar Peterson.** Other Canadian jazz artists include trumpeter Maynard Ferguson, be-bopper Moe Kaffman, Claude Ranger and mainstream musician James Galloway. Quebec's widely-acclaimed **Cirque du Soleil** (Circus of the Sun) delights audiences around the world with its innovative and enchanting blend of traditional music, circus entertainment, theatre and dance.

Canada's **classical music** tradition was under way in colonial times, with concert announcements appearing in newspapers as early as 1751. Quebec City had a concert hall by 1764 and Halifax audiences were delighted by performances of the music of Handel, Bach and Mozart. The 1840s exposed Canadians to international touring performers such as singer Jenny Lind. Local and regional musical societies—the precursors of today's philharmonic orchestras—sprang up around the country. The years between the world wars saw Canada's first musician to achieve national stature (and the only Canadian musician ever knighted): noted conductor Sir **Ernest Macmillan** (1893-1973). He founded one of Canada's first string quartets, and his composition *Two Sketches for Strings* became a Canadian classic. Other Canadians of renown included singer Rodolphe Plamondon, pianist Léo-Pol Morin and violinist Kathleen Parlow. Conductor **Wilfrid Pelletier** (1896-1982) launched Montreal's dynamic music scene while Claude Champagne (1891-1965), composer of the *Symphonie gaspésienne,* opened the way for numerous other composers. Internationally renowned Canadian pianist **Glenn Gould** (1932-82) retired from concert tours in 1964, concentrating on studio recordings; he is noted in particular for his recordings of Bach's *Goldberg Variations.* Yet another classical genre was internationally popularized by guitarist Liona Boyd (b.1950), who branched into New Age music via her 1986 recording *Persona.*

Several outstanding Canadian voices—contralto **Maureen Forrester** and father and son baritones Louis and Gino Quilico among them—are heard on the **opera** stages of Milan, New York, Paris and London, as well as in home-town concert halls in Vancouver, Toronto and Montreal. Composer **R. Murray Schafer's** *Ra* premiered in 1983 and at 11 hours in length remains Canada's most experimental theatrical-music experience. The country sustains several opera companies, including the Canadian Opera Company in Toronto, Opera du Québec, Opera du Montréal, and companies in Vancouver, Calgary, Edmonton. Opera Lyra performs in the nation's capital of Ottawa.

Canada's **folk music** boasts a varied tapestry of prominent singer-songwriters: balladeers Ian Tyson (Ian and Sylvia), **Anne Murray,** Stan Rogers (1949-83) and **Gordon Lightfoot** (his *Canadian Railroad Trilogy* became a classic); Alberta-born folk-jazz singer

Royal Winnipeg Ballet

Joni Mitchell; Celtic songster Loreena McKennitt; and Quebec "chansonneur" **Gilles Vigneault,** whose song *Mon Pays (Gens de mon pays)* became the separatist movement's anthem in the late 1960s. Incidentally, the originators of Canada's national anthem, *O Canada,* were two French-Canadians; Adolphe-Basile Routhier (1839-1920) wrote the lyrics and Calixa Lavallée (1842-91) composed the music.

The **rock music** of Robert Charlebois reflected a more critical social outlook typical of the 1960s. At that time, large-scale shows and a recording industry heavily influenced by American culture were adding a whole new dimension to Canada's music scene. The California counterculture was echoed in the music of groups such as Harmonium and Beau Dommage. During the early 1970s, bands like the **Guess Who** burst on the scene with their now-classic *American Woman,* whose lyrics became the anthem for the anti-Vietnam War movement. The Quebec rock group Offenbach also rose to prominence in the 1970s and Ginette Reno is considered one of the province's most acclaimed pop singers. In 1987 lead singer Robbie Robertson of The Band established his solo career as a rock singer-songwriter of world note. The 1990s witnessed the phenomenal rise of Quebec's diva **Céline Dion,** whose acclaim today extends worldwide. Cana-

da's contemporary rock bands include **Bare Naked Ladies,** Nickelback and the Maritime's Great Big Sea. Contemporary popular single artists include Bryan Adams, **k.d. lang,** Colin James, country-western crooner **Shania Twain** and jazz artist **Diana Krall.**

DANCE

Early European explorers, such as John Cabot, chronicled the traditional dances of the aboriginal peoples. Later, in the early 19C, Edmond Curtis photographed West Coast native peoples; his remarkable footage of Native Americans dancing in their war canoes makes for unforgettable viewing. It was not until the early 20C, when Anna Pavlova toured the country several times, that **ballet** truly arrived in Canada. The country's first professional company was the renowned **Royal Winnipeg Ballet,** founded in 1949. British dancer Celia Franca established the National Ballet of Canada in 1951 in Toronto. Montreal's Les Grandes Ballets Canadiens followed in 1958. All of these companies continue to stage splendid performances throughout Canada and abroad. Canadian ballerinas **Karen Kain** and Evelyn Hart have endeared themselves to their fellow countrymen, and choreographers Brian Macdonald and James Kudelka have gained wide recognition.

Modern dance in Canada owes its existence to European and American dancers and choreographers who established schools and troupes in the country. The **Toronto Dance Theatre** (1968) was established by Patricia Beatty, Peter Randazzo and David Earle, who trained in the techniques of American dance pioneer Martha Graham. In the early 1970s, former member of the Winnipeg Ballet Rachel Browne founded the dance company **Winnipeg's Contemporary Dancers** (WCD). Also in the 1970s, Montreal became a centre for the genre, following the opening of the experimental troupe La Groupe de la Place Royale. Vancouver-based Karen Jamieson and choreographer Conrad Alexandrowicz explored new forms of expression. Today Canadian modern dance continues to evolve, becoming less dependent upon the external influences that initiated it.

Cinema

Although most films shown in Canada are imported from the US, Canadians factor significantly in a surprising number of major films—as actors, directors and animators. Canadian locations are frequently chosen for their lower production costs and visual similarity to the US. Vancouver and Toronto have thriving production companies and employ many actors as extras in international films. Quebec has long had a vibrant film industry, with both a local and international market for French-language films.

Founded in 1939, the National Film Board of Canada (NFB), a federal institution, has acquired an international reputation for animated films, such as *Crac!* in 1982 by two-time Oscar-winner Frédéric Back (*The Man Who Planted Trees,* 1988). In 1999 the NFB's *When the Day Breaks* (by Wendy Tilby) won the Palme d'or prize for Best Short Film at Cannes. The NFB is also known for its documentary tradition, which evolved into a new genre known as "cinéma-vérité," a widely recognized trend in Quebec's film industry, best seen in the works of **Pierre Perrault** (*The Moontrap,* 1963; *Wake up, mes*

bons amis!, 1970) and Michel Brault (*Les Ordres,* 1974). Reflecting the growing importance of animation in cinema, the Ottawa International Animation Festival has become North America's largest and most important showcase for the genre and the second largest in the world since its founding in 1976.

Canada produces about 40 feature films per year with budgets of $3.5 million or more. Almost 40 percent of financing for English-language features and some 80 percent of funding for French-language features is provided by government.

Noted Canadian **directors** include **Claude Jutra,** who won international fame for *Mon Oncle Antoine* (1971) and *Kamouraska* (1973), based on Anne Hébert's novel; **Denys Arcand** reached European and American audiences with his films *The Decline of the American Empire* (1986) and *Jesus of Montreal* (1989), the latter receiving nominations at Cannes and Hollywood. Once reviled in Canadian Parliament as a public menace, director **David Cronenberg** has unnerved film-goers with his gripping treatment of dark subjects—from his first commercial breakthrough, *Scanners* (1981) to *The Fly* (1986), then *Crash* (1996) and *A History of Violence* (2005). The films of Toronto-based director **Atom Egoyan** are more works of art than traditional movies; with *The Sweet Hereafter* (1997), he became a player in American commercial cinema. In 2002 his film *Ararat* premiered at the Cannes Film Festival. *The Statement* (2004) is the most recent in a string of award-winning films by **Norman Jewison** that include his Oscar-winning *The Russians Are Coming, The Russians Are Coming* (1966), *Fiddler On The Roof* (1971) and *Moonstruck* (1987). Best known as the director of *Titanic* (1997), **James Cameron** also wrote and directed *The Terminator* (1984) and directed a series of successful science-fiction action films like *Aliens* (1986) and *Terminator 2: Judgment Day* (1991). Paul Gross' directorial debut, *Men with Brooms* (2002), became the top-grossing English-Canadian film of the last 20 years. Numerous awards for Western-Canadian director Gary Burns' *waydowntown* (2002) followed the critical success of his *Kitchen Party* (1998).

THE COUNTRY TODAY

Since the mid 1990s, fiscal management and rising natural resource prices—particularly for fossil fuels—has buoyed the economy, and Canada ranks high in the world's wealthiest nations.

See also the introduction for each province.

The Economy

The following is a very general account of economic activity in Canada. Additional information can be found in the regional introductions. Statistics Canada provides electronic publications for readers seeking detailed information (fees may apply): www.statcan.ca. Another source is the Canadian government's website http://canada.gc.ca, which provides links to all government publications.

Canada's great strength lies in its wealth of natural resources—forests, minerals and energy fuels that contribute greatly to its economy. Mining and agriculture are part of the country's highly diversified economy, whereas energy is among the top-performing sectors, along with transportation and telecommunications.

With nearly 70 percent of Canadians living within 300km/186mi of the US border, it is not surprising that the US is Canada's largest trading partner. Increased trade contributed to a gross domestic product (GDP) growth rate of 4.3 percent by 2000—the highest of the major industrialized countries. The country has not been able to sustain that rate, averaging 2.6 per cent annually since 2000, but steady growth and strong fiscal management has enabled the federal government to apply some of its budget surpluses to reducing Canada's large public-sector debt by 7.4 per cent.

LAND OF FORESTS

Forests are of prime importance to Canada; trees in one form or another are among the country's most valuable assets. Over half the total land area is forested, and the forest-products industry exists in every province. Although no longer dominant in British Columbia, which is best known for its sawed lumber, the industry is still important there, and Quebec is a major producer of **newsprint**. Canada is the world's larg-

Wheatfield near Waterton Lakes National Park

est exporter of the latter commodity, supplying nearly a third of total world consumption.

TRADITIONAL OCCUPATIONS

Despite Canada's tough climate and terrain, **agriculture** occupies an important position in the economy, making up 2.3 percent of the country's GDP. Wheat has long been the leader in agricultural exports from the Prairie provinces, challenged in more recent years by canola, a relatively new oilseed crop. Beef cattle are also raised in the Prairie provinces, whereas dairy products, poultry and hogs are more important in British Columbia, Ontario and Quebec. Potatoes, which have been a mainstay of the Maritime provinces, are of growing significance in the prairie lands. Apples, grapes and several hardy small fruits are harvested in the southernmost areas of the country, especially in Ontario and British Columbia.

Fishing and **trapping** were for centuries Canada's primary industries. Today, Canada is still a leading exporter of fish in the world, although the country's east and west coasts have seen declines in fish stocks in recent years. The Atlantic Coast supplies the vast majority of this resource, while 15 percent of the value is provided by the Pacific salmon fishery. Canada remains one of the largest suppliers of animal pelts in the world. The country's total exports have increased significantly in recent years; new and emerging markets for Canada's fur products include China and Greece.

RICHES BENEATH THE SOIL

Although in decline in some parts of the country, mining has played an important economic role in every region of Canada; it is a particularly active industry in the Northwest Territories and the Yukon. The country is a leading international producer of metals including nickel (Ontario, Manitoba), zinc (New Brunswick, Northwest Territories, Quebec, Ontario), molybdenum (British Columbia), uranium (Saskatchewan, Ontario), gold (Ontario, Quebec, Northwest Territories, Yukon) and lead (New Brunswick, British Columbia, Northwest Territories). Leading non-metals are potash (Saskatchewan, New Brunswick) and asbestos (Quebec). Iron ore is produced in the Labrador Trough (Quebec and Newfoundland) and in Ontario.

Alberta is the leading province for **fossil fuels.** Alberta possesses immense reserves awaiting exploitation in its Athabasca oil sands, and shares substantial coal reserves with British Columbia. Although fossil fuel production is almost entirely restricted to western Canada at present, offshore oil developments such as the Hibernia project on the continental shelf off Newfoundland, is changing this imbalance.

TRANSPORTATION

Because of Canada's size, transportation has always been of prime importance. Until about 1850, waterways commanded the country's economic growth. Since then, wheat farming, mining, and pulp and paper industries have grown largely dependent on rail transport. Even in these industries, movement of goods by water is not insignificant. The network of locks and canals known as the **St. Lawrence Seaway** significantly boosted Canada's economy: in particular, the country became an exporter of iron ore after the seaway facilitated exploitation of Labrador and Quebec's huge deposits. The road network has expanded since World War II with the completion of the Trans-Canada Highway and the opening of the great northern roads—the Alaska and the Dempster highways. Aviation plays an important role, especially in the North.

"Few Englishmen are prepared to find it [Canada] what it is. Advancing quietly; old differences settling down, and being fast forgotten; public feeling and private enterprise alike in a sound and wholesome state; nothing of flush or fever in its system, but health and vigour throbbing in its steady pulse: it is full of hope and promise."

Charles Dickens, *American Notes*, 1842

Container ship in Halifax Port

HYDROELECTRIC GIANT

The abundance and power of Canada's water sources offer exceptional opportunities for generation of hydroelectricity. Almost two-thirds of the country's electricity comes from this source. Generating stations operate in every province except Prince Edward Island, and Quebec's massive **James Bay Hydroelectric Project,** with a capacity of more than 12,000 megawatts, is one of the largest hydroelectric engineering projects in the world. In Labrador a huge generating station is located on the Churchill River. Other examples are in British Columbia on the Peace and Columbia rivers, in Quebec on the Manicouagan and Outardes rivers, in both Ontario and Quebec on the St. Lawrence, in Saskatchewan on the South Saskatchewan, and in Manitoba on the Nelson.

Electricity produced by such projects powers industries engaged in natural resource utilization such as smelting businesses and pulp mills. Plentiful and inexpensive hydroelectricity has attracted other industries, such as the aluminum industry to British Columbia and Quebec. Canada's energy is transported via high-voltage power lines to southern Canada and surplus electricity is exported to the US.

MANUFACTURING AND THE NEW ECONOMY

Canada's manufacturing industry, traditionally based on resource-processing (forest products, minerals, food and beverages, for example), has largely shifted into secondary manufacturing. A significant petrochemical industry exists in Alberta, Manitoba, Ontario and Quebec. Automobile and auto parts manufacturing and electrical and electronics industries are based mainly in Ontario and Quebec. British Columbia's Vancouver and Ontario's Toronto are centres for telecommunications, pharmaceuticals and biotechnology as well as film and video production. In Atlantic Canada commercial medicine, environmental industries and information technologies (the latter most notably in New Brunswick) complement traditional industries.

Gross Domestic Product

Formerly known as the GNP (gross national product), the GDP is a measurement (traditionally an annual one) of the monetary value of goods and services produced in Canada. Closely linked to such variables as productivity and the unemployment rate, the GDP is the most commonly used, and widely considered the best, indicator of the country's economic performance. Calculated by deducting imports from total spending, the GDP actually presents an estimate of the value of goods and services.

Source: *Statistics Canada*

INFORMATION AND COMMUNICATIONS TECHNOLOGIES

On a per capita basis, Canada is next only to the United States in the number of personal computers, with 669 per 1,000 inhabitants in 2005. Long considered one of the best-wired countries, Canada boasts comprehensive and inexpensive **telecommunications services**—no doubt a contributing factor to the nation's top ranking in worldwide Internet use per capita. Canada's long-distance telephone services were deregulated in 1992. Deregulation of the local telephone market in 1998 resulted in alternative carriers and resellers entering the market with new competitive services, although downturns in the worldwide telecommunications industry in 2001 led to consolidation and layoffs within Canada. Several Canadian companies are world leaders in the telecommunications equipment market.

INVESTMENT AND BANKING

In the past decade, Canada's economy has sustained steady growth. By 2007 inflation was at 2.2 percent and the unemployment rate was at 6.1 percent. The S&P/TSX Composite Index , which accounts for 95 percent of all equity trading in Canada, reached record levels in mid-2000, but fell back sharply in 2001. Since then, steady growth in energy and manufacturing stocks has pushed it well past the 2000 levels. Consumers have been quick to adopt new technologies and services introduced by Canadian financial institutions. In 2004 Canada ranked first in debit card usage, with 88.2 transactions per inhabitant. Use of the Internet for banking continues to grow: while only 8 percent of Canadians used it in 1999, 58 percent used it for banking by 2005.

Government

Canada is a **federal state** with 10 provinces and three territories. Each province has its own elected legislature controlling regional affairs. Canada's three territories—the Yukon, the Northwest Territories (which is only one territory despite its name) and newly created Nunavut (1999)—have elected legislative assemblies to govern their respective territories. Nunavut, in addition, has a number of joint resource-management bodies composed of Inuit, federal and territorial government appointees who play important decision-making roles. The central government in **Ottawa,** the federal capital, assumes responsibility for such matters as defence, foreign affairs, transportation, trade, commerce, money and banking, and criminal law.

Though officially part of the Commonwealth, Canada functions in actuality as an independent nation. The Canadian head of state is the **British monarch.** Her authority is exercised by the **governor general,** who was at one time appointed by the monarch but today is chosen by the elected representatives of the Canadian people. However, the governor general is little more than a figurehead as actual power lies in the hands of the Canadian **prime minister,** the leader of the majority party in Canadian **Parliament.** This latter institution consists of an elected legislature called the **House of Commons** and an appointed Senate, members of which are chosen by the governing party. The prime minister rules through a cabinet drawn from elected representatives (and sometimes from members of the Senate), and must submit his or her government for re-election after a maximum of five years, or if he or she is defeated in the House of Commons.

INTERNATIONAL RELATIONS

After World War II Canada was catapulted to global leadership as a founding country in the United Nations and as a member of the North Atlantic Treaty Organization (NATO). The country retains diplomatic missions in over 150 countries and has earned respect as an international peacekeeper. In addition, Canada is a regular participant in international conferences, including the yearly economic summit of the eight major industrialized democracies, known as the G8. In 1994, Canada, Mexico and the

Scottish Bagpiper

Inuit Hunter

Acadian Woman

Ukrainian Woman

Native American

US implemented the **North American Free Trade Agreement** (NAFTA), a pact designed to increase trade and investment among the three countries largely by eliminating tariffs and other barriers. This has contributed to a sharp increase in Canadian exports in recent years.

Population

This immense country is inhabited by a relatively small number of people: just under 32 million in 2006, compared to more than 300 million in the US. Overall population density is only 3.5 persons per sq km compared to 246 per sq km in the United Kingdom. Canada's inhabitants are largely concentrated in a band about 160km/100mi wide immediately north of the Canadian/US border. The regional distribution is approximately as follows: British Columbia, Rockies, Yukon 13 percent; the Prairie provinces 17 percent; Ontario 38 percent; Quebec 24 percent; the Atlantic provinces 8 percent; Northwest Territories 0.2 percent. Although 62 percent of the population lives in Ontario and Quebec, mainly between Quebec City and Windsor, Canada is strongly characterized by regional distinctions.

Back Bacon Dinner

Food and Drink

Food in Canada has many regional specialties. Staples of the Plains Indians, such as **buffalo stew** with bannock (bread), still provide sustenance for Canada's First Nations people today. British Columbia is famous for its **seafood,** especially king crab and salmon. The country produces a variety of fruit, such as apples, peaches, cherries, and its own wine in the Okanagan Valley in British Columbia and from Niagara in Ontario to Quebec's Eastern Townships. In the Prairies the **beef** is excellent, along with fresh lake fish in the north, wild rice, berries of all types, and the heritage of many immigrant cultures—cabbage

rolls, pierogies (dumplings) and borscht, for example.

Quebec's French heritage provides it with a fine culinary tradition, and many restaurants serve traditional French-Canadian cuisine—pork dishes, meat pie *(tourtière)*, soups, thick stews (ragout) and a generous quantity of maple syrup. Quebec's Beauce region is well known for its maple products: sugar pie, maple syrup, ice cream and taffy. The Atlantic provinces are another great **seafood** region, especially oysters, lobster, scallops, and mussels. In Newfoundland **screech,** a heady dark rum, or one of the country's fine **beers** is popular with meals. New Brunswick is famous for **fiddleheads,** the new shoots of ferns available fresh in May and June, and for **dulse,** an edible seaweed. **Moose meat** and fresh lake fish are available in the Northwest Territories, as is **Arctic char,** a delicacy similar to trout and salmon in taste.

Canadian Lobsters

Toronto Skyline
©iStockphoto.com/Vertex IS

BRITISH COLUMBIA, ROCKIES, YUKON

Known as the **Canadian Cordillera**, this region consists of the province of British Columbia, part of the province of Alberta, and the Yukon Territory. Covering the extreme west, it stretches from the Pacific Ocean to the Rockies and from the Canadian/US border to the Beaufort Sea. The high snowcapped peaks, massive glaciers, rugged ranges, mighty rivers, wild streams and tranquil lakes of this land of beauty attract millions of tourists every year.

Don't Miss: Vancouver, Victoria, and at least one of the Canadian Rockies parks.

Organizing Your Time: If you plan to drive, allow plenty of time to cover the long distances and the many stops you'll want to make. *See the Regional Driving Tours at the front of the guide for itinerary ideas.*

Kids Especially for Kids: The Aquarium and Science World in Vancouver.

A Bit of Geography

Mountainous Terrain – From the west, the **Coast Mountains** rise steeply out of the deeply indented and heavily forested Pacific Coast to over 3,000m/10,999ft. North of this chain in the Yukon are the St. Elias Mountains, which peak with **Mount Logan** at 5,959m/19,520ft, the highest point in Canada.

To the east of the coastal ranges, an immense **plateau** nearly 300km/200mi wide contains the Cariboo ranch lands and the irrigated Okanagan fruit-growing belt. The **Columbia Mountains** define the plateau's eastern edge. In the north, it changes to an area of rugged mountains—the Skeena and Cassiar ranges—before spreading out into the vast Yukon Plateau, a basinlike area of rolling uplands, encircled by high mountains and drained by the Yukon River and its tributaries.

Travel Alberta

Trail riding in Jasper National Park

East of this interior plateau and the Rocky Mountain Trench, the Canadian **Rockies** stretch north from the 49th parallel. Rugged, with numerous peaks over 3,000m/10,000ft, the Rockies' front ranges rise abruptly above the foothills and prairie lands of Alberta. At the Yukon/British Columbia boundary, the **Liard River**, a tributary of the Mackenzie River, carves a channel between the Rockies and the **Mackenzie Mountains**. North of the Mackenzies, the Richardson and British mountains stretch almost to the Beaufort Sea.

Climate – Tremendous variation marks the climate of this region, which extends from latitude 49° to north of the Arctic Circle and has coasts on two oceans—the cool Pacific and the icy Arctic.

The climate of coastal British Columbia is influenced by the temperate waters of the Pacific, the prevailing westerly winds and the high Coast Mountains. Winters are mild (0°–5°C/30°–40°F) and summers warm, though not hot (15°–24°C/ 60°–75°F). Rainfall can be low in protected areas, but among the heaviest in the world in locations exposed to

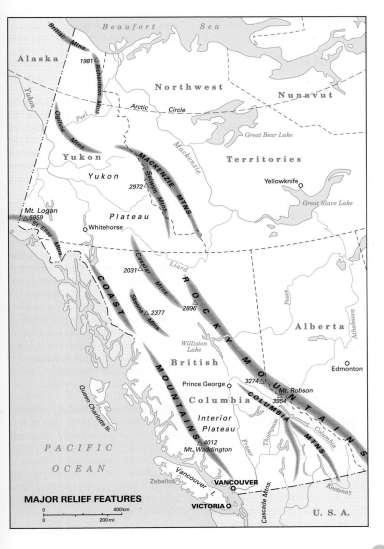

MAJOR RELIEF FEATURES

0 ———— 400km
0 ———— 200mi

the moisture-laden winds off the Pacific. Greater extremes of temperature and lower rainfall are found to the east, with winters averaging –5°C/23°F and summers 22°C/72°F. Irrigation is needed in the Okanagan Valley to allow cultivation of its famous fruits.

In the north the St. Elias Mountains shield the Yukon from the moderating influences of the Pacific, but also from the high precipitation of the coast. Summers are pleasantly warm (nearly 21°C/70°F) and dry with long hours of daylight (an average of 20 hours). Winters are dark and cold, though temperatures vary widely (Dawson City –27°C/–16°F, Whitehorse –15°C/–5°F).

A Bit of History

The First Inhabitants – Native cultures of this region fall into three basic groups: the wealthy, artistic tribes of the Pacific Coast; the tribes of hunters and fishermen who inhabited the British Columbia interior (known as the Cordillera Indians); and the Athapaskan-speaking tribes of the Yukon.

The Arrival of the Europeans – European discovery of the region occurred from two directions. Small ships explored the coast, while fur traders, seeking new supplies and transportation routes, approached the interior. Capt. **James Cook** made the first documented landing during his voyage of 1778, sailing up the coast of British Columbia. To reinforce its claims, the British government sent an expedition under the command of Capt. **George Vancouver**, who had been a midshipman on the Cook voyage, to map the coast between 1792 and 1794.

Fur-Trading Empire – The first European to glimpse the Canadian Rockies was **Anthony Henday** of the Hudson's Bay Company (HBC) in 1754. **Alexander Mackenzie** of the rival North West Company completed the first crossing of the continent north of Mexico in 1793. Other "Nor'westers" sought alternative routes through the Rockies to the rich fur area west of the mountains. By following the Columbia and Kootenay rivers,

David Thompson explored the Howse and Athabasca passes, the southeast corner of British Columbia and northern Washington state between 1804 and 1811. **Simon Fraser** retraced Mackenzie's route in 1808 and descended the river that now bears Fraser's name.

An American fur-trading company created by **John Jacob Astor** founded a post at the mouth of the Columbia, beginning the American challenge to British ownership of the Oregon territory. In 1846 the rivalry was settled with the 49th parallel designated as the US frontier. The HBC moved its western headquarters from the Columbia River area to **Vancouver Island**, which was declared a crown colony in 1849 with Victoria as its capital. The rest of the territory (known as New Caledonia) remained the domain of the company.

Gold – The discovery of gold in California in 1848 attracted people seeking a fortune. Nine years later the gold was gone, and many prospectors moved north to New Caledonia. In 1858 news spread of gold in the lower Fraser River. **Victoria** (pop. 400) saw 20,000 people pass through en route to the goldfields.

Afraid the influx of Americans would lead to an American takeover (as had occurred in California), the governor of the island colony, **James Douglas**, stepped in quickly to assert British sovereignty. The mainland was declared a British colony and named British Columbia, with Douglas as its first governor. Poor transportation routes made control of the new territory difficult. When rich gold strikes in the Cariboo brought even more people, Douglas planned construction of a wagon road—the famous **Cariboo Road**, built between 1862 and 1865—which helped ensure British control of the area.

Confederation and a Railway – The two western colonies united in 1866 as British colonies in the east were discussing confederation (which became a reality in 1867). The US purchase of Alaska in 1867 raised new fears of an American takeover and prompted negotiations to become part of the new Canada, located 3,200km/2,000mi away.

British Columbia entered Confederation in 1871 on the condition that a railway be built to connect the province with the east within 10 years. The birth pains of the project nearly led to British Columbia's withdrawal; but initiated in 1881, it was completed within only four years. The railway brought tourists, settlers and capital to the impoverished region, and encouraged the search for mineral wealth.

"Ho for the Klondike" – When the Cariboo goldfields were exhausted, prospectors again moved north. The long-hoped-for big strike was made in 1896 on a small creek renamed "Bonanza," which drained into the Klondike River, a tributary of the Yukon. As news spread, thousands of men and women set off for the Klondike. In eight years $100 million worth of gold was shipped out, providing an enormous stimulus for this western frontier.

Population – The population of **British Columbia** increased from just over 50,000 at the dawn of the 20C to 4 million by the 21C (2006), 13 percent of Canada's total. The great majority of these inhabitants live in the southwest corner of the province, nearly half in the Vancouver metropolitan area. Today, the population of 30,372 in the **Yukon** is just slightly greater than in 1900. Two-thirds of the residents live in the territorial capital of Whitehorse.

Economy

British Columbia – The turn of the 19C brought on the resource-extraction economy that dominated British Columbia for most of the 1900s. A second national rail line reached the lower mainland, and the decline of timber supplies elsewhere made the province's huge reserves more valuable. Construction of the **Panama Canal**, opened in 1915, stimulated exploitation and export of the province's minerals by providing a cheap means of transport to Europe. The Great Depression and World War II slowed economic growth, but the postwar boom across North America brought renewed demand for BC's forest products. The second half of the 20C garnered increased trade with Asia and a huge influx of new residents, whose arrival created new economic growth.

Timber – Once paramount, the forest-products industry remains crucial but not dominant. Virtually all the wood cut is softwood, with lodgepole pine, spruce, hemlock and Douglas fir the leading species. Mills convert about 20 percent of this wood into pulp and paper products; the vast majority is exported to the rest of Canada, the US and overseas.

Trade – Vancouver is by far Canada's most active port, shipping huge exports of forest products, grain and mine ores,

Fly fishing

Travel Alberta

Practical Information

GETTING THERE

BY AIR

International and domestic flights to Vancouver International Airport (*15km/9mi south of downtown;* ☎*604-207-7077; www.yvr.ca*) via Air Canada (☎*888-247-2262; www.aircanada.ca*), WestJet (☎*888-937-8538; www.westjet.ca*) and other major carriers. Various carriers offer connections to other cities in the region. Taxi to downtown Vancouver (*approx 25min; $20–$30*). Airport **shuttle** Vancouver Airporter ☎*604-946-8866* (*$13.50*). Airport Limousine Service (☎*604-273-1331* (*$41.35*). Major car rental agencies at the airport. Travellers pay a Airport Improvement Fee upon departure from Vancouver (*$5 for BC and Yukon destinations; $15 for all others*).

BY BUS AND TRAIN

Greyhound **bus** service to BC and the Yukon: ☎*604-482-8747* (in Vancouver); www.greyhound.ca. **VIA Rail** Canada operates the Skeena route from Jasper to Prince Rupert, connects Victoria to Courtenay and links Vancouver to Toronto ☎*800-561-8630* (in BC), or ☎*800-561-3949* (US).

BY BOAT

BC Ferries operates year-round scheduled ferries linking Vancouver Island, the mainland, and many of the islands. Expect heavy traffic during summer months, on weekends and over holidays. BC Ferries, ☎*250-386-3431* or 888-BCFERRY, www.bcferries.bc.ca. ♿ For ferries from the US to British Columbia *see VANCOUVER ISLAND*.

GENERAL INFORMATION

ACCOMMODATIONS AND VISITOR INFORMATION

Government tourist offices produce annually updated guides on accommodations, camping, fishing, skiing and vacations. The *BC Vacation Planner* suggests driving tours and gives general travel tips, and the *Accommodations Guide* is a comprehensive catalog of hotels, inns, B&Bs and campgrounds. All publications and a map are available free of charge from: **Tourism British Columbia** (*Parliament Buildings,*

Victoria, BC, V8V 1X4; ☎*604-435-5622 or 800-435-5622; www.hellobc.com*). The *Yukon Vacation Guide*, updated annually, provides details about facilities and attractions, entertainment, adventure travel, outdoor activities and gives travel tips. This publication and a road map are available free of charge from **Tourism Yukon** (*Box 2703, Whitehorse, YT, Y1A 2C6;* ☎*800-789-8566; www.touryukon.com*).

Both British Columbia and the Yukon maintain extensive networks of provincial and territorial **campgrounds** containing more than 10,000 campsites along major highways. Many BC campgrounds are booked well in advance during summer holidays and weekends. Fees range from $12 to $18 per night, and reservations are advisable; contact Discover BC Reservations: ☎*800-689-9025 (Apr 1-Sept 15), www.discovercamping.ca*. In the Yukon, the nightly fee for government-run campgrounds is $12; travellers must stop at visitor centres to purchase camping permits.

ROAD REGULATIONS

BC, Alberta and the Yukon have good paved roads. Although there are few freeways, major roads are built to high-speed standards and passing lanes are common. Secondary roads vary in quality; it's a good idea to ask locally about road conditions before leaving the main highway.

Throughout the north in BC and the Yukon, summer brings considerable road repair and construction; be alert and patient.

Unless otherwise posted, speed limits are: in British Columbia and the Yukon 90km/h (55mph) on provincial highways and 50km/h (30mph) in cities; in Alberta 100km/h (60mph) on provincial highways and 50km/h (30mph) in cities. For road conditions in British Columbia ☎*900-565-4997* (toll call) or *www.drivebc.ca*. For road conditions in the Yukon ☎*867-456-7623* or *www.gov.yk.ca/roadreport*. **Seat belt** use is mandatory. Not mandatory, but practically universal, is courtesy—horn-honking is almost never heard in Vancouver.

TIME ZONES

Alberta and the BC Rockies region are on Mountain Standard Time. The rest of BC and the Yukon are on Pacific Standard Time. Daylight Saving Time is observed from the second Sunday in March to the first Sunday in November. The northeast corner of BC is on Mountain Standard Time year-round.

TAXES

In addition to the national 5% GST, BC levies a 7% provincial sales tax, and an 8% accommodation tax (10% in some communities).

LIQUOR LAWS

The legal drinking age is 19. Liquor is sold in government stores.

PROVINCIAL/TERRITORIAL HOLIDAYS

BC Day: 1st Monday in August
Discovery Day, Yukon: 3rd Monday in August

RECREATION

OUTDOOR ACTIVITIES

The rivers, mountains and many parks of this vast and sparsely populated region offer outdoor enthusiasts a variety of recreational activities: hiking, horseback riding, fishing, river rafting, canoeing and kayaking.

Many **fishing** lodges arrange fly-in packages to remote lakes that attract anglers from around the world. Separate licenses are required for saltwater and freshwater fishing, and can be obtained locally. For more information, contact the BC Fishing Resorts & Outfitters Assn. ☎866-374-6836 or www.bcfroa.ca.

The many navigable waterways, especially in the Shuswap Lake district, offer a host of water sports as well as houseboating. Marine adventures and **cruises** that include nature observation are popular along the coastline. Whistler, north of Vancouver, is one of the world's top ski resorts, with first-class accommodations and facilities, including glacier skiing from June through October. The three ski resorts in the Rockies offer a variety of **winter activities**. For information on recreation, contact Tourism British Columbia (ⓒ *above*) or www.hellobc.com/ski.

SPECIAL EXCURSIONS

The **Rocky Mountaineer** journeys through some of the most spectacular mountain scenery in North America during a two-day rail trip from Vancouver to Jasper or Banff. The train travels in the daylight hours only; passengers spend the night in Kamloops. Eastbound, westbound and round-trip travel is possible (*departs from Vancouver Apr–Oct Mon, Wed & Sat 7am; one-way $789–$1,919/person, double occupancy; cost of lodgings in Kamloops included; reservations required;* ✕ ♿ 🅿; *Rocky Mountaineer Vacations;* ☎604-606-7245 or 877-460-3200; *www.rockymountaineer.com*). **Pack trips** and trail ride excursions are offered (*1-10 days*) for all levels of riding ability. Warner Guiding and Outfitting (☎800-661-8352; *www.horseback.com*) leads rides (*1-7 hrs*) from Banff into the surrounding wilderness. Tonquin Valley Adventures (☎780-852-1188; *www.tonquinadventures.com*) guides small groups to a remote lake within the Jasper backcountry, overnighting (*2-6 nights*) in a rustic lodge. Contact Travel Alberta for information about outfitters (☎800-252-3782; *www.travelalberta.com*).

PRINCIPAL FESTIVALS

FEB	**Sourdough Rendezvous,** *Whitehorse, YT*
	Yukon Quest Sled Dog Race, *Whitehorse, YT*
MAY	**Swiftsure Yacht Race Weekend,** *Victoria, BC*
JUN–JUL	**Stampede,** *Williams Lake, BC*
JUN–AUG	**Festival of the Arts,** *Banff, AB*
AUG	**Loggers' Sports Day,** *Squamish, BC*
	Peach Festival, *Penticton, BC*
	Discovery Day, *Dawson City, YT*
AUG–SEPT	**Pacific National Exhibition,** *Vancouver, BC*
SEPT	**Classic Boat Festival** *Victoria, BC*
SEPT–OCT	**International Film Festival** *Vancouver, BC*
OCT	**Okanagan Wine Festival** *Penticton, BC*

Kayaking on Lesser Slave Lake

and handling significant imports of cars, electronic goods and other finished products. The port handles about 76 million tonnes of cargo a year; most of which is in bulk commodities such as wheat (from the Prairie provinces), ore and timber products.

Mining – Although gold is still mined in British Columbia, the focus long ago shifted to lesser-value commodities. The overall value of mineral production is more than $5.6 billion; coal, natural gas, and copper all exceed gold in revenues.

Agriculture – Despite only 3 percent of land available to British Columbia farmers, the province leads Canada in production of apples, peaches, pears, grapes and numerous other fruits; the greenhouses of the Fraser delta ship tomatoes and other produce throughout North America. The great interior plateau is cattle-raising country; and the Peace River country east of the Rockies is British Columbia's chief grain-growing area. Agriculture constitutes a $2.4 billion industry in British Columbia.
Fisheries contribute another $250 million to the provincial economy, with more than 80 species of fish, shellfish and marine plants harvested.

Film and Tourism Industries – Cheaper production costs and tax breaks for foreign-film investors are factors in Vancouver's popularity as a filmmaking capital.

Both the film and tourism industries benefit from the province's scenery and diversity. Vancouver's and Victoria's attractions and British Columbia's islands, coast, mountains and wildlife draw more than 22 million visitors each year, who pour almost $10 billion into the provincial economy. Ecotourism and outdoor adventure are key activities in British Columbia, which boasts some of the world's best fishing, camping, hiking, canoeing and kayaking opportunities. Serving almost 17 million passengers a year, Vancouver International Airport ranks as the West Coast's second busiest (after Los Angeles, California). And the port of Vancouver is a major debarkation point for cruise ships, with nearly 840,000 passengers utilizing British Columbia docks annually.

BC Today – Newer industries are assuming ever greater roles. Fueled by growth in trade and population, Vancouver is booming and Victoria thrives on tourism and government. Elsewhere, the decline in mining, logging and fishing has led to more than 20 percent unemployment in some isolated areas, though growth in tourism is beginning to help.

The Rockies – The Canadian Rockies remain major tourist magnets, drawing some 6 million sightseers a year. The Rockies attract hordes of outdoor adventurers and sports enthusiasts. The proper balance between mankind and nature continues to be elusive.

The Yukon – The golden years of the Klondike Stampede were followed by years of economic stagnation. Construction of the Alaska Highway during World War II led to increased exploitation of the Territory's mineral wealth. Mining entered a steep decline in the 1990s, though, with only gold still a significant resource. Today tourism and energy development are the brightest stars in the Yukon's future.

ALASKA HIGHWAY★★
BRITISH COLUMBIA, YUKON, ALASKA

This great road to the North passes through a land of mountains and lakes of rare beauty, largely untouched by mankind except for a scattering of small communities. Beginning at Dawson Creek in British Columbia, the highway parallels the Rocky Mountains, enters the Yukon along the valley of the Liard, touches the Cassiar and the Coast mountains of British Columbia, and follows the St. Elias Mountains to enter Alaska, finally terminating in Fairbanks.

- **Information:** *The Milepost* is an annually updated directory of natural and historic sights, eating establishments and overnight accommodations mile by mile. Available at bookstores or directly from ☎800-726-4707 *(Canada/US)* or *www.themilepost.com.*
- ▶ **Orient Yourself:** The Alaska Highway starts in Dawson Creek—a nine hour drive from Edmonton or an 18-hour drive from Vancouver—and requires some 28 hours to drive to the border between the Yukon and Alaska .
- **Don't Miss:** Liard Hot Springs
- **Organizing Your Time:** The parks at Muncho Lake and Liard River Hot Springs are good halfway stopping points for the 22 hour drive between Dawson Creek and Whitehorse.
- **Also See:** YUKON CIRCUIT.

A Bit of History

When the Japanese bombed Pearl Harbor in 1941 and landed in the Aleutian Islands, Americans feared an imminent invasion of mainland Alaska. After a joint agreement between Canada and the US, a land route was pushed through muskeg swamps, over rivers and mountain ranges from Dawson Creek to Alaska in only nine months during 1942. The 2,451km/1,523mi highway has become a legend in the annals of road construction. Upgraded after World War II and opened to civilian traffic, it now transports the region's resources and the tourists who travel its length.

From Dawson Creek to Fort Nelson

483km/300mi

The Alaska Highway begins at **Dawson Creek**, BC, in the most northerly corner of the Great Plains that stretch all the way south into Mexico. The descent into the Peace River valley is lengthy and somewhat winding, crossing the river at **Taylor**, in the midst of a vast natural gas and oil field. Gas processing plants can be seen along the highway, and oil pipelines run beneath fields of crops all the way to **Fort St. John**.

After the junction with Highway 29, the Alaska Highway passes through flat and heavily wooded country, dominated by spruce muskeg and threaded by gas pipelines, that gradually becomes more mountainous until the road reaches **Fort**

Alaska Highway

Nelson. This busy lumber centre and base for oil and gas exploration is also the junction of the Liard Highway to Fort Simpson (Northwest Territories), and access to spectacular Nahanni National Park Reserve.

From Fort Nelson to Whitehorse★★

991km/616mi (not including excursion)
After leaving Fort Nelson, the highway turns west into aspen parkland and boreal forest as it climbs into the Rocky Mountains. The countryside is very open, affording many sweeping views of largely flat-topped mountains.

Muncho Lake Provincial Park★★
KM 688/mi 427. ⟲*Open mid-May–Sept.* ⚠ *☎250-787-3411. www.bcparks.ca.*
This park is one of the most beautiful and geologically interesting parts of the drive. From the wide rocky valley of the Toad River, the vista widens and more mountains come into view, many of them snow-capped. Stone sheep can often be seen licking salt from the roadbed. Held in a high valley between two towering ranges, **Muncho Lake**★★ mirrors the surrounding folded mountains as the road traverses the many alluvial fans of eroded material washed down from the peaks. This provincial park has two good campgrounds and several lodges.

Liard River Hot Springs Park★
KM 765/mi 478. Exit highway right to parking area; follow boardwalk. ⟲*Open year-round daily;* ⊜*$5 ($10/family).* ⚠ *☎250-776-7000. www.bcparks.ca.*
This small park consists of large, hot sulphur pools (temperature averages 42°C/107°F) in bucolic, forested surroundings. One pool is deep enough for swimming; the lower, hotter pool draws the largest crowds. Both have been developed with boardwalks and changing rooms. The park is one of the most popular overnight stops on the Alaska Highway; during summer months the campground fills up in early afternoon (*reservations are highly advisable*).
About 10km/6mi past the hot springs, the highway enters a massive burn area, testimony to the frequency and ecological significance of wildfire in the north. The 1982 fire burned 182,725 hectares, the second-largest conflagration in BC history; the landscape is now being reclaimed by aspen, willow and fireweed, the pioneering species that typically follow a fire.
The **Liard River** is crossed at KM 788/mi 490. This wild and turbulent river flows south from the Yukon before turning north near here to join the Mackenzie River. Its valley marks the northern limit of the Rocky Mountains.
At KM 947/mi 588 the highway crosses the 60th parallel, entering the Yukon Territory. The exit from British Columbia is not yet final, however, as the highway

Practical Information

DRIVING THE HIGHWAY

The Alaska Highway is paved over its entire length, and navigable year round. Snowfall is inevitable in fall, winter and spring and possible even in May and August. Driving conditions can also be difficult during spring thaw, and road repair is endemic in summer; however, highway advisories are broadcast promptly. Vehicles should be in good mechanical condition before starting out, but service stations are situated at regular intervals. The speed limit varies from 80km/h (50mph) to 100km/h (60mph); watch posted signs. Headlights should be kept on at all times. For the latest road conditions, call ☎900-565-4997 (toll) or www.drivebc.ca (BC); ☎867-456-7623 (YT) or www.gov.yk.ca/roadreport.

DISTANCES

Alaska Highway distances were derived from a destination's mileage from Dawson Creek in British Columbia—the official starting point of the highway. Canada's conversion to the metric system and constant highway improvement have complicated the distance measurements, although many businesses still use the original mileage indicators of their location.

Along the Canadian portion of the highway, distances are now marked by kilometre posts from Dawson Creek; on the US side, distances are given in miles.

ACCOMMODATIONS AND VISITOR INFORMATION

Overnight accommodations and visitor information are provided in *The Milepost* (☉above). Most travellers divide the journey from Dawson Creek to Whitehorse with a stop halfway at Muncho Lake Provincial Park or Liard River Hot Springs, where there are campgrounds and small inns and motels. Reservations are strongly advised for provincial park campsites in BC ☎800-689-9025.

crosses and recrosses the boundary several times. Travellers along this road are rewarded with fine views of the **Cassiar Mountains.**

Watson Lake
KM 1,016/mi 632.

This transportation and communications centre for southern Yukon is famous for its collection of **signposts**. In 1942 a homesick soldier, employed in the highway's construction, erected a sign with the name of his hometown and its direction. Tourists have kept up the tradition. Today over 30,000 signs from all over the continent and abroad are stacked on posts in a wide field in the middle of town near the visitor centre. From the south the **Stewart-Cassiar Highway** (Route 37) joins the Alaska Highway at KM 1,044/mi 649. Winding 800km/500mi through western British Columbia, this road provides an alternate route to the Yukon. After this junction the Alaska Highway begins to cross the Cassiar Mountains, with pretty views of snowy peaks on both sides of the road.

At KM 1,162/mi 722 a rise of land is traversed that marks the divide between two great river systems, the Mackenzie and the Yukon, which empty into the Beaufort and Bering seas respectively.

ADDRESS BOOK

Accommodations along the Alaska Highway are mostly quite rudimentary, on the order of vintage roadside motels. Two of the nicest inns are located about halfway between Dawson and Whitehorse. **$$Northern Rockies Lodge** (☎250-776-3481 or 800-663-5269; www.northern-rockies-lodge.com) is a lakeshore, spruce-log structure within Muncho Lake Provincial Park, with 45 tidy rooms, every modern convenience and highly efficient staff. Across the road from the hot springs park is **$Trapper Ray's Liard River Lodge** (☎250-776-7349). One cabin and 12 comfortable wood-panelled rooms at Trapper Ray's feature upscale rustic furnishings. The hot springs are a 10-minute walk from the lodge.

Liard River Hot Springs Park

Teslin Lake

KM 1,290/mi 802.

The name of this stretch of water means "long lake" in local native dialect. The highway crosses Nisutlin Bay and hugs the shore for about 48km/30mi. Frequently the mountains and lake are bordered by clusters of the Yukon's adopted emblem, the pinkish purple flower called **fireweed**, common throughout the region. The climate here is dry (less than 305mm/12in of precipitation) and warm in summer.

At the head of the lake, the road crosses the Teslin River by a high bridge.

Atlin★

Excursion: 196km/122mi round-trip from Jake's Corner at KM 1,392/mi 865; take road south. An isolated drive on unpaved road. Visitor centre (in the Atlin Museum, 3rd & Trainor Sts.) ⊙open mid-May–mid-Sept daily 10am–6pm. ☎250-651-7522.

An old gold-mining centre, this small community in British Columbia has a pretty **site** overlooking beautiful Atlin Lake, backed by majestic snow-covered peaks. The excursion boat *MV Tarahne* is beached in town, a remnant of Atlin's more prosperous days, and the local historical society occasionally offers tours in summer. From Warm Bay Road, Llewellyn Glacier can be seen beyond the lake on a clear day. The town is a set-off point for adventures in the spectacular wilderness of Atlin Provincial Park.

Marsh Lake★★

KM 1,428/mi 887.

Surrounded by mountains, this lake is an arm of the much larger **Tagish Lake** to the south. At the end of the lake, the road crosses the Yukon River at a dam. At KM 1,445/mi 898 there is a **view**★ from above of the steep, white cliffs and clear green water of the fabled **Yukon River**, which rises only 24km/15mi from the Pacific Ocean and meanders nearly 3,200km/2,000mi, crossing the Arctic Circle before reaching the Bering Sea.

Whitehorse★

KM 1,474/mi 916. ⓖSee Entry Heading.

THE CARIBOO ★
BRITISH COLUMBIA

The Cariboo is the name given to the region centred in the valley of the Fraser River north of the Thompson River. Part of the central plateau of British Columbia, this region is a vast rolling upland of low arid hills, lakes, sagebrush, and lodgepole and fir forests bounded to the east by the Cariboo Mountains—from which the area gets its name—and to the west by the Coast Mountains.

- **Information:** ☎800-663-5885 or 250-392-2226; www.landwithoutlimits.com.
- **Orient Yourself:** Williams Lake, the center of the region, is an eight hour drive north of Vancouver through the scenic Fraser Canyon.
- **Organizing Your Time:** The most interesting places to visit require excursions from Highway 97, and may require backtracking to return to the main highway. Plan to spend a night near Barkerville so you can spend a full day exploring it.
- **Especially for Kids:** Barkerville Historic Town.

A Bit of History

The Cariboo Gold Rush – Opened by fur traders, the Cariboo first reached prominence with the gold rush of 1861, which led to the building of the Cariboo Road. Gold was first found in this area in 1859 by prospectors who had made their way from California to the lower Fraser and then north, following the gold trail. Large quantities were being extracted from the upper part of Williams Creek by 1862, when **Billy Barker**, a Cornish sailor who had jumped ship at Victoria to try his luck, hit pay dirt in its lower reaches. Within 48 hours he had extracted $1,000 worth of gold. The area boomed and towns such as Barkerville (named for Billy), Camerontown and Richfield sprang up.

Within ten years, the easily-accessible gold was gone, and the towns of the Cariboo were almost deserted. Barkerville was uninhabited until 1958, when the provincial government transformed the site into a museum-town, carefully restoring it to its former splendor.

Cattle Country – After the boom of the gold rush, the rail and road links that had been built for mining brought wood and ranch products to market in Vancouver, and today the main economic activities are timber harvesting and cattle raising (some of the largest ranches in Canada are found in this region). The annual stampede held in **Williams Lake** during the first week of July is considered the premier rodeo of the province, with cowboys from all over North America vying for trophies. A popular tourist area, the region is known for its sports fishing, game hunting, dude ranches and other traditional features of "Western" living,

SADDLE SORE

Often thought of as ghosts of the past, **cattle drives** still take place in Western Canada, where ranchers send herds into the high country to graze in spring and bring them down in the fall. An annual summer event in the Cariboo replicates the more amiable aspects of a drive for riders of all types. All you need is moderate riding experience; horses and tack can be rented. Based in cattle capital Williams Lake, the **Great Cariboo Ride** is no-frills and bovine-free (no cows) but traverses spectacular countryside and includes high-country hiking, swimming and fishing (☎250-395-3120; www.greatcaribooride.org). The schedule, route and costs for the trip vary from year to year. Several guest ranches in central BC offer experienced riders an opportunity to come along on roundups *(for more information, contact the BC Guest Ranchers' Assn. ☎877-278-2922; www.bcguestranches.com).*

Address Book

BC GUEST RANCHES

Below is a selection of the best-known ranches.

For more information, contact them individually or the BC Guest Ranchers' Assn. (☎ 877-278-2922; www.bcguestranches. com).

$$$ Big Bar Ranch – ☎*250-459-2333. www.bigbarranch.com.* This down-home family-style guest ranch offers economical lodging, riding and fishing in the Marble Mountain uplands near Clinton. Accommodations are available in the main ranch house, log cabins or teepees.

$$$$ Douglas Lake Ranch – ☎*250-350-3344 or 800-663-4838. www.douglaslake.com.* Canada's largest working cattle ranch embraces half-million acres of bunchgrass-prairie upland. Lodges, camp sites, remote cabins and yurts, plus horseback riding and fishing.

$$$$ Echo Valley Ranch – ☎*250-459-2386 or 800-253-8831. www.evranch. com.* Founded in 1994 by a high-tech entrepreneur, Echo Valley features spruce-log lodges and cabins, a full-service spa, indoor pool, gourmet meals, and guided rides along the Fraser Canyon rimrock.

$$ Wells Gray Ranch – ☎*250-674-2792; www.wellsgrayranch.com.* This wilderness compound has 10 log cabins, bunkhouses, and room to pitch tents for the more economy-minded. Trail rides take in the rim of Clearwater Canyon. The ranch's saloon is a popular nightspot.

$$ Helmcken Falls Lodge – ☎*250-674-3657; www.helmckenfalls.com.* This historic lodge (1948) and guest ranch near Wells Gray Park overlooks Trophy Mountain. Guests can stay in 8 log cabins, 11 double units in chalets or twin cottage units. This soft-adventure lodge offers guided hiking, canoeing and riding tours.

$$$$ Elkin Creek Ranch – ☎*604-513-5008 or 877-870-0677. www.elkin-creekranch.com.* Set in a pristine valley in the far Chilcotin region, shadowed by the Coast Range, Elkin Creek is spectacular. Handsome log cabins are set in an aspen grove, and fishing in nearby lakes is usually superb.

$$$ Flying U Ranch – ☎*250-456-7717. www.flyingu.com.* The Flying U is Canada's oldest guest ranch, in operation since the 1920s. Famed for its laissez-faire ambience, guests here saddle their own horses and set off by themselves through peaceful aspen/fir forests. Lodgings are comfortably funky.

$$ Hills Health Ranch – ☎*250-791-5225. www.spabc.com.* Devoted equally to fitness and riding, the Hills offers guests the choice of being pampered or pummelled (or both). The ranch offers excellent spa cuisine and wonderful riding through verdant Cariboo hay meadows. Rosehip oil treatments are a specialty.

$$$ Sundance Guest Ranch – ☎*250-453-2422. www.sundance-ranch.com.* Just four hours from Vancouver, Sundance offers amenities Club-Med style. Perched on a bend above Thompson Canyon near Ashcroft, the resort has guided horseback rides, tennis courts, a billiards room, a heated pool and other amenities that appeal especially to singles.

and for the restored gold rush town of **Barkerville**.

The Cariboo Road – To facilitate transportation to the boomtowns of the gold rush, the government of British Columbia built a wagon road to Barkerville from the lower Fraser River near Yale, some 650km/403mi away. Following the wild rocky canyon of the Fraser, the road, opened in 1864, was a remarkable engineering achievement. The old road has been transformed into the Trans-Canada Highway, the Cariboo Highway (97) and Highway 26.

Highway 97 from Cache Creek first climbs out of the Thompson Canyon desert into the Cariboo uplands—a scenic, rolling plateau of aspen, fir and spruce forest interspersed with broad meadows. The rest stop at **108 Mile Ranch** in the heart of this region incorporates a half-dozen historic buildings from a century-old roadhouse. A two-storey 1908 log barn built for the Clydesdales that once trod the highway is the largest wood barn in Canada, and functions today as a community dance hall. After passing through Williams Lake, the highway continues north to Quesnel, a timber-mill centre. The **drive**★ from Quesnel to Barkerville (*Hwy. 26*) penetrates the Cariboo Mountains, passing **Cottonwood House**★ (*open mid-May–Sept daily 10am–5pm; $4.50; 250-992-2071*). One of the few remaining roadhouses (lunch is served) on the old wagon road, the house was constructed in 1865 of cottonwood logs and is still sound. The mining community of **Wells** neighbors Barkerville. Several small inns in the area, such as the Wells Hotel, or the St. George Inn in Barkerville, offer overnight accommodations to modern travellers (*contact the district Chamber of Commerce: 877-451-9355; www. wellsbc.com*).

Barkerville Historic Town★★

90km/56mi east of Quesnel by Hwy. 26. *Open year-round daily 8am–8pm. $13. 250-994-3332. www.barker ville.ca.*

The old gold-mining centre has a fine **site**★ surrounded by mountains in the valley of Williams Creek. The restored buildings of Barkerville include the stores, hotels, saloons and assay office of a mining community. In the **visitor centre** the video shows and displays on the town, the Gold Rush and methods of mining are a good introduction. Note the rather unusually shaped **St. Saviour's Anglican Church**, a structure of whipsawed timber and square nails. At the far end of the street is the Chinese section, with its **Chinese Freemasons' Hall** (the Chinese followed the other gold rushers north from California but tended to stay within their own community). **Billy Barker's claim** is marked, and the **Theatre Royal** stages typical Gold Rush-era shows (*mid-May–Labour Day, call for hours; $10; reservations suggested; *). Visitors can also pan for gold in the Eldorado Mine *(fee)*.

St. Saviour's Anglican Church

R.Corbel/MICHELIN

Wells Gray Park★★

204km/127mi east of Williams Lake to Clearwater by Hwy. 97 South, Hwy. 24 West and Hwy. 5 North. At Clearwater, proceed 35km/22mi north to the park entrance. Hiking, canoeing, swimming, fishing and horseback riding. Park open year-round. Visitor centre open Jul–Aug daily 9am–5pm; rest of the year, call for hours. Maps available at visitor centre. 250-674-2646. www.wellsgray.ca.

Spread across a spectacular mountain canyon and the western flanks of the southern Cariboo range, Wells Gray Provincial Park is a huge (one million acres) scenic and recreational treasure, with excellent hiking through its forests and extensive backcountry, as well as water sports in its four main lakes.

Wells Gray's best-known attraction is **Helmcken Falls** (*accessible via Clearwater Road*), where the Murtle River plunges 137m/452ft over a wide basalt cliff. **Clearwater Lake** is the site of a popular campground, and the departure point for daylong or weeklong wilderness canoe treks. **Murtle Lake**, sheltered in a mountain bowl on the park's southeast fringe, is the largest lake in North America reserved for nonmotorized boat travel.

DAWSON CITY★★
YUKON TERRITORY
POPULATION 2,022

Set on a dramatic site on the east bank of the wide Yukon at its confluence with the Klondike, this historic frontier town—the heart of the gold rush—is truly a delight. Remarkably like a Western movie set, the former destination of thousands of fortune seekers now hosts thousands of tourists, yet retains its unpaved streets, pedestrian boardwalks and false facades, which enhance the feeling of a bygone era. Several Dawson City buildings compose the Dawson Historical Complex, a National Historic Site of Canada.

- **Information:** Tourist Office ☎867-993-5575 or www.dawsoncity.ca.
- **Orient Yourself:** Stop first at the Parks Canada visitor centre (*Front & King Sts.*) for a map and tour times. Take the 1hr guided tour (*see Visiting box*).
- **Don't Miss:** Panning for gold (*contact Klondike Visitors Assn. ☎867-993-5575; www.dawsoncity.ca*).
- **Organizing Your Time:** Allow an hour for Downtown Dawson City. The Robert Service cabin and Jack London centre will need 2hrs. Allow a day for the Excursions.

A Bit of History

The Great Stampede – On August 16, 1896, **George Carmack** and his Indian brothers-in-law, Skookum Jim and Tagish Charlie, found gold on **Bonanza Creek**, a tiny stream emptying into the bigger **Klondike River**, itself a tributary of the mighty Yukon. When news of their find reached the outside world, an estimated 100,000 people left their homes from as far away as Australia to begin the long, arduous trek to Dawson City, the town that sprang up at the mouth of the Klondike. Stories of their travels and travails are legion. Many never made it; of those who did, few made a fortune.

The Routes of '98 – Of several routes to Dawson City during the gold rush, the longest, yet easiest, was by sea to the mouth of the Yukon and then by riverboat the 2,092km/1,300mi upstream. But this passage was only for the rich. A few people tried an overland course from Edmonton through almost impassable muskeg and bush, following more or less the present-day Alaska Highway route. The majority, however, sailed up the Pacific Coast via the Inside Passage to Skagway or Dyea, tiny way stations on the Alaska Panhandle, and trudged into the Yukon across the Coast Mountains.

Home of the Klondike – Soon after the discovery, the whole area near Bonanza Creek was staked by prospectors. Instead of making a claim, a trader named **Joe Ladue** laid out a townsite on the level swampland at the mouth of the Klondike, amassing a fortune from his foresight. Lots were soon selling for as much as $5,000 a front foot on the main street. The heyday of Dawson was under way. Prices were sky-high: eggs $1 each, nails $8 a pound; but everything was available, from the latest Paris fashions to the best wines and foods. At the many saloons, drinks were normally paid for in gold dust.

Dawson had a unique feature: despite being the biggest and richest of all the mining boomtowns, it was the most law-abiding. The North West Mounted Police maintained tight control. Everything was closed down on Sundays. No one carried a gun except the police. Offenders were given a "blue ticket" (i.e., run out of town).

Decline and Revival – The heyday was short-lived. By 1904 the rich **placer** fields were exhausted: $100 million in gold had been shipped out. Complicated machinery was needed to exploit any gold that remained. People left; the glamor departed.

Once the largest Canadian city (pop. 30,000) west of Winnipeg, Dawson City maintained its preeminence until World War II, when Whitehorse—connected to the outside world by road (Alaska Highway), rail and air—took over, growing as Dawson shrank. In 1953 Whitehorse was made the capital of the Yukon. With this blow and the end of commercial gold mining in 1966, Dawson might have become a ghost town were it not for the tourist boom reviving the city. People still make a living mining the creeks, but little gold is found in comparison to the $66 million discovered in 1898.

The year-round population of just over 2,000 swells in summertime with the arrival of tourists and seasonal residents. Situated less than 300km/200mi south of the Arctic Circle on fertile soil untouched by the last Ice Age, Dawson enjoys hot summers with nearly 24 hours of daylight. Vegetables are cultivated in gardens, and flowers sprout through cracks along the streets. Many old buildings tell the story of a grandeur and wealth seen nowhere else so far north. Some lean sideways, however, because of permafrost. A Canadian government restoration project is returning the town to some of its former splendor.

Festivities – On June 21, the midnight sun barely dips down behind the Ogilvie Mountains, and the third weekend in August, the anniversary of **Discovery Day** is celebrated.

Downtown★★

Laid out in a grid pattern, the town lies in the shadow of the huge hill known as the Midnight Dome. On its face is **Moosehide Slide**, a natural landslide thought to be the result of an underground spring.

On **Front Street** (also called 1st Avenue) stands the **SS Keno**, a stern-wheeler once used to transport silver, lead and zinc on the Stewart River from the mines in the Mayo district. Built in Whitehorse in 1922, the steamer also made trips to Dawson. After its last voyage in 1960, it was permanently dry-docked there. The extensive damage caused by the flood of 1979 led to the building of a dike along the riverbank where the steamers once docked. Next to the *Keno* is the former **Canadian Imperial Bank of Commerce**, a stately building with a pressed-tin facade made to imitate stone. The plaque on the exterior refers to its famous teller Robert Service.

The former **British North American Bank** (*guided tour*), with its handsome polished-wood teller enclosure, occupies the corner of Queen Street and 2nd Avenue. South on 2nd Avenue is **Ruby's Place** (*window display*), formerly a brothel, and now one of several restored town buildings.

At Princess Street and 3rd, the renovated **Harrington's Store** (*open mid-May–mid-Sept daily*), built in 1900, contains the comprehensive photo exhibit, "Dawson As They Saw It." Across the street is **Billy Bigg's** blacksmith shop (*window display*) and north on 3rd, note the **KTM Building** (*window display*), which served as a warehouse for the Klondike Thawing Machine Co. in 1912.

Formerly a Carnegie Library, the Neoclassical **Masonic Temple** corners 4th and Queen, while diagonally across the street is **Diamond Tooth Gertie's Gambling Hall**. Named for a notorious female resident, this establishment boasts a legalized casino (*open May–*

VISITING DAWSON CITY

Dawson's sights and tourist activities are numerous, so stop first at the Parks Canada visitor centre (*Front & King Sts.; open Jun–mid-Sept daily 8am–8pm; 867-993-7200; www.pc.gc.ca*) for a schedule of events and guided tours as well as a map. Informative audiovisuals and displays are also in the centre. Sights that can be visited by one-hour guided tour only (*Jun–mid-Sept daily; $5*) are indicated below by "(*guided tour*)." An audio-tape tour is available to rent (*$5*). Historic buildings not open to the public usually have a window display depicting the structure's history. Additional information can be obtained from the Klondike Visitors Association (*867-993-5575; www.dawsoncity.ca*).

Sept daily 7pm–2am; floor shows nightly; ≋$6; ✕ ♿ ☎867-993-5525).

Back on 3rd Avenue are the **Dawson Daily News** (1898-1953), and **Madame Tremblay's Store**, restored to its 1913 appearance (*both window displays*). Opposite, a clapboard building with a squat tower houses the original 1900 **Post Office** (⏱*open Jun–mid-Sept daily*), designed by **Thomas W. Fuller**, who served as Canada's chief architect for 15 years. He also designed the Government House and the Old Territorial Administration Building (🛈*below*). Across King Street stands a replica of the **Palace Grand Theatre**★ (👄🔊*guided tour*), a distinctive pinewood structure with an elaborate false front. Built in 1899, the theatre offered everything from opera to Wild West shows. Draped with Old Glory and Union Jacks, the colorful two-tiered, U-shaped interior seats audiences in rows of padded "kitchen chairs."

One street over is aptly named Church Street, site of the clapboard **St. Paul's Anglican Church**, built in 1902 with money collected from miners in the creeks.

Southward, double-porticoed **Commissioner's Residence**, where the Yukon's commissioner, or governor, lived in the early 1900s, overlooks Front Street. The original residence had a more ornate exterior than the present structure, a replacement after a house fire in 1906. The house and grounds, abundant with flowers, were the centre of Dawson's social life—host to afternoon teas,

dinner receptions and summer garden parties (⏱*open Jun–mid-Sept daily; ≋$5*). To the rear are the remains of **Fort Herchmer** (*grounds open to the public*), a former North West Mounted Police barracks complete with married quarters, stables, jail and commanding officer's residence. The renovated St. Andrews **Presbyterian Manse** stands behind **St. Andrews Church**, at 4th Avenue.

Additional Sights

Dawson City Museum★

595 Fifth Ave. ⏱*open mid-May–mid-Sept daily 10am–6pm. Rest of the year by appointment.* ≋*$7.* ✕☎*867-993-5291.*
Dominating the upper section of 5th Avenue, the impressive Neoclassical styled Old Territorial Administration Building (1901, T.W. Fuller) houses the museum. The South Gallery has exhibits and re-creations of Dawson's gold rush; the North Gallery features early-20C city life in Dawson City. Locomotives of the short-lived Klondike Mines Railway are on display in an outdoor shelter.

Robert Service Cabin

8th Ave. at Hanson St.
Overlooking the town from the southeast is a two-room log cabin with moose antlers over the door—the residence from 1909 to 1912 of the "poet of the Yukon" (1874-1958). Here he wrote his only novel, *The Trail of Ninety-Eight*, and his last Yukon verses, *Songs of a*

Bards of the North

Jack London and **Robert Service** were the two writers who helped make the Klondike gold rush an enduring part of the history of adventure. Both men had residences in or near Dawson City. London, a young Californian, arrived in the Yukon in 1897 to seek his fortune. Back in California, he discovered a more valuable Yukon treasure when he sold, in 1903, *Call of the Wild*, the tale of a Northland sled dog who returns to the wilderness. London became the most famous and best-paid American author of his time. Robert Service arrived in the Yukon in 1904. *Songs of a Sourdough*, his first success (1907), was a popular collection of his Yukon tales set to verse, including the famous "The Shooting of Dan McGrew."

"Back of the bar, in a solo game,
sat Dangerous Dan McGrew,
And watching his luck was his light-o'-love,
the lady that's known as Lou."

Dawson City

Rolling Stone. Though he arrived in Dawson shortly after the gold rush, his poetry—*Songs of a Sourdough* in particular—vividly re-creates the atmosphere of the times. Outdoor **recitals** (*1hr*) of his poems are presented on the grounds (*Jun–mid-Sep daily 9am–5pm; $5;* ♿).

Jack London Interpretive Centre
8th Ave. at Firth St.

The cabin of another writer who spent time in Dawson City during its heyday, American author **Jack London** (1876–1916), has been reconstructed on the property. His stories of the North, *Call of the Wild* and *White Fang* are among his best-known works. The adjacent centre (🕐 *open late May–mid-Sept daily 11am–6pm; $2;* ☎*867-993-6317*) houses a photo exhibit of London's life in the Klondike. There are also **readings** (*30min*) of his works (*twice daily*).

Excursions

Midnight Dome
9km/5mi by Dome Rd., a steep, winding road.

So named because of the midnight sun visible here on June 21, this mountain rises 884m/2,900ft behind the townsite. From the summit the **view**★★ is splendid day or night. Below lies Dawson at the junction of the Yukon and Klondike rivers—and Bonanza Creek can be seen entering the Klondike. The devastation of the whole area caused by the dredges is evident. There are mountains in all directions; to the north, the Ogilvie Mountains are particularly impressive.

Bonanza Creek★★
4km/2.5mi by Klondike Hwy. from town to Bonanza Creek Rd.

The unpaved road (*maintained for 16km/10mi*) along Bonanza Creek winds through huge piles of **tailings**, or washed gravel refuse, left by mining dredges. The largest remnant of earlier

---

ADDRESS BOOK

$$$ Bombay Peggy's – *2nd & Princess St.* ☎*867-993-6969. www.bombaypeggys.com.* Named for a legendary Dawson madam of the 1950s, this property was a largely abandoned, but still handsome 3-storey Victorian house (1900), until two enterprising Dawson residents bought it in 1998. They moved it downtown and transformed it into an opulent 10-room inn. The current owners have restored what they could and refurbished the rest with burgundy wallpaper and period furnishings like claw-foot tubs and canopy beds—there's even a player piano in the sitting room. The inn's lounge proffers appetizers and alcoholic beverages to guests and the public.

mining equipment is **No. 4 dredge** (⏱*Jun–mid-Sept;* 🎫*$5; tickets available from visitor centre*) on Claim 17BD.

Signs designate a claim provided by the Klondike Visitors Assn. for those who wish to **pan for gold** (☎*867-993-* *5575*). A simple plaque marks the place where the Klondike Stampede began: **Discovery Claim** itself (*14.5km/9mi from junction with Klondike Hwy.*).

FORT ST. JAMES ★
BRITISH COLUMBIA
POPULATION 1,927

In a lovely setting beside Stuart Lake, this town, 154km/96mi northwest of Prince George, is one of the oldest settlements in western Canada. Simon Fraser founded a trading post here that became the chief Hudson's Bay Company post in New Caledonia after 1821. It remained in operation until 1971. Since the site is still fairly remote today, it's easy to imagine how isolated early traders posted here must have felt.

▶ **Orient Yourself:** Fort St. James is at the end of Highway 27, an hour's drive north of Vanderhoof.

🕐 **Organizing Your Time:** The fort and its grounds can be explored in 3–4 hours. There is a picnic ground at the fort and campgrounds nearby.

A Bit of History

Today a National Historic Site, Fort St. James, restored to the year 1896, is a testament to life in a fur-trading post.

Canada's fur trade at the beginning of the 19C was largely in the hands of the Hudson's Bay Company and its rival, the North West Company. In 1806 Simon Fraser, a member of the North West Company, established a trading post at Stuart Lake as an administrative hub for the fur trade west of the Rockies. Upon the merger of the two companies in 1821, the post, by then named Fort St. James, fell under the supervision of the "new" Hudson's Bay Company.

Visit

Beside lake in town. ⏱*Open mid-May–Sept daily 9am–5pm.* 🎫*$6.50.* 🍴♿ ☎*250-996-7191, ext. 25. www.pc.gc.ca.* The National Historic Site contains several restored Hudson's Bay Company buildings that date from 1884 to 1889. The **men's house** and officer's dwelling with their meticulously restored furnishings can be visited, as can a reconstruction of the original trading store. Built off the ground, the **fish cache** holds displays of dried fish and pork, and the log **general warehouse** contains a priceless **collection** of furs. Throughout the site, costumed interpreters offer entertaining and knowledgeable tales about 19C wilderness life and perform chores common to fort life. In the visitor centre, displays and artifacts are on view and an excellent film (*9min*) about the fort's history is shown.

FRASER CANYON COUNTRY★★
BRITISH COLUMBIA
MAP PP 100-101

Between the city of Vancouver and Shuswap Lake, the Trans-Canada Highway (Highway 1) follows deep valleys, cut by two of the most powerful rivers in the province, through the rocky Coast Mountains and the dry, hilly scrubland of central British Columbia: the Fraser River and the Thompson River.

- **Information:** Vancouver Coast and Mountains Tourism (☎800-667-3306; www.coastandmountains.bc.ca) or Thompson Okanagan Tourism (☎800-567-2275; www.totabc.com
- **Don't Miss:** Hell's Gate.
- **Organizing Your Time:** Shuswap Lake is an 8hr drive from Vancouver, so stay overnight at a campground or motel between Lytton and Kamloops.
- **Especially for Kids:** Hat Creek Ranch.

A Bit of History

The first European to see the Fraser River was **Alexander Mackenzie** on his epic journey to the Pacific in 1793. His partner in the North West Company, **Simon Fraser**, descended and reascended the river's entire length in 1808. Fraser gave the river his name and that of **David Thompson**, geographer and another North Westerner, to its major tributary. Too wild for a fur-trading route, the Fraser was little used until gold was discovered at **Hill's Bar** near Yale in 1858. The canyons were selected in the 19C for the Canadian Pacific Railway's route, now traversed by a second railway and the Trans-Canada Highway.

1 Fraser Canyon★★ – From Hope to Lytton

109km/68mi (not including excursion)

Hope★

The mountains close in around this community as the valley narrows and swings northward. The wildness and unpredictability of the region were well demonstrated by the **Hope Slide**★ of 1965. One January day an immense amount of rock from Johnson Peak (*18km/11mi east by Rte. 3*) slid into the valley, filling a lake and forcing its waters up the other side. Route 3 had to be rebuilt more than 45m/148ft above its original level.

Manning Provincial Park

Excursion: 136km/84mi round-trip from Hope by Rte. 3 East. After entering the park (☉*open year-round; hiking, horseback riding, bicycling, cross-country skiing;* ⚠), Route 3 traverses an area called **Rhododendron Flats**★, where these wild plants flower in profusion in mid-June. This park is one of only two places in Canada where visitors can drive to extensive subalpine meadows (*the other is Mt. Revelstoke*).

After Hope, mountains close in abruptly. Surrounded by impressive cliffs, the tiny hamlet of Yale was a town of 20,000 during the gold rush when it was the terminus of river navigation and the beginning of the Cariboo Road. To the north the cliffs are sheer, the valley is narrow, tunnels are frequent and the river below seethes along, around and over rocks. Just after Spuzzum, the road crosses the river and continues on the east side.

Hell's Gate★★

The canyon here is 180m/600ft deep, but the river, rushing past at 8m/25ft per second, is only 36m/120ft wide. The river was once wider, but during construction of the Canadian National Railway in 1914, a rockslide occurred, narrowing the gap. Thereafter, upstream passage was almost impossible for the salmon, their spawning grounds being the lakes and streams throughout British Columbia's interior. A sharp decline in the Pacific salmon fishing industry occurred until

Pacific Salmon

Every summer and autumn British Columbia's five salmon species—sockeye, pink, coho, chinook and chum—leave the ocean and swim far inland up the province's rivers and streams to spawn. In none are their numbers greater than in the Fraser River—which contains 10 million or more salmon in good years—where they travel as far as 48km/30mi a day. Spawning grounds lie as far north as Stuart Lake, near Fort St. James. Soon after spawning, they die. Their offspring remain in fresh water for about two years before heading to the ocean, where they mature in two to five years. Then the epic return journey to their spawning grounds occurs.

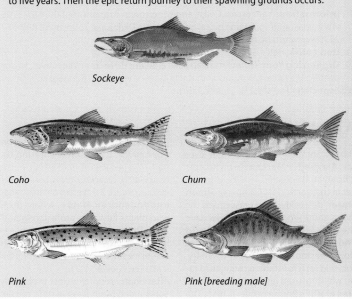

Sockeye

Coho

Chum

Pink

Pink [breeding male]

"fishways" were constructed during the 1940s to enable the salmon to bypass the turbulent water.

An **airtram**★ (*mid-May–Labour Day daily 10am–5:30pm; mid-Apr–early May and rest of Sept–mid-Oct daily 10am–4pm;* ⊚ *$15;* ♿ ☎ *604-867-9277; www.hellsgateairtram.com*) descends 150m/500ft to river level, where the canyon and the incredible speed of the water can be appreciated. There are displays on the salmon and the fishways as well as a film (*20min*). Visitors can also hike down a steep road (*.5km*) just south of the airtram parking lot to take a look at the narrow defile.

After Hell's Gate, the canyon becomes less dark and formidable, and there are fewer trees on its rocky slopes. From **Jackass Mountain** there is a fine **view**★ of the canyon from high above the river.

Lytton

This community regularly registers the highest temperatures in Canada; its record, shared with the town of Lillooet farther north, is 44°C/112°F. At this point the clear blue waters of the Thompson River surge into the muddy brown Fraser, making a streak visible for a short distance downstream.

②Thompson Canyon★ – From Lytton to Shuswap Lake

230km/143mi (not including excursion)
The Trans-Canada Highway and the two railways leave the valley of the Fraser and turn east along the Thompson, passing through a dry, treeless and steep-sided canyon. The road winds and weaves

Address Book

HORSTING'S FARM MARKET
2km/1mi north of Cache Creek on Rte. 97. ☎250-457-6546; www.horstingfarms. com. Freshly made bread goes into the oven early every morning at Horsting's, followed by fresh fruit pies. All are done in time for lunch, a bountiful selection of thick-sliced sandwiches, hearty soups and irresistable plates of homemade pie. Virtually all the produce is grown on the farm. Many travellers stock up here for their journeys north.

GORT'S GOUDA CHEESE
Salmon River Rd., 2km/1mi south of Hwy. 1, just west of Salmon Arm. ☎250-832-4274. www.gortsgoudacheese.bc.ca. Nestled in a pastoral valley beneath the Monashee Mountains, Arie Gort's Gouda cheese factory uses locally produced organic milk to make Gouda, Swiss and other European cheeses, including savory well-aged wheels that will serve the average family for an entire month. Tours to explain the cheese-making process are available to the public.

QUAAOUT LODGE
$$ *North shore of Little Shuswap Lake, across the Squilax Bridge from Hwy. 1. ☎250-679-3090 or 800-663-4303. www. quaaout.com.* One of the few native-owned hotels in British Columbia, this lodge is a peaceful resort set amid ponderosa pines along the best beach on Little Shuswap Lake. Quaaout's massive carved fir doors are works of art in themselves. Summer visitors may choose to sleep in one of the 72 rooms or in teepees by the lake. All guests have access to the on-site sweat lodge, indoor pool and Jacuzzi.

along, making sharp bends. At Spences Bridge, where the road crosses the river, the river **valley**★ gradually widens into a semidesert area, where scrub vegetation and sagebrush predominate.

Hat Creek Ranch★★
Excursion: 22km/14mi round-trip from Cache Creek via Rte. 97. ◷Open May–mid-Oct daily 9am–5pm. ☞$8. ☎800-782-0922; www.hatcreekranch.com. Once a way station along the Cariboo Road, this provincial heritage site offers an impressive collection of restored 19C buildings. The **Hat Creek House** is a handsome Victorian, once a hotel; the **Freight Horse Barn** is still floored with well-worn original timbers. Visitors enjoy wagon rides, drawn by draft horses, around the pretty site. Just upstream, a local First Nations band demonstrates a traditional **summer encampment**.

Just before Savona the Thompson expands to form **Kamloops Lake**. From the Trans-Canada Highway there are some pleasant **views**★ of this blue lake set in rocky arid hills. The highway bypasses the rapidly growing commercial and government centre city of **Kamloops**★, which hosts one of Western Canada's best native heritage sites.

Secwepemc Museum and Native Heritage Park★★
355 Yellowhead Hwy. (Rte. 5), in Kamloops. ◷Open mid-Jun–Labour Day daily 8:30am–4:30pm; rest of year Mon–Fri 8:30am–4:30pm. ◷Closed major holidays. ☞$6. ✕♿🅿☎250-828-9749. www.secwepemc.org/museum. The museum in this heritage park shows how the native Shuswap people lived, and signage in the ethnobotanical gardens explains how they used the plants of the five ecosystems in this region. The Trans-Canada Highway follows the south branch of the Thompson River to its headwaters in **Shuswap Lake**. Here the country changes from dry barrenness to verdant green with sparkling waters. Many salmon spawn in this region after their long swim up the turbulent Fraser and Thompson rivers. The short stretch of water extending north from Shuswap Lake is home to one of the world's largest salmon runs. As many as 2 million sockeye return in October in the "dominant run" years. To celebrate the event, area residents and fisheries

officials sponsor a colorful **festival**★. At **Adams Lake Provincial Park** (*7km/4mi north of Hwy. 1*), visitors can watch the salmon spawn and learn about their fascinating life cycle. Shuswap Lake's warm summer waters draw thousands of vacationers, many of whom rent **house-**

boats to ply the lake's unpopulated back channels (called "arms"). (*For houseboat rental information contact Twin Anchors ☎250-836-2450 or 800-663-4026; www.twinanchors.com*).

INSIDE PASSAGE★★
BRITISH COLUMBIA

This protected inland waterway, the result of past glaciation, cuts between the wildly indented northwest coast and the myriad islands that stretch 1,696km/1,060 mi from Puget Sound in Washington state to Skagway, Alaska. The Inside Passage route extends 507km/314mi from Port Hardy on the northern tip of Vancouver Island to Prince Rupert on the northwest coast of British Columbia, ushering visitors into a world of lush, tranquil beauty.

▶ **Orient Yourself:** The Inside Passage route starts at Port Hardy, a 6 hour drive north of Nanaimo on Vancouver island, or from Prince Rupert, 1,500km/925mi by road from Vancouver.

🕓 **Organizing Your Time:** By using the ferries, you can make a loop from Vancouver to Vancouver Island, then north to take the Inside Passage to Prince Rupert. From there, return to Vancouver via the scenic Cariboo and Fraser Canyon regions. Since the Inside Passage ferry leaves from Port Hardy early in the morning, plan to arrive there the night before.

👣 **Also See:** Vancouver Island

KING PACIFIC LODGE

$$$$$ *Barnard Harbour, BC. ☎604-987-5452 or 888-592-5464. www.kingpacificlodge.com.* This luxurious floating retreat is moored in a quiet bay on Princess Royal Island, and can only be reached by a float plane. Guests enjoy spectacular scenery, wildlife viewing and outdoor adventure along British Columbia's famed Inside Passage. The three-storey wood lodge has amenities ranging from a communal sauna and steam room to soaking tubs and floor-to-ceiling windows in each of the 17 spacious guest rooms. Gourmet chefs prepare all meals, which highlight local seafood. Fishing, kayaking, canoeing and watching for whales, sea lions, bears and wolves occupy daylight hours. Helicopters and motorboats provide access to the island's breathtaking scenery of deep fjords, soaring granite mountains and remote inland lakes.

Cruise

Departs Port Hardy mid-May–Sept every other day 7:30am, arrives Prince Rupert 10:30pm (odd-numbered days Jun, Jul & Sept; even-numbered days May & Aug). Reservations required. One-way ⊜$275/car plus $116 each adult passenger (summer rate). Check-in 1hr before sailing. ✕👣⮾ *BC Ferries ☎250-386-3431 or 888-223-3779. www.bcferries.com.*

From Port Hardy the ferry crosses the open sea at Queen Charlotte Strait, then enters the sheltered waters of Fitz Hugh Sound. The remainder of this voyage through the narrow, spectacular Inside Passage offers close-up **views**★★, weather permitting, of islands to the west and BC's fjord-slashed coast to the east. The densely forested, mountainous terrain drops steeply into the sea. Several abandoned cannery communities are passed during the cruise.

Eagles and seabirds, as well as such marine mammals as seals, dolphins,

The Spirit Bear

Although it is technically just a rare color variation of Canada's ubiquitous black bear, the **Kermode bear** of British Columbia's central coast has long been considered spiritually significant by the area's First Nations inhabitants. Found only in the coastal rain-forest islands and valleys south of Prince Rupert, these bears are rare—there may be just 60 to 100 such creatures left in the world. Ranging in color from pale white to light cinnamon, the "Spirit Bears," as they are known to the native peoples, are most often glimpsed in the early autumn near coastal salmon streams. Conservationists are pressing the government of British Columbia to preserve the bears' homeland, forestalling massive logging proposed for areas along the central coast.

orca and humpback whales, may be sighted during spring and fall migration. The highlight of the voyage comes near its northern end as the ferry enters the 40km/25mi **Grenville Channel**★★. At its narrowest the channel measures only 549m/1,800ft across, with a maximum depth of 377m/1,236ft.

THE KOOTENAYS ★
BRITISH COLUMBIA

Rising in the Rockies, the Kootenay River winds throught the southeast corner of British Columbia, joining the Columbia River at Castlegar. Kootenay Lake, 92km/60mi long, is surrounded on all sides by towering glacier-clad peaks in the Purcell and Selkirk ranges. At the south end of the lake, the valley around **Creston** holds grainfields and orchards. The **Crowsnest Pass** region has some of the largest soft-coal deposits in North America. Farther west, copper, lead, zinc and silver are mined and processed in the huge smelter at **Trail**. Kootenay National Park, on the Alberta border, is one of the four Rocky Mountain Parks.

- **Information:** Kootenay Lake Chamber of Commerce, Box 120 Crawford Bay, British Columbia, V0B 1E0. www.kootenaylake.bc.ca.
- **Orient Yourself:** The Kootenays stretch from the British Columbia-Alberta border, north of Montana, westwards to Kootenay Lake, north of Idaho.
- **Don't Miss:** The SS Moyie in Kaslo is a wonderfully restored paddlewheeler.
- **Organizing Your Time:** The Kootenay area encompasses several provincial and national parks that offer spectacular scenery as well as recreation.
- **Especially for Kids:** At Fort Steele you can ride a steam locomotive and attend the rip-roaring Wildhorse Theatre.
- **Also See:** *ROCKY MOUNTAIN PARKS, THE OKANAGAN VALLEY, CALGARY*

A Bit of History

Gold brought the first settlers to the valley of the Wild Horse River in 1864. When land disputes with the Kootenay Indians erupted, a detachment of the North West Mounted Police under the famed Mountie **Sam Steele** (1849-1919) restored peace, and the settlement took the name Fort Steele.

Sights

Fort Steele Heritage Town★

Kids *16km/10mi northeast of Cranbrook by Rte. 95.* Open early May–June & early Sept–early Oct daily 9.30am–5pm; July–Aug daily 9.30am–6pm; Oct–Apr 10am–4pm (shops and attractions closed). *$13 adult.* 250-417-6000. www.fort steele.bc.ca.

Fort Steele, a fine **site** at the foot of the Rockies, flourished in the early 1890s

Alpenglow in Kimberley

until the railway over Crowsnest Pass bypassed it. The provincial government began restoration in 1961.

The **museum** is set in a reproduction of the old hotel. Live entertainment is provided in the **Wildhorse Theatre** (*July–Labour Day daily 2pm;* ◎*$8 adult ticket.* ☎*250-417-6000*). An old steam locomotive offers rides (*July–Aug. 20min.* ◎*$6 adult*). Costumed staff portray townspeople while shops and cafes offer goods and food.

Kimberley
43km/27mi west of Fort Steele via Rtes. 95 & 95A. www.city.kimberley.bc.ca
A former mining centre a half-hour from Fort Steele, Kimberley has golf courses,

a nature park, a ski centre and summer festivals. The town's main square, the **Platzl**, has a Bavarian touch. **Kimberley Alpine Resort** (*www.skikimberley. com*) has 80 runs, 5 lifts and dependable snow.

Nelson
234km/145mi west of Kimberley via Rtes. 95 South, 3 West & 6 North.
www.city.nelson.bc
This former mining centre has more than 350 lovingly restored buildings and houses, many in granite. The town's historic charm is familiar to those who have seen Steve Martin's film *Roxanne*, made here in 1984.

Kaslo
66km/41mi north of Nelson via Rtes. 3A & 31. www.kaslo.com
This small lake town prospered a century ago as a shipping centre for Kootenay silver ore. Today it offers tree-lined streets, well-preserved buildings and an incomparable lakeside site.

SS Moyie National Historic Site
On the lakeshore on Front St. ◷*Open mid-May–mid-Oct daily 9am–5pm.* ◎*$5 adult.* ☎*250-353-2525. http://community. netidea.com/klhs/home.htm.* This vessel is the world's oldest intact passenger sternwheeler. In its heyday it carried passengers, supplies and silver ore in velvet comfort downlake to the railhead at Creston.

The Gentleman Bandit

Billy Miner (c.1847-1913), an American, gained notoriety when, in September 1904, he robbed the Canadian Pacific Railway's Transcontinental Express. During a later holdup near Kamloops, Miner and his cohorts were apprehended by the North West Mounted Police. He escaped and fled back to the US, where he died in a Georgia prison after robbing banks as well as more trains. Known for his courtesy, he is believed to have originated the command, "Hands up!" The award-winning 1983 film, *The Grey Fox*, starring Richard Farnsworth, is an affectionate tribute.

MONASHEES AND SELKIRKS★★

BRITISH COLUMBIA
MAP P 96

The Trans-Canada Highway crosses the the Monashee and Selkirk ranges by an often spectacular route through Eagle and Rogers passes.

🛈 **Information:** Glacier National Park ☎250-837-7500; Mount Revelstoke National Park ☎250-837-7500. www.parkscanada.gc.ca.

▶ **Orient Yourself:** The Monashee and Selkirk ranges are located in southeastern British Columbia between the central plateau and the Rockies.

☺ **Don't Miss:** Meadows-in-the-Sky Parkway, in Revelstoke National Park, has spectacular views.

⊙ **Organizing Your Time:** Abundant snowfalls can block roads; check conditions before making plans.

✎ **Also See:** ROCKY MOUNTAIN PARKS, CALGARY, THE KOOTENAYS

From Sicamous to Golden

219km/136mi by Trans-Can Hwy.
From the small town of **Sicamous**, the Trans-Canada begins to climb the valley of the Eagle River. After 26km/16mi the highway reaches **Craigellachie** where, on November 7, 1885, the last spike of the Canadian Pacific Railway, linking east and west, was driven (*note the plaque off the road on the right*). The valley narrows before the road reaches **Three Valley Gap**★ (*47km/29mi*), occupying a lovely **site**★ beside Three Valley Lake, edged with sheer cliffs. Soon afterward the road arrives at the top of Eagle Pass (55km/34mi) and then begins a steep descent to the Columbia in the valley of Tonakwatla Creek.

Eagle Pass★
71km/44mi from Sicamous to Revelstoke.
According to legend, this pass through the Monashee Mountains was discovered in 1865 when **Walter Moberly** fired his gun at an eagle's nest and saw the birds fly up a valley pass, which eventually became the route of the Canadian Pacific Railway as well as the Trans-Canada Highway.

Revelstoke★★
🛈 ☎toll-free 1-800-487-1493. www.city-ofrevelstoke.com. Set on the east bank of the Columbia River at its junction with

the Illecillewaet, this small community has a picturesque **site**★. It has become a summer-winter sports centre because of its proximity to **Mount Revelstoke National Park** (*Hiking, fishing, skiing, cross-country skiing.* ⊙*Open daily year-round.* ☎*$6.90/day.* ☎*250-837-7500; www.parkscanada.gc.ca*).

The **Revelstoke Mountain Resort**, known for helicopter, snowcat and back-country skiing, in 2007 announced purchase of a gondola and high-speed lift that will make it North America's longest skiable vertical at 1 829m/6 000 ft. Just to the north, the **Revelstoke Dam** can be seen rising 175m/574ft above the Columbia River. A visitor centre (*4km/2.5mi north by Rte. 23.* &⊙*Open early May–mid-Oct daily 9am–5pm.* ☎*250-814-6697*) features displays of Columbia River power projects.

Meadows-in-the-Sky Parkway★★
27km/16mi of paved road, unsuitable for trailers. Begins on Trans-Can Hwy. 1.6km/1mi east of Revelstoke turnoff. 45min ascent (visitors must board free park shuttle for last 1.5km/.9mi). ⊙*Open daylight hours in snowfree season only. Shuttle runs 10am–4.20pm, late July–Sept.* ☺*Be sure to verify if road is open.* This road ascends Mt. Revelstoke in a series of switchbacks, with a **viewpoint**★ of the town of Revelstoke.

At the summit the **view**★★ extends to the Columbia valley and the Clachna-

Giant Cedars Trail, Mount Revelstoke

cudainn Range. Paths at the summit descend into the **alpine meadows**. Farther up Highway 1, some 20km/12mi east of Revelstoke, the park's **Giant Cedars Trail** is a short (.5km) boardwalk among ancient Western red cedars.

Rogers Pass★★

148km/92mi from Revelstoke to Golden. In 1881 a determined surveyor, **Albert Rogers**, followed the Illecillewaet River and discovered the pass through the Selkirk, through which the railroad was routed.

From Rogers Pass to Golden★★

⚡ *May be temporarily closed when avalanche control is under way. Winter travellers must follow instructions by park wardens.* The Trans-Canada Highway follows the high-walled valley of the Illecillewaet River into the Selkirks and soon passes through snowsheds that provide winter protection for the road. After 48km/30mi the highway enters **Glacier National Park** (*Hiking, fishing, skiing, cross-country skiing, campsites.* ♿⊙*Open daily year-round.* 🚌*$6.90 adult/day;* ☎*250-837-7500; www.pc.gc. ca*). Ahead, the four pointed peaks of the **Sir Donald Range** are visible *(left to right)*: Avalanche Mountain, Eagle Peak, Uto Peak and Mt. Sir Donald itself. To the north is of **Mount Cheops**.

The road swings around the Napoleon Spur of Mt. Cheops to reach the summit of the pass *(72km/45mi)*. The **Rogers Pass Discovery Centre**★ has displays, models and films that explain the history of the pass and the annual battle against avalanches (♿⊙*Open summer daily 7:30am–8pm; spring and fall 8:30am–4:30pm; winter 7am–5pm.* ⊙*Closed Christmas Day and Tue and Wed late Oct–mid Nov.* ☎*250-837-7500; www.pc.gc.ca*). The **view**★ includes the slide-scarred peaks of **Mount Tupper** and **The Hermit**.

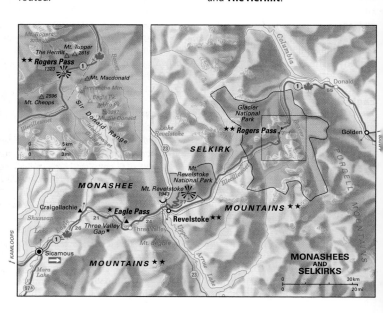

Address Book

RECREATION

Waterborne adventures in the Golden area range from running rapids on the famed Kicking Horse River to watching wildlife while floating on the Columbia wetlands. Outfitters and guides as well as lodges are listed on www.tourism-golden.com. Here's a sampling:

Kicking Horse Mountain Resort –☎250-439-5424. www.kickinghorse-resort.com) 13km/8mi west of Golden This four-season recreational haven is accessible by an 8-person gondola that transports visitors high above the valley floor. Summer hiking trails offer spectacular views. Mountain bike trails, and rentals. Skiing and snowboarding in winter. Area accommodations.

The Alpine Rafting Company – ☎888-599-5299; www.alpinerafting. com) Rafting guides will take you down the Kicking Horse River.

Golden Kayaking Club – ☎250-344-2204. feelfree@rockies.net. Contact Larry Sparks for expert local advice on the fast area rivers. **The Whitewater Kayaking Association of British Columbia** has information at www. whitewater.org.

Columbia River Safaris – ☎1-866-344-4931, www.columbiariversafaris. ca. Wetland eco-tours on rafts or boats with naturalist-guides.

WHERE TO STAY AND EAT

$$$ Alpine Meadows Lodge – ☎250-344-5863; 1- 888-700-4477. www. alpinemeadowslodge.com. 6km/4mi west of Golden. 10 rooms and a chalet. ▭. Situated on mountain slopes above the Columbia River and wetlands, the lodge is perfectly positioned for hiking, golfing, canoeing, skiing and fishing adventures, all minutes away.

$$$ Eagle's Eye Restaurant – ☎250-439-5400. At 3,433m/11,266ft (access by gondola), the restaurant of the Eagles's Eye Suites complex is reputedly Canada's highest dining room. Try the salmon baked in a saffron-vanilla cream.

The road descends under the looming form of **Mount Macdonald**. Passing through a series of reinforced concrete snowsheds, it swings into the valley of the Beaver River, then leaves the park, crosses the Columbia at the town of Donald and follows the river south to **Golden** in the Rocky Mountain Trench.

Golden

🛈☎1-800-622-4653. www.town.golden. bc.ca. www.tourismgolden.com. This rail centre in the heart of the upper Columbia Valley is renowned for its many river rafting, hiking, skiing, mountain climbing and wildlife-watching outfitters. The ski gondola at the new **Kicking Horse Resort** rises to 7,705 ft/ 2,350m. Many inns and lodges offer accomodation.

Touring Rogers Pass

Don Weixl/KootenayRockies.com

OKANAGAN VALLEY★★
BRITISH COLUMBIA

Lots of sunshine and intensive use of lake water for irrigation have made vineyards as well as apple, peach, plum, grape, cherry, apricot and pear growing possible in this area of low rainfall, arid hills and sagebrush. Beautiful lakes, sandy beaches, warm summers and intensive golf course development have made the valley a popular resort that gets quite crowded in season.

- **Information:** Individual towns have tourist offices, given below. For general information go to www.okanaganbritishcolumbia.com; www.okanagan.com; www.okanagan-bc.com. www.sunnyokanagan.com.
- **Orient Yourself:** This valley in south-central British Columbia extends some 200km/125mi north from Washington State, taking in Lake Okanagan, several smaller lakes, and the Okanagan River (in the US, it is spelled Okanogan).
- **Don't Miss:** There are some 60 wineries in the area, and nearly all offer tours.
- **Organizing Your Time:** This area of British Columbia is relatively compact and well-served by roads open reliably all year round.
- **Especially for Kids:** The O'Keefe Ranch near Vernon offers a glimpse of ranch life.
- **Also See:** THE KOOTENAYS; ROCKY MOUNTAIN PARKS; MONASHEES AND SELKIRKS

Osoyoos to Vernon

177km/110mi by Rte. 97.

Osoyoos

Town of Osoyoos, 8707 Main St, Osoyoos, BC, V0H 1V0. ☎250-495-6515. www.osoyoos.ca. The arid hills around **Osoyoos Lake** contrast sharply with the green orchards on the lakeshore. **Anarchist Mountain** (*6km/4mi east by Rte. 3*) provides a fine **view**★★ of the area.

The **Desert Centre**★ (*4km/2.5mi north off Rte. 97;* Open daily 9am–9pm; guided tours (1hr) available May–Oct daily 10am, 11am, noon and 2pm; night tours Mon, Wed, Fri 7pm; self-guided tours daily 9am–8pm. $6 adults. ☎250-495-2470, or toll-free 1-877-899-0897; www.desert.org*) offers tours along a boardwalk through the desert-like foothills.

Similkameen River Valley

Excursion: 138km/86mi round-trip from Osoyoos by Rte. 3 West. The drive from Osoyoos to **Keremeos** (*www.keremos.net*) climbs up to a low pass and descends into the verdant Similkameen River Valley, between the ramparts of the Cathedral Mountains. The area around Cawston (*36km/22mi northwest of Osoyoos*), is particularly dense with fruit stands. Near Keremeos is an 1877 heritage **gristmill**★ (*about 3km/1.5mi northeast of Keremeos off Rte. 3A; follow signs to Upper Branch Rd. ☎250-499-2888*). Southwest of Keremeos (22km/14mi), along a mostly gravel road, is **Cathedral Provincial Park**★, a premier hiking area explorable only by foot (*Open May–Oct daily dawn–dusk;*

CATHEDRAL LAKES LODGE

Open mid-May–mid-Oct. 6 rooms in lodge, 4 in bungalow, and 7 cabins. Rates include all meals, boats, transport. ☎toll-free 1-888-255-4453 (US and Canada only); 01-250-226-7560 (overseas) or 250-492-1606 (lodge). www.cathedral-lakes-lodge.com. $$$ (2 nights minimum stay). Situated on Quiniscoe Lake, across from the provincial park's campground, this wilderness resort welcomes many park visitors, especially hikers, for whom it serves as a base camp. It is accessible only by foot or via the resort's four-wheel-drive shuttle (1hr), which also transports campers. Hearty meals fortify adventurers for a day's exersions. The resort's isolation – and lack of TV and radio – provide total peace.

Touring the Wineries

The best way to see a selection of the Okanagan Valley's 60-some wineries is to use Kelowna or Penticton as a base and devote an early autumn day to touring and tasting. (In summer, tour buses sometimes overwhelm the major wineries.) You can find lists of area wineries, maps and wine country tours on local websites (*www.penticton.ca, www.osoyoos.ca, www.tourismkelowna.com*). Tourism offices can also help plan a travel itinerary and provide maps but highway signs indicate major wineries. Almost all wineries offer tastings and special-purchase bargains; many also serve food. Children can visit as well, but those under 19 cannot taste wine. Nearly all wineries have websites, or you can telephone for information.

Among the most notable Kelowna area wineries are Quail's Gate, Mission Hill, Summerhill, Gray Monk, St. Hubertus, Cedar Creek, Hainle Vineyards and Calona. Penticton highlights include Sumac Ridge, Stag's Hollow, Jackson Triggs, Tinhorn Creek, Gehringer Brothers, Hester Creek and Inniskillan.

Okanagan late-harvest ice wine (the grapes are picked frozen) is a well-regarded desert wine.

www.bcparks.ca). Cathedral Lake Lodge provides jeep transport from its property on the Ashnola River to its resort near the Quiniscoe Lake campground (*$90 return, booked 48hrs in advance*); day trips are possible. The heart of the park is a high alpine basin containing the five Cathedral Lakes. There are campgrounds by three of the lakes.

Route 97 to Penticton★★
Through orchards, Route 97 follows the Okanagan River from Osoyoos to Oliver. As the road approaches **Vaseux Lake**★, huge rocks and barren slopes appear. Watch for bighorn sheep, while the lakeshore is a waterfowl preserve. In contrast, the sandy hills surrounding lovely blue **Skaha Lake**★ are covered with sagebrush.

Penticton
🛈 *Wine Country Visitor Centre, 553 Railway St. Penticton BC, V2A 8S3. ☎250-493-4055. Toll-free 1-800-663-5052. www.penticton.ca.* Set on a pleasant **site**★ on narrows between Okanagan Lake and Skaha Lake, Penticton is a tourist resort.

Mission Hill Family Estate

Mission Hill Family Estate

Beside Okanagan Lake lies the **SS Sicamous**, a stern-wheeler once used on the lake (○*Open mid-Jun–mid-Sept daily 10am–9pm; Nov–Mar weekdays 10am–4pm; May–mid-Jun daily 10am–4pm.* ○*Closed mid-Sept–Oct.* ☎*$5 adult.* ☎*250-492-0403; toll-free 1-866-492-0403. www.sssicamous.com*).

Route 97 to Kelowna★★

Leaving Penticton, Route 97 follows **Okanagan Lake★★**, offering lovely views. According to local Indian legend, the monster **Ogopogo** lives beneath the cliffs. Like his name, Ogopogo is said to look the same viewed from either end; a popular statue in Kelowna's City Park purports to represent the creature.

Kelowna★

🛈*Visitor Info Centre, 544 Harvey Ave, Kelowna, BC V1Y 6C9.* ☎*toll-free 1-800-663-4345. www.tourismkelowna.com.* Route 97 crosses the narrows of Lake Okanagan by a floating bridge.
In 1859, **Father Pandosy**, an Oblate priest established a **mission★**, which still stands at Benvoulin and Casorso roads in south Kelowna.
The **Wine & Orchard Museums**, (*1304 Ellis St.* ☎*250-763-0433. www.kelownamuseum.ca*) hold compact exhibits about these signature local industries.

Route 97 to Vernon

After Kelowna the road skirts Wood Lake and winds along the eastern edge of **Kalamalka Lake★★**.

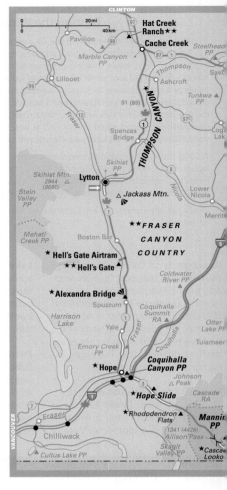

Vernon★

🛈*Vernon Tourism, 701 Hwy 97S, Vernon BC V1T 3W4.* ☎*250-542-1415. www.vernontourism.com.* Along Highway 97 the town's central **Polson Park** stretches along Vernon Creek.

Kettle Valley Railway

Railroad enthusiasts have launched the **Kettle Valley Steam Railway**, which runs regular trips over the remaining 16km/10mi of track on a 1912 steam locomotive, the "3716," out of the Prairie Valley Station in Summerland. (○*Mid-May–early Oct, Sat–Mon 10:30am and 1:30pm; late June–early Sept Thu–Sat*). ☎*$19 adult. www.kettlevalleyrail.org*). The train traverses the spectacular Trout Creek Trestle Bridge.

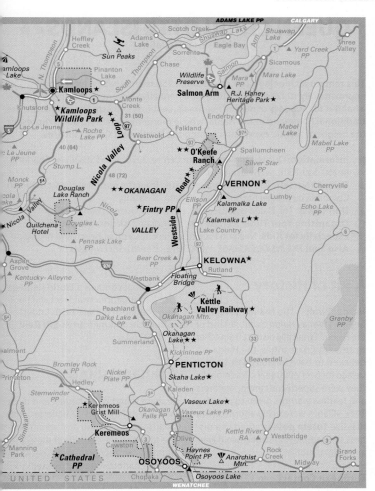

O'Keefe Ranch★★

Kids In Spallumcheen, 12km/7.5mi northwest of Vernon on Rte. 97; turn toward Kamloops, continue 4km/2.5mi. ◷Open May–Oct daily 9am–6pm. ➔$12 adult. ✗ ☎250-542-7868. www.okeeferanch.ca.
In 1867, Cornelius O'Keefe founded a cattle ranch that remained in the family until 1977. Every summer, the **Cowboy Festival** showcases riding and roping contests over a weekend.

Historic fruit label, BC Orchard Industry Museum

QUEEN CHARLOTTE ISLANDS★★
BRITISH COLUMBIA
POPULATION 5,083

This remote archipelago comprises some 150 islands with a total landmass of approximately 10,126sq km/3,910sq mi. Essentially wilderness, the islands remain a habitat for a variety of marine mammals, seabirds and fish. The islands are the traditional homeland of the Haida, whose monumental totem poles represent the height of artistic expression among the **Northwest Coast cultures.**

🄸 **Information:** Queen Charlotte Visitor Centre, 3220 Wharf St, Queen Charlotte. ☎250-559-8316. www.qcinfo.ca
▶ **Orient Yourself:** The islands are separated from the northwest coast of British Columbia by the Hecate Strait (50–130km/ 31–81mi).
⊛ **Don't Miss:** The Haida Gwaii Heritage Centre in Queen Charlotte City.
🕓 **Organizing Your Time:** A cruise takes in isolated islands rich in wildlife.
Kids **Especially for Kids:** Naikoon Provincial Park has a great beach and hiking.
⚲ **Also See:** *THE INSIDE PASSAGE, VANCOUVER ISLAND, SKEENA VALLEY*

A Bit of History

Haida Gwaii – The islands have long been known as *Haida Gwaii*, "Island of the Haida." Ethnically distinct from other Northwest Coast tribes, the Haida are believed to have inhabited this archipelago for over 7,000 years. Traditionally they were superb craftsmen, seafarers and fearless warriors given to plunder. Their villages were richly adorned with massive **totem poles** carved in a distinct style employing strong ovoid lines and animal motifs.

European Contact – In 1774 Spanish navigator Juan Perez Hernandez was the first European to sight these islands. The British named them for **Queen Charlotte**, wife of King George III.
European contact introduced the Haida to iron tools that facilitated their wood carving. By the end of the 19C, however, diseases had decimated the population and by the early 20C the Haida had relocated to Graham Island.

The Islands Today – Though located only 55km/34mi south of the Alaska panhandle, the islands enjoy a temperate climate, thanks to the warm Kuroshio Current. High annual rainfall and fertile soil support forests of Sitka spruce, hemlock and cedar. The southern third of the archipelago is a national park reserve that contains a World Heritage Site. A resurgence of Haida art and traditions, begun in the late 1950s under the leadership of famed artist **Bill Reid**, is evident today.

Graham Island

Graham Island is the largest and most populated of the Queen Charlottes, with small logging, fishing and administrative towns on the east side of the island. Highway 16 runs north–south between Queen Charlotte City and Masset.

Queen Charlotte City
Catering to tourists from the mainland, many of whom arrive by ferry at nearby **Skidegate** (SKID-eh-get) **Landing**, the town's centre offers hostelries, restaurants, and shops along Skidegate Inlet.

Haida Gwaii Heritage Centre★
At Qay'llnagaay, 1km/.6mi from ferry landing. 🕓*Open year-round. Summer hours weekdays 10am–6pm, weekends and holidays 10am–5pm.* ⊛*$12 adult.* ♿ ☎*250-559-7885. www.haidaheritagecentre.com*
This complex of 10 longhouses, completed in 2007, offers exhibits, a museum, meals, shops and tours, as well as the Bill Reid Teaching Centre and Canoe House, housing the stunning **Loo**

Taas, an ornate 15m/50ft hand-crafted dugout canoe produced in traditional Haida style for Expo '86 in Vancouver.

Skidegate
1.5km/.9mi from ferry.
Facing Rooney Bay, this is the seat of the Haida Skidegate Band Council; the elaborate **totem pole**★★ in front of the Council's cedar longhouse was carved by the renowned Haida artist Bill Reid.

Masset
Located on Masset Sound, near its entrance to the open waters of McIntyre Bay, the town attracts sports anglers and beachcombers.

Haida
Adjacent to Masset, Haida boasts several totem poles, notably one in front of St. John's Anglican Church by acclaimed Haida artist Robert Davidson. Craft shops sell works of Haida artists.

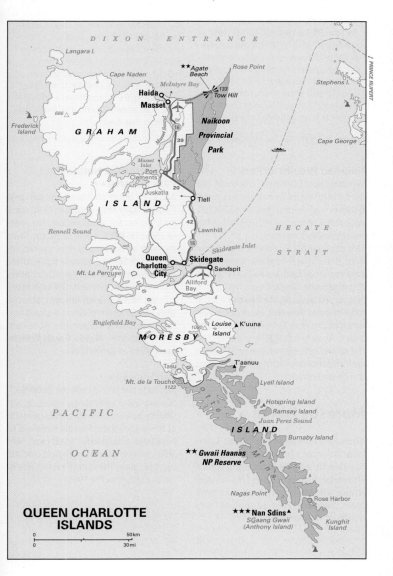

Practical Information

GETTING THERE

By Air: Air Canada Jazz (☎toll-free 1-888-247-2262. www.flyjazz.ca) provides daily flights from Vancouver to Sandspit while **North Pacific Seaplanes** (☎250-627-1341, toll-free 1-800-689-4234. www.northpacificseaplanes.com) offers floatplane service from Prince Rupert to Masset and to Sandspit. **Pacific Coastal Airline** (☎604-273-8666, toll-free 1-800-663-2872. www.pacific-coastal.com) flies from Vancouver to Masset.

By Sea: BC Ferries (☎250-386-3431, toll-free 1-888-223-3779. www.bcferries.bc.ca) offers year-round service from Prince Rupert to Skidegate-Alliford Bay; book well in advance.

You can also arrive in your own boat, docking at Sandspit, Queen Charlotte City or Masset. Arriving from the south, contact the Gwaii Haanas National Park (☎250-559-8818. www.pc.qc.ca)

Car and RV rentals are available in Sandspit, Queen Charlotte City and Masset. For a list of companies, contact the Queen Charlotte Visitor Centre.

TOURIST INFORMATION

To visit sites not accessible by road, including the Gwaii Haanas National Park and Heritage Site, you are advised to use an outfitter. Lists of licensed outfitters are provided by Parks Canada (☎250-559-8818; www.pc.qc.ca), or contact the Queen Charlotte Visitor Centre (☎250-559-8316; www.qcinfo.com). Independent travellers must reserve and take an orientation session. (☎1-800-435-5620 in North America; 250-387-1642 from elsewhere; 604-435-5622 from the Vancouver area.)

Naikoon Provincial Park

9km/6mi east of Masset. Unpaved, but well-maintained beach access road. ⏱*Open year-round.* ☎*250-557-4390. Park visitor centre in Tlell. Hiking, fishing, beachcombing, camping.*

This park, with a 110km/62.5mi beach-front, encompasses the low-lying north-east corner of Graham Island. The two campgrounds operate on a first come, first served basis; **Agate Beach**★★ is the most popular. **Tow Hill**, a forested basalt outcropping, rises 133m/436ft above the beach. An easy trail (⏱1hr round-trip) to the summit affords **views**★ of the beach and, weather permitting, Alaska across the Dixon Entrance.

Moresby Island

Abundant rainfall in the Queen Charlotte Mountains has nourished impressive **rain forests**★★ of towering spruce and cedar, luxuriant ferns and mosses, where wildlife is abundant. The only town, **Sandspit**, is a 20-minute ferry ride from Graham Island.

Gwaii Haanas National Park Reserve★★

Access by sea or chartered aircraft only. ⏱*Open daily May–Sept.* ⊗*$19.80 adult daily access fee. Reservations required.* ☎*250-559-8818; www.pc.qc.ca. Touring with an outfitter is strongly recommended.*♿*See the Address Book. There are no maintained hiking trails; campsites and facilities are primitive.* Though many villages have reverted to forest, at some sites Haida totem poles still stand and ruins are clearly discernible. At several important sites, **Haida Gwaii Watchmen** serve as caretakers.

Nan Sdins★★★

Added to the World Heritage list in 1981, SGaang Gwaii (or Anthony Island), accessible by boat, occupies a spectacular site at the edge of the Pacific. Believed to have been occupied for 1,500 years, Nan Sdins, where several totem poles are still upright, gives the visitor a rare taste of Haida culture in the 19C.

ROCKY MOUNTAIN PARKS★★★
ALBERTA, BRITISH COLUMBIA

Internationally known for spectacular mountain scenery, this chain of four national parks with their diverse topography, vegetation and wildlife, is the jewel of western Canada. Modern parkways dissect the region's wide river valleys, and hiking trails crisscross the backcountry, allowing access to an awesome landscape of soaring peaks, alpine lakes, waterfalls and glaciers.

The major parks in the Canadian Rockies are Banff, Jasper, Yoho and Kootenay national parks and Mt. Robson Provincial Park. They form one of the largest mountain parklands in the world, covering over 22,274sq km/8,600sq mi.

- **Information:** Each park has a visitors' centre. Parks Canada: www. pc.gc.ca
- **Orient Yourself:** The parks are connected by excellent roadways. **Highway 93**, starting at Radium Hot Springs, BC, stretches north to link the Kootenay, Banff and Jasper parks. East-west, Highway 1, the **Trans-Canada Highway**, links Calgary to Banff, then turns north to Lake Louise, where it again turns west, crossing Yoho park to emerge at Golden, BC. In the north, Route 16, the **Yellowhead Highway**, also runs east-west, linking Edmonton to Jasper, crossing the park and emerging at Tête Jaune Cache, BC.
- **Parking:** When hiking or skiing, park only in designated lots: police ticket cars parked on the roadside. Never get out of your car to photograph or feed wildlife, a potentially ticketable offence.
- **Don't Miss:** Icefields Parkway between Lake Louise and Jasper offers spectacular views of glaciers; in the autumn during elk rutting season, you can hear male elks bugle; Parks Canada promises that if you visit Yoho in May or June, you'll see a bear; you can stand astride the Continental Divide at the Vermillion Pass in Kootenay National Park.
- **Also See:** *THE KOOTENAYS, CALGARY, EDMONTON*

Geographical Notes

Canada's Rooftop – Frequently rising over 3,000m/10,000ft, the Canadian Rockies stretch roughly 1,550km/900mi from the US border through western Alberta and eastern British Columbia. To the north the range is bounded by the broad plain of the Liard River; to the east by the Interior Plains; and to the west by the **Rocky Mountain Trench**, one of the longest continuous valleys in the world. The spine of the Rockies forms part of the **Continental Divide**.

Fauna and Flora – Still largely wilderness, the Rockies are inhabited by a variety of animal and plant life. Even along roadways black bear, coyote, elk, moose, mule deer, mountain sheep, squirrels and chipmunks are often seen. Mountain goats and bighorn sheep may be sighted, and in more remote areas, grizzly bears roam.

Plant life varies greatly due to drastic changes in elevation. Wildflowers follow the snowmelt up the mountainsides from late June through early August. Stands of Douglas fir, lodgepole pine, white spruce and trembling aspen in the valleys gradually give way to alpine fir, Lyall's larch and Engelmann spruce on the higher slopes. Just below the tree line lies a band of krummholz vegetation—trees dwarfed by the severe conditions. Above the tree line (normally 2,200m/7,200ft on south-facing slopes, lower on north facing), only the mosses, lichens, wildflowers and grasses of the alpine tundra survive.

A Bit of History

Archaeological evidence indicates nomads traversed this region 10,000 years ago. The Indians living here were overwhelmed, prior to European contact, by the **Stoney tribe**, who moved

Canmore

This former coal-mining town just off Highway 1, a half-hour east of Banff (*22km/13mi*), was propelled into tourism by the 1988 Alberta Olympics, when it was the venue for Nordic events. Accommodation is modern and varied. Outdoor activities include golf, hiking, biking, soaring, climbing, kayaking and river rafting. Nearby are 5 alpine ski centres, as well as opportunities for Nordic skiing and snowshoeing. Set in a wide vale in the Bow River Valley, Canmore is also a gateway to Kananaskis Country, the popular Alberta recreation and wilderness reserve. Good for strolling and less hectic than Banff, downtown Canmore is a tidy district of shops, cafes and small inns. *Tourism Canmore, 907-7th Ave., Canmore, AB, T1W 2V3. ☎403-678-1295, toll-free 1-666-226-6673 or www.tourismcanmore.com.*

into the Rockies in the early 1700s. During the 18C, the **fur trade** burgeoned in the Rockies, and by the mid-19C, mountaineers and explorers had arrived.

By 1885 the **Canadian Pacific Railway** (CPR) line had reached the West Coast. Recognizing the mountains' tourist potential, the CPR convinced the government to establish "preserves"– the origin of the parks. During the late 18C and early 19C, the railway company built fine mountain chalets and hotels, a number of which are still in operation. By the 1920s all four Rocky Mountain

national parks had been established. In 1984 the combined four parks were designated a World Heritage Site.

1 Banff National Park★★★

Canada's first and most famous national park, Banff encompasses impressive peaks, scenic river valleys and the popular resort towns of Banff and Lake Louise. In the 1880s construction of the transcontinental railroad and discovery of natural hot springs on Sulphur Mountain elevated Banff to national prominence. Canadian Pacific president **George Stephen** called the springs Banff after his native Banffshire, Scotland.

The Banff Hot Springs Reserve was established in 1885 around Cave and Basin Hot Springs. In 1888 the CPR opened what was then the world's largest hotel, the **Banff Springs Hotel**.

Town of Banff and Environs★★

Banff Town Hall, 110 Bear Street, Box 1260, Banff AB T1L 1A1. ☎403-762-1200. www.banff.ca. www.banfflakelouise. com. This well-known resort town on the Bow River sits at an elevation of 1,380m/4,534ft amid breathtaking mountains. Though bustling with visitors, the community maintains the

Bow River Valley, Banff National Park

Address Book

GETTING THERE

BY AIR

Canadian, US and international air carriers serve Calgary International Airport (*17km/11mi from downtown Calgary*), and Edmonton International Airport (*30km/19mi from downtown Edmonton*). Banff is 128km/79mi west of Calgary via the Trans-Canada Highway and Jasper is 366km/227mi west of Edmonton via Hwy. 16. Scheduled van and bus services connect Banff and Lake Louise to the Calgary airport, with frequent departures daily, as do chartered shuttle and bus services. Buses also connect the Calgary airport with Jasper, while regular bus service by Greyhound and Sun Dog Tour Company connects Edmonton with Jasper. *See below.*

Air Jasper offers charter service out of Jasper Hinton Airport (*780-865-3616. www.airjasper.com*)

CAR RENTAL

Major car-rental agencies serve the Calgary and Edmonton airports, as well as Banff and Jasper. Since Banff and Jasper, as well as Field, BC (Yoho), are within national parks, you will need to pay entry fees at the gate: $9 per person per day, or $18 per day for a car with 2-7 passengers. Yoho and Kootenay parks are less well served by public transport.

BY BUS

Greyhound provides **bus** service between Calgary and the Banff/Lake Louise area and between Edmonton and Jasper; it has Canada's most extensive inter-city bus service. (*toll-free 1-800-661-8747. www.greyhound.ca*).

Sun Dog Tour Company provides bus connections among Calgary, Banff, Lake Louise and Jasper as well as sight-seeing tours. (*780-852-4056, toll-free 1-888-786-3641. www.sundogtours.com.*)

BY TRAIN

VIA Rail runs the **Skeena** between Jasper and Prince Rupert, with an overnight stop in Prince George, year-round. The **Canadian**, running between Toronto and Vancouver, passes through Edmonton and Jasper (*604-669-3050 or 800-561-8630. www.viarail.ca*); www.viarail.ca. The **Snow Train** (*www.snowtraintojasper.com*) takes skiers to Jasper from Edmonton, Vancouver or Toronto, and points along the way. There is no passenger rail service to Banff. (*Toll-free 1-888-8422-7245. www.viarail.ca.*) **Rocky Mountaineer Vacations** offers spectacular train rides on three routes that take in Vancouver, Whistler, BC; Banff; Jasper; and Calgary (*Toll-free 1- 877-460-3200, or international toll-free 1-604-606-7245; www.rockymountaineer.com*)

GENERAL INFORMATION

WHEN TO GO

The Rocky Mountain parks are open year-round. The **summer season** is June to mid-September, peak season being July and August, when daylight extends to 10pm. Visitors should be prepared for cold weather even in summer, since snowfall in August and September is not unusual. Throughout the **winter**, most park roads remain open. Parkways are regularly cleared, but snow tires are strongly recommended from November to April.

VISITOR INFORMATION

Each national park has a visitor centre, operated by Parks Canada, where schedules, pamphlets, maps and permits are available. Go to the Parks Canada website, www.pc.gv.ca, and select the specific website you wish to access. A park pass (*$9 per person per day, valid until 4pm the next day*) is interchangeable among national parks (multiday passes available) and can be obtained from park visitor centres, entrance gates or campground kiosks. *For specific information about each park, consult the white portion of this section.*

ACCOMMODATIONS

The Canadian Rockies are known for their **back-country lodges**, sometimes accessible only by hiking, skiing or helicopter. These wilderness hostelries range from rustic cabins to comfortable alpine chalets with fine food. Primitive cabins that rent for $25-$32 per night per person can be reserved in both national and provincial parks through The Alpine Club of Canada (*PO Box 8040, Indian Flats Road, Canmore, AB, T1W 2T8.*

☎403-678-3200. www.alpineclubof-canada.ca). Campgrounds are located throughout the national parks. At least one campground in each park offers powered sites and showers. All sites are offered on a first-served basis. Hotels, resorts, motels, B&Bs, chalets and condominiums abound in the area. For lodging information, contact the Banff/Lake Louise Tourism Bureau (☎403-762-8421; www.banff-lakelouise.com) or the Jasper Chamber of Commerce (☎780-852-3858, www.jaspercanadianrockies.com)

RECREATION

All four national parks, as well as many provincial parks, offer **hiking, backpacking, bicycling, horseback riding, canoeing, fishing, swimming** (except Yoho) and **winter sports**. Banff and Jasper have facilities for **tennis** and **golf**; Banff has **bowling**; boat tours and canoe rentals are also available. For details contact Parks Canada (See above).

Fairmont Banff Springs, Fairmont Lake Louise and Fairmont Jasper Lodge hotels offer **guided hikes/snowshoe/ski excursions.** Skilled naturalist guides explain the history, ecology, and legends of the mountains. Available for everyone, not only hotel guests. Reservations can be made with the hotel concierge: Fairmont Banff Springs ☎403-762-2211; The Fairmont Chateau Lake Louise ☎403-522-3511; Jasper Park Lodge ☎780-852-3301.

The Fairmont Banff Springs and the Jasper Park Lodge have renowned golf courses, while Kananaskis Country Golf Course has two 18-hole courses (☎403-591-7272). Other popular golf courses are located at Canmore and Radium Hot Springs, BC.

Outfitters specializing in **wilderness excursions** provide equipment, guides and transportation. Flightseeing is not permitted within the national parks. Canmore-based Alpine Helicopters Ltd. offers sightseeing and heli-hiking (☎403-678-4802. www.alpinehelicopter.com). For more information, contact the Banff/Lake Louise Tourism Bureau (☎403-762-8421. www.banfflakelou-ise.com) or The Jasper Chamber of Commerce (☎780-852-3858. www.jaspercanadianrockies.com)

The Canadian Rockies offer **winter sports** from mid-November to mid-May including downhill skiing, snowboarding, ice-skating, dogsledding and cross-country skiing. Three **ski resorts** are near Banff: **Lake Louise** (☎403-522-3555, toll-free 1-800-258-7669. www.skilouise.com); **Sunshine Village** (☎403-277-7669, toll-free 1-877-542-2633. www.sunshinevillage.com); **Ski Banff @ Norquay** (☎403-762-4421. www.banffnorquay.com). **Marmot Basin** is near Jasper (☎780-852-3816, toll-free 1-866-952-3816 www.skimarmot.com). Amenities include restaurants, ski rentals, ski schools and day-care services. An adult lift tickets at these resorts runs to $50-$70 a day, but there are many packages. The multi-day Tri-Area pass at Banff includes free transport between your hotel and the

Hiking in Banff National Park

slopes. Buses shuttle skiers from lodgings to the slopes for $5–$10 one-way. For **Nordic skiers**, there are 80km of trails around Banff, while the parks, notably Kananaskis, have vast networks.

The **Canmore Nordic Centre Provincial Park** (☎403-678-2400, wwwcanmoreadventures.ca) on the site of the 1988 Olympic Nordic events, has 70km/43mi of trails for the intermediate and advanced cross-country skier. Facilities include ski rentals, lessons and a day lodge. The centre was recently extensively renovated.

USEFUL NUMBERS

Area Codes: Banff 403, Jasper 780, Yoho and Kootenay 250.

RCMP (Police): 403-762-2226

Park Weather Forecasts: 1-900-565-5555 (charged per minute), 1-888-292-2222 (from cell or pay phones, credit card required) or www.weatheroffice.gc.ca

Trail Conditions: Banff: 403-522-1264; Jasper 780-852-6177, toll-free 1-877-423-7433. Look on Parks Canada website, www.pc.gc.ca.

Avalanche Hazard (winter): Look on Parks Canada website, www.pc.gc.ca, or consult www.avalanche.ca

♿ *For dollar sign categories and symbols, see the Legend on the cover flap.*

WHERE TO STAY

♿*Almost all hotels in the parks area offer access to outdoor activities, guides and outfitters. The Fairmont hotels also offer Mountain Heritage Guide programs.*

$ HI-Lake Louise Alpine Centre – *203 Village Rd., PO Box 115, Lake Louise AB, T0L 1E0.* ☎403-670-7580 *or toll-free 1-866-762-4122. www.hihostels.ca. 36 rooms, including family rooms, 164 beds.* ♿▣ This hostel's stylish wood-framed appearance and high standards make budget travel a pleasant experience. Dorm-style rooms are spotless and come with two to six beds. Private rooms are also available. Guests have access to a kitchen, a reading room, laundry facilities, a café and wireless Internet. Other Hostelling International facilities in the region are located in Banff, Jasper and Yoho parks, Golden, BC, and along the Icefields Parkway.

$$ Blue Mountain Lodge – *137 Muskrat St. PO Box 2763, Banff AB, T1L 1C4.* ▣☎403-762-5134. www.bluemtnlodge. com. 10 rooms. Minimum 2-night stay. Built in 1908, this small bed-and-breakfast offers affordable rooms, all with a private bath, cable TV and wireless Internet. The rate includes an ample cold breakfast buffet. Guests also have use of a communal kitchen and a ski-storage area.

$$$ Num-Ti-Jah Lodge – *40km/25mi north of Lake Louise on Hwy 93 North, PO Box 39, Lake Louise AB, T0L 1E0.* ☎403-522-2167. www.num-ti-jah.com. 25 rooms. ♿▣. The original lodge was built some 80 years ago by Jimmy Simpson, a mountain guide. Refurbished and expanded, the timber-frame inn overlooks Bow Glacier and Bow lake, in a splendid setting. The Elkhorn Dining Room offers a table d'hôte. Comfortable lounge and library. No TV or phone, although a satellite phone is available.

$$$ Baker Creek Chalets – *PO Box 66, Lake Louise AB, T0L 1E0.* ☎403-522-3761. www.bakercreek.com. 33 cabins and suites. ♿▣. Situated between Lake Louise and Banff on the Bow Valley Parkway, Baker Creek's cozy log chalets provide well-priced accommodations. The chalets all have balconies and kitchenettes. Suites in a newer building are done up in warm, earthy tones. Plan to eat at the **Baker Creek Bistro ($$$)**, an unpretentious dining room that serves up hearty Canadian-style meals.

$$$ Brewster's Mountain Lodge – PO Box 2286, *208 Caribou St., Banff AB T1L 1C1.* ☎403-762-2900 or toll-free 1-888-762-2900. www.brewsteradventures.com. 60 rooms, 17 suites. ♿▣. This western-style hotel, with its distinctive peeled-log exterior,is just one block from downtown Banff. A timber stairway leads upstairs to spacious, updated bedrooms. Bountiful breakfasts in an inviting downstairs dining room.

$$$ Paradise Lodge and Bungalows – *Lake Louise Dr., Lake Louise AB, T0L 1E0. Closed Oct –May.* ♿▣. ☎403-522-3595. www.paradiselodge.com. 45 cabins and suites. The undeniable charm of this heritage property, located between the valley floor and Lake Louise, attracts the same guests year after year. Well-tended gardens surround the tidy cabins, built in the 1930s, some of which feature vaulted ceilings and claw-foot tubs. Larger than the cabins, the suites contain fireplaces and offer the best views; some have kitchens, equipped with basic amenities. No pets.

$$$ Spruce Grove Inn – *Banff Ave, PO Box 1540, Banff AB, T1L 1B5.* ☎*403-762-3301 or toll-free 1-800-879-1991. www. banffvoyagerinn.com. 114 rooms.* ♿ 🅿. Built in 2002, this lodging is spanking new by the venerable standards of many park hotels. It is on a strip of motels that leads into downtown Banff from the Trans-Canada Highway. Although the inn keeps rates relatively low by offering fewer amenities, its rooms are spacious and comfortable. Ski storage and heated underground parking are included in the rate. Many restaurants lie within a 10-minute walk.

$$$ Tekarra Lodge – *1.6km/1mi south of Jasper. Hwy 93A South, Jasper AB, T0E 1E0.* ☎*780-852-3058 or toll-free 1-800-709-1824. www.tekarralodge. com. 52 cabins. Closed Nov–Apr.* ♿ 🅿. After 1913, when motor vehicles were permitted in the Rocky Mountain parks, "bungalow camps" such as this one sprang up. Tekarra dots the open forest above the Athabasca River with rustic cabins featuring comfortable beds, cooking facilities and wood-burning fireplaces. There is a telephone at the front desk, but no TV. The Tekarra restaurant (**$$**) serves a varied menu, on the hearty side.

$$$$ Buffalo Mountain Lodge – *PO Box 1326, Tunnel Mountain Rd., Banff AB, T1L 1B3.* ☎*403-762-2400 or toll-free 1-800-661-1367. www.crmr. com. 108 rooms.* ♿ 🅿. This sprawling lodge offers a peaceful retreat from the bustle of Banff, just a short walk away. The sizable bedrooms include a fireplace, and a balcony or patio. Some bathrooms feature claw-foot bathtubs and heated floors. The renowned Sleeping Buffalo Restaurant (**$$$$**) specializes in local produce and game raised on a ranch nearby. As well as the customary strenuous activities, the hotel offers a comfortable lounge with excellent single-malt Scotch.

$$$$$ Emerald Lake Lodge – *In Yoho National Park. PO Box 10, Field, BC, V0A 1G0.* ☎*403-410-7417 or toll-free 1-800-663-6336. www.crmr.com. 85 rooms in 24 chalets.* ♿ 🅿. Set among towering evergreens, this quintessential mountain getaway overlooks one of the region's most picturesque lakes. Large comfortable rooms with fieldstone fireplaces, pine furnishings and private entrances, promote a restful stay. Take your meals in the main lodge or at the casual lakeside cafe. A wide range of summer and winter activities, and a free shuttle connects to the Lake Louise ski resort.

$$$$$ Fairmont Banff Springs – *405 Spray Ave., Banff AB T1L 1J4.* ☎*403-762-2211 or toll-free 1-800-257-7544. www. fairmont.com. 778 rooms.* ♿ 🅿 🆂🅿🅰. This turreted château overlooking the Bow River is one of the world's best-known mountain playgrounds. First opened in 1888, "The Springs" has since been thoroughly modernized. Rooms are smartly decorated, although on the smallish side. The real attractions are the opulent ambience and an abundance of facilities, including its luxurious Willow Stream Spa, a 27-hole golf course and riding stables. No less than 11 restaurants range from an intimate wine bar to the top-drawer **Banffshire Club ($$$$),** the latter specializing in roasted Alberta lamb and beef, bison carpaccio, venison and other Canadian classics. Visitors are welcome at all hotel eateries.

$$$$$ Fairmont Chateau Lake Louise – *111 Lake Louise Drive, Lake Louise AB T0L 1E0.* ☎*403-522-3511, toll-free 1-800-257-7544. www.fairmont.com. 489 rooms.* ♿ 🅿 🆂🅿🅰. This famous mountain resort's stunning view of turquoise-blue Lake Louise is perhaps the most renowned in the Canadian Rockies. Restaurants include the Fairview Room (**$$$**), offering fine contemporary fare accompanied by dramatic views. Outside, colourful gardens lead to a paved walkway bordering the lakeshore. Activites offered range from rock-climbing to barn dancing.

$$$$$ Fairmont Jasper Park Lodge – *Old Lodge Rd, Jasper AB, T0E 1E0.* ☎*780-852-3301 or toll-free 1-800-257-7544. www.fairmont.com. 446 rooms in a complex of cabins and lodges.* ♿ 🅿 🆂🅿🅰. Sprawling along turquoise-colored Beauvert Lake, this historic property boasts its own championship golf course as well as extensive sports facilities. Accommodations range from chalet-style cottages to log cabins that have hosted royalty, including Queen Elizabeth II. Dining spots include the illustrious **Edith Cavell Room ($$$$)**, (named for a nearby mountain) with a menu of Canadian game and seafood.

$$$$$ Lake O'Hara Lodge – *In Yoho National Park. PO Box 55, Lake Louise AB T0L 1E0. ☏250-343-6418, 403-678-4110 (off-season). www.lakeohara.com. 23 cabins and rooms. (Rates include all meals and shuttle to the lodge.) Closed Oct–Jan, early-Apr–mid-June.* Originally built by the Canadian Pacific as a back-country lodge, this site on Lake O'Hara is one of the most splendid in Canada. The main lodge holds a restaurant and eight standard guest rooms, but the the lakeside cabins are more coveted. Access to the property is by shuttle; no private cars are allowed on the site (*parking is 15km/9mi east of Field*). In the winter season (*early-Feb–early-Apr*), guests ski or snowshoe 12km/7.5mi to the lodge. No TV, radio or Internet connections. ☏Parks Canada and the Alpine Club of Canada (☏*see above*) have far less pricey sites on Lake O'Hara.

$$$$$ Post Hotel – *PO Box 69, 200 Pipestone Rd, Lake Louise AB, T0L 1E0. ☏403-522-3989 or toll-free 1-800-661-1586. www.posthotel.com. 94 rooms.* ☏☏. A short walk from the village, this stylish retreat, part of the French Relais & Châteaux group, is set along the tumbling waters of the Pipestone River. Spacious guestrooms feature polished logwork, luxurious bathrooms and balconies; many feature a hot tub and fireplace. The **dining room ($$$$)** is renowned for its Canadian cuisine.

WHERE TO EAT

$$ Becker's Gourmet Restaurant – *Hwy 93, PO Box 579, Jasper AB, T0E 1E0. ☏780-852-3535. www.beckerschalets. com. Open May–Oct for breakfast and dinner.* Diners can look across the Athabasca River to distant mountains while enjoying cuisine prepared from fresh local products such as Alberta beef, lamb, bison, venison and rainbow trout.

On colder evenings, a fire crackles in the riverstone fireplace. Repeat customers ask for a bowl of housemade ice-cream.

$$ Lake Louise Railway Station and Restaurant – *200 Sentinel Rd., Lake Louise AB T0L 1E0. www.lakelouisestation.com. ☏403-522-2600.* This former Canadian Pacific Railway station, built in 1910 and furnished with Arts and Crafts furniture, offers eclectic lunch and dinner menus with foreign touches: Asian, Italian and Mexican. The restored 1925 Canadian Pacific dining car offers a more limited dinner menu only. For authenticity, CPR freight trains still rumble past.

$$ Jack Pine Bistro and Lodge – *In Rundlestone Lodge, 537 Banff Ave., PO Box 481, Banff AB, T1L 1A6. ☏403-762-2201, toll-free 1-800-661-8630. www.rundlestone.com. Breakfast and dinner only.* Many tourists miss this fine restaurant, located away from the town centre, but it's worth seeking out because the contemporary cuisine is excellent in all regards. The kitchen serves Canadian game such as bison rib-eye, as well as Pacific-coast seafood, Québec duck, Atlantic lobster and, of course, Alberta beef. Knowledgeable wait staff and a good representation of Canadian wines (try a glass of British Columbia ice wine with your dessert) round out a pleasant dining experience.

$$$ Maple Leaf – *137 Banff Ave., PO Box 3150, Banff AB, T1L 1C8. ☏403-760-7680, toll-free 1-866-403-7680. www.banffmapleleaf.com.* This popular dining room, faced in cedar and presided over by a moose head, offers imaginative Canadian cuisine. Lunch features local favorites such as paninis, fish-and-chips and bison or elk-burgers. The dinner menu offers a more refined menu of fresh seafood as well as lamb, beef, bison and game. There is a children's menu. Request an upstairs table for the best views and a quieter dining experience.

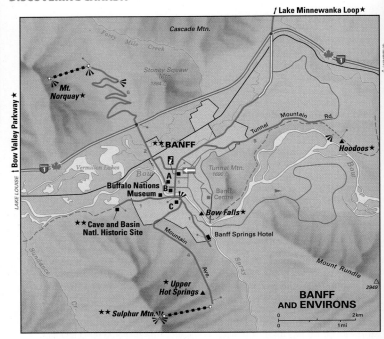

charm of a small alpine town. June through August, it hosts the **Banff Arts Festival**.

Operated by Parks Canada, the **Banff Information Centre** (*224 Banff Ave. Box 900, Banff AB T1L 1K2* Open mid-Jun–Labour Day daily 8am–8pm; rest of the year 9am–5pm. Closed Dec 25. *403-762-1550. www.pc.gc.ca*) provides information on park activities and services. Next door, find Friends of Banff

National Park (*403-762-8918. www. friendsofbanff.com*), where topographic maps, books and gifts are sold. Both places offer free guided nature walks.

Whyte Museum of the Canadian Rockies★ (A)

111 Bear St, PO Box160, Banff AB T1L 1A3. Open year-round daily 10am–5pm. Closed Jan 1, Dec 25. $6 adult. *403-762-2291. www.whyte.org.*

This contemporary building displays historical items and Stoney Indian artifacts, art exhibits and archives. The museum also gives tours of 7 historical local houses and offers regular lectures.

Banff Park Museum★ (B)

93 Banff Ave, PO Box 900, Banff AB, T1L 1K2. Open mid-May–September daily 10am–6pm. Rest of the year 1pm–5pm. Closed Dec 25-26 and Jan 1. Tours in summer daily 3pm; rest of year Sat-Sun 2.30pm. $4 adult. *403-762-1558. www.pc.gc.ca.* Constructed in the "railway pagoda" style in 1903, this national historic site displays minerals and stuffed animals of the Rocky Mountains. Among the collections is a series of prints by renowned artist **Robert Bateman**.

FLOAT YOUR OWN BOAT

Summertime crowds in downtown Banff can be daunting, but a remarkably serene interlude lies the corner of Bow Ave. and Wolf St. **Rocky Mountain Raft Tours** (*PO Box 1771, Banff AB, T1L 1B6.* *403-762-3632*) offers one- or two-hour tours on oar-powered rafts down the Bow river, led by a guide. $24 for one hour, $40 for two hours, children half price. You can also rent a canoe and paddle yourself. A quiet two-hour trip leads up the valley along Echo Creek to the three Vermilion Lakes and back, amidst hushed forests. You are likely to see elk, deer, bears and eagles.

Cascade Gardens★ [C]

At the south end of Banff Ave., across Bow River Bridge. 🕐*Open Jun–Sept daily.* 🚫*No charge.* These terraced gardens provide an excellent **view**★ of **Cascade Mountain**, the 2,999m/9,840ft peak that towers above the north end of Banff Avenue. The stone 1935 Gothic Revival building houses the park administration offices.

Buffalo Nations Museum

[Kids] ♿*On the south bank of the Bow River. 1 Birch Ave., PO Box 850, Banff AB, T1L 1A8.* 🕐*Open mid-May–early Oct daily 11am–6pm. Rest of the year daily 1pm–5pm.* 🚫*$8 adult.* ☎*403-762-2388. www.buffalonationsmuseum.ca.*
A replica of a log fur-trading fort, this museum displays native artifacts and life-size dioramas depicting aspects of Plains Indian life.

Bow Falls★

At the foot of the Fairmont Banff Springs Hotel, the Bow River tumbles over a wide, low lip, just before its confluence with the Spray River.

Cave and Basin National Historic Site★★

♿🕐*Open mid-May–Sept daily 9am–6pm. Rest of the year Mon–Fri 11am–4pm, weekends 9:30am–5pm.* 🕐*Closed Jan 1, Dec 25-26.* ☞*Tours in summer 11am, 2pm, 4pm. Rest of the year Sat-Sun at 11am.* 🚫*$4 adult.* ☎*403-762-1566. www.pc.gc.ca.*
The 1914 stone building surrounds an open-air swimming pool (🚫*not open for swimming*) of hot springs water (average temperatures 30–35°C/86–95°F).

Sulphur Mountain★★

3.5km/2.2mi from downtown. ♿🕐*Access by gondola (8min ascent) year-round daily. Hours vary.* 🚫*$25 adult.* ☎*403-762-2523; www.banffgondola.com.*
The 2,285m/7,500ft summit allows a splendid 360-degree **panorama**★★★ of the Bow Valley and surroundings.

Upper Hot Springs★

♿[Kids] *3.5km/2.2mi from downtown; follow Mountain Ave.* 🕐*Open mid-May–early Sept daily 9am–11pm. Rest of the year Sun–Thu 10am–10pm, Fri–Sat 10am–11pm.* 🚫*$7.50 adult.* ☎*403-762-1515, toll-free 1-800-767-1611. www.pc.gc.ca.*
Discovered a year after the Cave and Basin hot springs, the mineral waters (average temperature 38°C/100°F) now feed a large public pool perched on the mountainside overlooking Bow Valley.

Hoodoos★

These naturally sculpted pillars of cemented rock and gravel can be viewed from a scenic nature trail above Bow River (*1km/.6mi; trailhead off Tunnel Mountain Rd.*).

Elevated boardwalk along Sulphur Mountain's ridge, Banff National Park

©iStockphoto.com/Vera Bogaerts

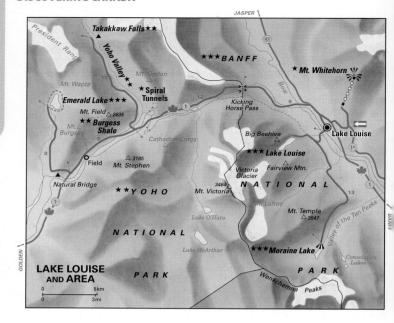

Lake Minnewanka Loop★

Begins 4km/2.4mi from downtown.
Along this 16km/10mi drive are three lakes known for water sports: Johnson, Two Jack and Minnewanka, a reservoir. Tour boats offer cruises *(90min)* down to Devil's Gap *(mid-May–Sept, sailings daily 10:30am, 12:30pm, 3pm and 5pm; late June–Sept 7 pm.* ☎*$40 adult. Minnewanka Tours* ☎*403-762-3473; www. minnewankaboattours.com).* The road passes **Bankhead**, an abandoned early-20C coal-mining operation. An interpretive trail explains the the site.

Bow Valley Parkway to Lake Louise (Highway 1A)★

48km/30mi. Begins 5.5km/3.5mi west of town.
Running along the north bank of the Bow River parallel to the Trans-Canada Highway, this scenic parkway was the original 1920s road connecting Banff and Lake Louise. The route offers **views**★ of the Sawback Range to the northeast—in particular, crenellated Castle Mountain—and of the Great Divide peaks to the southwest. At **Johnston Canyon**★★ *(17km/11mi)* a paved pathway over the narrow limestone canyon leads to the **lower falls**★★ *(about 1km/.6mi)* and the **upper falls**★★ *(about 1.6km/1mi).* The Inkpots, a collection of cold springs, are beyond the upper falls *(6km/4mi).*

▶ *At Castle Junction, Hwy. 93 leads west from Bow Valley Parkway to Kootenay National Park.*

Lake Louise and Area★★★

Smaller and less congested than Banff, this township and the park's west-central section encompass massive, glaciated peaks and pristine lakes, most notably Lake Louise, named for Queen Victoria's daughter, Princess Louise, wife of a Governor-General. By the early 1900s a road had been built to the lake, a large chalet had been constructed and guests were flocking there. In 1925 the CPR completed the **Château Lake Louise**.

Lake Louise Village

The resort is located just off the Trans-Canada Highway. A park **visitor centre** (🕐*Open year round. Late Jun–Labour Day daily 9am–8pm. Rest of the year hours vary.* 🕐*Closed Dec 25;* ☎*403-522-*

3833; www.pc.gc.ca) features excellent **displays** on the natural history of the area, including the Burgess Shale.

Lake Louise★★★
4km/2.5mi from village.

Set in a hanging valley backdropped by the majestic mountains of the Continental Divide, this beautiful glacier-fed lake remains one of the most iconic sites in the Canadian Rockies.

Fed by glacial meltwater, the lake (maximum temperature 4°C/40°F) changes color with light conditions and as the summer progresses. Known as glacial flour, fine powdery silt suspended in the water refracts the green rays of the spectrum and emits hues ranging from bluish-green to emerald.

The far end of the lake is dominated by **Mount Victoria** (3,464m/11,362ft) and **Victoria Glacier**. To the left of Victoria stands **Fairview Mountain** (2,744m/9,000ft), and to the right rises **Big Beehive**. A 2km/1.2mi trail leads along the lake's north shore. Two popular day hikes lead to teahouses: one at Lake Agnes (*3.5km/2.2mi from the lake*) and another at the Plain of Six Glaciers (*5.5km/3.3mi from the lake*).

Moraine Lake★★★
13km/8mi from village.

Smaller and less visited than Lake Louise, Moraine Lake occupies a splendid **site** below the sheer walls of the Wenkchemna peaks.

Moraine Lake Road climbs above Bow Valley, offering a very impressive **view**★★ of ice-capped **Mount Temple** (3,547m/11,644ft) and of the glaciated **Wenkchemna** or **Ten Peaks**. A short walk leads up the rock pile damming the north end of the lake, providing the best **view**★ of the surroundings. Other trails lead to the end of the lake and to nearby back-country lakes and valleys.

Mount Whitehorn★
Access by gondola (15min ascent) mid-May–Sept daily 9am–4.30pm (last ride 4pm). Restaurant at base. ☞$24 adult. ☎403-522-3555. www.skilouise.com.

From the top of the Friendly Giant gondola, a **panorama**★★ of Bow Valley spreads out: the Wenkchemna peaks

Lake Louise

Travel Alberta

and Mt. Temple, with Lake Louise to the west below the Victoria Glacier.

2 Yoho National Park★★

Smallest and most compact of the parks, Yoho (a native word meaning "awe") is a place of raging rivers and waterfalls and the site of the Burgess Shale, one of the most important fossil beds ever discovered.

The Trans-Canada Highway cuts across the park, passing over **Kicking Horse Pass** (1,625m/5,330ft), a point on the Great Divide which is also the boundary between Alberta and British Columbia and between Banff and Yoho national parks. Here, geologist **James Hector** of the Palliser Expedition (1857-60) was kicked by his horse, fell unconscious and, mistaken for dead, was almost buried by his men.

The **visitor centre** at **Field** features displays on the Burgess Shale and other park attractions (&⊘*Open late Jun–Labour Day daily 9am–7pm. Rest of the year daily 9am–4pm.* ⊘*Closed Dec 25.* ⊛*$9 adult park fee.* ☎*250-343-6783; www.pc.gc.ca*).

Spiral Tunnels★

In the shape of an elongated figure eight, these tunnels allowed trains to make the treacherously steep, 4.5 percent descent down "the big hill" leading into the valley of the Kicking Horse River.

Yoho Valley★★

Access road of 13km/8mi with switchbacks; no trailers allowed. Situated between Mt. Field and Mt. Ogden, lovely Yoho Valley is accessed by a climbing road that includes a lookout above the confluence of Yoho and Kicking Horse rivers. Near the road's end Yoho Peak and Glacier can be seen straight ahead, with Takakkaw Falls to the right.

Takakkaw Falls★★

One of the highest waterfalls on the continent, this torrent of meltwalter from the Daly Glacier cascades in two stages for a combined total of 254m/833ft to join the Yoho River. A short paved walk leads to the base of the falls.

Burgess Shale★★

The public can visit by guided hike only. 6km/3.5mi round-trip to Mt. Stephen's fossil beds; 20km/12mi round-trip to Burgess Shale. ⊛*Both are strenuous all-day hikes on steep trails. Reservations required. Contact Randie Robertson, Yoho-Burgess Shale Foundation Mon–Fri 9am–3pm.* ☎*1-800-343-3006. www.burgess-shale.bc.ca.*

Located on **Mount Field** (2,635m /8,6432ft), the Burgess Shale, considered the richest Cambrian site in the world, contains evidence of multicellular life in the oceans 515 million years ago. The challenging trail to the Burgess Shale offers excellent **views**★★ of Emerald Lake and the President Range.

Emerald Lake★★★

Accessible via 8km/5mi road off Trans-Can Hwy. Food and lodging available.

This beautiful lake at the foot of the President Range is fed by glacial runoff that colours the water a striking green.

The road to the lake offers views, from a parking area, of a **natural bridge** of limestone cut by the Kicking Horse River. The **site** is lovely, with Mt. Stephen rising to the northeast and the mountains of the Van Horne Range visible downstream. At the southeastern end of the lake, Emerald Lake Lodge traces its beginnings to a 1902 CPR chalet. Mt. Wapta lies to the northeast and the peaks of the President Range to the west. A pleasant **trail** (*5km/3mi*) circles the lake. After the turnoff to Emerald Lake, the Trans-Canada Highway follows the scenic **lower gorge** of the Kicking Horse River to its junction with the Columbia River and the town of Golden.

③Icefields Parkway★★★

233km/145mi (Trans-Canada Hwy. junction to Jasper).

Designed expressly to dramatize the incredible landscape, this unequalled parkway (Highway 93) runs below the highest mountains in the Canadian Rockies. Following the valleys of five rivers, the road angles northwesterly along the eastern flank of the Continental Divide, connecting Banff and Jasper parks. Glaciers, lakes and waterfalls are abundant along the route.

Hector Lake★

16km/10mi.

The lake is set below the Waputik Range (south), Mt. Hector (east) and Bow Peak (north).

Crowfoot Glacier★★

33km/20mi.

After rounding Bow Peak the parkway reaches a viewpoint from which this glacier spreads across the lower rock plateaus of Crowfoot Mountain.

Bow Lake★★

37km/23mi. Directly by the road, this lovely lake is best seen from the lookout leading to historic, red-roofed Num-ti-jah Lodge. The Bow Glacier hangs above the lake between Portal and St. Nicholas peaks.

Passing through a green meadowland of birch and willow, the parkway reaches Bow Summit (2,069m/6,786ft), the highest pass on the route.

Peyto Lake★★★

40km/25mi to spur road. ⓟ*Park in the lower lot; a short trail leads to a viewpoint.*

The striking turquoise waters of this lake are fed by Peyto Glacier. **Mistaya Mountain** rises sheerly from the opposite side of the lake, with Peyto Peak on its left. The road descends to the valley and passes a series of lakes. At **Lower Waterfowl Lake** lookout (*56km/35mi*), there is a fine **view**★ of the Great Divide peaks, especially towering Howse Peak (3,290m/10,791ft) and pyramidal Mt. Chephren (3,307m/10,847ft).

Mistaya Canyon★

72km/45mi to spur road for parking; follow trail into valley for 400m/.3mi.

This narrow gorge, cut by the Mistaya River, has sculpted limestone walls. Continuing northward, the parkway passes Mt. Murchison (3,337m/10,945ft),

which rises to the east, and the steep cliffs of Mt. Wilson (3,261m/10,696ft), looming above the road. After the road descends into the valley of the North Saskatchewan River, a lookout (*76km/47mi; trail through trees*) affords a **view** of the Howse River Valley.

After the junction with Highway 11, the parkway runs below the massive cliffs of Mt. Wilson (to the east), with views of Survey Peak and Mt. Erasmus to the west and then the facade of **Mt. Amery**.

The road hugs the base of Cirrus Mountain, whose sheer cliffs are known as the **Weeping Wall** because streams cascade down them. The parkway rounds "the big bend" and climbs quickly above the valley to a lookout with a spectacular **view**★★ of the North Saskatchewan Valley. A second lookout faces the filmy spray of **Bridal Veil Falls**.

Parker Ridge★★

118km/73mi.

This ridgetop affords a magnificent **view**★★★ of glaciated backcountry, particularly the Saskatchewan Glacier, part of the Columbia Icefield *(below)*. A switchback trail *(2.4km/1.5mi)* ascends through dwarf, subalpine forest and then through treeless tundra.

At 122km/76mi the parkway crosses Sunwapta Pass (2,035m/6,675ft) to enter Jasper National Park.

Travel Alberta

Athabasca Glacier

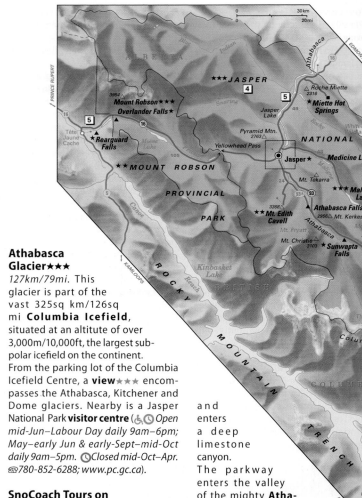

Athabasca Glacier★★★

127km/79mi. This glacier is part of the vast 325sq km/126sq mi **Columbia Icefield**, situated at an altitude of over 3,000m/10,000ft, the largest sub-polar icefield on the continent. From the parking lot of the Columbia Icefield Centre, a **view**★★★ encompasses the Athabasca, Kitchener and Dome glaciers. Nearby is a Jasper National Park **visitor centre** (♿⏰*Open mid-Jun–Labour Day daily 9am–6pm; May–early Jun & early-Sept–mid-Oct daily 9am–5pm.* ⏰*Closed mid-Oct–Apr.* ☎*780-852-6288; www.pc.gc.ca).*

SnoCoach Tours on the Glacier★★

😊*Expect long lines in Jul & Aug especially 10:30am–3pm).* ♿⏰*Tours (90min) depart from Icefield Centre mid-Apr–mid-Oct daily 9am–5pm.* 👓*$34 adult. Brewster Tours* ☎*877-423-7433; www.sightseeing tourscanada.ca.*
These ultra-terrain vehicles travel a short distance onto the upper end of the Athabasca Glacier and allow passengers to get off to briefly on the glacial surface.

Sunwapta Falls★

176km/109mi; 400m/.3mi spur road to parking.
The Sunwapta River plunges over a cliff, turns around an ancient glacial moraine

and enters a deep limestone canyon. The parkway enters the valley of the mighty **Athabasca River** and follows it to Jasper. On the west is the distinctive off-centre pyramidal shape of **Mount Christie** (3,103m/10,180ft) and the three pinnacles of the Mt. Fryatt massif (3,361m/11,024ft). **Mount Kerkeslin** (2,956m/9,696ft) towers over the parkway to the east.

Athabasca Falls★★

199km/123mi; turn left on Rte 93A for 400m/.3mi.
The silt-laden waters of the Athabasca River roar down a canyon smoothed by the force of the rushing waters. Backdropping the cataract is Mt. Kerkeslin.

As the parkway approaches Jasper, the Whistlers can be seen to the west. Straight ahead rises Pyramid Mountain, and to the east, the pinnacled peak of **Mount Tekarra**.

4 Jasper National Park★★★

The largest and northernmost of the four Rocky Mountain parks, Jasper National Park covers 10,878sq km/4,200sq mi, most of which is remote wilderness.

Town of Jasper and Environs★

This pleasant town sits in the valley of the Athabasca River near its confluence with the Miette River, surrounded by small and very beautiful lakes: **Pyramid, Patricia, Annette, Edith** and **Beauvert**. The peak of Mt. Edith Cavell is visible to the south and rugged **Pyramid Mountain** (2,763m/9,063ft) to the north. Jasper, which grew from a Grand Trunk Pacific Railway construction camp set up in 1911, is the site of the park **visitor centre** (500 *Connaught Dr.* ♿ 🕐*Open daily mid-Jun– Labour Day daily 8:30am– 7pm; rest of the year daily 9am, closing hours vary.* 🕐*Closed Jan 1, Dec 25;* ☎ *780-852- 6176; www. pc.gc.ca*).

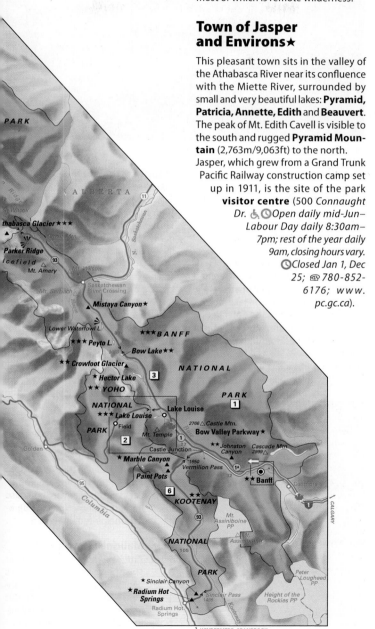

Jasper National Park

The Whistlers★★

Access by tramway (7min ascent) ○*Late June–late Aug daily 9am–8pm, mid-Apr – late June & late Aug –early Oct, 10am, closing hours vary.* ☞*$24 adult.* ☎*toll-free 1-866-850-8726. www.jaspertram way.com.*

The tramway ascends more than 900m/3,000ft to the terminal perched on the ridge. The **panorama**★★★ takes in the townsite, the lake-dotted Athabasca Valley and the Colin Range to the northeast, and Mt. Yellowhead and the Victoria Cross Ranges to the northwest.

Mount Edith Cavell★★

24km/15mi from townsite. Access via Ice-fields Pkwy. to junction with 93A, then Mt. Edith Cavell Rd.

This massif (3,368m/11,047ft) was named for an English nurse executed by the Germans in World War I.

The narrow, twisting access road climbs steeply into the high country, paralleling the dramatic Astoria River Valley. A short walk to **Cavell Lake** from the parking area for the Tonquin Valley Trail (*26km/17mi*) leads to a **view** of the mountain. The lake's bright-green waters feed from **Angel Glacier**. At the end of the road (*2km/1.2mi drive*), is the trailhead for the Path of the Glacier Trail, which follows the toe of this ice river.

Maligne Valley★★★

96km/60mi round-trip by Hwy. 16 and Maligne Lake Rd.

This valley cradles a magnificent lake and canyon, both also named Maligne (Ma-LEEN), or "mean-spirited" in French.

Maligne Canyon★★

7km/4mi from Hwy. 16 junction.

This spectacular gorge reaches depths of 50m/164ft, while spanning widths of less than 3m/10ft in some places. A paved trail follows the the canyon rim.

★ **Miette Hot Springs** \ EDMONTON

Pyramid Lake

★★ **Maligne Canyon**

Edith Lake

★★★ **Maligne Valley**

Annette Lake

Patricia Lake

◆ Jasper Park Lodge

Maligne Lake ★★★, Medicine Lake ★

★**JASPER**

Beauvert Lake

TÊTE JAUNE CACHE

JASPER AREA

0 ——— 2km
0 ——— 1mi

★★ **The Whistlers**★★

★★ **Mt. Edith Cavell** \ LAKE LOUISE

Medicine Lake★

22km/14mi.

The Colin Range to the north and the Maligne Range to the south hem in this lovely lake. After the snowmelt of early summer, the lake gradually shrinks, sometimes becoming only mud flats. The road follows the lake for 8km/5mi.

Maligne Lake★★★

For boat rentals, hiking trips or whitewater rafting, contact Maligne Tours in Jasper. ☎780-852-3370, toll-free 1-866-625-4463. www.malignelake.com.

At 23km/14mi long, Maligne is the largest natural lake in the Rockies and one of the most spectacular. From the road, the twin peaks of **Mounts Unwin** (3,300m/10,824ft) and **Charlton** (3,260m/10,693ft) loom prominently.

Boat Trip★★★

Departs from chalet at Maligne Lake from early June until ice forms in the fall, hourly 10am–4pm (5pm late-Jun–early Sept). 90min. ☞ $43 adult. Maligne Tours ☺See above. The water color changes from green to deep turquoise because of the presence of suspended glacial silt. Passengers can disembark near tiny **Spirit Island** to enjoy the **view**★★★ of the peaks at the south end of the lake.

⑤ The Yellowhead Highway★★

This major thoroughfare, Highway 16, runs east-west through Jasper and Mt. Robson parks and continues westward to the Pacific at Prince Rupert.

From Jasper to Miette Hot Springs★★

60km/37mi

East of Jasper the highway enters the broad valley of the Athabasca River, offering breathtaking **views**★★★. The road passes between **Talbot Lake** (east) and **Jasper Lake**, which is backdropped by the **De Smet Range**. At the Disaster Point **animal lick**, small pools on the east side of the road attract mountain sheep and sometimes mountain goats.

The drive holds fine views of **Roche Miette** (2,316m/7,599ft).

Miette Hot Springs★

42km/26mi to junction with Miette Hot Springs Rd. ♿ ☉Open late June–Labour Day 8:30am–10.30pm, May–late June & early Sept–early Oct 10:30am–9pm. ☉Closed early Oct–April. ☞ $6.15 adult. ☎780-866-3939, toll-free 1-800-767-1611.

The springs are high in natural minerals and the hottest in the Canadian Rockies (maximum temperature 54°C/129°F). The mountainous **setting**★★ for the springs makes this the most spectacular location of the park bathhouses.

From Jasper to Rearguard Falls★

100km/62mi

At **Yellowhead Pass**, the road leaves Jasper National Park (*24km/15mi*) and enters Mt. Robson Provincial Park.

Mount Robson Provincial Park★★

East boundary at 24km/15mi. ☉Open year-round. ☎250-566-9174. Campground reservation 1-800-689-9025.

This 224,866ha/555,650 acre park is named for its greatest attraction: 3,954m/12,972ft **Mt. Robson**★★★, the highest peak in the Canadian Rockies. Just beyond **Overlander Falls**★ (*88km/55mi; accessible by trail*) is the park *visitor centre*. (*♿ ☉Open mid-May–early Oct daily 9am–5pm. www.env.gov.bc.ca*).

Rearguard Falls★

🚶 *3.2km/2mi walk.*

Here, chinook salmon leap upstream during the August spawning season, having made a 1,200km/744mi journey inland from the Fraser outlet on the Pacific.

⑥ Kootenay National Park★★

Kootenay, founded in 1920, extends 8km/5mi from both sides of the highway. ☺Due to forest fires in 2003, some park trails may still be closed. Check with

Peaks of the Parks

Numerous mountains of the Canadian Rockies approach or exceed the 3,000m/10,000ft mark. Here are some of the high risers, in order of elevation, mentioned in this guide:

Mount Kerkeslin: 2,956m/9,696ft

Cascade Mountain: 2,999m/9,840ft

Mount Christie: 3,103m/10,180ft

Mount Stephen: 3,185m/10,447ft

Mount Charlton: 3,260m/10,693ft

Mount Wilson: 3,261m/10,696ft

Howse Peak: 3,290m/10,791ft

Mount Unwin: 3,300m/10,824ft

Mount Chephren: 3,307m/10,847ft

Mount Murchison: 3,337m/10,945ft

Mount Fryatt: 3,361m/11,024ft

Mount Edith Cavell: 3,368m/11,047ft

Mount Victoria: 3,464m/11,362ft

Mount Temple: 3,549m/11,644ft

Mount Robson: 3,954m/12,972ft (highest peak in the Canadian Rockies)

Kootenay National Park Visitor Centre, *7556 Main Street East, Radium Hot Springs, BC. ☎250-347-9505. ◷Open mid-May–early Oct 9am–5pm (Jul–Aug 6pm). In off-season, contact Yoho National Park Visitor Centre ☎250-343-6783.*

From Castle Junction to Radium Hot Springs

105km/65mi by Rte. 93

This picturesque **route**★★ through Kootenay National Park leaves the Trans-Canada Highway at Castle Junction and climbs steeply to the summit of **Vermilion Pass** (1,650m/5,412ft). The pass marks the Great Divide.

Marble Canyon★

17km/11mi from junction.

The rushing waters of Tokumm Creek charge through this narrow limestone gorge on their way to meet the Vermilion River. The **visitor centre** (&.&*For hours, see above. ☎403-762-9196, or 250-347-9615/winter*) for the park's north entrance is located here.

Paint Pots

20km/12mi from junction; trail of 1.2km/.7mi.

This area contains pools of ochre clay used as body paint and dyes by Indians and later mined by Europeans. Native tribes considered the three cold **mineral springs**★places of spiritual power.

At 89km/55mi a lookout provides a sweeping **view**★ of the wide, wooded **Kootenay Valley** and the **Mitchell Range** flanking its west side. After topping Sinclair Pass (1,486m/4,874ft), the

Kootenay National Park

road follows Sinclair Creek's tumbling descent through **Sinclair Valley**★.

Radium Hot Springs★
103km/64mi.

Kids ♿ 🕐 *Open mid-May– early Oct daily 9am–11pm. Rest of the year Sun–Thu noon–9pm, Fri–Sat noon–10pm.* 🎫*$6.50 adult.* ☎*250-347-9485, toll-free 1-800-767-1611. www.pc.gc.ca.*The waters of Radium Hot Springs (average tem-perature 47°C/117°F) feed the swim-ming pools in the park complex. A park **information centre** is located at the corner of Main Street East and Redstreak Campground Road. ☎*250-347-9505 or 250-347-9615/winter; www.pc.gc.ca).* After the hot springs, the highway passes through **Sinclair Canyon**★ before reaching the park's southern entrance gate.

SKEENA VALLEY★★
BRITISH COLUMBIA

This verdant river valley holds the second-largest river in the province. Rising in the Skeena Mountains of the interior, the 565km/350mi "river of mists" flows south to the town of New Hazelton, then southwest to the Hecate Strait, following a massive channel cut by Ice Age glaciers. The valley is noted for its rich Tsimshian culture of the Gitxsan tribe, which still inhabits the riverbanks. The river itself is famed worldwide for its steelhead trout; fishing lodges are situated along its banks.

- ℹ **Information:** Northern British Columbia Tourist Association. ☎250-561-0432, 1-800-663-8843. www.nbctourism.com
- ▸ **Orient Yourself:** The western portion of Route 16 between Prince George and Prince Rupert takes you through the Skeena Valley, lying between New Hazelton and Kitwanga.
- 👁 **Don't Miss:** The totem poles and reconstructed K'san village near New Hazelton; the Cow Bay waterfront area in Prince Rupert.
- Kids **Especially for Kids:** The area around New Hazelton is rich in aboriginal culture.
- 👣 **Also See:** ALASKA HIGHWAY, INSIDE PASSAGE, QUEEN CHARLOTTE ISLANDS

A Bit of History

Ancestral Home – The Skeena River and its tributaries have been the terri-tory of the Gitxsan Indians for close to 10,000 years. The Gitxsan subsisted on salmon, berries and western red cedar, which was used for their longhouses, canoes, clothing and elaborate totem poles. Pole-raisings and important occa-sions were accompanied by great feasts called **potlatches**.

European Contact – In the 19C Euro-pean fur-trading posts, dominated by the Hudson's Bay Company, were established along the river. In the 1880s stern-wheelers came to the Skeena. In 1912 the Grand Trunk Pacific Railway was completed. Today the Yellowhead

Chilkat blanket

Highway follows the Skeena from east of Prince Rupert to New Hazelton.

Native Decline and Renewal – The Gitxsan Indians were greatly affected by the arrival of Europeans. Old patterns of hunting and gathering were curtailed in favor of supplying furs to the new immi-grants; missionary zeal and European

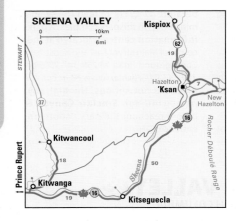

SKEENA VALLEY

misapprehensions about the potlatch led to its ban between 1884 and 1951; totem poles were destroyed; and the introduction of diseases such as smallpox significantly reduced the native population. In the 1970s a renaissance of native culture began. Today their language, Tsimshian, is taught in reserve schools, and traditional crafts have been revived. Silk-screening, introduced in the past few decades, has allowed artists to develop innovative approaches to classic designs.

Prince Rupert

Served by BC Ferries (⊙ See Inside Passage). 🛈*Atlin Terminal, 100-215 Cow Bay Road, Prince Rupert BC, V8J 1A2.* ☎*250-624-5637, 1-800-667-1994.www.tourismprincerupert.com.* Situated on Kaien Island near the mouth of the Skeena, this maritime city faces a deepwater harbor dotted with islands. Located just south of the Alaska Panhandle, Prince Rupert was established in 1906 as the terminus of the Grand Trunk Pacific. With its ice-free harbor, the city today is a fishing and fish-processing centre as well as a port. Prince Rupert receives an annual rainfall of 2,564mm/100in. Reproductions of Tsimshian and Haida **totem poles**★ are scattered throughout the city.

The **Cow Bay** area has a dockside, with cafes, small inns and shops. A Grand Trunk Pacific station removed to the waterfront, the small **Kwinitsa Railway Station Museum**★ has displays of railroading artifacts and old photographs

(⊙*Open Jun–Aug Mon–Sat 9am–noon, 1pm–5pm.* ⊚*Contribution requested.* ☎*250-624-5637*).

Museum of Northern British Columbia★★

100 First Ave. W, Prince Rupert BC, V8J 3S1. ♿⊙*Open Jun–Aug daily 9am–8pm (Sun 5pm). Rest of the year Mon–Sat 9am–5pm.* ⊚*$5 adult.* ☎*250-624-3207. www.museumofnorthernbc.com.*

The museum is known for native Northwest basketry, argillite and wood carvings. The Tsimshian **mortuary frog** is the only remaining item of its kind. The museum building is constructed of massive red cedar posts and beams. At the carving shed visitors can watch First Nations craftspeople at work.

From Prince Rupert★★ to 'Ksan

307km/184mi by Hwy. 16

North Pacific Historic Fishing Village★★

22km/14mi east of Prince Rupert, southeast of Port Edward. 1889 Skeena Dr., PO Box 1109, Prince Edward BC, V0V 1G0. ♿⊙*Open Jul–mid-Aug daily 10am–7.30pm, mid-May–mid-June & mid-Aug–mid-Sept Tue-Sun 10am–5pm.* ⊚*$12 adult.* ☎*250-628-3538. www.district.portedward.bc.ca.*

Built in 1889 on an arm of the Skeena, the complex is the oldest surviving cannery village on the north coast. Fishing and canning methods are explained on guided tours. There is a bed-and-breakfast inn, a restaurant specializing in seafood and a cafe offering light meals.

East of Port Edward Hwy 16 meets the Skeena River, following it through its magnificent valley. The entire route provides excellent views of the broad, turbulent river and of the cloud-shrouded, snowy Coast Mountains rising to 2,000m/6,000ft. In the town of **Terrace**, the **Heritage Park**, a collection of eight old log buildings moved here from outlying areas, depicts pioneer life in the region. The river waters around the town and around nearby Kitimat to the south (*52km/31mi*) provide excellent sportfishing for trout and salmon. After Terrace, where the valley widens briefly, the road winds through the Hazelton Mountains. East of Terrace (*12km/7mi*) at the village of **Usk**, a small cable ferry breasts the treacherous waters of the Skeena.

Tour of the Totems★★

Self-guided driving tour.

New Hazelton Visitor Centre, Hwy. 16, 4070 9th Ave., POBox 40, Hazelton BC, V0J 1Y0. ⓒ*Open Jun–Sept daily.* ☎*250-842-6071. www.village.hazelton.bc.ca.*
Today the Gitxsan still inhabit five ancient villages along the Skeena and its tributaries. Four of these villages have impressive stands of **totem poles**★★★ that date from the late 19C. The weathered poles, devoid of paint, range in height from 5m/15ft to 9m/30ft.

Kitwanga

▶ *Junction of Hwy. 16 and Hwy. 37 North, after crossing the Skeena River; then turn right on Bridge St.*

Situated beside the Skeena River, a fine stand of about a dozen 19C totem poles graces a flat, grass-covered field against a backdrop of the impressive **Seven Sisters** Mountains (2,755m/9,039ft).

Kitwancool

Hwy. 37, 18km/11mi north of Kitwanga.
This village has the oldest existing stand of Gitxsan totem poles, though several of its most venerable ones are now stored in a shed at the rear of the totem field for preservation.

▶ *Return to Hwy. 16 and continue east.*

Kitseguecla

Hwy. 16, 19km/12mi east of junction with Hwy. 37.
The original totem poles in this village were destroyed by fire (1872) and by flood. New poles, however, now stand throughout.

▶ *Continue east to New Hazelton and turn left on Hwy. 62.*

'Ksan

Hwy. 62, 7km/4mi northwest of New Hazelton. PO Box 326, Hazelton BC, V0J 1Y0. ⓒ*Open Apr–Sept daily 9am–5pm.* *Guided tours available. Museum & gift shop also open Oct–Mar Mon–Fri 9:30am–4:30pm.* *$2 adult.* ☎*250-842-5544, toll-free 1-877-842-5518. www. ksan.org.*
A complex of totem poles and longhouses re-created in the traditional style, this historical village museum provides an insight into the Gitxsan culture. 'Ksan, the Gitxsan name for the Skeena, consists of seven major buildings, including a carving house and a silk-screen workshop as well as a museum and gift shop. An extensive **collection**★★ of native artifacts is used to explain the culture and lifestyle of these First Nations people. The acclaimed 'Ksan dancers perform July to mid-August (*Fri 7pm.* *$8*).

Kispiox

19km/12mi north of 'Ksan on Kispiox Valley Rd.
Situated near the confluence of the Skeena and Kispiox rivers, this large village boasts a dozen totems in a field by the waters of the Kispiox.

For dollar sign categories, see the Legend on the cover flap.

WHERE TO EAT

$$$ Cow Bay Café– *205 Cow Bay Rd., Prince Rupert BC V8J 1A2.* ☎*250-627-1212. cbcafe@citytel.net.* ⓒ*Closed Sun and Mon.* This small waterfront café offers creative cuisine and an exceptional site overlooking Prince Rupert's harbor. Fresh local seafood, wonderful crab cakes (*in season*), great deserts. Reservations advised. along with housemade desserts and a good selection of wines.

VANCOUVER★★★
BRITISH COLUMBIA
METRO POPULATION 1,986 865

Canada's third-largest metropolis, this West Coast city has a magnificent **site**★★★ on a peninsula protruding into the Strait of Georgia. A protected deep-sea port, accessibility to the Pacific Ocean, and a virtually snow-free climate have contributed to Vancouver's rapid growth and attracted a multi-ethnic population bringing a cultural diversity and liveliness matched by few cities anywhere. The city is almost surrounded by mountains. To the north the Coast Mountains rise steeply; to the west across the Strait of Georgia stand the mountains of Vancouver Island and to the southeast rises the Cascade Range. Heavy snowfall in the mountains provides the superb skiing conditions that prompted Vancouver's selection as host city for the 2010 Winter Olympics and Paralympics.

- **Information:** Tourist Info Centre, Plaza level, 200 Burrard St., ☎604-683-2000. www.tourismvancouver.com.
- **Orient Yourself**: Downtown Vancouver sits on a peninsula, with Stanley Park on the northwest end. To the southwest, walking and cycle paths connect the beaches of English Bay. To the south, Yaletown and new residential towers are rapidly filling the space along the False Creek waterfront. To the east, BC Place stadium and Chinatown are separated from the shops of Gastown by the seedy East Hastings area (☺*best avoided*).
- **Parking:** Garage and metered street parking is available downtown, but elusive during working hours. Consider walking, cycling or taking public transit.
- **Don't Miss:** Stanley Park's trails and seawalks; the Aquarium; University of British Columbia's Museum of Anthropology.
- **Organizing Your Time:** A good way to start your visit is to take the elevator to the Observation Deck atop the Harbour Centre Tower, from which the city spreads out clearly below.
- **Especially for Kids:** Kids will love the Aquarium, especially the beluga performances, and Science World. There are also many free outdoor activities.
- **Also See:** VICTORIA, VANCOUVER ISLAND

A Bit of History

Early History – The shores of the Strait of Georgia were the preserve of the Coast Salish Indians until 1791, when Spanish captain José Maria Narvaez entered its waters. (English explorer Francis Drake had likely visited two centuries earlier.) A year later, British Capt. **George Vancouver** explored Burrard Inlet, while in 1808 Simon Fraser saw the area from the land side. During the 1860s, entrepreneurs built a brickyard, sawmills to process the area's rich timber, and a saloon. The village known as Gastown became Granville in 1869, when government surveyors laid out a townsite.

The Coming of the Railway – When it was finally decided to route the Canadian Pacific Railway (CPR) down the Fraser Valley to Burrard Inlet, land prices skyrocketed, prompting **William Van Horne** in 1884 to extend the line farther down the inlet to Granville, which he renamed Vancouver. In 1887, the new city welcomed the first trans-Canadian passenger train.

World Exposition – At the conclusion of its centennial world exposition, **Expo '86**, the city of Vancouver sold the site to Concord Pacific Group, Inc, which is investing $3billion in a planned community for 15,000 people with 61ha/150 acres of public parks and a 3km/1.5mi seawall walkway. (*www.concordpacific.com*).

Totem poles in Stanley Park

Vancouver Today – The financial, commercial and industrial centre of British Columbia, Vancouver is also Canada's **largest port**, trading some $43 billion in goods annually, chiefly with Japan and other Pacific Rim countries.

Vancouver is a centre for forest products and fishing as well, although **technology** is now a bigger employer; areas of strong growth are biotechnology, environmental businesses, software, new media and telecom/wireless businesses. Tourism is still a major employer.

Vancouver is also a **film industry** centre, particularly foreign productions attracted by scenic locations, excellent production facilities and a highly qualified workforce.

2010 Winter Olympics

Vancouver will host the Winter Olympic Games in February 2010. The venues stretch over a 120km/75mi zone from Richmond, south of Vancouver, through the city centre and up into the mountain resort of Whistler. Some 5,500 athletes from 80 countries will participate; shortly after, the Paralympic Games will bring in another 1,350 participants. Typically of Vancouver, organisers have set high standards for environmental impact and social responsibility.

Stanley Park★★★

This 405ha/1,000 acre park has a magnificent **site** at the end of a peninsula that almost closes Burrard Inlet at **First Narrows**. The park contains several fine restaurants and family attractions.

Visiting the Park

Kids ✕ 🚻 ⏱ *Open daily year-round.* ☎604-257-8400. www.parks.vancouver.bc.ca. (🐾*it is illegal to feed Stanley Park's wild animals.*) To access the park by car, stay in the far right lane of Georgia Street and follow the overhead sign. Coin-operated parking metres (*summer rates: $2/hr or $7 all day*) are located throughout the park but the city encourages visitors to cycle, roller-blade or take the bus (No.19) to the park, or to park their car and use the **free shuttle** (⏱*Mid-Jun–late Sept 10am–6:30pm; passes every 12-15min*) that circles the park. Numerous walking trails crisscross the forested interior, and a path known as the **seawall** rims the shoreline. Facilities include cricket grounds, tennis and shuffleboard courts, picnic areas, children's playgrounds, and a swimming pool at Second Beach. Horse-drawn carriage tours (*1hr*) depart from Coal Harbour parking lot near the Georgia Street entrance (🚻⏱*Mar–Oct, schedule varies.* ☜*$25 adult. Stanley Park Horse-Drawn Tours Ltd.* ☎604-681-5115. www.stanleyparktours.com).

VANCOUVER

Abbott Street	EV
Alexander Street	EV
Barclay Street	CV
Beach Avenue	CV, DX
Beatty Street	DX
Bidwell Street	CV
British Columbia Place	DEX
Broughton Street	CV
Burnaby Street	CV
Burrard Street Bridge	CX
Burrard Street	CX, DV
Bute Street	CV
Cambie Bridge	DEX
Cambie Street	DX
Cardero Street	CV
Carrall Street	EV
Chestnut Street	CX
Chilco Street	CV
Comox Street	CV
Cornwall Avenue	CX
Creekside Drive	CX
Cypress Street	CX
Davie Street	CV, DX
Denman Street	CV
Drake Street	DX
Dunsmuir Street	DV
Dunsmuir Viaduct	EVX
Expo Boulevard	EVX
Georgia Street	CDV
Georgia Viaduct	EX
Gilford Street	CV
Granville Bridge	CX
Granville Street	DVX
Hamilton Street	DEV
Haro Street	CV
Harwood Street	CV
Hastings Street	DV
Homer Street	DVX
Hornby Street	DV
Howe Street	DVX
Jervis Street	CV
Johnston Street	CX
Keefer Street	EV
Main Street	EX
Manitoba Street	EX
Marinaside Crescent	DX
Melville Street	DV
Nelson Street	CV, DX
Nicola Street	CV
Pacific Street	CVX
Pacific Boulevard	DEX
Pender Street	DEV
Powell Street	EV
Quebec Street	EX
Richards Street	DX
Robson Street	CDV
Seawall Walk	CVX
Seymour Street	DVX
Smithe Street	DX
Spyglass Place	DX
Station Street	EX
Thurlow Street	CDV
Union Street	EVX
Water Street	EV
1st Avenue	CEX
2nd Avenue	EX
3rd Avenue	EX

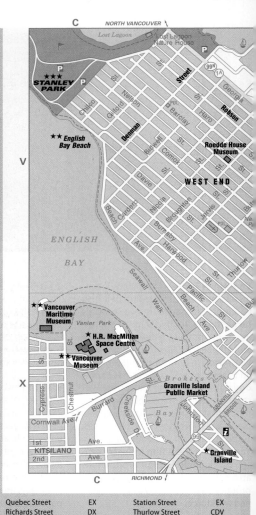

Scenic Drive★

10km/6mi.

Circling the park in a counterclockwise direction, the drive begins and ends at Georgia Street. The route follows the edge of Coal Harbour, offering views of the yacht clubs, port and city as far as **Brockton Point**. Just before the point note the display of brightly painted **totem poles**★, the work of the Northwest Coast Indians. The road continues to **Prospect Point**★ where ships pass through First Narrows. Then the road turns inland, but paths lead to the seawall near **Siwash Rock**★. From **Ferguson Point** there are **views** of **Third Beach**★. The **Sequoia Grill** ($$$ ☎604-669-3281. www.vancouverdine. com) at Ferguson Point features fresh local cuisine and fine vistas. The road continues past Second Beach, various sports facilities and Lost Lagoon.

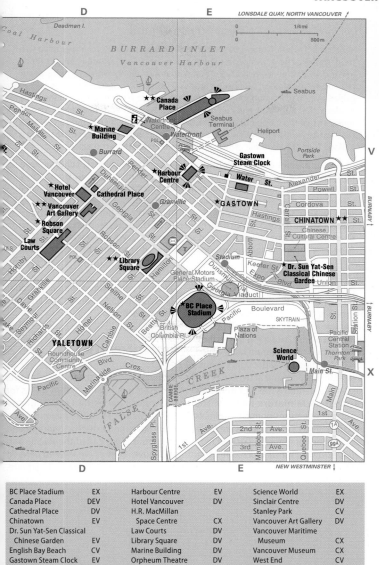

BC Place Stadium	EX	Harbour Centre	EV	Science World	EX
Canada Place	DEV	Hotel Vancouver	DV	Sinclair Centre	DV
Cathedral Place	DV	H.R. MacMillan		Stanley Park	CV
Chinatown	EV	Space Centre	CX	Vancouver Art Gallery	DV
Dr. Sun Yat-Sen Classical		Law Courts	DV	Vancouver Maritime	
Chinese Garden	EV	Library Square	DV	Museum	CX
English Bay Beach	CV	Marine Building	DV	Vancouver Museum	CX
Gastown Steam Clock	EV	Orpheum Theatre	DV	West End	CV
Gastown	EV	Robson Square	DV	Yaletown	DX
Granville Island	CX	Roedde House	CV		

The Park on Foot

Circumnavigating Stanley Park by the 9km/5.5mi **seawall**★★ takes about two hours, but allow extra time for attractions along the way, such as the totem poles, aquarium and Siwash Rock. 😕The pleasant forest trails should not be travelled after dark.

Vancouver Aquarium★★

Kids ✕ ♿ 🅿 🕐 *Open July–Labour Day daily 9:30am–7pm. Rest of the year daily 9:30am–5pm.* 💲 *$20 adult.* 📞 *604-659-3474. www.vanaqua.org.*

This aquarium is known for its marine mammal centre featuring whales, seals and sea otters. Dolphins and **beluga whales** perform daily, while sea otters entertain during feeding times.

West Coast Seafood

Vancouver's location along the north Pacific Ocean provides for superlative seafood. Oysters, clams, Dungeness crabs, halibut and a half-dozen kinds of salmon are grown and/or harvested in British Columbia, along with the more exotic prawns, sea cucumber, squid and octopus. Traditional recipes are simple: salmon grilled over maple-wood, clams steamed in big pots, halibut roasted in the oven. Modern chefs add Asian and European influences—curried salmon filets, for example, or seafood cioppino, cooked with tomatoes, wine, herbs and spices. Note that lobster, which many visitors expect to find, must be shipped clear across Canada from the Maritime provinces—there is no Northwest species.

The major species of native Northwest salmon include chinook, coho, sockeye, pink, chum and steelhead (actually a sea-running form of rainbow trout). Farm-grown salmon is usually Atlantic salmon; the "farms" are pens in protected inland waters along the central British Columbia coast and Vancouver Island. Wild chinook (or king) salmon is widely considered the top choice, but many connoisseurs prefer sockeye or coho, which have higher natural oils, greater color and stronger flavor. Halibut is moist and mild, cod smoky and oily. Whatever you order, if it's fresh, of Northwest origin and properly prepared, it's certain to be memorable.

A highlight is the walk-in **Graham Amazon Gallery**, where crocodiles, anacondas, turtles, lizards and two-toed sloths live in a jungle environment with brightly colored birds and butterflies. The new Clownfish Cove area is designed for children under 8, with puppet shows, an animal hospital and activities.

Near the aquarium is the Kids **Children's Farmyard & Miniature Railway**. The petting zoo features domestic animals and the railway's locomotives are replicas of historic engines. (&⊙*Open Jun–Labour Day daily, train 10:30am–5pm, farmyard 11am–4pm. Rest of the year schedule varies: phone info line ☎604-257-8531. ⊜$5.50 adult, $2.75 child for each attraction*).

Downtown★★

Granville Street, the commercial centre, is closed to all traffic except buses for a six-block pedestrian thoroughfare known as The Mall. The major department stores and extensive underground shopping areas called the Pacific and Vancouver centres are located here. At the northern end is Granville Square,

Canada Place

a plaza with views of port activities on the wharves below. Steps lead to the rail station from which the SeaBus crosses Burrard Inlet to Londsdale Quay in North Vancouver (*See green address box*), offering good **views** of the harbor and city.

Canada Place★★

Designed by architect Eberhard Zeidler as the Canada Pavilion for Expo '86, the complex consists of a hotel, office tower and convention centre. Exhibition halls are enclosed by the "sails" of fibreglass yarn coated with Teflon, tensioned to appear as though they are catching the ocean winds.

Marine Building★

355 Burrard St.
Open during business hours.
Opened in 1930, this 21-storey landmark is one of the finest Art Deco buildings in the world. The decorative terra cotta work depicts marine scenes to honour Vancouver's ties to the sea.

Vancouver Lookout★

Atop the Harbour Centre Tower, 555 West Hastings St.,Vancouver BC V6B 4N6.
Observation deck open May–mid-Oct daily 8:30am–10:30pm. Rest of the year daily 9am–9pm. $13 adult. 604-689-0421. www.vancouverlookout.com.
Visitors ascend this distinctive office building via exterior elevators to arrive at the circular observation deck, 167m/553ft above ground, with its magnificent **view**★★★ of the city, mountains and ocean. Recently renovated.

Vancouver Art Gallery★★

750 Hornby St., Vancouver BC, V6Z 2H7.
Open daily 10am–5:30pm (Tue, Thu 9pm). $19.50 adult. 604-662-4719. www.vanartgallery.bc.ca.
The Neoclassical building was converted by Arthur Erickson so that galleries open off the central rotunda with its glass-topped dome.
A highlight are the paintings and drawings by British Columbian **Emily Carr**, whose West Coast themes are striking. Works on display include *Big Raven* (c.1931) and *Scorned as Timber, Beloved of the Sky* (c.1936).

Vancouver Art Gallery

The art gallery's north-side lawn and south-side steps are often ground zero for political protests in Vancouver.

Robson Square★

Stretching from Nelson Street almost to Georgia Street, this complex was also designed by **Arthur Erickson**. Now housing the provincial **law courts**, the seven-storey building with a spectacular slanted-glass roof complements a series of terraced gardens with waterfalls and plants on top of offices (*between Smithe and Robson Sts.*). A plaza under Robson Street contains outdoor cafes, a skating rink and a conference centre.

Library Square★★

350 W. Georgia St., Vancouver BC, V6B 6B1.
Open Mon–Thu 10am–9pm, Fri–Sat 10am–6pm, Sun noon–5pm. Closed public holidays. 604-331-3603. www.vpl.vancouver.bc.ca.
Moshe Safdie's breathtaking 1995 building, with its nine-storey office tower, houses the main branch of the Vancouver Public Library. Punctuated with small shops and cafes, the atrium courtyard is a popular gathering place. Built over a two-year period at a cost of $156 million, the 36,270sq m/390,000sq ft library is the largest publicly funded project in Vancouver history.

Address Book

GETTING AROUND

BY PUBLIC TRANSPORTATION

Vancouver Regional Transit System operates an integrated network of rapid transit, ferries (*below*) and buses. Hours of operation vary among the different services. **SkyTrain**, the city's rapid transit, serves Downtown, Burnaby, New Westminster and Surrey (*daily 5:08am–1:15am; every 2–4 min*). Fares are based on zones travelled, with discounts in evening and on weekends. Buses require exact fare; SkyTrain accepts coins, bills, debit and credit cards. Keep your ticket: you may be asked to show it to an agent. FareSaver books of 10 tickets (*$18–$36*) and a DayPass (*$8*) are available from ticket machines and outlets. Transfers are free for 90min of unlimited travel. **Bus** service connects SkyTrain and SeaBus at all stations. Buses operate 7 days/wk. *A Transit Guide* map (*$1.50*) is sold at Fare Dealer outlets and convenience stores. The entire system is accessible. For route information and schedules: ☎604-521-0400; www.translink.bc.ca.

BY CAR

Use of public transportation or walking is strongly encouraged within the city as roads are often congested and street parking may be difficult to find. Metered and garage parking available.

BY BOAT

SeaBus, passenger harbor ferries, operates between Vancouver and the North Shore (*12min one-way; departing Vancouver Mon–Sat 6:16am–1:22am, Sun 8:16am–11:16pm; every 15–30min*). Adult fare is $3; exact fare is required. Bus service connects SkyTrain and SeaBus at all stations: ☎604-953-3333; www. translink.bc.ca.

A **harbour tour** by paddlewheeler takes in Vancouver's busy port (*departs from Harbour Cruises Marina early-May– late Sept daily 11:30am, 1pm & 2:30pm; mid- Apr–early May & mid-Sept–Oct daily 2:30pm. Round-trip 1hr 15min. $25. ☎604-688-7246 or toll-free 1-800-663-1500. www.boatcruises.com*).

BY TAXI

Black Top & Checker Cabs ☎604-681-2181; Yellow Cabs ☎604-681-1111.

North Shore: North Shore Taxi Ltd. ☎987-7171; Sunshine Cabs ☎604-988-8888

ON FOOT

Vancouver is an excellent city to tour on foot, as most major sights are within 15-20 minutes' walk of virtually all the downtown hotels (many hotels offer shuttle service to Stanley Park and Granville Island). *Visitors should avoid the stretch of Hastings Street between Cambie and Main, a dangerous drug-dealing district. To reach Chinatown, follow Pender Street.*

GENERAL INFORMATION

ACCOMMODATIONS AND VISITOR INFORMATION

For **hotels/motels**, contact **Tourism Vancouver**, 200 Burrard St., Vancouver, BC V6C 3L6. ☎604-683-2000. www. tourismvancouver.com. Reservation services: Best Canadian B&B Network ☎604-327-1102. www.bc-bed-and-breakfast.com. Advance reservations strongly recommended in peak travel months (*Jun–Aug*) and even for May and Sept.

LOCAL PRESS

Daily: *The Vancouver Sun* and *The Province*. Weekly: *Business in Vancouver*, business news.

ENTERTAINMENT

The Georgia Straight and the *Westender* provide entertainment and activity listings, as does *West Coast Life,* in the Thu issue of the *Vancouver Sun*. On-line, go to *Where.ca/vancouver*. Ticketmaster ☎604-280-4444. www.ticketmaster. ca (major credit cards accepted). For last-minute and half-price tickets, go to www.ticketstonight.ca, ticket booth at Plaza level, 200 Burrard St, open daily 10am–6pm. ☎604-684-2787. The Alliance for Arts and Culture is an arts clearinghouse, with information on many events (*938 Howe St. Vancouver BC V6Z 1N9. ☎604-681-3535. www. allianceforarts.com*).

SPORTS

BC Lions Football Club: home games at BC Place Stadium. Season Jun–Nov; ticket office ☎604-589-7627 or www. bclions.com. **Vancouver Canadians**

(baseball): home games at Nat Bailey Stadium. Season Jun–Sept. ☎604-872-5232 or www.canadiansbaseball.com. **Vancouver Canucks** (ice hockey): home games at General Motors Place. Season Oct–Apr. Info line ☎604-899-4610 or http://canucks.nhl.com. Tickets for all events are sold through the venues or through Ticketmaster ☎604-280-4444. www.ticketmaster.ca (major credit cards accepted).

USEFUL NUMBERS

Callers must dial all 10 digits (area code plus the phone number) when making local calls.

Area Codes: 604 and 778
Police: 911(emergency) or 604-717-3535
VIA Rail *1150 Station St.(Pacific Central Station)*: 604-640-3756, toll-free 1-888-842-7245
Amtrack *Pacific Central Station*: 1-800-872-7245
BC Ferries toll-free 1-888-223-3779
Greyhound Lines of Canada (bus): 604-661-0328, toll-free 1-800-661-8747
Vancouver International Airport: general inquiries: 604-207-7077
Canadian Automobile Assn. *999 W. Broadway*: 604-268-5600
CAA Emergency Road Service (24hr): 604-293-2222, cell users *222
Shoppers Drug Mart (24hr pharmacy), *1125 Davie St.*: 604-669-2424
885 W. Broadway: 604-708-1135
2302 W. 4th St: 604-738-3138
Road Conditions : 1-800-550-4997
Weather (24hr) : 604-664-9010
♿ *For dollar sign categories, see the Legend on the cover flap.*

WHERE TO STAY

$ Hostelling International Vancouver –*1114 Burnaby St., Vancouver BC, V6E 1P1.* ☎604-684-4565, toll-free 1-888-203-4302. *226 beds. www.hihostels. ca.* ⌨ Not only is this clean, economical lodging the best choice for budget travellers in downtown Vancouver, its West End location is convenient to both Stanley Park and Granville Island. The hostel lies just off the busy Davie Street district with its myriad small shops and cafes. Other HI hostels are located in the Granville St entertainment area and at Jericho beach.

$$ Sylvia Hotel – *1154 Gilford St., Vancouver BC, V6Z 2L9.* ☎604-681-9321. *www.sylviahotel.com. 119 rooms.* ╳♿. This ivy-covered, 1912 brick and terra-cotta landmark borders English Bay. Many rooms here have kitchenettes; the larger units are an exceptional value for families, who can prepare all their meals in-room and enjoy the recreational opportunities a mere two blocks away at Stanley Park.

$$$ Edgewater Lodge – *8841 Rte. 99, Whistler.* ☎604-932-0688, toll-free 888-870-9065. *www.edgewater-lodge.com. 12 rooms.* ╳♿▣. Exceptional lake and mountain views characterize this quiet Whistler retreat set on 17ha/42 acres on the shores of Green Lake, 3km/2mi from Whistler. The property is well outside the ferment of the main resort, and all rooms front the lake.

$$$ Hotel Georgia – *801 W. Georgia St., Vancouver BC, V6C 1P7.* ☎604-682-5566, toll-free 1-800-663-1111. *www.hotelgeorgia.bc.ca. 313 rooms. Hotel may be closed for renovation.* ╳♿▣. The Art Deco lobby of this historic property (1927) is a decorative marvel, with its hand-carved mahogany panelling and shiny brass fixtures. Guest rooms have high ceilings and deep bathtubs. Once the social centre of Vancouver, the Hotel Georgia is ideally located for shoppers.

$$$ Residences on Georgia and The Palisades– *100-1288 W. Georgia St, Vancouver BC, V6E 4R3. vancouverextended-stay.com. 100 units.* ♿▣. Popular with the film industry, these sophisticated high-tech twin towers are just the thing for extended stays (there's even an on-site screening room). Units are smartly furnished with compact kitchens, small offices and breakfast nooks. Upper-floor units boast expansive views of the mountains and the harbor.

$$$ Thistledown House – *3910 Capilano Rd., North Vancouver BC , V7R 4J2.* ▣⌨. ☎604-986-7173, toll-free 1-888-633-7173. *www.thistle-down. com. 5 rooms.* Set in a half-acre of serene lawns and gardens, the superbly renovated 1920 Craftsman-style mansion offers elegant, quiet rooms near Grouse Mountain and Capilano Canyon. Sumptuous multicourse breakfasts feature such entrées as alder-smoked-salmon omelettes and crepe primavera in chantilly sauce. Room rates include breakfast, tea and evening sherry.

$$$$ The Fairmont Chateau Whistler – *4599 Chateau Blvd., Whistler BC, V0N 1B4. ☎604-938-8000, toll-free 1- 800-257-7544. www.fairmont.ca. 558 rooms.* ⚓♿️🅿️ Spa 🏊 Located right next to the ski lifts at the foot of Blackcomb Mountain, the Chateau Whistler envelops guests in upscale elegance with country-style furnishings and large bathrooms. Most rooms include sleeper-sofas and window seats for taking in the great views of lovely Whistler Valley. **The Wildflower ($$$$)** dining room serves innovative West Coast cuisine.

$$$$ Listel Vancouver – *1300 Robson St., Vancouver BC V6E 1C5. ☎604-684-8461, toll-free 1-800-663-5491. www.listel-vancouver.com. 129 rooms.* ⚓♿️🅿️🏊 With a location close to West End and Stanley Park, yet within walking distance of the financial hub, this well-run 6-storey hotel, built for the 1986 World Exposition, attracts business travellers and tourists alike. The Museum Floors showcase Northwest Coast-inspired decor and art; the Gallery Floors feature original or limited-edition works from nearby Buschlen Mowatt Galleries; the Artist Series Suites each feature a different artist and design movement.

$$$$ Metropolitan Hotel – *645 Howe St., Vancouver BC, V6C 2Y9. ☎604-687-1122, toll-free 1-800-667-2300. www.metropolitan.com. 197 rooms.* ⚓♿️🅿️🏊 A high-style small hotel, the Metropolitan caters to business travellers with an exceptional health club featuring a heated indoor pool, steam room and squash court. Angular but spacious rooms include luxuries such as Italian linens, down duvets and pillows, marble baths and deep soaking tubs. The hotel's location provides convenient access to shopping, Canada Place and the theatre district. A favorite pre-theatre stop for Vancouverites, **Diva ($$$)** has gained renown for its innovative West Coast cuisine served amid a glitzy decor of brass and crystal.

$$$$ Sutton Place Hotel Vancouver – *845 Burrard St., Vancouver BC, V6Z 2K6. ☎604-682-5511, toll-free 1-866-378-8866. www.suttonplace.com. 396 rooms.* ⚓♿️🅿️🏊 Spa . A pink-sided modern high rise set just a half-block off Robson Street, Sutton Place is favored by members of the film industry, whose limousines are constantly pulling up to the porticoed entrance. Service is expert and discreet. Next door, **La Grande Résidence** offers 164 suites for those staying a week or more.

$$$$ Wedgewood – *845 Hornby St., Vancouver BC V6Z 1V1. ☎604-689-7777, toll-free 1-800-663-0666. www.wedgewoodhotel.com. 83 rooms.* ⚓♿️🅿️ Spa . Comfortable and spacious guest quarters, distinctively designed by owner Eleni Skalbania with antiques and original artwork, characterize this boutique hotel, constructed in 1984 on Robson Square. The recently opened spa offers a full list of treatments. Mediterranean accents spice the French cuisine at **Bacchus ($$$)**, and the hotel lounge is a popular after-work gathering spot, with piano music nightly.

$$$$$ The Fairmont Hotel Vancouver – *900 W. Georgia St., Vancouver BC, V6C 2W6. ☎604-684-3131, toll-free 1-800-257-7544. www.fairmont.ca. 555 rooms.* ⚓♿️🅿️ Spa 🏊. This copper-roofed landmark chateau welcomed King George VI and Queen Elizabeth after it opened in 1939. Renovated in the mid-1990s, the Hotel Vancouver now boasts a sleek Art Déco-style lobby and quiet rooms with period reproduction furnishings. The popular bistro, **Griffins ($$)**, serves lavish buffets. In the evening, **900 West ($$$$)** serves up celebrated martinis and live jazz, as well as prime or Angus beef and fresh seafood. Try the expansive Sunday brunch at **Fleuri ($$$)**, which features tables of seafood and rich delights like croissant bread pudding. The adjacent lounge, **Gerard's**, is a film-industry haunt with notable martinis.

$$$$$ The Fairmont Waterfront – *900 Canada Place Way, Vancouver BC, V6C 3L5.* ⚓♿️🅿️ . *☎604-691-1991 or toll-free 1-8866-540-4509. www.fairmont.ca. 489 rooms.* A classy, modern business hotel, the Fairmont Waterfront is linked by a covered walkway to Canada Place and the Cruise Ship Terminal. Rooms are tastefully decorated in warm pastels and light-colored woods; more than half the rooms overlook Vancouver Harbour. The third-floor fitness facility enjoys view of nearby Stanley Park and the North Shore mountains.

WHERE TO EAT

$ Buddhist Vegetarian Restaurant – *137 E. Pender St.,Vancouver BC, V6A 1T6. Chinatown.* ☎604-683-8816. **Asian**. ♿After a fire, this restaurant has re-opened under new management, offering both regular Chinese cuisine and the nourishing vegetarian fare for which it was famous, with menus for special diets (gluten-free, salt-free, MSG-free etc.). A meal here is a great value for the money.

$ Stepho's Souvlakia – *1124 Davie St., Vancouver BC, V6E 1N1.* ☎604-683-2555. **Greek**. ♿Locals love this West End restaurant for its dependable food and good value—lines often wind out the door and down the street.

$ Sawasdee – *4250 Main St., Vancouver BC V5V 3P9.* ☎604-876-4030. **Thai**. ♿Vancouver's first Thai restaurant has been called its best, with highly flavored curries and soups, and exotic desserts such as banana fritters. An excellent pad thai is only the beginning here, and the green curry chicken is a standout.The basic dinner platter heaps up lamb, rice, potatoes, salad and rolls—a full meal for less than $10.

$$$ Blue Water Cafe – *1095 Hamilton St., Vancouver BC, V6B 5T4. Yaletown.* ☎604-688-8078. *www.bluewatercafe. net.* ♿**Seafood**. This glamorous seafood shrine has been the centrepiece of Vancouver's newly gentrified warehouse district since 2000. Warm woods and soft lighting enhance Blue Water's wide selection, including its famed Blue Water Tower, a structure of chilled fresh fish, shellfish, sushi and Dungeness crab. Entrées focus on regional offerings: miso-crusted BC sablefish, Chinook salmon with artichokes in saffron consomé, kobe style beef short ribs, white sturgeon with braised cucumber and watercress.

$$$ LaRua – *4557 Blackcomb Way, Vancouver BC, V0N 1B4, in the Le Chamois Hotel, Whistler, BC.* ☎604-932-5011. *www.larua-restaurante.com.*

♿**Pacific Northwest**. Savory regional cuisine with international accents on the menu at this Whistler standout. Choose a table in one of two distinct dining rooms connected by an arched entryway (*la rua*, in Spanish). Inspired fare, such as BC red deer loin with oven-dried blueberries, and BC halibut in a pumpkin seed and leek crust, delights the eye as much as the palate.

$$$$ Bishop's – *2183 W. 4th Ave.,Vancouver BC, V6K 1N7. Kitsilano. Dinner only.* ☎604-738-2025. *www. bishopsonline.com.* **Contemporary Pacific West Coast**. Impeccable service and an intimate atmosphere mark this high-end Vancouver institution. Owner John Bishop was one of the originators of West Coast cuisine, which, in Bishop's case, is based on organic regional ingredients. Artfully presented dishes on the weekly changing menu incorporate such local bounty as Saltspring Island goat cheese, Dungeness crab, wild sockeye salmon and local chanterelles.

$$$$ C Restaurant – *1600 Howe St., on False Creek.* ☎604-681-1164. *www. crestaurant.com.* **Seafood**. ♿Inside this striking industrial-chic dining space with floor-to-ceiling windows overlooking False Creek, chef Robert Clark's creative Northwest seafood takes on Asian accents. Lavender-cured halibut or albacore tartare might precede an entrée of seared salmon with summer squash tart and eggplant purée. Delicious fruit-based deserts. Fortunately, there is a tasting menu if you can't make up your mind..

$$$$$ Lumiere – *2551 W. Broadway. Dinner only.* ☎604-739-8185. *www.lumiere.ca.* **French.** In an elegant, subdued decor, executive chef Robert Feenie sets off electricity with his innovative continental cuisine, often judged the best in the province. The nightly changing prix-fixe menu offers entrées such as braised pork belly and tiger prawns, Qualiicum Bay scallops with compressed watermelon and Thai basil. There is a tasting menu as well. The restaurant is part of the French Relais & Châteaux organization.

Address Book

DIM SUM

As a North American capital for Chinese culture, Vancouver enjoys a sterling collection of restaurants that offer dim sum, the small platters of bite-size delights that take literally hundreds of forms, many based on seafood. Usually the focus of leisurely lunches or brunches, a dim sum meal takes at least two hours–and be ready to try anything. Among the best-known dim sum palaces are: the **Pink Pearl Chinese Restaurant** (1132 E. Hastings St. ☎604-253-4316. www.pinkpearl.com), a venerable 700-seat hall, hugely popular with government officials; **Imperial Chinese Seafood Restaurant** (355 Burrard St.. ☎604-688-8191. www.imperialrest.com), which melds superb food with a match-

less location in the Marine Building; and **Sun Sui Wah Seafood Restaurant** (3888 Main St. ☎604-872-8822, toll-free 1-800-872-8822. www.sunsuiwah.com), which earns consistent raves from food critics.

SIKORA'S CLASSICAL RECORDS

432 West Hastings St., Vancouver BC. Open Mon–Sat 10am–6pm, Sun noon–5pm. ☎604-685-0625, toll-free 1-866-685-0625. www.sikorasclassical.com. An inconspicuous storefront at the edge of the Gastown district conceals a treasure trove of recordings, almost exclusively of classical music: 25,000 CDs, 50,000 vinyl LPs, plus DVDs and videos. The knowledgable staff is happy to answer questions. Smaller sections are devoted to Celtic and New Age music.

BC Place Stadium★

Main entrance Robson & Beatty Sts. 777 Pacific Blvd, Vancouver BC, V6B 4Y8. ♿ 🅿 ⟿ Guided tours (1hr 30min) mid-Jun–Labour Day Tue 11am & 1pm, event schedule permitting. ⟿$8 adult. ☎604-669-2300. www.bcplacestadium.com. Resembling an enormous quilted marshmallow, this stadium is the largest air-supported domed amphitheatre in the world. Designed by Phillips Barratt, it opened in 1983 and hosts football games (the BC Lions), soccer

matches, trade shows and concerts. A glass-enclosed concourse on the upper level offers a city **panorama**. The stadium will be the site for ceremonies of the 2010 Winter Olympics

Chinatown★★

Pender St. between Carrall St. and Gore Ave.

This colorful quarter is the centre of Vancouver's large Chinese community. Many restaurants and shops sell Asian foods and wares. The neighborhood is is a wonderful place for a daytime stroll.

Maps Galore

Over 25 years, Jack Joyce has worked with a succession of innovative cartographers to create maps for trackless stretches of South America, Asia and far-away places generally. Today, International Travel Maps publishes more than 250 titles encompassing the world, and is working on more. The Vancouver store (530 W. Broadway; ☎604-879-3621; www.itmb.com) is stuffed with maps, globes and guidebooks. Note especially the 65-inch by 90-inch silk-screen map of the world, the largest ever published, centering on the Pacific rather than the Atlantic. Jack, a seasoned traveller, offers knowledgeable conversation.

Dr. Sun Yat-Sen Classical Chinese Garden★

578 Carrall St.,Vancover BC, V6B 5K2. Behind Chinese Cultural Centre on Pender St. ♿ 🕐Open mid-Jun–Aug daily 9:30am–7pm. Rest of the year daily 10am–6pm (Oct–Apr 10–4.30pm). ⟿Guided tours daily included in ticket price. ⟿$8.75 adult. ☎ 604-662-3207. www.vancouverchinesegarden.com.

Modelled after classical gardens of the Ming dynasty (14-17C), this is a small oasis of contemplative calm. Next door to the garden is the equally serene **Dr. Sun Yat-Sen Park**, graced by a large, placid pond.

Gastown★

This attractive area between Carrall and Richards streets combines restored late 19C buildings with modern structures constructed to blend with their surroundings. The area was named for a garrulous English saloonkeeper, **Gassy Jack**, whose statue stands on Maple Tree Square.

Nearby Attractions

Vancouver Museum★★

In Vanier Park. 111 Chestnut St., Vancouver BC, V6J 3J9. ♿ 🅿 🕐*Open year-round Tue–Sun 10am–5pm (Thu 9pm)* 🕐*Closed Mon Sept–June and Dec 25.* 🎟*$10.* ☎*604-736-4431. www.vanmuseum.bc.ca.*

This museum specializes in the history and art of Vancouver and of Canada's native cultures. It also has a fine collection of Asian artifacts. From the parking area there is an excellent **view**★★ of the city and North Shore mountains.

To the left of the museum rises the distinctive conical dome of the **MacMillan Planetarium**, part of the **H.R. MacMillan Space Centre**★ that houses a space station, flight simulator and other interactive exhibits and displays on space research (*1100 Chestnut St., Vancouver BC, V6J 3J9.* 🄺 ♿ 🅿 🕐*Open Jul–Labour Day daily 10am–5pm. Rest of the year Tue–Sun 10am–5pm.* 🎟*$15 adult.* ☎*604-738-7827; www.hrmacmillanspacecentre.com*).

Maritime Museum★★

In Vanier Park. 1905 Ogden Ave., Vancouver BC, V6J 1A3. 🄺 🅿 🕐*Open late May–Labour Day daily 10am–5pm. Rest of the year Tue–Sat & holidays 10am–5pm, Sun noon–5pm.* 🕐*Closed Dec 25.* 🎟*$10.* ☎*604-257-8300. www.vancouvermaritimemuseum.com.*

The highlight is the **St. Roch**, a Royal Canadian Mounted Police patrol ship, the first ship to navigate the Northwest Passage in both directions, 1940-45.

Granville Island★

Accessible by car from Granville Bridge & West 4th Ave. (follow signs; pass under the bridge), or by ferry from Vancouver Aquatic Centre on Beach Ave. or from Maritime Museum. ✕ ♿ 🅿 . *www.granville-island.net.*

This onetime industrial area under Granville Bridge has been renovated to house art galleries and studios, boutiques, restaurants, theatres and a hotel. The Emily Carr Institute of Art and Design populates the island with students. The island's highlight is the **public market** (🕐*Open daily 9am–7pm*), where stalls of fresh produce vie with products of Vancouver's many ethnic groups. Edible British Columbia offers market tours. (🍴*8:30am Wed &Sat, book ahead on website.* ☎*604-662-3606. www.ediblebritishcolumbia.com*)

Address Book

FALSE CREEK FISHERMEN'S WHARF

East end of W. 1st St. near Granville Island. Though there are many places in Vancouver to buy fresh seafood, here you can buy *fruits de mer* from the folks who actually catch it. Seafood is available in all seasons, and often includes crab and salmon as well as shrimp, octopus and rockfish.

ROUNDHOUSE COMMUNITY CENTRE

181 Roundhouse Mews, Vancouver BC, V6Z 2W3 (Davie St. and Pacific Blvd.), *in Yaletown.* ☎*604-713-1800. www.roundhouse.ca.* The Engine 374 Pavillion (🚂no charge) next to the Roundhouse community centre, houses the Canadian Pacific steam engine that brought the first transcontinental train into Vancouver on May 23, 1887. The centre also holds a small gallery that focuses on the work of Yaletown artists and craftspeople. Concord Pacific, the surrounding residential development, largely occupies the site of Expo '86.

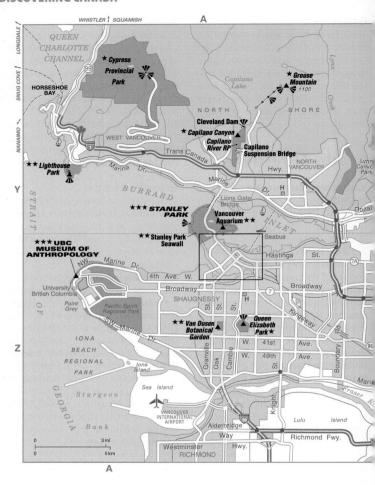

Science World

1455 Quebec St.,Vancouver BC, V6A 3Z7.
Kids ✕ & P ○*Open daily 10am–6pm.*
○*Closed Labour Day & Dec 25.* ⊚*$16
adult.* ☎*604-443-7443. www.science-world.bc.ca.*
Situated on the Expo '86 site overlooking False Creek, this complex features interactive exhibits and includes an Omnimax theatre and Kidspace, a gallery for young children.

West End

Downtown northwest of Broughton St. City fathers proudly advertise the West End as the most densely populated urban neighborhood in North America, with its towering apartment and condominium complexes overlooking Stanley Park, False Creek and the North Shore. **Denman Street**, a hive of small stores and cafes, is worth a stroll. At **English Bay Beach**★★ (*Beach Ave. and Denman St.*) parks officials maintain palm gardens.

Roedde House Museum

1415 Barclay St., Vancouver BC, V6G 1J6.
⊶*Visit by guided tour (45min) only, Tue–Fri 10am–5pm, Sun 2pm–4pm.* ○*Closed public holidays.* ⊚*$4 ($5 Sun, includes tea).*
☎*604-684-7040. www.roeddehouse.org.*
This Queen Anne-style house was built in 1893 for Vancouver bookbinder Gustav Roedde. Furnished to the period, nine rooms on the ground and second floors can be visited.

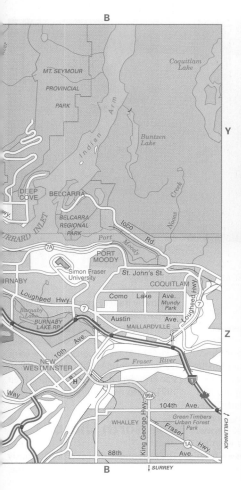

VANCOUVER

Alderbridge Way	AZ
Austin Avenue	BZ
Boundary Road	AZ
Broadway	AZ
Cambie Street	AZ
Como Lake Avenue	BZ
Dollarton Highway	ABY
Fraser Highway	BZ
Granville Street	AZ
Hastings Street	AZ
Ioco Road	BYZ
King George Highway	BZ
Kingsway	AZ
Knight Street	AZ
Lougheed Highway	BZ
Marine Drive	AY
Marine Way	ABZ
North West Marine Drive	AZ
Oak Street	AZ
Richmond Freeway	ABZ
St John's Street	BZ
Southwest Marine Drive	AZ
Trans Canada Highway	AY
4th Avenue West	AZ
West 41st Avenue	AZ
West 49th Avenue	AZ
Westminster Highway	AZ
10th Avenue	BZ
88th Avenue	BZ
104th Avenue	BZ
Capilano Canyon	AY
Capilano River Regional Park	AY
Capilano Suspension Bridge	AY
Cleveland Dam	AY
Cypress Provincial Park	AY
Grouse Mountain	AY
Horseshoe Bay	AY
Lighthouse Park	AY
Queen Elizabeth Park	AZ
Stanley Park	AY
Stanley Park Seawall	AY
UBC Museum of Anthropology	AZ
Van Dusen Botanical Garden	AZ
Vancouver Aquarium	AY

Sights Outside Downtown

UBC Museum of Anthropology★★★

6393 N.W. Marine Dr, Vancouver BC, V6T 1Z2. ✕ ♿ 🅿 🕐*Open mid-May–early Oct daily 10am–5pm, Tue 9pm. Rest of the year closed Mon.* 🕐*Closed Dec 25–26.* 💳*$9 (no charge Tue 5pm–9pm).* ☎*604-822-5087. www.moa.ubc.ca.*
The University of British Columbia campus overlooks the Strait of Georgia and Vancouver Island. Opened in 1976, the **museum building**—the work of Arthur Erickson—is a glass and concrete masterpiece. Glass walls of the **Great Hall** rise 14m/45ft around the magnificent collection of Haida and Kwakwaka'wakw totem **poles**.

Van Dusen Botanical Garden★★

5251 Oak St, V6M 4H1. ✕ ♿ 🅿 🕐*Open June–August daily 10am–9pm. Rest of the year closing times vary.* 🕐*Closed Dec 25.* 💳*$8.25 (Oct–Mar $6).* ☎*604-878-9274. www.vandusengarden.org.*
This rolling 22ha/55-acre expanse was acquired by the Van Dusen Botanical Garden Assn. and transformed into a remarkably rich and mature garden holding 7,500 kinds of plants, in arrangements ensuring that something is in bloom every month.

Haida Totem pole fragments, UBC Museum of Anthropology

Queen Elizabeth Park★

West 33rd Ave. and Cambie St.
This beautiful park lies at the geographic centre and highest point (150m/500ft) of Vancouver. The road from the entrance climbs through an arboretum to the **Bloedel Floral Conservatory**, a geodesic-domed structure of glass and aluminum (✕&🅿️🕘*Open daily 9am–8pm, weekends 10am–9pm.* 🕘*Closed Dec 25.* ✆*$4.50.* ☎*604-257-8584. www.city.vancouver.bc.ca*). In clear weather there are extraordinary **views**★★ from the conservatory's plaza of the city and mountains by day and night.

The lovely **quarry gardens** offer winding pathways, waterfall and views. The on-site restaurant, **Seasons in the Park** (**$$$** ☎*604-874-8008, toll-free 1-800-632-9422. www.vancouverdine.com*), hosted US President Bill Clinton and Russian President Boris Yeltsin during their 1993 Vancouver summit.

The North Shore

The mountains descend precipitously toward Burrard Inlet on its north side, cut by deep fiords and the steep valleys

View from Queen Elizabeth Park

of several small rivers. Scenic Highway 1 (which becomes Route 99) follows the North Shore slope, 12km/7mi west to **Horseshoe Bay**, from where BC Ferries depart for Vancouver Island, Bowen Island and the Sunshine Coast, north of Howe Sound.

Lighthouse Park★★

10km/6mi west of downtown West Vancouver along Marine Dr. 604-925-7200 (Parks & Community Services). www.westvancouver.net.
Situated on a headland protruding into Howe Sound, this West Vancouver park offers excellent hikes 🚶 through the finest old-growth forest in the metropolitan area. Rocky headlands provide spectacular **views**★★★ across the Strait of Georgia and of Stanley Park, the Vancouver skyline and Mt. Baker in the distance. Numerous trails lead down to the lighthouse (1912), the best place to watch sunsets over Georgia Strait. The park is often used as a film set.

Cypress Provincial Park★

12km/7mi from downtown by Lions Gate Bridge and Hwy. 1/Rte. 99. ♿🅿🕐*Open year-round (gates 🕐closed 11pm–7am). Hiking, picnicking, biking, skiing. 604-924-2200. www.env.gov.bc.ca.*
This 3,000ha/7,400-acre park includes Cypress Mountain (*604-419-7669. www.cypressmountain.com*), a popular ski area that will host freestyle skiing and snowboarding for the 2010 Winter Olympics. The access road leads to Highview Lookout, which permits a breathtaking **view**★★★ of the Vancouver area.

Capilano Canyon★

9km/6mi from downtown by Lions Gate Bridge and Capilano Rd.
This deep canyon can be crossed by the narrow pedestrian **suspension bridge** 70m/230ft above the Capilano River (🅿🕐*Open mid-May–Labour Day daily 8:30am–8pm (Jul–mid-Aug 9pm). Rest of the year daily 9am (mid-Dec–early Jan 10am), closing times vary. 🕐Closed Dec 25. May–Oct $27 adult. Rest of the year $24 adult. 604-985-7474. www.capbridge.com*). Built in 1889, the bridge is 137m/450ft long and sways as visitors

walk across it. On the opposite side is a pleasant glade of evergreens.
Farther along Capilano Road, **Capilano River Regional Park** offers pleasant walks and views of the canyon. At the northern end of the park (*access from Nancy Greene Way*) are Cleveland Dam and Capilano Lake. Across the lake is a **view**★ of the twin peaks of The Lions.

Grouse Mountain★

3km/8mi from downtown by Lions Gate Bridge, Capilano Rd. and Nancy Greene Way. ✖♿🅿🕐*Tram operates year-round daily 9am–10pm. $33 adult. 604-980-9311. www.grousemountain.com.*
The aerial tram rises to an elevation of 1,100m/3,700ft, offering, as it ascends, a splendid **view**★★ of the city. At the top is a resort, recreation area and attractions. The **Grouse Grind**, 🚶one of Vancouver's most popular trails, ascends the mountain (*3km/2mi*).

Excursions

Sea to Sky Highway★★

Route 99, the 102km/63mi highway that runs from **Horseshoe Bay**, a picturesque ferry port west of Vancouver, past Squamish to Whistler, takes in a remarkable coast-to-range **panorama**★★★. It hugs a narrow shelf

Capilano Suspension Bridge

HIWUS FEASTHOUSE

Atop Grouse Mountain; access by aerial tram. 6400 Nancy Greene Way, North Vancouver BC, V9J 1B3. ☎604-980-9311. www.grousemountain. com. Featuring massive cedar beams, totem poles and posts hand-carved by First Nations artists, this mountaintop retreat is architecturally impressive. In the evening, guests enjoy a six-course feast including cedar-plank salmon, forest mushrooms, berries and other traditional dishes, accompanied by native chants, songs and tales performed by Coast Salish dancers.

School groups are also brought to the Feasthouse to learn about nature and the Coast Salish culture.

along **Howe Sound**, then casts upward into the Coast Range peaks.

BC Museum of Mining★★

In Britannia Beach, 38km/24mi north of Horseshoe Bay. ◔Open early May–mid-Oct daily 9am–4:30pm. Rest of the year Mon–Fri 9am–4:30pm. ◔Tours (1hr30min) every 40min. ◔$15 adult. ☎604-896-2233, toll-free 1-800-896-4044. www.bcmuseumofmining.org.
The Britannia mine was once the largest copper producer in the British empire. Mining equipment is demonstrated. The mining house (*three levels*) has displays on mining in British Columbia.

Shannon Falls★

45km/28mi. These impressive falls cascade 335m/1,100ft over a cliff in pleasant surroundings.

As travellers approach the town of Squamish, an outdoor activity centre popular with hikers, bikers, climbers, sailboarders and kayakers, the 700m/2,296ft granite monolith known as **Stawamus Chief** comes into view.

Whistler★★

🛈Visitor Centre, 4030 Gateway Drive, Whistler BC, V0N 1B4. ☎604-395-3357 Activity Centre, 4010 Whistler Way, Whistler BC V0N 1B4. ☎604-938-2769, toll-free 1-800-9988. www.tourismwhistler.com.
Whistler, among the world's top ski resorts, is the venue for alpine, nordic, ski-jumping and sliding events of the 2010 Winter Olympics. All Paralympic events will be held here. The three alpine hamlets (Whistler Village, Village North and Upper Village) are dominated by two massive peaks, **Blackcomb Mountain** (2,284m/7,494ft) and **Whistler Mountain** (2,182m/7,160ft).

Warm-weather recreation is plentiful: boating, swimming, fishing, horseback riding, tennis and golf. Hiking and biking trails abound. The resort village offers fine shops, accommodations, restaurants and nightclubs.

The **Whistler Museum and Archives** (*4329 Main St. ◔Open Jul– Aug daily 10am–4pm (Thu 8pm). Rest of the year Fri–Sun 10am–4pm (Thu 8pm). ◔$5*

Skiing at Whistler

Paul Morrison/Whistler Resort Assn.

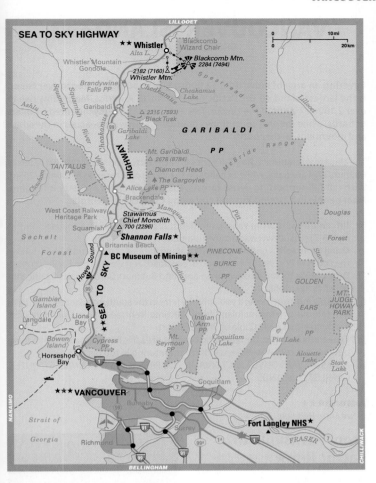

SEA TO SKY HIGHWAY

adult. ☎604-932-2019. www.whistlermu-seum.org) depicts the area's early history as a logging and fishing camp, and its astounding growth as a ski resort. The **Whistler Interpretive Forest** (*Rte. 99, 5km/3mi west of main village*) holds numerous short and long hiking trails. Nearby **Garibaldi Provincial Park**, a hike-in only park, offers additional trails of varying difficulty as well as campsites (*Open year-round; parking area accessible by paved road from Whistler Village; park map available from Whistler visitor centre, or contact BC Parks ☎604-898-3678. www.env.gov.bc.ca*).

Fort Langley National Historic Site★

56km/35mi southeast of Vancouver by Trans-Can Hwy, PO Box 129, 23433 Mavis Ave., Fort Langley BC, V1M 2R5. Kids ☐ Open Jul–Labour Day daily 9am–8pm. Rest of the year daily 10am–5pm. Closed Dec. 25-6 and Jan 1. $7.15 adult. ☎604-513-4777. www.pc.gc.ca.

The fort was one of a network established by the Hudson's Bay Company in the early 19C. The storehouse, the only structure original to the site, has a fine **collection** of furs and the trading goods once exchanged for them. Costumed staff demonstrate blacksmith's skills.

VANCOUVER ISLAND ★★★
BRITISH COLUMBIA
MAP P 146-147

Covering an area of more than 32,000sq km/12,000sq mi, Vancouver Island is the largest island off the Pacific Coast of North America. Mountains rise to over 2,100m/7,000ft in the centre. The west coast is deeply indented by inlets or fiords, while the east coast slopes gradually, with wide beaches in the south and mountains farther north.

The climate is temperate. Rainfall varies greatly: Victoria in the southeast receives 680mm/27in annually, while Zeballos on the west coast receives 6,480mm/255in. With rainfall supporting dense forests, the island's major industry is logging. Most people live around Victoria and along the Strait of Georgia.

- **Information:** Tourism Vancouver Island, 203-335 Wesley St, Nanaimo. ☎250-754-3500. www.vancouverisland.travel
- **Orient Yourself:** A good highway runs along the east of the island from Victoria in the south to Port Hardy in the north. Few roads run west to the Pacific coast.
- **Don't Miss:** Victoria's downtown area and Butchart Gardens; the Pacific Rim beaches near Tofino.
- **Organizing Your Time:** If you arrive by ferry in the south, consider driving north and returning to the mainland from Nanaimo (central) or from Port Hardy (far north) to either Bella Coola or Prince Rupert.
- **Especially for Kids:** The hard sand beaches of Pacific Rim are warm and inviting, but the very cold water keeps kids from venturing in too far.
- **Also See:** VANCOUVER, VICTORIA, INSIDE PASSAGE, SKEENA VALLEY, QUEEN CHARLOTTE ISLANDS

Victoria ★★★
See Entry Heading.

From Parksville to Pacific Rim ★

154km/95mi by Rte. 4
This winding route traverses the mountain backbone of the island through lovely scenery. Some parts are wild and untouched; others are bustling, particularly with logging activity.

Englishman River Falls ★
From Parksville, take Rte. 4.

- *After 5km/3mi, turn left and continue 8km/5mi.*

This river tumbles over two sets of falls. The upper ones are narrow and deep, dropping into a gorge. A path bridges the river, leading to the lower falls through a dense forest. The lower falls drop around a rock into a deep pool. Route 4 enters the mountains.

Cathedral Grove

Tourism Vancouver Island

Address Book

ACCESS

Vancouver Island is served by several ferry services

Washington State Ferries – Anacortes WA to Sidney BC (Victoria). ☎206-464-6400, www.wsdot.wa.gov/ferries

Black Ball Transport – Port Angeles WA to Victoria BC, ☎360-457-4491(Port Angeles). 250-386-2202 (Victoria). www.cohoferry.com

BC Ferries – British Columbia mainland to Vancouver Island, ☎250-386-3431, toll-free 1-888-223-3779, cell-phone*223. www.bcferries.bc.ca

Clipper Navigation, Inc.– Seattle WA to Victoria BC, ☎206-448-5000 or 800-888-2535, www.victoriaclipper.com

WHERE TO STAY

The myriad bays, inlets and fiords along Vancouver Island's west coast lack roads but are quite accessible by boat. Two remote lodges offer visitors the opportunity to enjoy marine scenery and view wildlife in comfort.

$$$$$ Eagle Nook Ocean Wilderness Resort – *Barkley Sound. 120 W. Dayton, B-6, Edmonds WA 98020 (mailing address).* ☎*250-728-2370, toll-free 1-800-760-2777. www.eaglenook.com. Closed Oct–May. 23 rooms.* ✕ Spa This luxury hotel occupies a spectacular setting in serene Jane Bay in Barkley Sound. Guests pass the time kayaking, beachcombing, fishing and swimming, and enjoying hearty meals of local seafood. Rooms are spacious and quiet. You can take a seaplane from Seattle or Vancouver, or a water taxi from Tofino/Ucluelet.

$$$$$ Clayoquot Wilderness Resorts – *Box 130, Tofino BC.* ☎*250-726-8235, toll-free 1-888-333-5405. www.wild-retreat.com. Closed Oct–Apr. 23 tents.*

✕ Spa. Guests stay in tent cabins on wooden decks at the Outpost on Bedwell River, within 8km/5mi of Tofino, or 30min by boat. Lounge tents offer a taste of luxurious camps of a century ago. Horseback riding and hiking complement various marine activites. The cuisine is West Coast gourmet, and Chef Timothy May offers informal cooking classes.

WHERE TO EAT

$$$$ Sooke Harbour House, *1528 Whiffen Spit Rd., Sooke BC, V0S 1N0.* ☎*250-642-3421, toll-free 1-800-889-9688. www.sookeharbourhouse.com. Reservations essential.* **West Coast.**Fredrica and Sinclair Philip's famed Sooke Harbour House is a 45min-drive west of Victoria. Gardens provide much of the provender; the rest comes from island farms and ranches and nearby waters. Meals are among the most memorable in North America. Menus change daily and list such appetizers as warm albacore tuna on a salad of garden greens. Seafood includes Hecate Strait halibut with a sweet pepper and fruit relish. The inn's 28 rooms are luxurious.

JUAN DE FUCA TRAIL 🚶

You don't have to brave the legendary (and notorious) West Coast Trail to enjoy the Pacific Coast of Vancouver Island. The new Juan de Fuca Trail is designed for moderate to easy day hikes or strenuous two- to five-day treks. Reached from China Beach, a half-hour west of Sooke, and several other points along Route 14, the trail offers wide breezy beaches, rocky headlands, tidepools and lots of wildlife-watching opportunities. *For information, maps and permits:* ☎*250-391-2300 or www. bcparks.ca.*

Little Qualicum Falls★

▶ *26km/16mi from Parksville; turn right to parking area.*

The Little Qualicum River descends over two sets of falls connected by a gorge. The lower falls are small, but the walk through forest to the upper falls is pleasant, providing views of the canyon. The **upper falls** are on two levels, with a pool between them.

Route 4 follows the south side of **Cameron Lake**, glimpsed through the trees.

Cathedral Grove★★

35km/22mi from Parksville, part of MacMillan Provincial Park.

Parking beside highway. Cathedral Grove was preserved by the MacMillan Bloedel Paper Co. and donated to the province.

Many of these firs rise to 60m/200ft or more and the largest trees are 800 years old. A viewing platform affords a look at damage wrought by a storm in the early 1990s.

Route 4 descends to the coast and bypasses **Port Alberni**, an important lumber and boating centre at the head of Alberni Inlet, the departure point for the *MV Lady Rose*, a small freighter that has served Alberni Inlet and Barkley Sound for more than half a century (*Departs from Argyle St. dock in Alberni Jun–late Sept Mon–Sat 8am, additional departure Jul–Labour Day Sun 8am. Rest of the year Tue, Thu & Sat 8am; round-trip 8-10hrs. Reservations required. $58–$64 round trip adult. Alberni Marine Transportation ☎250-723-8313, toll-free 1-800-663-7190; www.ladyrosemarine.com*). The Lady Rose feries visitors to the Broken Group Islands (*below*) or Bamfield.

After leaving Port Alberni, Route 4 follows Sproat Lake with good views of glacier-clad Klitsa Mountain and Mt. Gibson. Logging activity is evident along the road, from cut areas to huge logging trucks. After leaving the lake, Route 4 begins to climb Klitsa Mountain along the valley of the Taylor River.

After crossing a low pass, the road begins its winding descent to the Pacific along the Kennedy River, offering **views**★ of snow-capped peaks. The river widens into **Kennedy Lake**, the largest stretch of fresh water on the island. The road follows the lake, rising above it and dipping to water level. Pacific Rim National Park Reserve is reached near the junction with the Tofino-to-Ucluelet road. The park's Long Beach Unit Visitor Centre is located here.

Pacific Rim National Park Reserve★★★

Open year-round. Hiking, canoeing, kayaking, sailing, cycling, swimming, camping. Park office open year-round; call for hours. $7/adult, $17.50/family or group for 24hr. Park Office 2185 Ocean Terrace Rd, PO Box 280, Ucluelet BC V0R 3A0. ☎250-726-7721. www.pc.gc.ca. This reserve is a long, narrow strip of rocky islands and headlands, stretching intermittently for about 130km/80mi between Port Renfrew and Tofino. The park consists of the 75km/47mi **West Coast Trail** for backpackers between Port Renfrew and Bamfield (*Each end is accessible by road. Orientation session required. Hiking/camping fees $128.75 per person, reservation fees $24.75,*

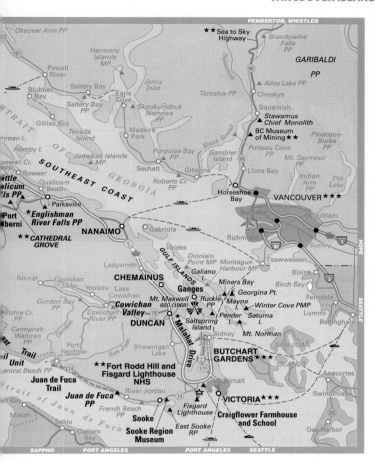

ferries *$15 each*.), about 100 islands and rocky islets in Barkley Sound known as the **Broken Islands Group** and famous **Long Beach**.

Long Beach★★

Visitors can surf and swim. However the water is cold (10°C/50°F) and can be extremely dangerous due to tides and currents. For details contact the park office. Pounded by the surf, this 11km/7mi curve of sand and rock is backed by a dense rain forest and mountains rising to 1,200m/4,000ft. Offshore, sea lions bask on the rocks, and Pacific gray whales are often spotted.

There are several points of access to Long Beach. The **Schooner Trail** *(2km/1mi)* takes hikers through old-growth forest and down to a lovely, iso-

Pacific Whale Watching

Whale watching is one of the Pacific Northwest's top visitor activities, but marine biologists now suspect excess attention may adversely affect the whales, especially orcas. Visitors who patronize whale-watching services can help by demanding that tour operators maintain a healthy distance from whales (at least 100 yards), and refrain from chasing or harassing any marine species. For information, contact The Whale Museum in Friday Harbor, Washington state. (*62 First St., PO Box 945, Friday Harbor WA, 98250.* ☎360-378-4710, toll-free 1-800-946-7227. www.whale-museum.org).

Tofino

WHERE TO STAY

$$$$$ Wickaninnish Inn – *Box 250, Tofino BC V0R 2Z0. Osprey Lane at Chesterman Beach.* ☎*250-725-3100, toll-free 1-800-333-4604. www.wick-inn.com. 75 rooms.* ✕ 🅿 🆂🅿🅰. While summer is lovely along Long Beach, Nov–Mar is spectacular at this luxurious lodge built on a rocky headland facing Pacific storms. Each of the airy, wood-panelled rooms offers ocean views from floor-to-ceiling windows and private balconies. Guests can watch whales from Mar–Jun. Cuisine is based on fresh seafood and regional produce. Enjoy European spa services while waves crash, rain pelts and winds roar.

WHERE TO EAT

$ Common Loaf Bake Shop – *180 1st St., Tofino BC.* ☎*250-725-3915.* The bulletin board at Common Loaf is news central for Tofino's counter-cultural types, but visitors of all persuasions are drawn to the cafe's savoury homemade muffins, pastries and breads, along with strong coffee drinks. In summer, there are pizzas and East Indian dishes. Soups, wraps, sandwiches and daily specials are on the menu for lunch. The eclectic mix of second-hand chairs, tables and lamps lends a relaxed informality and bargain-basement comfort to the place.

lated beach. The **Wickaninnish Trail** (*3km/1.5mi*) leads to Florencia Bay.

Radar Hill★★

22km/14mi from Ucluelet junction. 🚶*Take road to left, climbing 1.6km/1mi to a viewpoint.*
A splendid **panorama**★★ (*telescope available*) opens of mountains, as well as the wild and rocky coastline.

Tofino★

ℹ*Tourism Tofino, PO Box 249 Tofino BC V0R 2Z0.* ☎*250-725-3414. www.tourismtofino.com.* Quiet and low-key in the winter, Tofino is a busy staging area the rest of the year for exploring Pacific Rim National Park Reserve, charter fishing, sailing, surfing, kayaking and hiking.
The **Rainforest Interpretive Centre** (*451 Main St. Tofino BC, V0R 2Z0* ☎*250-725-2560. www.longbeachmaps.com*) offers information on Clayoquot Sound and its ecology. Tofino is also the departure point for **whale-watching** and sightseeing cruises into Clayoquot Sound, including day trips to the memorable waterside bathing pools at Hot Springs Cove. One popular tour operator is Jamie's Whaling Station (*606 Campbell St, PO Box 129, Tofino BC, V0R 2Z0.* ☎*250-725-3919, toll-free 1-800-667-9913. www.jamies.com*).

VICTORIA★★★
BRITISH COLUMBIA
POPULATION 78,057

"If I had known of this place before, I would have been born here," observed humourist Stephen Leacock. Facing the **Juan de Fuca Strait** and the **Olympic and Cascade mountains** of Washington state, the capital of British Columbia is famous for its mild climate, spectacular views, beautiful gardens, and British traditions.

🛈 **Information:** Tourist Office, 812 Wharf St. ☎250-953-2033 or www.tourismvictoria.com

▶ **Orient Yourself:** From the Art Déco tower of the Tourist Office on Wharf St, you can get a good view of central Victoria.

🅿 **Parking:** Meters are enforced Mon–Sat 9am–6pm, and both indoor and outdoor lots are available in the downtown area.

🚗 **Don't Miss:** The scenic Marine Drive takes you through old neighbourhoods and offers views across the Straits of Juan de Fuca. You may even see whales.

🕐 **Organizing Your Time:** The downtown area is quite compact, and walking is the best way to explore it.

Kids **Especially for Kids:** The Royal BC Museum has been a favourite destination for school groups for many years.

♿ **Also See:** VANCOUVER ISLAND, VANCOUVER, INSIDE PASSAGE

A Bit of History

The Hudson's Bay Company built a trading post in 1843 on the site of present-day Victoria, naming it after the Queen of England. Gold rushes brought prosperity, and eventually the settlement became capital of British Columbia. Other than the Canadian Forces' Pacific base in nearby **Esquimalt**, major employers for the Victoria area are the government and the tourism industry. The city's pleasant climate has attracted a large retirement population.

Downtown★★

The city centre is situated along Government Street, the main shopping area, and around the James Bay section of the harbour, where ferries from Port Angeles and Seattle dock. Shops, restaurants and cafés line intriguing little squares and alleys such as **Bastion Square** and Trounce Alley. Just north, vibrant **Market Square**, a collection of older renovated buildings, has shops around courtyard gardens. Fort Street is an extensive antiques district.

To the south, off Belleville Street, is Heritage Court, which houses the Royal British Columbia Museum. The narrow columns and arches on the ground floor of these striking modern buildings add a distinct Islamic flavor. The Netherlands Carillon Tower, an open-sided 27m/88ft campanile containing 62 bells, was given to the province by Canadians of Dutch origin (*concerts seasonally*).

Royal BC Museum Corp.

Woolly Mammoth,
Royal British Columbia Museum

Address Book

 For dollar sign categories, see the Legend on the cover flap.

WHERE TO STAY

$$ Bedford Regency – *1140 Government St., Victoria BC, V8W 1Y2.* ☎250-384-6835, toll-free 800-665-6500. *www.bedfordregency.com. 40 rooms.* ✕🅿. This five-storey boutique hotel is located a short walk from the Inner Harbour and Government Street shops. Guest rooms have large cushy chairs and goose-down duvets. Some rooms feature fireplaces, Jacuzzis and views of James Bay. Pub fare is served in the English-style Garrick's Head **($)**.

$$ Fairholme Manor – *4638 Rockland Pl., Victoria BC, V8S 3R2.* 🅿 Spa ☐. ☎250-598-3240, toll-free 1-877-511-3322. *www.fairholmemanor.com. 5 suites.* Built in 1885, the Italianate mansion occupies a bucolic hilltop in Victoria's Rockland district. Annex apartments are done in light woods, while the suites have fireplaces, bay windows and expansive baths; some have decks and Jacuzzis. Breakfast features fresh bakery goods.

$$$ Laurel Point Resort – *680 Montreal St., Victoria BC V8V 1Z8.* ☎250-386-8721 or 800-663-7667. *www.laurelpoint.com. 200 rooms.* ✕🅿☐. This glitzy glass-and-steel complex occupies a small peninsula at the entrance to Victoria's Inner Harbour, giving it expansive bay views. Spacious, bright rooms feature balconies and cozy down comforters. Exercise and leisure facilities include a pool, saunas and hot tubs. Outside, guests can relax in the Japanese garden, graced with a reflecting pond and waterfall.

$$$$ Haterleigh Heritage Inn – *243 Kingston St., Victoria BC, V8V 1V5.* ☎250-384-9995, toll-free 1-866-234-2244. *www.haterleigh.com. 7 rooms.* 🅿☐. Light pours through huge stained-glass windows in this elegant 1901 home near Victoria's Inner Harbour and downtown. All rooms have private baths and are furnished with antiques; most have Jacuzzi tubs. Delicious breakfasts, afternoon tea and evening sherry.

$$$$$ The Aerie – *600 Ebedora Lane, PO Box 108, Malahat BC V0R 2L0.* ☎250-743-7115, toll-free 1-800-518-1933. *www.aerie.bc.ca. 35 rooms.* ✕🅿 Spa ☐.

A Relais & Chateaux property, The Aerie's exotic stucco complex sprawls across the Malahat hillside high above Victoria, with exceptional views of Finlayson Arm and the Saanich Peninsula far below. Opulent ooms have eclectic furnishings that suggest Roman villas; many have private decks, Persian carpets and canopy beds. There's even a helicopter landing pad! The Aerie's **dining room ($$$$)** offers imaginative cuisine, featuring regional products.

$$$$$ The Fairmont Empress – 721 Government St., Victoria BC, V8W 1W5 ☎250-384-8111, toll-free 1-800-257-7544. *www.fairmont.ca. 476 rooms.* ✕🅿⬛ Spa. The Empress has welcomed distinguished guests from Rudyard Kipling to Queen Elizabeth II since it opened in 1908. After renovation in 1989, the public areas are splendid: the Palm Court, the Crystal Ballroom, the Empress Dining Room and the Tea Lobby. Guest rooms are richly appointed. The Tea Lobby, with its immense potted palms, serves afternoon tea **($$$)** daily starting at noon; reservations (☎250-389-2727) and appropriate attire required. The Willow Stream Spa, (🕘*Open daily 9am–9pm, Thu–Sat 10pm*) offers services fit for a queen.

WHERE TO EAT

$ Blue Fox – *919 Fort St., Victoria BC V8V 3K3.* ☎250-380-1683. **Canadian.** Crowds line up to get into this antiques-district bistro, which offers breakfast all day. The draw? Huge platters of "very fat French toast," huevos rancheros and three-egg omelettes. Expansive sandwiches, burgers and wraps round out the simple menu.

$ Murchie's –*1110 Government St., Victoria BC, V8W 1Y2.* ☎250-383-3112. *www.murchies.com.* **Canadian.** Known as purveyors of fine teas and coffees since 1894, the Murchie family presents a smorgasbord of delectables for breakfast and lunch. Enjoy afternoon tea, then browse the adjacent shop for specialty teas, coffee and all the accoutrements (down to the tea cozy).

$$ Da Tandoor – *1010 Fort St., Cictoria BC V8V 3K4.* ☎250-384-6333. *Dinner only.* **Indian.** Tandoori (clay-oven baked) lamb and chicken dishes are the signature at this popular Victoria eatery. The dining room features opulent, gilded decor, and the menu includes Indian and Pakistani specialties such as vindaloo stews and curries.

$$ Paprika Bistro – *2524 Estevan Ave. Victoria BC, V8R 2S7* ☎*250-592-7424.* ♿*Dinner only. Closed Sun.* **International**. This sleek dining spot melds French-Hungarian cuisine with Vancouver Island ingredients. Duck is a specialty, either confit with herb-roasted potatoes or roast with a sour-cherry sauce. For dessert, the vanilla-bean crème brûlée is a favourite. The wine list is international, with good BC vintages.

$$ Spinnaker's Gastro Brewpub – *308 Catherine St., Victoria BC, V9A 3S8. Kitsilano.* ☎*250-386-2739 or toll-free 1-877-838-2739. www.spinnakers.com. Open daily 11am–10.30pm.* **Canadian**. This brew pub occupies a Tudor-style building on the Inner Harbour. High-class pub fare such as pork tenderloin with yam fritters, or local seafood with herbs and local vegetables. Guesthouse rooms also.

$$$ Cafe Brio – *944 Fort St. Victoria BC. V8V 3K2. Dinner only.* ☎*250-383-0009, toll-free 1-866-270-5461. www.cafe-brio. com.* **Pacific Northwest**. The decor in this sunny yellow building along antiques row is discreet, with wood floors and fine art lining the stucco dining room walls. Tuscan-inspired dishes include braised short ribs with gorgonzola polenta or salmon with Dugeness crab-eggplant involtini; the accompanying dishes are especially original. Reservations recommended.

WHERE TO SHOP

Munro's Books – *1108 Government St., Victoria BC V8W 1Y2.* ☎*250-382-2464, toll-free 1-888-243-2464. www.munrobooks.com. Open daily 9am–7.30pm (Thu-Fri to 9pm, Sun to 6pm).* Housed in a Neoclassical stone building, this bookshop has more than 50,000 titles.

Rogers Chocolates –*913 Government St., Victoria BC, V5W 1X5.* ☎*250-384-7021. www.rogerschocolates.com. Open daily 9am–9pm.* This 1903 heritage building houses a fine chocolate shop, which dates to 1885. Many visitors refuse to leave Victoria without a box of Rogers Chocolates.

Parliament Buildings★

501 Belleville St. 🕐*Open late May–Labour Day daily 9am–5pm. Rest of the year Mon–Fri 8.30am–5pm.*🚶*Guided tours (30-60min) 9am–4pm.* 🕐*Closed major holidays.* ☎*250-387-3046, toll-free 1-800-663-7867. www.leg.bc.ca*

On the south side of James Bay stands a long, squat stone building with a central dome, topped by a gilt statue of Capt. George Vancouver, which houses the British Columbia Legislative Assembly. In front is a bronze statue of **Queen Victoria**. At dusk thousands of small lights outline the buildings' exterior.

Royal British Columbia Museum★★★

675 Belleville St. ✕♿🕐*Open year-round daily 9am–5pm (Jul–mid-Oct 6pm, Fri-Sat 10pm).* 🕐*Closed Jan 1, Dec 25.* 🎫*$14 adult ($34 adult museum & IMAX).* ☎*250-356-7226, toll-free 1-888-447-7977. www.royalbcmuseum.bc.ca.*

One of the top museums in the world, this institution focuses on the natural and human history of the province.

At the north end of the hall, the **Glass House** contains a collection of totem poles from all over the province. On the second floor is a series of spectacular **dioramas** of the coastal forest and sea-

Parliament and Inner Harbour

Tourism Victoria©Photosure.com

ALCHERINGA GALLERY

665 Fort St., Victoria BC, ☎250-383-8224. www.alcheringa-gallery.com. This gallery focuses on aboriginal art from the entire Pacific Rim, and not just the Northwest. Note the striking similarities among New Zealand, New Guinea and British Columbia coastal works. Shapes and designs found in Haida totems reappear in ceremonial masks from Papua New Guinea, for instance. Most works are modern, evidencing a resurgence of traditional art along the Pacific Rim.

shore regions. An unusual **Open Ocean** exhibit is based on William Beebe's deep-sea dive in 1930. The third floor

First Peoples exhibit displays native art, arranged in striking dioramas. **Nisga'a: People of the Nass River**, a new exhibit, focuses on contemporary life and cultural objects.

Bordering the museum, small **Thunderbird Park** has a fine collection of original and replica totem poles.

Next to Thunderbird Park stands an 1852 clapboard dwelling, **Helmcken House**★ (🕐*Open summer only, contact Royal BC Museum ☎250-356-7226)*, the home of Dr. John Helmcken, physician to the Hudson's Bay Company.

Empress Hotel★

👜*See Fairmont Empress in the Address Book.*

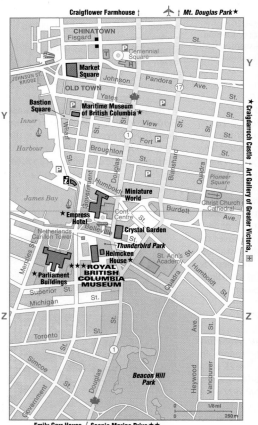

VICTORIA

Belleville Street	Z
Blanshard Street	Y
Broughton Street	Y
Burdett Avenue	YZ
Douglas Street	YZ
Fisgard Street	Y
Fort Street	Y
Government Street	YZ
Heywood Avenue	Z
Humboldt Street	YZ
Johnson Street Bridge	Y
Johnson Street	Y
Menzies Street	Z
Michigan Street	Z
Pandora Avenue	Y
Quadra Street	YZ
Simcoe Street	Z
Superior Street	Z
Toronto Street	Z
Vancouver Street	Z
View Street	Y
Wharf Street	Y
Yates Street	Y
Bastion Square	Y
Beacon Hill Park	Z
Chinatown	Y
Crystal Garden	Z
Empress Hotel	Z
Helmcken House	Z
Inner Harbour	Y
Maritime Museum of British Columbia	Y
Market Square	Y
Miniature World	Y
Old Town	Y
Parliament Buildings	Z
Royal British Columbia Museum	Z
Thunderbird Park	Z

The Fairmont Empress Hotel

The Fairmont Empress Hotel

Miniature World

Kids ⚊ ⏲ *Open mid-Jun–Labour Day daily 8:30am–9pm. Rest of the year daily 9am–5pm.* ⚊*$9 adult.* ☎*250-385-9731. www. miniatureworld.com.* Located in the Empress Hotel complex, on the Humboldt Street side, is **Miniature World**, featuring small-size re-creations ranging from the Battle of Waterloo to the Canadian Pacific Railway.

Maritime Museum of British Columbia★

28 Bastion Sq. ⚊ ⏲ *Open year-round daily 9:30am–4:30pm (mid-June–mid-Sept 5pm). Closed Dec 25.* ⚊*$8.* ☎*250-385-4222. www.mmbc.bc.ca.*
Of special interest are the *Tilikum*, a converted Indian dugout canoe that sailed from Victoria to England in the early 1900s, and the Trekka, a 6m/20ft sailing boat built in Victoria that sailed around the world from 1955 to 1959.

Scenic Marine Drive★★

13km/8mi

This beautiful marine drive enables visitors to appreciate Victoria's grand site and lovely gardens.

▶ *Leave from Thunderbird Park and take Douglas St.*

Skirting the large, flower-filled **Beacon Hill Park**, the road passes a plaque marking the initial kilometre of the nearly 8,000km/5,000mi **Trans-Canada Highway**, which stretches to St. John's, Newfoundland.

▶ *Turn left on Dallas Rd.*

From Finlayson and Clover points, there are fine **views**★★ of the Olympic Mountains.

▶ *Continue to Hollywood Crescent. Turn right on Ross St. (at Robertson St.); Ross becomes Crescent Rd. Bear left at King George Terrace and ascend the hill.*

The drive enters the community of **Oak Bay**, a wealthy suburb with beautiful gardens, pretty views and a very English population. Harling Point provides a good **view** of the rocky coastline and the houses perched along the shore. Directly below on the right, Gonzales Bay is visible and the Trial Islands can be seen offshore to the left.

▶ *Take Beach Dr.*

The drive continues around McNeill Bay. Bisected by the road, the Oak Bay golf course on Gonzales Point has **views**★★ of the sea *(weather permitting)*, the San Juan Islands and the snow-clad peaks of the Cascades, dominated by Mt. Baker. The drive then passes through **Uplands Park**, a pleasant section of Oak Bay. From **Cattle Point** there are views of the coast.

153

Sanctuary and Solitude

Swan Lake Christmas Hill Nature Sanctuary (*3873 Swan Lake Rd.;* ☎*250-479-0211; www.swanlake.bc.ca*). This peaceful 45ha/110-acre preserve includes wetlands, fields forest and a lily pad-filled lake that provides refuge for waterfowl and nesting birds. Nature House features displays and activities for children. The trail (*2.5km/1.5mi*) up Christmas Hill crosses residential streets, but the summit reveals a wonderful panorama of Victoria and its environs, including Elk Lake to the north.

▶ *Go south on Beach Dr. Turn right onto Bowker Ave., left onto Cadboro Bay Rd. and then Fort St. to return to downtown.*

Additional Sights

Craigdarroch Castle★

1050 Joan Crescent. ◷*Open mid-Jun–Labour Day daily 9am–7pm. Rest of the year daily 10am–4:30pm.* ◷*Closed Jan 1, Dec 25-26.* ◒ *$10.* ☎*250-592-5323. www.craigdarrochcastle.com.*
Built by Robert Dunsmuir, a Scot who made a fortune from coal, the huge 1880s stone mansion has dozens of stained-glass windows that create rainbows of light. From the top of the tower there is a good view of Victoria.

Art Gallery of Greater Victoria

1040 Moss St. ♿ ⊡ ◷*Open year-round Mon–Sun 10am–5pm (Thu 9pm).* ◷*Closed Good Friday & Dec 25.* ◒*$12.* ☎*250-384-4101; www.aggv.bc.ca.*

ENGLISH INN AND RESORT

429 Lampson St., in Esquimalt. ☎*250-388-4353 or 866-388-4353. www.oldenglandinn.com.* This 16C Tudor-style complex includes an inn, replica historic houses, and five acres of landscaped gardens. Dine on roast beef with Yorkshire pudding in the **Knight's Dining Room**, served by staff in period costume. **Anne Hathaway's** thatched-roof **cottage** is a replica of the home of William Shakespeare's wife; Stratford-upon-Avon has been re-created on the premises too. Inn guestrooms follow the Old English theme with antique furnishings and canopy beds; some have fireplaces and kitchenettes.

Housed in a Victorian mansion (1889), the gallery offers an eclectic blend of East and West, as well as paintings by Emily Carr. The highlight of the gallery's collection of Asian art is the Shinto Shrine (1899-1900) in the small Japanese outdoor garden.

Fort Rodd Hill★★

14km/9mi west by Rtes. 1, 1A and Ocean Blvd. ⊡ ◷*Open Mar–Oct daily 10am–5:30pm. Rest of the year daily 9am–4:30pm.* ◷*Closed Dec 25.* ◒*$4.* ☎*250-478-5849. www.pc.gc.ca.*
Set on 18ha/44 acres of land at the southwest corner of Esquimalt's harbor, the fort contains the remains of three coastal artillery-gun batteries which, until 1956, protected the approaches to the naval base at Esquimalt. From beside **Fisgard Lighthouse**, there are fine **views**★ of Juan de Fuca Strait, the Olympic Mountains and the naval base.

Craigflower Farmhouse

Hwy. 1A (Craigflower Rd.) at Admirals Rd. ⊡ ◷*Open May–Sept Wed–Sun 1pm–5pm.* ◒*$5.* ☎*250-356-5137. www. craigflower.ca.*
This Georgian clapboard house (1856) was constructed by Kenneth McKenzie, bailiff for Puget Sound Agricultural Co., the first organization to develop the island for farming. Most of the manor is original and contains period furnishings.

Excursions

Butchart Gardens★★★

800 Benvento Ave. in Brentwood Bay, 21km/13mi north by Rte. 17 and Keating X Rd. or by Rte. 17A. ✗♿⊡ ◷*Open year-round daily 9am (Jan 1 & Dec 25 1pm). Closing times vary.* ◒*$23 mid-Jun–Sept ($14-$18 rest of the year).* ☎*250-652-5256*

Butchart Gardens

Gwen Cannon/MICHELIN

or toll-free 1-866-652-4422. www.butchart gardens.com.

These internationally famous gardens (20ha/50acres) were started in 1904 by Jennie Butchart to beautify the quarry pit resulting from her husband's cement business. The floral showpiece is the beautiful **sunken garden** with its green lawns, trees and exquisite flower arrangements. Set in a huge pit with ivy-covered sides, the garden is best viewed from above or from the rock island at its centre. The other gardens include the **Ross Fountain;** the **Rose Garden**; the dark, secluded **Japanese Garden**; and the formal **Italian Garden**.

Malahat Drive★

▸ *Take Douglas St. north to Hwy. 1 (Trans-Can Hwy.). The drive begins about 18km/11mi north of Victoria.*

This attractive stretch of road (*some 19km/12mi between Goldstream Provincial Park and Mill Bay Rd.*) crosses Malahat Ridge with good **views**★ of Finlayson Arm, Saanich Inlet, the Gulf Islands, and the mainland. On a clear day Mt. Baker is visible through the trees.

Quw'utsun Cultural and Conference Centre

In Duncan, about 60km/37mi north by Hwy. 1. ◐*Open daily 9am–5pm.* ◓*$13.* ✖&. ☎ 250-746-8119. www.quwutsun.ca.

This complex is operated by the Cowichan tribes, BC's largest single native group. Enclosed by a high fence, the village is a tranquil setting of paved walkways and wooden buildings. The crafts shop features exquisite masks, cedar baskets, jewellery, Cowichan sweaters etc. At the large **carving shed**, native craftsmen transform red cedar poles into totems and war canoes.

BC Forest Discovery Centre★

65km/40mi north by Hwy. 1, just after Duncan. &.◐*Open daily mid-May–Labour Day daily 10am–6pm. Mid-Apr–early May & rest of Sept–mid-Oct daily 10am–4pm.* ◓*$9.* ☎250-715-1113. www.bcforestmuseum.com.

Visitors can walk through a forest of Douglas fir trees, visit a logging museum, see a reconstructed logging camp and ride the narrow-gauge steam railway (May–Labour Day).

Chemainus

78km/48mi north by Hwy. 1. Visitor centre at 9796 Willow St. ☎250-246-3944. www.muraltown.com.

This small waterfront town has gained fame for over 30 **murals** painted on its buildings. Especially fine are *Native Heritage*, symbolizing the three tribes of the Coast Salish Nation, and *Arrival of the 'Reindeer' in Horseshoe Bay*, featuring a native woman in a colorful robe watching a ship enter the bay.

WATERTON LAKES NATIONAL PARK★★

ALBERTA

This Rocky Mountain preserve "where the prairies meet the mountains," forms an International Peace Park with Glacier National Park in Montana. The mountains have been sculptured by erosion and glaciation into sharp peaks, narrow ridges and interlocked U-shaped valleys. The three Waterton Lakes lie in a deep glacial trough. Formerly a Blackfoot Indian stronghold, the area was explored by the Palliser Expedition in 1858; the lakes were named for 18C English naturalist **Charles Waterton**. The area was designated a national park in 1895.

- **Information:** Visitor Information Centre. ☎403-859-2220. www.pc.gc.ca. Open early May–early Oct.
- ▶ **Orient Yourself:** Waterton Lakes lies in southwest Alberta, near the border with British Columbia. Take Highway 2 from Calgary to Lethbridge.
- **Don't Miss:** A cruise on the Waterton lakes.
- **Organizing Your Time:** The Waterton townsite, located at the centre of the park, has extensive tourist facilities. www.watertonchamber.com.
- **Kids Especially for Kids:** The Buffalo Paddock is near the park entrance.
- **Also See:** CARDSTON, FORT MACLEOD, THE KOOTENAYS

Visit

Park open year-round, but very few facilities open late fall–early spring. Hiking, camping, horseback riding, fishing, boating, golf, winter sports. $7 adult/day use fee. www.pc.gc.ca.

Waterton Townsite

The town has a lovely **site**★★ near the point where Upper Lake narrows into the Bosporus Strait, which separates it from Middle Lake. Just south behind the townsite, **Mount Richards** can be distinguished. Beside it stands **Mount Bertha**, marked by pale green streaks caused by snowslides that swept trees down the mountainside. Across the lake rise **Vimy Peak** and **Vimy Ridge**. Upper Lake stretches south into Montana, separating the mountains of the Lewis and Clark Range. In summer **tour boats** make trips down the lake to the US ranger station at the southern end (*depart from Waterton Marina Jul–Aug 10am, 1pm,4pm,7pm. Mid-May–June &*

Prince of Wales Hotel, Waterton Lakes National Park

Bison or Buffalo?

While most people use the words interchangeably, purists will opt for the term bison when referring to the North American animal. Early settlers in the US called bison buffalo, since they saw a similarity to the buffalo of Asia and Europe. In fact, the ancestors of modern bison are thought to have migrated from Asia to North America across the Bering Strait thousands of years ago when the two continents were united by a land bridge. Some 200 years ago Plains bison inhabited the grasslands of the prairies. The larger wood bison, fewer in number, made the forested fringes of the northwestern prairie their home. Bison are wild bovids, members of the same family as cattle and sheep. An adult male can weigh as much as 2,200 pounds but can charge at a speed of 40mph. Calves weigh up to 70 pounds when born and can walk within 20 minutes. Mature at three years, a bison can live as many as 30 years.

Source: Parks Canada

Sept 10am, 1pm, 4pm. May & late Sept– early Oct 10am and 1pm. Round-trip 2hrs 15min; commentary. $30 adult. Waterton Inter-Nation Shoreline Cruise Co. Ltd., Box 126, Waterton park AB, T0K 2M0. 403-859-2362. www.waterton-cruise.com). Behind the townsite, **Cameron Falls** can be seen dropping over a layered cliff.

Cameron Lake★★
17km/11mi from townsite by Akamina Hwy.
The lake is set immediately below the Continental Divide and, like Upper Waterton, spans the international border. Across the lake are, left to right, **Mount Custer** and **Forum Peak**.

Red Rock Canyon★
19km/12mi from townsite; turn left at Blakiston Creek.
The drive to this small canyon offers good **views**★ of the surrounding mountains. A **nature trail** follows the narrow canyon *(2km/1.2mi),*.

Buffalo Paddock★
Kids *400m/.2mi from park entrance. Auto circuit 3km/2mi.*
A small herd of buffalo occupies a large enclosure on a fine **site** backed by Bellevue Mountain and Mt. Galway.

WHITEHORSE★
YUKON TERRITORY
POPULATION 24,041

Situated on the Yukon River, Whitehorse is the capital of the Yukon Territory. Today the city is a centre for tourism. Proud of its part in the Klondike Stampede, the community stages a celebration called the **Sourdough Rendezvous** every February, when people dress in the costumes of 1898 and race dog teams on the frozen Yukon River. This time of year is also the height of Northern Lights (*Aurora Borealis*) viewing season, an event that draws thousands of visitors, from Japan especially.

- **Information:** Tourist Office, 100 Hanson St., ☎867-667-3084. www.whitehorse.ca
- **Orient Yourself:** Whitehorse lies in southwestern Yukon; to the west stretches the Alaskan panhandle.
- **Parking:** For road conditions, call ☎867-456-7623 or toll-free within the Yukon 1-877-456.7623. www.gov.yk.ca.

- **Don't Miss:** The Frantic Follies revue is locally produced, and great fun.
- **Organizing Your Time:** Besides a day visiting the town, you'll want to devote a few days to the excursions.
- **Especially for Kids:** There are numerous hiking opportunities in the spectular surroundings.
- **Also See:** ALASKA HIGHWAY, DAWSON CITY, YUKON CIRCUIT

A Bit of History

The city owes it existence to the difficulty encountered by the Dawson City-bound **Klondike Stampeders** negotiating Miles Canyon. The White Pass and Yukon Route Railway changed area transport; its decision to end its line at Whitehorse made the site a bustling centre for transferring goods to riverboats or overland stages bound onward to Dawson City. In 1953 the territorial capital was moved here.

Sights

Whitehorse retains some historic structures, notably: the old **log church** on Elliott at Third Avenue, built in 1900; the "**skyscrapers**" on Lambert between Second and Third avenues, built after World War II; and the log **railway station** on First Avenue at Main. In contrast is the modern steel and aluminum Yukon government **Administration Building** on Second Avenue, opened in 1976. The Yukon Permanent Art Collection installed here consists of contempo-rary as well as traditional native art. The **Philipsen Law Centre**★ at Second and Jarvis houses a significant collection of contemporary regional art.

MacBride Museum★

1st Ave. at Wood St. Open mid-May–Labour Day daily 9am–6pm. Rest of the year Thu–Sat 10am–5pm. $6. 867-667-2709. www.macbridemuseum.com. Situated in a log building (1967) with a sod roof, this museum features gold-rush memorabilia, Indian cultural objects and a splendid collection of old **photographs** of the Yukon. Outside are relics of Yukon transport, early machinery, the cabin of legendary Sam McGee (immortalized by Robert Service) and a government telegraph office c.1900.

SS Klondike★★

6 Robert Service Way. Open mid-May–mid-Sept daily 9am–5pm. $5. 867-667-3910. www.pc.gc.ca. Upper decks not wheelchair accessible. This 1937 craft, now designated a National Historic Site, is the only steamboat open to the public in the Territory.

Address Book

WHERE TO EAT

$ The Chocolate Claim *(305 Strickland St. Whitehorse YK, Y1A 2J9. 867-667-2202)* This spacious coffee house sells scrumptious pastries and chocolates, light lunches and coffee roasted by a Whitehorse company, Bean North.

WHERE TO STAY

$$$$$ Tincup Wilderness Lodge – *On Tincup Lake. Box 30049, Whitehorse YK, Y1A 3M2. 604-762-0382 or 600-700-0654 (in summer). www.tincup-lodge. com. Open mid-Jun–mid-Sept. 4 cabins.* Guests are flown into this wilderness site on Tincup Lake. *(Pickup is usually in Whitehorse.)* Trout fishing, hiking and berry picking during the day precede splendid evening meals of fresh fish or Canadian beef prepared by chef and co-owner (along with Larry and Ernie Nagy) José Janssen, after which guests can relax in the wood-heated sauna or hot tub. Guests can even take cooking classes during their stay. The four comfortable red-roofed cedar cabins are deluxe by wilderness standards, with showers and wood stoves. The main lodge contains the dining room, a lounge and large deck.

Yukon Cancans

Although it's unlikely gold-rush miners ever saw shows quite like these, the separately operated dance-hall extravaganzas in Whitehorse and Dawson City are among the Yukon's most popular attractions.

In Dawson, **Diamond Tooth Gertie's Gambling Hall** – Canada's oldest legal casino – presents nightly shows including a boisterous cancan performed in colorful costumes. The midnight show is the liveliest. (*Open May–Sept nightly 7pm–2am, weekends June–Labour Day 2pm–2am. Shows at 8.30pm, 10:30pm, 12.30am. $6. 867-993-5525. www.dawsoncity.ca*).

Whitehorse's **Frantic Follies Vaudeville Revue,** which has toured Canada and the US, is a more sophisticated production staged in a local hotel. A lively cancan performance is also included (*Mid-May–mid-Sept nightly. $20. 867-668-2042. www.franticfollies.com. Reservations essential.*).

It is now in the midst of major restoration, which visitors can observe.
Cross the river via Robert Campbell Bridge and stop to see the **fish ladder** at **Whitehorse Dam**, built to enable the chinook salmon to circumnavigate the dam and reach their spawning grounds upriver (*usually occurs in August*). The dam is best viewed from the fishway's observation deck.

Miles Canyon★
9km/6mi south of Whitehorse via Canyon Rd.
Following the edge of Schwatka Lake, **Canyon Road** passes the MV Schwatka dock (*below*) and climbs above the canyon (sharp curves and steep grades), where there is a **view**★ from the lookout. Near the parking lot above Miles Canyon is another **view**★.
Canyon **cruises** afford good **views**★ of the deep green waters of the Yukon and the steep canyon walls. (*MV Schwatka departs May 25–early-Sept daily 2pm; Jun 15–Aug 15 2pm & 4pm. Round-trip 2hrs. Reservations required. $25adult. Yukon Wings Ltd., 68 Miles Canyon Rd, Whiteyorse YK, Y1A 6L4. 867-668-4716. www.yukon-wings.com*).

▶ *To access cruise boat landing, take South Access Rd. toward centre of Whitehorse and turn right onto unpaved road immediately past railroad tracks.*

Gwen Cannon/MICHELIN

SS Klondike

Chilkoot Pass

Starting in Dyea, this route climbed at an angle of 35° in places. Raw rock in summer, the pass became slick ice and snow in winter, and with temperatures of minus 50°C/minus 58°F, it was a nightmare to climb. Yet over the winter of 1897-98, some 22,000 people scaled it, not just once but 30 to 40 times! The North West Mounted Police at the Canadian border insisted that anyone entering Canada have a year's supply of food and equipment. To carry this "ton" of goods over the pass, stampeders had to make numerous trips. Today the **Chilkoot Trail** (*53km/33mi*) starts for hikers at the abandoned site of Skagway's former rival, **Dyea** (*15km/9mi north of Skagway by dirt road*) and ends at Bennett Lake. The 54km/33mi trek can take up to five days (*for maps & trail & permit information, contact the National Park Service in Skagway.* ☎*907-983-2921. www.nps.gov/klgo*).

Beringia Interpretive Centre★

Next to Transportation Museum on Alaska Hwy. ♿🕐*Open mid-May–late Sept daily 9am–6pm. Rest of year Sun 1–5pm, or by appointment.* ➤*$6.* ☎*867-667-8855. www.beringia.com.*

The centre offers a colorful scientific look at the region's prehistoric past. Beringia is the name given the Siberia/Alaska/Canada North 40,00-20,000 years ago when the Bering Strait land bridge was open.

Yukon Transportation Museum

Alaska Hwy. near airport.30 Electra Crescent, Whitehorse YK, Y1A 6E6. ♿🕐*Open May–Aug daily 10am–6pm.* ➤*$6.* ☎*867-668-4792. www.yukontransportation museum.com*

There is a replica of the 1920s mail plane, **Queen of the Yukon**, as well as dogsleds and early cars.

Yukon Arts Centre

300 College Dr., northwest end of Whitehorse, PO Box 16, Whitehourse YK X1A 5X9. 🕐*Open Tues–Fri noon–6pm, weekends noon–5pm.* 🕐*Closed Mon.* ☎*867-667-8575. www.yukonartscentre.org.*

This public art gallery displays the work of regional artists.

Excursion To Skagway★★

Note: Skagway is in Alaska. Canadian citizens need passports to enter the US. Other visitors need US visas, available from any US consulate, but not in Whitehorse.

An impressive trip in the Yukon is the traverse of the Coast Mountains to Skagway—terminus of the Klondike Highway—on the Alaska Panhandle.

Most gold seekers en route to Dawson City sailed up the Pacific Coast to Skagway or **Dyea** (*below*) and trudged into the Yukon across the Coast Mountains. From Skagway the trail followed the **White Pass**, a climb of 888m/2,914ft. When this route was closed in 1897, stampeders turned to the more difficult **Chilkoot Pass**.

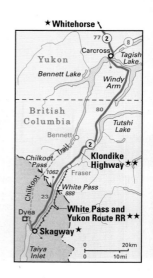

Klondike Highway to Skagway★★

180km/112mi by Alaska Hwy. and Klondike Hwy. (Rte. 2). US border open year-round daily 24hrs. Canada Customs in Fraser open Apr–Oct daily 24hrs. Nov–Mar daily 8am–midnight. ☎867-821-4111 (Canada Customs) or 907-983-2325 (US Customs).

Adjoining the Alaska Highway south of Whitehorse, the Klondike Highway passes through forest and gradually enters the mountains. At **Carcross**— where the final rail was laid for the White Pass and Yukon Route—the road follows the shores of **Tagish Lake**, **Windy Arm** and **Tutshi** (TOO-shy) **Lake**. After leaving Tutshi Lake the road begins the traverse of the desolate White Pass. The steep descent to Skagway offers views of the **Taiya Inlet** of the Lynn Canal.

Skagway★

The "Gateway to the Klondike" is a small busy port, the northern terminus of the southeast ferry system. The Klondike Highway from Skagway to Carcross was laid in 1978, and the railway restored in 1988.

The Town

Skagway Visitor Centre in Arctic Brotherhood Hall, 240 Broadway, PO Box 1029, Skagway AK 99840. ☎907-983-2854. www.skagway.com).

The area along **Broadway** from First to Seventh avenues contains several restored 19C wooden structures.

The former railroad depot (1898) serves as the Park Service **visitor centre** (*2nd & Broadway.* Open May–Sept daily 8am–6pm. Town tours (45min) daily 9am,10am, 11am, 1pm, 2pm,3pm. ☎907-983-2921. www.nps.gov/klgo).

White Pass and Yukon Route Railroad★★

White Pass Summit Excursion departs from 2nd & Spring Sts. May–Sept daily 8:15am & 12:45pm (additional departure Mon–Thu 4:30pm). Round-trip 3hrs. US$95. ☎907-983-2214 or toll-free 1-800-343-7373. www.whitepassrailroad.com. Reservations essential. Several other excursions also offered.

This narrow-gauge railroad originally linked Skagway to Whitehorse. The refurbished railroad cars climb to an elevation of 873m/2,865ft, providing views★ of Skagway and the rugged peaks dominating the town. The train concludes its thrilling 45km/28mi run at the Canadian station in Fraser, BC.

White Pass & Yukon Route/John Bush

White Pass and Yukon Route Railroad

YUKON CIRCUIT★★
YUKON TERRITORY, ALASKA
MAP OPPOSITE

This scenic journey through the Yukon rewards travellers willing to traverse a relatively isolated frontier to witness nature's grandeur and mankind's diversions. The majestic Yukon River, a silent but ever-present companion, dominates half the circuit.

- **Information:** Dept of Tourism and Culture, Government of Yukon. ☎1-800-661-0494. www.travelyukon.com.
- ▶ **Orient Yourself:** The Yukon Territory covers a 483,450sqkm/186,660sq mi triangle in Canada's northwest corner.
- **Parking:** Check out road conditions at ☎867-456-7623 or toll-free within the Yukon 1-877-456-7623. www.gov.yk.ca
- **Don't Miss:** Museums in Mayo and Keno City offer a poignant look at bygone boom times and at native culture.
- **Organizing Your Time:** Those in a hurry can arrange air transport at Haines Junction.
- **Also See:** DAWSON CITY, WHITEHORSE, ALASKA HIGHWAY

A Bit of History

During the gold rush thousands of stampeders travelling from Skagway ended their winter trek through Chilkoot Pass at **Bennett Lake**. In the spring, they constructed boats to complete the journey via the Yukon and its tributaries to Dawson City, a distance of some 800km/500mi. Today thousands of people follow the route alongside the river to discover the wild northland.

Driving Tour

About 1,500km/930mi from Whitehorse via Klondike, Top of the World, Taylor and Alaska Hwys. Lengthy drive over stretches of gravel road. Several roads in the Yukon, notably Silver Trail and Top of the World Highway, contain lengthy stretches of oiled gravel, which can be quite slick when wet. It is advisable to check road conditions in advance. In some sections, service facilities are few and infrequent. Prepare for emergencies with food, warm clothing and vehicle supplies. Know how to protect yourself from bad weather and wild animals.

From Whitehorse to Dawson City★

540km/335mi by Klondike Hwy. (Rte. 2), not including excursion.

Whitehorse★
See WHITEHORSE.

The **Klondike Highway** skirts Lake Laberge (*barely visible from the road*), through which the Yukon River runs. At the end of the unpaved access road to the campground, there is a lovely **view** of this lake and the mountains beyond. The highway rejoins the river at **Carmacks** (*178km/110mi*), named for the discoverer of Klondike gold. After 196km/122mi, just beyond a bend in the Yukon, small rock islands have divided the river into five fast-flowing channels, known as **Five Finger Rapids**★.

In the vicinity of Minto, about 2km/1.4mi past Minto Resorts, an unpaved road leads to the riverside (*1.6km/1mi*). Here a sign marks the Overland Trail, a wagon road built in 1902 from Whitehorse to Dawson City. The **view**★ of the Yukon from the bank is grand.

Leaving the Yukon Valley, the highway crosses the central plateau and bridges the Pelly and Stewart rivers. At Stewart Crossing, Route 11 (*unpaved between Mayo and Keno*), designated the Silver Trail, begins its 112km/69mi northeast

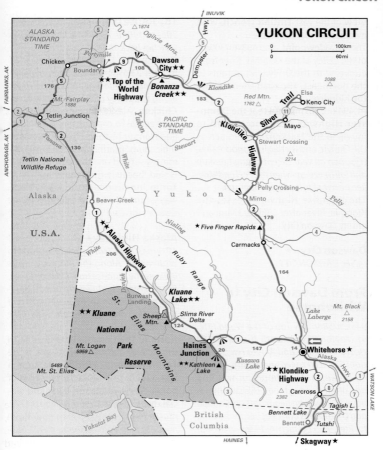

traverse through the villages of Mayo and Elsa to Keno City.

Silver Trail

Excursion: 224km/138mi round-trip from Klondike Hwy.

This byway into Yukon mining country offers landscapes typical of the subarctic interior. The first stop, **Mayo** *(53km/33mi)*, experiences extreme climates. Summer temperatures have hit 36°C/98°F (a Yukon record), while winter lows have dropped to –62°C/–79°F. The **Binet House Interpretive Centre** presents an explanation of permafrost, and photos of First Nations life *(Center St. & Second Ave. ⏱Open May–Sept daily 10am–6pm. ☎867-996-2926)*. **Keno City** *(112km/69mi)* was a thriving town until the last mine closed in 1989. **Keno City Mining Museum** *(Elsa-Mayo Rd. ⏱Open*

June–Sept daily 10am–6pm. ✎$4. ☎867-995-2792. www.kenocity.info) has a collection of 1950s-era **photographs**★ by a miner and photographer.

From the designated lookout about 61km/38mi south of Dawson City, is a

The Mighty Yukon

One of the longest rivers in North America, this giant of the remote North—its Loucheux Indian name *Yu-kun-ah* means "great river"—traverses 3,185km/1,975mi of rugged territory. Originating in Tagish Lake on the Yukon/British Columbia boundary, the greenish-blue river flows northward through the Yukon Territory and Alaska to empty into the Bering Sea.

view of the vast **Tintina Trench,** vivid evidence of plate tectonics.

There is a **viewpoint,** after 483km/300mi, of the valley of the Klondike River from above, with the Ogilvie Mountains to the northeast. The road then follows the Klondike.

At 494km/307mi note that the **Dempster Highway** heads northward to Inuvik in the Mackenzie Delta across the Ogilvie and Richardson mountains. (*Open all year except spring breakup and fall freeze-up when the Peel and Mackenzie river ferries do not operate*).

The Klondike Highway crosses the Klondike River after 538km/334mi and enters Dawson City.

Dawson City★★
See DAWSON CITY.

From Dawson City to Whitehorse

945km/586mi by Top of the World (Rte. 9), Taylor (US 5) (both highways closed in winter) and Alaska Hwys. Caution: Reduced speeds necessary, usually 40–64km/h/25–40mph on winding and often unpaved road (Alaska Hwy. is paved). Drive with headlights on. Canada and US Customs offices at border crossing for Rtes. 9 & 5 Open mid-May–mid-Sept daily 9am–9pm (8am–8pm Alaska time). Alaska Hwy. border open year-round daily 24hrs. ☎867-862-7230 (Canada Customs). 907-774-2252 (US Customs).

Top of the World Highway★★
108km/67mi to Alaska border. Road closed in winter. Entry only when US Customs open (above).

Route 9 is called Top of the World Highway it is mostly above the tree line, allowing magnificent **views★★★**. It leaves Dawson by the ferry across the Yukon (*continuous 24hr service May–Sept*). For about 5km/3mi, the road climbs to a **viewpoint** at a bend in the road. After 14km/9mi there is another **viewpoint** of the Ogilvie Mountains, the Yukon Valley and, visible to the north, the Tintina Trench. The road then follows the ridgetops for 90km/50mi.

The Route in Alaska
306km/190mi. At Alaska border, set watches back 1hr.

Route 9 joins the Taylor Highway (US 5) after 23km/14mi (*services available at Boundary, Alaska*) and heads south along the valley of the Fortymile River. **Chicken**, Alaska (*food and fuel. www.chickenalaska.com*), offers local color and frontier history. Wanting to name their camp "ptarmigan" for a local bird, miners settled on "chicken" instead, it is said, because they could spell it! At **Tetlin Junction** take the Alaska Highway south to the Canadian border (*Set watches forward 1hr*).

Alaska Highway★★
491km/305mi from Alaska border to Whitehorse. Along the highway, posts indicate the distance from Dawson Creek, BC, where the highway begins. Kilometres/miles in this section are shown in descending order to conform with these post readings.

North of the Canadian/US border, in the vicinity of Northway, Alaska, is the **Tetlin National Wildlife Refuge**, a 384,620ha/730,000-acre preserve of boreal forest, wetlands, lakes and glacial rivers (*Visitor Centre, Milepost 1229, Alaska Highway. Open mid-May–mid Sept daily 8am–4:30pm. ☎907-883-5312. http://tetlin.fws.gov*). After crossing the Canada/US border (*KM1969/mi 1221*), the highway (caution: intermittent bumps) passes through flat muskeg country and crosses the White and then the Donjek rivers. From the latter (*KM1810/mi 1125*), there is a **view** of the **St. Elias Mountains**.

Kluane Lake★★
Just before Burwash Landing (*KM1759/mi 1093*), the road approaches this vast lake, paralleling it for 64km/40mi and offering excellent **views★★**. To the south and west lie the **Kluane Ranges**, to the north and east the **Ruby Range**. In Burwash Landing, the **Kluane Museum of Natural History** is housed in a six-sided log building. **Dioramas★** of native wildlife line the building's interior. (*Open May 15–Sept 15 daily 9am–6:30pm. www.yukonmuseums.ca. $4.75. ☎867-841-5561*).

Descent towards Haines Junction from Kluane National Park

Kluane National Park Reserve★★

♿⏰*Park open year-round. Hiking, camping, rafting, fishing, cross-country skiing.* 🎫*User fees. Park office and visitor centre in Haines Junction; visitor centre also near Sheep Mountain. PO Box 5495, Haines Junction YK, Y0B 1L0. ☎867-634-7208. www.pc.gc.ca.* ⏰*Open mid-May–mid-Sept daily 9am–5pm (Sheep Mountain until 4pm) and by appointment rest of year. Limited 4-wheel-drive vehicle access to park's interior (streams must be forded). Arrangements to visit interior must be made in advance with park authorities. Sifton Air offers charters and tours year-round. Box 5419 Haines Junction YK, Y0B 1L0. ☎867-634-2916. TransNorth Helicopter offers heli-tours and charters year-round. Box 8, Whitehorse YK, Y1A 5X9. ☎867-634-2242. www.hainesjunctionyukon.com*

From the Alaska Highway the Kluane Ranges *(as high as 2,500m/8,000ft)* can be seen. Behind them are the **Icefield Ranges**, which contain many peaks exceeding 4,500m/15,000ft. Best known are **Mount Logan** *(5,959m/19,550ft)* and **Mount St. Elias** *(5,489m/18,008ft)*. Mt. Logan is second in height only to **Mount McKinley** *(6,194m/20,320ft)* in Alaska, the highest point on the continent.

At KM 1707/mi 1061 the Alaska Highway passes **Tachal Dhal (Sheep Mountain)**, a rocky and barren peak so named for the white Dall sheep on its slopes. The Alaska Highway crosses the large **Slims River Delta** *(km 1707–2/mi 1061–58)*, .

Haines Junction

KM 1635/mi1016.

At the junction of the Alaska and Haines (Route 3) highways, this community sits at the foot of the Auriol Range.

Haines Highway crosses the Chilkat Pass before entering Alaska. About 20km/12mi south of Haines Junction via Route 3, there is a **view★★** of **Kathleen Lake★★**. Returning to Haines Junction, drivers can continue to Whitehorse *(KM 1474/mi 916)* on the Alaska Highway.

Prairie Provinces

Alberta, Saskatchewan and Manitoba, known collectively as the Prairie provinces, are often thought of as flat and monotonous. But there is something awe-inspiring about the wide open spaces, extensively cultivated, yet sparsely populated (just over 6 million people). In places, rivers have cut deep valleys into the soft soil of the prairie and in Alberta and Saskatchewan have formed the sculpted buttes of **badlands**. The countryside is a patchwork of colors: massive rectangles of wheat, green in the spring, turn gold before harvest. Flax has a small blue or white flower, canola a yellow one. Tall brightly painted **grain elevators**—the "cathedrals of the plains"—rise beside railway tracks. Above extends an infinite blue sky, dotted with puffy white clouds, sometimes black as a thunderstorm approaches.

- **Information:** Each prairie province has a tourist office: Travel Alberta, Tourism Saskatchewan, Travel Manitoba. See the green Address Book in this section.
- **Orient Yourself:** The three prairie provinces cover a vast region of 1,963,00sq km/758,000sq mi (larger than Alaska), in the centre of Canada.
- **Don't Miss:** Try to take in at least one agricultural fair or stampede.
- **Organizing Your Time:** A few days can be devoted to an adventure tour.
- **Especially for Kids:** Farm or ranch vacations are a thrill for youngsters.
- **Also See:** The following 17 sections describe the prairie provinces.

Geographical Notes

Diverse Region –The French word *prairie* was given to the large area of grassland in the interior of the North American continent where the bison, roaming in huge herds, were hunted by Plains Indians. In Canada the term "Prairies" now applies to all three provinces.

Semiarid Southwest – The southernmost part of Alberta and Saskatchewan is a relatively dry land of short grass. Widespread use of irrigation has brought much of the region into cultivation today. The native grasses provide pasture for cattle and this region, especially the vicinity of Cypress Hills.

Grain-Growing Crescent – To the north of the arid lands lies a crescent-shaped region of fertile soil, graced with more abundant rainfall. This is the grain belt, the prairie of many people's imagination. Prim farm buildings dot the enormous fields of wheat, barley, canola and flax. The old grain elevators, easily visible for miles, serve as town landmarks.

Aspen Parkland – North of the wheat belt is another roughly crescent-shaped region, where trees grow in good soil and mixed farming flourishes. This is a region of rolling parkland, a transitional zone between the prairie and the forest of the north. Most inhabitants of the three provinces live in this region.

Boreal Forest and Tundra – The northern halves of the three provinces lie directly on the Precambrian rock of the Canadian Shield. This expanse is a pristine land of countless lakes, trees and rock outcroppings, dotted by small towns and First Nations communities.

Prairie "Steps" – Apart from deep valleys cut by rivers, the Prairies rise gradually in three main levels, or steps, from sea level at Hudson Bay to nearly 1,200m/4,000ft west of the Rockies. The first step ends with the **Manitoba Escarpment**, which rises to a maximum 831m/2,726ft. Encompassing the flattest lands, the second step ends with the **Missouri Coteau**, rising to a maximum 879m/2,883ft and visible from Moose

Canola Field

Jaw. The third step borders the Rockies. The Prairies are also broken by numerous ranges of small hills in the north and by the Cypress Hills and the Pembina Valley in the south.

Climate – The Prairies experience a climate of extremes that varies from year to year, making average conditions difficult to gauge. Winter is generally long and cold; summer is short and hot. Precipitation is low (380-500mm/15-20in a year), sometimes arriving in the form of blizzards in winter and violent thunderstorms in summer. July is the driest and hottest month (mean maximum for Calgary is 24°C/76°F, Regina 27°C/81°F, Winnipeg 27°C/80°F). In the southwest winter is alleviated by the chinook winds, which blow warm air from the Pacific through the Rockies. In a few hours temperatures can rise as much as 28°C/82°F.

A Bit of History

Indians of the Plains – The Assiniboine, Blackfoot, Cree, Gros Ventre and Sarcee Indians lived almost exclusively on bison, which were driven over cliffs or stampeded into pounds. Their meat was often dried and made into **pemmican**—a nutritious mixture of pounded meat, animal fat and some-times saskatoon berries—which could be preserved for up to a year. Bison hides were used to make moccasins, clothing and winter robes. Home was a **teepee**, a conical structure of poles (some almost 12m/40ft tall) covered with buffalo hides.

Existing warfare among the tribes grew more lethal when fur traders began supplying guns. Their use by Plains Indians and incoming homesteaders resulted in the gradual extinction of the great herds. By the 1880s European settlers had arrived and fenced the once-open prairie.

Fur Traders – Eager to reduce the long journey by canoe between present-day Montreal and Lake Superior, two traders, **Pierre Radisson** and **Sieur des Groseilliers,** proposed a quicker way to transport furs to Europe via Hudson Bay. France showed little interest in the scheme, but Charles II of England In 1670 granted a royal charter to the "Governor and Company of Adventurers of England trading into Hudson's Bay." The **Hudson's Bay Company** (HBC), as it became known, held sole right to trade in the vast watershed that drains into the bay. Forts and factories were established on its shores .

The Métis and the Creation of Manitoba – A consequence of the fur trade

Practical Information

PRACTICAL INFORMATION

GETTING THERE

By Air – Major airlines such as Air Canada (☎514-393-3333 or toll-free 1-888-247-2262 (Canada/US). www.aircanada.ca) service Calgary, Edmonton, Regina, Saskatoon and Winnipeg. Regional carriers include Westjet Airlines (☎403-444-2552 or toll-free 1-800-538-5696 (Canada/US). www.westjet.com).

By Train – VIA Rail Canada has regularly scheduled service to all three provinces (☎514-989-2626 or toll-free 1-888-842-7245 (Canada/US). www.viarail.ca.)

By Bus – Greyhound services communities across the Prairies: ☎toll-free 1-800-661-8747 (Canada), ☎toll-free1-800-231-2222 (US). www.greyhound.ca.

GENERAL INFORMATION

ACCOMMODATIONS AND VISITOR INFORMATION

The government tourist offices produce annually updated guides listing approved accomodations. Contact:

Travel Alberta (PO Box 2500, Edmonton AB, T5J 2Z4. ☎780-427-4321 or toll-free 1-800-252-3782 (Canada/US). www.travelalberta.com).

Travel Manitoba (155 Carlton St., 7th floor, Winnipeg MB, R3C 3H8. ☎204-927-7800 or toll-free 1-800-665-0040 (Canada/US). www.travelmanitoba.com).

Tourism Saskatchewan (1922 Park St., Regina SK, S4N 7M4. ☎306-787-9600 or toll-free 1-877-237-2273 (Canada/US). www.sasktourism.com).

Most major hotel chains have facilities in these provinces. Independent hotels and B&B lodgings can be found along major routes. **Farm vacations** are offered in all three provinces. Alberta in particular boasts many **guest ranches**.

ROAD REGULATIONS

Unless otherwise posted, speed limits on provincial highways are: Alberta 100km/h (60mph), or 90km/h (55mph) in parks; Manitoba 100km/h (60mph); Saskatchewan 110km/h (70mph). Use of **seat belts** is compulsory.

TIME ZONES

Alberta: Mountain Standard Time. Manitoba: Central Standard Time. Both observe Daylight Saving Time from the 2nd Sunday in March to the 1st Sunday in November. Most of Saskatchewan remains on Central Standard Time all year. Some border communities keep the same time as the neighboring province all year.

TAXES

In addition to the national 5% GST, Manitoba levies a 7% and Saskatchewan a 5% retail sales tax on all items. In Alberta there is a 5% hotel tax but no sales or restaurant tax.

LIQUOR LAWS

The legal drinking age is 18 in Manitoba and Alberta, 19 in Saskatchewan. In Manitoba and Saskatchewan, liquor and wine can be purchased only in government liquor stores and approved retail outlets. In Alberta liquor can be bought in privately owned liquor stores. In isolated parts of the North where no government stores exist, grocery stores are licensed.

PROVINCIAL HOLIDAYS

Family Day (Alberta only) – 3rd Monday in February
Civic Holiday – 1st Monday in August

RECREATION

OUTDOOR ACTIVITIES

Water sports—boating, sailing, canoeing, waterskiing and swimming—are popular because of the many lakes and river systems. Saskatchewan offers **white-water rafting,** especially along the Clearwater River, and Alberta offers rafting trips.

The region has many national and provincial parks, offering hiking, biking, horse trails and campsites in summer, and downhill and cross-country skiing, snowshoeing and snowmobiling in winter. Wildlife viewing includes whooping cranes in Saskatchewan, polar bears in Manitoba and bighorn sheep in Alberta. Northern Manitoba and Saskatchewan are famous for their fly-in fishing lodges. Lac la Ronge in Saskatchewan is well known for sportfishing. Anglers and hunters must have a valid license, obtainable in most sporting-goods stores. Fishing and hunting guidebooks are available free from provincial tourist offices (🔵*opposite*).

SPECIAL EXCURSIONS

Birding trips *(May–Jun)* and **beluga-whale** *(Jul–Aug)* and **polar-bear** *(Oct–Nov)* watching in Churchill, MB, are offered by such companies as Natural Habitat Wildlife Adventures (☎*303-449-3711 or toll-free 1-800-543-8917. www. nathab.com)*, or Sea North Tours (☎*204-675-2195. www.seanorthtours.com)*. Contact Travel Manitoba (🔵*opposite*) for a complete list of adventure tour operators. **Paddling trips** on Saskatchewan's historic Churchill River are popular (☎ *877-511-2726. www.churchillrivercanoe. com)*. **Trail rides and horse-pack trips** are exciting options. Contact Travel Alberta (🔵*opposite*) for specifics.

PRINCIPAL FESTIVALS

FEBRUARY
Northern Manitoba Trappers' Festival The Pas MB. *www.trappersfestival. com*
Festival du Voyageur Saint-Boniface MB. *www.festivalvoyageur.mb.ca*
Winter Festival Prince Albert SK. *www.princealbertwinterfestival.com*

JUNE
Manitoba Summer Fair Brandon MB. *www.brandonfairs.com*
Western Canada Farm Progress Show Regina SK.*www.wcfps.com*
Red River Exhibition Winnipeg MB. *www.redriverex.com*

JULY
Folk Festival Winnipeg MB. *www.winnipegfolkfestival.ca*
Manitoba Threshermen's Reunion Austin MB. *www.ag-museum.mb.ca*
Calgary Exhibition and Stampede Calgary AB. *www.calgarystampede.com*
Klondike Days Edmonton AB. *www. capitalex.ca*
Craven Country Jamboree Craven SK. *www.cravencountryjamboree.com*

AUGUST
Saskatoon Exhibition Saskatoon SK. *www.saskatoonexhibition.ca*
Manitoba Highland Gathering Selkirk MB. *www.manitobahighlandgathering. org.*
National Ukrainian Festival Dauphin MB. *www.cnuf.ca*
Pioneer Days Steinbach MB. *www.communityprofiles.mb.ca*
Buffalo Days Regina SK. *www.ipscoplace.com*
Whoop-up Days and Rodeo Lethbridge AB. *www.exhibitionpark.ca*
Icelandic Festival Gimli MB. *www.icelandicfestival.com*
Corn and Apple Festival Morden MB. *www.communityprofiles.mb.ca*
Folklorama Winnipeg MB. *www.folklorama.ca*
Folkfest: Saskatoon, SK. *www.saskatoon.com/folkfest*

NOVEMBER
Canadian Western Agribition Regina SK. *www.agribition.com*

Klondike Days, Edmonton

Travel Alberta

was the creation of a new ethnic group, the Métis—offspring of the native women and French coureurs des bois (and later of Scots and English traders). Though mainly French-speaking Roman Catholics, the Métis preserved the traditional lifestyle of their native forebears. The first threat to them came with the arrival of settlers along the Red River in 1812. In 1870 the situation escalated when the new Dominion of Canada decided to take over the vast lands of the Hudson's Bay Company. The Métis saw their traditional life disappearing with the arrival of more settlers.

The Métis turned to 25-year-old **Louis Riel**, who set up his own provisional government to recognise Métis rights. Riel gained no sympathy from English Métis and other settlers. After foiling a plot to assassinate him, Riel executed an adventurer from Ontario, **Thomas Scott,** an act that he was long to regret. Nevertheless his plea on behalf of his people was heard. In July 1870 the new province of Manitoba was created.

A Human Mosaic – Treaties negotiated with the residents of the region proved unsuccessful, as the Northwest Rebellion of 1885 showed. Some means of enforcing law and order was needed. In 1873 the **North West Mounted Police** force was created. Additionally, land had to be distributed. The **Dominion Lands Act** of 1872 allowed prospective homesteaders to register for a quarter section (65ha/160 acres). When construction of the **Canadian Pacific Railway** was completed in 1885, the population of the Prairies was about 150,000; by 1914 it had reached 1.5 million.

The prospect of free land attracted inhabitants of an overcrowded Europe- and religious refugees. The Canadian government under **Sir Wilfrid Laurier** advertised the Prairies all over the world. Millions indeed came. The provinces of **Alberta** and **Saskatchewan** were created in 1905. The population today stands around 6 million (Alberta 3, 375,763; Manitoba 1,777,765; Saskatchewan 985,386).

Economy

Agriculture – Between 1876 and 1915, the land where the fur trade once reigned supreme suddenly developed a wheat economy. In 1842 David Fife of Ontario developed a strain of wheat that later proved ideal for cultivation on the prairies. Called **Red Fife** for its rich color, it is the ancestor of all the strains used today.

Today about 80 percent of Canada's agricultural land is in Alberta, Manitoba and Saskatchewan. Wheat, canola and flax are major crops. Mixed farming—including beef farming—and poultry, egg and pork production are also important.

Cattle Country – Although grain is the major economic staple of the Prairies, ranching is a secondary industry. Southern Alberta and Saskatchewan are "cowboy country." and rodeos abound, including the internationally renowned Calgary Stampede.

Manufacturing – Although agriculture is Saskatchewan's top industry, it is second to manufacturing in Manitoba and third after petrochemical production and mining in Alberta. Manitoba has a broad-based manufacturing sector, which includes food processing, equipment, printing, clothing and furniture. Alberta's petrochemical production is surpassed by Quebec and Ontario.

Riches Below the Earth – Alberta produces most of Canada's oil and **natural gas.** Its **Athabasca oil sands** are said to be the largest known hydrocarbon accumulation in the world. **Coal** was found in Lethbridge, Alberta, in 1869.

Saskatchewan is the largest producer of **potash**—used for fertilizer— in the world. Oil and **sodium sulphate** are found in the Lloydminster, Swift Current and Estevan. The giant **zinc, cadmium** and **copper** field at Flin Flon, Manitoba, was established in 1915. Copper was discovered near Lynn Lake, Manitoba, and **gold** in the Lake Athabasca area of Saskatchewan. **Uranium** was found in the late 1940s in Saskatchewan, and in the 1960s the giant **nickel** field of Thompson, Manitoba, came into production.

ALBERTA BADLANDS★★★
ALBERTA

The meltwaters of the last continental glacier eroded a deep valley across Southern Alberta, through which the Red Deer River now flows, and exposed rocks formed during the Cretaceous period (64 million-140 million years ago). This area is the Alberta Badlands, a striking panorama of steep bluffs and fluted gullies.

In Cretaceous times, the area was a subtropical lowland inhabited by dinosaurs, and it now holds one of the world's richest deposits of fossils. Several hundred complete skeletons have been unearthed since the first discovery in 1884.

🛈 **Information:** Information Centre, 60 1st Ave. West, Drumheller. ☎403-823-8100 toll-free 1-866-823-8100. www.traveldrumheller.com

▶ **Orient Yourself:** Drumheller is 138km/86mi northeast of Calgary. The Dinosaur Trail extends northwest along both sides of the Red Deer River.

🅿 **Parking:** All of the attractions along the Dinosaur Trail have parking areas.

⊛ **Don't Miss:** The Royal Tyrrell Museum and the Hoodoos.

🕐 **Organizing Your Time:** Give yourself a half day to tour the Dinosaur Trail and visit the Royal Tyrell Museum. Then drive southeast along the Red Deer River to see the Hoodoos and Dinosaur Provincial Park.

Kids **Kids:** How can you go wrong with dinosaurs? The Royal Tyrrell Museum is a must and the Dinosaur Trail offers weird rock formations holding fossil remains.

⚹ **Also See:** CALGARY

Dinosaur Trail

51km/32mi circular drive. See map.

Connecting the sights of the Drumheller area, this loop on the plain above Red Deer River offers good views of the badlands.

Drumheller★
Visitor centre. ⚹For address see above. 🕐Open Jul–Aug daily 9am–9pm. Rest of the year daily 10am–5pm.
Dominating the entrance to the visitor centre is an 86ft-high replica of a *Tyrannosaurus rex* which contains a stairwell

that leads to a viewing platform (⊛*$3. Same hours as visitor centre).* The **view**★ of the river valley is worth the climb (106 steps).

Badlands Historical Centre
335 1st St. East, PO Box 2135,Drumheller AB, T0J 0Y0. ⚹🕐Open June–Sept daily 10am–6pm. Rest of the year by appointment. ⊛$4. ☎403-823-2593. The centre features exhibits, interactive displays, artifacts and dinosaur fossils.

Royal Tyrrell Museum★★★
Kids *6km/4mi northwest of Drumheller by Hwy. 838 (North Dinosaur Trail). PO Box*

Defining Dinosaurs

The word *dinosaur* is derived from Greek, meaning "terrible lizard." In fact, some were small and most were plant eaters, but the biggest weighed as much as 27 tonnes/30 tons and grew to 24m/80ft in length. The **duckbilled dinosaur** walked on its hind feet, which were webbed for swimming, and sported a snout resembling a duck's bill. The **horned dinosaur** walked on four feet and had horns—usually one over each eye and one on the nose. The **armored dinosaur** was equipped with a row of bony plates on its back and spikes on its tail as a form of protection. All these were herbivorous, slow moving and prey to the ferocious **carnivorous dinosaur** with its sharp claws and teeth, and muscular hind legs for running.

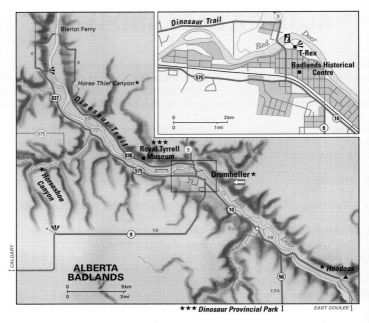

★★★ *Dinosaur Provincial Park* | EAST COULEE |

7500, Drumheller AB, T0J 0Y0. ✕&⌚Open mid-May–Labour Day daily 9am–9pm. Rest of Sept–early Oct daily 10am–5pm. Rest of the year Tue–Sun 10am–5pm. ⌚Closed Jan 1, Dec 24-25. ⊚\$10. ☎403-823-7707 or toll-free 1-888-440-4240 (Canada/US). www.tyrrellmuseum.com.
The highlight is the enormous **Dinosaur Hall**, where the huge *Tyrannosaurus rex*, *Albertosaurus*, the armored *Stegosaurus* and smaller birdlike dinosaurs can be seen. One area represents Bearpaw Sea, which covered the western Canadian interior 70 million years ago.

Dinosaur Trail provides a good view of the badlands from **Horse Thief Canyon★**, with its rounded, almost barren hills stretching to the river. The trail crosses the river by the **Bleriot cable ferry** and climbs to a fine **view★** of the valley.

Additional Sights

Horseshoe Canyon★
18km/11mi southwest of Drumheller by Rte. 9.
Paths leading through the hillocks to the river provide some of the best **views** of the badlands in the area.

Hoodoos★
17km/10mi southeast of Drumheller by Rte. 10.
These strange rock formations illustrate the work of erosion in the valley.

Dinosaur Provincial Park★★★
174km/108mi southeast of Drumheller by Rte. 56 & Trans-Can Hwy. east to Brooks. Take Hwy. 873 for 10km/6mi, then turn right on Hwy. 544, and left on Hwy. 551. ⌚Open daily year-round. Visitor Centre open mid-May–Labour Day daily 8:30am–7pm, Sept–early Oct 10am–5pm. Rest of year hours vary. ☎403-378-4342. www.tprc.alberta.ca.
The park is set in the most spectacular part of the Red Deer River Valley and the richest fossil area, which UNESCO placed on the World Heritage list in 1979.
Immediately upon entrance to the park, an excellent **viewpoint★★★** overlooks nearly 3,000ha/7,000 acres of badlands cut by the Red Deer River. The road then descends to the valley.
A **circular drive** *(5km/3mi)* takes the visitor through this wild and desolate landscape. At several points, short walks lead to dinosaur bones preserved where they were found. Most of the park, however, is accessible only by a special

Hunting Fossils

Look for fossils where sedimentary rocks are exposed such as in quarries, along road cuts, cliffs and seashores. **Always get permission** from local authorities or landowners before you begin your search. ☺**Be aware of legal restrictions:** in Alberta, it is illegal to remove fossils from provincial and federal parks or to sell or take fossils out of the province without a government certificate. Check with the Royal Tyrrell Museum regarding excavation permits.

Whether surface collecting or excavating, you need a map, compass, magnifying glass, notebook, small paintbrush, knife, trowel and geological hammer. Safety gear includes gloves, goggles and a hard hat. Take paper towels or newspaper to wrap the fossil and plastic bags for carrying it.

Give the specimen a number and handle it properly to maintain the scientific information held within. Record the location and date of your find in your note-book. Also describe the color and texture of the rocks in which the fossil was found (e.g., hard limestone block).

In Drumheller, you can buy fossils and related materials at the **Badlands Historical Centre** or **The Fossil Shop** (*61 Bridge St., Drumheller AB, T0J 0Y0.* ☎*403-823-6774. www.thefossilshop.com*) or the **Museum Shop** in the Tyrrell Museum. The Tyrrell offers day-long and week-long field research courses (*You must be age 18 or older; contact the museum for details*).

R. Corbel/MICHELIN

bus tour (*2 hrs. Departs from the Visitor Centre plaza mid-May–Labour Day daily Mon–Friday 9am–noon, 1pm–4pm, weekends 10am–noon, 1pm–4pm. 1-day advance reservations required.* ☎*$8.* ☎*403-378-4344*) or by **conducted hikes** (*reservations* ☎*403-378-4344*). ♿*Wheelchair access to bus by arrangement and on some trails. Ask ahead.*

Travel Alberta

Dinosaur Provincial Park

AUSTIN ★
MANITOBA

Set in the centre of a rich agricultural region, this pleasant rural community is renowned for its collection of operating vintage farm machinery and an annual reunion celebration.

- **Information:** Manitoba Agricultural Museum, ☎204-637-2054. www.ag-museum.mb.ca
- ▶ **Orient Yourself:** Austin lies 123km/76mi west of Winnipeg on Hwy 1.
- Ⓟ **Parking:** Museum parking lot.
- **Don't Miss:** The Threshermen's Reunion, if possible; the Homesteaders Village.
- Ⓞ **Organizing Your Time:** Nearby Brandon MB is a good-sized town (pop 43,000) with accomodation and restaurants.
- **Also See:** WINNIPEG

Sight

Manitoba Agricultural Museum ★
Kids *On Hwy. 34, 3km/2mi south of Trans-Can Hwy.PO Box 10 Austin MB, R0H 0C0. ⓈⓄOpen May–Sept daily 9am–5pm. ☜$5 adult. ☎204-637-2354. www.ag-museum.mb.ca.*
This museum has a splendid collection of "prairie giants"—steam trac

tors, threshing machines and gasoline machines. In late July, these machines are paraded and demonstrated in the Manitoba **Threshermen's Reunion and Stampede**, held on the grounds of the museum. The **homesteaders' village** illustrates life at the end of the last century.

THE BATTLEFORDS ★
SASKATCHEWAN
POPULATION 16,875

Surrounded by rolling country, the twin communities of **Battleford** and **North Battleford** face each other across the valley of the North Saskatchewan River. North Battleford has a fine **site** overlooking the river.

- **Information:** ☎306-445-2000, toll-free 1-800-243-0394. www.battlefordstourism.com
- ▶ **Orient Yourself:** The Battlefords are on the Yellowhead Highway (Hwy 16) 153km/96mi northwest of Saskatoon.
- Ⓟ **Parking:** The sites provide ample parking.
- **Don't Miss:** Battleford has several other interesting tourist attractions near the Fort.
- Ⓞ **Organizing Your Time:** Fort Battleford will take 2-3hrs to visit, especially with children.
- **Kids** **Especially for Kids:** At Fort Battleford, children can dress up and take part in police drills.
- **Also See:** SASKATOON

Curling: Canada's Other Ice Sport

More than a million Canadians enjoy this winter activity, which became an Olympic sport at Calgary in 1988. Here's how the game works:

During 8 to 10 rounds ("ends"), two four-person teams (wearing rubber-soled shoes, not ice skates) take turns "throwing" their 20kg/42lb granite stones along the ice toward a **bull's-eye** at the opposite end of a 42m/138ft by 4.3m/14ft rink. "Sweepers" use brooms to alter the ice in front of a teammate's stone in order to increase its speed or help determine its path. The captains signal their players to knock the opponent's stones away from the target area. A point is awarded for each stone resting closer to the centre mark than the nearest of the opponent's stones.

Curling probably developed in the 16C in **Scotland**, and was introduced to Canada in the 18C by Scottish troops. Clubs were established by 1807, and the Canadian Curling Association was formed in 1935. **Manitoba** is Canada's curling centre. Many clubs have a visitors' viewing gallery, and important matches are televised.
For more information, contact the Canadian Curling Assn. www.curling.ca.

A Bit of History

Fur traders established posts on the Battleford (south) side of the river in the 18C, but it was not until 1874 that the first settlers arrived. A North West Mounted Police post was established in 1876. Then the Canadian Pacific Railway Co. routed its line to the south, and in 1883 the territorial capital was moved from Battleford to Pile O'Bones Creek (later Regina). During the Northwest Rebellion of 1885, Battleford was looted and burned by Poundmaker Crees. In 1903 the Canadian Northern Railway was built along the opposite side of the river, creating North Battleford, which grew as Battleford shrank.

Sights

Fort Battleford★
Central Ave., PO Box 70, Battleford SK, S0M 0E0. Kids *Open mid-May–Labour Day daily 9am–5pm. $7.15 adult. ☎306-937-2621. www.pc.gc.ca.*
This North West Mounted Police post, attacked during the Northwest Rebellion, was abandoned in 1924. Today restored, this National Historic Site provides insight into police life in the late 19C. At the **interpretation centre**, children are invited to dress up in Mountie uniforms and take part in police drills.

Western Development Museum★
On Hwy. 16 at junction with Rte. 40, PO Box 183, North Battleford SK, S9A 2Y1. Open mid-May–Labour Day daily 9am–5pm. Rest of the year Mon–Fri 10am–4pm. $8.50 adult. ☎306-445-8033. www.wdm.ca.
This branch of the Western Development Museum—one of four in the province (the others are in Moose Jaw, Saskatoon and Yorkton)—displays agricultural machinery and domestic artifacts from the 1920s.
Outside, a **heritage farm and village** of 1925 is set out with homes and churches reflecting the diverse origins of the peoples who settled this province.

ALLEN SAPP GALLERY
1 Railway Ave. East, Box 460, North Battleford SK, S9A 2Y6. ☎306-445-1760. www.allensapp.com. Images of the Northern Plains Cree painted by Cree artist Allen Sapp are on view in a large building located just off Highway 16 (Yellowhead Highway). A descendant of Chief Poundmaker, Sapp (b.1928) was born on an Indian reserve south of the city. His paintings vividly record Cree traditions and the rugged frontier life. Limited and open editions of his prints are on sale in the gift shop.

CALGARY★★
ALBERTA
POPULATION 988,079

Calgary is Canada's fastest-growing metropolis, its prosperity due largely to Alberta's vast oil wealth, favorable business climate (no sales tax) and importance as a transportation hub. Blessed with a pleasant climate (moderate rainfall, low humidity, lots of sunshine and a moderately cold winter, tempered by warm chinook winds), this tourist mecca is known for its renowned Stampede and remembered fondly as host of the 1988 Winter Olympic Games.

- **Information:** Tourist Office 200-238 11 Ave SE. ☎403-263-8510, or toll-free 1-800-661 1678. www.tourismcalgary.com
- ▶ **Orient Yourself:** Calgary is set in the foothills of the Canadian Rockies, at the confluence of the Bow and Elbow rivers. The Transcanada Highway passes here.
- **Parking:** Parking meters operate from 9am–6pm daily; rates range from $1 to $3.50 per hour. The Light Rail Transit (LRT) is free in downtown Calgary.
- **Don't Miss:** The Glenbow Museum and the Calgary Zoo.
- **Organizing Your Time:** To attend the Stampede, book up to a year ahead.
- **Especially for Kids:** Heritage Park and the Bar-U Ranch are surefire winners.
- **Also See:** LETHBRIDGE, CARDSTON, WATERTON LAKES, FORT MACLEOD

A Bit of History

Origins – In 1875 a North West Mounted Police post was built on this site and named Fort Calgary by Col. James Macleod, police commander in the Northwest, for his home in Scotland.

Then, in the 1880s, the Canadian Pacific Railway Co. routed its railway through Calgary, bringing a huge influx of settlers to the lush grazing lands of the region. The Dominion Lands Act encouraged the movement of cattle herds northward from the US. Well-to-do Englishmen arrived to establish ranches.

"Black Gold" – The discovery of oil in 1914 at Turner Valley, southwest of Calgary, marked the birth of western Canada's petroleum industry. Then in 1947 a great discovery was made at Leduc, launching Calgary on its phenomenal growth. As well, Calgary has become a financial centre, second only to Toronto in attracting corporate head offices.

Downtown See map p180.

Attractive, glass-fronted high rises such as the Calgary Tower and Canadian bank offices as well as the brown marble headquarters of **Petro-Canada** dominate Calgary's glittering skyline; a pedestrian **mall** stretches along 8th Avenue. Most of downtown lies along a network of sky bridges that allow pedestrians to escape winter's cold.

The easterly stretch of the 8th Avenue mall, known locally as the Stephen Avenue Walk, is filled with early-1900s Alberta sandstone buildings now converted to small shops and cafes. At 7th Avenue and Macleod Trail SE is the 1907 Romanesque Revival city hall building. The tiered, blue reflecting-glass structure east of city hall is Calgary's **Municipal Building,** rising around a 12-storey atrium. Across 2nd Street SE stands the **Centre for the Performing Arts**.

On the fourth floor of Toronto Dominion Square is an indoor greenhouse, the **Devonian Gardens★**, with some 20,000 tropical plants, plus fountains and sculptures (☉Open year-round daily 9am–9pm. ☎403-268-2489).

Glenbow Museum★★

130 9th Ave. SE, Calgary AB, T2G 0P3. In Convention Centre complex. ☉Open daily 9am–5pm (Thur 9pm). ☉Closed Dec 25. ☞ $14 adult. ☎ 403-268-4100. www. glenbow.org.

The **Nitsitapiisinni Gallery** (third floor), reflects the colorful history of the Black-

The Calgary Stampede

Hailed as "the Greatest Outdoor Show on Earth," the **Calgary Stampede** is a grand 10-day event held in early July that attracts hundreds of thousands of spectators and competitors every year *(reservations recommended)*. Almost the entire population of Calgary dons western garb (boots, jeans and hats) and joins the festivities. There are flapjack breakfasts, street dances, and a huge parade in the city. Livestock shows and the famous **rodeo** and **chuckwagon races** are held in Stampede Park, where a lengthy midway features rides, games, live musical entertainment and food galore. Invented in Calgary, the chuckwagon races recall the wagon races held by cowboys after a roundup and are an exciting part of the stampede. Near the South Gate, the Indian Village showcases several colorful tee-pees and offers native arts and crafts for sale. ☎403-261-0101 or toll-free 1-800-661-1260 (Canada/US). www.calgarystampede.com.

Travel Alberta

foot Indians. Exhibits focus on the fur trade, the North West Mounted Police, missionaries, the Canadian Pacific Railway, farming and ranching, Métis life, and the discovery of oil.

Calgary Tower★★

In Palliser Square, 101 9th Ave. SW. Calgary AB, T2P 1J9. Observation deck ✕&🅿🕙*Open daily 7am–11pm. Hours adjusted seasonally; deck sometimes closed for events – call to confirm hours.* ☞*$13 adult.* ☎*403-266-7171. www.calgary tower.com.*

This 191m/626ft tower provides an excellent **view**★★ of the city and its site. To the west the snowy peaks of the Rockies rise above rolling, arid foothills.

Additional Sights

Crescent Road Viewpoint

Rising above the Bow River and Prince's Island Park, this road offers a fine view of downtown and the snow-clad Rockies.

Fort Calgary

750 9th Ave. SE. PO Box 2100, Sation M (#106), Calgary AB, T2P 2M5. ✕&🅿 🕙*Open daily 9am–5pm.* 🕙*Closed Jan 1, Good Friday, Dec 24-26.* ☞ *$10.50 adult.* ☎*403-290-1875. www.fortcalgary.com.*

An **interpretation centre** on the site of the original North West Mounted Police post recounts the history of the city. The adjacent **Deane House** (&*See green address box*), former home of the NWMP superintendent, is now a popular restaurant. Paths afford **views** of the Bow River, and a pedestrian bridge allows access to St. George's Island and the zoo.

Calgary Zoo★★

🄺🄸🄳🅂 *1300 Zoo Rd. NE, Calgary AB, T2E 7V6. On St. George's Island , directly north of Fort Calgary.* ✕&🅿🕙*Open year-round daily 9am–5pm.* 🕙*Closed Dec 25.* ☞*May–Aug $18, rest of the year $14.* ☎*403-232-9300, or toll-free 1-800-588-9993. www. calgaryzoo.ab.ca.*

Address Book

For dollar sign categories, see the Legend on the cover flap.

WHERE TO STAY

$ Westways B&B – *216 25th Ave. SW. Calgary AB, T2S 0L1.* ☎*403-229-1758 or toll-free 1-866-846-7038. www. bedandbreakfast.com. 5 rooms.* 🅿️💻. Built in 1912 in the Arts and Crafts style, this pleasant inn is a 20min walk from downtown. All rooms come with a private bath and high-speed Internet connection. For couples, either of the two largest rooms—each with a king bed and gas fireplace—is more than adequate. Copious breakfast.

$$ Big Springs Estate B&B – *35km/22mi northwest of city limits along Hwy. 567. RR#1, Airdrie AB, T4B 2A3.* ☎*403-948-5264 or toll-free 1-888-948-5851. www.inntravels.com. 5 rooms.* 🅿️💻. A stay at this modern ranch house will give you a taste of life under the big sky. The friendly hosts make guests feel at home on their 35-acre spread. The comfortable bedrooms have private baths, duvets and robes and slippers. Evening snacks and breakfast in a cheery dining room.

$$ Inglewood B&B – *1006-8th Ave. SE., Calgary AB, T2G 0M4.* ☎*403-262-6570. www.inglewoodbedandbreakfast.com. 3 rooms.* 🅿️💻. A pleasant backyard and simply furnished rooms with private baths make this bed-and-breakfast lodging a good choice for travellers looking for a simple alternative to a regular hotel. The property is within easy walking distance of Stampede Park and other major attractions.

$$ Lord Nelson Inn – *1020 8th Ave. SW. Calgary AB T2P 1J2.* ☎*403-269-8262 or toll-free 1-800-868-9218. 56 rooms.* 🍴🅿️. Rooms in this renovated hotel are modest but comfortable, providing excellent value right downtown. Despite the busy location, noise is not a problem. The restaurant offers breakfast and lunch, while the bar serves inexpensive pub-style fare.

$$$$ Fairmont Palliser – *133-9th Ave. SW. Calgary AB, T2P 2M3.* ☎*403-262-1234 or toll-free 1-800-257-7544. www. fairmont.com. 405 rooms.* 🍴♿🅿️🚇 Spa. Although not as conspicuous as its famous sister properties in the Canadian Rockies, this historic, 12-storey hotel is an elegant oasis amid Calgary's urban bustle. The Alberta sandstone landmark (1914) sits close to the financial district, attracting business travellers as well as vacationers. Many rooms are on the small side, but each comes with plush duvets and bathrobes, as well as modern conveniences such as high-speed Internet access.

$$$$ Kensington Riverside Inn – *1126 Memorial Dr. NW, Calgary AB, T2N E3E.* ☎*403-228-4442 or 877-313-3733. www. kensingtonriversideinn.com. 19 rooms.* ♿🅿️💻. Situated in the Kensington district across the Bow River from downtown, this boutique hotel offers perks such as Egyptian cotton towels, heated towel bars and polar fleece bathrobes. Rooms feature high ceilings and some have private balconies, garden patios or gas fireplaces. Rates include evening hors d'oeuvres, free local calls, wireless Internet, a daily newspaper and a gourmet breakfast.

WHERE TO EAT

$ Deane House – *806-9th Ave. SE. PO Box 2100, Station M #106, Calgary AB, T2P 2M5. Lunch only.* ♿ ☎*403-269-7747. www.fortcalgary.com.* **Contemporary**. Built in 1906 for the commanding officer of the North West Mounted Police, this two-storey wooden house is perfect for a light lunch after visiting adjacent Fort Calgary or the zoo. Innovative salads are a staple, but daily offerings range from quiche to pan-fried Arctic char. The screened-in porch provides the best views.

$ Thai Sa-On – *351-10th Ave. SW. Calgary AB. T2R 0A5.* ☎*403-264-3526.* **Thai**. The diversity and complexity of Thai cuisine make for an extensive menu, but everything at this unpretentious, family-run restaurant is authentically fresh and flavorful. Hearty eaters love the whole snapper, spiced and served with savory vegetables and coconut rice. Vegetarians can choose from the likes of pad paq tua, a peanut-based curry.

$$ Buzzards Cowboy Cuisine – *140-10th Ave. SW. Calgary AB, T2R 0A3.*

☎403-264-6959. www.cowboycuisine. com.♿ **Steaks.** A rustic timber interior decorated with authentic ranching relics and a menu of western specialties make this eatery a popular spot. While fried prairie oysters raise eyebrows, most diners stick to what the city is famous for—Alberta beef.

$$$ The Ranche – *Bow Bottom Trail SE.* ☎403-225-3939. www.crmr.com.♿ **Canadian**. At this beautifully restored 1896 ranch house, set in Fish Creek Provincial Park, the imaginative menu is based on local products. Fresh and smoked game (buffalo, elk, caribou), Alberta beef, lamb and pork and a variety of seafood are creatively partnered with berries and organic vegetables. For example, medaillions of caribou are served with blueberry sourdough bread. Sunday brunch on the veranda is a real treat.

$$$ River Café – *Prince's Island Park, 200 Barclay Parade SW, PO Box 193, Calgary AB, T2P 4R5. www.river-cafe. com.* ☎403-261-7670. **Canadian**. With the ambience of a rustic fishing lodge, this restaurant, set on an island in central Calgary, offers seasonal cuisine focusing on Canadian ingredients such as buffalo, Alberta beef, maple syrup, cranberries, salmon and prairie grains. Access is by footbridge from the Eau Claire Market parking lot.

WHERE TO SHOP

Callebaut Chocolate, *1313-1st St. SE, Calgary AB T2G 5L1.* ☎ *403-265-5777 or 800-661-8367. www.bernardcallebaut. com.* Bernard Callebaut came to Calgary from Belgium 25 years ago and set about creating the best chocolates in Canada, using fresh Alberta dairy products. Now, Callebaut confections are available in 28 retail outlets in Canada, 4 in the US and through catalog sales. Specialties include nut clusters, truffles and nougats. Daily factory tours *(call ahead)* and, best of all, free samples.

Eau Claire Market, *2nd Ave. & 2nd St. SW. 202-200 Barclay Parade SW, Calgary AB, T2P 4R5.* ☎403-264-6450. *www.eau-clairemarket.com.* 🅿You'll find plenty to keep you busy at the bright red, green and yellow buildings housing Eau Claire Market, located adjacent to Prince's Island Park on the Bow River. More than 60 shops, restaurants and services and 5 Cineplex screens vie for attention, including an IMAX theatre that projects films on a 5½-storey screen. Find unique gift items and imports, prints, books and clothing. A food court and more than a dozen restaurants offer everything from Cajun-Creole, Thai and Lebanese cooking to Italian cuisine.

PEARL SNAPS AND BOOT STRAPS

As you would expect, Calgary has a great selection of stores offering Western wear and gear. **Alberta Boot** *(614-10th Ave. SW, Calgary AB, T2R 1M3.* ☎403-263-4605. www.albertaboot. com)* specializes in fine handmade Western boots (the Mounties' footwear of choice). With hundreds of pairs, the selection is vast and prices range from economical to astronomical. **Lammle's Western Wear** *(209-8th Ave. SW Calgary AB, T2P 1B8.* ☎503-266-5226 or toll-free 1-877-526 6537. www.lammles.com)* is an Alberta chain offering ranch wear, boots and hats. Locations include a 1911 heritage storefront on Stephen Avenue Walk. **Chase Cattle Co.** *(Willow Park Village, 10816 Macleod Trail SE #100, Calgary AB, T2J 5N8.* ☎403-269-6450)* sells upscale ranch dress wear, including highly decorated shirts, skirts and jackets.

ROYAL CANADIAN PACIFIC TRAIN

Luxury train travel reached its peak in the late 19C and early 20C in the railcars built specially for Canadian Pacific executives. Long retired, these cars are being returned to the rails for leisurely tours through the Rockies. Departing from downtown Calgary, the Royal CP train is pulled by historic locomotives through spectacular mountain scenery. Four- and five-day excursions feature comfortable staterooms, gourmet meals in the well-appointed dining cars, and overnight stops in such popular destinations as Banff and Lake Louise, AB and Golden, BC. Limited summer and fall schedule. *For information:* ☎403-508-1400 or toll-free 1-877-665-3044 (North America, UK & Germany). www.cprtours.com.

SPRUCE MEADOWS

Southwest of downtown via MacLeod Trail, then west along Hwy. 22X. RR 9

Calgary AB, T2J 5G5. ☎403-974-4200. www.sprucemeadows.com. One of the finest show-jumping facilities on earth, Spruce Meadows is an oasis of perfect turf on the city outskirts. The 120 ha/300 acre site encompasses outdoor rings, indoor arenas, stables for 700 horses and a three-storey tournament centre. Major annual events include The Masters *(2nd weekend of Sept)*, the world's richest show-jumping tournament in prize money ($2M), attracting some 50,000 spectators daily and a television audience of millions. Other outdoor tournaments are the National *(1st week of Jun)*; Canada One *(last weekend of Jun)*; and the North American *(early Jul)*, coinciding with the Calgary Stampede.

Located partly on an island in the Bow River, this attractive zoo houses a variety of animals and a tropical greenhouse. The prehistoric park re-creates western Canada as it looked when dinosaurs roamed. The **Canadian Wilds** section, adjacent to the park, admirably reproduces habitats of western Canada.

Grain Academy★

In the Roundup Centre, Stampede Park, on the plus 15 level. 17th Ave. and 2nd St. SE. PO Box 1060 ST.M, Calgary AB T2P 2K8. ♿🅿 ($10/vehicle) ⊙*Open year-round Mon–Fri 10am–4pm.* ⊙*Closed major holidays.* ⊜ *No charge.* ☎403-263-4594. www.grainacademymuseum.com

This museum presents a working model of a prairie grain elevator, a model railway and a film *(12min)* about grain. It is located in Stampede Park near the distinctive 20,240-seat **Saddledome★,** constructed in 1983 *(Pengrowth Saddledome, 555 Saddledome Rise, Calgary AB, T2G 2W1.* ⊙*Open year-round Mon–Fri 8:30am–5pm.* ☛⊶*Tours Jun–Aug on non-event days Mon–Fri 11am–2pm. Last departure 1pm. Reservations required* ☎777-1375). ☎403-777-4636.www.pengrowthsaddledome.com).

Heritage Park★

📷*16km/10mi southwest of downtown. Take Macleod Trail SW. 1900 Heritage Dr. SW, Calgary AB, T2V 2X3.* ✕🅿 ⊙*Open*

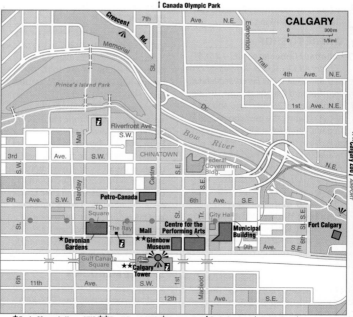

★ Rocky Mountain House NHS, ★★ Bar U Ranch NHS, ★ Heritage Park ┊ Grain Academy ★, Saddledome ★

Heritage Park

mid-May–Labour Day daily 9am–5pm. Rest of Sept–early-Oct weekends only 9am–5pm. ☜$14 adult (rides $3 extra).☎403-268-8500. www.heritagepark.ca. Occupying a pleasant site overlooking Glenmore Reservoir, this park re-creates prairie life of a bygone era. A steam train gives tours, a replica paddlewheeler sails on the reservoir *(every 35min)* and the antique **midway** has great rides.

Canada Olympic Park
12km/7mi west by Trans-Can Hwy. 88 Olympic Road SW, Calgary AB, T3B 5R5.

✕♿🅿🕐*Open July–Labour Day daily 9am–5pm, mid-May–June and Labour-day–early Nov daily 10am–4pm.Rest of year times vary.* 🕐*Closed Dec 25.* ☜*Prices depend on activity.*☎403-247-5452. www. coda.ab.ca.

This large facility was developed to host ski-jumping, luge, bobsled and freestyle-skiing events during the 1988 Winter Olympic Games. During summer, a chair lift provides access to the 90-meter ski-jump tower; a new ride simulates a ski jump.

Calgary City Hall and Olympic Park

Bar U Ranch

Excursions

Bar U Ranch★★

[Kids] *92km/57mi south of Calgary via Rtes. 2 South (Macleod Trail), 22X West and 22 South. PO Box 168, Longview AB, T0L 1H0. ✕ ♿ ⏰ Open Jun–early-Oct daily 9am–5pm. ⊘ $7.15 adult. ☎ 403-395-2212 or toll-free 1-800-773-8888 (Canada/US). www.pc.gc.ca.*

This National Historic Site preserves early 20C ranch buildings. On Sundays, there are Cowboy Bruches and demonstrations of ranch activities. Highway 541, which intersects Route 22 north of the ranch, offers a spectacular 210km/130mi loop **drive**★ to the west to return to Calgary. Climbing into the Rockies, the road becomes Route 40 and traverses **Kananaskis Country,** an Alberta recreational reserve.

Rocky Mountain House National Historic Site★

225km/139mi northwest of Calgary via Rtes. 8 West and 22 North. From Rocky Mountain House take Rte. 11A West (7km/4mi). Site 127 Comp 6, RR4, Rocky Mountain House, AB T4T 2A4. ♿ ⏰ Open mid-May to Labour Day daily 10am–5pm. ⊘ $2.50 adult. ☎ 403-845-2412. www.pc.gc.ca.

On the banks of the North Saskatchewan River, this post, founded in 1799, was David Thompson's headquarters for exploring western Canada. **Highway 11** continues on into the Rockies, joining the Icefields Parkway 174km/108mi west of Rocky Mountain House and affording an alternate route to either Jasper or Banff.

CARDSTON
ALBERTA
POPULATION 3,452

This small town was founded in 1887 by **Charles Ora Card**, a son-in-law of Brigham Young, leader of the Church of Jesus Christ of the Latter-Day Saints, also known as Mormons, who established Salt Lake City in 1847.

🛈 **Information:** Tourist Information, 67 3rd Ave W. ☎ 403-653-3366. www.town.cardston.ab.ca

▶ **Orient Yourself:** Cardston lies in southwest Alberta, near Waterton Lakes National Park, 25km/16mi north of the Montana (US) border.

🅿 **Parking:** Parking lots provided.

- 🤍 **Don't Miss:** The Remington Carriage Museum is among the world's best.
- 🕐 **Organizing Your Time:** Take time to visit lovely Waterton Lakes.
- 🧒 **Especially for Kids:** Carriage rides at the Remington Museum.
- ⚲ **Also See:** WATERTON LAKES, FORT MACLEOD, LETHBRIDGE

Sights

Remington Carriage Museum★★

🧒 *623 Main St. Po Box 1649, Cardston AB, T0K 0K0.* ✕⚲🕐 *Open mid-May–mid Sept daily 9am–6pm. Rest of year daily 10am–5pm.* 👓 *$9 adult.* ☎ *403-653-5139. www.remingtoncarriagemuseum.com.* Carriage rides (👓*$4 adult*) seasonally. This museum houses one of the most comprehensive collections of horse-drawn vehicles in North America.

Cardston Alberta Temple

348 Third St. West. PO Box 700, Cardston AB, T0K 0K0. ⚲*Temple not open to the public. Visitor centre* ⚲🕐*Open mid-May–Labour Day daily 9am–9pm.* ☎*403-653-3552.*

This imposing white granite structure was completed in 1923 and is one of the few Mormon temples in Canada.

CHURCHILL★★

MANITOBA

POPULATION 923

Canada's most northerly deep-sea port, Churchill is bleak in winter, but during the summer months, a carpet of wildflowers covers the tundra. In autumn, polar bears wander near, and sometimes into, the townsite on their seasonal migration northward, and in early July **beluga whales** arrive to feed and calve in the river. The aurora borealis here is the most intense in the world, drawing researchers and thousands of tourists.

- 🛈 **Information:** Town of Churchill, ☎204-675-8871 or toll free 1-888-389-2327 (Canada/US). www.townofchurchill.com
- ▶ **Orient Yourself:** Churchill lies on Hudson Bay, on the east side of the Churchill River estuary, some 1000km/625mi north of Winnipeg.
- 🅿 **Parking:** You can't drive to Churchill, but you can rent a truck or van to park (see the Churchill website).
- 🤍 **Don't Miss:** From Prince of Wales Fort, you can view many types of wildlife.
- 🕐 **Organizing Your Time:** The Churchill website has a thorough list of tour companies, stores, transport, accomodation etc.
- 🧒 **Especially for Kids:** Polar bears and northern lights.
- ⚲ **Also See:** KIVALLIQ (KEEWATIN) REGION

A Bit of History

In 1717, after a false start, the Hudson's Bay Company (HBC) established a fur-trading post on the Churchill River, named for the governor of the company, **John Churchill**, the future Duke of Marlborough and ancestor of Winston Churchill. Prompted by demands for a Prairie port, the railway was built in 1929 and port facilities soon after.

The Hudson Bay and Strait are navigable only four months a year *(mid-Jul–mid-Nov)*, when trains arrive constantly and ships take on Prairie grain.

Access

Two airlines offer regularly scheduled flights from Winnipeg. Calm Air Inter-

Polar Bears Up Close

Abruptly, the large white bear sat down, completely upright in the snow, to nurse her cubs. Scanning the horizon, she stopped from time to time to poke her nose into the air and check for scents. Cameras whirred. "Ahhhh!" chorused the human observers who had come from far and wide to see these massive creatures (adult females weigh 300kg/660lbs on average, males 600kg/1,300lbs).

These observers were enclosed within heated, bathroom-equipped Tundra Buggies®—wide, rectangular "buses" equipped with 6ft-high all-terrain tires to keep windows (and passengers) out of reach of curious bears. From the vehicle's rear viewing platform, visitors can photograph polar bears as they chew on the tires, curl up behind a boulder or splay themselves on the snow.

In spring, these great sea bears float along the western coastline on huge ice floes blown by prevailing winds. The bears spend the summer on shore dozing and eating grass and seaweed. From mid-October to mid-November, the water normally freezes first on the points and capes near Churchill, where polar bears congregate, making this the perfect viewing point. One operator, Frontiers North Adventures, offers a tour that includes accommodations in the **Tundra Buggy Lodge**, a train-like series of sleeping, dining and utility cars, linked by viewing decks.

Travel Manitoba and the Churchill Chamber of Commerce maintain lists of tour operators. Tundra Buggy Lodge program: contact Frontiers North Adventures, PO Box 40063 RPO Nairn, Winnipeg, MB, R2L 2G2. ☎204-949-2050 or toll-free 1-800-663-9832. www.tundrabuggy.com).

Watching polar bears

national, 90 Thompson Dr., Thompson MB R8N 1Y8. ☎204-778-6471 or toll-free 1-888-225-6247 (Canada & US). www.calmair.com.
Kivalliq Air (a division of Keewatin Air), #15, Hangar Line Road, Winnipeg, MB, R3J 3Y8. 204-888-5619 or toll-free 1-877-855-1500. www.kivalliqair.com.
Also accessible from Winnipeg by VIA Rail (☾see Planning Your Trip).

Sights

The Town

Churchill consists of a dozen paved streets filled with houses, shops and hotels; the grain elevator towers over the town. Health and recreational facilities, a library, cafeteria, theatre, high school, and business offices are housed in the **Town Centre Complex** (1976), which offers good **views** of the bay. The Parks Canada **visitor centre** is located at the train station (*PO Box 107 Churchill MB, R0B*

0E0. &. ⓘHours seasonal. Call for information. ☎204-675-8863. www.pc.gc.ca). It offers information on area wildlife and history, including Prince of Wales Fort (👆 below) and **York Factory National Historic Site**, the remains of an earlier HBC trading post located 240km/149mi to the southeast, near the mouth of the Hayes River (accessible only by canoe or charter plane). Kelsey Boulevard runs through town to the **Arctic Trading Co.**, a charming store filled with northern crafts, clothing and souvenirs. The **Northern Study Centre**, located east of town (24km/15mi), the offers courses on Arctic ecology, ornithology and other subjects (☎204-675-2307. www.church illscience.ca).

Eskimo Museum★★

Beside Roman Catholic Church. ⓘOpen Jun–early-Nov Mon 1pm–5pm, Tue–Sat 9am–noon & 1pm–5pm. Rest of the year Mon–Sat 1pm–4:30pm. ⓘClosed Sun and major holidays. Contribution requested. ☎204-675-2030.

This museum houses a fine **collection** of Inuit carvings in stone, ivory and bone collected over 50 years by the Oblate fathers.

Prince of Wales Fort★

Across Churchill River estuary from town. Access by helicopter or by boat. 👆 Visit by guided tour (1hr) only, Jul–Aug daily. ⓘ$8. ☎204-675-8863. www.pc.gc.ca. This stone HBC fortress took 40 years (1731-71) to complete. In 1782 commander Samuel Hearne surrendered to a French fleet without firing a shot, but returned the next year.

The boat trip to the fort is an excellent way to see beluga whales in July and August.

Across from the fort, on the east shore of the Churchill River, the remnants of an 18C stone battery at **Cape Merry National Historic Site** provide a good vantage point for wildlife viewing (☎204-675-8863).

CYPRESS HILLS★★
ALBERTA-SASKATCHEWAN

These verdant hills, watered by lakes and streams, rise prominently in the midst of otherwise unbroken, sunbaked, short-grass prairie. On their heights grow the tall, straight lodgepole pines favored by Plains Indians for their teepees or lodges—thus the name. The trees were probably mistaken by early French voyageurs for the jack pines (cyprès) of eastern Canada. A bad translation further compounded the error, and the name Cypress Hills was born.

- **Information:** Parks Canada and Alberta-Saskatchewan operate visitor centres. 👆See below.
- **Orient Yourself:** Cypress Hills lies on the Alberta/Saskatchewan border, 70km/43mi north of the state of Montana.
- **Don't Miss:** The highest point in Saskatchewan, 1468m/4,816 ft.
- **Organizing Your Time:** The park is a detour off the TransCanada Highway.
- **Especially for Kids:** Farwell's Trading Post at Fort Walsh re-creates frontier life.
- **Also See:** LETHBRIDGE, CARDSTON, FORT MACLEOD, MOOSE JAW, REGINA

Geographical Notes

Oasis in the Desert – In 1859 John Palliser, touring the western domains for the British government, described this area as "A perfect oasis in the desert we have travelled." Later, settlers found the hills ideally suited for **ranching**, a vocation the area maintains today.

The hills present unique geographical features. The highest elevations in Canada between Labrador and the Rockies,

Sitting Bull in Canada

In 1876 a force of Sioux warriors under their great chief, Sitting Bull, exterminated an American army detachment under Gen. **George Custer** on the Little Big Horn River in southern Montana. Fearing reprisals from the enraged Americans, Sitting Bull crossed into Canada with nearly 5,000 men. Inspector **James Walsh** of the North West Mounted Police was given the difficult task of trying to persuade the Sioux to return, in order to avoid war between the Sioux and their traditional enemies, the Cree and the Blackfoot, who inhabited the region. Riding into the sizable Sioux encampment near Wood Mountain *(350km/217mi east of Fort Walsh)* with only four constables and two scouts, he informed Sitting Bull that he must obey Canadian law. Although this act of bravery won the respect of the chief, it was four years before Sitting Bull consented to return to the US to live on a reservation.

they rise to nearly 1,500m/5,000ft. A 200sq km/80sq mi area was untouched by the last Ice Age, which covered the rest of this vast area with ice more than 1km/.6mi deep. The hills form a divide between two great watersheds: Hudson Bay and the Gulf of Mexico. Streams flow south to the Missouri-Mississippi system and north to the South Saskatchewan River, Lake Winnipeg and Hudson Bay. The flora and fauna of the hills offer remarkable diversity.

A Bit of History

Cypress Hills Massacre – In the early 1870s several trading posts were established in the Cypress Hills by Americans from Montana. In exchange for furs, they illegally traded "firewater," an extremely potent brew. During the winter of 1872-73, Assiniboine Indians camped near two of these posts were joined by a party of Canadian and American wolf-hunters, whose horses had been stolen by Cree raiders. Thinking the Assiniboines were the thieves, the drunken "wolfers" attacked the Indian camp, killing 36 people.

When news of this massacre reached Ottawa, Prime Minister Sir John A. Macdonald acted quickly. He created the **North West Mounted Police** (renamed the **Royal Canadian Mounted Police** in 1920) and dispatched them to the Northwest to stop such border incursions and end the illegal whisky trade. The perpetrators of the massacre were arrested but later acquitted for lack of evidence. However, the fact that white

men had been arrested impressed the Indians and helped establish the force's reputation.

Sights

Cypress Hills Interprovincial Park★★

In Alberta, 65km/40mi southeast of Medicine Hat by Trans-Can Hwy. and Hwy. 41 South. Park office at Elkwater Lake. For road conditions check at park office ☎ *403-893-3777(Alberta) or 306-662-5411 (Saskatchewan).* Park ◷ *Open year-round. Visitor centre* ♿✕◷*Open mid-May–Labour Day daily 9am–5pm.* ☎*403-893-3833. www.cypresshills.com.*

This park encompasses the highest part of the Cypress Hills. From Elkwater Lake an interesting drive *(40km/25mi)* leads past **Horseshoe Canyon** to **Head of the Mountain,** which affords pleasant views of coulees and hills as far as the Sweet Grass Hills and Bear Paw Mountains of Montana. The drive proceeds to Reesor Lake and the park boundary. This road continues to Fort Walsh, approximately 18km/11mi south.

Fort Walsh National Historic Site★

In Saskatchewan, 52km/32mi southwest of Maple Creek by Hwy. 271. PO Box 278, Maple Creek, SK, S0N 1N0. ✕♿◷*Open mid-May–Labour Day daily 9:30am–5:30pm (in Sept, call post for hours).* ◷*Closed Oct–mid-May.* ☞*$9.15 adult.* ☎*306-662-3590. www.pc.gc.ca.*

Reached from Cypress Hills Provincial Park or from Maple Creek, this North

Hiking in Horseshoe Canyon

West Mounted Police post, named for its builder, James Walsh, lies near the site of the Cypress Hills Massacre. From 1878 to 1882 it was the force's headquarters. At the **visitor centre** displays and films provide a good introduction. The fort can be reached by foot or by park bus service. The whitewashed log buildings include barracks, stables, a workshop and the commissioner's residence. At Farwell's Trading **Post**★ Kids *(2.5km/1.5mi south of the fort, access by park bus. Visit by 45min guided tour only)*, visitors are shown around by costumed guides who depict historical figures of the trading post's past.

EDMONTON★★
ALBERTA
POPULATION 730,372

The capital of Alberta, long associated with the energy and agricultural industries, today enjoys a more diversified economy, marked by manufacturing and advanced technologies. Edmonton prides itself on its lively cultural scene, with museums, theatres and festivals as well as the dazzling attractions of the Edmonton Mall.

- **Information:** Visitor Centre, 9990 Jasper Ave. (World Trade Centre). ☎780-496-8400 or toll-free 1-800-463-4667. www.edmonton.com
- **Orient Yourself:** Edmonton spans the valley of the North Saskatchewan River in the centre of Alberta; downtown lies on the steep northern bluffs.
- **Parking:** City parking meters charge from $2/hr to $1/hr depending on the area and day of the week. Sundays, parking is free.
- **Don't Miss:** Fort Edmonton is a lively introduction to Western history.
- **Organizing Your Time:** Plan a visit during one of Edmonton's many festivals.
- **Especially for Kids:** The West Edmonton Mall has attractions galore.
- **Also See:** ROCKY MOUNTAIN PARKS, ALBERTA BADLANDS

A Bit of History

From Post to Provincial Capital – By the end of the 18C, posts near present-day Edmonton were trading blankets, guns and other goods to Cree and Blackfoot Indians in exchange for animal pelts. In 1821, **Edmonton House** emerged as the Hudson Bay Company's most important post in the West.

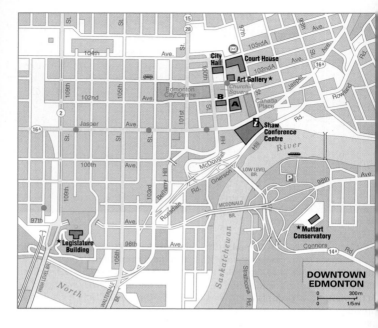

DOWNTOWN
EDMONTON

0   300 m
0   1/5 mi

The settlement grew as goods arrived by York boat from York Factory or overland from Winnipeg by Red River cart. The decision of the Canadian Pacific Railway Co. to route its line through Calgary was a blow, but other rail lines were built at the end of the century. During the Klondike Stampede of 1896-99, Edmonton became a "gateway to the North." Due to its strategic location between central farmland and northern energy resources, the city became Alberta's capital in 1905.

Petroleum Centre – Edmonton might have remained a quiet administrative centre had oil not been discovered in 1947 in **Leduc**, a small community to the south, followed by other discoveries. The city is the major service and distribution centre for the vast Athabasca oil sands to the north. The largest percentage of the province's producing oil wells are concentrated in the Edmonton area.

Downtown

Edmonton's downtown centres on Sir Winston Churchill Square and Jasper Avenue. The square is surrounded by modern buildings including **City Hall**,

Klondike Days

Every year in July Edmonton stages a frenzied, citywide celebration of the great **Klondike Stampede**, when gold prospectors came through Edmonton to begin their trek north to Dawson City, Yukon. Formally called the Capital City Exhibition, or Capital EX, the celebration attracts entertainment from far and wide, such as acrobats from China, as well as home-grown glitter. Bedecked in costumes of the 1890s, residents and visitors alike strut in the kick-off parade and Sunday Promenade and in general whoop it up for 10 days. Chuckwagon races, a big midway, a food fair, a craft show, and nightly vaudeville shows and fireworks are traditions. Many activities, such as Fun Town Farm, are aimed at families and children. *Capital EX, c/o Northlands, PO Box 1480, Edmonton AB, T5J 2N5. ☎780-471-7210, toll-free 1-888-800-7275. www.capitalex.ca*

the **Court House**, the Art Gallery *(below)*, the elegant glass and brick **Citadel Theatre (A)**, the attractive **Stanley A. Milner Library (B)**, and Edmonton Centre with its shops, restaurants and offices. Two blocks south, the steel and glass structure of Edmonton's **Shaw Conference Centre** rises opposite Canada Place, which houses offices of the federal government.

Art Gallery of Alberta★

Interim location: Enterprise Square, 100-10230 Jasper Ave, Edmonton AB, T5J 4P6. 🕐*Open year-round Mon–Fri 10:30am–5pm (Thu 8pm), weekends 11am–5pm.* 🕐*Closed major holidays.* 💰*$10 adult (no charge Thu evening).* ☎*780-422-6223. www.artgalleryofalberta.com.*
The gallery is undergoing a renovation that will double its exhibition space.

Address Book

🌟*For dollar sign categories, see the Legend on the cover flap.*

WHERE TO EAT

$$$ Hardware Grill, *9698 Jasper Ave. Edmonton AB, T5H 3V5.* ☎*780-423-0969. www.hardwaregrill.com. Dinner only. Closed Sun, holidays, 1st 10 days Jul.* Located downtown in Edmonton's historic Goodridge Block, the 5,000sq ft space was transformed from a hardware store into an award-winning restaurant known for its regional and staunchly seasonal Canadian cuisine. Bison carpaccio (with wild rice and oyster-mushroom salad) is a popular choice. Or, you may want to try the cedar-plank salmon with chanterelles.
$$$ Jack's Grill, *5842-111th St., Edmonton AB, T6H 3G1.* ☎*780-434-1113. www.jacksgrill.ca.* Despite its unlikely strip-mall setting in Edmonton's southern Lendrum neighborhood, this restaurant offers relaxed chic with oak floors, sand-colored walls and well-spaced tables. The modern bistro fare includes grilled duck breast in black currant sauce, or rack of lamb with vegetable lasagne. The menu changes often.Save room for Jack's famous bread pudding with raisins and caramelized rum sauce.

OLD STRATHCONA

Just across the river from downtown, beautifully restored buildings line Whyte (82nd) Avenue in Edmonton's historic Old Strathcona, a vibrant 10-block hub packed with coffeehouses, restaurants, pubs and some 300 shops (☎*780-437-4182. www.oldstrathcona.com).* Look for Canadian and native art at **Fort Door** *(10308-81st Ave. T6E 1X2.*☎*780-432-7535)* or fair-trade handicrafts at **The Ten Thousand Villages** *(10432-82nd St. T6E 2A2.* ☎*780-439-8349).* For a break, sip a latté one of the dozen coffee or tea shops, or enjoy an Italian lunch at **Chianti's** *(10501-82nd Ave. T6E 2A3.* ☎*780-439-9829)* in the Old Post Office. **O'Byrnes Irish Pub** *(10616-82nd Ave. T6E 2A7.* ☎*780-414-6766)* is a fine place to sample Irish beers and whiskies. **The King & I** *(8208 107th St. T6E 6P4.* ☎*780-433-2222)* serves excellent Thai cuisine – the Rolling Stones have stopped in; and **Blues on Whyte** *(10329-82nd Ave. T6E 1Z9.* ☎*780-439-3981)* features live blues from bands performing nightly. Every August the district hums when Canada's largest fringe theatre festival *(10330-82nd Ave. T6E 2G9.* ☎*780-448-9000. www.fringetheatreadventures.ca)* draws crowds to venues such as the Fringe Theatre and Walterdale Playhouse. Every Saturday year-round, the Old Strathcona **farmers' market** displays local produce and crafts *(🅿10310-83rd Ave. T6E 5C3. Sat 8am–3pm.* ☎*780-439-1844.www.osfm.ca).*

WELLNESS

🅂🄿🄰**EvelineCharles Salon and Spa,** *Second level, near the ice palace in West Edmonton Mall. #2151 8882-170 St. T5T 2J2.* ☎*780-424-5666. www.evelinecharles.com. Mon–Sat 9am–9pm, Sun 10am–5pm.* Within the huge mall, the attraction for tired shoppers may well be this spacious spa, offering a full slate of aesthetic services. Stop in for a 45min neck and back massage or a pedicure. More time? Take the hydrotherapy or try the Hydro Tub with its 144-jet massage. Packages of treatments available. *Reservations suggested (required for packages).*

Travel Alberta

Fort Edmonton Park

Until late 2009, when it will move back to Sir Winston Churchill Square, it is housed in the former Hudson Bay Building, but with a full program of temporary exhibitions and displays from its 7,000-item permanent collection.

Muttart Conservatory★

9626-96A St, Edmonton AB, T6C 4L8.
✕ ♿ P ⊙ *Open year-round Mon–Fri 9am–5:30pm, weekends and holidays 11am–5:30pm.* ⊙ *Closed Dec 25.* ⊙ *$8.75 adult.* ☎*780-496-8755. www.edmonton. ca/muttart.*

The four glass pyramids of this striking architectural ensemble shelter some 700 plant species. Behind the conservatory is the landing for the paddlewheeler Edmonton Queen, which offers a **cruise** on the North Saskatchewan River *(*✕ P ⊙*Departs May–mid-Sept Thu–Sat noon & 3pm, dinner cruise 7.30pm. Sun brunch 1pm, family cruise 3.30pm, dinner cruise 7.30pm. Round-trip 1hr. Reservations required.* ⊙ *$18 adult.* ☎*780-424- 2628. www.edmontonqueen.com).*

Legislature Building★

Visitor centre, 10800-97th Ave., Edmonton AB, T5K 2B6. ✕ ♿ P ☜ *Visit by guided tour (45min) only, May–mid-Oct daily hourly 9am–noon, every 30min 12:30pm– 4pm, weekends hourly 9am–5pm. Rest of the year Mon–Fri tours hourly 9am–3pm, weekends hourly noon–4pm.* ⊙*Closed*

Jan 1, Good Friday & Dec 25. ☎*780-427- 7362. www.assembly.ab.ca.*

Set in pleasant gardens overlooking the North Saskatchewan River, the yellow sandstone Alberta Legislature building (1912) occupies the original site of Fort Edmonton.

Additional Sights

Fort Edmonton Park★★

Kids *Fox Dr. at Whitemud Dr., 7000 143 St, Edmonton AB.* ✕ ♿ P ⊙*Open mid- May–Jun Mon–Fri 10am–4pm, weekends & holidays 10am–6pm. July–Labour Day daily 10am–6pm. Sept* ☜ *Mon–Sat guided wagon tours, Sun 10am–6pm, Nov–Dec weekends 11am–4pm.* ⊙ *$13 adult.* ☎*780-496-8787. www.ftedmonton park.com.*

This park re-creates the history of settlement in Edmonton. Board the vintage train *(free; continuous service)* to reach **Fort Edmonton**, the 1846 fur-trading post. Among other reconstructed buildings is the chapel built for Rev. **Robert Rundle**, the first missionary in Alberta, who spent the years 1840 to 1848 at Fort Edmonton. Wagon tours available on the hour *(⊙Mon–Sat 11am–3pm).*

The **prerailway village** contains a reconstruction of Jasper Avenue in 1885. The McDougall Church, built in 1873 by Rev. **George McDougall,** was the first Protestant church in Alberta. The village gradually becomes **1905** Street, which shows Edmonton at a time of great growth. A street car *(free, continuous service)* runs down the middle of the road, which is lined with a penny arcade, Eventually 1905 Street becomes **1920 Street**.

West Edmonton Mall

170th to 178th Sts., 87th to 90th Aves., Offices #2472, 8882-170 St, Edmonton AB, T5T 4M2. Kids ✕ ♿ P ⊙*Shopping hours Mon–Sat 10am–9pm, holidays 10am– 6pm, Sun 11am–5pm. Hours and fees vary for waterpark and rides.* ☎*780-444-5200. www.westedmontonmall.com.*

Covering over 483,000sq m/5.3 million sq ft, this leviathan shopping/entertainment complex is the largest in the world, enclosing an amusement park, full-size skating rink, waterpark, movie theatres, a casino, two hotels and more than 800 stores and 100 restaurants.

Royal Alberta Museum★★

Kids *12845-102nd Ave, Edmonton AB, T5T 4M2.* ✗♿🅿️⏰*Open year-round daily 9am–5pm.* ⏰*Closed Dec 24–25.* ☞ *$10.* ☎ *780-453-9100. www.royal albertamuseum.ca.*

On the main floor is the **Habitat Gallery**, which features **dioramas** of the wildlife of the province.

On the second floor, the **Gallery of Aboriginal Culture** details the life of the Plains Indians in western Canada. The **Natural History Gallery** encloses the popular Bug Room, filled with live creatures; the Bird Gallery, featuring the largest collection of mounted birds in the country; Reading the Rocks, which explains geological forces; and Treasures of the Earth, a display of colorful gems and minerals.

Telus World of Science Edmonton★

Kids *11211-142nd St., Edmonton AB T5M 4A1.* ✗♿🅿️⏰*Open late Jun–Labour Day daily 10am–9pm. Rest of the year Sun–Thur and holidays 10am–5pm, Fri–Sat 10am–9pm).* ⏰*Closed Dec 25.* ☞ *$13.* ☎*780-452-9100. www.telusworldof scienceedmonton.com.*

Resembling a large spaceship, the centre houses an IMAX theatre and a planetarium, in addition to exhibit areas on the environment, the body, space, and forensics. Exhibits are designed particularly for young people.

Housed separately, an **observatory** offers a close-up view of the stars and planets *(weather permitting, call for hours).*

Excursions

St. Albert

19km/12mi north by Rte. 2.

In 1861 a Roman Catholic mission was founded here on the banks of the Sturgeon River by Father **Albert Lacombe**

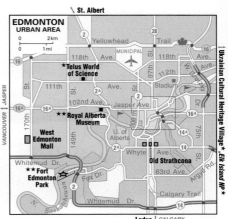

(1827-1916). The simple log chapel is the oldest building in Alberta (*St. Vital Ave. St Albert MB. Contact Father Lacombe Chapel Provincial Historical Site, c/o 8820-112 St, Edmonton AB T6G 2P8.* ♿🅿️⏰*Open mid-May–Labour Day daily 10am–6pm.* ☞*$2.* ☎*780-459-7663. www.tprc.alberta.ca).*

The crypt of the modern-day church contains the tombs of Father Lacombe and Bishop **Vital Grandin** (1829-1902), whose adjoining residence can also be visited.

Elk Island National Park★

On Hwy. 16, about 35km/22mi east. Site 4, RR#1, Fort Saskatchewan T8L 2L7. ♿⏰*Open daily year-round. Hiking, camping, canoeing, cross-country skiing, golfing.* ☞*$7.* ☎*780-992-5790. www.pc.gc.ca. Visitor centre* ⏰*Open May–Jun weekends only, Jul–Aug daily.* One of the smallest of Canada's national parks, the 194sq km/75sq mi Elk Island nevertheless abounds with wildlife. Herds of Plains bison stand or sit in the road in the early hours of the day; elk, moose, beaver and coyote are routinely sighted. At Tawayik Lake myriad waterfowl crowd the skies, and the rare trumpeter swan has been seen at Astotin Lake. Some 100km/60mi of nature trails punctuate the park's wetlands, aspen forests and meadows.

Ukrainian Cultural Heritage Village★

On Hwy. 16, about 50km/30mi east. Contact 8820-112 St NX, Edmonton AB T6G

Elk Island National Park

2P8. ✕ ℗ ⏰ *Open mid-May–Labour Day daily 10am–6pm. Rest of Sept–early Oct weekends only 10am–6pm.* ☞ *$8.* ☎ *780-662-3640. www. tprc.alberta.ca.*
Some 30 historic buildings have been moved to this site, which is staffed by costumed interpretors who explain the mass migration of Ukrainian people to the Canadian Prairies starting in the 1890s, and their lives before 1930. Special events are held throughout the year.

FORT MACLEOD ★
ALBERTA
POPULATION 3,072

This small town was the site of the first North West Mounted Police post in the West. In 1874 Col. James Macleod and his men were dispatched to stop the illegal whisky trade and border incursions, such as the one leading to the Cypress Hills Massacre. Today Fort Macleod is an agricultural community. Grain is grown and cattle are raised on the ranch land of nearby Porcupine Hills.

🛈 **Information:** ☎403-553-4425. www.fortmacleod.com
▶ **Orient Yourself:** Fort MacLeod lies on the Oldman River, 165km/102mi south of Calgary.
℗ **Parking:** Both sights have designated parking.
Especially for Kids: The Musical Ride at the Fort should thrill kids.
⏱ **Also See:** LETHBRIDGE, CARDSTON, WATERTON LAKES, CALGARY

Sights

Fort Museum ★
On Hwy. 3, one block from centre of town. PO Box 776, Fort MacLeod AB T0L 0Z0. ♿ ⏰ *Open Jul–Labour Day daily 9am–6pm. Mid-May–Jun & Labour Day–Oct Wed–Sun 10am–4pm.* ☞ *$7.50.* ☎403-553-4703, toll-free 1-866-273-6841. www.nwmpmuseum.com.
The **Kanouse House** with its sod roof is devoted to the early settlers of the region. **The Mounted Police Building** houses a model of the original fort

Teepee Camping

If you've always wondered what it would be like to sleep in a teepee (or tipi), here's your opportunity to find out. Overnight and two-night teepee camping is available April through October at Head-Smashed-In Buffalo Jump. The site is remote enough to assure a starry night, if the weather is clear. Bring your own sleeping bag or rent one there ($15/night). Canvas teepees, air mattresses, camping stoves and flashlights are supplied, and showers are available at the interpretive centre. You'll help set up a teepee, dine on buffalo burgers and buffalo stew with bannock, listen to Blackfoot legends around the campfire, and take a guided walk before a breakfast of fry bread and Saskatoon jam. Lunch and a guided hike to a nearby archaeological dig site revealing aboriginal petroglyphs are included in the two-night package *(90-day advance reservations requested; for information ☎ 403-553-2731 or www.head-smashed-in.com).*

and exhibits on the police. **The Indian Artifacts Building** contains a sizable collection of native arts and crafts.

In summer students dressed in the police uniforms of 1878 (red jackets, black breeches, white pith helmets) perform a musical ride *(Jul–Labour Day daily except Tue, 10am, 11:30am, 2pm, 3:30pm, weather permitting).*

Head-Smashed-In Buffalo Jump★★

18km/11mi northwest by Hwy. 785 (Spring Point Rd.) PO Box 1977, Fort Macleod AB, T0L 0Z0. ✕ ♿ ◷ *Open mid-May–mid-Sept daily 9am–6pm. Rest of the year daily 10am–5pm.* ◷ *Closed Jan 1, Easter Sunday, Dec 24–25.* ☜ *$9.* ☎ *403-553-2731. www.tprc.alberta.ca.*

This buffalo jump, a UNESCO World Heritage Site, has the most extensive deposits of bones (9m/30ft deep) of any jump in North America.

For over 5,000 years, buffalo were driven to their deaths over this cliff. Built into the cliff, a dramatic **visitor centre** contains excellent displays on five floors as well as films. Outside, paths lead to the top of the cliff, where visitors are afforded a spectacular **view**★★ of the largely treeless surroundings.

Head-Smashed-in Buffalo Jump

Alberta Economic Development and Tourism

LETHBRIDGE★
ALBERTA
POPULATION 81,692

Lethbridge was founded in 1870, after coal deposits were discovered in the valley. Today widespread irrigation and the relatively mild winters moderated by the warm chinook winds have made the cultivation of grain and vegetables, especially canola and sugar beet, very profitable. Livestock are also raised here. Constructed into the side of Oldman riverbed are the striking buildings of the University of Lethbridge, and crossing it is the High Level Railway Bridge (about 1.5km/1mi long and 96m/314ft high).

- **Information:** City offices, 910-4th Ave S. ☎403-329-7355. www.lethbridge.ca
- **Orient Yourself:** Lethbridge is in southern Alberta, 216km/134mi southeast of Calgary, overlooking the wide riverbed of the Oldman River.
- **Parking:** Permitted parking times vary in the downtown area; check signage.
- **Don't Miss:** Lethbridge has lovely parks, trails and walking paths.
- **Organizing Your Time:** Lethbridge is a pleasant place to stop for a night.
- **Especially for Kids:** Fort Whoop-up, proudly "Founded by Scoundrels."
- **Also See:** FORT MACLEOD, CARDSTON, WATERTON LAKES, CYPRESS HILLS

Sights

Nikka Yuko Japanese Garden★
In Henderson Lake Park on Mayor Magrath Dr., PO Box 751, Lethbridge AB, T1J 3Z6. ⚅🕐Open Jul–Labour Day daily 9am–8pm. Mid-May–Jun & Sept daily 9am–5pm. ⌨$7. ☎403-328-3511. www. nikkayuko.com.

The city built this lovely garden in 1967 as a symbol of Japanese-Canadian amity *(Nikka Yuko* means "Japan-Canada friendship"). When Canada declared war on Japan in 1941, about 22,000 Japanese-Canadians living on the West Coast were placed in internment camps in central British Columbia and Alberta. About 6,000 of these were resettled in Lethbridge, where they chose to stay after the war.

Fort Whoop-up★
In Indian Battle Park by river, access from Hwy. 3.PO Box 1074, Lethbridge AB, T1J 4A2. ⚅🕐Open Jul-Aug Tue–Sun 10am–5pm. Rest of year hours vary. 🕐Closed holidays. ⌨$7. ☎ 403-329-0444. www. fortwhoopup.com.

In the deep valley of the Oldman River stands a replica of this once-notorious whisky trading post. Founded by Americans from Fort Benton, Montana, the post attracted Indians from far and wide to trade buffalo skins, furs and indeed almost anything for a particularly lethal brew.

Such illegal liquor forts sprang up all over Southern Alberta and Saskatchewan in the early 1870s. The creation of the North West Mounted Police and the founding of Fort Macleod, and later Fort Calgary ended the illegal trade and brought law and order to the West.

MOOSE JAW ★
SASKATCHEWAN
POPULATION 32,132

The city is reputedly named for a sharp turn in the river that resembles a protruding moose jaw, but the Cree word *Moosegaw*—meaning "warm breezes"—is a more credible source for the appellation. Moosejaw is an important railway junction, industrial centre and proud home of the Snowbirds, the precision flying team of the Canadian Air Force; 30 giant murals recall its colourful past.

Information: Tourism Moose Jaw,450 Diefenbaker Drive, Moose Jaw SK, S6J 1N2. ☎306-693-8097, toll-free 1-866-693-8097. www.moosejaw.ca.

Orient Yourself: Located in southern Saskatchewan, Moose jaw is 71km/44mi due west of Regina via the TransCanada Highway

Parking: Parking meters cost only $0.50- $1/hr.

Don't Miss: The Kinsmen International Band and Choral Festival, held every May.

Organizing Your Time: You will need a full day to enjoy the city.

Especially for Kids: Burrowing Owls Interpretive Centre; the Main St. tunnels.

Also See: REGINA, SASKATOON, CYPRESS HILLS

Sights

Board a replica of a 1911 streetcar for a guided tour of the city (Moose Jaw Trolley Co. Box 81, Moose Jaw SK S6H 4N7. May–Oct daily. $12 adult . ☎306-693-8537).

Tunnels

Tours year-round. 18 Main St. N. ☎306-693-5261. www.tunnelsofmoose jaw.com.

During Prohibition, Moose Jaw became the rum-running capital of the Prairies: its tunnels, carved beneath Main Street to stoke the furnaces of town businesses, were used, among other purposes, for bootlegging.

Western Development Museum ★

50 Diefenbaker Dr., Moose Jaw SK, S6J 1L9. Open Apr–Dec daily 9am–5pm. Rest of the year Tue–Sun 9am–5pm. Closed Jan 1, Dec 25-26. $7.25. ☎ 306-693-5989. www.wdm.ca. One of four provincial museums on Western development (North Battleford, Saskatoon, Yorkton), this one is devoted to transportation. Displays include a Canadian Pacific locomotive, a reconstructed train station and a 1934 Buick converted to run on rails and used as an inspection vehicle for 20 years; several Canadian

planes, including a 1927 Red Pheasant; and the Snowbird gallery, highlighting the history of this renowned aerobatics team. *Railway rides mid-May–Labour Day $2.*

Burrowing Owl Interpretive Centre

In Exhibition Grounds, 250 Thatcher Dr. East, Moose Jaw SK, S6J 1L7. Open mid- May–Labour Day Tue–Sun 10am–

WHERE TO SHOP AND RELAX

Yvette Moore's Gallery–*76 Fairford St. West, Moose Jaw SK, S6H 1V1. Mon–Sat 10am–5pm, Sun noon–5pm (mid-May–Dec). ☎306-693-7600. www.yvettemoore.com.* Housed in a heritage building, this gallery sells Ms. Moore's paintings of Prairie life and landscapes, as well as crafts from the region. The tiny Copper Cafe serves lunches and Saskatoon berry pie.

Temple Gardens Resort Hotel *– 24 Fairford St. East, Moose Jaw SK S6H 0C7. ☎306-694-5055, toll-free 1-800-718-7727. www.templegardens. sk.ca.* Soak in a mineral pool, filled with hot water drawn from ancient seabeds 1,350m/4,500ft below the earth. A variety of spa treatments are also available to the public.

6pm. ⊙Closed Mon. Rest of the year by appointment only. ⊛Donation requested. ☎306-692-8710. www.sboic.ca.

Visitors can walk through a giant reconstructed burrow and an open field to see this endangered species in captivity as well as in the wild.

Sukanen Ship Pioneer Village and Museum

13km/8mi south on Hwy. 2, PO Box 2071, Moose Jaw SK, S6H 7T2. ⊙Open mid-May–mid-Sept Mon–Sat 9am–5pm, Sun noon–6pm. ⊛$6. ☎306-693-7315. www.sukanenmuseum.ca.

Vintage cars and some 30 original and re-created buildings comprise a village of the early 1900s. The highlight is the restored ship built by Finnish settler Tom Sukanen, in which he planned to return to his homeland by way of the Saskatchewan River and the Hudson Bay.

A replica of the **Diefenbaker Homestead**, a three-room pioneer dwelling, home to John George Diefenbaker, prime minister of Canada from 1957 to 1963, has been moved here from Regina.

PRINCE ALBERT NATIONAL PARK★
SASKATCHEWAN

This large park is a fine example of Canada's southern boreal plains, an area where the aspen forest of the south mixes with the true boreal wilderness. Bison roam in isolated pockets of grassland near the southern boundary that also support prairie animals—coyotes, badgers and ground squirrels. The northern forests are home to wolves, moose, elk, black bears, beavers, red foxes and a small herd of woodland caribou. In the extreme north, white pelicans nest on Lavallée Lake, the second-largest white pelican colony in North America.

- **Information:** Northern Prairies Field Unit, Waskesiu Lake. ☎306-663-4522. www.pc.gc.ca.
- ▶ **Orient Yourself:** The park sits in central Saskatchewan, 80km/50mi north of Prince Albert by Hwys 2 and 264.
- **Parking:** On-site parking available.
- **Don't Miss:** Either a hike in the park or one of the interpretive boat tours.
- ⊙ **Organizing Your Time:** You will surely need to spend the night in the park, where there is a range of accommodation, from resorts to campgrounds.
- **Kids Especially for Kids:** Older children will enjoy a hike to Grey Owl's hideaway.
- ⊙ **Also See:** THE BATTLEFORDS, SASKATOON

Visit

⊙*Open year-round. Hiking, camping, canoeing, swimming, cycling, golf, tennis, winter sports. ⊛ $7/day. Map available at visitor centre (♿⊙Open late May–Labour Day daily 8am–8pm. Rest of the year hours vary. ☎306-663-4522. www.parkscanada.gc.ca.) Accommodations and services available in the town of Waskesiu Lake (Chamber of Commerce, PO Box 216, Waskesiu Lake, SK. ☎306-663-5410. www.waskesiulake.ca).*

The Parks Canada Nature Centre in Waskesiu Lake provides an introduction to the park, as well as information about day hikes and paddle trips in the area (*Lakeview Dr. ⊙Open mid-May–Sept daily 10am–5pm*). The roads follow both shores of Waskesiu Lake. The Waskesiu Marina Adventure Centre, with sites at 3 locations, offers watercraft rentals and interpretive tours on pontoon boats and canoes (*☎306-663-1999 in summer or 306-763-1278 in winter. www.waskesiu-marina.com*).

Grey Owl

"Grey Owl," who posed as an Indian, dressing in buckskins and wearing his long hair in braids, travelled throughout North America and Europe with a conservation message, even lecturing to the British monarch George VI in 1937. Trying to reestablish beaver colonies, he worked for Canada's national park service, living first in Riding Mountain National Park with his pet beavers Rawhide and Jelly Roll, and then in Prince Albert. At his death in 1938, he was exposed as an Englishman, **Archie Belaney**, who had taken the Indian name Wa-sha-Quon-Asin ("the Grey Owl") about 1920. Though an impostor, Grey Owl remains one of Canada's finest nature writers and among the first to promote preservation of the wilderness. His most famous books are *Tales of an Empty Cabin*, *Pilgrims of the Wild* and *Sajo and Her Beaver People*. A 1999 film, *Grey Owl*, directed by Richard Attenborough and starring Pierce Brosnan, is a respectful tribute to his accomplishments.

Hiking trails and canoe routes crisscross the park. One interesting hike takes the visitor to the cabin and grave of Grey Owl on the shores of Ajawaan Lake (19km/12mi).

REGINA★★
SASKATCHEWAN
POPULATION 194,971

Set in an extensive, fertile wheat-growing plain and located on the main line of the Canadian Pacific Railway and the Trans-Canada Highway, this provincial capital has long been an important agricultural centre. Regina is the headquarters for the Saskatchewan Wheat Pool, one of the largest grain cooperatives in the world.

- **Information:** ☎306-789-5099, or toll-free 1-800-661-5099. www.tourismregina.com
- ▶ **Orient Yourself:** Regina lies on the TransCanada Highway, in south central Saskatchewan.
- **Parking:** Meters operate Mon-Fri until 6pm, and cost $1.50 for 2hrs. On Sat, 2hrs are free, and on Sun parking is free. Meters are strictly patrolled.
- **Don't Miss:** Wascana Centre is a vast and varied parkland.
- ○ **Organizing Your Time:** Take time to see Moose Jaw, only 1hr away.
- **Kids Especially for Kids:** Candy Cane Park at the Wascona Centre offers lots of playground space and climbing opportunities.
- **Also See:** MOOSE JAW, YORKTON

A Bit of History

Pile O' Bones –In the early 1880s, the Canadian Pacific Railway Co. decided to build its line across the southern plains. The Dominion government, in collaboration with the CPR, chose to locate the new territorial capital at a place where the rail line would cross a creek long favored by Indians and Métis for running buffalo into pounds to slaughter them, hence the Cree name Oskana, translated as "pile o' bones." In August 1882 when the first train arrived, Princess Louise, wife of Canada's governor general, rechristened it Regina ("Queen" in Latin) after her mother, Queen Victoria.

Queen City of the Plains – When Saskatchewan became a province in 1905, Regina became the capital. As immigrants poured in, the city burgeoned. To solve the water problems, Wascana Creek was dammed, creating an artificial lake. Trees were planted and carefully

Royal Saskatchewan Museum exhibit

Tourism Saskatchewan

nourished, defying the notion of a tree-less wilderness.

Though the city's development in the 20C has been precarious, Regina has experienced steady growth since World War II. The downtown core has been revitalized, and imposing buildings constructed. Today, Regina rises above the flat, treeless prairie like a mirage, the "Queen City of the Plains."

Downtown

Royal Saskatchewan Museum★★

2445 Albert St., Regina SK, S4P 4W7. ♿🅿🕐 Open May–Labour Day daily 9am–5:30pm. Rest of the year daily 9am–4:30pm. 🕐 Closed Dec 25. ⬤$2. ☎306-787-2815. www.royalsaskmuseum.ca.

This long, low building of Tyndall stone houses one of the finest museums of natural history in Canada. On the upper level, the **Life Sciences Gallery** features remarkable dioramas that depict the wildlife and habitats of Saskatchewan. Exhibits in the **Earth Sciences Gallery** showcase dinosaurs and woolly mammoths, volcanoes and glaciers. The **First Nations Gallery** displays art and artifacts of the native cultures of the region.

Legislative Building★

2405 Legislative Dr., Regina SK, S4S 0B3. ✕♿🅿☎Visit by guided tour (30min) only, late May–Labour Day daily 8am–9pm. Rest of the year daily 8am–5pm. 🕐Closed Jan 1, Good Friday, Dec 25. ☎306-787-5358. www.legassembly.sk.ca.

Completed in 1912, this graceful building of Tyndall stone occupies a fine **site** overlooking gardens and Wascana Lake.

Wascana Centre★

2900 Wascona Dr., PO Box 7111, Regina SK, S4S 3S7. Kids 🅿🕐Open daily year-round. Picnicking, swimming, boating. ☎306-522-3661. www.wascana.sk.ca.

Park information centre at Wascana Place (off Broad St.) within the park. This 930ha/2,300 acre park, Regina's pride and joy, is reputedly the largest urban park in North America. Formal gardens of beautiful flowers and trees surround the western part of the artificial Wascana Lake. **Willow Island** is a picnic site accessible by ferry *(Victoria Day–Labour Day Mon–Fri noon–4pm. ⬤$4. Reservations required for evenings and weekends ☎306-522-3661).*

MacKenzie Art Gallery★

3475 Albert St., Regina SK , S4S 6X6. ♿🅿🕐 Open year-round Mon–Sat 10am–5:30pm (Thu & Fri 10pm), Sun and

Historic Court Case of Louis Riel

After the defeat of the Northwest Rebellion in 1885, the Métis leader Louis Riel was taken to Regina for trial. The court immediately became a centre of controversy. To Quebeckers, Riel—a Catholic Métis who had studied for the priesthood in Montreal—was a patriot. To Ontarians, he was a common rebel who had gone unpunished after murdering Thomas Scott during the Red River Rebellion. Defence counsel pleaded that Riel was insane: he had spent several years in asylums and had wished to set up a new Catholic state on the Saskatchewan River, with Bishop Bourget of Montreal as Pope. Riel himself rejected the plea and convinced the jury he was sane. But if sane, he was guilty: the verdict was death by hanging. Prime Minister Sir John A. Macdonald was inundated with petitions from both sides. The sentence was delayed while doctors studied Riel's mental health. The prime minister weighed the political consequences of hanging Riel and decided the sentence had to be carried out. Riel lost his life on November 16, 1885.

Every summer the Schumiatcher Theatre at the MacKenzie Art Gallery (◉ See below) is the setting for a dramatic reenactment of the **Trial of Louis Riel**, based on actual court transcripts (◔Mid-Jul–mid-Aug Wed–Fri 7:30pm. Tickets available at door or ☎306-728-5728).

holidays 11am–5:30pm. ◔Closed Jan 1, Good Friday, Dec 25–26. ∞No charge. ☎306-584-4250. www.mackenzieartgallery.sk.ca.

Occupying the western end of the T.C. Douglas Building in Wascana Centre, this expansive art gallery features seven viewing rooms devoted largely to Canadian historical and contemporary art.

Additional Sights

Royal Canadian Mounted Police Training Academy★

5600-11th Ave., RCMP Academy, Depot Division, PO Box 6500, Regina SK, S4P 3J7. ☎306-780-5900. www.rcmp-grc.gc.ca. Sunset Retreat Ceremony Jul–mid-Aug, Tue 6:30pm.

People who know nothing else about Canada have heard of the **Mounties**, the country's federal police force who "always get their man." Visitors may no longer wander the academy grounds, but the nearby new **Heritage Centre**★ (5907 Dewdney Ave.; ♿ P ◔open mid-May–Labour Day daily 10am–6pm, 8pm Thu and Tue when Musical Rides; rest of the year Mon–Sat 10am–4:30pm; ∞$12 adult; ◔closed Jan 1, Dec 25; ☎306-522-7333, toll-free 1-866-567-7267; www.rcmpheritagecentre.com), opened in 2007, brings the history of the Mounties up

to date with exhibits on community policing, counter-terrorism activities and forensics. The vivid past of the force is not neglected, with exhibits on favourite characters such as Sitting Bull and the Mad Trapper of Rat River.

Excursion

Qu'Appelle Valley★

See Map of Principal Sights. From Lake Diefenbaker to the Manitoba border, the Qu'Appelle (kap-PELL) Valley cuts a deep swath across the otherwise flat prairie. As much as 120m/400ft deep in places, with several sparkling lakes, the valley presents a complete contrast to the surrounding plains.

The Fishing Lakes★

73km/45mi east of Regina by Trans-Can Hwy., northeast by Rte. 10.

The Fishing Lakes—Pasqua, Echo, Mission and Katepwa — lie along the valley. North of Lake Echo, an attractive stretch of road on Route 56 leads to Echo Valley Provincial Park★, a delightful place to camp (PO Box 790, Fort Qu'Appelle SK, S0G 1S0. ♿◔Open year-round, campgrounds closed in winter. Visitor centre open mid-May–Labour Day, hours vary. ∞$7/day vehicle fee. ☎306-332-3215. www.se.gov.sk.ca).

RIDING MOUNTAIN NATIONAL PARK★★

MANITOBA

This diverse park is a rolling plateau of aspen parkland, bogs, grasslands and hardwood forests that attract the province's heaviest concentrations of wildlife. Given the large populations of moose and elk, sightings of these creatures, as well as of bears or foxes, are highly probable.

- **Information:** Park Office, Wasagaming. ☎204-848-7275. www.pc.gc.ca.
- **Orient Yourself:** The park lies in southwestern Manitoba, 197km/122 mi west of Winnipeg via the TransCanada Highway then 91km/56mi north of Brandon by Rte. 10.
- **Parking:** Do not get out of the car to approach wildlife on the roads.
- **Don't Miss:** At Lake Audy you can see a bison herd.
- **Organizing Your Time:** To find out about accommodation, events and services, contact the Wasagaming Chamber of Commerce at Box 222, Wasagaming MB, R0J 2H0. 204-848-2742 (May–Oct). www.discoverclearlake.com.
- **Especially for Kids:** The park visitor centre offers an excellent introduction to the park's geology and wildlife.
- **Also See:** YORKTON, AUSTIN, WINNIPEG

Geological Notes

The park rises 457m/1,500ft above the surrounding countryside (756m/2,480ft above sea level).

Early fur traders named it "Riding" Mountain, the place where they exchanged canoes for horses to continue west. It is part of the **Manitoba Escarpment,** a jagged 1,600km/1,000mi ridge winding across North Dakota, Manitoba and Saskatchewan. The park is also a crossroads where northern, western and eastern environments and habitats meet. High areas are covered with an evergreen forest of spruce, pine, fir and tamarack. Lower sections support a deciduous forest of hardwoods, shrubs, vines and ferns. In the west wildflowers thrive on meadows and grassland *(Jul and Aug)*, forming some of the only true prairie left on the continent.

Visit

Open daily year-round. Hiking, camping, boating, fishing, biking, horseback riding, golf, winter sports. Visitor centre *Open Jul–Aug daily 9:30am–8pm, late May–Jun & Sept–mid-Oct daily 9:30am–5:30pm. Closed mid-Oct–mid-May. Map available at visitor centre.$7/day adult.* ☎204-848-7275. *www.pc.gc.ca. Accommodations in Wasagaming.*

The **visitor centre** in Wasagaming features excellent displays and films on the park's geological history, different habitats, and native wildlife.

Trails are popular among hikers and cyclists in the summer, and cross-country skiers in the winter. Birders come from around the world to see great grey owls and the many species of songbirds and other birds (some 260 species) that converge here. Wolf howls and elk-bugling trips are organized by the park office; on these group excursions, guides imitate wolf howls or use high-pitched bugles to coax the animals into view.

Near Lake Audy *(47km/29mi from Wasagaming)*, a herd of bison roams a large enclosure *(accessible by Lake Audy Rd. off Rte. 10).* From an interpretive viewpoint above the Audy plain, these animals can be seen in their true prairie environment.

There are good **views**★ of the Manitoba Escarpment from an observation tower off Route 10 near the park's north gate.

Address Book

WHAT TO DO

National Ukrainian Festival, *In Selo Ukraina, 60km/36mi north of Wasagaming and 12km/7mi south of Dauphin, near intersection of Hwys. 5 and 10. Ukrainian Festival, 1550 Main St, PO Box 368, Dauphin MB, R2N 2V2.* ☎*204-622-4600 or toll-free 877-474-2683. www.cnuf. ca.* Held annually in early August near Riding Mountain National Park, this is a three-day celebration of traditional and contemporary Ukrainian dancing, music and food. Among the festival highlights are a parade, street dances, arts and crafts displays, a bread-baking contest, beer gardens and a children's fest. On-site camping is available (*reservations essential*) and there are bus transport packages from Saskatchewan, Alberta and Winnipeg.

Triangle Ranch – *Triangle Ranch Ltd., Mooswa Dr. E, Onanole MB, R0J 1N0.* ☎*204-848-4583 Reservations advised.* Located adjacent to the Elkhorn Ranch Resort, the riding stables of Triangle Ranch are open to the public for one- and two-hour as well as full-day trail rides in the immediate vicinity of the ranch or within Riding Mountain National Park itself. In the summer, hayrides and wiener roasts are offered, and in winter, sleigh rides and cutter rides (for two) are a relaxing way to enjoy the outdoors. Horses are available for all levels of riding ability and experienced guides accompany each outing.

SASKATOON★
SASKATCHEWAN
POPULATION 202,340

The largest city in Saskatchewan, this manufacturing and distribution centre is set in a fertile wheat-growing area, amid the province's vast potash reserves. Surrounding prairie landscape is dominated by the "heights" of Mount Blackstrap (91m/300ft), an artificial ski hill rising south of the city (40km/25mi).

- **Information:** 6-305 Idlywyld Dr. ☎306-242-1206 or toll-free 1-800-567-2444. www.tourismsaskatoon.com
- **Orient Yourself:** On the banks of the South Saskatchewan River, Saskatoon lies 259km/161mi northwest of Regina.
- **Parking:** Parking meters operate Mon–Sat, 9am–6pm. Time limits vary from 30min to 3hrs.
- **Don't Miss:** The Wanuskewin Heritage Park is a fascinating look at 6,000 years of human habitation in the area.
- **Organizing Your Time:** If you continue on to Prince Albert by Rte 11, the site of the Métis' last stand, Batoche, is not far out of your way.
- **Especially for Kids:** There is plenty for kids in Boomtown at the Western Development Museum.
- **Also See:** THE BATTLEFORDS, PRINCE ALBERT NATIONAL PARK, REGINA, MOOSE JAW

A Bit of History

Founded in 1883 by Methodists from Ontario, the city was named for the Saskatoon, a small purplish berry native to the region. Starting in 1908, German, Scandinavian, Ukrainian and British settlers arrived by the new train line and transformed the city; early Methodist temperance ideals were laid to rest. Today the settlers are honored once a year in July during Pioneer Days.

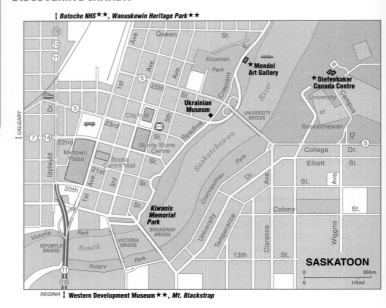

↑ *Batoche NHS*★★, *Wanuskewin Heritage Park*★★

SASKATOON

REGINA | *Western Development Museum*★★, *Mt. Blackstrap*

Sights

Mendel Art Gallery★

950 Spadina Crescent East, PO Box 569, Saskatoon SK, S7K 3L6. ✕ ♿ 🅿 🕒 *Open year-round daily 9am–9pm.* 🕒 *Closed Dec 25.* 🎫 *No charge.* ☎ *306-975-7610. www. mendel.ca.*

This attractive gallery overlooking the river is named for **Fred Mendel**, a wealthy Saskatoon meatpacker of German origin who spent much of his time and money developing the gallery.

The permanent collection includes works by the Group of Seven, Emily Carr and David Milne in the Canadian section, as well as Feininger, Chagall, Utrillo and Pissarro and other European painters. There is also a small, attractive conservatory of exotic flowers and plants.

Ukrainian Museum

910 Spadina Crescent East, Saskatoon SK. S7K 3H5. ♿ 🕒 *Open year-round Tue–Sat 10am–5pm, Sun & holidays 1pm–5pm.* 🕒 *Closed Jan 7 & Orthodox Easter Friday.* 🎫 *$4 adult.* ☎ *306-244-3800. www.umc. sk.ca or www.tourismsaskatoon.com.*

This museum presents displays of traditional costumes, tapestries, pioneer tools, musical instruments, wood-inlaid objects, and other handicrafts. Manne-

quins are garbed in male and female Ukrainian folk attire, including headdresses and footwear.

Boat Trip

The Saskatoon Princess departs from Riverside Park (behind Mendel Art Gallery) ♿ 🕒 *May–Sept daily 1:30pm, 3pm, 4:40pm. Round trip 1hr.* 🎫 *$15 adult. Shearwater Properties Ltd., Hafford SK, S0J 1A0.* ☎ *toll-free 1-888-747-7572 (Canada/ US). www.shearwatertours.com. Reservations recommended.* This cruise on the South Saskatchewan River is a pleasant way to discover the scenic beauty of the area and view the city from the waterside.

Diefenbaker Canada Centre★

University of Saskatchewan, 101 Diefenbaker Pl., Saskatoon, SK, S7N 5B8. ♿ 🅿 🕒 *Open year-round Mon–Fri 9:30am–4:30pm (Tue and Thu to 8pm), weekends and holidays noon–4:30pm.* 🎫 *$5 adult ($2 Tue evening).* 🕒 *Closed Jan1, Dec 25-26, Good Friday, Remembrance Day.* ☎ *306-966-8384. www.usask. ca/diefenbaker.*

The 13th prime minister of Canada, John G. Diefenbaker (1895-1979) left his papers and collections to the university. A lawyer by training, well known for his defence of the "little man," "Dief" was a strong proponent of Western Canadian ideas in the Conservative Party. Elected party leader in 1956, he served as prime minister from 1957 to 1963, remaining influential in federal politics until his death.

In addition to displays on his life and works, the centre features a replica of the office of the prime minister and the cabinet chamber as they existed in the Diefenbaker era.

Western Development Museum★★

Kids *In Prairieland Exhibition Grounds, 8km/5mi south of downtown by Rte. 11/16. 2610 Lorne Ave., South Saskatoon SK, S7J 0S6.* ✕ ♿ 🅿 🕐 *Open daily 9am–5pm (schedule may vary –contact museum).* 🕐 *Closed holidays.* 💰$8.50 adult. ☎306-931-1910. www.wdm.ca.*

The grand attraction of the Saskatoon branch of this museum (other branches in North Battleford, Moose Jaw and Yorkton) is **Boomtown**, a faithful reconstruction of an entire street of 1910 vintage, complete with its Western Pioneer Bank, garage, stores, Chinese laundry, school, pool hall, theatre, hotel, church and railway station. Separate halls house automobiles and agricultural equipment, including steam tractors. Enjoy a light meal or a piece of fruit pie in the Victorian-styled Boomtown Cafe.

Wanuskewin Heritage Park★★

5km/3mi north of downtown by Hwy. 11. RR#4 Penner Rd, Saskatoon SK, S7K 3J7. 🕐 *Open mid-May–Labour Day daily 9am–9pm. Rest of the year daily 9am–5pm.* 🕐 *Closed Dec 25–Jan 1.* 💰$8.50 adult.* ✕ ♿ 🅿 ☎306-931-6767, or toll-free 1-877-547-6546 (Canada/US). www.wanuskewin.com.*

Translated from Cree as "seeking peace of mind," *Wanuskewin* was a meeting place and hunting ground for nomadic Indians for more than 6,000 years until their removal to reserves in the 1870s. Several trails in the 120ha/300 acre park link the prehistoric sites, including a **buffalo jump** and the remains of a rare **medicine wheel**. A striking **visitor centre** features displays and demonstrations of native culture and allows observation of archaeological excavations and laboratory work. A special treat is a performance by the Wanuskewin Dance Troupe, founded in 1997, which presents both traditional and contemporary styles. *Call ahead for schedule* ☎306-931-6767.

Excursion

Batoche National Historic Site★★

88km/55mi northeast of Saskatoon by Rte. 11 to Rosthern, Rte. 312 East and Rte. 225 North. PO Box 999, Rosthern SK, S0K 3R0. ✕ ♿ 🕐 *Open early May–Sept daily*

Batoche National Historic Site

Tourism Saskatchewan

The Northwest Rebellion

The seeds of the last armed conflict on Canadian soil were sown in Manitoba's Red River Valley early in the 19C when the Métis learned that land did not necessarily belong to them. The uprising led to Louis Riel's provisional government of 1869, the formal creation of the province of Manitoba (1870) and the allocation of 567,000ha/1.4 million acres of land for the Métis settlement.

Unfortunately, the Métis, left leaderless when Riel was banished for five years, were prey to speculators who bought their land for a fraction of its worth. Many moved northwest to the valley of the South Saskatchewan River, hoping to lead traditional lives and to avoid European settlers. However the Métis again found they had no right to the land they farmed. The Dominion government consistently ignored their petitions. In 1884, they sent for Riel.

Riel hoped to repeat his earlier victory at Red River. He allied the Métis with the Cree Indians, also discontent with changes in their lifestyle. An unfortunate incident resulting in the deaths of some members of the North West Mounted Police at **Duck Lake** destroyed all hope of a peaceful solution. A military force was quickly dispatched to the West under Maj. Gen. **Frederick Middleton.**

Under their military leader, **Gabriel Dumont** (aka **Poundmaker),** an experienced buffalo hunter, the Métis made a stand at Batoche. It was a heroic defence against overwhelming force that lasted four days, May 9–12, 1885. Riel surrendered and was taken to Regina to stand trial for murder. He was found guilty and hanged. Dumont fled to the US, though he was later pardoned and returned to Batoche. The struggle was not in vain, however, for in the wake of the rebellion, the Métis were offered the land title they had sought for such a long time.

9am–5pm. $7.15 adult. 306-423-6227. www.pc.gc.ca.

At this quiet and beautiful **site** on the banks of the South Saskatchewan River, the Métis made their last stand in 1885.

Little remains of the village except the white, steepled **church** dedicated to St. Anthony of Padua, the **rectory** with its bullet holes and a cemetery of Métis graves, including Gabriel Dumont's burial place.

The **visitor centre** offers a moving audiovisual presentation on the rebellion and displays on Métis history and culture.

The return trip to Saskatoon can be made by the St.-Laurent cable ferry (10km/6mi north of Batoche), past the small community of Duck Lake on Route 11, where the rebellion had its beginnings.

WINNIPEG★★★
MANITOBA
POPULATION 633,451

For over a century, Winnipeg was the traditional first stop for immigrants to the West. Although challenged by Vancouver, Calgary and Edmonton in recent years, it retains a huge **commodity exchange** (the most important in Canada), vast stock and railway yards, a manufacturing industry and headquarters of the Hudson's Bay Company. Winnipeg is rich in cultural institutions—the Manitoba Theatre Centre, the Winnipeg Symphony Orchestra, the Manitoba Opera Company and, most famous of all, the Royal Winnipeg Ballet.

- **Information:** Visitor centre, Main floor, 259 Portage Ave., ☎204-943-1970 or toll-free 1-800-665-0204. www.destinationwinnipeg.ca
- **Orient Yourself:** Winnipeg, "Where the West begins," is at the geographic heart of Canada, on the banks of the Red and Assiniboine rivers.
- **Parking:** New solar-powered city parking meters issue a ticket that you leave in the windshield. In no-parking periods, meters display a menacing tow-truck.
- **Don't Miss:** The grounds of The Fork; the Manitoba Museum; the shopping area around Corydon Avenue.
- **Organizing Your Time:** Winnipeg is famed for its cultural activities; plan to take in at least one event if you can.
- **Especially for Kids:** Assiniboine Park, with its zoo and statue of Winnie the Bear, inspiration for the Pooh.
- **Also See:** RIDING MOUNTAIN NATIONAL PARK

A Bit of History

Named for the large and shallow lake to the north called *win-nipi* ("muddy water") by the Cree, Winnipeg's future was assured when the Canadian Pacific Railway Co. chose the site as a major maintenance and repair centre and built a rail line through town. Waves of immigrants poured in by train. The city's skyline, dotted with spires, towers and domes of Catholic, Protestant and Orthodox churches, reflects this diversity. Every August the city's varied cultural background is celebrated in **Folklorama,** a festival held in pavilions throughout Winnipeg. The Folk Festival held in July is also a popular event.

Travel Manitoba

Folklorama

Downtown

The intersection of **Portage Avenue** and **Main Street** has traditionally been considered the centre of Winnipeg. It was said these streets were wide enough for 10 Red River carts to rush along side by side. Today this corner, long known as the windiest in Canada, is dominated by tall buildings, all connected underground by an attractive shopping area, **Winnipeg Square**. Extending for three blocks to the west, between Vaughan and Carlton streets, is **Portage Place**★, a shopping and office complex with restaurants, movie theatres, a giant-screen IMAX theatre and the Prairie Theatre Exchange.

Just south of the intersection at Portage and Main, in a small park below the Fort Garry Hotel, stands a stone gateway, all that remains of **Upper Fort Garry**, once the local headquarters of the Hudson's Bay Company. The present-day headquarters **(A)** rises a block away.

The Forks, 26ha/65 acres of riverfront property refurbished by the city, includes a **public market** housed within former stables, restaurants, shops, a children's museum and a waterside walkway *(boat rentals)*. Riverboat cruises on the Red River depart near the Provencher Bridge *(Paddlewheel River Rouge Tours* ✕🅿🕐*May–October, departures 1pm & 3pm.* ✎*$17 adult.* ☎*204-944-8000. www. paddlewheelcruises.com)*.

Walking tours (2hrs) of the downtown area depart from the ViaRail station. 🕐*Late May–Sept, Thu–Fri, 10am.* ✎*$8 adult.* ☎*204-997-8687. www.muddy watertours.ca. Call for reservations.*

North of the intersection lies the historic **Exchange District**, which has some remarkable examples of early-20C architecture *(Walking tours (1hr30min)depart from Old Market Sq., look for sign.* 🕐*Daily June–Labour Day 10am & 2pm; specialty tours (45min) at noon.* ✎*$6.* ☎ *204-942-6716.www.exchangedistrict.org)*, and boutiques and restaurants around the **Old Market Square** *(King, Albert and Bannatyne Sts.)*. Close by is **Centennial Centre**, a complex enclosing a concert hall, theatre, museum and planetarium. Just north is Winnipeg's **Chinatown**. Another interesting area for shopping and dining is **Osborne Village**, south of the Assiniboine River between River and Stradbrook avenues.

Manitoba Museum★★★

🅺🆂190 Rupert Ave., Winnipeg MB, R3B 0N2, across from City Hall. ♿🅿🕐Open Jun–Aug daily 10am–6pm. Rest of the year Tue–Fri 10am–4pm, weekends & holidays 11am–4pm. ✎$8 adult. ☎204-956-2830. www.manitobamuseum.mb.ca.

On entering this remarkable museum, the visitor first sees the magnificent diorama of a Métis rider, his spear poised, chasing several bison. The **Earth History Gallery** includes an explanation of the geological creation of Manitoba. The

The Red River Settlement

In the early 19C Thomas Douglas, Earl of Selkirk, obtained title from the Hudson's Bay Company to **Assiniboia**, a large piece of land covering much of present-day Southern Manitoba. In 1811 he began resettling some of his poverty-stricken compatriots from the Scottish Highlands there in the Red River Valley. The success of this colony was slow in coming, mainly because of the Red River's tendency to flood, plagues of crop-eating grasshoppers and rivalry between the great fur-trading companies—the Hudson's Bay and the North West. The latter allied with the Métis, who had seen their traditional lifestyle disrupted by settlers.

During the **Seven Oaks Massacre** of 1816, the Métis nearly succeeded in wiping out the colony: Some 20 settlers were killed and the rest temporarily abandoned the settlement. Selkirk reestablished his colony, however, and it gradually grew in size as a commercial centre, with brigades of Red River carts going to and from St. Paul, Minnesota, and steamboats chugging along the Red River. The settlement's connections below the border made annexation by the US seem likely, but the Northwest Rebellion and the creation of Manitoba in 1870 prevented it.

Address Book

For dollar sign categories, see the Legend on the cover flap.

WHERE TO STAY

$ Beechmount B&B – *134 West Gate, Winnipeg MB, R3C 2E1. Minimum two-night stay Jun–Aug.* ☎204-775-1144. *www.beechmount.ca. 5 rooms.* P♨☕. Two acres of shady elms and oaks surround this riverbank 1890s Victorian mansion in a quiet yet central neighborhood just west of Osborne Village. Large rooms and an outdoor pool in a garden setting make this an attractive accommodation. Generous breakfast.

$ HI Downtowner – *330 Kennedy St., Winnipeg MB, R3B 2M6.* ☎204-943-5581 *or toll-free 1-866-762-4122. www.hihostels.com. 120 beds.* ✕♿. This brand-new hostel is located in downtown Winnipeg, near The Forks, the museums, the shopping and nightlife. All rooms with washroom and shower and air conditioning. Family rooms available. Restaurant and bar on premises.

$ Maison Grosvenor B&B – *824 Grosvenor Ave, Winnipeg MB R3M 0N2.* ☎204-475-9630. *www.bbcanada.com. 3 rooms.* P☕. This 1912 Queen Anne Revival-style house lies within a five-minute walk of Corydon Avenue (the shopping and restaurant district of Little Italy) and Osborne Village. Guests can choose a continental or vegetarian breakfast, or a traditional meal of fruit, muffins, spinach omelette and bacon.

$$ Best Western Charter House Hotel – *330 York Ave. Winnipeg MB, R3C 0N9.* ☎204-942-0101 *or toll-free 1-800-782-0175. www.bwcharterhouse.com. 90 rooms.* ✕♿P. This five-storey hotel, half a block from the Winnipeg Convention Centre and not far from The Forks, features friendly service and well-equipped, if conventional, rooms. The **Rib Room Restaurant ($$)**, whose affordable menu includes veal ribs and a variety of seafood dishes, attracts the downtown business crowd.

$$ Delta Winnipeg – *350 St. Mary's Rd., Winnipeg MB, R3C 3J2.* ☎204-942-0551 *or toll-free 1-888-311-4990. www.deltahotels.com. 393 rooms.* ✕♿P☕. A great location across from shopping and restaurants in Citi Place and the connecting skywalk to Winnipeg Convention Centre make this a favorite for conference delegates and travellers alike. The Delta has two pools (indoor and outdoor) as well as high-speed internet access. The **Blaze Bistro ($$)** offers a well-priced menu, while the pub, **The Elephant & Castle ($)**, offers British pub fare and a game of darts.

$$$ The Fairmont Winnipeg – *Two Lombard Pl., Winnipeg MB, R3B 0Y3.* ☎204-957-1350 *or toll-free 1-800-257-7544. www.fairmont.com. 340 rooms.* ✕♿P Spa ☕. Winnipeg's premier downtown hotel towers over the famous corner of Portage and Main. Well-appointed, spacious rooms provide views of the historic Exchange District. **The Velvet Glove ($$$)**, the hotel's renowned restaurant, offers seasonal Manitoba specialties such as chateaubriand or Manitoba ostrich.

$$$ Fort Garry Hotel – *222 Broadway, Winnipeg MB, R3C 0R3.* ☎204-942-8251 *or toll-free 1-800-665-8088. www.fortgarryhotel.com. 246 rooms.* ✕♿P☕Spa☕. A few blocks south of Portage and Main, this imposing landmark has graced Winnipeg's skyline since 1913. A five-minute walk from The Forks, shopping areas and the major business district, the hotel offers spacious rooms, a fitness centre and spa, an indoor pool and a 24-hour deli. With its marble walls and crystal chandeliers, the lobby is especially noteworthy. The **Broadway Room ($$)** is known for its bounteous Sunday brunch.

WHERE TO EAT

$$$ Café La Scala – *725 Corydon Ave., Winnipeg MB, R3M 0W4.* ☎204-474-2750. **Italian**. Art brightens the walls of this narrow restaurant. Start with La Scala's portabella mushroom dumplings with cilantro chili garlic sauce or mussels Sambuca, and move on to a pasta course such as vermicelli with tiger shrimp in black bean sauce. Arugula salad with Asiago cheese, pine nuts and a balsamic-vinegar reduction wins consistent raves.

$$$ Amici – *326 Broadway, Winnipeg MB, R3C 0S5.* ☎204-943-4997. *www.amiciwpg.com.* **Northern Italian**. For more than a decade, Chef Heinz Kattenfeld's Tuscan-inspired dishes have been a downtown draw for business people as well as celebrities such as Mick Jagger, Jane Seymour and Keifer Sutherland. In an elegant linen-and-silver ambience enjoy an inspiring menu of antipasti, pasta and risotto, and roasted veal, lamb or fowl with imaginative sauces and vegetable dishes. Downstairs at the ever-popular and less expensive **Bombolini** (**$$** ☎204-943-5066), enjoy pizza, pasta and simple meat dishes.

$$$ Restaurant Dubrovnik – *390 Assiniboine Ave.Winnipeg MB,R3C 0Y1* . ☎*204-944-0594. www.resstaurantdubrovnik.com.* **Fusion**. One of Canada's best, this restaurant in a turn-of-the-century riverfront mansion features up-to-date dishes such as venison with chestnuts, cabbage and lingonberry sauce, or rack of lamb with harissa and Algerian eggplant jam, as well as inventive salads. There is an extensive wine list.

$$$ Tavern in the Park – *55 Pavilion Crescent, Winnipeg MB, R3P 2N6. (Assiniboine Park-Shaftesbury entrance off Corydon Ave.). Closed Mon.* ☎*204-896-7275. www.taverninthepark.ca.* **Continental**. Enjoy splendid views of lushly treed Assiniboine Park while you enjoy dishes such as weiner schnitzel with lingonberrys and spaetzle, or rack of lamb. This restored historic building offers meals in the elegant sunlit dining room or outside on the stone terrace.

$$ Chutneys – *101-102 The Forks Market at the Forks.* ☎*204-957-7767.* **Indian**. Dine on dishes like creamy mussels Masaladar or Chinese/Indian dried-chili chicken—rated one-pepper mild to five-pepper hot—in Chutney's lavish, yet casual, atmosphere. Can't decide? Try the buffet, where you can sample a host of traditional dishes. Marble-topped tables and Indian antiques add an authentic touch.

$$ Civita – *691 Corydon Ave.Winnipeg, MB, R3M 0W4* ☎*204-453-4616.* **California/Italian.** Locals frequent this neighborhood hot spot for its thin-crusted gourmet pizza, baked in a clay wood-burning oven. During the summer, diners on the lively streetfront patio can sample pizza or creative pasta dishes while not missing a beat from the Corydon Avenue scene. Those wanting a quieter venue can choose the secluded side garden porch.

$$ Pasta La Vista – *66-333 St. Mary Ave, Winnipeg MB, 3RC 4A5.* ☎*204-956-2229. www. wowhospitality.ca. Second location at 1715 Kenaston Blvd.* ☎*204-398-2229.* **California/Italian**. Modern, trendy and frequented by businesspeople and conference delegates, this downtown restaurant serves up creatively-named pasta and pizza such as Simpatico goes Tuscan (linguine with shrimp, peppers and vegetables) or Spice is the Variety of Life pizza (complex, involving jalpenos, pepperoni and feta).

WHERE TO SHOP

Winnipeg's Little Italy – In summer, an eight-block stretch of Corydon Avenue between Stafford and Osborne fills with people roaming the table-filled sidewalks, enjoying gelato and shopping along this popular restaurant row. If you're looking for home decor items, **Room for Style** (*875 Corydon, Winnipeg MB, R3M 0W7.* ☎*204-287-8833. www.roomforstyle.ca*) carries interior furnishings and unusually beautiful wrought-iron accent pieces. The store also stocks interesting frames, hooks and shelves, among other things. When you're done with housewares, slip into **Radiance Books & Treasures,** which sells New Age items next door (*875 Corydon, Winnipeg MB, R3M 0W7.* ☎*204-284-4231. www.radiencegifts. com*), if only to marvel at the soothing tabletop fountains.

Winnipeg Outfitters, *250 McPhillips St., Winnipeg MB, R3E 2K4.* ☎*204-775-9653 or toll-free 1-800-665-0193. www. outfitters.ca.* A stuffed musk-ox greets browsers at the entrance to this rambling brick building, situated five minutes west of downtown. For more than 30 years, people have turned to the exchange, or its 7,000-item catalogue, to dress themselves in outdoor, hunting, and extreme cold-weather wear, such as boots that keep feet toasty at minus 40 degrees Celsius. It's also the place to go for outdoor equipment such as binoculars, air-guns, and fur hats, including the Mountie model.

The Forks

Arctic/Subarctic Gallery is devoted to the northernmost part of the province. In the **Boreal Forest Gallery**, dioramas present the area's indigenous animals. The highlight of the museum is the **Nonsuch Gallery**, a large, walk-through diorama that houses a replica of the *Nonsuch,* which sailed from England to Hudson Bay in 1668 in search of beaver pelts. The successful expedition led to the creation of the Hudson's Bay Company two years later. Relics of Sir John Franklin's ill-fated Arctic expedition are also on view.

The **Grasslands Gallery** is devoted to the southern part of Manitoba. Displays describe the Assiniboine Indians and first European settlers. There is an example of the famous pioneer **Red River cart**.

The **Urban Gallery** captures a fall evening in Winnipeg in the 1920s. A **planetarium** *(daily shows. $6.50)* and the **Science Gallery** are located on the lower level *(same hours as museum. $6.50).*

Ukrainian Cultural and Educational Centre★

184 Alexander Ave. East., Winnipeg MB, R3B 0L6. Open year-round Mon–Sat 10am–4pm (Sun 1pm–4pm during Jul–Aug). Closed major holidays. 204-942-0218. www.oseredok.org.

The **museum** *(5th floor)* features exquisite examples of Ukrainian traditional embroidery, wood carving, ceramics and beautifully painted *pysanky* (Easter eggs). The centre includes an art gallery, library, archives and museum shop.

Costume Museum of Canada★

109 Pacific Ave., Winnipeg MB, R3B 0M1. Open Mon–Sat 10am–5pm (Thu 8pm), Sun noon–4pm. $5 adults. 204-989-0072. www.costumemuseum.com.

The museum, recently moved downtown near the Manitoba Museum, illustrates 400 years of North American apparel via mannequin-filled *tableaux.* The 35,000-piece collection *(seasonally displayed)* spans 400 years of costumes worn by ordinary Canadians, as well as those made by great couturiers.

Art Gallery★

300 Memorial Blvd. Winnipeg MB, R3C 1V1. Open Jun–Labour Day daily 10am–5pm (Wed 9pm). Rest of the year Tue–Sun 11am–5pm (Wed 9pm). $6 adult. 204-789-1760. www.wag.mb.ca.

Designed by Winnipeger Gustavo Da Roza, this unusual wedge-shaped structure contains a beautiful art gallery. The gallery is best known for its **Inuit art** and for the Lord and Lady Gort Collection of Gothic and Renaissance panel paintings *(displayed periodically).*

Legislative Building★

450 Broadway, Winnipeg MB, R3C 0V8. Open daily 8am–8pm. Closed Dec 25. Guided tours available hourly July–Labour Day 9am–4pm. Rest of year

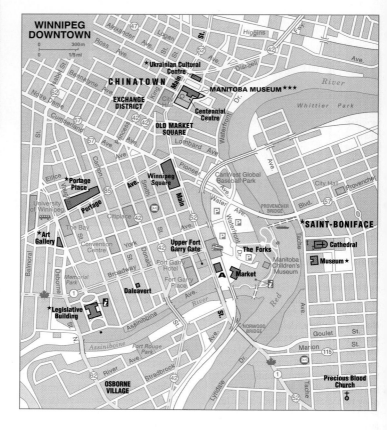

by appointment. ☎204-945-5813. www.
gov.mb.ca/legtour.
This harmonious Neoclassical building
stands in an attractive park. Completed
in 1920, the Tyndall stone building forms
an "H" with a dome at its centre. Above
the dome stands the **Golden Boy**, cast
by Charles Gardet, a bronze gold-plated
statue clutching a sheaf of wheat.
Across Assiniboine Avenue stands a
striking **statue** of Louis Riel by Miguel
Joyal.

Dalnavert

61 Carlton St.Winnipeg MB,R3C 1N7.
🅿️💬Visit by guided tour (45min) only,
🕐 Wed–Fri 10am–5pm, Sat 11am–6pm,
Sun noon–4pm. 💲$5. ☎204-943-2835.
www.mhs.mb.ca.
This beautifully restored Victorian house
was built in 1895 by Sir Hugh John Macdonald, the only son of Sir John A. Macdonald, Canada's first prime minister.

Saint-Boniface★

In 1818 Fathers Provencher and Dumou-
lin arrived from Quebec to establish a
Roman Catholic mission on the banks of
the Red River. Saint-Boniface retains its
distinctive French character. Every February a **Festival du Voyageur** is held,
celebrating the early fur traders.
*Walking tours of St. Boniface in sum-
mer. Tourisme Riel, 219 Provencher Bld.
Winnipeg MB, R2H 0G4. 204-233-8343,
or toll-free 1-866-808-8338. www.tour-
ismeriel.com*

Museum★

494 Ave. Taché, Winnipeg MB, R2H 2B2.
♿🕐Open mid-May–Sept Mon–Fri 9am–
5pm (Thur 8pm), weekends noon–4pm.
Rest of the year Mon–Fri 9am–5pm, Sun
noon–4pm. 💲$5 adult. 💬Tours availa-
ble. ☎204-237-4500. www.msbm.mb.ca
This attractive convent was built for
the Grey Nuns in 1846, making it the

oldest building in Winnipeg. Inside are mementos of Saint-Boniface residents, in particular of Louis Riel.

Cathedral

Six churches have stood on this site since 1818. Designed by Étienne Gaboury, the new cathedral features an attractive wooden interior. The **cemetery** contains the grave of Louis Riel.

Precious Blood Church

Also the work of Gaboury, this brick, shingle-roofed church is built in a shape that resembles a teepee.

Additional Sights

The Royal Canadian Mint★

Trans-Can Hwy. at Hwy. 59. 520 Lagimodière Blvd. Winnipeg MB, R2J 3E7. ♿🅿🕐*Open mid-May–Labour Day Mon–Sat 9am–5pm. Rest of the year Mon–Fri 9am–5pm. Reservations recommended.* 🕐*Closed major holidays.* ☞*$5 weekdays, $3.50 weekends.* ☎*204-983-6429. www.rcmint.ca.*

Visitors to this spectacular half-pyramid structure of rose-colored reflecting glass can view the coin-minting process.

Riel House

330 River Rd., St. Vital, PO Box 73,R2N 3X9. 👣*Visit by guided tour (30min) only.* ♿🅿🕐*Mid-May–Labour Day daily 10am–6pm.* ☞ *$4 adult.* ☎ *204-257-1783; www.pc.gc.ca.*

The tiny wooden house was built in 1881 by the Riel family who occupied it until 1968. Although Louis Riel never actually lived in the house, his body lay in state there after his execution in November 1885.

Seven Oaks House Museum

115 Rupertsland Ave. East, PO Box 25176, Winnipeg MB, R2V 4C8. 🅿🕐*Open mid-May–Labour Day daily 10am–5pm.* ☞*Contribution requested.* ☎*204-339-7429.www.geocities.*

*com/sevenoaksmuseum.*This nine-room log structure, believed to be the oldest remaining habitable house in Manitoba, was completed in 1853 by John Inkster, a wealthy merchant. It lies near the site of the Seven Oaks Massacre of 1816.

Zoo

Kids *In Assiniboine Park. Mailing address City Hall, 510 Main St, Winnipeg MB, R3B 1B9.* ✕♿🅿🕐*Open Jul–Labour Day daily 9am–7pm, late May–Jun daily 9am–6pm, early-Sept–early Oct & late Mar–mid-May daily 10am–4pm (weekends to 6pm). Rest of the year daily 10am–4pm.* ☞*$4.50 adult.* ☎*204-986-2327. www.winnipeg. ca/cms/ape/zoo.*

This large and pleasant zoo offers a **tropical house,** home to a variety of monkeys and birds.

Not far from the zoo, and within Assiniboine Park, is the **Leo Mol Sculpture Garden**. The Winnie the Bear sculpture (named for Winnipeg) is said to be the inspiration for A.A. Milne's character Winnie the Pooh.

Western Canada Aviation Museum★

Kids *At airport, Ellice and Ferry Rds., Hangar T-2, 958 Ferry Rd, Winnipeg MB, R3H 0Y8.* ♿🅿🕐*Open year-round Mon– Fri 9:30am–4:30pm, Sat 10am–5pm, Sun noon–5pm.* 🕐*Closed major holidays.* ☞*$7.50.* ☎*204-786-5503. www.wcam. mb.ca.*

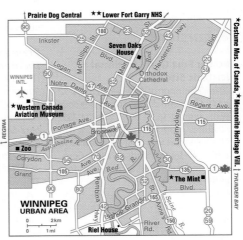

Lower Fort Garry National Historic Site

THE LIVERY BARN RESTAURANT

Take a break from touring the **Mennonite Heritage Village** to sample Russian Mennonite recipes in The **Livery Barn Restaurant (($)**. Begin with borscht, a type of Russian vegetable soup (no beets). Pair it with wheat bread baked on the premises from the village's own stone-ground flour. Or try the *pluma moos*, a cold soup made from three kinds of dried fruits. With your sausage and coleslaw, order some *vareniki,* also known as *perogies*. For dessert, try the rhubarb platz or a slice of fruit pie.

Over 20 aircraft are on display, ranging from early bush planes to jets. A second-floor observation deck allows views of the airport runways.

Excursions

Lower Fort Garry National Historic Site★★

32km/20mi north of Winnipeg by Hwys. 52 and 9. ○*Open mid-May–Labour Day daily 9am–5pm.* ⊛ *$6.50.* ✕&🅿 ☎*204-785-6050 or 877-534-3678. www.pc.gc.ca.*

This stone fort was built between 1830 and 1847 by the Hudson's Bay Company and remained a company post until 1911.

Mennonite Heritage Village★

In Steinbach, 61km/38mi southeast of Winnipeg by Trans-Can Hwy. and Hwy. 12. 23 PTH 12 N, Steinbach, MB, R5G 1T8. ✕&🅿○*Open Jul–Aug Mon–Sat 10am–6pm, Sun 10am–6pm; May–Jun & Sept, Mon–Sat 10am–5pm, Sun noon–5pm. Rest of the year Tue–Fri 10am–4pm, weekends by appointment.* ⊛ *$8.* ☎ *204-326-9661. www.mennoniteheritagevillage.com.*

This village presents the life of the first Mennonites who settled in Manitoba about 1874. Two groups of Mennonites exist in Canada: the Swiss-Germanic of Ontario and the Russian Mennonites of the West. Extreme pacifists who refuse to fight in any war, both are descended from the Protestant sect led by **Menno Simons**.

Of particular interest is the farmhouse built in characteristic style with the kitchen and stove in the centre (to heat all rooms) and a barn on one end.

Prairie Dog Central

Departs from Inkster Junction in Winnipeg (1km/.6mi north of Inkster Blvd. between Sturgeon Rd. & Metro Rte. 90) Vintage Locomotive Society Inc., PO Box 33021 RPO Polo Park, Winnipet MG, R3G 3N4. ○*Early May–Sept weekends departs 11am, return 3pm.* ⊛*$22. Reservations required.* ☎*204-832-5259 or through Ticketmaster* ☎*204-253-2787 www.pdcrailway.com.*

This vintage steam train, with its late-19C coaches, makes weekly excursions from Winnipeg to Warren. Along the way, the train stops at small towns so visitors can browse at local markets.

YORKTON
SASKATCHEWAN
POPULATION 15,038

This city was first settled by farmers from York County, Ontario. They were soon followed by other nationalities, especially Ukrainians. Today Yorkton is known as a manufacturing centre for agricultural equipment and for its stockyards.

- **Information:** Tourist Office, Junction Hwys 9 & 16, PO Box 460, Yorkton SK, S3N 2W4. ☎306-783-8707, toll-free 1-877-250-6454. www.tourismyorkton.com
- **Orient Yourself:** Yorkton is 187km/116mi northeast of Regina on the Yellowhead Highway.
- **Parking:** Yorkton has metered parking.
- **Don't Miss:** The Western Development Museum
- **Organizing Your Time:** Near Yorkton are four provincial parks, as well as numerous golf courses.
- **Especially for Kids:** In Yorkton, there is a sample of original prairie as the early settlers saw it.
- **Also See:** RIDING MOUNTAIN NATIONAL PARK

Sight

Western Development Museum★

PO Box 98, Hwy 16 West, Yorkton SK, S3N 2V6. ⚫⚫Open mid-May–June Mon–Fri 9am–5pm, weekends noon–5pm; July–Labour Day daily 9am–5pm. Rest of the year Mon–Wed 2pm–5pm. ⚫ *$8.50.* ☎306-783-8361. www.wdm.ca.

The Yorkton branch of this museum (other branches in North Battleford, Moose Jaw and Saskatoon) is devoted to the various ethnic groups found in Saskatchewan: Ukrainian, German, Scandinavian, English and American. There is a collection of antique steam and gas-traction engines on exhibit outdoors.

A Sampling of Canada's Collections of Native Culture and Art

Banff	Buffalo Nations Luxton Museum★
Calgary	Glenbow Museum★★
Churchill	Eskimo Museum★★
Edmonton	Provincial Museum★★
Fort Macleod	Head-Smashed-In Buffalo Jump★
Hull	Canadian Museum of Civilization★★
'Ksan	Gitksan artifacts collection★★
Midland	Huron Indian Village★
Montreal	McCord Museum of Canadian History★★
Prince Rupert	Museum of Northern British Columbia★★
Queen Charlotte	Haida Gwaii Museum★
Regina	Royal Saskatchewan Museum★★★
St. John's	Newfoundland Museum★
Toronto	Royal Ontario Museum★★★
Vancouver	UBC Museum of Anthropology★★★
	Vancouver Museum★★
Victoria	Royal British Columbia Museum★★★
Winnipeg	Manitoba Museum★★★
	Art Gallery★
Yellowknife	Prince of Wales Northern Heritage Centre★★

ONTARIO

Canada's richest and most populous province (12,160,282 inhabitants), Ontario is the country's industrial, economic, political and cultural heartland. Stretching from the Great Lakes in the south to Hudson Bay in the north, the province encompasses a wide variety of scenery, the majority of its natural beauty spots being in or near water. Possessing nearly 200,000sq km/70,000sq mi of lakes, Ontario takes its name from the Iroquoian word meaning "shining waters."

- **Information:** Ontario Tourism Marketing, 10th floor, Hearst Block, 900 Bay St., Toronto ON, M7A 2E1. ☎toll-free 1-800-668-2746. www.ontariotravel.net
- ▶ **Orient Yourself:** Ontario lies between Québec and Manitoba, stretching from the Great Lakes to Hudson's Bay. To the south are the states of New York, Pennsylvania, Ohio, Michigan and Minnesota.
- ☺ **Don't Miss:** Ontario's vast system of lakes and rivers offers any number of attractions for vacationers, but Toronto and Ottawa are also well worth your while.
- ◷ **Organizing Your Time:** Ontario has many interesting sights, but distances are vast; plan your itinerary realistically.

Geographical Notes

A Land Shaped by Glaciers – When North America's last Ice Age receded about 10,000 years ago, it left the region that is now Ontario scarred and completely reshaped. Great holes gouged out of the earth had gradually filled with water and over much of the land the geological core of the continent was revealed. The Precambrian rocks of this forested, lake-filled terrain known as the Canadian Shield are still exposed over a large part of the province today, producing a landscape of rock, water and rock-clinging trees. Only in the north and in the extreme south have sedimentary deposits allowed more varied surface features.

The Great Lakes – These vast expanses of freshwater are one of the most extraordinary legacies of the glaciers. **Lake Superior,** the largest, deepest and

Niagara Falls

	January		July	
	low	high	low	high
Ottawa	−15°C/5°F	−6°C/21°F	15°C/59°F	26°C/79°F
Toronto	−7°C/18°F	−1°C/30°F	17°C/63°F	27°C/81°F
Thunder Bay	−21°C/-6°F	−8°C/16°F	11°C/52°F	23°C/75°F
Windsor	−9°C/16°F	−1°C/30°F	17°C/63°F	28°C/82°F

coldest of the lakes, was created before the ice ages by a fault in the Shield. The other four (Lakes **Huron, Michigan, Erie** and **Ontario**) were formed by erosion of the original sediment over millions of years. Today their waters flow northeast down the St. Lawrence to the Atlantic. All but Lake Michigan border Ontario, giving the province a freshwater shoreline of 3,800km/2,360mi, which greatly affects its climate.

The North – The large region north of an imaginary line from the Ottawa River to Georgian Bay via Lake Nipissing is referred to as "Northern Ontario." Sparsely populated except in areas of rich mineral deposits, the land rarely rises above 460m/1500ft. Northern Ontario provides wood for the pulp and paper mills, and its many lakes have created a sportsman's paradise.

The South – The smaller region south of the Ottawa River–Georgian Bay dividing line is the most densely populated and industrialized part of Canada, especially the area at the western end of Lake Ontario, known as the **Golden Horseshoe**.
To the east lies a small agricultural triangle in the forks of the Ottawa and St. Lawrence rivers. To the west are the fertile farmlands of the Niagara Peninsula and the region called **Southwestern Ontario**.

Climate – The climate varies widely in this province. Northern Ontario experiences long, bright but cold winters, and sunny summers with hot days and cool nights. In the south the winters are less severe because of the moderating

influence of the Great Lakes. The summers are longer than in the north but much more humid, again due to the Great Lakes.

A Bit of History

Before the Europeans – Northern Ontario was inhabited by Indians whose subsistence lifestyle was similar to that of the tribes in the Northwest Territories. The south, on the other hand, was the realm of Indians of the Algonquian and Iroquoian language groups known as the **Eastern Woodlands culture** (see *Introduction to Canada*). These tribes generally lived a fairly sedentary life in organized villages around which fields of beans, corn and squash were cultivated. Every 10 or so years when the land was exhausted, the village was moved to a new site. The men hunted and fished extensively, never staying away long from their palisaded villages.
Iroquoian society was matrilineal (descent was from the mother), and the women of these tribes wielded considerable power, selecting the male chiefs, for example. In contrast Algonquin society was patrilineal.
Composed of five tribes (Mohawk, Onondaga, Seneca, Cayuga, Oneida), the **League of the Iroquois** warred repeatedly with the early French settlers and defeated and dispersed the **Huron**, another Iroquoian group.

Part of New France – What is now Ontario was crisscrossed by most of the 17C and 18C French explorers, many in pursuit of furs. First to visit was **Étienne Brûlé,** followed by **Champlain, Radis-**

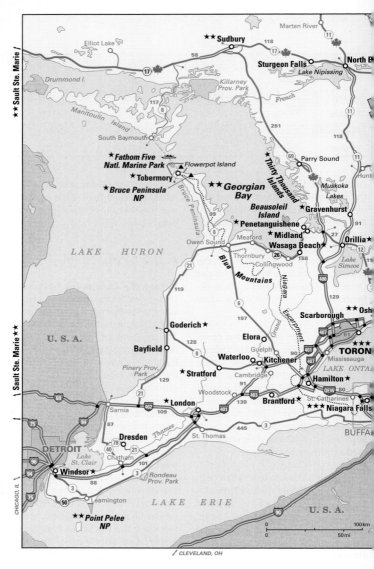

son and **Groseilliers** in their search for a route to Hudson Bay; Marquette and Jolliet in their search for a river flowing west from Lake Superior; and **Sieur de La Salle** on his famous trip down the Mississippi. In 1639 the **Jesuits** established a mission on the shores of Georgian Bay to convert the Huron to Christianity. In 1650 the settlement succumbed to attacks by the Iroquois, who martyred five of the Jesuit fathers. In the early 18C,

farms were laid out on the shores of the Detroit River in Southwest Ontario. At the same time, the **Hudson's Bay Company** was establishing itself in the province's northern section. In 1673 a post was founded at **Moosonee** on James Bay, which claims to be Ontario's oldest settlement.

Arrival of the Loyalists – When the American colonies revolted against British rule in 1775, many refused to join the

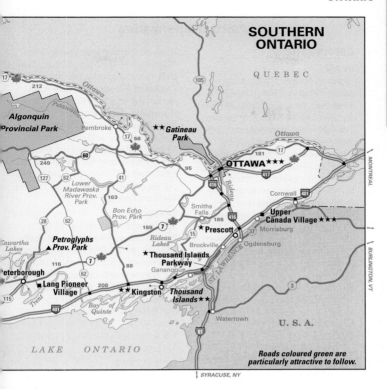

SOUTHERN ONTARIO

QUEBEC

Algonquin Provincial Park

Pembroke

★★ *Gatineau Park*

Ottawa

OTTAWA ★★★

Lower Madawaska River Prov. Park

Cornwall

Bon Echo Prov. Park

Smiths Falls

Upper Canada Village ★★★

Morrisburg

Petroglyphs Prov. Park

Rideau Lakes

★ **Prescott**

Ogdensburg

Brockville

Peterborough

★ **Thousand Islands Parkway**

Gananoque

■ **Lang Pioneer Village**

Bay of Quinte

★★ **Kingston**

Thousand Islands ★★

Watertown

U. S. A.

LAKE   ONTARIO

Roads coloured green are particularly attractive to follow.

SYRACUSE, NY

MONTREAL

BURLINGTON VT

rebels. Called Loyalists (or "Tories," to use the American term), most fled at the end of the Revolution.

An estimated 80,000 Loyalists settled in Canada—in Nova Scotia, New Brunswick, Prince Edward Island, the Eastern Townships of Quebec, the St. Lawrence Valley and the Niagara Peninsula. Among the Loyalists in Ontario were Indians of the Six Nations **Iroquois Confederacy** (the Tuscarora joined the five-nation Iroquois league in 1722) who, under their great chief **Joseph Brant**, had fought for the British. The arrival of such a great number of people—one of the largest mass movements of the time—created, almost overnight, the province of Upper Canada (Lower Canada being present-day Quebec).

American Invasion – In 1812 the Americans, infuriated by British high-handedness on the open seas, declared war and invaded Canada, hoping to seize it quickly while the British were preoccupied fighting Napoleon in Europe. The ensuing war was fought mainly in Upper Canada. Naval encounters occurred on the Great Lakes, during which Toronto was looted and burned. There was fighting in the Niagara Peninsula, where **Isaac Brock** and **Laura Secord** established their names in Canadian history, and along the St. Lawrence, particularly at **Crysler's Farm** (*see UPPER CANADA VILLAGE*).

Toward Confederation – The British government encouraged immigration to Upper Canada to bolster the population against further American attack. Approximately 1.5 million people crossed the Atlantic from 1820 to 1840 to seek a better life in Ontario.

Fresh from a struggle to promote electoral reform in England, immigrants found Canada backward. Real political power lay with the governor and a council dominated by several well-connected groups known as the **Family Compact.** Opposition to this system was led by a fiery Scot, **William Lyon Mackenzie**,

217

Practical Information

GETTING THERE

BY AIR

Flights to Toronto's Pearson International Airport *(25km/15mi west of downtown. Terminal 1 ☎416-247-7678, Terminal 3 ☎416-7765100 or toll-free 1-866-207-1690. www.gtaa.com)* are available via major domestic and international carriers. **Air Canada** *(☎toll-free 1-888-247-2262 Canada/US)* and its affiliates provide connections to regions throughout the province. **Public transportation** (bus and subway) links the airport to the greater metropolitan area *(☎416-869-3200 or toll-free 1-888-438-6646. www.gotransit. com).* **Taxis** generally offer a flat rate to downtown *(☜about $40).* Airport **shuttle service** to and from major downtown hotels, subway stops and landmarks: Airport Express Aeroport *(☜$17 one way. ☎905-564-3232. www. torontoairportexpress.com).* Major **car rental** agencies at the airport.

BY BUS AND TRAIN

The major intercity **bus** line is Greyhound *(☎416-367-8747, or toll-free 1-800-661-8747(Canada) or 1-800-231-2222(US). www.greyhound.ca).* **VIA Rail,** Canada's national passenger service, links many cities within the province *(☎toll-free 1-888-842-7245 (Canada/US). www.viarail.ca).*

GENERAL INFORMATION

ACCOMMODATIONS AND VISITOR INFORMATION

The government tourist office produces annually updated regional guides that list accommodations, camping facilities, attractions and travel centres. Contact **Ontario Tourism Marketing**, 10th Floor, Hearst Block, 900 Bay St, Toronto, ON, M7A 2E1. ☎toll-free 1-800-668-2746. www.ontariotravel.net. This website has a wealth of very useful information for travellers to Ontario.

ROAD REGULATIONS

The province has good paved roads. Speed limits, unless otherwise posted, are 100km/h (60mph) on freeways, 90km/h (55mph) on the Trans-Canada routes, and 80km/h (50mph) on most highways and rural roads. The speed limits in cities and towns range from 40km/hr to 60km/h (25–40mph). **Seat belt** use is mandatory. For listings of the **Canadian Automobile Assn. (CAA)**, consult the local telephone directory or the website *(www.caa.ca).*

Time Zones – Most of Ontario is on Eastern Standard Time. Daylight Saving Time is observed from the 2nd Sunday in March to the 1st Sunday in November. In the western third of the province (west of longitude 90°) Central Standard Time applies.

TAXES

In addition to the national 5% GST, Ontario levies an 8% provincial retail sales tax (RST), a 10% alcoholic beverages tax and a 5% accommodation tax. Non-residents can request rebates of the RST (a receipt must total $50 or more) from Retail Sales Tax, 5 Park Home Ave., Suite 200, North York, ON, M2N 6W8. ☎416-222-3226 or toll-free 1-800-263-7965 (Canada) or 1-905-432-3332 (outside Canada).

LIQUOR LAWS

The legal drinking age is 19. Liquor is sold in government stores.

PROVINCIAL HOLIDAY

Civic Holiday: 1st Monday in August

RECREATION

OUTDOOR ACTIVITIES

Water sports – Scenic routes to explore by boat are the Rideau Canal and lakes from Ottawa to Kingston, and the Trent-Severn system from Trenton to Georgian Bay via the Kawartha Lakes and Lake Simcoe. **Canoeing** is one of the most popular outdoor activities, ranging from lake and river to whitewater canoeing.

Many outfitters offer an array of excursions that include transportation, lodging, equipment and the service of experienced guides. The best-known regions are **Algonquin Provincial Park** *(☎705-633-5572. www.algonquinpark.on.ca),* which has 1,500km/900mi of canoe routes, and **Quetico Provincial Park** *(☎807-597-2735. www.ontarioparks.com),* through which the Boundary Waters Fur Trade Canoe Route passes with 43 portages along 523km/325mi. For additional information, contact Paddle Canada. *(PO Box 20069 RPO Taylor-Kidd, Kingston ON, K7P 2T6. ☏1-888-252-6292. www.paddlingcanada.com).*

Hiking – The famous Bruce Trail follows the Niagara Escarpment for 692km/430mi across the southern part of the province. Hikers pass through wilderness on the Coastal Trail along the shores of Lake Superior in **Pukaskwa National Park** *(☏807-229-0801; www.pc.gc.ca).*

Fishing – Ontario is a fisherman's paradise, particularly in the north, where many fly-in lodges arrange expeditions. Nonresidents must obtain a license, available from local sporting good stores. For information on seasons, catch and possession limits contact the Natural Heritage Information Centre, *(300 Water St., Peterborough, ON, K9J 8M5. ☏416-314-2000. www.mnr.gov.on.ca/mnr/fishing).*

Skiing – Thunder Bay, Blue Mountain (Collingwood), and the Gatineau Hills (Ottawa) are popular alpine skiing and snowboarding areas. Cross-country skiing is widely practiced in parks and centres across the province. Contact the Ontario Snow Resorts Association, 125 Napier Street, PO Box 757 Collingwood, ON. L9Y 4E8. ☏705-443-5450. www.skiontario.on.ca.

SPECIAL EXCURSIONS

Several **white-water rafting** excursions, led by experienced guides, are available on the Ottawa River *(May–Sept; round-trip 4-6hrs. From ☞$105, including equipment & meals. Accommodations extra. Reservations required. Wilderness Tours, Box 89, Beachburg, ON, K0J 1C0 ☏613-646-2291 or toll-free 888-723-8669. www.wildernesstours.com).*

A fascinating all-day train trip, the **Polar Bear Express**, takes the traveller across terrains of giant forests, bushland and muskeg through the Arctic watershed to Moosonee on Hudson Bay. Arriving at midday, visitors have ample time to tour Ontario's oldest English settlement, founded by the Hudson's Bay Co. in 1673. *(Departs from Cochrane late Jun–Labour Day Mon-Fri 9am, returns to Cochrane 10pm. Reservations required. Round trip ☞$90 adult. ✕ & ☐. Ontario*

Northland, 200 Railway St, Cochrane ON, P1B 8L3. ☏ 705-472-5338 or toll-free 1-800-268-9281. www.polarbearexpress.ca).

Luxury steamboat cruising can be enjoyed aboard **MV Canadian Empress**. Cruises include shore visits to historic sites and to Ottawa, Montreal, Quebec City and other cities. Trips of 5–7 days available *(Depart from either Kingston of Quebec City. Mid-May–late Oct.Reservations required. Contact St. Lawrence Cruise Lines, Inc., 253 Ontario St., Kingston, ON, K7L 2Z4; ☏613-549-8091, toll-free-1-800-267-7868. www.stlawrencecruiselines.com).*

PRINCIPAL FESTIVALS

Feb	**Winterlude,** Ottawa	
Apr	**Maple Syrup Festival,** Elmira	
Apr–Nov	**Shaw Festival,** Niagara-on-the-Lake	
May	**Blossom Festival,** Niagara Falls	
	Canadian Tulip Festival, Ottawa	
May–Nov	**Stratford Festival,** Stratford	
Jun	**Metro International Caravan,** Toronto	
Jun–Jul	**International Freedom Festival,** Windsor	
Jul	**Great Rendezvous,** Thunder Bay	
	Molson Indy, Toronto	
Jul-Aug	**Caribana,** Toronto	
Aug	**Rockhound Gemboree,** Bancroft	
	Glengarry Highland Games, Maxville	
	Six Nations Native Pageant, Brantford	
	Summerfolk, Owen Sound	
Aug–Sept	**Canadian National Exhibition,** Toronto	
Sept	**Internatonal Film Festival,** Toronto	
	Niagara Grape and Wine Festival, St. Catharines	
Oct	**Oktoberfest,** Kitchener-Waterloo	
Nov	**Royal Agricultural Winter Fair,** Toronto	
Nov–Jan	**Winter Festival of Lights,** Niagara Falls	

who eventually resorted to armed revolt in 1837. While the uprising was quickly suppressed, it did persuade Britain to grant "responsible government." In 1841 Upper and Lower Canada were reunited as the Province of Canada. This union fostered a movement to unite all British colonies in North America, led by Ontario politician **John A. Macdonald** and his Quebec colleague **George-Étienne Cartier.** When union (Canadian Confederation) was achieved in 1867, Upper Canada officially took the name of Ontario.

Economy

Agriculture – The southern part of the province boasts some of the richest soil in Canada as well as the province's longest frost-free season. Dairy farming is the predominant activity in the southeast corner. Soybean and field corn are the staple crops of the southwest. The section of the Niagara Peninsula on the shores of Lake Ontario sheltered by the Niagara Escarpment is Ontario's most important **fruit-growing** region and a **wine-making** industry thrives.

Mining – No other province is as rich in minerals as Ontario, one of the world's largest suppliers of nickel, and a major producer of gold, silver, platinum, uranium, zinc, copper and a range of structural materials. The **Sudbury Igneous Complex** is the largest single source of nickel in the world. Platinum, copper, cobalt, silver, gold, selenium, sulphur compounds and tellurium are also extracted from the ore.

Forests, Fishing, Furs and Hydroelectricity – The province is still largely covered with forest, despite harvesting in the last century. Today pulp, paper and sawn lumber are the main products, and Ontario ranks third after British Columbia and Quebec in the value of total production. Ontario leads the rest of Canada in the value of fish taken from inland waters, thanks to the province's 250,000 lakes, and four of the Great Lakes. Fur production is still carried on both by trapping and fur farms. The harnessing of the Niagara River, the St. Lawrence and other waters was essential for industrial development. Today Ontario ranks third after Quebec and British Columbia in hydroelectric output.

Manufacturing – Motor-vehicles and parts manufacturing is a major industry in Ontario, but also important are the production of telecommunications systems, electronics and electrical machinery, primary and fabricated metals, rubber, chemical goods and food products, as well as printing and publishing. Most of these industries are concentrated in the Greater Toronto Area and along the Highway 401 corridor from Windsor to Kingston. Other industrial regions of significance include Sarnia (petrochemicals), Niagara (auto parts), Sault Ste. Marie (steel and paper) and Ottawa-Carleton (telecommunications, high technology).

Great Lakes/St. Lawrence Seaway System – Completed in 1959, this network of lakes, rivers, locks and canals extends 3,790km/2,350mi from the Atlantic Ocean to the western end of the Great Lakes.

Cheap water transportation on this system has been of unparalleled importance to the development of Ontario.

The New Economy – Biotechnology and information and communications technologies in Ontario are centred primarily in Toronto and Ottawa, although the provincial economy is still dominated by the manufacturing sector. Toronto is a leader in new media and in **film and television** production as well. Tourism in Ontario is the country's largest such industry; the province attracts some 48 percent of visitors to Canada and generates about 37 percent of the nation's income from this source.

BRANTFORD ★

POPULATION 90,192 – MAP P 242

Named for Six Nations chief Joseph Brant, this manufacturing city, located on the banks of the Grand River, is also famous as the family home of inventor **Alexander Graham Bell** and birthplace of hockey great **Wayne Gretzky.**

- **Information:** Tourist Centre, 399 Wayne Gretzky Parkway, ☎519-751-9900, toll-free 1-800-265-6299. www.visitbrantford.ca
- **Orient Yourself:** Brantford is southwest of Toronto, lying on Hwy 403 between Hamilton in the east and Woodstock in the west.
- **Don't Miss:** The Grand River provides canoeing opportunities, and the Trans-Canada hiking and biking trail runs through town. Ask at the Tourist Centre.
- **Organizing Your Time:** Brantford is about an hour's drive from Toronto, and about the same distance to Niagara Falls.
- **Especially for Kids:** The Wayne Gretsky Sports Centre.
- **Also See:** HAMILTON, LONDON, KITCHENER-WATERLOO, NIAGARA FALLS

A Bit of History

Brantford stands in the valley of the Grand River on land given to the Six Nations Indians in 1784 by the British government. Led by Chief **Joseph Brant** (1742-1807), these Native Americans, like other Loyalists, fled the US after the Revolution. European settlers purchased land from the Indians in 1830, and the present city was founded, retaining the old name, Brant's Ford. The Indian reserve to the south is the scene every August of the **Six Nations Native Pageant**.

Sights

Bell Homestead National Historic Site★

From downtown, take Colborne St. West across Grand River, turn left on Mt. Pleas-ant St. and left again on Tutela Heights Rd. Bell Homestead National Historic Site, 94 Tutela Heights Rd., Brantford ON, N3T 1A1. Visit by guided tour (45min) only. Open year-round Tue–Sun 9:30am–4:30pm. Closed Jan 1 & Dec 24-26. $5 adult. ☎519-756-6220. www.bellhomestead.on.ca.

In 1870 Alexander Graham Bell (1847-1922) left Scotland and took a job in Boston as a teacher of the deaf. While trying to reproduce sounds visibly for his deaf pupils, he discovered how to transmit speech along an electrified wire, hence the telephone. The first "long distance" call was made from his parent' home in Brantford when Bell, in Paris, Ontario *(about 11km/7mi away)*, was able to hear his father's voice.

This house (1858) is furnished much as it would have been in Alexander Graham Bell's day. Next door is an early tel-

The Great Gretzky

Born in Brantford, Ontario, **Wayne Gretzky** (b.1961) is revered in Canada and beyond as the National Hockey League's greatest player. A backyard ice-skater at age two, first coached by his father, he went on to become NHL's most valuable player eight years in a row. For four seasons in the 1980s, he led his team, the Edmonton Oilers, to victory in Stanley Cup competitions. For seven consecutive years, he was awarded the leading NHL scorer trophy. His native city adores him: Wayne Gretzky Parkway, the annual Wayne Gretzky International Hockey Tournament, and the **Wayne Gretzky Sports Centre** are all named in his honor. The Centre has three ice rinks, an Olympic swimming pool and many other facilities. *(254 North Park St., Brantford ON, N3R 4L1. ☎519-756-9900. www.visitbrantford.ca).*

Address Book

WHERE TO EAT

$$ John Peel Steak and Seafood – 48 Dalhousie St., Brantford ON, N3T 2H8 ☎519-753-7337. www.johnpeel.ca. A fixture since 1974, John Peel's serves fine steaks along with the area's best wine selection. Hot apple beignets with ice cream or crème caramel tempt diners for dessert. In spring and summer, live jazz on selected Wednesdays.

$$$ Olde School Restaurant – 687 Powerline Rd., Brantford ON, N3T 5L8. 2km off Hwy 403. ☎519-753-3131 or 888-448-3131. www.theoldeschoolrestaurant.ca. ♿📺. This 19C brick school building is now a popular eating spot, awash in Victorian details like stained-glass windows and ornate light fixtures. It is a bit out of the way, toward the town of Paris, but the Queen visited in 1997. The extensive menu is resolutely conventional.

ephone exchange and displays on the development of the telephone.

Woodland Cultural Centre

184 Mohawk St., PO Box 1506, Brantford ON, N3T 5V6. ♿🕐*Open year-round Mon–Fri 9am–4pm, weekends 10am–5pm.* 🕐*Closed major holidays.* 💲*$5 (museum).* ☎*519-759-2650. www.woodland-centre. on.ca.*

The **museum**'s highlight is the Constitution of the League of Five Nations (1452)

made of shell beads and string. The interior of a 19C longhouse depicts the life of the Eastern Woodlands Indians.

A short drive away stands the oldest Protestant church in Ontario, **Her Majesty's Royal Chapel of the Mohawks**. (*Mailing address: PO Box 22074, 794 Colborne St. E., Brantford ON, N3S 7V1.* ♿🕐*Open July–Labour Day daily 10am–6pm, May–Jun & Sept–Oct Wed–Sun 1pm–5pm.* 💲*Contribution requested.* ☎*519-756-0240). www.mohawkchapel.ca*

DRESDEN

MAP P 216

The country around this small manufacturing centre was first settled by black slaves who fled the US for freedom in British North America. **Josiah Henson**, arriving in Ontario with his family in 1830, purchased land in the Dresden area, established a refuge for other fugitives and founded a school. Unable to write, Henson dictated the story of his life *(The Life of Josiah Henson—Formerly a Slave)*, which so impressed **Harriet Beecher Stowe** that she used him as the model for her influential novel *Uncle Tom's Cabin*.

🔲 **Information:** www.dresden.ca

▶ **Orient Yourself:** Dresden is in southwestern Ontario, between Windsor and London. Leave Hwy 401 (TransCanada Hwy) at exit 101, and follow signage to Hwy 21, then to Dresden. Dresden is about an hour from London.

🕑 **Also See:** LONDON, WINDSOR. POINT PELEE NATIONAL PARK

Sight

Uncle Tom's Cabin Historic Site★

1.6km/1mi west off Hwy. 21. 29251 Uncle Tom's Road, Dresden ON, ♿🕐*Open mid-May–Oct Tue–Sat 10am–4pm, Sun noon–4pm (July–Aug open daily).* 💲*$6.25.* ☎*519-683-2978. www.uncletomscabin.org.*

This collection of wooden buildings includes Henson's house (Uncle Tom's Cabin), a simple church of the same era as the one in which he preached and a fugitive slave's house. In the museum there are items recalling the era of slavery such as posters advertising slave sales.

GEORGIAN BAY★★

MAP P 216

Named for George IV of England, this immense bay off Lake Huron is a popular vacation spot; summer cottages line its shores and islands. More than a resort area, however, the region supports considerable light industry. Owen Sound, Collingwood, Midland, Port McNicoll and Parry Sound are fair-size ports with grain elevators.

- **Information:** Chamber of Commerce, Tobermory, ☎519-596-2452. www.tobermory.org.
- ▶ **Orient Yourself:** The Georgian Bay is almost a lake in itself, cut off from the rest of Lake Huron by the Bruce Penninsula and Manitoulin Island.
- **Don't Miss:** One of the cruises around the islands.
- **Organizing Your Time:** You will need a few days to tour the bay area.
- **Kids Especially for Kids:** Wasaga Beach, especially the Super Slide.
- **Also See:** SUDBURY, NORTH BAY, ORILLA, GRAVENHURST

Geographical Notes

Immortalized by the Group of Seven painters, the eastern and northern shorelines are wild and rocky with thousands of islands. The western and part of the southern shores form a section of the **Niagara Escarpment;** this ridge of limestone crosses Ontario from Niagara Falls, mounts the Bruce Peninsula, submerges and then resurfaces to form Manitoulin and other islands, and ends in Wisconsin. In contrast, the coast along the western side of the Midland Peninsula has long sandy stretches, especially in the region of Wasaga Beach. In the southeast corner of the bay is Georgian Bay Islands National Park, established in 1929.

A Bit of History

Étienne Brûlé, one of Champlain's men, visited Georgian Bay in 1610. Fur traders and Jesuits soon followed, arriving via the 1,300km/800mi canoe route from Quebec. Jesuits built a mission post called Sainte-Marie near the present site of Midland in 1639. At this time, the Huron were under attack from the Iroquois tribes to the south. Caught in the middle, several Jesuit fathers were killed after suffering incredible torture. The atrocities led to the abandonment of Sainte-Marie in 1649. After the Jesuits'

return to Quebec and the Huron's defeat, peace was restored until the early-19C when warfare erupted between the British and Americans over control of the Great Lakes.

Historical Sights

Midland★

This busy city on the bay is well known for its numerous historical and natural attractions.

Sainte-Marie among the Hurons★★

Hwy. 12 E. Midland ON, L4R 4K8. ✗🅿️⏱️*Open mid-May–early-Oct daily 10am–5pm. Early May and late Oct, Mon–Fri 10am–5pm.* 💲*$11.25 adult.* ☎*705-526-7838. www.saintemarie-mongthehurons.on.ca.*

The mission established by the Jesuits in 1639 and destroyed by them before their retreat in 1649 has been reconstructed.

An audiovisual presentation *(17min)* explains the mission's history and should be viewed before the rest of the visit. The chapel, forge, saw pit, carpentry shop, residences and native area are peopled by guides in 17C costume.

Beside Sainte-Marie is the **Wye Marsh Wildlife Centre**, with nature trails, a boardwalk and an observation tower

223

(16160 Highway 12 E, PO Box 100, Midland ON, L4R 4K6. ♿⏰Open daily year-round 9am–5pm. ⌖$10 adult. ☎705-526-7809. www.wyemarsh.com).

Martyrs' Shrine★

5km/3mi east of Midland on Hwy. 12 near Wildlife Centre. PO Box 7, Highway 12, Midland ON, L4R 4K6. ✕♿⏰Open mid-May–early-Oct daily 8:30am–dusk. ⌖$3. ☎705-526-3788. www.martyrs-shrine.com

This twin-spired stone church was built in 1926 as a memorial to the eight Jesuit martyrs of New France killed by the Iroquois between 1642 and 1649 and declared saints in 1930. On the front portico stand **statues** of Jean de Brébeuf and Gabriel Lalemant. The church has a striking **interior** with wood panelling and a roof of sandalwood from British Columbia.

Huron Ouendat Village★

549 Little Lake Park, PO Box 638, Midland ON, L4R 4P4. ♿⏰Open May–Oct daily 9am–5pm. Rest of the year Mon–Fri 9am–5pm. ⏰Closed Good Friday & Dec 25–26. ⌖$8 adult (including museum). ☎705-526-2844. www.huroniamuseum.com.

This village is a replica of a 16C Huron community. A wooden palisade surrounds examples of the long, rectangular, bark-covered frame houses in which the Huron lived communally.

Located beside the village is the **Huronia Museum** *(same hours)*.

Penetanguishene★

12km/8mi west of Midland by Rtes. 12 and 93.

The southern entrance to this town, which has a large French-speaking community, is guarded by two angels symbolizing the harmony between the English and French cultures.

Discovery Harbour★

93 Jury Dr., Penetanquishene ON, L9M 1G1. ✕🅿⏰Open Jul–Labour Day daily 10am–5pm. Late May–Jun Mon–Fri 10am–5pm. ⏰Closed Victoria Day. ⌖$6 adult. ☎705-549-8064. www.discovery-harbour.on.ca.

On a pleasant site above Penetang harbour stands this reconstruction of a British Naval dockyard and military garrison established here after the War of 1812.

Wasaga Beach★

This popular resort is well known for its 14km/9mi stretch of white sand, its water parks and giant **Super Slide** Kids .

Nancy Island Historic Site★

In Wasaga Beach Provincial Park, on Mosley St. off Hwy. 92. 11-22nd St. N, Wasaga Beach ON, L9Z 2V9. ♿⏰Open mid-Jun–Labour Day daily 10am–6pm. Late May–mid-Jun weekends only 10am–6pm. Labour Day–early-Oct weekends 11am–5pm. ☎705-429-2728, ☎705-429-2516 (off-season). www.wasagabeachpark.com.

The museum stands on a small island near the mouth of the Nottawasaga River created by silt collecting around the hull of a schooner, the **Nancy**. During the War of 1812, the vessel was sunk by the Americans. In 1927 her hull was recovered from the silt and is now displayed in the museum.

Natural Sites

Thirty Thousand Islands★

An excellent way to see the natural beauty of Georgian Bay and its many islands is one of three boat cruises. From **Midland** town dock *(✕♿⏰departs May–Oct daily 1:45pm, additional cruises late Jun–Sept. Round-trip 2hrs 30min. ⌖$22 adult. Reservations suggested. Midland Tours Inc. ☎705-549-3388, toll-free 1-888-833-2628. www.midlandtours.com).* From **Penetanguishene** town dock *(✕⏰Departs mid-Jun–early Sept daily 2pm, also 7pm Wed & Thu, less frequently in spring and fall. Round-trip 3hrs 20min. Reservations suggested. ⌖$25. Argee Boat Cruises, Ltd. ☎705-549-7795 or toll-free 1-800-363-7447 Canada/US. www.georgianbaycruises.com).* From **Parry Sound** town dock *(✕♿⏰2hr morning cruises (Jul–Aug departs daily 10am ⌖$24) and 3hr afternoon cruises (Jun–mid-Oct daily 1pm ⌖$30). Reser-*

vations required. 30,000 Island Cruise Lines Inc. ☎705-746-2311 or toll-free 1-800-506-2628/Canada & US. www.island-queen.com).

Tobermory★

This small village, located at the tip of the Bruce Peninsula, surrounds its double harbour known as Big Tub and Little Tub. The clear blue-green waters, underwater rock formations and number of old shipwrecks also attract divers. Visitors can stroll around the marina and follow the lakeside boardwalk.

The 110m/365ft-long vessel **MS Chi-Cheemaun** provides regular ferry service to Manitoulin Island. The ship accommodates some 143 vehicles and 638 passengers and offers full meal service in its cafeteria (✕&🕒Departs late Jun–Labour Day daily 7am, 11:20am, 3:40pm & 8pm, early May–mid-Jun & rest of Sept–mid-Oct daily 8:50am & 1:30pm, additional departure Fri 6:10pm. One-way 1hr 45min. ⚲$33/car plus $14.20 adult. Owen Sound Transportation Co. ☎519-376-6601 or toll free 1-800-265-3163/Canada & US. www.ontarioferries.com).

Bruce Peninsula National Park★

PO Box Tobermory ON, N0H 2R0. &🅿🕒Open daily year-round. Visitor centre July–Labour Day daily 8am–8pm (Fri and Sat 9pm), Sept–Oct daily 9am–4pm (Sat 8am–4pm). Admin office Mon–Fri 8.30am–4pm. ⚲$10.40/car ☎519-596-2233. www.pc.gc.ca.

Established in 1987, this national park is known for its trails along the spectacular Niagara Escarpment.

Fathom Five National Marine Park★

🕒Same conditions as Bruce Penninsula National Park.

This "underwater" national marine park encompasses 20 islands and the treacherous waters off Tobermory, where lie 22 known wrecks of sail and steam vessels. Some of the islands and two of the wrecks can be seen on a **glass-bottomed boat tour** (✕&🅿Contact Blue Heron Co. ☎519-596-2999. www.blueheronco.com.

Tiny **Flowerpot Island** was at one time completely covered by the waters of

Lake Huron. Caves high up on the cliffs and two rock pillars, known as the **flowerpots**, can be closely approached by

Ontario Tourism Marketing Partnership Corp.

Halfway Rock Point, Bruce Peninsula National Park

Just east of Meaford lies the cross-roads village of Thornbury.

$$ SiSi on Main – *27 Bruce St. Thornbury ON, N0H 2P0.* ☎*519-599-7769.* Pasta, pizza, fish and excellent steaks behind this brick storefront.

$$$ White House on the Hill – *53 Bruce St., Thornbury ON, N0H 2P0.* ☎*519-599-6261)* This restaurant serves a mélange of Asian, Californian and Italian fare in a comfortable heritage house.

$$ Sterios Steak & Seafood –*81 King St. E, Thornbury ON, N0H 2P0.* ☎*519-599-5319.* Before you exit Thornbury en route to Meaford via Route 26, try the BBQ ribs here.

boat or on foot (☎*$2 day-use fee)* from the island. The tour boats afford good views of the flowerpots.

Beausoleil Island

Part of the Georgian Bay Islands National Park. Access by private boat or water taxi only from Honey Harbour (about 40km/25mi northeast of Midland via Rte. 12, Hwy. 400 and Rte. 5). ◷*Open daily year-round.* ☎*$5.45 adult day-use fee (mid-May–early Oct). Contact the park office in 901 Wye Valley Rd, Box 9, Midland, ON, L4R 4K6.* ☎*705-526-9804. www.pc.gc.ca).*

There are walking trails, a picnic area, camping and a visitor kiosk (♿◷*Open Jul–Labour Day Mon–Thu 11am–5pm, Fri–Sun 11am–7pm.)* on this island.

The Blue Mountains

56km/35mi from Wasaga Beach to Meaford by Rte. 26.

The waters of Georgian Bay lie on one side of the road and the Blue Mountains, the highest part of the Niagara Escarpment, on the other.

GODERICH ★

POPULATION 7,604 – MAP P 216

This town was founded in 1828 as the terminus of the Huron Road, a right-of-way built in the early 19C to encourage settlement. The town has wide, tree-lined residential streets that radiate like the spokes of a wheel from central, octagonal Court House Square.

- ℹ **Information:** 57 West St. ☎519-524-6600, or toll-free 1-800-280-7637. www.goderich.ca.
- ▶ **Orient Yourself:** The town sits on a bluff above the point where the Maitland River joins Lake Huron, midway between Port Elgin and Sarnia.
- ⌖ **Don't Miss:** The Queen called this "the prettiest town in Canada." Take time to stroll and admire the big houses and three beaches.
- ◷ **Organizing Your Time:** From Goodrich it is a pleasant drive north to Georgian Bay on Hwy 21.
- Kids **Especially for Kids:** The Huron Historic Gaol; harbour tugboat tours .
- ⌚ **Also See:** STRATFORD, KITCHENER

Sights

The Waterfront

- ▶ *Follow West St. from Court House Sq.*

In 1984, dredging deepened the lake to provide entry into the harbour for full-cargo vessels. Small craft berth at the city marina and a fleet of tugboats service freighters (Kids*Tugboat harbour tours (30min)* ☎*$5 adult.* ◷*May–Sept; for details, contact MacDonald Marine* ☎ *519-524-9551. www.mactug.com).* Residents and visitors alike are drawn to the sandy beaches, snack bars and extensive **boardwalk**.

Convictions and Penalties

Here's a sampling of charges and resulting fines for the quarter ending in June 1879, in the County of Huron, from the Clerk of the Peace's Office:

Nature of Charge	Amount of Penalty, Fine or Damage
Vagrancy	$ .25
Insulting Language	$1.00
An Affray	$2.00
Disorderly Conduct	$1.00
Telling Fortunes	$2.00
Fast Driving over Brussels bridge	$1.00

Huron County Museum

110 North St., Goderich ON, N7A 2T8. ♿🕐*Open mid-Apr–Dec Mon–Sat 10am–4:30pm, Sun 1pm–4:30pm. Rest of the year Mon–Fri 10am-4.30pm, Sat 1pm–4.30pm.* 🕐*Closed Sundays Jan–Mar.* 🚌$5 adult ($7.50 museum & gaol).* ☎519-524-2686. *www.huroncounty.ca/museum.*
Agricultural implements, military artifacts, and furniture are on view.

Huron Historic Gaol

181 Victoria St. North.(Mailing address same as Museum). Kids 🕐*Open mid-May–Labour Day daily 10am–4:30pm, Sept–Oct Sun–Fri 1pm–4pm, Sat 10am–4.30pm.* 🕐*Closed Nov–mid-May.* 🚌$5 ($7.50 museum & gaol).* ☎519-524-6971. *www.huroncounty.ca/museum.*
This unusual 150-year-old octagonal stone structure housed the county jail (gaol is the British spelling) until 1972. Visitors may enter the cells, library, kitchen, laundry room and outdoor yards. The top floor actually served as the courtroom (♿*see sidebar of sample penalties*).

Excursion

Bayfield

21km/13mi south by Hwy. 21. This small village near Lake Huron has a short but colorful main street, shaded by tall

WHERE TO STAY AND EAT

$$$ The Little Inn – *26 Main St., Bayfield ON, N0M 1G0.* ☎*519-565-2611 or toll-free 800-565-1832. www.littleinn. com. 28 rooms.* ✕ P Sms A former coach stop, this charming inn, operating since 1832, offers guests the simplicity of times past coupled with modern amenities such as whirlpools and working fireplaces. Rooms are individually decorated with country antiques. The airy dining room (**$$$**) is open to the public year-round. Menus change frequently here to reflect the freshest seasonal produce from Huron County. A typical summer menu might include rack of lamb, citrus-glazed pork tenderloin, or Lake Huron fish with new potatoes. Exensive wine list.

trees and brimming with interesting shops, restaurants, inns and places of worship. Surrounding tree-lined residential streets hold vacation cottages, well-kept houses, manicured gardens and trailered boats.

"The Americans are our best friends whether we like it or not."

Robert Thompson, in the House of Commons, 1960s

GRAVENHURST★

POPULATION 10,899 – MAP P 216

This attractive town with its tree-lined streets, elegant houses, and opera house (now a performing-arts centre) lies on picturesque Lake Muskoka, with its indented shoreline and numerous islands. A former logging settlement, Gravenhurst today serves as the gateway to the Muskoka Lakes area. It is also the birthplace of Dr. **Norman Bethune** (1890-1939), surgeon, inventor, advocate of socialized medicine and a national hero in China.

- **Information:** Municipal Offices 190 Harvey St. ☎705-687-3412. www.gravenhurst.ca.
- ▶ **Orient Yourself:** Gravenhurst lies at the southern end of the Muskoka lakes, east of the Georgian Bay, on Hwy 11 between Orillia and Bracebridge.
- **Don't Miss:** A lake cruise will help you appreciate why the Muskoka area is Ontario's most popular vacation region.
- **Organizing Your Time:** Gravenhurst and the Muskoka Lakes can be fit into a leisurely tour of the Georgian Bay.
- **Also See:** ORILLIA, THE GEORGIAN BAY

COTTAGE COUNTRY

Visitors to Ontario will inevitably hear references to "cottage country"—and for most Toronto residents that means the Muskoka Lakes and Georgian Bay. Other Ontarians think of area between Georgian Bay and the Ottawa River, all the way north to Algonquin Park. Some 1,600 lakes litter this largely forested landscape. During cottage season (traditionally Victoria Day to Thanksgiving) whole families abandon their homes to dwell in cabins, small houses and mansions (all called "cottages" by Canadians) around these deep-blue waters. Amenities range from the bare essentials to grandiose furnishings, a float plane and a water craft or two. The place to purchase the latest in cottage couture is the **Muskoka Store** *(Hwy. 11 N. of Gravenhurst, P1P 1R1. ☎705-687-7751. www.muskokastore.com).* This huge purveyor of stocks wooden furniture (including the ubiquitous Muskoka chair), casual clothing, canoes and kayaks, kitchen utensils, gardening tools and just about anything else cottagers need to enjoy their vacations.

Sights

Bethune Memorial House National Historic Site★

235 John St. N., Gravenhurst ON, P1P 1G4. Visit by guided tour (1hr) only, Jun–Aug daily 10am–4pm. Sept–Oct Sat–Wed 10am–4pm. *Closed Nov–May.* $4 adult. ☎705-687-4261. www.pc.gc.ca.

The son of a Presbyterian minister, Norman Bethune (1890-1939) studied medicine in Toronto, then practised in Detroit. Between 1928 and 1936, he worked as a chest surgeon in Montreal but, disillusioned with the lack of interest in socialized medicine in Canada, he departed for Spain to fight on the Republican side in the civil war. In 1938 he went to China and worked as a surgeon with the Chinese Communists fighting the Japanese, dying of blood poisoning late in 1939. Fame in his own country stemmed from Bethune's status as a hero to the Chinese.

The doctor's birthplace contains several rooms restored to their 1890s appearance, and an excellent **interpretive display** in three languages (English, French and Chinese) on his life and importance.

Steamship Cruises

Muskoka Lakes Navigation, 185 Chero-kee Lane, Gravenhurst ON, P1P 1Z9. ✕♿○Depart from Sagamo Park June–Labour Day daily. Call for departure times. Round trip 1hr–4hrs. Reservations required. ☞$16–$43 adult. ☎705-687-6667 or toll-free 1-866-687-6667. www.realmuskoka.com.

Visitors can board the **RMS Segwun** at Gravenhurst's wharf to appreciate the beauty of the lakes and see some of the summer homes along their shores.

Excursion

Algonquin Provincial Park

About 100km/60mi northeast of Graven-hurst by Rtes. 11 and 60. Park Superintend-ent, PO Box 209, Whitney ON, K0J 2M0 ✕○Open daily year-round. ☞Vehicle permit $13. ☎705-633-5572. www.algonquinpark.on.ca.

Encompassing 7,725sq km/2,983sq mi of forested wilderness in the eastern portion of the province, this popular recreation spot has hiking trails, canoe routes, camping facilities, fishing and swimming holes, winter ski runs and resident wildlife. Known as the Parkway Corridor, Route 60 traverses the southern portion of the park. Information centres are located at each entrance, and a **logging museum** near the East Gate features area history of the industry. Situated 13km/8mi northwest of the East Gate is the park's visitor centre, containing a cafe, bookstore, theatre, exhibits and an outdoor viewing deck. Two rustic resorts with dining rooms are **Killarney Mountain Lodge** *(Lake of Two Rivers, Killarney ON, P0M 2A0. ☎705-287-2242 or toll-free 1-800-461-1117 US/Canada. www.killarney.com)* and **Arowhon Pines** *(Little Joe Lake, PO Box 10001, Huntsville, ON, P1H 2G5. ☎705-633-5661 (winter 416-483-4393) or toll-free 1-866-633-5661. www.arowhonpines.ca).*

HAMILTON ★

POPULATION 504,559 – MAP P 216

The city of Hamilton has a fine landlocked harbour bounded on the lakeside by a sandbar. A canal has been cut through the bar to enable ships of the seaway to reach port with their loads of iron ore for Hamilton's huge steel mills. The sandbar is crossed by Burlington Skyway, part of the **Queen Elizabeth Way (QEW)**, which connects Toronto with Niagara Falls. Hamilton is set on the Niagara Escarpment, which swings around the end of Lake Ontario at this point, rising steeply to 76m/250ft in the city. Known locally as "the mountain," it provides pleasant parks and views.

- **Information:** Tourist Office, 34 James St. S. ☎905-546-2666 or toll-free 1-800-263-8590 or www.tourismhamilton.com
- **Orient Yourself:** Hamilton lies at the extreme western end of Lake Ontario, southwest of Toronto.
- **Parking:** Parking meters are enforced Mon–Sat, 8am–6pm. They cost $0.50 to $1/hr. There are also 19 lots and 2 covered garages.
- **Don't Miss:** The Royal Botanical Gardens offer lovely landscapes and pleasant restaurants.
- **Organizing Your Time:** Hamilton deserves at least a day of your time.
- **Especially for Kids:** The African Lion Safari Park.
- **Also See:** TORONTO, KITCHENER-WATERLOO, STRATFORD, NIAGARA FALLS, BRANTFORD

Address Book

WHERE TO EAT

$ The Gardens' Café – *In RBG Centre at the Royal Botanical Gardens.* ☎*905-527-1158, ext 540. www.rbg.ca. Open for lunch only 11am–3pm daily.* This pleasant restaurant on the grounds of the Royal Botanical Gardens overlooks Spicer Court with its seasonal plantings. Sandwiches, soups and salads and seasonally changing entrées.

$$$ Ancaster Old Mill Inn – *548 Old Dundas Rd., Ancaster ON, L9G 3J4. Exit Mohawk Rd. from Hwy. 403 West.* ☎*905-*648-1827. www.ancasteroldmill.com.* At Ancaster, just west of Hamilton, an 18C stone mill has been converted into an upscale restaurant with seven dining rooms, the most popular of which overlooks a waterfall through floor-to-ceiling windows. Two prix-fixe menus are prepared daily. An example: smoked trout and Bosc pear salad, venison on parsnip purée with seasonal vegetables and finally vanilla and plum soufflé for desert, with a selected wine for each course. A variety of breads made on the premises accompanies the meal.

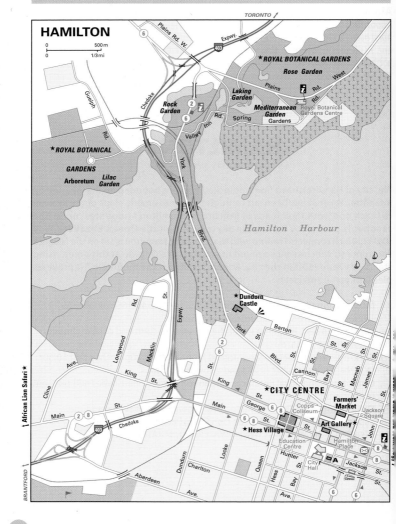

Sights

City Centre★

Downtown Hamilton has *(along Main St. between Bay and James Sts.)* several attractive buildings, in particular City Hall; the Education Centre; the Art Gallery; and Hamilton Place, a cultural centre with two theatres.

A few blocks west is **Hess Village**★ *(junction Hess and George Sts.)*, a district of older homes converted to fashionable boutiques, restaurants and cafes.

Also in the vicinity is the **farmers' market** *(55 York Blvd., Hamilton ON, L8P 4Y5. ♿🕐Open year-round Tue & Thu 7am–6pm, Fri 8am–6pm, Sat 6am–6pm. ☏905-546-2096)*, one of Ontario's largest indoor markets, selling the produce of the Niagara Peninsula.

Art Gallery★

123 King St. W., Hamilton ON, L8P 4S8. ♿✕🕐Open year-round from noon: Tue–Wed to 7pm, Thu–Fri to 9pm, Sat–Sun to 5pm. 🕐Closed Mon except holidays. ☏$12 adult. ☏905-527-6610. www.artgalleryofhamilton.on.ca.

This distinctive concrete structure stands across a plaza from City Hall.

Whitehern Historic House and Garden (A)

41 Jackson St. W., Hamilton ON, L8P 1L3. ✎Visit by guided tour (1hr) only. 🕐Mid-Jun–Labour Day Tue–Sun 11am–4pm. Rest of the year Tue–Sun 1pm–4pm. 🕐Closed Jan 1 & Dec 25–26. ☏$6 adult. ☏905-546-2018. www.myhamilton.ca.

In small but pleasant gardens surrounded by Hamilton's city centre, this Georgian house was the residence until 1968 of three generations of the McQuesten family, which inspired such projects as the Royal Botanical Gardens and the Niagara Parkway.

Dundurn National Historic Site★

610 York Blvd, L8R 3H1. ✎Visit by guided tour (1hr) only, ✕🕐July–Labour Day daily 10am–4pm. Rest of the year Tue–Sun noon–4pm. 🕐Closed Jan 1, Good Friday & Dec 25. ☏$10 adult. ☏905-546-2872. www.myhamilton.ca

This grand stone house with its Neo-classical portico entry stands on a hill in Dundurn Park, with a good **view** of the bay and city. The residence was completed in 1835 by Sir **Allan Napier MacNab**, prime minister of the Province of Canada from 1854 to 1856. Of particular interest is the basement, the domain of an army of servants.

Royal Botanical Gardens★

680 Plains Rd. W., Hamilton/Burlongton ON, L7T 4H4. ✕🕐RBG Centre open daily 10am–dusk. Outdoor gardens open May–mid-Oct. 🕐Closed Dec 25, Jan 1. ☏$8 adult. ☏905-527-1158. www.rbg.ca. Free shuttle bus May–Oct.

These gardens occupy 1,000ha/2,700 acres of land at the western tip of Lake Ontario. Much of this area is natural parkland with walking trails.

Museum of Steam and Technology★

900 Woodward Ave., Hamilton, ON, L8H 7N2. Just south of Queen Elizabeth Way (QEW). 🕐Open Jun–Labour Day Tue–Sun 11am–4pm. Rest of the year Tue–Sun noon–4pm. 🕐Closed Jan 1, Dec 25-26. ☏$6 adult. ☏905-546-4797. www.myhamilton.ca.

Hamilton's 1859 water-pumping station now provides a rare example of 19C steam technology with two Gartshore steam-powered beam engines in full working order.

Excursion

African Lion Safari★

Kids 32km/20mi northwest by Hwy. 8, right on Rte. 52 North after Rockton and left on Safari Rd. RR#1, Cambridge ON, N1R 5S2. ✕♿🕐Open late Jun–Aug daily 10am–5:30pm. Early May–Jun & Sept–early-Oct daily 10am–4pm. ☏$27. ☏519-623-2620 or toll-free 1-800-461-9453 (US/Canada). www.lionsafari.com.

Visitors drive their own cars *(safari tram available at additional cost)* through various enclosures of African and North American free-roaming animals. The monkey jungle contains about 100 African baboons that will climb over your car and steal any part they can.

KINGSTON AND THE THOUSAND ISLANDS★★

MAP P 217

This onetime capital of the Province of Canada owes its political and economic development to its location at the junction of Lake Ontario and the St. Lawrence River. The former colonial stronghold is home to several military colleges

- 🛈 **Information:** Tourist Office, 209 Ontario St. ☎613-548-4415, toll-free 1-888-855-4555. www.cityofkingson.ca/visitors
- ▶ **Orient Yourself:** The city of Kingston lies on the north shore of Lake Ontario, where the St. Lawrence River leaves the lake in a channel full of islands.
- 🅿 **Parking:** Meters operate downtown Kingston Mon–Sat 9.30am–5.30pm, 2hr limit, $1.50 per hour. In city parking lots with attendants, the first hour is free.
- ⊘ **Don't Miss:** Take a cruise around the 1000 islands.
- 🕐 **Organizing Your Time:** If you plan to visit an American island, be sure to carry proper documents. *♿see Know Before you Go.*
- ♿ **Also See:** PETERBOROUGH, OTTAWA

Kingston★★

A French fur-trading post established here in 1673 was abandoned when New France fell. The settlement established by Loyalists soon became an important British naval base and dockyard, and a fort was built to protect it during the War of 1812. The Rideau Canal increased the town's importance. Kingston served as capital of the Province of Canada from 1841 to 1843.

Today the **Royal Military College** (Fort Frederick), the Canadian Army Staff College and the National Defence College are located here. Kingston is a pleasant city, with tree-lined streets, parks, and public buildings constructed of local limestone. Among these is the handsome **City Hall**★ in Confederation Park on the harbour; the **Court House**★ with a small dome similar to that of City Hall; the **Cathedral of St. George,** which is reminiscent of Christopher Wren's London churches; the **Grant Hall** building of Queen's University; and some of the buildings of the Royal Military College.

Sights

Marine Museum of the Great Lakes★
55 Ontario St, Kingston ON, K7L 2Y2. ♿✕🕐Open May–Oct daily 10am–5pm. Rest of the year Mon–Fri 10am–4pm. 🕐Closed major holidays. ☞$6.50. ☎613-542-2261. www.marmuseum.ca.
Set in old shipbuilding works beside Lake Ontario, this museum has displays on sail and steam vessels.

Pump House Steam Museum
23 Ontario St. Mailing address: City hall, 216 Ontario St, Kingston ON, K7L 2Z3. 🕐Open Jun–Labour Day daily 10am–4pm. ☞$3.75. ☎613-542-0543. www.cityofkingston.ca.
Two enormous 1897 steam pumps once used in Kingston's 1849 pumping station have been restored.

Murney Tower
West of harbour. 🕐Open mid-May–Labour Day daily 10am–5pm. ☞$2. ☎613-544-9925. www.cityofkingston.ca or www.pc.gc.ca
This 1848 squat stone tower in a pleasant park beside the lake is one of Kingston's Martello towers, a National Historic Site. Inside, living quarters of the garrison have been re-created.

Ontario Tourism Marketing Partnership Corp.

Kingston Harbour, with City Hall visible in the background.

Address Book

WHERE TO STAY

$$ Hotel Belvedere –*141 King St. E., Kingston ON, K7L 2Z9.* ☎613-548-1565 or toll-free 1-800-559-0584. www.hotelbelvedere.com. 20 rooms. 🅿 🖵. This well-situated hotel, built in 1880, exudes Edwardian elegance throughout, from its antique-appointed sitting room to its fireplace- and duvet-equipped guest quarters. On the patio are umbrella-shaded tables and seasonal plantings.

$$ The Rosemount Inn and Spa – *46 Sydenham St. S., Kingston ON, K7L 3H1.* ☎613-531-8844 or toll-free 1-888-871-8844. www.rosemountinn.com. Two night minimum on weekends. 9 rooms, 2 suites. 🅿 🆂🅿🅰 🖵.Guests at this stately Italianate stone house (c.1848) enjoy its wicker-furnished porch, lovely gardens, gourmet breakfasts and convenient walking distance to the downtown core.

WHERE TO EAT

$ Chez Piggy–*68-R Princess St., Kingston, ON, K7L 1A5.* ☎613-549-7673. www.chezpiggy.com. In a restored livery stable, Piggy's offers lunch, dinner and Sunday brunch, served indoors or on the popular garden patio. The delicious bread comes from the owners' next-door bakery, Pan Chancho.

$$ Le Chien Noir Bistro – *69 Brock St., Kingston ON, K7L 1R8.* ☎613-549-5635. www.lechiennoir.com. This bistro serves up honest French fare for lunch, dinner

and Sunday brunch. One surprise: a gourmet version of *poutine*, the Québécois snack staple.

AFTER HOURS

The Kingston Brewing Company–*34 Clarence St., Kingston ON,* .☎613-542-4978) Open Mon–Sat 11am–1am, Sun 11:30am–12:30am. Behind the Victorian storefront, house-brewed beer.

$ Tir nan Og Irish Pub –*200 Ontario St. Kingston ON, K7L 4H1.* ☎613-544-7474. Sun–Tue 11am–1am, Wed–Sat 11am–2am. Irish beer, food and song.

WHERE TO SHOP

Earth to Spirit Trading Company –*340 King St. E., Kingston ON, K7L 3B6.* ☎613-536-5252. www.earthtospirit.com. Fair-trade baskets, crafts, jewellery and other gift items from around the world.

A-1 Clothing Ltd. – *358 King St. E., Kingston ON, K7L 3B6.* ☎613-548-8732. www.aoneclothing.com. Rugged gear, attire and footwear for outdoor adventurers—especially the city's many sailing enthusiasts.

LEISURE

Dolce Bella Spa – *8 Cataraqui St., Kingston ON, K7? 1Z7.* ☎613-544-1166 or toll-free 1-877-424-4417. www.dolcebellaspa.com. A restored woolen mill overlooking the Cataraqui River, this polished day spa and hair salon provides treatments for men and women.

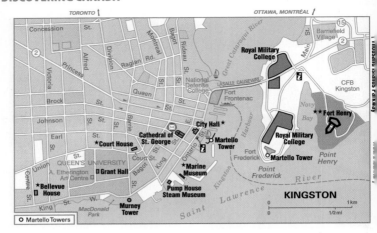

Bellevue House★

25 Centre St., Kingston ON, K7L 4E5. ♿ⓉOpen Jun–Labour Day daily 9am–6pm. Apr–May & Sept–Oct daily 10am–5pm. ⓉClosed Nov–Mar. ⚲$4. ☎613-545-8666. www.pc.gc.ca.

From 1848 to 1849 this 1840 Italian-styled villa was the residence of Canada's first prime minister, **Sir John A. Macdonald** (1815-91), who spent much of his youth in Kingston and opened his first law office in the city in 1835. The house is furnished to reflect Macdonald's time of residence.

Fort Henry★★

County Road 2, east of downtown. Contact Rideau Canal National Historic Site, 43A Beckwith St. S., Smiths Falls ON, K7A 2A8. ✕ⓉOpen mid-May–Sept daily 10am–5pm. ⚲$11. ☎613-542-7388. www.forthenry.com. or www.pc.gc.ca.

Completed in 1837, this stone fortress is set on a peninsula above Lake Ontario. Restored in 1938 and now a National Historic Site, it is best known today for the **Fort Henry Guard**, a troop of students who re-create the life of the 19C British soldier and guide visitors. In particular, the **garrison parade** *(daily)* should not be missed.

The Thousand Islands★★

🛈*1000 Islands Tourist Office, PO Box 69, Lansdowne ON, K0E 1L0.* ☎315-482-2520. www.visit1000islands.com

The Thousand Islands

Tour boat, The Thousand Islands

Gwen Cannon/MICHELIN

As it leaves Lake Ontario, the St. Lawrence River is littered, for an 80km/50mi stretch, with about 1,000 islands. All of the islands are of Precambrian rock, the remnants of the **Frontenac Axis**, which links the Canadian Shield with the Adirondacks of New York state. The international border passes among them.

Visit

Boat Trips★★

Several companies offer cruises among the islands. **From Kingston**: *Kingston 1000 Islands Cruises* ☎613-549-5544, *toll-free 1-800-848-0011. www.1000islandscruises.ca.* **From Gananoque** or **from Ivy Lea**: *Gananoque Boat Line* ☎613-659-2293, *or toll-free 1-800-171-4837. www.ganboatline.com.* **From Rockport**: *Rockport Boat Line*

☎613-659-3402 or toll-free 1-800-563-8687. www.rockportcruises.com.

Thousand Islands Parkway★

Begins 3km/1.8mi east of Gananoque at Interchange 648 (Hwy. 401). 37km/23mi to Interchange 685 (Hwy. 401), south of Brockville.
This scenic drive follows the shore of the St. Lawrence. **Skydeck** (&⊙*Open mid-April–Oct daily 9am–dusk.* ⊛*$9.* ☎613-659-2335. www.1000islandsskydeck.com) on Hill Island provides a fine **view**★ of the islands *(take bridge to island, toll $2; do not enter US).*
At Mallorytown Landing is the visitor centre for **St. Lawrence Islands National Park** *(2 County Rd 5, RR3, Mallorytown ON,K0E 1R0.* &⊙*Open daily Mid-May–early Oct 10am–4pm.* ⊛*Parking $7/day.* ☎613-923-5261. www. pc.gc.ca).*

KITCHENER–WATERLOO

POPULATION 302,143 – MAP P 216

Orderly and clean, these twin industrial cities in Southern Ontario reflect their German heritage. The skills and industriousness of their immigrant founders created a diverse economy still evident today. Every fall there is a nine-day **Oktoberfest** featuring German food and drink, oompah-pah bands and dancing (*Oktoberfest Inc., 17 Benton St., Kitchener ON, N2G 3G9.* ☎*519-570-4267 or 1-888-294-4267. www.oktoberfest.ca*)

- 🛈 **Information:** Kitchener-Waterloo Tourism, 191 King St W., Kitchener. ☎519-745-3536 or toll-free 1-800-265- 6959. www.kwtourism.ca
- ▶ **Orient Yourself:** Kitchener and Waterloo are separate cities that, together with the town of Cambridge, form an urban agglomeration. They lie southwest of Toronto, between Toronto and London.
- 🅿 **Parking:** Parking at the farmers' markets is free.
- 🚫 **Don't Miss:** The farmers' markets in Kitchener and nearby St. Jacobs.
- 🕐 **Organizing Your Time:** The area is a cluster of big and small towns; take your map with you.
- **Kids Especially for Kids:** The Elora Quarry swimming hole has ice-cold water.
- 👣 **Also See:** HAMILTON, STRATFORD, LONDON, BRANTFORD

Sights

Woodside National Historic Site

528 Wellington St. N., Kitchener ON, N2H 5L5. 🕐*Open mid-May–Dec 23 daily 10am–5pm.* 🕐*Closed Dec 24–mid-May.* 🎟*$4 adult.* ☎*519-571-5684. www.pc.gc.ca.*

This 1853 brick Victorian house was the boyhood home of **William Lyon Mackenzie King**, prime minister of Canada 1921-30 and 1935-48. The house has been restored to reflect the period of King's residence in the 1890s. The influence of his grandfather, the rebel leader William Lyon Mackenzie, is of particular note.

Joseph Schneider Haus Museum

466 Queen St. South, Kitchener ON, N2G 1W7. 🕐*Open Jul–Aug Mon–Sat 10am–5pm, Sun 1pm–5pm. Mid-Feb–Jun & Sept–Dec 24 Wed–Sat 10am–5pm, Sun 1pm–5pm.* 🕐*Closed Christmas–mid-Feb.* 🎟*$2.25.* ☎*519-742-7752. www.region. waterloo.on.ca.*

This Georgian frame house was built around 1820 by Kitchener's founder, Joseph Schneider. It is restored and furnished to the period of the mid-1850s. An added wing displays decorative arts and German folk art.

Doon Heritage Crossroads

Kids *About 3km/2mi from Hwy. 401. Take Exit 275 and turn north. 10 Huron Road, Kitchener ON, N2P 2R7.* 👣🕐*Open May–Labour Day daily 10am–4:30pm.* 🎟*$6.* ☎*519-748-1914. www.region.waterloo. on.ca.*

This site depicts a small rural Waterloo village c.1914. The two-storey frame house at the **Peter Martin Farm**, originally constructed c.1820, permits an overview of Mennonite family life.

Excursion

Elora

About 37km/23mi northeast via Regional Rds. 22 and 18.

🛈*Welcome Centre, 5 Mill St., PO Box 814, Elora ON, N0B 1S0.* ☎*519-846-9841. www. elora.info.* In this charming 19C mill town on the banks of the Grand River, stone buildings house shops and restaurants. Elora's spectacular attraction is its 21m/70ft **gorge**, above which perches the Elora Mill Inn, a five-floor former feed and lumber mill which overlooks the thunderous falls of the river as it meets the gorge. In summertime villagers enjoy a dip in the cold waters of the **Elora Quarry** **Kids**, just east of the vil-

Address Book

WHERE TO EAT

$ Desert Rose Café –130 Metcalfe St., Elora ON, N0B 1S0. ☎519-846-0433. This restaurant serves vegetarian food in a casual atmosphere. Savour soups, salads or sandwiches inside or on the outdoor patio out back.

$ E.J.'s – 39 Snyder's Rd. West, Baden ON, N3A 2M1. ☎519-634-5711. www.ejsatbaden.com. This restaurant, built as a hotel in 1874, dishes up pork schnitzel, baby back ribs and locally producedOktoberfest sausage, as well as pub grub. 15 beers on tap.

$ Kennedy's Restaurant – 1750 Erb's Rd. West, St. Agatha ON, N0B 2L0. ☎519-747-1313, or toll-free 1-800-250-5953. www.kennedycatering.ca. This old-fashioned Irish pub is known for its rolled ribs, complete with all the fixings.

$ Olde Heidelberg Restaurant and Brew Pub – 3006 Lobsinger Line (RR#15), Heidelberg ON, ☎519-699-4413. www.oldhh.com. This 1860 stage coach stop near the St. Jacobs market serves hearty German fare. Photos of dishes posted on the wall to help diners make their selection.

$$$ Elora Mill Inn – 77 Mill St., Elora ON, N0B 1S0. ☎519-846-9118 or toll-free 1-866-713-5672. www.eloramill.com. Within the stone walls of the inn's large dining room, guests can hear the rush of the waterfall below. The menu has fusion touches such as coriander pesto on the veal chop. 32 guest rooms with colorful bed quilts and antique furnishings.

MARKETS

Farmers' markets offer not only produce, but local German and ethnic specialties.

Kitchener –300 King St. W. ☎519-741-2287. www.kitchenermarket.ca. Year-round Sat 7am–2pm & Jun–Sept Wed 8am–2pm. Shops and restaurants Tue–Fri 10am–6pm and Sat 7am–4pm.

St. Jacobs – At Weber St. N. and Farmers' Market Rd, north of Waterloo. ☎519-747-1830. www.stjacobs.com. Year-round Thu & Sat 7am–3:30pm, Jun–Labour Day Tue 8am–3pm, June–Dec Sun 10am–4pm.

The Mennonites in St. Jacobs Country

The first settlers in this area, the **Mennonites** were members of a Protestant sect that grew out of the Anabaptist movement (whose members believed in adult baptism) during the reformation of 16C Europe. The Mennonites were persecuted in Europe and began coming to America in the early 18C. Many emigrated to Pennsylvania, but during the American Revolution the group's commitment to nonviolence (members refused to serve in any army) made them unpopular. Some Mennonites moved North with the Loyalists, settling in the Kitchener area.

Ontario Tourism Marketing Partnership Corp.

Old Order Mennonites eschew electricity, modern machinery, cars and telephones. They can sometimes be seen in the country north and west of Kitchener–Waterloo, driving horse-drawn buggies that display a fluorescent triangle on the back as a safety precaution. Mennonite men wear black suits and wide hats; the women wear ankle-length black dresses and small bonnets. To learn more about Ontario's Mennonites and their way of life, catch the 15min video at the visitor centre in St. Jacobs (1408 King St.N., St. Jacobs ON, N0B 2N0. ☎519-664-3518. www.stjacobs.com). Contact the centre about tours of Mennonite country. ÍRemember, Mennonites are not a tourist attraction; they want to stay separate from "English" life.

lage (318 Wellington Country Rd. 18, Elora ON, N0B 1S0. ☎519-846-5234. ◔Open mid-Jun–Labour Day. ◔$4 adult). The Elora Festival (33 Henderson St, PO Box 370, Elora ON, N0B 1S0. ☎519-846-0331. www.elorafestival.com. ◔Mid-Jul–Aug), is a popular celebration of classical and contemporary music.

LONDON ★

POPULATION 352,395 – MAP P 216

In 1792 **John Graves Simcoe,** lieutenant-governor of Upper Canada (now Ontario), named the site for the British capital and called the river on which it stood the Thames.

Today London is a bustling industrial and insurance centre, but with quiet tree-lined streets, attractive houses and expansive green spaces, notably **Springbank Park,** a hub of outdoor activity west of the downtown core, offers an oasis. The University of Western Ontario, one of Canada's most distinguished, is located here.

- **Information:** Tourist Office, 696 Wellington St. South. ☎519-661-5000 or toll-free 1-800-265-2602. www.londontourism.ca
- **Orient Yourself:** London lies between Toronto and Windsor on Hwy 401, in the rich agricultural south of Ontario.
- **Parking:** Parking in the downtown core and on the campus can be difficult. In city parking lots, time limits are strictly enforced.
- **Don't Miss:** Western Ontario University offers tours of its attractive campus: ☎559-661-2100. www.welcome.uwo.ca
- **Organizing Your Time:** London International Airport is well served by regular carriers.
- **Especially for Kids:** Storybook Gardens, a park with animals and games.
- **Also See:** DRESDEN, STRATFORD, KITCHENER-WATERLOO

Address Book

WHERE TO EAT

$ Café Milagro – 1271 Commissioners Rd. West, London ON, N6K 1C9. ☎519-473-0074. Before strolling in nearby Springbank Park, fortify yourself at this small, Euro-style bistro, open for breakfast, lunch and casual dining.

$ Miestro – 352 Dundas St., London ON, N6B 1V7. ☎519-439-8983. An intimate nook near the Delta London Armouries Hotel specializes in rijstaffel, owner Mies Bervoets' version of the ten-course Dutch-Indonesian meal.

$$ Michael's on the Thames –1 York St., London ON, N6S 1A1. ☎519-672-0111. www.michaelsonthethames.com. This smart dining room overlooking the river has an extensive menu, with emphasis on fine local steaks, lamb and duck. Flambéed desserts prepared tableside are the house specialty.

$$ The Riverview Restaurant – 284 Wonderland Rd. S., London ON, N6K 1L3. ☎519-471-4662. Here, overlooking the Thames near Springbank Park, you can watch rowing and canoe club members hurtle by as you enjoy a leisurely meal of seafood specialties.

$$ Villa Cornelia – 142 Kent St. , London ON, N6A 1L3. ☎519-679-3444. www.villacorneliarestaurant.com. In a turreted 1892 Queen Anne house, enjoy a romantic atmosphere. The menu offers meat and fish with few surprises.

Sights

Museum London★★

421 Ridout St. North, London ON, N6A 5H4. ✕ ⚘ ◷ Open year-round Tue–Sun noon–5pm (June-Labour Day 11am). ⊙ Contribution requested. ☎ 519-661-0333. www.londonmuseum.on.ca.

Set in a park overlooking the river Thames, this spectacular museum is remarkable chiefly for its design by Toronto architect Raymond Moriyama. The structure of concrete barrel vaults contains skylights which provide indirect natural lighting without damaging the art. The collection includes portraits by London's native son Paul Peel, who maintained a studio on Richmond Street.

Eldon House★

481 Ridout St. North (see Museum address) ◷ Open Jun–Sept Tue–Sun noon–5pm, Jan–Apr Sat–Sun noon–5pm, May & Oct–Dec Wed–Sun noon–5pm. ⊙ $5 (by donation Wed). ☎ 519-661-0333. www. londonmuseum.on.ca

Just north of a series of restored Georgian houses stands London's oldest house, constructed in 1834. The library and drawing room are particularly noteworthy.

Excursions

Fanshawe Pioneer Village

Kids *In Fanshawe Conservation Area, 15km/9mi northeast. 2609 Fanshawe Park Rd. E. London ON, N5X 4A1. ✕ ◷ Open Mid-May–mid-Oct Tue–Sun and holiday Mon 10am–4:30pm. ⊙ $5. ☎ 519-457-1296. www.fanshawepioneervillage.ca.*

This reconstructed 19C Presbyterian community is set in a park beside Fanshawe Lake. The village has an Orange Lodge. A Protestant fraternity founded in Ireland in 1795 and named for William III (of Orange), the militantly Protestant **Orange Order** had considerable influence in the founding of Ontario. Costumed guides lend life to the village.

Ska-Nah-Doht Iroquoian Village

In Longwoods Road Conservation Area, 32km/20mi southwest by Hwy. 401, then Hwy. 402, Exit 86. 8449 Irish Drive, RR#1, Mount Brydges ON, N0L 1W0. ⚘ ◷ Open mid-May–Labour Day daily 9am–4:30pm. Rest of the year Mon–Fri 9am–4:30pm. ◷ Closed holidays. ⊙ $3. ☎ 519-264-2420. www.lowerthames-conservation.on.ca. ⊙ Insect repellent recommended.

This village is a re-creation of the type inhabited by Iroquois in Ontario 800 to 1,000 years ago. The park visitor centre at the entrance features audiovisual programs and displays. The village is surrounded by a wooden palisade with a complicated entrance to make it easy to defend.

NIAGARA FALLS★★★

MAP P 216

Roughly halfway along its course from Lake Erie to Lake Ontario, the Niagara River suddenly plunges over an immense cliff, creating one of earth's great natural wonders. These famous falls are the most visited in the world, attracting more than 12 million people a year.

The Province of Ontario and the State of New York have created beautiful parks full of flowers on both sides of the river adjacent to the falls.

- **Information:** Tourist Office, 5400 Robinson St. ☎905-356-6061 or toll-free 800-563-2557. www.niagarafallstourism.com
- **Orient Yourself:** The Skylon tower offers an excellent view of the region.
- **Parking:** Free parking is available at all Niagara Parks locations outside the main Falls/Queen Victoria park area. Consider using the People Mover bus system.
- **Don't Miss:** Drive at least one way along the Niagara Parkway.
- **Organizing Your Time:** Visit to The Falls at night to see them illuminated. There are also fireworks displays summer and winter. Contact the Tourist Office.
- **Kids:** Scary but fun, White Water Walk shows the full force of The Falls. The Botanical Gardens and butterfly conservatory offer a more relaxing time.
- **Also See:** HAMILTON, BRANTFORD

Geographical Notes

Two Cataracts – There are, in fact, two sets of falls separated by tiny Goat Island, which stands at their brink. The **American Falls** (on the US side of the river) are 300m/1,000ft wide and more than 50m/160ft high. The Canadian or **Horseshoe Falls** (named for their shape) are nearly 800m/2,600ft wide, about the same height, and contain 90 percent of the water allowed to flow down the river. It is the Horseshoe Falls that people think of as Niagara.

Diverting the Waters – The river's water volume varies by hour and season. Major power developments divert up to 75 percent of the water above the falls and the flow of water over the falls is reduced at night when additional electricity is needed to illuminate them. In winter so much water is diverted that the falls partially freeze—a spectacular sight. Visitors should consider today's water diversion and try to imagine the cataract's appearance in 1678 when **Louis Hennepin** was the first European to view them. Hennepin heard such a mighty noise on Lake Ontario that he followed the river upstream to discover its source.

Erosion of the Falls – In geological terms the falls are not old. At the end of the last Ice Age, the waters of Lake Erie created an exit channel for themselves over the present-day Niagara Escarpment into the old Lake Iroquois. The water's force immediately began to erode the underlying soft shale, creating a gorge.

Today the Niagara River has cut a gorge some 11km/7mi back from the edge of the escarpment at Queenston to the present position of the falls. In another 25,000 years or so, the gorge will extend back to Lake Erie, and unless we find a solution, and the falls as we know them will practically cease to exist.

Sights

Operated by Niagara Parks Commission, the People Mover buses stop at more than 20 attractions along Niagara Parkway from the falls to Queenston Heights Park. Buses run every 20min May–Oct. Hours of operation vary, check at ☎877-642-7275 (Canada/US). www.niagaraparks.com. Tickets available at main terminal, 7369 Niagara Parkway (southwest of the falls) or, in summer, from People Mover booths along the parkway. ☎$7.50 adult

Niagara Falls

(unlimited boarding throughout the day. includes Falls Incline Railway). Parking available in summer at Rapids View Parking Lot ≈$6.50/car, rest of the year at Falls Parking Lot ≈$10/car.

The Falls★★★

The falls can be viewed from the riverbank level, from the water level at the bottom of the cataract and from the summit of various viewing towers.

The Walk from Rainbow Bridge to Table Rock★★★

About 1.6km/1mi. From Rainbow Bridge visitors can wander along the bank beside the river,

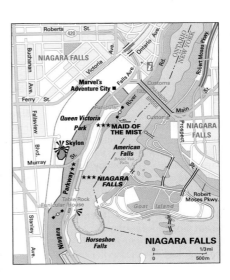

passing **Queen Victoria Park**. The American Falls are in view, and it is possible to stand on the brink of Horseshoe Falls at Table Rock. In Table Rock House, elevators descend to enable visitors to walk along **tunnels** to see this immense curtain of falling water (♿ ◷*Open daily 9am, closing hours vary.* ◷*Closed Dec 25.*⊚*$12 adults.* ☎ *877-642-7275 Canada/US.* *www.niagaraparks.com).*

Maid of the Mist★★★

Access from River Rd. Elevator & boat ride (weather permitting). ♿◷*Departs from Maid of the Mist Plaza early May–late Oct daily, 9 or 9:45am, closing hours vary.* ◷*Closed Oct 24 until ice-free. Round-trip 30min.* ⊚*$14 adult. Maid of the Mist Steamboat Co. Ltd.* ☎ *905-358-5781. www.maidofthemist.com.*

This boat trip is exciting, memorable and wet *(visitors are equipped with raincoats and hoods).* The boat goes to the foot of the Horseshoe cataract.

The View from Above★★★

Three towers in Niagara Falls provide a spectacular elevated view of the cataract. The best view is from the **Skylon** *(5200 Robinson St., Niagara Falls ON, L2G 2A3.* ✕♿◷*Open Jun–Oct daily 8am–midnight. Rest of the year daily 9am–10pm.* ⊚*$11 adult.* ☎*905-356-2651. www.skylon.com),* ascended by exterior elevators known as yellow bugs.

Additional Sights

Niagara Parkway (North)★★

follows the river to its junction with Lake Ontario. From the falls the parkway passes under Rainbow Bridge, through a pleasant residential area and past the Whirlpool Bridge.

White Water Walk★★ (formerly Great Gorge Adventure)

◷*Open daily Apr–late fall, 9am–closing times vary.* ◷*Closed winter.* ⊚*$8.50*

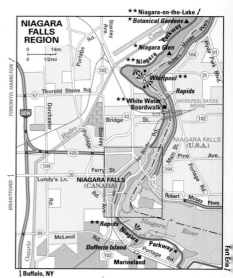

adults. ☎*1-877-642-7275 (Canada/US). www.niagaraparks.com.*

An elevator descends to the bottom of the gorge where visitors can see some of the world's most hazardous water thundering, roiling and rising into huge **rapids**.

The Whirlpool★★

A colorful antique Spanish aerocar *(weather permitting,* ◷ *opens early-Mar–June daily 10am, July–late November 9am, closing times vary.* ⊚*$11 adult.* ☎*877-642-7275 Canada/US. www.niagaraparks.com)* crosses the gorge high above the river, with excellent **views**★★ of the water as it swirls around the whirlpool and the rocky gorge. Thompson's Point scenic look provides a fine **view**★.

Niagara Glen★

There is a view of the river from above. Trails lead to the water's edge *(15min to descend, 30min to ascend).*

Niagara Parks Botanical Gardens★

✕♿◷*Open year-round daily dawn–dusk.* ◷*Closed Dec 25.*⊚*No charge.* ☎*877-642-7275 (Canada/US). www.niagaraparks.com.*

The 1,022sq m/11,000sq ft **butterfly conservatory** shelters some 2,000 butterflies in climate-controlled comfort (◷*Open mid-June–Labour Day 9am–9pm. Rest of the year closing times vary.* ◷*Closed Dec 25.* ◉*$11*).

About 1.6km/1mi from the botanical gardens, across the river on the US side, the immense **Robert Moses Generating Station** can be seen. Later, on the Canadian side, the **Sir Adam Beck Generating Station** is visible. They use water diverted from the river above the falls to generate electricity.

Just after the power stations, be sure to note the large **floral clock**.

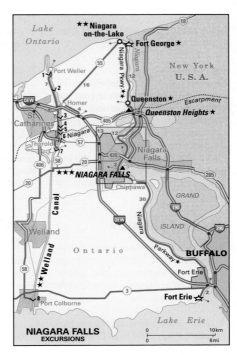

NIAGARA FALLS
EXCURSIONS

Queenston Heights★

◷*Open daily year-round.*

These heights are part of the Niagara Escarpment and were once the location of Niagara Falls. Today they are a pleasant park that provides good views of the river. In the park stands a monument to Gen. Sir **Isaac Brock**, the Canadian military hero of the War of 1812.

Excursions

From Queenston to Niagara-on-the-Lake

12km/7mi.

Queenston★

This village at the foot of the escarpment has attractive houses and gardens.

Laura Secord Homestead

29 Queenston St., Queenston ON. ✎*Visit by guided tour (30min) only.* ◷*July–Labour Day daily 11am–5pm, early May–June weekdays 9:30am–3:30pm, weekends 11am–5pm, Sept–early Oct Wed–Sun 11am–5pm.* ◉*$4.50 adult.* ☎*877-642-7275 (Canada/US). www.niagaraparks.com.*

In 1813 Laura Secord walked 30km/19mi from her home to warn the British of a surprise attack planned by the Americans. Her rather plain house has been beautifully restored by the candy company named after this Canadian heroine. For the remainder of the drive to Niagara-on-the-Lake, there are several parks with picnic tables, and occasional fine views of the river. In summer, stalls selling the produce of the Niagara Peninsula line the route.

Niagara-on-the-Lake★★

12km/7mi. ℹ*Chamber of Commerce 29 Queen St., PO Box 1043, Niagara-on-the-Lake ON, L0S 1J0. www.niagaraonthelake.com.*

Pleasant shops, restaurants, teahouses, hotels and the **Niagara Apothecary**, an 1866 pharmacy (♿◷*Open May–Labour Day daily noon–6pm, Sept–mid Oct weekends noon–6pm. www. niagaraapothecary.ca*) line a wide, main thoroughfare, **Queen Street**★, with a clock tower at its centre. Niagara-on-the-Lake is also a cultural centre, home to the **Shaw Festival**, a season (*Mar–Nov*) of theatre featuring the works of the Irish playwright **George Bernard Shaw** (1856-1950).

Other works are also performed. *Box office: ☎toll-free 1-800-511-7429 (Canada/US). www.shawfest.com.*

Fort George★

On River Rd. near the theatre. PO Box 787, 26 Queen St., Niagara-on-the-Lake ON, L0S 1J0. ⚐⚐◷Open Apr–Oct daily 10am–5pm, Nov weekends 10am–5pm. ☜$11 adult. ☎905-468-4257. www.friendsoffortgeorge.ca. or www.pc.gc.ca

Built by the British in the 1790s, this fort played a key role in the War of 1812. Costumed staff demonstrate activities of the period.

Welland Canal★★

▶ *From Niagara-on-the-Lake, take Niagara Stone Rd. (Rte. 55) to its end; turn left on the south service road, right on Coon Rd. to Glendale Ave.; turn right and cross the canal.*

▶ *From Niagara Falls, take Queen Elizabeth Way (QEW) to St. Catharines; exit at Glendale Ave. interchange, follow Glendale Ave. and cross the canal by the lift bridge; turn right or left on canal service road (Government Rd.).*

Navigation of large watercraft between Lakes Ontario and Erie was impossible until canals and locks were built in the 19C. The present canal, which is part of the St. Lawrence Seaway system, is 45km/28mi long, crossing the Niagara Peninsula between St. Catharines and Port Colborne. The canal's eight locks raise ships a total of 99m/326ft—the difference in the levels of the two lakes.

The Drive along the Canal★★

▶ *About 14km/9mi from Lake Ontario to Thorold on Government Rd.*

There are fine views of the huge ships on the seaway negotiating seven of the eight locks of this section. Just north of the lift bridge at Lock 3, the visitor centre (*PO Box 312, St Catharines ON, L2R 7C2. ✕⚐◷Open daily 9am–5pm. ◷Closed Dec 24–Jan 5. ☜$4.25 ☎905-984-8880 or toll-free 1-800-305-5134. www.stcatharineslock3museum.ca*) includes a convenient **viewing platform** of the seaway.

From the Falls to Fort Erie

32km/20mi

Rushing along at 48km/h (30mph), Niagara River is impressive, revealing its **rapids**★★ as it prepares to plunge over the cliff. **Niagara Parkway (South)**★ crosses to **Dufferin Island**, where a pleasant park (◷ *Open year-round. ☎877-642-7275. www.niagaraparks.com)* has hiking trails, streams and a swimming area. The river slowly becomes a broad, quietly flowing stream.

At the city of **Fort Erie**, the Peace Bridge crosses the river to the large American city of **Buffalo**. There are good **views**★ of the Buffalo skyline.

Old Fort Erie

✕⚐ *Open early-May–early-Oct daily 10am–4pm. Rest of the year, call for hours. ☜$9. ☎905-871-0540. www.niagaraparks.com.*

A reconstruction of the third fort built on this site, the star-shaped stone stronghold is set at the mouth of Lake Erie. Students in early-19C uniforms perform manoeuvres and serve as guides.

NORTH BAY ★

POPULATION 53,966 – MAP P 216

This resort centre on the shores of **Lake Nipissing** was located on the old canoe route to the West. North Bay is still the centre of a rich fur-trapping industry. Four times a year *(Jan, Feb, May, Sept)* beaver, mink, muskrat and other furs are auctioned at Fur Harvesters Auction, Inc., which ranks among the largest in the world *(1867 Bond St. PO Box 1455, P1B 8K6. ☎705-495-4688. www.furharvesters.com)*.

- **Information:** Tourist Office, 200 McIntyre St. E. ☎705-474-0400.
- ▶ **Orient Yourself:** North Bay lies on Lake Nipissing, between the Georgian Bay and the Quebec border.
- **Don't Miss:** In late Sept the Dreamcatcher Express train heads to Temagami for the fall colours (555 Oak St. E., North Bay On, P1B 8L3. ☎1-800-268-9281. www.northlander.ca).
- **Especially for kids:** The Sturgeon River fur museum has programs for children.
- ⊘ **Organizing Your Time:** North bay has a vibrant cultural life, with festivals, theatre and events. Check with the tourist office
- **Also See:** SUDBURY, GEORGIAN BAY, ALGONQUIN PARK

Sights

Quints' Museum

Hwy. 11/17 at Seymour St. ⟳Open July–Aug 9am–7pm, mid-May–June & Sept–mid Oct daily 10am–4pm. ⊛$3.50 adult. ☎705-472-8480. www.city.north-bay.on.ca.

On May 28, 1934, the **Dionne quintuplets** were born in this house. These five little girls quickly became the world's sweethearts.

The Waterfront

Memorial Dr. below Main St.

The sidewalk bordering Memorial Drive bustles with joggers, walkers, cyclists, pet owners and tourists. From the government dock, there are scenic **cruises** aboard the 300-passenger, twin-hulled *Chief Commanda II* on Lake Nipissing around the Manitou Islands. ╳⟳Depart daily Jun–Labour Day, mid-May–mid-June weekends only, Sept Sat only. Round trip 1.5hrs. Reservations required. ⊛$18. Georgian Bay Cruise Co. ☎705-494-8167 or toll-free 1-866-660-6686. www.chiefcommanda.com).

Excursion

Sturgeon Falls

37km/23mi west by Hwy. 17. Follow signs.

Southwest of this community is the **Sturgeon River House Museum** ⟨Kids⟩, which tells the story of the fur-trapping industry in Northern Ontario *(250 Fort Rd.;* ⟳Open Jul–Labour Day daily 9am–5pm. Rest of the year Mon–Fri 9am–4pm. ⊘Closed major holidays. ⊛$3; ☎705-753-4716. www.sturgeon-riverhouse.com)*. Exhibits include a Hudson's Bay Company trading post. A variety of nature trails thread the riverside property.

WHERE TO EAT

$$$ Churchills – *631 Lakeshore Dr. North Bay ON, P1A 2E7.* ☎705-476-7777. For fine dining in the North Bay area, head to Churchill's. The fastidious menu includes pan-fried lake pickerel as well as dishes from farther afield such as beef tenderloin with tiger shrimp, all accompanied by cleverly presented seasonal produce. Upstairs is Chumbolly's bar, while Winnie's Pub is just at hand.

ORILLIA

POPULATION 30,259 – MAP P 216

This small resort town has a reputation out of all proportion to its size. Orilla served as the model for "Mariposa" in *Sunshine Sketches of a Little Town* by famed humourist and author **Stephen Leacock** (1869-1944). This professor of political economics at McGill University spent his summers here.

- **Information:** 50 Andrews St. S. ☎705-325-1311. www.city.orillia.on.ca
- **Orient Yourself:** Ortillia is set on the narrows between Lake Couchiching and Lake Simcoe.
- **Don't Miss:** The Leacock Museum.
- **Organizing Your Time:** Take time to stroll around Orillia, a picturesque town with lovely walking paths.
- **Also See:** GEORGIAN BAY, GRAVENHURST

Sight

Stephen Leacock Museum★
50 Museum Dr. Near Old Brewery Bay off Hwy. 12 Bypass. From the bypass, turn left onto Forest Ave., then right on Museum Dr. 20 Museum Drive, PO Box 625 Orillia ON, L3V 6K5. ✕◷*Open May–Sept daily 9am–5pm. Rest of the year Mon–Fri 9am–5pm.* ﹪*$5 adult.* ☎*705-329-1908. www.leacockmuseum.com.*

Set amid pleasant grounds overlooking Brewery Bay, this attractive house was designed and built by Leacock in 1928.

OSHAWA★★

POPULATION 141,590 – MAP P 216

This industrial city on the north shore of Lake Ontario is a centre of Canada's automobile industry. Its name has long been synonymous with industrialist and philanthropist **Robert S. McLaughlin** (1871-1972).

- **Information:** Tourist Information. ☎905-725-4523, or toll-free 1- 800-667-4292 or www.oshawa.ca
- **Orient Yourself:** Oshawa lies on the north shore of Lake Ontario, 39km/24mi east of Toronto.
- **Parking:** All the sights have designated parking.
- **Don't Miss:** The Canadian Automotive Museum, for rare cars.
- **Organizing Your Time:** Lunch at the Parkwood estate, in either the garden or the greenhouse tearoom, is very pleasant.
- **Also See:** TORONTO, PETERBOROUGH

Sights

Parkwood Estate★★
270 Simcoe St. North, Oshawa ON, L1G 4T5. 4km/2.5mi north of Hwy. 401. ✕✦⚲*Visit by guided tour (1hr) Jun–Sept Mon–Sun10:30am–4pm. Rest of the year Tue–Sun 1:30pm–4pm.* ◷*Closed Mondays & major holidays.* ﹪*$7adult.* ☎*905-433-4311. www.parkwoodestate.com.*

This gracious, imposing residence was built by Robert S. McLaughlin in 1917. he converted his father's carriage business into a motor company, and used an American engine in his famous **McLaughlin Buick**. In 1918 he sold the company to the General Motors Corp.

of the US, but remained chairman of the Canadian division, whose main plant is in Oshawa. The house is set in beautiful **gardens**.

Canadian Automotive Museum★

99 Simcoe St. South, Oshawa ON, L1G 4G7. ◔*Open year-round Mon–Fri 9am–5pm, weekends 10am–6pm.* ◔*Closed Dec 25.* ◔*$5.* ☏*905-576-1222. www.oshawa.ca*
Primarily from the 1898-1981 period, about 70 automobiles, in mint condition, are on display, including the 1903 Redpath Messenger built in Toronto, the

1912 McLaughlin Buick and the 1923 Rauch and Lang electric car.

Robert McLaughlin Gallery

72 Queen St. Civic Centre, Oshawa ON L1H 3Z3. ✕&◔*Open year-round Mon–Fri 10am–5pm (Thu 9pm), week-ends noon–4pm.* ◔*Closed Jan 1, Dec 24–26. Admission by donation.* ☏*905-576-3000. www.rmg.on.ca.*
The gallery designed by Arthur Erickson displays the works of the **Painters Eleven**, a group of Toronto abstract artists.

OTTAWA★★★

POPULATION 808,391

MAP P 217

This seat of national government charms visitors with its handsome rivers, expansive parklands, miles of bicycle paths, colorful springtime tulips and the world's longest skating rink: the Rideau Canal.

The city sits on the south bank of the **Ottawa River** at the point where it meets the **Rideau River** from the south and the **Gatineau River** from the north. The Ottawa River marks the boundary between the provinces of Ontario and Quebec, but the National Capital Region spans the river, encompassing a large area that includes both the cities of Ottawa and Gatineau.

- **Information:** Tourist Office ☏ 613-237-5150 or 800-363-4465 or www.ottawatourism.ca
- ▶ **Orient Yourself:** The capital is due west of Montreal, about 160km/100mi upstream from the confluence of the Ottawa and St. Lawrence rivers.
- **P** **Parking:** No public parking is permitted on Parliament Hill. Pay lots and metered parking are available in the downtown area south of Wellington Street. Many museums and other sights provide parking lots, as do hotels.
- ☺ **Don't Miss:** The many trails and parks where you can walk or bicycle among spectacular views, particularly along the Rideau Canal.
- ◔ **Organizing Your Time:** Ottawa's truly spectacular natural setting is best appreciated through the Scenic Drives such as Ottawa River Parkway and Rideau Canal drive, which take at least two hours.
- **Kids** **Kids:** The Canada Agriculture Museum where they can see and pet some rare breeds of domesticated animals. Many museums offer exhibits for children.
- ☺ **Also See:** GATINEAU, UPPER CANADA VILLAGE, MONTREAL

A Bit of History

The First Settler – In the winter of 1800, American **Philemon Wright** travelled by oxcart on frozen waterways from New England and harnessed the **Chaudière**

Falls to power gristmills and sawmills on the Quebec side of the river. He floated the first raft of squared timber to Quebec in 1806, beginning what was to become a vast industry.

Changing of the Guard, Parliament Buildings

The Rideau Canal – The War of 1812 exposed the dangers of using the St. Lawrence as a military communications and supply route from Montreal to Upper Canada. After the war the **Duke of Wellington** sent men to Canada to look for a safer passage. The route selected followed the Ottawa, Rideau and Cataraqui rivers and a series of lakes to reach the Royal Navy base at Kingston on Lake Ontario. Construction of the necessary canals and locks was entrusted in 1826 to Lt.-Col. **John By** of the Royal Engineers, who established his base at the present site of Ottawa, named Bytown. By 1832 the canal system was completed, but its cost was so great that By returned to England unemployed and penniless.

Lumbertown – The completion of canal construction did not signal the end of Bytown's boom. Using the power of Chaudière Falls, residents built sawmills on the Bytown side of the Ottawa River. Having never been used militarily, the Rideau Canal blossomed briefly as a means of transporting the lumber south to the US. Bytown became a rowdy centre for lumberjacks and rivermen skilled at negotiating the rapids.

Westminster in the Wilderness – The 1850s saw great rivalry among Montreal, Toronto, Kingston and Quebec City over selection as the capital of the newly united Canada. The government asked **Queen Victoria** to decide the issue. She chose Bytown, which had hastily changed its name to Ottawa as a more suitable appellation for a capital. The choice did not please everyone: "the nearest lumber village to the north pole" wrote Torontonian **Goldwin Smith**. Despite such quips, in 1867 the parliament buildings were used by representatives of the new confederation.

Ottawa Today – A city of parks, scenic roads and bicycle paths, Ottawa is also a city of flowers, especially in May when thousands of tulips bloom—a gift from the Dutch, whose future queen spent the war years in Ottawa. It is a city that has capitalized on the cause of its founding—the **Rideau Canal**. Flanked by tree-lined drives, this waterway is a recreational haven: canoeing, boating, jogging, strolling, biking in summer,

Address Book

For dollar sign categories, see the Legend on the cover flap.

WHERE TO STAY

$ Hostelling International Ottawa: Ottawa Jail – *75 Nicholas St., Ottawa ON, K1N 7B9. ☎613-235-2595, toll-free 1-866-299-1478. www.hihostels.ca. 154 beds.* ☐Housed in the 1863 Carleton County Gaol near ByWard Market, this hostel offers beds in renovated jail cells, as well as dormitories and semi-private rooms. Rooms for couples are available, as are laundry facilities, lockers, Internet access and, it is said, ghosts. Historic tours show off the gallows and the cells.

$$ A Rose on Colonel By B&B – *9 Rosedale Ave. Ottawa ON, K1S 4T2. ☎ 613-291-7831. www.rosebandb.com. 3 rooms.* ☐☐. This 1925 red-brick abode in a quiet, tree-filled neighborhood is only steps away from the Rideau Canal. Coffee, tea and hot chocolate are available around the clock in the lounge. Two airy rooms overlook the canal; the third is shaded by a 200-year-old oak tree. Vegetarian breakfasts.

$$ Auberge McGee's Inn – *185 Daly Ave., Ottawa ON, K1N 6E8. ☎613-237-6089 or toll-free 1-800-262-4337. www.mcgeesinn.com. 12 rooms.* ☐☐. This sprawling brick mansion (1886) in Sandy Hill was built for John McGee, brother of Thomas D'Arcy McGee, a father of Confederation assassinated in Ottawa in 1868. Two themed rooms—one with a canopy bed—have gas fireplaces and double Jacuzzis. Every room has air conditioning, Internet access, small fridge and cable television.

$$ Auberge The King Edward – *525 King Edward Ave., Ottawa ON, K1N 7N3. ☎613-565-6700 or 800-841-8786. www.bbcanada.com/464.html. 3 rooms.* ☐☐. Asymmetrical turrets and bull's-eye windows characterize this Victorian terrace house in Sandy Hill, with a restored interior featuring moldings, archways, fireplaces and bay windows. Spacious guest quarters feature 3m/10ft ceilings, antique furnishings, air-conditioning and wireless Internet. Framing the grounds is a cast-iron fence built in the 1870s to deter the neighbors' cows and pigs.

$$ Gasthaus Switzerland Inn – *89 Daly Ave., Ottawa ON, K1N 6E6. ☎613-237-0335 or toll-free 1-888-663-0000. www.gasthausswitzerlandinn.com. 22 rooms.* ☐☐. Located in the Sandy Hill neighborhood east of the city centre, this heritage limestone house (1832) sits adjacent to Ottawa University and close to cinemas and theatres. Guests enjoy well-lit rooms with duvets, large windows, wireless Internet and possibly a working fireplace. In summer, enjoy breakfast in the garden.

$$$ Lord Elgin Hotel – *100 Elgin St. K1P 5K8. ☎ 613-235-3333 or toll-free 1-800-267-4298. www.lordelginhotel.ca. 355 rooms.* ✕☐☐☐. Named for James Bruce, 8th Earl of Elgin and governor general of British North America from 1847–54, this Ottawa institution near Confederation Square is well located for sightseeing and shopping. Exensive fitness facilities. Guestrooms are decorated with pastel fabrics and blond furnishings. The restaurant, **The Elgin Café ($$$)**, offers international cuisine in its bright, contemporary dining room.

$$$$ Fairmont Château Laurier – *1 Rideau St., Ottawa ON, K1N 8S7. ☎ 613-241-1414 or 800-441-1414. www.fairmont.ca. 429 rooms.* ✕☐☐☐☐. Named after former Canadian prime minister Sir Wilfrid Laurier, this massive limestone chateau has been an Ottawa landmark since 1912 and enjoys an enviable location next door to Parliament. Immense leaded-glass windows pierce the oak-panelled lobby and adjoining rooms. Guest rooms have been renovated with luxurious decor; some boast views of Parliament Hill and the Rideau Canal. Services include baby-sitting. A favorite local meeting spot, **Wilfrid's ($$$)** restaurant serves regional Canadian cuisine. [Spa] The Holtz Health and Beauty Spa is located across the street.

WHERE TO EAT

$ Blue Cactus – *2 ByWard Market, Ottawa ON, K1N 7A1. ☎613-241-7061. www.firestonerestaurantgroup.com.* ♿ **American Southwest.** Sample some of Ottawa's best margaritas, the house-blend Sangria, or choose from a selection of nine regional micro-brewed beers while you ponder the large menu at this marketside cafe. Start with the ever-popular Blue Cactus nachos, or the Voodoo Chicken with searing Creole mustard sauce. In summer, the floor-to-ceiling windows become patio-style doors.

$ Roses Café – *523 Gladstone Ave., Ottawa ON, K1R 5N9.* ☎613-233-5574. **Indian.** Popular with locals, this cozy eatery features spicy Southern Indian cuisine and specializes in dosas (a type of semolina pancake stuffed with spiced meats and vegetables). There is also an Indian restaurant on Wellington called Roses, which leads to confusion; it's good, too.

$ Yang Sheng – *662 Somerset St. W.Ottawa ON, K1R 5K4.* ☎613-235-5794. **Asian.** This casual eatery is always crowded with a local Asian clientele, students among them. Yang Sheng's spicy cuisine includes dim sum, and ample servings of delicacies like hot and sour soup, barbecued duck and spicy Szechwan eggplant.

$$ Canal Ritz – *375 Queen Elizabeth Dr., Ottawa ON, K1S 5M5.* ☎613-238-8998. **Italian.** ♿Patrons can literally paddle here by canoe, tie up at the dock and drop in at this renovated boathouse perched on a bend in the Rideau Canal (or else walk or cycle to the restaurant along the bike paths). The floor-to-ceiling windows and patio place diners seemingly atop the canal. The Ritz specialty is thin-crust pizza, but people come here more for the view than for the food.

$$ Papagus Taverna – *281 Kent St.,Ottawa ON, K2P 2A3.* ☎613-233-3626. **Greek.** Be prepared for large portions at this lively and quite authentic taverna. Try the bakalaos, an Icelandic codfish served with mashed potatoes and garlic, and horta, a cabbagelike vegetable.

$$ Trattoria Zingaro – *18 Beechwood Ave. Ottawa ON, K1L 8L9.* ☎613-744-6509. **Italian.** Enjoy imaginative Tuscan cuisine in a setting of royal blue, gold and scarlet walls, tables, chairs and lamps. The chef of this trendy bistro prides himself on meals prepared to order, using only fresh ingredients. Try the antipasto. The homemade bread varies daily. Call ahead to reserve a street-side window seat.

$$$ Le Café – *In National Arts Centre, 53 Elgin St. PO Box 1534, Station B, Ottawa ON, K1P 5W1.* ☎613-594-5127. *www.nac-cna.ca.* **Canadian.** ♿Overlooking the Rideau Canal, this upscale restaurant is known for its well-presented regional Canadian cuisine, created by renowned chef Kurt Waldele. In summer, patrons enjoy the airy patio and the passing parade of "canalites."

$$$ Empire Grill – *47 Clarence St., Ottawa ON, K1N 9K1.* ☎613-241-1343. *www.empiregrill.com.* **Asian.** A patio spilling out onto bustling market streets in summer, an Art Deco-style martini bar and comfortable indoor booths entice diners to linger at this friendly, relaxed bistro. Besides the fusion fare, there is a good selection of grilled steaks. The Empire sponsors live jazz on Sunday evenings.

$$$$ Le Jardin – *127 York St., Ottawa ON, K1T 5T4. In ByWard Market. Dinner only.* ☎613-241-1424. **French**. Since 1976 this elegant restaurant, located in a red-brick Victorian house, has catered to a loyal Ottawa clientele devoted to Le Jardin's excellent French cuisine. The house specialty is rack of lamb with mustard, garlic and rosemary-mustard sauce. Desserts are sheer temptation, most with a light fruit-based theme.

PUBS APLENTY

Heart and Crown – *67 Clarence St., Ottawa ON, K1N 5P5. At Parent in ByWard Market.* ☎613-562-0674. *www.irishvillage.ca.* This Irish pub serves shepherd's pie and Guinness beef stew in a lively, casual setting. 16 taps promise a wide selection of brews. In summertime the pub's outdoor tables afford great people-watching in the heart of the market. Wednesday through Saturday bring live Celtic music.

D'Arcy McGee's Irish Pub – *44 Sparks St. K1P 5A8.* ☎613-230-4433. *www.darcymcgees.ca/ottawa.* The high-gloss wood interior with detailed scrollwork around the bar, was hand-carved in Ireland for authenticity's sake. Draft beer and a fine array of Irish whisky, cognac, bourbon, port, Cuban cigars and, well, plenty of craic (good times and fun) complement the corned beef and cabbage. Entertainment Wed and weekends: Celtic, blues, whatever.

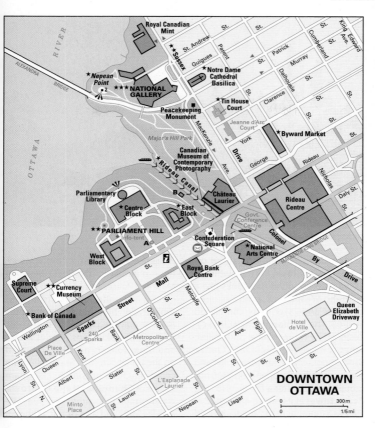

DOWNTOWN OTTAWA

0		300m
0		1/5mi

and ice-skating and cross-country skiing in winter, when little "chalets," set on the ice, offer food and skate rentals. The canal can be followed its entire 200km/125mi length to Lake Ontario through picturesque countryside with lovely lakes. Scenic roads follow the Ottawa and Rideau rivers.

High rises contain government departments and ministries, the most dominant being **Place du Portage** across the river in Gatineau.

Finally, Ottawa is a cultural centre, with a fine selection of museums and music, dance and drama at the **National Arts Centre**. The city is particularly lively in February during the winter festival titled **Winterlude**, in May for the **Canadian Tulip Festival,** and from late June to early July, when **Canada Day** is celebrated in style on Parliament Hill.

In 2001, the City of Ottawa absorbed 12 former municipalities to become a

megacity, overseen by one mayor, one city manager and nearly two dozen city executives.

Parliament Hill and Area★★

Parliament Hill, with its three Gothic-style parliament buildings, dominates the northern side of **Confederation Square**. In the middle of the square stands the towering granite archway of the **National War Memorial (1),** which was dedicated in 1939 by King George VI. Neighboring "the Hill," as it is familiarly known, is **Château Laurier**, a distinguished hotel recognizable by its turrets and steeply pitched copper roofs. The government conference centre stands opposite. Bordering the southern tip of Confederation Square is the National Arts Centre.

Rideau Canal and the Parliament

The parliament buildings stand on the hill. **East Block,** with its whimsical windowed tower that looks like a face, and **West Block**, both designed by Strent and Laver, were completed in 1865. The **Parliamentary Library**, designed by Thomas Fuller and Chilion Jones, was finished only in 1877. **Centre Block**, originally designed by Fuller and Jones, was officially opened in 1866 but rebuilt in 1920 after a fire in 1916. The **Peace Tower** at its centre was added in 1927 as a monument to Canadians killed since Confederation. Today Centre Block contains the Houses of Parliament—the Commons and the Senate. West and East blocks contain the offices of senators and members of Parliament.

Visiting Parliament Hill

Since Parliament Hill's tourist activities are numerous during peak season *(mid-May to Labour Day)*, it is advisable to stop first at the large white tent **(Infotent)** located between Centre Block and West Block for a schedule of the day's events.(◷*Mid-May–Labour Day, 9am–5pm, 8pm weekdays late Jun–Labour Day*) Information is also available at the National Capital Commission's **Capital Infocentre** at 90 Wellington St (corner Metcalfe St. (◷*Open early-May–Labour Day daily 8:30am–9pm.Rest of the year daily 9am–5pm.* ◷*Closed Jan 1 & Dec 25–26.* ☎*613-239-5000 or toll-free 1-800-465-1867. www.canadascapital.gc.ca).*

Parliament Hill is "guarded" by the Mounties—members of the Royal Canadian Mounted Police, attired in their famous ceremonial uniforms of stetsons, red tunics, riding breeches, boots and spurs *(summer only).* Regiments of Foot Guards wearing bearskin caps, scarlet tunics and blue trousers are also stationed on the Hill in summer. Resembling the ceremony held outside Buckingham Palace, a **Changing of the Guard**★★ is performed in summer *(late Jun–late Aug 9:45am)* and a seasonal, bilingual **sound and light show** *(30min)* presents Canada's history (⚿◷*9:30 and 10:30pm mid-Jul–mid- Aug, 9pm and 10pm mid-Aug–Sept. in case of rain, show may be cancelled). Nightly Christmas lights show mid-Dec–mid-Jan.* ☎*613-239-5000).*

Sights

Ottawa River Boat Trip★★

✕⚿◷*Departs from Ottawa locks mid-May–mid-Oct daily 11am, 2pm, 4pm,evening cruises 7pm late June–Labour Day. Cruise departs from Gatineau dock (Hull) 30min earlier. Round-trip 1hr 30min.* ◷*$18 adult. Paul's Boat Lines.* ☎*613-225-6781. www.paulsboatcruises.com.*

This is an excellent trip, especially at dusk, affording close-up views of Parliament Hill, the Rideau Falls and the houses along Sussex Drive overlooking the river, in particular the prime minister's residence. The sheer size and force of the Ottawa River are impressive.

Centre Block★

♿ 🚶‍♂️ *Visit by free guided tour (45min) only, mid-May–Labour Day daily 9am–8:30pm. Rest of the year daily 9am–4:30pm.* 🕐*Closed Jan 1, Jul 1 & Dec 25.* ☎613-239-5000 or 800-465-1867. www.canadascapital.gc.ca.

Tours enable visitors to enter the Senate, the House of Commons and the **Parliamentary Library**, the only part of the original structure to escape the 1916 fire. Separately, the Peace Tower can be ascended for a fine **view**★ of the sprawling capital. Parliamentary proceedings are open to the public if the House or Senate is in session. Each sitting begins with the **Speaker's Parade.**

East Block★

♿ 🚶‍♂️ *Visit by guided tour (45min) only, Jul–Labour Day daily 10am–6pm.* 🕐*Closed Jul 1.* ☎613-239-5000 or toll-free 1-800-465-1867. www.canadascapital.gc.ca.

The interior of this mid-19C building has been restored to its 1872 appearance. In summer students role-play these historical figures to enliven the visit.

The Grounds

In front of the parliament buildings is a low-lying fountain called the **Centennial Flame (A)** because of the natural gas always burning at its centre. Symbolizing the first 100 years of Confederation, it was lit at midnight on New Year's Eve, 1966.

The walk around Centre Block is pleasant, affording **views**★ of the river and of Gatineau. A notable collection of statues, many by Quebec sculptor **Louis-Philippe Hébert** (1850-1917), commemorates Canadian prime ministers, as well as Queen Victoria and Queen Elizabeth II.

Rideau Canal★

Heritage Canal. From Wellington Street visitors can descend into the small gorge where the Rideau Canal begins. Eight **locks** raise boats from the Ottawa River to the top of the cliff. There is also a **boat trip** on the canal *(*♿ 🕐*Departs*

from Ridean Canal Dock, behind Conference Centre, mid-May–mid-Oct daily 10am, 11.30am, 1.30pm, 3pm, 4:30pm. Late Jun–Labour Day cruises also at 7pm and 8:30pm. Round-trip 1hr 15min. 🚢*$16. Paul's Boat Lines.* ☎ 613-225-6781. www.paulsboatcruises.com).

Beside the locks stands the **Old Commissariat Building (B)**, completed by Colonel By in 1827, which now houses the **Bytown Museum**, with a display on the canal builders *(*🕐*Open mid-May–early Oct daily 10am–5pm (8pm Jul–Aug), April–mid-May & Sept–Oct Mon–Fri 10am–2pm.* 🕐*Closed November–March.* 🚢*$5.* ☎613-234-4570. www.bytownmuseum.com).

Above the canal, and next to Château Laurier, the **Canadian Museum of Contemporary Photography,** an affiliate of the National Gallery *(*🕐*Temporarily closed for construction.* ☎613-990-8257; http://cmcp.gallery.ca). South of Wellington and facing the canal, the handsome **National Arts Centre**★ contains theatres and a celebrated cafe with an outdoor terrace located beside the waterway *(*🍴 ♿ 🅿 🚶‍♂️ *visit by 45min guided tour only, leaving from main lobby July–Aug, Tues, Thur & Sat 11am & 2pm.* 🚢*$2 adult.* ☎613-947-7000. www.nac-cna.ca). Across the canal stands the

Rideau Canal

ByWard Market

Rideau Centre, a hotel, convention and shopping complex.

ByWard Market★

✕ 🄿 🕒 *Open May–mid Oct daily 6am–6pm. Rest of the year daily 8am–5pm.* 🕒 *Closed Jan 1 & Dec 25.* ☎ *613-562-3325. www.byward-market.com.*
Stretching over several blocks, this colorful market (primarily indoors in winter) has existed since 1846. The ByWard Market Building holds restaurants, craft shops and coffeehouses.

Tin House Court★

This pleasant cobblestone square, bordered by stone buildings and graced by a fountain, is home to Art Price's 1973 sculpture, once part of the actual facade of tinsmith Honoré Foisy's whimsical house.
To the south, across Clarence Street, Nunavut artist Pauta Saila's bronze sculpture of a dancing bear energizes cobblestoned Jeanne d'Arc Court.

Notre Dame Cathedral Basilica★

385 Sussex Dr.K1N 5H5 ♿ 🄿 🕒 *Open Mon 11:30am–6pm, Tue–Sat 7:30am–6pm, Sun 8am–6pm.* 👥 *Guided tours available.* ☎ *613-241-7496.*
This church with twin spires is a Roman Catholic cathedral built between 1841 and the 1880s. To the right of the basilica, there is a statue of Joseph-Eugene Guigues, the first bishop of Ottawa.

The very fine **woodwork** of the interior was carved in mahogany by Philippe Parizeau. Around the sanctuary there are statues crafted in wood by Louis-Philippe Hébert, which have been painted to look like stone.

Peacekeeping Monument

Across the street, and adjacent to the basilica, is a prominent memorial to Canadians who have served as international peacekeepers. Titled *The Reconciliation*, the monument was dedicated in 1992.

Nepean Point★

Situated high above the river beside Alexandra Bridge, this point offers a splendid **view**★★ of Parliament Hill, Gatineau and the Gatineau Hills across the river. Overlooking the river facing west is a statue of **Samuel de Champlain (2)**, who paddled up the Ottawa River in 1613 and 1615.

Sparks Street Mall

South of Parliament Hill stretches this pleasant pedestrian mall with trees, seating and cafe tables between the shops. Note the **Royal Bank Centre** and, at the opposite end of the mall, the attractive **Bank of Canada**★, designed by Arthur Erickson and opened in 1980. Outside the east tower in a small park stands a bronze sculpture by Sorel Etrog titled *Flight* (1966).

Supreme Court

301 Wellington St., Ottawa ON, K1A 0J1. Visit May–Aug daily 9am–5pm. *Tours continual throughout day. Sept–April Mon–Fri 9am–5pm, book tour in advance.* 613-995-4330. www.scc-csc.gc.ca.

Canada's Supreme Court occupies a building with green roofs overlooking the Ottawa River. The court itself consists of nine judges, five of whom constitute a quorum. Visitors can listen to a hearing of an appeal if the court is in session, and see the building's interior.

The Museums★★★

Several of Ottawa's numerous fine museums are concentrated within the city core. Others, such as the Aviation Museum and the Agriculture Museum, are on the outskirts of the city proper.

National Gallery of Canada★★★

380 Sussex Dr, Ottawa ON, K1N 9N4. Open May–Sept daily 10am–5pm *(Thu 8pm). Rest of the year Wed–Sun 10am–5pm (Thu 8pm), open Mon when holiday.* Closed Christmas Day, New *Year's Day and Good Friday.* $6 adult. *(special exhibits additional fee)* 613-990-1985. www.gallery.ca.

This magnificent glass, granite and concrete building (1988, Moshe Safdie), capped by prismatic glass "turrets," rises on the banks of the Ottawa River across from the Gothic parliament buildings.

Canadian Art

Second floor. Both the **garden court**, with its colorful plantings, and the restful **water court** add grace and beauty to the transition from gallery to gallery. Highlights include the reconstructed chapel of the Convent of Our Lady of the Sacred Heart (1888); early Quebec religious art; the works of Paul Kane and Cornelius Krieghoff; paintings by Tom Thomson and the Group of Seven, Emily Carr, David Milne, Marc-Aurèle Fortin, Jean-Paul Lemieux, Alfred Pellan *(On the Beach)*, Goodridge Roberts, Guido Molinari and Claude Tousignant. Mondeern and ontemporary works are also featured.

Galleries devoted to Inuit art *(accessed from second-floor level)* feature work by artists such as Jessie Oonark and Pudlo.

European and American Art

Third floor. Among the highlights are Simone Martini's *St. Catherine of Alexandria*, Lucas Cranach the Elder's *Venus*, Rembrandt's *The Toilet of Esther*, El Greco's *St. Francis and Brother Leo Meditating on Death*, Bernini's fine bust of *Pope Urban VIII* and Benjamin West's *Death of General Wolfe*. Impressionists are 20C masters are well represented.

Canadian Museum of Civilization★★★ (Quebec)

See Entry Heading Gatineau.

National Gallery of Canada

Ontario Tourism Marketing Partnership Corp.

Canada Aviation Museum★★★

Rockcliffe Airport, 11 Aviation Pkwy, Ottawa ON, K1K 4R3. ✕ ⚐ 🅿 🕐*Open May–Labour Day daily 9am–5pm. Rest of the year Wed–Sun 10am–5pm.* 🕐*Closed Dec.25.* ⟿*$6 adult.* ☎613-993-2010. www. aviation.nmstc.ca.

There is a replica of the Silver Dart, the first aircraft to fly in Canada. There are fighters and bombers used in both world wars: a Spad 7, a Sopwith Snipe, Hawker Hurricane, Supermarine Spitfire and a Lancaster Bomber. Early "bush" float planes include the De Havilland Beaver, first flown in 1947. The **RCAF Hall of Tribute** honors men and women of the Royal Canadian Air Force.

Canadian Museum of Nature★★

240 MacLeod St., PO Box 3443, Station D, Ottawa ON, K1P 6P4. 𝕂𝕚𝕕𝕤✕ ⚐ 🅿 🕐*Open May–Labour Day daily 9am–5pm (Wed & Thu 8pm). Rest of the year Tue–Sun 10am–5pm (Thu 8pm).* 🕐*Closed Dec 25 & 2nd week in Jan.* ⟿*$5 adult. (No charge Sat before noon).* ☎613-566-4700. www. nature.ca.

The museum contains exhibits on the creation of oceans and continents, particularly North America, and an outstanding display on **dinosaurs**.

The **Birds in Canada** gallery features lifelike dioramas. Dioramas of **Canadian mammals** include the musk-ox of Northwest and Nunavut territories, the pronghorn of Saskatchewan, British Columbia's grizzly bear and the moose of New Brunswick. Children will enjoy the **Creepy Critters** exhibit, with cockroaches, slugs, spiders and snakes.

Currency Museum★★

In Bank of Canada complex, 245 Sparks St. Ottawa ON, K1A 0G9. ⚐🕐*Open May–Sept Mon–Sat 10:30am–5pm, Sun 1pm–5pm. Rest of the year Tue–Sat 10:30am–5pm, Sun 1pm–5pm.* 🕐*Closed major holidays.* ⟿*No charge.* ☎ 613-782-8914. www. currencymuseum.ca.

This museum presents the history of money from early China, Greece, Rome, Byzantine, Medieval and Renaissance Europe to its introduction and use in North America, with examples of wampum, the card money of New France, Hudson's Bay Company tokens, and the first banknotes.

Canada Science and Technology Museum★★

𝕂𝕚𝕕𝕤*1867 St. Laurent Blvd. Ottawa ON, K1G 5A3.* ✕ ⚐ 🅿 🕐*Open May–Labour Day daily 9am–5pm. Rest of the year Tue–Sun 9am–5pm.* 🕐*Closed Dec 25.* ⟿*$6 adult.* ☎ 613-991-3044. www.sciencetech. technomuses.ca.

The flashing beacon of the old Cape North (Nova Scotia) lighthouse marks the museum's location.

The hall of **steam locomotives** is impressive because of the sheer size of the vehicles. Exhibits on early automobiles (1900-30) in Canada and the ocean liner Titanic are also featured.

Canadian War Museum★★

1 Vimy Place, Ottawa ON, K1A 0M8. ✕ ⚐ 🕐*Open Jul–Labour Day daily 9am–6pm (Thu & Fri 9pm). May–June & Sept daily 9am–6pm (Thu 9pm). Rest of the year Tue–Sun 9am–5pm (Thu 9pm).* 🕐*Closed Dec 25.* ⟿*$10 adult. (No charge Thu after 4pm).* ☎819-776-8600 or toll-free 1-800-555-5621. www.warmuseum.ca.

Canada's brand new (2005) museum honours the nation's military involvements and peacekeeping efforts throughout the ages. Don't miss paths over the museum's roof, allowing superb **views**★ of the Ottawa River. The Military History Research Centre (🕐*Open May–mid–Oct Mon–Fri 9am–4:30pm. Rest of the year Tues–Fri 9am–4:30pm.* 🕐*Closed weekends and holidays.* ☎819-776-8652) includes important national collections documenting Canada's military history.

Royal Canadian Mint

320 Sussex Dr, Ottawa ON, K1A 0G8. ⚐⟿*Visit by guided tour (40min) only, mid–May–Labour Day Mon–Fri 9am–7pm, weekends 9am–5:30pm. Rest of year Mon–Sun 9am–5pm.* 🕐*Closed Jan 1, Dec 25.* ⟿*$5 adult. Weekends $3.50. Reservation recommended.* ☎613-993-8990, toll-free 1-800-276-7714. www.mint.ca.

Canada's circulating money is created at the the Royal Canadian Mint in Winnipeg. Commemorative and collector

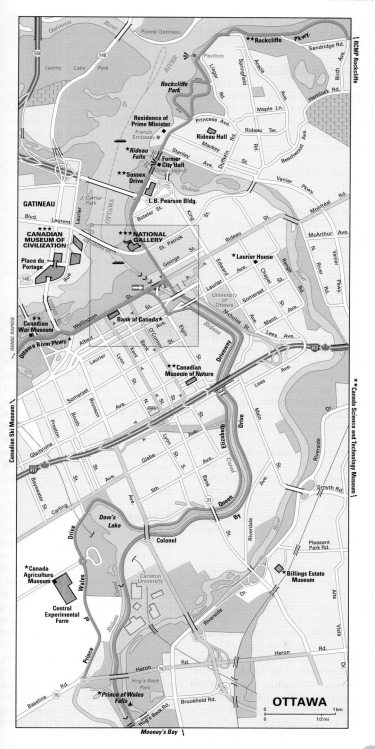

★★ Rockcliffe Pkwy.

Sandridge Rd.

Pointe Gatineau

Pavilion

Leamy Lake Park

Rockcliffe Park

Residence of Prime Minister

French Embassy

★ Rideau Falls

★★ **Former City Hall**

Green Island

★★ Sussex Drive

L. B. Pearson Bldg.

GATINEAU

Boteler St.

J. Cartier Park

★★★ CANADIAN MUSEUM OF CIVILIZATION

Place du Portage

★★★ NATIONAL GALLERY

St. Patrick

George

★ Laurier House

University of Ottawa

Bank of Canada ★

★★ Canadian War Museum

Ottawa River Pkwy.

Wellington

★★ Canadian Museum of Nature

Driveway

★ Canada Science and Technology Museum

Canadian Ski Museum

Somerset

Elizabeth Drive

Glebe

Dow's Lake

Colonel

★ Canada Agriculture Museum

Central Experimental Farm

Carleton University

★ Billings Estate Museum

Pleasant Park Rd.

Riverside

Heron Rd.

Hog's Back Park

★ Prince of Wales Falls

Brookfield Rd.

OTTAWA

0   1 km

0   1/2 mi

Mooney's Bay

Rideau Hall

Princess Ave.

Residence of Prime Minister

Rideau Falls

Rideau Hall

Rideau Ter.

Beechwood Ave.

Vanier Pkwy.

Montréal Rd.

McArthur Ave.

Rideau

Edward

Chapel

Range Rd.

River Rd.

Vanier Pkwy.

Nicholas St.

Lees Ave.

Mann

Lees Ave.

Lees

Main

Riverside Dr.

Smyth Rd.

Queensway

Baseline Rd.

Prince of Wales

(numismatic) coins are made at this Ottawa location. There's a new (2005) interactive coin museum.

Canadian Ski Museum

1960 Scott St., Ottawa ON, K1Z 8L8. ⏰*Open year-round Mon–Sat 9am–5pm, Sun 11am–5pm.* ⏰*Closed Dec 25.* ✆*Contribution suggested.* ☎*613-722-3584. www.skimuseum.ca.*

Archival photographs and equipment depict the history of the sport. A Hall of Fame features history's great Canadian skiers.

Laurier House★

335 Laurier Ave. East, Ottawa ON, K1N 6R4. ☛*Visit by guided tour (1hr) only,* ⏰*Open mid-May–early Oct daily 9am–5pm. Rest of year Mon–Fri 9am–5pm.* ⏰*Closed Easter holidays.* ✆*$4 adult.* ☎*613-992-8142. www.pc.gc.ca.*

In 1897 Canada's first French-speaking prime minister, **Sir Wilfrid Laurier**, in office from 1896 to 1911, moved into the house. Canadian prime minister **William Lyon Mackenzie King,** grandson of the rebel William Lyon Mackenzie resided here until his death in 1950.

The visit includes a reconstruction of the study of **Lester Bowles Pearson,** 1957 Nobel Peace Prize winner and prime minister from 1963 to 1968.

Canada Agriculture Museum★

Kids *Building 88, Prince of Wales Drive, on grounds of the Central Experimental Farm.* ♿🅿⏰*Main exhibition area open Mar–Oct daily 9am–5pm.* ⏰*Closed Nov–Feb. Barns open all year round 9am–5pm.* ✆*$6 adult.* ☎*613-991-3044. www.agriculture. technomuses.ca.*

The machinery displayed, the techniques, even the smells, evoke farming in times past. Old breeds of sheep, cattle, pigs and horses can be seen. (☛*Guided tours of animal barns year-round.* ☎*613-991-3053).* Seasonally, visitors can take wagon rides *(Jun–Sept, Wed–Sun.* ✆*$2.50)* on the premises.

The 425ha/1,050-acre **Central Experimental Farm** is the headquarters of Canada's Agriculture and Agri-Food department. On the grounds are splendid ornamental gardens. There is also a tropical greenhouse and a large

arboretum bordering the Rideau Canal (♿🅿*Grounds open year-round daily dawn–dusk. Greenhouse open year-round daily 9am–4pm.* ☎*613-759-6900).*

Billings Estate Museum★

2100 Cabot St. ♿🅿⏰*Open mid-May–Oct Wed–Sun noon–5pm.* ☛*Tours Wed–Sun 12pm–5pm.* ✆*$2.50.* ☎*613-247-4830. www.friendsofbillingsestatemuseum. org.*

This attractive home is a national historic site. Built in 1829, it is the oldest frame house in Ottawa.

Drives around the Capital★★

Ottawa is well known for its lovely drives beside the river, along the canal and in the Gatineau Hills to the north.

Sussex Drive and Rockcliffe Parkway★★

8km/5mi from Confederation Square. This drive along the river and through the prestigious residential area of Rockcliffe passes the Basilica of Notre Dame and the Canadian War Museum, and the **Lester B. Pearson Building**, which houses the Department of Foreign Affairs and International Trade. The road then crosses the Rideau River to Green Island past **Ottawa's former city hall;** from the top floor, there's a pleasant **view**★ of the river.

Rideau Falls★

🅿 *Park beside the French Embassy.* On both sides of Green Island, the Rideau River drops over a sheer cliff into the Ottawa River. The falls are said to resemble a curtain, hence their name, which means "curtain" in French. To see the second set of falls, visitors can cross the first set by a bridge. There are good views of the Ottawa River and Gatineau.

Along Sussex Drive, the entrance to the official residence of Canadian prime ministers, **24 Sussex Drive**, is seen on the left. Around the corner is the gate to **Rideau Hall,** official residence of the governor general, set amid landscaped grounds. The grounds can be visited (🕐 *Open year-round daily 8am–one hour prior to sunset.* 👁 *Tours Sept–June 9am–4pm. Call for reservations.* ☎ *613-991-4422 or toll-free 1-866-842-4422.* There are guided **tours** of the residence (45 minutes) (♿ 👁 *guided tours July–Labour Day daily 10am–1pm self-guided, 1-4pm guided. May–June weekends 10am–4pm, Sept–Oct & Feb noon–4pm. Other times, reserve at 1-866-842-4422. www.gg.ca).* The road then passes through **Rockcliffe Park** via a one-way route. On the return there are good views of the river. Farther on, however, there are excellent **views**★★ from a covered pavilion of Pointe Gatineau on the Quebec shore and of the Gatineau Hills. The steepled church in Pointe Gatineau is St. François de Sales, built in 1886.

Rockcliffe is an area of large stone mansions, tree-lined streets and lovely gardens. The drive ends at **RCMP Rockcliffe** (Royal Canadian Mounted Police), where members of the famous **musical ride** and their horses are trained. When the troop is not on tour (generally May – October) the horses can be seen in training (♿ 🕐 *May–Aug daily*

9am–3:30pm. Sept Mon–Fri 9am–3:30. Rest of the year Tue & Thu 10am–2pm. ☎ 613-998-8199. www.rcmp-grc.gc.ca or www.canadascapital.gc.ca).

Rideau Canal Driveways★

Each drive is about 8km/5mi from Confederation Square.

The **Queen Elizabeth Driveway** follows the canal's west bank; the **Colonel By Drive** parallels the east bank. The University of Ottawa is soon passed on the left. Later on, Carleton University is also seen. At **Dow's Lake**, where the canal widens out, canoes and paddleboats can be rented. At this point the two drives diverge, the Colonel By continuing along the canal, the Queen Elizabeth entering the Central Experimental Farm. From Colonel By Drive, there are views of Prince of Wales Falls and the Rideau Canal locks before the drive ends at Hog's Back Road.

Prince of Wales Falls★

Free parking in Hog's Back Park. **Mooney's Bay** marks the end of the Rideau Canal; thereafter, the Rideau River is navigable. After leaving the bay, the river drops over these falls and rushes

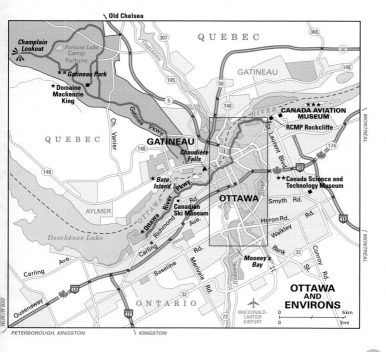

through a small gorge. The dam was built by Colonel By in 1829. Mooney's Bay *(access from Riverside Dr.)*, is one of Ottawa's main recreational areas.

Ottawa River Parkway★

1km/7mi from Confederation Square. Wellington Street passes the parliament buildings, the Bank of Canada and the Supreme Court, and becomes the parkway just south of Portage Bridge. The drive beside the Ottawa River offers several lookout points for the Remic Rapids.

The best view is from **Bate Island**★ *(take Champlain Bridge to Gatineau and exit for island)*. The parkway continues, affording other good viewpoints.

Gatineau Park★★ (Quebec)

www.canadascapital.gc.ca Circular drive of 55km/34mi from Confederation Square. Cross Portage Bridge and proceed to Gatineau, turn left on Rte. 148 for just over 2km/1.2mi, then turn right on the Gatineau Parkway. Ꮬ *see GATINEAU*

PETERBOROUGH

POPULATION 74,898 – MAP P 217

This pleasant city is set on the Trent Canal, part of the Trent-Severn Waterway, which links Lake Ontario with Georgian Bay. Boating, especially canoeing, is a popular activity in the region, particularly on the Kawartha Lakes to the north and, farther north, along the canoe routes in Algonquin Provincial Park. The area is also known for its sizable number of petroglyphic Indian relics.

🛈 **Information:** Peterborough and the Kawarthas Tourism, 1400 Crawford Dr. ☎705-742-2201, toll-free 1-800-461-6424. www.thekawarthas.net

▶ **Orient Yourself:** Peterborough lies between Toronto and Kingston on the Otonabee River where it widens into Little Lake.

⊛ **Don't Miss:** Take a cruise to observe the locks in action.

🕐 **Organizing Your Time:** You may want to time your visit to enjoy one of the many festivals and events organized to draw tourists.

Kids **Especially for Kids:** Lang Pioneer Village for make-believe.

Ꮬ **Also See:** OSHAWA, TORONTO

Sights

Lift Lock★

🕐*In operation mid-May–mid-Oct.* This hydraulic lift lock built in 1904 is one of only eight in the world. Its operation is explained in the **Trent-Severn National Historic Site Visitor Centre** *(PO Box 567 Peterborough ON, K9J 6Z6.* ♿🅿🕐*Open daily mid-May–early-Oct.*🕐*Closed Good Friday. contribution requested.* ☎*705-750-4950.www.pc.gc.ca)*. Visitors can experience the lift lock by taking the **boat cruise** *(Departs from Del Crary Park, next to Holiday Inn downtown.* ✕♿🕐*July–Aug 3 times daily. Mid-May–June & Sept–mid-Oct twice daily.* ᎐*$16.50 adult. Reservations suggested. Liftlock Cruises* ☎*705-742-9912, toll-free 1-888-535-4670. www.liftlockcruises.com)*.

Canadian Canoe Museum★

910 Monaghan Rd., Peterborough ON, K9J 5K4. 🅿♿🕐*Open Mon–Sat 10am–5pm, Sun noon–5pm.* 🕐*Closed Dec 24–27, Dec 31–Jan 1 and major holidays.* ᎐*$7.50 adult.* ☎*705-748-9153 or 866-342-2663. www.canoemuseum.net.*

A former factory houses this fascinating array of more than 600 canoes, kayaks

Child's birchbark canoe by William Commanda

and rowing craft of all types and construction. The newest exhibit is devoted to the paddling accoutrements of the late prime minister **Pierre Elliott Trudeau**.

Excursions

Lang Pioneer Village

Kids *104 Lang Rd, Keene, ON (Mailing address:470 Water St., Peterborough ON, K9H 3M3). 16km/10mi southeast of Peterborough by Rte. 7 and Country Rd. 34. ○Open mid-June–Labour Day daily 10am–4pm, late May–mid June Mon–Fri 10am–3pm, 1st 2 wks Sept Mon–Fri 10am–4pm guided tours only. ⊜$7 adult. ☎705-295-6694, toll-free 1-888-289-5264. www.langpioneervillage.ca.*

In a delightful rural setting, this 19C village contains reconstructed buildings and an original gristmill (1846), still in working order. Costumed staff demonstrate daily chores and trades.

Petroglyphs Provincial Park

55km/34mi northeast of Peterborough via Hwy. 28. Mailing address: General Delivery, Woodview ON, K0L 3E0.&○Open mid-May–mid-Oct daily 10am–5pm. ⊜$9/car. ☎ 705-877-2552. www.ontarioparks.com.

The largest concentration of petroglyphs anywhere in Canada is protected in this park, located near Stony Lake. About 900 carvings of between 500 and 1,000 years of age can be seen.

POINT PELEE NATIONAL PARK★★

MAP P 216

This park is one of the few places where the true deciduous forest of eastern North America still exists. Well known to ornithologists across the continent, the southernmost tip of the Canadian mainland possesses a unique plant and animal life, largely due to its latitude of 42°N, the same as that of Rome.

- **Information:** Visitor Centre, 407 Monarch Lane, Leamington. ☎519-322-2365. www.pc.gc.ca
- ▶ **Orient Yourself:** Point Pelée lies on a pointed peninsula extending into Lake Erie, south of Windsor near the Michigan border.
- **Parking:** There are several parking areas. Cars parked on the roads are towed.
- **Don't Miss:** Even if you don't know birds, the guides make them easy to spot.
- **Organizing Your Time:** You need a full day to enjoy this park.
- Kids **Especially for Kids:** Many trails are short and easy. There are also beaches.
- **Also See:** WINDSOR, DRESDEN

Geological Notes

The peninsula took its shape 10,000 years ago when wind and lake currents deposited sand on a ridge of glacial till under the waters of **Lake Erie**. The sand spit today is mantled with a lush forest of deciduous trees. Beneath them, many species of plants thrive, including the prickly pear cactus with its yellow flower.

An Ornithologist's Paradise – Point Pelee's location at the convergence of two major flyways, its extension into Lake Erie and its lack of cultivation have combined to foster large bird populations. In spring and fall migrations, as many as 100 species have been sighted in one day. September is the month of the southern migration for the monarch butterfly. Visitors can see trees covered with these beautiful insects.

Access

About 10km/6mi from Leamington. Follow the ⊕ (beaver) signs.

Rose-Breasted Grosbeak

R. Corbel/MICHELIN

Visit

✕🚹🕙*Open year round: Apr–Oct 6am–10pm. (Opens 5am during May migration). Rest of the year daily 7am–7pm. Hiking, fishing, canoeing, bicycling (bicycle & canoe rentals), swimming, ski trails, ice-skating.* 🚌*$7/day.* ☎*519-322-2365.*

www.pc.gc.ca. For recorded information on migration, weather conditions and events ☎*519-322-2371.*

V**isitor centre**–*7km/4mi south of park entrance.* 🚹🕙*July–Labour Day 9am–7pm, 1st 3 wks May 7am–5pm, June & Sept 10am–6pm, Oct & April 10am–5pm. Rest of the year weekends only 10am–5pm.* Be sure to buy a Checklist of Birds to keep track of birds you see.

Transit to the tip of the peninsula departs from the visitor centre *(every 20min, Apr–Nov).* Paths lead in both directions along the park's 19km/11mi of fine sandy beaches *(swimming prohibited at the tip; swimming beaches accessible from picnic areas).*

Marshland between the sandbars can be toured by a **boardwalk** *(1km/.6mi),* where two lookout towers provide good **panoramas**★ of the marsh.

Eastern Kingbird

Northern Oriole

PRESCOTT★

POPULATION 4,228 – MAP P 217

This small industrial town on the St. Lawrence is the only deepwater port between Montreal and Kingston. It was the site of the **Battle of the Windmill** in 1838 when rebel supporters of William Lyon Mackenzie were dislodged from a windmill on the riverbank. Today an international bridge spans the river near the town, one of 13 linking Ontario with the US.

🛈 **Information:** Town of Prescott. ☎613-925-2812. www.prescott.ca

▶ **Orient Yourself:** Prescott lies halfway between Kingston and Cornwall.

🔄 **Don't Miss:** Prescott is an old Loyalist town, with heritage buildings, a renovated waterfront and walking paths.

🕙 **Organizing Your Time:** Spend a half day here, to see the town and fort.

Kids **Especially for Kids:** The fort is full of Redcoats; children seem to like them.

🕯 **Also See:** KINGSTON, OTTAWA

Sight

Fort Wellington

On Hwy. 2, just east of town. PO Box 479, Prescott ON, K0E 1T0. ⏰*Open mid-May–Sept daily 10am–5pm.* 🎟*$4 adult.* ☎*613-925-2896. www.pc.gc.ca.*
Built during the War of 1812, this small earthen fort includes officers' quarters and a three-storey stone **blockhouse**. Costumed interpreters include those attired in British regimental uniforms of the period.

East of the fort *(1.5km/1mi)*, between Highway 2 and the river, stands the **windmill** of battle fame. It features displays on the battle and offers a pleasant **view** of the river *(picnic tables)*.

SAULT STE. MARIE ★★

POPULATION 74,566

Connected to Michigan's city of the same name by road and railway bridges, this Ontario city is an industrial centre with huge steelworks and a pulp mill. The "Soo," as it is commonly called, lies on the north side of St. Mary's River, the international boundary and waterway that connects Lakes Superior and Huron, forming an important link in the Great Lakes/St. Lawrence Seaway system.

- 🛈 **Information:** Tourism office. 99 Foster Dr. ☎705-759-5432. toll-free 1-800-461-6020. www.saulttourism.com
- ▸ **Orient Yourself:** Sault Ste. Marie lies between lakes Huron and Superior.
- ⊛ **Don't Miss:** A train ride into the wilderness with the Algoma Central Railway.
- ⏱ **Organizing Your Time:** The surrounding area is wilderness punctuated by parks, with some lovely drives.
- ⚑ **Also See:** GEORGIAN BAY

A Bit of History

Étienne Brûlé visited the rapids in 1622, as did many of the great explorers of New France: Nicolet, Radisson, Groseilliers, Marquette, Jolliet, La Salle, the La Vérendrye family and others. In 1668 Père Marquette established a mission here, calling it Sainte Marie du Sault (sault means "rapids" in French).

Gateway to the wild and uninhabited Algoma wilderness, a favoured subject of the Group of Seven painters, Sault Ste. Marie is also the birthplace of Canada's first woman astronaut, **Roberta Bondar**, for whom several city properties are named.

Sights

Sault Ste. Marie Canal National Historic Site ★

Visitor centre at 1 Canal Dr., Sault Ste-Marie ON, P6A 6W4. Lock ⏰*open early-Jun–Labour Day daily 9am–9pm, mid-May–early Jun & early Sept–mid-Oct daily 11:30am–7:30pm.* 🚶*Jul–Aug site tours 11am and 2pm.* ⏰*Closed mid-Oct–mid-May.* ☎ *705-941-6262. www.pc.gc.ca.*
The enormous ships of the Great Lakes bypass the rapids through four parallel locks on the American side of the river, one of the busiest sections of the entire seaway system. A lock on the Canadian side to handles recreational craft *(mid-May–mid-Oct)*. The vast lock system can be appreciated by taking a **boat trip** that passes through one of the large American locks *(*✕⏰*Departs from Roberta Bondar Park mid-May–mid-Oct daily 12:30pm & 3pm, Jul–Labour Day also at 6pm. Round-trip 2hrs.* 🎟*$26 adult. Lock Tours Canada* ☎*705-253-9850, toll-free 1-877-226-3665. www.locktours.com).*

City Hall ★

Sault Ste. Marie has a pleasant riverfront area dominated by its attractive City Hall, built of copper-coloured reflecting glass. Nearby stands the permanently berthed **MS Norgoma (B)**, the

263

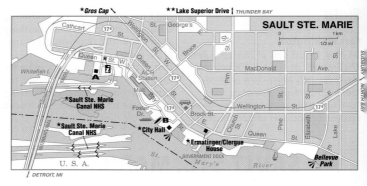

SAULT STE. MARIE

last overnight passenger ship used on the Great Lakes *(Docked next to Roberta Bondar Pavilion. ⊙Open Jun–Aug daily 10am–8pm.Sept–Oct hours vary. ⊆$5. ☎705-256-7447. www.norgoma.org).*

Ermatinger/Clergue House★

831 Queen St. East, Sault Ste-Marie ON, P6A 2A8. ⊙Open Mid-April–Nov Mon–Fri 9am–5pm . ⊙Closed Jan–mid-May. ⊆$5. ☎705-759-5443. www.ssmcoc.com.
This attractive Georgian stone house was built in 1814 by Charles Oakes Ermatinger, a partner in the North West Company, and his Ojibway wife, Charlotte.

Bellevue Park

From this park on the river, there are fine **views**★ of the ships using the locks and of the bridge to the US.

Excursions

Gros Cap★

26km/16mi west by Hwy. 550.
From this headland there is a good **view**★ of Lake Superior and the beginning of the St. Mary's River.

Train Trip to Agawa Canyon

29 Bay St., Sault Ste-Marie ON, P6A 6Y2. 183km/114mi. Departs from Bay St. depot ✕⎔⊙Late Jun–mid-Oct daily 8am, return 5:30pm. Also Wed–Fri last 2 wks Jun. 1 Round-trip 9hrs. ⊆$65 (summer), $85 (fall). Also late Jan–early Mar Sat 8am, return 5pm. ⊆$65. Reservations required. Algoma Central Railway Inc. ☎705-946-7300 or toll-free 1-800-242-9287 (Canada/US). www.agawacanyontourtrain.com.
At a stopover in Agawa Canyon (2hrs), travellers can climb to a lookout for a fine view★ of the canyon and the Agawa River.

Lake Superior Drive★★

⎔ *Map of Principal Sights. 230km/143mi by Trans-Can Hwy. (Rte. 17) to Wawa.*
The road cuts through some of the oldest rock formations in the world, the Canadian Shield. The drive is especially fine around **Alona Bay** *(viewpoint after 108km/67mi)* and **Agawa Bay** *(viewpoint after 151km/94mi).* Lookouts have been built beside the road.
For 84km/52mi the road passes through **Lake Superior Provincial Park** *(swimming, hiking, camping, boat rentals. ℗⊙Open daily early May–late Oct.*

Roberta Bondar, Astronaut

Born in Sault Ste. Marie in 1945, Roberta Bondar later became a neurologist and biologist and trained as a pilot. In 1992, Dr. Bondar crewed on the American space shuttle *Discovery,* becoming Canada's first woman in space. *MacLean's* magazine included her in 1998 among the top 10 heroes in the history of the nation. A popular public speaker and avid environmental photographer, Dr. Bondar has seen her photos exhibited in the Canadian Museum of Nature in Ottawa and the Royal Ontario Museum in Toronto. Her birthplace has named a city park, marina and government office building in her honour.

$10/vehicle. ☎705-856-2284. *www.ontarioparks.com).* The park is known for its Indian **pictographs**—rock paintings. After 153km/95mi a side road leads to a parking lot from which a rugged trail descends to the lake. A series of pictographs can be found on **Agawa Rock**, a sheer rock face rising out of the water *(accessible only when lake conditions are favourable; extreme caution advised).* The **view**★ of the lake is excellent.

STRATFORD★

POPULATION 30,461 – MAP P 216

This community is home to the annual **Stratford Festival**, a major theatrical event that attracts people from all over North America. Though the focus is Shakespearean, the festival offers a wide variety of drama and music as well as behind-the-scenes tours, lectures and workshops.

Information: Tourism Alliance, 47 Downie St. ☎519-271-5140, toll-free 1-800-561-7926 or www.welcometostratford.com

▶ **Orient Yourself:** Stratford is north of London and west of Kitchener, a 2hr drive west from Toronto.

Parking: The Tourism Alliance office gives a one-day free-parking pass to visitors (*see above*). There is a parking lot at the Festival Theatre ($8) and at the Tom Patterson Theatre. No overnight parking on city streets.

Don't Miss: Take in a play.

Organizing Your Time: Book ahead for your restaurant.

Also See: LONDON, KITCHENER, BRANTFORD

Address Book

WHERE TO EAT

Picnics – Several local restaurants will prepare picnics for theatre-goers.

$ Festival Fare – *In the Festival Theatre's South Lobby's atrium*. Offers sandwiches, beverages, ice cream etc. before performances and during intermissions.

$$$$ Church Restaurant – *70 Brunswick St., PO Box 724, Stratford ON, N5A 6V6.* ☎519-273-3424. *www.churchrestaurant.com.* Menus are sophisticated, with unusual items such as poached skate, roast loin of red deer, or various pork parts, barbecued. A prix fixe option expedites matters for theatre-goers. The restaurant also serves lunch, Sunday brunch, and après-theatre supper on weekends. A bistro, **The Belfry ($$)**, shares the premises, offering the same high standard with a simpler menu.

$$$$ The Old Prune – *151 Albert St.Stratford ON, N5A 3K5.* ☎519-271-5052. *www.oldprune.on.ca.* Four cozy dining rooms include the Garden Room, which overlooks a serene reflecting pool. Chef Bryan Steele designs an intriguing menu, with a prix-fixe option for theatre-goers, that might include a warm duck-breast salad or lamb with wild leeks.

FESTIVAL THEATRE TOURS

Costume Warehouse Tour – *Meet at 350 Duoro St. Early June– early Nov daily 10am & 11.30am. 45min.* $7. Visitors can admire hundreds of stored costumes and props.

Garden Tour –*Meet at Festival Theatre's William Shakespeare sculpture. Early June–Labour Day , Wed–Sat 11am.* $7. A guided stroll through the landscaped grounds around the Festival Theatre. ☎519-273-1600, toll-free 1-800-567-1600. *www.stratfordfestival.ca. Advance reservations advised.*

A Bit of History

In 1952 local journalist **Tom Patterson** dreamed of creating a festival to celebrate the works of the Bard. The festival has since grown to a seven-month season *(May–Nov)* in three theatres—the Festival, the Tom Patterson and the Avon. Offerings have branched out from Shakespeare, and standards are very high.

For performance schedule & reservations, contact the Stratford Festival box office: P.O. Box 520, Stratford, ON, N5A 4M9. ☎519-273-1600, toll free 1-800-567-1600 (Canada/US); www.stratford-festival.ca.

Visit

Festival Theatre

This modern development of the Elizabethan stage used in Shakespeare's day was revolutionary in the 1950s (but much copied since) because no elaborate scenery could be used and no member of the audience was more than 20m/65ft from the stage.

The theatre is set at the edge of a pleasant park that stretches down to the river, dammed at this point to form **Victoria Lake**, the home of many swans. Before evening performances in the summer, the beautifully manicured lawns and the small island in the lake are covered with picnicking theatregoers.

SUDBURY ★★

POPULATION 157,857 – MAP P 216

Located on the largest single source of nickel in the world, Sudbury is the biggest and most important mining centre in Canada. The city is also a principal centre of Francophone culture in Ontario; about a quarter of the population of the region is Franco-Ontarian. Laurentian University, which serves the northeastern part of the province, is bilingual. The Sudbury region is typical Canadian Shield country, with beautiful lakes, rocks and trees. A number of lakes are encompassed within city limits, including Lake Ramsey, which has enough yellow pickerel (walleye) to supply local fishermen, and beaches just a short walk from the civic centre.

🛈 **Information:** Sudbury Tourism, City Hall, 200 Brady St. ☎705-688-7570 or, toll-free 1-877-304-8222. www.mysudbury.ca

▶ **Orient Yourself:** Sudbury lies east of Georgian Bay, between North Bay and Sault Ste. Marie, at the edge of a vast wilderness. Sudbury is at the northern end of the Georgian Bay Coastal Route, opposite Manitoulin Island.

😊 **Don't Miss:** Science North, a modern science centre with dramatic exhibits.

👶 **Also See:** NORTH BAY, GEORGIAN BAY

Sights

Science North ★★★

🧒 *About 1.5km/1mi south of Trans-Canada Hwy. From Hwy. 69 bypass, take Paris St. to Ramsey Lake Rd. 100 Ramsey Lake Rd, Sudbury ON, P3E 5S9.* ✕🚻🕐 *Open late Jun–Labour Day daily 9am–6pm. Rest of Sept–early May daily 10am–4pm. Rest of the year daily 9am–5pm.* 🕐 *Closed Jan 1 & Dec 24–26 and 1 week in Jan.* 💲*$18 adult. ☎705-535-4629, toll-free 1-800-461-4898. www.sciencenorth.on.ca.*

Perched on a rock outcropping on the shores of Lake Ramsey, this dramatic science centre was designed by Raymond Moriyama in association with local architects. A hexagonal exhibit building resembling a snowflake (to represent the glacial action that shaped Northern Ontario) is set over a cavern blasted out of the rock (to represent the probable creation of Sudbury Basin by a meteor).

Visitors enter a large admissions area and proceed to the centre proper via a **rock tunnel**. Raw rock is exposed as it is

Ontario Tourism Marketing Partnership Corp.

Science North and Lake Ramsay

in the impressive **rock cavern** (9m/30ft high by 30m/100ft in diameter), where a 3-D film and laser shows highlight geological history on a giant screen. Exhibit floors are reached via an ascending spiral ramp that zigzags over the **Creighton Fault**. This fault, a geological fracture within the Canadian Shield active more than 2 billion years ago, left a groove 4m/13ft deep at this point. Hanging over the fault is a 23m/72ft fin whale skeleton, weighing 1800kg/4,000 pounds, recovered from Anticosti Island. The glass walls of the ramp permit views of Lake Ramsey outside. Nature Exchange allows kids to swap their finds for items from the centre's nature collection. There are exhibits about the weather and fossils, among others, and in the Discovery Theatre, science shows are presented regularly.

Sudbury's Strata

The nickel-bearing rock strata are part of the **Sudbury Igneous Complex**, a geological formation about 60km/37mi long and 27km/17mi wide located within a 200km/125mi wide crater created by a meteor or comet impact some 1.85 billion years ago. The area's wealth (platinum, copper, cobalt, silver and gold, in addition to nickel) was discovered in 1883 during the construction of the Canadian Pacific Railway. A blacksmith named Thomas Flanagan noticed a rust-colored patch of rock while working with a crew in a recently blasted area just west of the present city.

Today the discovery is commemorated by a plaque *(on Hwy. 144 near the Murray Mine),* and Sudbury claims the world's largest integrated nickel mining, smelting and refining complex. The Super Stack, an enormous smokestack rising 380m/1,250ft above the surrounding countryside, tops the complex. **Super Stack** was built in 1970 to reduce the local impact of emissions of sulphur dioxide. Some 90 percent of the sulphur in the ore is successfully contained.

From the dock **boat tours** of the lake can be taken (🚻🕐*Depart late May–Sept daily.Round trip 1hr.* 🚢*$9.95. Cortina Cruise.* ☎*705-523-4629, toll-free 1-800-461-4898).*

Dynamic Earth★★

5km/3mi west of Science North by Regent and Lorne Sts. 122 Big Nickel Road, Sudbury ON, P3E 5S9. 🕐*Open Mar–Oct daily 9am (closing times vary)* 🕐*Closed Nov–Feb. $16 (combo pass with Science North is $30).* ☎*705-522-3701.*

Operated in conjunction with nearby Science North, this attraction enables visitors to descend deep into the old Big Nickel Mine to learn about geology and, in particular, how mining shaped this part of Northern Ontario.

Long a Sudbury landmark, the **Big Nickel**, a replica of the 1951 Canadian commemorative five-cent piece, has stood near the mine for more than 40 years.

THUNDER BAY★★

POPULATION 109,140

Situated almost in the centre of Canada on the shores of Lake Superior, the city of Thunder Bay is an important port and the Canadian western extremity of the Great Lakes/St. Lawrence Seaway system. Prairie grain arriving by rail is cleaned and stored in the port's grain terminals for transfer to the huge ships of the Great Lakes fleet. Port facilities also include two terminals for coal, potash and other dry-bulk commodities, a malting plant, a bagging facility for specialty grains and a general cargo facility noted for its ship/rail heavy lift transfers.

- 🛈 **Information:** Tourism Thunder Bay, 500 Donald St. E. ☎ 807-625-2149, toll-free 1-800-667-8386. www.visitthunderbay.com
- ▶ **Orient Yourself:** The nearest city to Thunder Bay is Duluth, Minnesota, to which it is linked by Hwy 61.
- 🔆 **Don't Miss:** The harbour as seen from Marina Park is an awesome sight.
- 🕐 **Organizing Your Time:** Sights lie mostly along the lake to the east of the city; the Isle Royale National Park in the US lies just opposite the city.
- 🧒 **Especially for Kids:** Fort William offers a look the life of northern fur traders and explorers. In July, the "great rendezvous" is re-enacted.
- 👣 **Also See:** SAULT STE. MARIE

Sights

The Waterfront

To appreciate the impressive port, and the sheer size of the grain terminals and ships, view them from **Marina Park** *(end of Red River Rd.* 🕐*Open daily year-round).* The largest of these ships is 222m/728ft by 23m/75ft, capable of carrying up to a million bushels of grain—the yield of 20,650ha/51,000 acres of land. The breakwater protecting the harbour from the storms of Lake Superior can also be seen. Waves can reach 12m/40ft in height in autumn. In summer the lake is calmer, and sailboat races are held weekly within and outside of the breakwater.

Viewpoints★

Thunder Bay is surrounded by the hills of the Canadian Shield. The city is hemmed in across the bay by a long peninsula that forms a cape called **Sleeping Giant** because it resembles the prone figure of a man.

Mt. McKay★

At end of Mountain Rd. on Indian reserve. This prominent flat-topped peak is the highest (488m/1,600ft) of the Norwestern Chain. From a ledge 180m/600ft high, there is a fine **view** on clear days of the city, port and Sleeping Giant.

Ontario Tourism Marketing Parnership Corp.

Kakabeka Falls

Hillcrest Park★

High St. between John Sreet Rd. and Red River Rd. Located on a cliff above Port Arthur, this park provides a good **view** of the port, elevators, ore dock and, in the distance, Sleeping Giant and the islands that close the harbour mouth.

Fort William Historical Park★★

Kids *16km/10mi south by Broadway Ave. Map below. 1350 King Rd, Thunder Bay ON, P7K 1L7.* ✕♿🕐 *Open mid-May–mid-Oct daily 9am–5pm (mid-June–Labour Day 6pm).* 🎫*$14.* ☎*807-473-2344. www. fwhp.ca.* 🕐*The park was closed for repairs after flooding, but is scheduled to re-open in May 2008.*

Located on the Kaministikwia River, part of the trade route to the northwest, the fort of the great rendezvous has been superbly reconstructed. From the visitor centre, visitors can walk through the woods to the palisaded fort. Inside is a large square of log buildings, two raised above the ground on stilts (the river still floods). Some 42 structures represent all aspects of early-19C fur-trade society. Costumed guides help re-create fort life. The North West Company partners can be seen discussing business in the council house; birchbark canoes, tinware and barrels are being crafted by hand.

Excursions

Kakabeka Falls★★

29km/18mi west by Trans-Canada Hwy. (Rte. 17). PO Box 252, Kakabeka Falls, ON, P0T 1W0. Provincial park 🕐*open year-round. Park* 🕐*open to vehicles mid-May–early Oct daily.* 🎫*$10/vehicle. Hiking, camping, fishing, canoeing.* ☎*807-473-9231. www.ontarioparks.com.*

The Kaministikwia River, crossed by a bridge, plunges 39m/128ft over a cliff around a pinnacle of rock into a narrow gorge. These falls were the first obstacle negotiated by the fur traders of the North West Company when they left Fort William on the return trip to the northwest.

North Shore Lake Superior★★

211km/131mi to Schreiber by Trans-Canada Hwy.
This route passes several interesting features northeast of Thunder Bay.

Terry Fox Monument and Scenic Lookout

1km/.6mi east of Hodder Ave.
The fine bronze monument commemorates the heroic efforts of **Terry Fox** to raise money to fight cancer. Deprived of his right leg by the disease at age 18, he

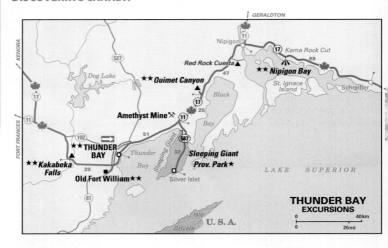

undertook a cross-Canada run in 1980, starting in Newfoundland. Two months later, he was forced to abandon his run close to this spot because of recurring cancer from which he died in 1981. The monument overlooks Lake Superior.

Sleeping Giant Provincial Park★

After 51km/32mi, take Rte. 587. Pass Lake ON, P0Y 2M0. ♿🕐Open daily late-May–mid-Oct. Cross-country ski trails accessible Jan–Mar. ⌬$10/car. ☎807-977-2526. www.ontarioparks.com.

Occupying most of the peninsula that has the Sleeping Giant at its end, this pleasant park features trails, high cliffs, fine **views**★ of Lake Superior and the remains of the village of Silver Islet. This community was formed in 1868 when a rich silver vein was discovered on the tiny islet offshore.

Amethyst Mine

After 56km/35mi, take E. Loon Rd. for 8km/5mi. Mailing address: Amethyst Gift Centre, 400 Victoria Ave. E., Thunder Bay ON, P7C 1A5. ♿🕐Open Jul–Aug daily 10am–6pm. Mid-May–Jun & Sept–mid-Oct daily 10am–5pm. ⌦Guided tours daily. ⌬$3. ☎807-622-6908. www.amethystmine.com.

This open-pit mine is a rock hound's delight as pieces of anethyst can be collected (charge per pound) and polished stones purchased.

Ouimet Canyon★★

After 76km/47mi, take road for 12km/8mi. Mailing address:c/o Sleeping Giant Park, Pass Lake ON, P0Y 2M0. 🕐Open late May–mid-Oct daily dawn–dusk. ⌬$2. ☎807-977-2526. www.ontarioparks.com.

This incredible canyon was gashed out of the surface of the Canadian Shield during the last Ice Age. It is 100m/330ft deep, 150m/500ft across and more than 1.6km/1mi long. Just after the Red Rock turnoff on the Trans-Canada Highway is a cliff of layered limestone colored red by hematite, the **Red Rock Cuesta**. nearly 210m/690ft high and about 3km/2mi long.

Nipigon Bay★★

88km/55mi from Nipigon to Schreiber. After crossing the Nipigon River, the Trans-Canada Highway runs along the shore of this bay, offering **views**★★ of rocky islands covered with conifers and rocks worn smooth by Lake Superior.

The **view**★★ of Kama Bay through the Kama Rock Cut *(27km/17mi from Nipigon)* is particularly fine. Rock such as this posed problems during the construction of this highway in 1960, and in the building of the Canadian Pacific Railway.

TORONTO ★★★

METROPOLITAN AREA POPULATION 5,113,149

MAP P 216

The country's largest metropolis, the capital of Ontario enjoys a buoyant economy driven by finance, telecommunications, biotechnology, aerospace, film and television production and media. Major Canadian corporations have their head offices here. A vibrant, multicultural city with a liveable downtown core, Toronto offers a vigourous cultural scene, professional sports teams, great shopping, and many recreational activities. The city possesses a fine harbour, punctuated with a chain of offshore islands that provide the city with its major parkland.

- **Information:** Toronto Visitors Centre, 207 Queens Quay W. ☎416-203-2600, toll-free 1- 800-499-2514. www.torontotourism.com
- **Orient Yourself:** Set on the broad north shore of Lake Ontario, Toronto is the hub of the Golden Horseshoe, the 60km/100m-wide arc stretching from Oshawa to Hamilton, where at least a quarter of Canada's manufacturing is based. The **Humber River** borders Toronto to the west, and the **Don River** to the east.
- **Parking:** Street metered parking is available but hard to find; timed parking (signed) and permit-only parking is strictly enforced. It is prudent to park in lots. Museum parking, when available, must be paid for, often in cash only.
- **Don't Miss:** CN Tower and the Royal Ontario Museum. For classical music, spend an evening at the Roy Thomson Hall. And, since this is Canada, why not visit the Hockey Hall of Fame?
- **Organizing Your Time:** Public transportation (Toronto Transit Commission or "TTC" as locals call it) with its network of subway trains, buses, and streetcars (trams) is efficient, safe and inexpensive. When driving, avoid the crowded north-south artery, Yonge St.; try Avenue Road, Bathurst or Don Valley Parkway.
- **Especially for Kids:** The Ontario Science Centre, the amusement parks at Toronto Islands, Ontario Place, and of course the Toronto Zoo.
- **Also See:** OSHAWA, HAMILTON, KITCHENER

A Bit of History

"Toronto Passage" – Prior to 1600, the **Huron** and **Petun** peoples abandoned their north shore lands to the warlike **Iroquois Confederacy**, which dominated the fur trade. The Iroquois in turn ceded to French traders control of the "Toronto Passage" of trails and canoe routes between Lakes Huron and Ontario.

The French Regime – As early as 1615 the site of Toronto was visited by **Étienne Brûlé**, one of Champlain's men. Years later French traders met native and English traders on the Humber River in what is now Toronto, a Huron word for "meeting place." The French began construction in 1720 of forts around Lake Ontario; remains of **Fort Rouillé** have been found in Toronto's Exhibition Grounds. The Seven Years' War (1756-63) brought an end to French presence in the area.

York – In 1787, **Sir Guy Carleton**, the governor of British North America, arranged to buy land from the **Mississaugas**, who had occupied the Toronto area after the Iroquois. Loyalists fleeing the US had also settled along the lake; their demands for English law led to the formation of Upper Canada (now Ontario) in 1791. Colonel **John Graves Simcoe**, lieutenant-governor of the new territory, chose the site for a temporary capital, because of its fine harbour and distance from the American border. It was called **York**, after the Duke, a son of George III. In 1813 an American fleet set fire to the legislative and other buildings. In retaliation, the British set fire to part of Washington, DC, including the White House, in 1814.

CN Tower

Montreal was the site of an armed rebellion, also in 1837, against British rule. Although crushed, the insurgence subsequently resulted in representative government for Quebec.

A City of Neighbourhoods – As late as 1941 Toronto was 80 percent Anglo-Saxon, but since World War II, the city has opened its doors to immigrants from around the world. Today Toronto benefits from a stimulating mix of cultures. **Kensington Market** *(Kensington Ave., east of Spadina and north of Dundas)* is the realm of the Portuguese and East Indian communities *(best time to visit is Mon–Sat mornings)*. One of the largest Chinese districts in North America, **Chinatown** *(Dundas St. from Elizabeth to Spadina)* is also vibrant with street vendors. The **Italian** districts *(College St. and St. Clair Ave., west of Bathurst)* evoke the mother country. **Greektown** *(Danforth Ave. between Coxwell and Broadview; ● Chester)* offers numerous cafes, specialty shops and fruit markets featuring Greek food. The **India Bazaar** on on Gerrard St E. offers restaurants, produce, art, clothing and street food from Southeast Asia. **Koreatown** on Bloor St W. is renowned for barbecue and karaoke. **Roncesvalles Village** is where the Polish community comes to shop and eat. Particularly active between Spadina and John Streets, **Queen Street West** has become a colourful area of trendy bistros, and boutiques.

The Family Compact – After 1814, immigrants flooding in from Britain began to challenge the power of what was called "the Family Compact," a small group of weathy men who dominated the government of York and Upper Canada. An outspoken Scot named **William Lyon Mackenzie** (1795-1861) attacked the group in his newspaper, *The Colonial Advocate*. He was elected to the legislative assemby (although not allowed to take his seat) and in 1835 was elected the first mayor of the City of Toronto (the name was changed as the Duke of York continued to lose in battle). In 1836, Gov. **Sir Francis Bond Head** dissolved the legislature.

The Rebellions of 1837 – Mackenzie turned to armed rebellion in 1837. When Toronto's garrison was away in Lower Canada, he gathered supporters and marched toward the city. British reinforcements arrived under Col. Allan MacNab, the revolt collapsed and Mackenzie fled to the US. Although two of Mackenzie's men were publicly hanged, the revolt was effective in that "responsible government" was granted and the united Province of Canada was created. Mackenzie was permitted to return in 1849.

Toronto Today – With a municipal population of nearly 2.6 million, the metropolis now ranks among the continent's largest cities. One project that will define the city is a multimillion-dollar development of a somewhat derelict waterfront. Highlights of the megaproject include creating new city-core neighbourhoods, a waterfront park and promenade and, most significantly, reconfiguration of the elevated Gardiner Expressway, a 1950s eyesore that divides the city from its waterfront.

At the corner of Dundas and Yonge streets, **Dundas Square**, opened with great fanfare in May 2003, has become Toronto's top visitor destination. The centrepiece is an "urban beach," an array

Ontario Tourism Marketing Partnership Corp.

Address Book

AREA CODES

Since the Greater Toronto Area has several area codes, you will need to dial all 10 digits (area code plus the phone number) when making local calls. For more information: ☎1-800-668-6878 or www.bell.ca.

GETTING AROUND

BY PUBLIC TRANSPORTATION

The Toronto Transit Commission (TTC) operates an extensive public transit system of buses, streetcars and subway lines. Hours of operation: **Subway** Mon–Sat 6am–1:30am, Sun 9am–1:30am. **Buses and trams** 5am–1.30 am Mon–Fri, reduced service weekends. Blue Night buses and trams daily 1am–5:30am. Adult fare $2.75 one way for unlimited travel with no stopovers. Day Pass $8.50. Tokens 10 for $5.50, 10 for $21. Exact fare required. Purchase tickets & tokens in subway stations. Free transfers between buses & streetcars. System maps & timetables available free of charge. Route information ☎416-393-4636 or www.ttc.ca.

BY CAR

Use of public transportation or walking is strongly encouraged within the city as streets are often congested and street parking may be difficult to find. Toronto has a strictly enforced tow-away policy. Motorists should park in designated **parking** areas which are identified by a sign with a green 'P'; there is a 3hr limit; public, off-street parking facilities are located throughout the city. For a free map and information about parking fees, call ☎416-393-7275. www.toronto.ca/faq/parking. Parking is serious enough to merit a website, www.greenp.com, devoted to finding parking lot space, parking services, and latest parking news.
Car rentals: Avis ☎416-777-2847. Hertz ☎416-979-1178. National ☎1-800-227-7368.

BY TAXI

Co-op ☎416-504-2667. www.co-opcabs.com. Diamond ☎416-366-6868. www.diamondtaxi.ca. Beck Taxi ☎416-751-5555.

BY MOTORCOACH

Gray Line Tours ☎416-594-3310, toll-free 1-800-594-3310. www.grayline.ca.

GENERAL INFORMATION

ACCOMMODATIONS

For a listing of suggested hotels, see the Address Book in this chapter. For **hotels/motels** contact Tourism Toronto (☎416-203-2600, toll-free 1-800-499-2514/Canada & US. www.torontotourism.com). Reservation services: Hotels.com ☎1-800-224-6835 (Canada/US) http://deals.hotels.com. Abodes of Choice B&B Assn. of Toronto, ☎416-537-7629. www.redtoronto.com. Downtown Toronto Assn. of B&B Guest Homes ☎416-410-3938. www.bnbinfo.com.

CITY PASS

Ask about **CityPass** wherein six major attractions are packaged together (CN Tower, Royal Ontario Museum, Casa Loma, Ontario Science Centre, Toronto Zoo, Hockey Hall of Fame) for a lower total price ($56). ☎1-888-330-5008. http://citypass.com/city/toronto.html.

LOCAL PRESS

Daily: The Toronto Star, The Toronto Sun, The Globe and Mail, The National Post. **Weekly:** L'Express (Francophone news) **Monthly** Toronto Life magazine, and free guides to entertainment, shopping, and restaurants (www.torontolife.com): Eye (www.eyeweekly.com), Now (weekly. www.nowtoronto.com), Where (monthly. www.wheretoronto.com).

ENTERTAINMENT

Consult the arts and entertainment supplements in local newspapers (Thursday edition) for schedules of cultural events and addresses of principal theatres and concert halls. Ticketmaster (☎416-870-8000 for concerts or 416-872-1111. www.ticketmaster.ca.) sells tickets for theatre and the arts. Try www.martiniboys.com (☎ 416-536-6468) for half-price, same-day tickets for theatrical, dance and musical events. Tickets must be purchased in person at Eaton Centre (Yonge St., north end, subway leve. Major credit cards accepted). Royal Alexandra and Princess of Wales theatres: ☎416-872-1212, www.mirvish.com. Useful web sites: www.torontolife.com (current events, restaurant and nightlife guide), www.martiniboys.com (overview of trendy restaurants, clubs and pubs).

SPORTS

Toronto Blue Jays (baseball).Season Apr–Oct at Rogers Centre (☎416-341-1234. http://toronto.bluejays.mlb.com). **Toronto Maple Leafs** (ice hockey): season Oct–Apr at Air Canada Centre (☎416-815-5500 (schedules). ☎416-872-5000 (Ticketmaster). http://.mapleleafs.nhl.com.) **Toronto Argonauts** (football). Season mid-Jun–Nov at Rogers Centre (☎416-489-2745 (schedules). www.argonauts.on.ca. ☎416-872-5000 (Ticketmaster)). **Toronto Raptors** (basketball): season Nov–Apr at Air Canada Centre, (☎416-366-3865. www.nba.com/raptors/).

USEFUL NUMBERS ☎

* **Police: 911 (emergency) or 416-808-2222 (non-emergency)**
* **Union Station** (VIA Rail) – *Front & Bay Sts. 65 Front St. W., Toronto ON, M5J 1E6.* Travellers Aid Society 416-366-7788. VIA Rail 1-888-842-7245.
* **Metro Coach Terminal** – *610 Bay St.,* Toronto ON, M5G 1M5. 416-393-7911
* **Toronto (Pearson) International Airport** – *416-766-3000 Terminal 1 & 2:* 416-247-7678 *Terminal 3:* 416-776-5100 *Toll Free:* 866-207-1690
* **Canadian Automobile Assn.:** *461 Yonge St.,* Toronto On, M4Y 1X4. 416-221-4300
* **CAA Emergency Road Service** (24hr): 416-222-5222
* **Shoppers Drug Mart** (24hr pharmacy) *various locations:* 416-979-2424
* **Post Office Station A** – *25 The Esplanade,* Toronto M5E 1W5. 416-979-8822
* **Road Conditions** – 416-599-9090
* **Weather** (24hr) – 416-661-0123

STAYING IN TORONTO

$ The Residence College Hotel – *90 Gerrard St. W., Toronto ON, M5G 1J6.* ☎416-351-1010. www.hostels.com. *420 rooms (only 30 are double).* 🛏 A former nurses' residence, this high rise adjacent to Toronto Hospital offers very modest rooms with single beds, desk, telephone and climate control. Two

washrooms per floor. Communal TV lounge, equipped kitchen and laundry facilities on each of 15 floors. The best features are the location and the fitness centre with its swimming pool.

$$ Cawthra Square – *10 Cawthra Square, Toronto ON, M4Y 1K8.* ☎416-966-3074 , toll-free 1-800-259-5474. www.cawthrasquare.com. *32 rooms.* 🅿 Spa. A few blocks from Church Street Village (Toronto's gay community), these inviting B&Bs offer lodgings in three restored period houses: an Edwardian at Cawthra Square, and Victorians at 512 and 514 Jarvis Street. A two-minute walk apart, the properties offer rooms at several levels of comfort; most have private baths and terraces. Rates include tea each afternoon, and guests have 24-hour access to beverages and snacks. Full-service spa at Cawthra Square.

$$ Hotel Victoria – *56 Yonge St., Toronto ON, M5E 1G5.* ☎416-363-1666 or 800-363-8228. www.hotelvictoria-toronto.com. *56 rooms.* ✗🅿. Situated only a few blocks from theatres, shopping and restaurants, this small boutique hotel is dwarfed by Yonge Street skyscrapers. Small standard rooms, nicely decorated in dark woods and warm peach and grey tones, include standard amenities and high-speed internet access as well as access to a health club.

$$ Strathcona Hotel – *60 York St., Toronto ON, M5J 1S8.* ☎ 416-363-3321 or 800-268-8304. www.thestrathconahotel.com. *194 rooms.* ✗🅿 Spa. Situated across the street from Union Station, smack in the middle of the Financial District, the Strathcona has a pleasant lobby facing busy York Street. Recently renovated rooms are on the small side, but are cheery and comfortable, with modern amenities; corporate rooms are equipped with data ports and dual-line phones. Guests here have access to a nearby fitness club and spa.

$$$ Metropolitan – *108 Chestnut St., Toronto ON, M5G 1R3.* ☎416-977-5000, toll-free 1-800-668-6600. www.metropolitan.com. *422 rooms.* ✗🅿. Sleek, clean lines and Asian influences permeate this fine downtown hotel. Guest rooms have blond woods, glass, and neutral colour schemes as well as down duvets, Italian linens, in-room safes, Internet access and windows that oen. The award-winning **Lai Wah Heen** (**$$$**) restaurant, whose name means "luxurious meeting place," serves some of the best Cantonese cuisine in the city.

$$$$ The Fairmont Royal York – *100 Front St., Toronto ON, M5J 1E3.* ☎*416-368-2511, toll-free 1-800-866-5577. www. fairmont.ca. 1,365 rooms.* ✕⛄🅿🛏 Spa. Its noble facade a familiar part of the city skyline, Toronto's landmark hostelry is palatial. From its imposing chande-liered lobby to its grand ballrooms, the hotel exudes an aura of majesty. Kings, prime ministers, three generations of Britain's Royal Family, not to mention countless celebrities, have stayed here. Elegant guest rooms offer all the ameni-ties and data ports.

$$$$ Le Royal Meridien King Edward – *37 King St. E. Toronto ON,M5C 1E9.* ☎*416-863-9700 , toll-free 1-800-543-4300. www.starwoodhotels.com. 298 rooms.* ✕⛄🅿. The "King Eddie," as it's locally known, dates to 1903 and the reign of King Edward VII. Marble pillars, a vaulted ceiling, fine period pieces and lavish floral arrangements decorate the public areas. Edwardian guest-room decor is fit for a king, with mahogany furnishings and marble baths, but with modern amenities including data ports. Crowned by a baroque plasterwork ceil-ing, the airy, palm-studded **Café Victo-ria ($$$)** is a lovely spot for a meal.

$$$$$ Sutton Place – *955 Bay St., Toronto ON, M5S 2A2.* ☎*416-924-9221, toll-free 1-866-378-8866. www.sutton-place.com. 294 rooms.* ✕⛄🅿🛏. This stylish hotel in tony Yorkville is a favour-ite with visiting celebrities. Old World charm and discretion combine here with modern-day comforts. Marble floors, lush carpets, antique furnish-ings and big bouquets of fresh flowers adorn the lobby. Spacious well-lit guest quarters, all newly decorated, contain traditional furnishings in dark or blond woods and feature full amenities for business travellers.

$$$$$ Windsor Arms – *18 St. Thomas St., Toronto ON, M5S 3E7.* ☎*416-971-9666 or 877-999-2767. www.windsorarmshotel. com. 26 rooms.* ✕⛄🅿🛏 Spa. Near Bloor Street and neighbouring Yorkville, this high-end boutique hotel occupies a

1927 Gothic Revival structure. Inside, luxury meets high-tech in 26 suites (and 2 deluxe rooms) outfitted with fireplac-es, limestone baths and Frette linens as well as computer ports. The celebrated Tea Room becomes a champagne and caviar bar in the evening, and Club 22 features dancing, cocktails and a cigar lounge. In the **Courtyard Café ($$$$)** impeccable service complements fine continental cuisine.

WHERE TO EAT IN TORONTO

$ Shopsy's Deli – *33 Yonge St., Toronto ON,M5E 1G4.* ☎*416-365-3333. www. shopsys.ca.* ⛄**American.** A Toronto institution since 1921, this breakfast-lunch-dinner spot is famous for its all-beef hot dogs and corned beef sandwiches enjoyed in indoor booths, on the spacious patio or as a takeout order. There's a good range of sandwich platters, burgers and salads as well. Walls are lined with celebrity photos and caricatures.

$ Spring Rolls – *85 Front St E, Toronto ON, M5E 1B8.Also 2 locations in Missis-sauga.* ☎*416-365-3649. www.sprin-grolls.ca.* **Asian.** Sleek Asian decor and tasty, affordable Vietnamese, Chinese and Thai dishes attract students, a local office crowd and tourists. Entrée specials change daily and include soup and salad. Pad Thai, Thai red curry and stir-fries with Szechwan or black bean sauce top the list of the most popular dishes. And don't forget the spring rolls!

$$ The Red Tomato – *321 King St. W. M5V 1J5.* ☎*416-971-6626. www. fredsnothere.com. Happy hour and din-ner only.* **International.** One of many popular, bustling restaurants in the King Street entertainment district, this cozy lower-level eatery (its higher-priced sister, **Fred's Not Here**, resides upstairs) offers salads, gourmet pizza, pasta and grill-your-own tandoori dishes.

$$ Rodney's Oyster House – *469 King St. W, Toronto ON, M5V 1K4.* ☎*416-363-8105. www. Rodneysoysterhouse.com.* **Seafood.** The house specialty is fresh Malpeque oysters presented on the half shell with a wide choice of condiments, including homemade pepper sauces. A meal at Rodney's is a night of boister-ous, good old Maritime fun.

$$ Le Papillon – *16 Church St., Toronto ON, M5E 1M1.* ☎*416-363-3773. www.lep-apillon.ca. Closed Mon.* **French**. This is one of the few crêperies in Toronto, serving up French and Québécois fare on a quiet street close to Hummingbird Centre. Stucco walls and checkered tablecloths are resolutely France. In addition to a wide selection of crêpes—15 varieties, not including dessert—*plats principaux* include *tourtière* (a Québécois meat pie baked with seasoned pork, beef and veal), and steak au poivre. Le Papillon's onion soup, smothered with Emmenthal cheese and chunks of bread, is a meal in itself.

$$ Myth – *417 Danforth Ave, Toronto ON, M4K 1P1.* ☎*416-461-8383.* **Greek.** One of a conclave of restaurants in Greektown, Myth is an open, high-ceilinged eatery with video screens and pool tables. A Mediterranean-style menu is available inside or on the sidewalk patio. Entrées include creative dishes like balsamic glazed octopus, grilled vegetables with goat cheese, and lamb burger with Kaseri cheese and mint aïoli.

$$$ Sassafraz – *100 Cumberland St. Toronto ON, M5R 1A6.* ☎*416-964-2222. www.cafesassafraz.com.* **California/ French.** After a major renovation, this trendy eatery on one of Yorkville's prime corners (Cumberland & Bellair Sts.), has a new menu and outlook. For lunch, a bistro menu—steak-frites, salade Niçoise—is available on the sidewalk patio facing busy Cumberland Street. Inside, the sunny yellow garden room blooms year-round with herb trees under a 40ft atrium. Here you'll dine on creative cuisine such as bison carpaccio, or roasted lamb with eggplant croquant. Jazz sessions at 10pm several times a week.

$$$ Southern Accent – *595 Markham St., Toronto ON, M5G 2L7. Dinner only.* ☎*416-536-3211. www.southernaccent. com.* **Cajun/Creole.** Housed in a former Victorian residence, this funky Mirvish Village restaurant attracts a mixed crowd to its outdoor patio and small, mood-lit rooms on different levels. Start your meal with a Creole martini, made with Cajun pepper vodka. Favourites include Creole jambalaya and blackened chicken livers. Everything is à la carte, including the side dishes and yummy corn bread.

$$$$ Canoe – *66 Wellington St. W, Toronto ON, M5K 1H6.* ☎*416-364-0054. www.oliverbonacini.com.* **Canadian.** Overlooking the harbour and the Toronto Islands from its perch on the 54th floor of the Toronto Dominion Bank Tower, this perennial hot spot combines haute Canadian cuisine with excellent service. Signature dishes include venison loin, roast suckling pig and Maritime lobster salad. Minimalist decor mixes country pine and polished concrete.

$$$$ Splendido – *88 Harbord St, Toronto ON, M5S 1G5.* ☎*416-929-7788. www.splendido.ca.* **Canadian**. This Annex neighbourhood restaurant offers a unique selection of fresh Canadian ingredients with Mediterranean accents such as baked halibut filet with Tuscan bean ragoût or smoked pork belly with cauliflower tortellini. For dessert, perhaps the chocolate truffle cake.

TEA TREATS

Three historic hotels in downtown Toronto feature afternoon tea, complete with traditional accompaniments: finger sandwiches, scones with clotted cream, pastries, petits fours and a wide selection of loose-leaf teas.

At the sumptuous **Windsor Arms** hotel *(see above)*, afternoon tea is served in two daily sittings *(1pm & 3pm)* in the parlourlike Tea Room.

The landmark **Le Royal Meridien King Edward Hotel** *(see above)* offers a gracious tea service in its majestic **Café Victoria**. An elegant space with high ceilings, ornate mouldings, brocade-covered banquettes, and striking floral arrangements, it's one of the oldest dining rooms in the city.

Tea at the grande dame of hotels, **The Fairmont Royal York** *(see above))*, is served in EPIC, a sleek, modern restaurant space. *(Sun–Fri 2:30–4pm, Sat 1–4pm)* . A children's tea selection is available for little ones.

TORONTO SHOPPING

Whether your taste is chic or a bit more edgy, you'll find what you're looking for in Toronto's many shopping districts. The upscale shops at **Bloor/Yorkville**

(Bloor and Cumberland Sts., Yorkville and Hazelton Aves.) carry top designs—and the highest price tags. Offering everything from evening attire to frumpy weekend wear, **Yonge and Eglinton** caters to the yuppie crowd. Boutiques along **Queen Street West** (west of Bathurst St.) show off the latest fashion trends, while up-and-coming designers occupy **West Queen West** (Bathurst to Shaw St.), a bargain-filled bohemian hub where sophisticated buyers find haute couture at affordable prices. Finally, **College Street** (Bathurst to Shaw St.) attracts—what else—college students and others who want cutting-edge clothes and gear. For specifics, access www.city.toronto.on.ca/shoptoronto.

AHHHH!

After a day of shopping or sightseeing, treat yourself to a trip to one of Toronto's many spas. The three cited here offer a full menu of services, including hair care. The newly renovated and expanded **Elizabeth Milan Hotel Day Spa** (Arcade Level, The Fairmont Royal York. (♿ see above) ☎416-350-7500. www.elizabethmilanspa.com) offers professional treatments and services within a serene, Mediterranean-themed space, where the pace is deliberately slow. Skin care is a specialty and the Swedish massages are heavenly. Princess Margaret, the Duchess of York, Dame Edna and Jennifer Lopez are just a few of the celebrities who have been pampered here. With just seven treatment rooms, **The Spa at Windsor Arms** (♿ see above). ☎416-934-6031. www.windsorarmshotel.com) is as intimate and exclusive as the hotel itself. One unique treatment is Tui Na, a deep massage mixing Chinese and shiatsu techniques. The adjacent pool area with its poolside fireplace offers relaxation or invigoration. With an address in Crowne Plaza Toronto Centre, newly relocated **Victoria Spa** (225 Front St. W., 3rd floor, Toronto ON, M5V 2X3. ☎416-413-9100. www.victoriaspa.com) ushers patrons into a calm space accented with Asian artifacts. Victoria offers a full range of aesthetics and therapeutic massages, plus a juice bar, for men and women. After your treatment, take a dip in the sparkling pool or sun on the deck beneath tall CN Tower.

of 10 fountains that people can walk around or through. High-tech signage rather controversially surrounds the square. On the northeast corner of the intersection, **Metropolis**, a $100 million entertainment and retail complex, includes a venue for concerts, brand-name shops, restaurants, bars and 30 movie theatres.

As with all big, bustling cities, not everything looks bright and rosy. Toronto's downtown streets are often gridlocked, homelessness is visible and parking is expensive and often scarce. Still, Toronto is a great city to live in or to visit.

🚇 The ● symbol indicates a subway station.

The Waterfront★★

Built largely on land reclaimed in the mid-19C to mid-20C for the city's growing port installations, the area south of Front Street contains Toronto's foremost landmarks—the CN Tower and Rogers Centre—and its largest lakefront revitalization. Several quays were overhauled to house colourful shops, galleries, performance arenas, restaurants, sailing schools and an outdoor stage known as Molson Place. The grounds of both CN Tower and Rogers Centre can be reached on foot from Union Station by **Skywalk**, a large, glass-enclosed walkway containing eateries and souvenir shops.

CN Tower★★★

301 Front St. W.; Entrance at Front and John Sts. ●Union, then via Skywalk. ✕♿ 🕐Open June–Sept daily 9am–11pm. Rest of the year 9am–10pm. (Fri–Sat 10:30pm). Hours may vary; call to confirm. 🕐Closed Dec 25. 🎫$26 adult. ☎416-868-6937. www.cntower.ca.

The city's most prominent landmark, this concrete structure reaches 180 storeys (over 553m/1,815ft in height), the tallest freestanding structure in the world. It attracts some 2 million visitors a year. In only 58 seconds visitors are "beamed up" 346m/1,136ft (nearly the height of the Empire State Building) in one of six exterior glass-front elevators to the **look-out level**, a seven-storey-tall, circular steel "turban." From its observation decks, **views**★★ of the city and suburbs, the lake and shoreline are superb *(panels identify buildings and parks)*. One floor down, intrepid visitors can stand or sit on the **glass floor**, a section of thick glass panels that permit an impressive view 342m/1,122ft straight down to the ground below. There's also **360 Restaurant** *(reservations recommended; ☎416-362-5411)*, the world's highest revolving restaurant.

The sweeping **views**★★★ of the cityscape and Lake Ontario from the **Skypod**, a windowed ring 447m/1,465ft above the ground, are spectacular. If visibility is good, Niagara Falls and Buffalo, 120km/75mi away, can be seen.

Rogers Centre★★

●*Union, then via Skywalk.* ✕ ♿ 🅿 *☎416-341-2770. www.rogerscentre.com.*

This huge, domed sports/entertainment complex next to CN Tower is home to American League Baseball's Toronto Blue Jays. Designed by architect Roderick Robbie and engineer Michael Allen, the centre was built (1989) by a private consortium in partnership with local and provincial governments for over $570 million. The multipurpose stadium hosts rock concerts, conventions and trade shows as well as a variety of sports. Projecting from the Front Street facade 5m/16ft above street level, **Michael Snow's** 14 painted-fibreglass sculptures *(The Audience)* tower over arriving visitors. Rogers Centre boasts a 3ha/8-acre **retractable roof**, the 348-room Renaissance Hotel overlooking the playing field *(☎416-341-7100, toll-free 1-800-237-1512)*, a 150-seat cinema, several restaurants and underground parking.

Entertainment Galore

The centre of English-language culture in Canada, Toronto boasts the Toronto Symphony and the Mendelssohn Choir at Roy Thomson Hall, concerts at Massey Hall, the National Ballet of Canada, Toronto Dance Theatre, Harbourfront Centre's Premiere Dance Theatre, and the Canadian Opera Company at the Hummingbird Centre. The St. Lawrence Centre for the Arts, the Royal Alexandra, Princess of Wales Theatre, and the Elgin and Winter Garden Theatre Centre stage new and traditional plays and musicals.

Every fall the city hosts one of the world's premier film festivals, and summer brings a variety of outdoor entertainment. Several annual events draw visitors: the **Canadian National Exhibition** *(at the Exhibition Grounds late-Aug–Labour Day)*, reputedly the world's largest exhibition, now primarily a showcase for consumer goods; the **Metro International Caravan**, a festival of ethnic cultures *(mid-Jun)*; the **International Dragon Boat Festival**, a Chinese celebration *(Jun)*; and **Caribana**, a West Indies festival of steel bands and floating nightclubs on the lake *(mid-Jul–early Aug)*.

Spectator sports include Toronto Blue Jays baseball, an annual harbour regatta *(July 1)*, horse shows *(Royal Agricultural Winter Fair)*, soccer and auto racing. Air Canada Centre (1999) is home to Toronto Raptors basketball and Maple Leafs hockey.

Caribana Dancer

Harbourfront Centre★★

Info desk at York Quay Centre, 235 Queens Quay West, Toronto ON, M5J 2J8. Access from York, Spadina and Bathurst Sts. ●Union or Spadina, transfer to 510 LRT to York Quay Centre. ✗ ♿ 🅿 ⊙Open mid-Apr–mid-Oct daily10am–11pm (Sun & holidays 9pm). Rest of the year Tue–Sun 10am–6pm (Wed–Fri 8pm). Box office open Tues-Sat 1pm-6pm (8pm if there is an evening performance). ☎416-973-4000. www.harbourfront.on.ca.

A focal point of the city's cultural life, especially in summer, Harbourfront is also the scene of year-round recreational, educational and commercial activities.

Queen's Quay Terminal (1927), with its imposing clock tower, accommodates airy offices, plush living spaces, fashionable boutiques and eateries, the 450-seat Premiere Dance Theatre and, on the fifth floor, the offices of the Toronto Convention and Visitors Assn. Nearby, **York Quay Centre** houses an art gallery, a crafts studio and summer theatre. Next is the **Power Plant Contemporary Art Gallery (A)**, (♿⊙*Open year-round Tue–Sun noon–6pm, Wed 8pm. ⊙Closed Mon except holidays open noon–6pm. ☞$5 adult. ☎ 416-973-4949. www.thepowerplant.org*), the multipurpose **du Maurier Theatre Centre (B)**, with its glass-faceted foyer, evolved from a 1920s icehouse. The **concert stage (C)**, an open-air 1,750-seat concert facility, occupies the southwest corner of the quay. Sailing schools, nautical stores and restaurants are located at **Pier 4**, and the Marine Division of the Metro Police is based at John Quay. Just south of Pier 4 is **The Pier** Kids, a two-level interactive museum housing nautical exhibits, a children's discovery zone and videos on Toronto and harbour history.

Toronto Islands★★

Ferries depart from Queen's Quay to three points in summer (Centre Island, Ward's Island and Hanlan's Point mid-Apr–mid Oct) and two in winter (Ward's Island and Hanlan's Point mid-Oct–mid-Apr). Wards Island year-round daily 6:35am–11:45pm, other islands hours vary, consult schedule. ☞$6 round-trip. ♿ ☎416-392-8193. www.toronto.ca/parks/islands.

Harbourfront Centre

Ontario Tourism

These islands function as Toronto's principal public parkland. Extending 6km/3.7mi from end to end, they offer expansive lawns, age-old shade trees, sandy beaches, marinas and splendid **views**★★ of downtown Toronto. Attractions on Centre Island include restaurants, cafes, a beach (*on the Lake Ontario side*), a delightful theme/amusement park Kids for youngsters

GREEK ON DANFORTH

One of Toronto's most enjoyable walking neighbourhoods, the Danforth Avenue section known as Greektown (*www.greektowntoronto.com*) is lined with designer shops and restaurants, many with sidewalk patios. Popular eateries include **Myth** (💧*see Address Book*) and **Pappas Grill** (*440 Danforth Ave, M4K 1P4. ☎416-469-9595.*), best known for appetizers such as hummus and *tzatziki* dips and pizzas. **Romancing the Home** (*511 Danforth Ave. M4K 1P5. ☎416-461-4663*) stocks hand-painted dishware and herbal bath teas or imports from Africa such as hand-crafted mirrors, raffia, animal-print pillows and Moroccan tapestries. Kids love **Suckers** (*450 Danforth Ave.M4K 1P4. ☎416-405-8946*), a sweet shop brimming with candy, toys and premium ice cream. For great family fun, catch the annual **Taste of the Danforth** (*2nd weekend in Aug.www.tasteofthedanforth.com*), which turns this busy thoroughfare into a pedestrian walkway bursting with live entertainment, food stalls, music and fashion shows.

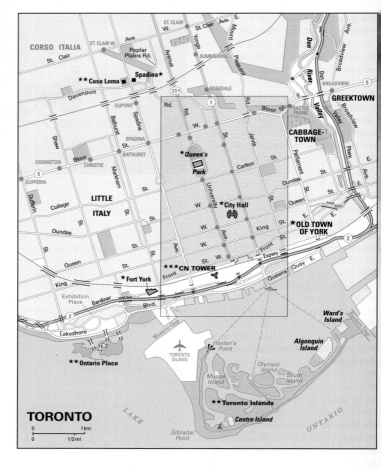

TORONTO

(⏰*Open mid-May–Labour Day, week-days 10:30am–5pm, weekends until 8pm.* ☎*416-203-0405. www.centreisland.ca*). Visitors can explore the islands on foot or by bike *(motor vehicles prohibited on the islands; bike rentals available)*, particularly **Algonquin** and **Ward's** Island, whose quaint roads lined with small, privately owned cottages have a decidedly rural charm. Near Toronto Island Airport on the islands' western end is **Hanlan's Point**, renowned for its **views** of the city *(a trackless train operates continuously between Centre Island and Hanlan's Point)*.

The hour-long **Inner Harbour & Island Cruise** offers fine **views** of downtown *(Departs from Pier 6, Queen's Quay West, York St. June–Aug every 30 min 10am–6pm, April–May & Sept–Oct, every hour 10am–5pm. Round-trip 1hr.* ⛴*$24 adult.* ℗*Toronto Harbour Tours:* ☎ *416-869-1372. www.we-know-toronto.com).*

Fort York★

🧒 *100 Garrison Road, Toronto ON, M5V 3K9. Access by Bathurst streetcar or by car: from Lakeshore Blvd. take Strachan St. just before Princes' Gate entrance to Exhibition Grounds, then right on Fleet St. and left on Garrison Rd. (under Gardiner Expressway).* ℗⏰*Open late-May–Labour Day daily 10am–5pm. Rest of the year daily 10am–4pm (weekends 5pm)* ⏰*Closed weekend before Christmas until Jan 2.* ⛴*$6 adult.* ☎*416-392-6907. www.fortyork.ca.* Constructed in 1793, Fort York was dev-astated in 1813 during American cap-ture. It was rebuilt, but peace meants its military importance diminished.

The **officers' barracks** is furnished to show the lifestyle of senior officers of the period. Costumed staff conduct tours and, in summer, stage military manoeuvres *(Jul–Aug)*. Events on Canada Day (July 1) and Simcoe Day *(Aug 1)* offer fife & drum, musketry and cannons.

Ontario Place★★

Kids *955 Lakeshore Blvd. W. Toronto ON, M5K 3B9. Access from Exhibition Grounds.* ✕ ♿ 🅿 🕐*Open Jul–Aug daily 10am–7pm. May–Jun & Sept call for hours. (Cinesphere* 🕐 *Open year-round.)* ✆ *$26 ($12.75 grounds only).* ☎ *416-314-9900. www.ontarioplace.com.*

This sprawling, innovative leisure complex designed by Eberhard Zeidler emerges from an extraordinary setting of lagoons, marinas and man-made islands on the lakefront bordering the Exhibition Grounds. With an emphasis on family entertainment and recreation, facilities include a water park, pedal and bumper boats, a water slide, mini-golf, helicopter rides, a children's village and restaurants.

Resembling a giant golf ball, **Cinesphere** features IMAX films on a screen six storeys high. The **amphitheatre** is is used to stage a variety of musical productions. The **water park** has wading pools full of water jets.

In winter, **Holiday Dreams** (🅿 🕐*Fri, Sat & Sun only, late Nov–early Jan. Call for hours. $12* ☎ *416-314-9900. www.holidaydreams.ca)* offers outdoor skating, petting zoo, riverboat café, live theatre and, at 8pm Sat, a firework display.

Old Town York★

Although little dates from the 1793 plans of Lieutenant-Governor Simcoe, some structures date from the early 19C, including an active marketplace, the **South St. Lawrence Market** *(92 Front St. E. at Jarvis St. Toronto On, M5E 1C4.* ●*King.* ✕ ♿ 🕐*Open year-round Tue–Thu 8am–6pm, Fri to 7pm, Sat 5am–5pm.* ☎*416-392-7120. www.stlawrencemarket.com)*, a cavernous brick building sheltering a two-storey food hall. the market is especially lively on Saturday morning when early-bird shopers converge on

Water park at Ontario Place

Ontario Tourism Marketing Parnership Corp.

fruit stands, bakeries, meat counters, and delicatessens. The market encases the surviving portion of the **Second City Hall** (1845-99). The former second-floor council chamber houses the **Market Gallery** of the City of Toronto Archives, which presents rotating exhibits of historical documents and artifacts (♿🕐*Open year-round Wed–Fri 10am–4pm, Sat 9am–4pm, Sun noon–4pm.* 🕐*Closed major holidays.* ☎*416-392-7604. www.toronto.ca/culture/the_market_gallery.htm)*.

Directly across the street is **North St. Lawrence Market**, a bustling farmers' market with many specialty vendors, housed in a smaller building. (✕♿ 🕐*Building open year-round. Farmers' market only Sat from 5am–5pm. Antique stalls hours vary – check Web site for days and times.* ☎*416-392-7219. www.stlawrencemarket.com)*. From the entrance there is a good view, to the west, of Toronto's **flatiron building**, the Gooderham (1892) on Wellington Street, against a backdrop of the towers of Brookfield Place.

Just behind the market via a charming walkway is the 1850 Neoclassical **St. Lawrence Hall** *(King and Jarvis Sts.)*, distinguished by its domed cupola. It now houses various commercial enterprises.

Just opposite is lovely St. James Park, a small manicured expanse that offers rest to passers-by.

Farther east is **Toronto's First Post Office**★ (Kids 260 Adelaide St. E., Toronto ON, M5A 1N1. Open year-round Mon–Fri 9am–4pm, weekends 10am–4pm. closed major holidays. ☎416-865-1833; www.townofyork.com), opened in 1833. Costumed staff demonstrate quill-and-ink letter-writing. Kids can write and post a letter the old-fashioned way for $1.

Downtown

Containing the city's formidable financial core, Toronto's downtown exudes a sense of momentum and prosperity. Site of the country's leading banks, legal, insurance and brokerage firms, and the Toronto Stock Exchange, the area of King and Bay streets constitutes Canada's "Wall Street."

The skyscrapers are connected by an **underground city** of shops, eateries, banks and concourses extending eight blocks from Union Station and the Fairmont **Royal York hotel** to City Hall, Eaton Centre and on up to Dundas

TAKING THE FIFTH

It has that Prohibition feel, but don't let the back-alley entrance fool you. **The Fifth Restaurant and Social Club** (225 Richmond St. W, M5V 1W2. ☎416-973-3000.), known as Easy and the Fifth, is no cheap date. Housed in a renovated factory in the city's buzzing Entertainment District, this nightclub/restaurant with the air of an upscale loft, attracts young professionals (ages 25 to 45) for weekend drinks and dancing. The recently opened Black Betty rock n' roll lounge bar is somewhat relaxed, though still swish (better dress up!). **The Fifth** ($$$) is one of the city's best restaurants, with skirted chairs, white linens, live piano music, and scrumptious French fare. In summer, enjoy your meal along with skyline views outside on **The Terrace,** a pretty rooftop patio. Restaurant reservations are a must.

Street. The PATH network of walkways, clearly marked, covers 10km/6mi.

One of the best-known and longest roads (1,896km/1,178mi) in Canada is **Yonge Street**, the city's east-west dividing line. Laid out by Simcoe in 1795 as a military route, this thoroughfare is lined with fancy boutiques, colourful flower stands, trendy restaurants, interesting stores and antiques shops.

Financial District★★

● King or St. Andrew

A stunning ebony-coloured ensemble covering an entire city block, the **Toronto-Dominion Centre**★★ was the first component of the current financial district. A fine example of the International style, the spartan black-glass towers, known locally as the T-D Centre, reflect the design of eminent 20C architect Mies van der Rohe, consultant for the project. The complex now includes five towers. Fronting Bay Street, the Ernst & Young tower (1992) incorporates the former Art Deco Stock Exchange Building (1937) within its base. On view throughout the centre are works by contemporary artists, predominantly Canadian.

The downtown abounds in other skyscrapers by noted architects, among them the adjacent **Royal Bank Plaza**★ **(D)**, designed by Boris Zerafa. Completed in 1976, the 41-storey and 26-storey gold reflecting-glass towers are linked by a 40m/130ft-high glass-walled banking hall, entry point to the underground city. A suspended sculpture of 8,000 aluminum tubes, the work of renowned Venezuelan artist Jesus Rafael Soto, dominates the interior of the hall.

The tiered, aqua-glass towers of **Brookfield Place**, (formerly BCE Place) designed by Spanish architect Santiago Calatrava, abut a lower central building bisected into matching office wings by an elaborate arched, aluminum **atrium**. The complex is also the home of the **Hockey Hall of Fame**★(E) Kids . Here, the original Stanley Cup is on display in the stately, domed lobby (1886) of the former Bank of Montreal building. (Take the escalator to lower level. Open daily Mon–Fri 10am–5pm, Sat 9:30am–

6pm, Sun 10:30am–5pm. ⏰Closed Dec 25, Jan 1. ☜$13. ☎416-360-7765. www. hhof.com).

Four buildings (1931 to 1972) form **Commerce Court**, a 57-storey stainless-steel tower, head office of the Canadian Imperial Bank of Commerce, designed by famed architect I.M. Pei.

Opposite Commerce Court, an "erector-set" canopy marks the entrance to the slender 68-storey **Scotia Plaza** (1988) by Boris Zerafa. It is distinguished by a V-shaped wedge at its summit.

First Canadian Place consists of a 72-storey white tower (1975) housing the Bank of Montreal and the 36-storey tower (1983) containing the **Toronto Stock Exchange (F)** (✖♿🅿⏰*Open year-round Mon–Fri 8:30am–5pm.* ⏰*Closed national holidays.* ☎416-947-4670. www.tsx.com). Stock Market Place, a ground-level interactive **visitor centre**, offers mock trader terminals, free Internet access and a giant wall of TV panels showing investment information. Connecting the towers is a three-level plaza with elegant shops and an attractive water wall. Under Adelaide Street, the PATH walkway leads to a grouping of shops known as the Lanes and another called the Plaza Shops, which extend to Sheraton Centre.

Designed by Boris Zerafa, the multifaceted glass towers of **Sun Life Centre**★ (1984) frame the east and west sides of University Avenue at King Street. Near the entrance to the 28-storey east tower, an outdoor sculpture by Sorel Etrog suggests a massive wheel-based tool.

Roy Thomson Hall★★
60 Simcoe St., Toronto ON, M5J 2H5. ●*St. Andrew.* ♿*Visit by guided tour (1hr) only, year-round, call for hours.* ☜*$5. Reservations required.* ☎416-593-4822. www.roythomson.com.

Resembling a large inverted bowl, this glass-sheathed concert hall, named for Canadian newspaper magnate Roy Thomson and designed by **Arthur Erickson**, dominates the corner of King and Simcoe streets. Opened in 1982 and the home of the Toronto Symphony, the hall retains is acoustical superiority. To insulate the performance area, a thick circular passageway with entry doors at intervals creates a "sound lock." Transparent at night when illuminated, the diamond-shaped exterior panels shimmer in daylight, their blue cast a reflection of the sky.

On Front Street, south of Roy Thomson Hall, the concrete box-shaped 10-storey **Canadian Broadcasting Centre**, built in the Deconstructivist style in 1992, was designed by Philip Johnson.

City Hall Area★
●*Osgoode or Queen*

With its crescent-shaped towers and mushroomlike council chamber, **City Hall**★, completed in 1965, was the sym-

Roy Thomson Hall and the Financial District

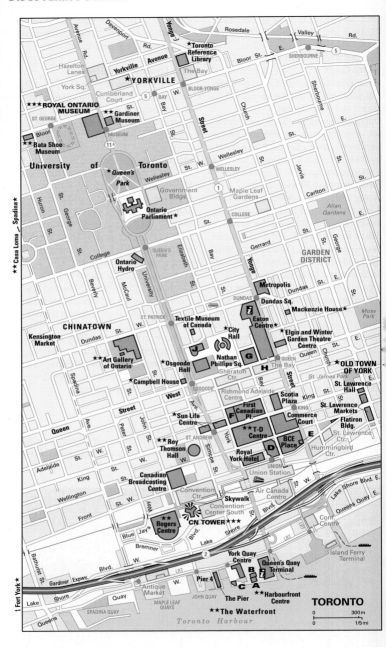

TORONTO

0   300m

0   1/5mi

bol of Toronto until supplanted by icons the CN Tower and Rogers Centre. The masterpiece by Finland's **Viljo Revell** remains a landmark nevertheless. Spacious **Nathan Phillips Square** (named for a former mayor), with its wide, arch-covered reflecting pool, attracts crowds of ice-skaters in winter. Henry Moore's outdoor bronze sculpture *The Archer* led to the sizable collection of his pieces in Toronto's Art Gallery of Ontario.

Occupying the east side of the square, **Old City Hall★ (G)**, designed by Toronto-born **Edward J. Lennox** (1855-1933), houses the provincial courts. Extending several blocks on Yonge Street between Queen and Dundas streets is **Eaton Centre★** (●*Queen.* ✕ ♿ 🅿 ⏱ *Open year-round Mon–Fri 10am–9pm, Sat 9:30am–7pm, Sun noon–6pm.* ☎*416-598-8560. www.torontoeatoncentre. com)*, a five-level office/shopping complex with trees, plants, fountains and natural lighting designed by Eberhard Zeidler.

The Hudson's Bay Company ("The Bay"), can be reached by a covered walkway across Queen Street.

Elgin and Winter Garden Theatre Centre★

189 Yonge St., Toronto ON,M5C 1J3. Opposite Eaton Centre north of Queen St. ●*Queen.* ♿☎•*Visit by guided tour (1hr 30min) only, Thur 5pm, Sat 11am.* ☎*$10. Box office Mon–Sat 11am–5pm, or until show time performance days.* ⏱*Closed Dec 25.* ☎*416-314-2871. www. heritagefdn.onca*

Reopened in 1989 after extensive restoration, this National Historic Site houses one of the few remaining double-decker theatres in the world. Designed by Thomas Lamb, the 1,500-seat Elgin and 1,000-seat Winter Garden opened in 1913 and 1914 respectively as vaudeville, and later, silent-film houses. The Elgin theatre is reached through a gilded lobby of Corinthian pilasters and arched mirrors. A seven-storey marble staircase leads to the fanciful Winter Garden, with its ceiling of hanging beech boughs.

Mackenzie House★

82 Bond St., Toronto ON, M5B 1X2 ●*Dundas.* ⏱*Open May–Labour Day Tue–Sun noon–5pm. Sept–Dec Tue–Fri noon–4pm, weekends noon–5pm. Rest of the year weekends noon–5pm.* ⏱*Closed major holidays.* ☎*$4 adult, holidays $5.50* ☎*416-392-6915. www.toronto.ca/culture/ mackenzie_house.htm.*

This 19C brick row house was the last home of William Lyon Mackenzie, the rebel leader and publisher. Rooms on the three floors have been restored to the 1850s period. In the modern annex at the rear is a replica of his **print shop** with a hand-operated flatbed press.

Osgoode Hall★

130 Queen St. W., Toronto ON, M5H 2N6. ●*Osgoode. Quiet is necessary, since courts may be in session.* ⏱*Free 45 min guided tours Jul–Aug only, Mon–Fri 1 pm.* ☎*416-947-3300, toll-free 1-800-668-7380. www. lsuc.on.ca.*

Home to the Supreme Court of Ontario and the Law Society of Upper Canada, this stately Neoclassical edifice is set on expansive lawns west of Nathan Phillips Square. Erected in 1867 allegedly to keep cows out, an ornate cast-iron fence isolates the judicial bastion from the bustle of the city.

Ontario Tourism Marketing Partnership Corp.

Ice skating at City Hall complex

Henry Moore Sculpture Centre, Art Gallery of Ontario

The two-tiered, arched interior courtyard induces admiration, as does the magnificent **Great Library**—said to be "perhaps the noblest room in Canada." North of Osgoode Hall stands the provincial **Court House (J)**, with its circular rotunda and walkway to Nathan Phillips Square.

Campbell House★

160 Queen St. W., Toronto ON, M5H 3H3. (University Ave. at Queen St.) ●*Osgoode.* ◗*Visit by guided tour (30min) only, mid-May–Labour Day Tue–Fri 9:30am–4:30pm, weekends 12pm–4:30pm. Rest of the year Tue–Fri 9:30am–4:30pm.* ◷*Closed Jan 1 & Dec 25–26.* ◉*$4.50.* ☎*416-597-0227. www.campbellhouse-museum.ca*

Once belonging to **Sir William Campbell** (1758-1834), chief justice of Upper Canada from 1825 to 1829, the Georgian brick mansion (built 1822) was moved to this site in 1972 from its location in historic York. The restored rooms contain some fine period pieces and surviving portraits of the Campbell family.

The headquarters of Canada Life Assurance Co. rise just behind Campbell House. A prominent landmark, the building is distinguished at night by its tower, the lights of which indicate the barometer reading.

Art Gallery of Ontario★★

317 Dundas St. W., Toronto ON, M5T 1G4. ●*St. Patrick.* ✕⅋◷*Open year-round Wed–Fri 10am–9pm, weekends 10am–5:30pm.* ◷*Closed Jan 1, Dec 25.* ◉*$15 adults.* ☎*416-979-6648. www.ago.net. May be closed for renovation.*

In 2008, the museum will re-open after a massive $250 million transformation designed by Toronto-born architect Frank Gehry. Major elements include a façade in glass and wood for Dundas St, a new 4-storey south wing for contemporary art, and a large new social gathering space with a two-storey museum store, a restaurant and cafe, a lecture hall, a members' lounge and space for temporary exhibits. Art viewing space will increase by 50 per cent. The museum closed in late 2007 in order to re-hang its collection in the new space. The project was propelled by businessman Kenneth Thomson's donation of nearly 2,000 works and $70 million.

The gallery retains the world's largest public collection of works by renowned British sculptor **Henry Moore** (1898-1986). The permanent collection ranges from 15C European paintings to international contemporary art and includes Canadian art from the 18C to the present.

Henry Moore Sculpture Centre★★

The centre owns more than 1,000 of Moore's works, including 689 prints, 139 original plasters and bronzes and 74 drawings. The centre was designed by the artist to use natural light from the glass-panelled roof. At night, the effect of artificial lighting, with its interplay of shadows on the sculpted shapes, is stunning.

Permanent Collection★★

The **European Collection** covers the Old Masters, Impressionism and early-20C movements. Displayed in several galleries, the **Canadian Collection** features 18C to contemporary works. . Contemporary **Inuit art** on exhibit dates from 1910 to the present. Contemporary art and 20C art are displayed in galleries on both levels.

The Grange★

Entrance through art gallery's Agora restaurant and sculpture atrium.

The Grange, closed since 2005 due to work on the gallery, will re-open in 2008. This Georgian brick mansion (c.1817) was the home of lawyer, politician and Family Compact stalwart, **Henry John Boulton** (1790-1870). In 1875 the Grange became the home of well-known scholar **Goldwin Smith**, Regius Professor of History at Oxford, who made it a centre of intellectual pursuits and progressive ideas. The mansion is meticulously furnished to give the aura of Family Compact days. Of special interest is the beautiful, curved staircase in the entry hall. The basement contains kitchens typical of a 19C gentleman's house.

The residence faces lovely Grange Park *(open to the public via street access)*, from which visitors can appreciate the mansion's gracious facade.

Textile Museum of Canada

55 Centre Ave., Toronto ON, M5G 2H5. ●*St. Patrick.* & ⏲*Open year-round daily 11am–5pm (Wed 8pm).* ⏲*Closed major holidays.* ◉*$12 adult.* ☎*416-599-5321. www.textilemuseum.ca.*

Occupying two floors of a high-rise hotel/condominium complex, the only Canadian museum devoted exclusively to textiles features traditional and contemporary works from around the world.

Queen's Park★

Based on E.J. Lennox's landscape scheme of 1876, this oval-shaped park is the setting for Ontario's Parliament and nearby government buildings. To the west and east sprawls the **University of Toronto**, Canada's largest university, perhaps best known for its medical school where, in 1921, **Frederick Banting** and **Charles Best** succeeded in isolating insulin. To the south, the curved, mirrored, multi-storied headquarters of **Ontario Hydro** (1975, Kenneth R. Cooper) rises above the surroundings. The building has no furnace or heating plant; instead, energy given off by artificial lighting, equipment and people is stored in thermal reservoirs in the basement and recirculated.

COLLEGE STRIP

If you want to know where U of T and Ryerson students hang out, College Street *(between Bathurst and Shaw Sts.)* is the place. Quirky boutiques beckon during daylight hours, while lively clubs and pubs draw in late-night revellers. **Motoretta** *(no.554)* sells vintage Vespas in flashy colours along with related paraphernalia (☎*416-925-1818. www.motoretta. ca).* Diner-style **Café Diplimatico** *(no. 594)* is a combo coffeehouse/ice-cream haunt *(☎416-534-4637.www. diplimatico.ca. Open 8am–2pm)*, where latte lovers lay back on the outside patio. **Brasserie Aix** *(no. 584)* offers inspired French cuisine amid high-ceilinged elegance *(☎416-588-7377).* Streamlined **Xacutti** *(no. 503)* offers "new Indian" food in a hip setting *(☎416-323-3957).* To begin or end your evening, enter **Souz Dal** *(no. 636)*, an intimate lounge specializing in flavored martinis *(☎416-537-1883).*

Ontario Parliament★

●*Queen's Park.* ✕♿🚻 *Tours (30min) leaving from information counter at front doors. Victoria Day–Labour Day daily 9am–4pm. Rest of the year daily 10am–4pm. View legislature in session (call to ensure government is in session) from public galleries Mon–Wed 1:30pm–6pm, Thu 10am–noon, 1:30pm–6pm.* ○*Closed major holidays.* ☎416-325-7500. www.ontla.on.ca.

Dominating the south end of the park, the imposing sandstone 1893 **Legislative Building** (also called Parliament Buildings) typifies Richardsonian Romanesque architecture.

The ponderous exterior belies the interior's elegant beauty, particularly the white-marbled **west wing**, rebuilt after a fire in 1909, and the stately **legislative chamber** with its rich mahogany and sycamore. On view is the 200-year-old mace *(ground floor)*, a ceremonial gold "club" mandatory at House proceedings. Taken by the Americans during their 1813 assault on York, it was returned years later by President F.D. Roosevelt.

Gardiner Museum of Ceramic Art★★

111 Queen's Park, Toronto ON, M5S 2C7 (Across from the Royal Ontario Museum). ✕♿○*Open year-round Mon–Fri 10am–6pm (Thu 9pm), weekends 10am–5pm.* ○*Closed Jan 1, Nov 20 & Dec 25.* ▱$12 *adults (no charge Fri 4pm–9pm and on 1st Fri of month).* ☎416-586-8080. www.gardinermuseum.on.ca.

Located in a modern granite building, this museum, the project of collectors George and Helen Gardiner, features pottery and porcelain from a variety of countries and cultures.

The Pottery Gallery *(ground floor)* showcases **pre-Columbian** works from Mexico, and Central and South America dating from 2000 BC to about AD 1500—primarily figurines, vessels and bowls of Olmec, Toltec, Aztec and other cultures. Also included is 15C and 16C **Italian majolica** and 17C English tin-glazed **delftware**.

The Porcelain Gallery *(2nd floor)* features **18C porcelains** of Du Paquier, Sèvres (characterized by bright yellows), the great English companies—Worcester, Derby, Chelsea—and others. Highlights are the Meissenware pieces. The new Bell collection of blue-and-white Chinese porcelain, attractively presented in glass wall cabinets, contains close to 200 pieces.

The restaurant, called Jamie Kennedy at the Gardiner after its chef, opened in 2006 and has gained a considerable reputation.

Royal Ontario Museum★★★

● *Museum.*

Renowned for extensive research, this enormous museum, commonly referred to as the ROM, is housed in an H-shaped, five-floor building at Avenue Road and Bloor Street. Maintaining over 20 departments in art, archaeology and the natural sciences, the museum, known especially for its East Asian holdings, possesses a remarkable collection of six-million-plus artifacts and artworks from around the world.

The ROM continues to expand. Expected completion of its $270 million **Renaissance project** is 2009. Part of that project, the Michael Lee-Chin Crystal, designed by Daniel Libeskind, opened in mid-2007. It includes a new entrance, main lobby on Bloor Street West, seven permanent galleries and a restaurant.

▶ **Orient Yourself:** Located on the southwest corner of Bloor Street and Avenue Road, the ROM is best reached by foot or subway. A live webcam accessible from the ROM Website offers various views of the grounds.

🅿 **Parking:** The closest municipal lot is at 9 Bedford Road (1 block west of Avenue Road) and offers a discount for a minimum 3-hour stay. Metered parking is available on nearby streets but can be difficult to find.

🏛 **Don't Miss:** The Hands-on Biodiversity gallery on the second floor; the permanent exhibit of Western Art and Culture; the Palaeobiology exhibit, with its extensive fossil collections.

⏱ **Organizing Your Time:** Plan to spend at least 3–4 hours.

🧒 **Especially for Kids:** The ROM always has special exhibits and activities for kids. Check "ROM Kids" on the Web site for current news.

Visit

100 Queen's Park, Toronto ON, M5S 2C6. ✕&⏱*Open year-round daily 10am–5.30pm (Fri 9:30pm. Dec 24 & 31 4pm).* ⏱*Closed Jan 1 & Dec 25.* ⬭*$20 adult (free 90min before closing).* ☎*416-586-8000. www.rom.on.ca.* ♿*Due to ongoing construction, these galleries will not reopen until 2009: 20th Century Design, Byzantium, Rome, Nubia, Earth & Early Life and Minerals & Gems. A 2008 re-opening is planned for: Africa, the Americas & Asia, the Pacific, the Middle East, Textiles and Costumes and South Asia. The museum's floor plan, available at the information desk in the entrance rotunda, is most useful.*

Ground Floor

The grand entrance **rotunda** is vaulted, with an exquisite domed **ceiling** of golden mosaic tessarae. Before entering the galleries, note the two **totem poles** in the stairwells. Crafted of red cedar by the Nisga'a and Haida peoples of British Columbia in the 19C, the poles are so tall that their upper sections can be viewed from the second and third floors. The taller pole depicts the family history of the chief who owed it.

The outstanding exhibit on this floor is the **Chinese collection**, one of the largest and most important of its kind outside China. Spanning nearly 6,000 years, the exhibits date from the Shang dynasty 1523 BC (the Chinese Bronze Age) to the overthrow of the Qing or Manchu dynasty (1644-1911).

The collection is noted for its clay **tomb figures,** small replicas of people and animals buried with the dead as their "servants," and dating from the 3C AD. The star attraction, however, is the **Ming Tomb,** the only complete example in the Western world. It is reportedly the burial place of Zu Dashou, a 17C general who served the last Ming emperors and lived into the Qing period.

A series of interconnected galleries is devoted to **Later Imperial China** (10-19C). Traditional room settings, a life-size Chinese courtyard and a moon gate re-create the life of the gentry during the Ming (1368-1644) and Qing dynasties.

Remarkable for its ink and colour clay wall paintings, the **Bishop White Gallery** simulates the interior of a Northern Chinese temple. Life-size polychromed and gilded statues of *bodhisattvas* (those enlightened, compassionate individuals destined for Buddha status) of 12-14C stand in the centre.

The Herman Herzog Levy Gallery is a dimly lit room displaying light-sensitive

Ming Tomb

East Asian works of art (12-14C), including murals, monumental statues and a collection of small Buddhist and Daoist bronzes. Among the most dramatic works in the gallery of **Korean Art** is an eight-panel colour and ink painting on silk titled *One Hundred Boys at Play*. The newest permanent exhibit is the Christopher Ondaatje **South Asian** Gallery, showcasing textiles, jewellry, sculpture, arms and other artifacts. Another new gallery, **Dynamic Earth**, with a host of interactive exhibits and presentations, including fossils and rocks that can be touched and examined. A highlight is the S.R. **Perren Gem and Gold Room**, where exquisite collections of smaller gems and jewellery are housed.

Second Floor

Kids Natural history exhibits occupy this floor, the highlight of which are the magnificent, reassembled **dinosaurs** in authentic settings. Many of these skeletons come from upper cretaceous rocks exposed in the badlands of the Red Deer River Valley in central Alberta. The glass atrium of the **Bird Gallery** is filled with Canadian geese, turkeys, owls, ducks and an assortment of smaller birds preserved in flight. The **Bat Cave** is a lifelike reconstruction of the St. Clair Cave in Jamaica, complete with hundreds of handmade bats.

Hands-On Biodiversity is a two-level interactive gallery that lets visitors crawl into a simulated wolf's den; identify leaves, sounds and tracks; and touch tusks, horns, bones, skulls and skins, among other activities. The **Discovery Gallery** is an innovative space wiht interactive exhibits for children.

Third Floor

The **Ancient Egypt** exhibit depicts daily life via tools, utensils, jewellery and miniature figures. The section on **religion** includes coffins, animal mummies, canopic jars, the remarkably preserved **Antjau mummy** and the upright mummy case of a female musician. The **Punt wall reliefs**, sculptural casts from the temple of Queen Hatshepsut (1503-1482 BC), illustrate her trade mission along the Nile. The exhibit on **Nubia**, a region in present-day lower Egypt and Northern Sudan, features pottery, glassware, arms and jewellry from 2000 BC to the 19C. Classic forms of marble sculpture, gold coins and decorated amphora are displayed in the **Greeks and Etruscans Gallery** (1100-100 BC), while the **Islamic** section reproduces a life-size Middle Eastern house and bazaar. The small exhibit devoted to **Byzantium** (AD 330–1453) includes a display of jewellry dating from AD 500-700.

The **Samuel European Galleries** concentrate on decorative arts from medieval times to the present. The **Lee Collection** assembles medieval and Renaissance wares of gold and silver. In the **Arms and Armour** gallery, armaments from medieval chain mail to modern-day weaponry can be seen. **Culture and Context** presents partial-

Foot Notes

England's Edward II is credited with initiating the measurement of the "foot" in 1320. His own foot measured 36 barley corns; each corn was a third of an inch, making the total of 12 inches equal to one foot. In England in the 14C, the length of a shoe's pointed toe was regulated by law and depended upon the wearer's social status. The height of a shoe's heel also conveyed the social importance of the wearer. Thus, the wealthy were, and still are, termed "well-heeled." The origin of calling someone a "square" is said to derive from the wearing of square-toed shoes long after they were in fashion.

Source: *Bata Shoe Museum*

"Shoes are such a personal artifact. They tell you about the owner's social status, habits, culture and religion. That's what makes them special."

Sonja Bata, founder, Bata Shoe Museum

room reconstructions, such as a Victorian parlour (1860-85). Art objects and furnishings from medieval times to the 20C are displayed in the South Wing.

Lower Level

In the **Ontario Archaeology Gallery**, human-scale dioramas capture the life of the early Algonquin and Iroquoian peoples.
The **Sigmund Samuel Canadiana Gallery** presents paintings and decorative arts from Canada's past. Note in particular the panelled room from the Bélanger House c.1820.
Two other galleries on the lower floor, the **Heritage Gallery of Canada's Peoples** and the **Gallery of Indigenous Peoples**, showcase rotating exhibits such as works by the Inuit and First Nations peoples.

Additional Sights

Bata Shoe Museum★★

327 Bloor St. W., Toronto ON, M5S 1W7. ●*St. George.* ⟨♿⟩⟨🕐⟩*Open year-round Mon–Sat 10am–5pm (Thu 8pm), Sun 12pm–5pm.* ⟨🕐⟩*Closed Dec 25, Good Friday.* ⟨⟩*$8. No charge Thu 5pm–8pm.* ☎*416-979-7799. www.batashoemuseum.ca.*
Housed in a five-storey building designed by renowned architect **Raymond Moriyama** to resemble a shoebox, this unique museum draws on its

Elton John's platform boots

10,000-piece collection to illustrate a 4,500-year history of shoemaking and mankind's footwear. Shoes in the permanent exhibit range from 3,550-year-old Theban funerary slippers and 1,500-year-old Anasazi sandals to Mahatma Gandhi's leather chappals (c.1940s) and Princess Diana's fuchsia kid pumps.

Yorkville★

●*Bay.* Once the hangout of drug addicts and dropouts, Yorkville today represents all that is chic in Toronto—and a remarkable transformation. Between Yonge Street and Avenue Road, **Yorkville Avenue** presents charming Victorian houses converted to expensive boutiques or trendy cafes sporting the latest architectural facades.

Yorkville

ALL THE BEST

1099 Yonge St., Toronto ON, M4W 2L7.
☎*416-928-3330. www.allthebestfine-foods.com. In Sept, 2008, the shops will re-open in the renovated Scrivener Square development. Until then, the cheese and gourmet food store remains on Yonge St., while the bakery and party store are at 5 Scrivener Sq.*
The Best's Bakery sells bounteous with berry crisps, tarts, cheesecakes, breads and pastries. The **Gourmet Foods and Cheese Store** offers ready-to-go food as well as an array of Canadian and imported cheese, exotic sauces and gourmet supplies. The **Party Store**, sells snazzy table linen, candles, cutlery, wine coolers and picnic packs. When you tire of shopping, step next door to **Patachou French pastry shop** *(1095 Yonge St., Toronto ON, M4W 2L7.* ☎*416-927-1105)* for an invigorating cup of espresso, and perhaps take home a baguette.

In York Square at the corner of Avenue Road and Yorkville Avenue, shops surround an interior brick courtyard where summer dining is alfresco. Behind the square lies posh Hazelton Lanes *(open during business hours)*, a labyrinthian shopping/office/condominium complex (1978) designed by Boris Zerafa . On the other side of Yorkville Avenue, Cumberland Court is a rambling enclosure of old and new shops, eateries and offices, with a passageway to Cumberland Street.

Toronto Reference Library★

789 Yonge St., Toronto ON, M4W 2G8. ●*Bloor-Yonge.* &🕐*Open Mon–Thu 9:30am–8:30pm, Fri 9:30am–5:30pm, Sat 9am–5pm.* 🕐*Closed Sun.* ☎*416-395-5577. www.tpl.toronto.on.ca.*

An architectural gem designed by Raymond Moriyama, this massive brick and glass building contains Canada's most extensive public library with 4.5 million items and 50 miles of stacks on 5 floors.

Rising from a wide, light-filled centre, the tiered balconies are bordered by solid undulating balustrades.

In a cozy corner on the fifth floor is a tiny room *(access from 4th floor)* brimming with the **Arthur Conan Doyle Collection**—famed Sherlock Holmes stories, Sherlockian criticism, Doyle's autobiography, historical novels, poetry and other writings. Worn Victorian furnishings complement mementos of the great detective's presence.

Casa Loma★★

1 Austin Terrace, Toronto ON, M5R 1X8. ●*Dupont, then climb steps.* ✕🅿🕐*Open year-round daily 9:30am–5pm (last*

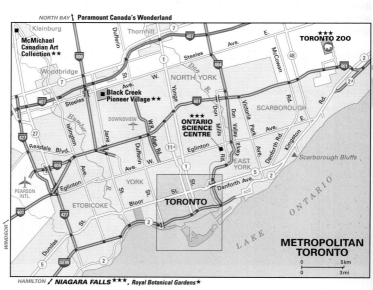

NORTH BAY \ **Paramount Canada's Wonderland**

Kleinburg

McMichael Canadian Art Collection ★★

Woodbridge

Thornhill

NORTH YORK

Black Creek Pioneer Village ★★

DOWNSVIEW

Rexdale Blvd.

PEARSON INTL.

YORK

ETOBICOKE

★★★ TORONTO ZOO

★★★ ONTARIO SCIENCE CENTRE

SCARBOROUGH

EAST YORK

Scarborough Bluffs

TORONTO

LAKE ONTARIO

METROPOLITAN TORONTO

0   5km
0   3mi

HAMILTON / **NIAGARA FALLS** ★★★, *Royal Botanical Gardens* ★

Mr. McGregor's House

10503 Eglinton Ave., Kleinburg ON, L0J 1C0. ☏905-893-2508. For a delightful afternoon tea, coffee break or lunch after visiting the McMichael gallery in the village of Kleinburg, enter this charming yellow house, named for the Beatrix Potter character, on the main street. McGregor's offers a bounty of tea cakes, cookies, tarts, fruit pies, nut breads, muffins, scones and other pastries—all labelled and set out on a large wooden table so guests can help themselves. An array of flavoured coffees and teas as well as juices and other beverages is also available. Eat inside in one of the whimsical dining rooms or outside at garden tables placed on the expansive backyard lawn, bordered with flowers and shaded by grand oaks.

admission 4pm). ⏰Closes 1pm Christmas Eve, closed Dec 25. ☜$16 adult. ☏416-923-1171. www.casaloma.org.

This enormous sandstone castle, completed in 1914, was the lavish 98-room residence of prominent industrialist Sir **Henry Pellatt**. Maintained since 1937 by the Kiwanis Club, the Medieval mansion is a popular tourist attraction.

Seven storeys in height, the castle boasts two towers—one open-air, the other enclosed—which offer good views of the city; secret passageways; and a 244m/800ft underground tunnel to the magnificent **carriage house** and stables. The palatial residence includes 21 fireplaces, a **great hall** (22m/70ft ceiling), a marble-floor conservatory, an oak-panelled drawing room and a library for 10,000 books. Especially well appointed are the **Round Room** with its exquisite Louis XV tapestry furnishings, the **Windsor Room** and Lady Pellatt's suite.

Spadina Museum★

285 Spadina Rd., Toronto ON, M5R 2V5. ●Dupont, then climb steps. ♿☜☜ Visit by guided tour (1hr) only, Apr–Labour Day Tue–Sun & holiday Mon noon–5pm. Sept–Dec Tue–Fri noon–4pm, weekends noon–5pm. Jan–Mar Sat noon–5pm. ⏰Closed Dec 25. ☜$6 adult ($6.75 on holidays). ☏416-392-6910. www.toronto.ca/culture/spadina.htm.

Spadina Museum is a historic house and garden that overlooks its 2.5ha/6-acre grounds in a fashionable residential district. The 50-room brick mansion was home to businessman **James Austin** and his heirs.

In 1866 Austin, a successful grocer who eventually headed Consumers' Gas and founded the Dominion Bank, acquired the estate. His son added the spacious billiard room in 1898 and, in 1907, the terraces and porte-cochere. The third floor, with its hipped roof and pedimented dormers, was built in 1912.

Reflecting the grandeur of Victorian and Edwardian styles, the spacious **drawing room** with its matching striped seating, and the airy wicker-furnished **palm room** show the comforts the Austin family expected.

Metro Sights

Ontario Science Centre★★★

Kids 770 Don Mills Rd. Toronto ON, M3C 1T3, 11km/7mi from downtown (22km/14mi by car via Don Valley Pkwy. to Eglinton Ave.). ●Eglinton and then no. 34 Eglinton East bus (to Don Mills Rd. stop). ✕♿🅿⏰Open year-round daily 10am–5pm. ⏰Closed Dec 25. ☜$17 adult ($25 with Omnimax). ☏416-696-1000. www.ontariosciencecentre.ca. Demonstrations and Omnimax films daily. For times and locations, check notice board at the bottom of escalator, level C.

Cascading down the Don River ravine, this sizable complex, designed by Raymond Moriyama, takes full advantage of its natural site. This popular attraction consists largely of interactive exhibits on science and technology.

The five levels are designated by letters, levels B, C, D and E being the exhibit/activity floors. Level C's **Earth/Food** section has a 5m/15ft-high stack of grocery-filled shopping carts to illustrate "Food for a Year," while **Space** includes a rocket chair, hydroponics, supergravity and other exhibits. Highlights of level D are the **Living Earth** exhibit, where visitors explore a limestone cave and experience an indoor rain forest; the **Hall of Transportation**, with its ascending model hot-air balloon, CA-3 powerboat and old-fashioned bicycles; the **Science Arcade**, with humorous electricity demonstrations; and **Communications**, where visitors can participate in papermaking. The **Hall of Technology** features, most recently, an Information Highway exhibit where visitors can access the Internet.

Toronto Zoo★★★

Kids *361A Old Finch Ave, Scarborough ON, M1B 5K7. 35km/22mi from downtown. ●Kennedy, transfer to bus 86A.* ✕ ♿ 🅿 *(free)* ◷*Open mid-May–Labour Day 9am–7:30pm, Jan–early Mar & early Oct–Dec 9:30am–4:30pm, early Mar–mid-May & Sept–early Oct 9am–6pm.* ◷*Closed Dec 25.* 🚌*$20 adult.* ☎*416-392-5929. www. torontozoo.com. Site map is available at the entrance. Begin by boarding the narrated shuttle, the Zoomobile (daily July–Labour Day 10am–7pm. Rest of the year Mon–Fri 10am–6pm, weekends 10am–6pm.* 🚌*$7 adult all-day pass), which provides an excellent overview of main attractions. Disembark at the Serengeti station and continue on foot.*

Opened in 1974, this world-class zoological park features a remarkable variety of wildlife on 287ha/710 acres of tableland and forest. The 5,000 animals are divided into six "zoogeographic" regions: Africa, Australasia, Eurasia, the Americas, Indo-Malaya and Canada. Among the 460 species represented are numerous endangered or rare animals such as the Siberian tiger, the snow leopard, the Malayan tapir, the pygmy hippopotamus and the Indian rhinoceros. Designed by Raymond Moriyama, harmoniously integrated glass and wood pavilions provide shelter for animals unadapted to Canada's climate.

The popular **Africa Pavilion**, abundant with tropical vegetation and exotic birds, is home to lowland gorillas and other primates as well as Canada's largest herd of African elephants. The **Edge of Night** exhibit *(in the Australasia Pavilion)* provides a journey into a nocturnal world

Spa Getaways

Hidden in the countryside an hour north of Toronto, **($$) High Fields Country Inn & Spa** *(PO Box 218,11568-70 Concession 3, Zephyr ON, L0E 1T0.* ☎*905-473-6132. www.highfields.com. Check website for updated rates.)* commands a hilltop overlooking Ontario's farmlands. A winding road leads to a large barn with horse pastures and the inn itself, complete with outdoor pool and tennis court. Paths groomed for guided nature walks or cross-country skiin thread the expansive property. The rambling main house holds overnight guest quarters, a dining area and treatment rooms. High Fields offers new-age techniques such as chakra and Japanese Reiki along with facials, wraps, massages and hydrotherapies. Breakfast, lunch and dinner **($)** are available.

Tucked away on 14 wooded acres in residential Port Hope, about an hour east of Toronto, **Ste. Anne's Country Inn & Spa,** a Haldimand Hills Spa **($$$$$)** *(175 Dorset St. W., RR#1, Grafton ON, K0K 2G0.* ☎*905-349-2493, toll-free 888-346-6772. www.haldimandhills.com)* welcomes guests to its grand porticoed mansion, appointed with Irish antiques, and surrounded by lushly landscaped grounds. Amenities include an outdoor pool, fitness room, sauna, chef-staffed kitchen, and dining room that affords a view of Lake Ontario. Body treatments include facials, manicures, pedicures, hydrotherapies, massages, wraps and exercise sessions.

Ste. Anne's Country Inn & Spa

Courtesy Haldimand Hills Spa

inhabited by seldom-seen species like the Tasmanian devil. Rides and special activities for kids are available: *Camel rides $6, Face painting $6, Pony rides $5, Safari Simulator $6, Airbrush tattoos $6.*

Black Creek Pioneer Village★★

Kids *1000 Murray Ross Parkway, Toronto ON, M3J 2P3. 29km/18mi northwest of downtown. ●Yonge and Finch, transfer to Steeles bus no. 60.* ✕🅿🕐*Open July–Labour Day Mon–Fri 10am–5pm, weekends & holidays 11am–5pm, May–June & Sept–Dec 9:30am–4pm, weekends & holidays 11am–4:30pm.* 🕐*Closed Dec 25, 26 and Jan–Apr.* ✆*$13 adult.* ☎*416-736-1733. www.blackcreek.ca. Site plan is distributed at the entrance.*

The village comprises 40 buildings, including 5 from the original farm established between 1816 and 1832 by Pennsylvania-German settlers, and a collection of 19C structures moved to the site.

Upon exiting the **orientation centre,** visitors enter mid-19C Ontario, among abundant greenery and dirt roads flanked by wooden sidewalks and split-rail fences. Highlights include the tinsmith shop; the **Stong farm;** the Half Way House, a spacious white inn with a two-tiered veranda; **Roblin's Mill,** a handsome four-storey water-powered stone gristmill; and the printing office, complete with a working flatbed press.

Costumed guides demonstrate traditional 19C crafts and trades.

Excursions

Canada's Wonderland

Kids *9085 Jane St, Vaughn, ON, L6A 1S6. 30km/19mi north by Hwy. 400 and Rutherford Rd. 9580 Jane St. GO TRANSIT from ●Yorkdale or York Mills.* ✕🕭🅿🕐*Open early May–early Nov daily 10am (closing times vary).* ✆*Admission packages vary. Consult website or phone.* ☎*905-832-8131. www2.cedarfair.com/canadas wonderland.*

This theme park features 200 attractions, including rides, both thrilling and less so, with lots of activities for children. There is an outdoor wave pool as well as shows, events and concerts.

McMichael Canadian Art Collection★★

10365 Islington Ave. Kleinburg ON, L0J 1C0. About 40km/25mi north. Hwy. 400 to Major Mackenzie Dr., then west about 6km/4mi to Islington Ave., then north 1km/.6mi. 🕐✕🕭🅿 *Open daily year-round Mon–Sat 10am–4pm, Sun 10am–5pm.* 🕐*Closed Dec 25.* ✆ *$15.* ☎*905-893-1121 or toll-free 1-888-213-1121 (Canada/US). www.mcmichael.com.*

Housed in log and fieldstone buildings among the wooded hills of the Hum-

Canada's Wonderland

Afternoon, Algonquin Park (1914) by Tom Thomson

ber Valley, this gallery features paintings by the first truly Canadian school—the **Group of Seven**. The gallery also owns a sizable collection of contemporary First Nations and Inuit art.

Though pioneer **Tom Thomson** (1877-1917) died before the group was formed, his influence was substantial. The original members were **Lawren Harris, A.Y. Jackson, J.E.H. MacDonald, Franklin Carmichael, Arthur Lismer, Frederick Varley** and **Frank Johnston**. Johnston left after the first exhibition; **A.J. Casson** joined the group in 1926. The group officially disbanded in 1932, but some members formed the Canadian Group of Painters, which had much the same aims. In 1952 **Robert and Signe McMichael** bought land in rural Kleinburg, decorating their home with Group of Seven paintings. In 1965 they donated their famed collection and property to the province of Ontario. Subsequent gifts by such individuals as R.S. McLaughlin have enlarged the collection.

Examples by artists influenced by the seven, notably **Clarence Gagnon, Emily Carr** and **David Milne**, are also displayed. On exhibit upstairs are fine works by contemporary Native artists such as Clifford Maracle, **Norval Morrisseau, Daphne Odjig** and **Arthur Shilling.**

Niagara Falls★★★
130km/81mi. ⚑*See Entry Heading.*

Parkwood Estate★★
61km/38mi. ⚑*see OSHAWA.*

Royal Botanical Gardens★
70km/44mi. ⚑*see HAMILTON.*

UPPER CANADA VILLAGE★★★

MAP P 217

The village was created in the late 1950s when plans were made to flood some 20,000 acres of farmland during construction of the St. Lawrence Seaway and the control dam at Cornwall. More than 500 houses, churches, offices, shops and other structures were moved to higher ground. Today some 25 of these heritage buildings can be visited in Upper Canada Village.

Information: Upper Canada Village, 13740 Country Road 2, Morrisburg. ☎613-543-4328, toll-free 1-800-437-2233. www.uppercanadavillage.com

▸ **Orient Yourself:** The village is located in Morrisburg, on the St. Lawrence upriver from Cornwall on Hwy 401. It is south of Ottawa on Hwy 31.

Parking: Leave your car at the large parking lot near the entrance.

Don't Miss: Beach's sawmill to see water-powered sawing of logs into boards; draft horses and oxen being used at Louck's Farm.

Organizing Your Time: Plan to spend 3–4 hours, but one- and two-hour tours are possible.

Especially for Kids: The costumed interpretors include children, so visiting kids can interact with their own ages.

Also See: OTTAWA, KINGSTON

Access

11km/7mi east of Morrisburg. From Hwy. 401, take Exit 758 (Upper Canada Rd.) and travel south. Turn left onto Country Rd. 2 and continue east 2km/1.25mi to the village. Parking lot is just past Crysler Farm Battlefield Park.

Visit

Open mid-May–early-Oct daily 9:30am–5pm. Horse-drawn transportation (free) on premises. $17 adult.

☎613-543-4328 or 800-437-2233. www. uppercanadavillage.com.

Costumed "inhabitants" walk the sawn boardwalks or are drawn by horses on sandy roads. They make cheese and bread, quilt, operate the mills and complete farm chores, among other activities.

Note in particular the elegant refinement of the **Robertson House**, a middle-class residence; the solid prosperity of the **Loucks Farm**, in contrast to the tenant farm; and **Crysler Hall** with its Greek Revival architecture. There are also churches and schools, a village

Upper Canada Village

Ontario Tourism Marketing Partnership Corp.

Address Book

WILLARD'S

$$ ☎ 613-543-3735. www.uppercana-davillage.com. A popular dining spot within Upper Canada Village, Willard's Hotel prepares authentic 19C fare for visitors to sample at lunch and tea time. Delectable dishes such as pan-fried perch in Rosemary and Robert's sauce, and sirloin steak smothered in wine-rich gravy issue forth from the busy kitchen. Homemade apple pie, bread pudding and lemon syllabub are good dessert choices. Afternoon tea is served upstairs on the wide front porch well shaded by the hotel's ample eaves, or indoors, in the upstairs parlour.

A NIGHT AT A FARMHOUSE

c/o Upper Canada Village, 13740 Country Rd 2, Morrisburg ON, K0C 1X0. ☎613-543-4328, toll-free 1-800-437-2233. Minimum 2 nights Jun–Aug. Families and groups of up to six people will find solitude at the **Upper Canada Guest House**, (**$$$**) a two-storey, late-19C farmhouse, which rents out as a complete accommodation. Its location on a grassy point that juts into the wide St. Lawrence River assures guests excellent views.

---

store, a doctor's surgery, a print shop and a tavern.

In the heart of the village stands **Willard's Hotel**, where patrons may enjoy an 1860s-style meal. (⟳ see Address Book) There's also the cafeteria-style Village Cafe and the Harvest Barn Restaurant. The **sawmill,** flour mill and **woollen mill** operate on water power and show the trend toward industrialization. The flour mill features a steam engine that dates to 1865.

A **children's activity centre** housed in a large barn offers educational activites.

Nearby Attractions

Battlefield Monument

Beside Upper Canada Village in the park. This monument commemorates the **Battle of Crysler Farm** in 1813, when British and Canadian troops routed a much larger American force. It stands beside the St. Lawrence River with a fine **view**. (Visitor Centre ⊜$3)

Long Sault Parkway

5km/3mi east of Upper Canada Village between Ingleside and Cornwall via Rte. 2. This scenic drive traverses a chain of connected islands in the St. Lawrence River. Activities along the way include fishing, boating (canoe rentals available), and picnicking. Bicycle and walking trails abound, and there are sand swimming beaches and bird-watching. Three campgrounds are administered by the St. Lawrence Parks Commission. Information and reservations: ☎613-543-3704.

WINDSOR ★

POPULATION 218,473 – MAP P 216SS

Like Detroit, this industrial centre is a major automobile manufacturer and a port on the Great Lakes/St. Lawrence Seaway system. Today Windsor is one of Canada's busiest points of entry. Every year an **International Freedom Festival** is celebrated (*Jun–Jul*) to include the national holidays of both countries: July 1st and July 4th.

Information: Tourist Office, 333 Riverside Dr. W., Suite 103. ☎519-255-6530. toll-free 1- 800-265-3633. www.visitwindsor.com

▸ **Orient Yourself:** The city of Windsor lies on the south side of the Detroit River opposite the American city of that name. A suspension bridge and tunnel connect the cities.

Parking: US quarters are accepted at parking meters and pay/display machines. Check signage very carefully. Overnight parking is prohibited on certain streets.

Don't Miss: Dieppe gardens, a place to watch boats pass in the Seaway.

Also See: POINT PELEE NATIONAL PARK, DRESDEN, LONDON

A Bit of History

The area was first settled by the French. In 1701 **Antoine de la Mothe Cadillac** built a post on the north side of the Detroit River that became the headquarters of the French fur trade in the Great Lakes/Mississippi River area. Captured by the British in 1760, the fort and town were handed over to the Americans after the Revolution, and the Detroit River became the international border.

Sights

Dieppe Gardens ★

The outstanding attraction of this park, which stretches several blocks along the river west of the main thoroughfare (*Ouellette Ave.*), is its **view** ★★ of the Detroit skyline across the water. It is also a good vantage point from which to watch the huge ships of the seaway.

Art Gallery of Windsor ★

401 Riverside Dr. West, Windsor ON, N9A 7J1. ✕ ♿ ⊙ *Open year-round Wed 11am–8pm, Thu–Fri 11am–9pm, weekends 11am–5pm.* ⊙ *Closed Mon–Tue.* ⊛ *$3.* ☎519-977-0013. www.artgalleryofwindsor.com.

Exhibits from the gallery's permanent collection of over 2,500 works of Canadian art dating from 1750 to the present include paintings from the Group of Seven.

Excursions

Fort Malden ★

PO Box 38, 100 Laird Ave., Amherstburg ON, N9V 2Z2. 25km/15mi south via Rtes. 2 and 20. ♿ ⊙ *Open May–Labour Day daily 10am–5pm, Sept–Oct Mon–Fri 1pm–5pm, weekends 10am–5pm.* ⊛ *$4 adult.* ☎519-736-5416. www.pc.gc.ca.

This fort, built by the British at the end of the 18C, occupies a fine **site** overlooking the seaway. In the **visitor centre** a video (*6min*) explains the fort's role in the War of 1812 and the Rebellions of 1837.

Route 50

31km/19mi from Malden Centre to Kingsville. This quiet road through the flat farmland that borders Lake Erie affords opportunities to view marshland birds and colourful market gardens.

Jack Miner's Bird Sanctuary

In Kingsville, 2km/1.5mi north of town centre via Rte. 29 (Division Rd.); then left on Rd. 3 West. ⊙ *Open year-round Mon–Sat 8am–5pm.* ☎519-733-4034. www.jack-miner.com.

Visit this sanctuary founded by conservationist **Jack Miner** (1865-1944) when an estimated 10,000 geese and ducks land to feed (*Nov-Dec*).

QUEBEC

This vast province encompasses an area of 1,540,680sq km/594,860sq mi, or one-sixth of Canada's total landmass. More than 75 percent of its population of 7.5 million is Francophone. The **Québécois** have maintained their own culture and lifestyle, creating a unique society in a North American milieu. About 8 percent of the population claims British origin and is concentrated largely on Montreal Island. About 1 percent claims native ancestry, primarily First Nations as well as Métis and Inuit, who live in small settlements in the Great North. A growing segment of Quebec's population hails from a wide variety of ethnic origins.

- ⚏ **Information:** Quebec Tourism. Montreal. ☎514-873-2015, toll-free 1-877-266-5687 (Canada/US). www.bonjourquebec.com
- ▶ **Orient Yourself:** East of Ontario and west of New Brunswick, Quebec borders the states of Maine, Vermont, New Hampshire and New York to the south.
- ✇ **Don't Miss:** Montreal and Quebec City are essential, but also plan at least one day by the side of a lake.
- 🕐 **Organizing Your Time:** Quebec City is about three hours from Montreal. In both cities, you are never more than an hour from forests, lakes and mountains.

Geographical Notes

Regional Landscape – Stretching almost 2,000km/1,240mi from the US border to Hudson Strait, Quebec is Canada's largest province. Three main physiographic regions can be distinguished in Quebec. The northern tundra and vast forested area lie on the **Canadian Shield**, a rocky expanse of extensive plateaus interrupted by a few mountain massifs. The extreme south of the province and the Gaspé Peninsula, on the other hand, are part of the **Appalachian Mountains**. These chains reach heights of 972m/3,188ft in the Eastern Townships and 1,288m/4,227ft in the Gaspé Peninsula. Lodged between these two regions, the **St. Lawrence Lowlands**, a triangular wedge graced with fertile soils

Parc National du Canada Forillon

and a moderate climate, support most of the province's agricultural production. Stretching some 1,197km/742mi in length, the **St. Lawrence River** flows in a northeasterly direction along Ontario and through Quebec to the Gulf of St. Lawrence and into the Atlantic Ocean.

Climate – Snowfall can accumulate up to 150cm/5ft in much of the central interior. Summer in the southern regions is hot and humid. Sometimes, in late October or early November, "Indian summer" returns briefly for a last fling.

January temperatures in Montreal average −9°C/16°F, with an average of 254cm/8ft of snowfall for the entire winter season. Located farther north, Sept-Îles registers the heaviest recorded snowfall in eastern Canada.

In July Montreal registers maximum means of 26°C/79°F, Quebec City 25°C/77°F and Sept-Îles 20°C/68°F. Temperatures in excess of 32°C/90°F are not uncommon.

A Bit of History

Birth of New France – Before the arrival of Europeans, Quebec's territory was inhabited by Indians of the **Eastern Woodlands** culture, including Algonquins and Montagnais. During the 15C Basque fishermen came to fish off the coast. French navigator **Jacques Cartier** (1491-1557) landed on the Gaspé Peninsula in 1534 and claimed this new land for the king of France. In 1608, **Samuel de Champlain** founded Quebec City. The **Iroquois Wars** (until 1701) and France's lack of interest in the colony, kept settlement to a minimum.

A Vast Empire – During the mid-17C the *coureurs des bois* (fur traders) and missionaries from New France explored the continent. Étienne Brûlé, Jean Nicolet and Nicolas Perrot reached Lake Superior. In the 1650s Pierre Radisson and the Sieur des Groseilliers travelled north perhaps as far as Hudson Bay.

The greatest explorers were the **La Vérendrye family**. Pierre Gaultier de Varennes explored Manitoba and Saskatchewan between 1731 and 1738, setting up trading posts. His sons François and Louis-Joseph reached the Rockies in present-day Montana in 1742.

Treaty of Paris – On September 13, 1759, British Gen. **James Wolfe** (1728-59) defeated French Gen. **Louis-Joseph de Montcalm** (1712-59) on the **Plains of Abraham** in Quebec City, signalling the end of the French colony. The colony was ceded to England in 1763 by the Treaty of Paris.

A British Colony – Faced with a Roman Catholic, French-speaking population, the new governor, **Sir Guy Carleton**, decided to recognize the rights of the Roman Catholic church, the seigneurial system and French civil law as a basis for government. These rights were enshrined in the **Quebec Act** of 1774. In 1791, the British divided the colony into Upper and Lower Canada. Public frustration over limits to self-government led to the **Rebellions of 1837** in both colonies. Led in Quebec by **Louis-Joseph Papineau** (1786-1871), the **Patriots** were defeated, but full representative government was granted.

In 1867 the British North America Act established **Canadian Confederation,** the foundation of modern Canada.

A Sovereign State – During the 1960s, under Premier **Jean Lesage** (1912-1980) a climate of social, economic and political change, labelled the "Quiet Revolution," emerged in Quebec. Spearheaded by the leader of the Parti Québécois (1968), **René Lévesque** (1922-87), Quebec sovereignty became a hotly debated topic. In 1980 and again in 1995, the PQ lost referendums on Quebec sovereignty, but the emotionally charged issue of the province's relationship to the rest of the country will likely dominate the political scene for some time.

Daniel Johnson Dam at Manic 5

Economy

Since the opening of the **St. Lawrence Seaway** in 1959, Quebec's economy has been tied to that of the US. Over 50 percent of the province's manufactured goods are exported, 80 percent to the US. Quebec is the Canadian leader in production of **pulp and paper**, manufacturing a third of the country's total output of **newsprint**. Abitibi and Témiscamingue contain large deposits of **copper**. The province has abundant **hydroelectric resources**. This low-cost energy has spurred the province's electro-metallurgic industries. Quebec has become a major producer of **aluminum**. **Agriculture** predominates in southern Quebec, and the major **fishing** centres are Gaspé Peninsula and Côte-Nord.

Practical Information

GETTING THERE

BY AIR

International and domestic flights arrive at Montreal's Pierre Elliott Trudeau International Airport airport (*22km/14mi west of downtown, in the town of Dorval.* ☎*514-394-7377, toll-free 1-800-465-1213. www.admtl.com*) and Quebec City's Jean-Lesage airport (☎*418-640-2600. www.aeroportdequebec.com*). Montreal's Mirabel airport (*55km/34mi north of downtown.* ☎*514-394-7377, toll-free 1-800-465-1213*) is used for cargo flights. Air Canada: ☎*514-393-3333, toll-free 1-888-247-2262 (Canada/US), www.aircanada.ca*. Affiliated carriers offer connections to many cities within Quebec. Major car rental agencies are located at the airports.

BY BUS AND TRAIN

Intercity **bus** service and connections throughout the Montreal–Quebec City–Gaspésie corridor are offered by **Autocars Orléans Express Inc.** (☎*514-*395-4000, 418-525-3043, toll-free 1-888-999-3977. www.orleansexpress.com*).
Amtrak links Montreal and the US with daily connections from Washington, DC, via New York City. For information in the US: ☎*1-800-872-7245 or www.amtrak.com*. **VIA Rail** train service is extensive within the province: ☎*514-989-2626, toll-free 888-842-7733 (Canada/US). www.viarail.com*.

BY BOAT

The province has an extensive **ferry** boat system. For schedules contact Tourisme Québec (♿ *below*).

GENERAL INFORMATION

ACCOMMODATIONS AND VISITOR INFORMATION

Tourism Québec publishes vacation brochures, regional guides and road maps that can be downloaded from the website or ordered free from: **Tourisme Québec**, (*PO Box 979, Montreal QC, H3C 2W3.* ☎*514-873-2015, toll-free 1-877-266-*

5687 (Canada/US).
www.bonjourquebec.com).
Major hotel chains can be found in urban areas. Small hotels and bed-and-breakfast lodgings offer quality accommodations at moderate prices throughout the province. **Farm holidays** may be especially appealing to families. The guide *Gîtes du Passant au Québec ($29.19 within Canada, $34.60 mail to US, $40.75 to Europe)* is available from Fédération des Agricotours du Québec *(4545 av. du Pierre-De Coubertin, PO Box 1000 Succursale M, Montreal QC, H1V 3R2. ☎514-252-3138. www.agrico-tours.qc.ca)* or Hôtellerie Champêtre, *(426 rue Sainte-Hélène, bureau 304, Montréal QC, H2Y 2K7. ☎514-861-4024, toll-free 1-800-861-4024. www.hotellerie-champetre.com).*

LANGUAGE
The official language of Quebec is French, spoken by 82% of the population. The second language is English. Many Quebecers in urban areas are bilingual. Tourist information is generally available in both languages. Telephone operators are bilingual. Road signs, except on the TransCanada Hwy, are in French.
Quebec websites appear initially in French, but an "English" button gives you an English version.

ROAD REGULATIONS
Quebec has a network of highways *(autoroutes)* and secondary roads. Road signs are in French only. The speed limit on highways, unless otherwise posted, is 100km/h (60mph), on secondary roads 90km/h (55mph), and 50km/h (30mph) within city limits. Turning right on red is prohibited on the island of Montreal. **Seat belt** use is mandatory. **Canadian Automobile Assn. (CAA),** Montreal ☎514-861-7111.

TIME ZONES
Quebec is on Eastern Standard Time, except the Magdalen Islands, which are on Atlantic Standard Time (1hr ahead of the rest of Quebec). Daylight Saving Time is observed from the 2nd Sunday in March to the 1st Sunday in November.

TAXES
In addition to the national 5% GST, Quebec levies a provincial sales tax of 7.5% for all goods and services. The Visitor Rebate Program for the federal GST was cancelled as of April 1, 2007. However, no GST is levied if the item is shipped directly by a Canadian business to the non-resident's home *(☎902-432-5608. www.cra-arc.gc.ca/visitors).* The Quebec sales tax is not refunded to visitors.

LIQUOR LAWS
The legal drinking age is 18. The sale of wine and liquor is regulated by the provincial government and sold in "Société des Alcools" stores. Beer and wine are also sold in grocery stores.

PROVINCIAL HOLIDAY
Saint-Jean-Baptiste Day: June 24

RECREATION

OUTDOOR ACTIVITIES
Parks Canada *(www.pc.gc.ca)* operates three **national parks** in Quebec (Forillon, La Mauricie, Mingan Archipelago) and the province operates 27 **provincial parks** (confusingly also called national parks.Consult Tourism Quebec.) which offer year-round activities such as hiking, backpacking, nature programs, biking, sailing, canoeing, fishing, camping and winter sports. You can download or order by mail useful brochures from the www.bonjourquebec.com site.
Canoeing is practised on most of the rivers except those used for logging. **Kayaking** is popular in the northern regions of Saguenay and Nunavik, where camps have been set up. Ranch vacations that include **horseback riding** are prevalent in the Eastern Townships, Gaspé Peninsula and Bas-Saint-Laurent regions. For further information on all outdoor activities contact Regroupement Loisir Québec ☎514-252-3126, toll-free 1-800-932-3735. www.loisirquebec.qc.ca.
Major ski areas offering alpine and cross-country **skiing** are the Laurentians *(Mt. Tremblant ☎819-425-8711. www.tremblant.ca)*, the Eastern Townships *(Bromont ☎450-534-2200; Mt. Orford ☎819-843-6548; Owl's Head ☎450-292-3342; Sutton ☎450-538-2545))* and the Quebec City region *(Mt. Ste-Anne ☎418-827-4561. www.mont-sainte-anne.com)*. For a list of resorts, go to www.bonjourquebec.com or

www.onthesnow.com/QU. **Snowmobiling** is a popular sport. A registration card is required to operate a snowmobile: contact the Fédératon des Clubs de Motoneigistes in Montreal ☎514-252-3076. www.fcmq.qc.ca.

Many regions in Quebec are known for **hunting** and **fishing**. Contact the Ministère des Ressources naturelles et de la Faune, *(418-627-8600, toll-free 1-866-248-6936. www.mrnf.gouv.qc.ca/ English/wildlife)*. An free publication on outfitters' lodges is available from the Fédération des pourvoyeurs du Québec *(☎418-877-5191, toll-free 1-800-567-9009. www.fpq.com)*.

SPECIAL EXCURSIONS

Canoeing, rafting, horseback riding, biking or hiking tours in the Montreal/ Ottawa region are offered through New World River Expeditions *(☎819-681-4535, toll-free 1-800-361-5033. www. newworld.ca)*. Rock climbing, dogsledding, canoeing and kayaking can be arrranged through CÉPAL *(☎418-547-5728, toll-free 1-800-361-5728. www. cepalaventure.com)*. Seal-watch excursions off Magdalen Islands depart from Halifax, Nova Scotia.

PRINCIPAL FESTIVALS

Feb	**Quebec Winter Carnival**: *Quebec City*
	Carnaval-Souvenir: *Saguenay*
	Winter Festival: *Hull*
Mar	**Maple Sugar Festival**: *Saint-Georges*
Jun	**Air Canada Grand Prix**: *Montreal*
Jul	**International Jazz Festival**: *Montreal*
	World Folklore Festival: *Drummondville*
	International Summer Festival: *Quebec City*
	International Swim Marathon: *Péribonka*
Jul-Aug	**Blueberry Festival**: *Mistassini*
	Festival Orford: *Magog*
Aug	**Hot Air Balloon Festival**: *Saint-Jean-sur-Richelieu*
	Montreal World Film Festival: *Montreal*

ÎLE D'ANTICOSTI★★

Some 222km/138mi in length and 56km/35mi at its widest point, Anticosti Island is mantled with coniferous forests, crisscrossed by rivers teeming with Atlantic salmon and trout, and known by deer hunters for its game. French industrialist **Henri Menier** purchased Anticosti for in 1895, and transformed it into his private paradise, importing white-tailed deer and other animals. The Quebec government acquired it in 1974; it is now part of a reserve (4,575sq km/1,766sq mi).

🖪 **Information:** Association touristique régionale de Duplessis, 312 av. Brochu, Sept-Îles QC, G4R 2W6. ☎418-962-0808, toll-free 1-888-0808 (Canada/US). wwwtourismeduplessis.com.

▶ **Orient Yourself:** The island lies where the St. Lawrence widens into the Gulf, downriver from Sept-Iles.

☻ **Don't Miss:** Port Menier is the only town. Tourist office: ☎418-535-0250.

🕒 **Organizing Your Time:** You will need at least two or three days.

👣 **Also See:** BAS ST-LAURENT, CÔTE-NORD, CÔTE DE CHARLEVOIS

Access

From Montreal, Quebec City or Sept-Îles contact SÉPAQ ☎418-890-6527, toll-free 1-800-665-6527 (US/Canada) www.sepaq.com. Boat service available through Relais Nordik Inc., from Rimouski and Havre-Saint-Pierre ☎418-723-8787, 1-800-463-0680. www.relaisnordik.com. Reservations 30 days in advance. A four-wheel-drive vehicle is indispensable on the island.

Visit

A tour of the island from **Port-Menier**, the island's only remaining permanent settlement, leads past such scenic wonders as the Chutes de Kalimazoo and Caverne à la Patate; **Chute et canyon de la Vauréal**★★, with a 70m/230ft waterfall; and **Baie de la Tour**★★, renowned for its spectacular limestone cliffs that plummet dramatically into the sea. Baie-Sainte-Claire provides an ideal setting for observing **white-tailed deer**, sometimes seen in herds of up to 100.

BAS-SAINT-LAURENT★★

MAP PP 306-307

On the south shore of the St. Lawrence River, between Quebec City and the Gaspé Peninsula, this region is characterized by peaceful farmlands along the shore, divided into long, narrow strips perpendicular to the river. To the north, the Laurentian Mountains plunge into the St. Lawrence.

- **Information:** Tourism Bas-St-Laurent, 148, rue Fraser, Rivière-du-Loup QC, G5R 1C8. ☎418-867-1272, toll-free 1-800-563-5268 (Canada/US). www.tourismebas-st-laurent.org/english
- ▶ **Orient Yourself:** Route 132 passes through the principal communities of this region, affording superb views of the St. Lawrence.
- ☺ **Don't Miss:** Kamouraska is one of the prettiest towns in Quebec.
- ◷ **Organizing Your Time:** You can cross the river on ferries at Rivière du Loup, Trois Pistoles and Rimouski.
- ⚑ **Also See:** CÔTE DE CHARLEVOIX, CÔTE NORD, ÎLE D'ANTICOSTI

Sights

Lévis★
250km/155mi east of Montreal by Rte. 20 or Rte. 132. A ferry connects Lévis to Quebec City.
Located opposite Quebec City, this city is noted for its port and its wood industries. The city is also the headquarters of the Desjardins cooperative savings and loan company (*Caisse populaire Desjardins*), founded in 1900 by journalist Alphonse Desjardins (1854-1920).
The white clapboard **Maison Alphonse-Desjardins**★ displays artifacts relating to Desjardins and the cooperative movement.
6, rue du Mont-Marie, Lévis QC, G6V 1V9. ♿️🅿️ ⟿ Visit by 45min guided tour only. Year-round Mon–Fri 10am–noon & 1pm–4:30pm, weekends noon–5pm. ◷Closed Jan 1-2, Dec 25-26 & 31. ☎418-835-2090, toll-free 1-866-835-8444 . www.desjardins.com).

Lieu historique national du Canada des Forts-de-Lévis★ (Lévis Forts National Historic Site of Canada)
41 du Gouvernement Rd, PO Box 10, Station B, Quebec City QC, G1K 7A1. ♿️🅿️ ◷Open early-May–Aug daily 10am–5pm. Sept weekends only 1pm–4pm. ⊜ $4 adult. ☎418-835-5182, toll-free 1-888-773-8888. www.pc.gc.ca.
Forming an irregular pentagon, the fort (1865-72) stands atop Pointe-Lévis, the highest point on the south shore of the St. Lawrence.

Lieu historique national du Canada de la Grosse-Île-et-le-Mémorial-des-Irlandais★ (Grosse-Île and the Irish Memorial National Historic Site of Canada)
2 d'Auteuil St, PO Box 10, Station B, Quebec City QC, G1K 7A1. ✕🅿️◷Open mid-May–mid-Oct daily 9am–6pm. ☎418-248-8888. www.pc.gc.ca. Ferry from Berthier-sur-Mer contact Les Croisières Lachance ☎418-259-2140, toll-free 1-

888-476-7734. www.croisiereslachance. com. From Quebec City, Lévis, Ste-Anne-de-Beaupré and Île-d'Orléans, contact Les Croisières Le Coudrier ☎418-692-0107, toll-free 1-888-600-5554. www.croisieres-coudrier.qc.ca. Reservations required. Visit & ferry ⬤ $44–$65.

Increasing European immigration prompted establishment, in 1832, of a quarantine station on Grosse-Île to limit the spread of cholera into Canada.

Route 132 continues through **L'Islet-sur-Mer**, the birthplace of famed Arctic explorer Capt. Joseph-Elzéar Bernier (1852-1934), and through **Saint-Jean-Port-Joli★**, the craft and wood-carving capital of Quebec.

La Pocatière★

60km/37mi from Montmagny. This community is a centre for agricultural research. The **Musée François-Pilote★** is a research centre for Quebec domestic architecture. (*100 4th Ave., La Pocatière QC, G0R 1Z0.* ▣ ⏲*Open Mon–Fri 9am–noon, 1pm–5pm, Sun 1pm–5pm.* ⬤*$4.* ☎*418-856-3145*).

Route 132 passes across a wide floodplain, affording expansive views of the Laurentian Mountains. From the pleasant community of **Kamouraska★**, lines of eel traps can be seen in the tidal flats.

Rivière-du-Loup★

72km/45mi from La Pocatière. Situated halfway between Quebec City and the Gaspé Peninsula, this town is a commercial and resort centre. Downtown are the imposing Gothic Revival **St. Patrick's Church and Presbytery**, surrounded by verandas, and the **Viatorian Clerics' Residence**. North of downtown, the Loup River drops over the cliff terrace in 38m/125ft-high falls. A lookout provides a view of the town and river.

Parc du Bic★ (Bic Park)

81km/50mi from Rivière-du-Loup. This provincial conservation park has both deciduous and boreal forests. The small town of **Bic** is known for its spectacular **setting★★** on the St. Lawrence.

Rimouski★

25km/16mi from Bic Park. This industrial city is a major metropolis of eastern Quebec. Note the **Maison Lamontagne★**, one of the few remaining examples of masonry half-timbering in North America. (*707, boul. du Rivage, Rimouski QC, G5L 7C3.* ✕ ▣ ⏲*Open mid-May–mid-Oct Thu–Sun 10am–6pm.* ⬤*$4*

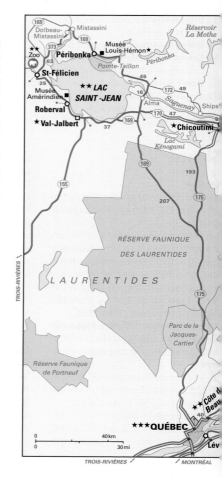

adult. ☎*418-722-4038. www.maison lamontagne.com).*

Located 10km/6mi from town, the **Musée de la mer et lieu historique national du Canada du phare de Pointe-au-Père**★ (Maritime Museum and Pointe-au-Père Lighthouse National Historic Site) at Pointe-au-Père display hundreds of artifacts recovered from the wreck of the *Empress of Ireland*, the "Titanic of the St. Lawrence": 1012 people died when she sank. (*1034 rue de la Phare, Rimouski QC, G5M 1L8.* ✕🅿🕒*Open early Jun–Aug daily 9am–6pm. Sept– early Oct daily 9am–5pm.* 👓*$10.50.* ☎*418-724-6214. www.shmp.qc.ca).*

HOW DO YOU EEL?

In the town of Kamouraska, take a guided tour at the Site d'Interprétation de l'Anguille de Kamouraska (*205 Ave. Morel, G0L 1M0.* ☎*418-492-3935*) and discover the secrets of traditional eel fishing. End the experience by sampling a smoked version of the snakelike fish, considered a delicacy by many cultures.

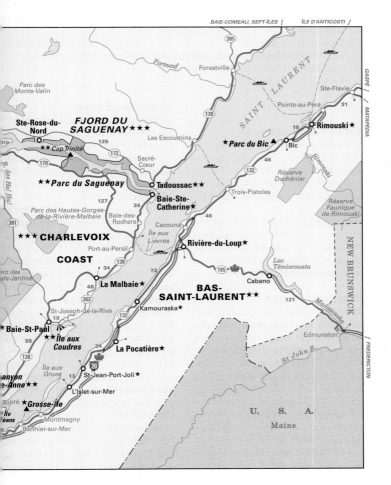

CÔTE DE CHARLEVOIX★★★

MAP PP 306-307

One of Quebec's loveliest, most varied regions, this rugged coast is best appreciated by following Routes 138 and 362, which weave up and down, affording magnificent clifftop or water-level views of forested hills, the pristine shore and mountains that sweep down into the mighty St. Lawrence. Named for Jesuit historian Pierre-François-Xavier de Charlevoix (1682-1781), this resort spot has long attracted and inspired painters, poets and writers.

Information: Tourism Charlevoix, 495, boul de Comporté, La Malbaie QC, G5A 3G3. ☎418-665-4454, toll-free 1-800-667-2276. www.charlevoixtourism.com

▶ **Orient Yourself:** The Charlevoix region lies about an hour's drive down the St. Lawrence northeast from Quebec City.

Don't Miss: The Île aux Coudres and whale-watching a the mouth of the Saguenay River.

Organizing Your Time: Watch for the "Route des Saveurs" signs marking places where you can eat or obtain local produce.

Kids Especially for Kids: The visitor centre just west of Baie-Saint-Paul has models and information about the the giant meteor impact that formed this region.

Also See: BAS SAINT-LAURENT, QUEBEC

Sights

Canyon Sainte-Anne★★

52km/32mi northeast of Quebec City.
✕♿🅿⏱Open Jun 24–Labour Day daily 9am–5:45pm. May–Jun 23 & rest of Sept–Oct daily 9am–4:45pm. ⬅$10. ☎418-827-4057. www.canyonste-anne.qc.ca.

Pleasant paths lead to this steep and narrow waterfall, which drops a total of 74m/243ft over the edge of the Canadian Shield, creating a mass of shattered rocks and whirlpools at its base.

Baie-Saint-Paul★★

95km/59mi northeast of Quebec City. Route 138 offers magnificent **views**★★ on the descent to this celebrated artists' haunt. Surrounded by rolling green hills, the charming community has many art galleries and an **arts centre** (23, rue Ambroise-Fafard, Baie-Saint-Paul QC, G3Z 2J2. 🅿⏱Open June 24–Labour Day Tue–Wed, Thu–Sun noon–8pm. Rest of the year Tue–Sun 11am–5pm. ⏱Closed – Dec & 31 Dec–3 Jan. ☎418-435-3681. www.centredart-bsp.qc.ca). Departing by Route 362, visitors will find an overlook that provides another splendid **view**★★ of the town, the St. Lawrence and the south shore.

Île aux Coudres★★

Free ferry service departs from Saint-Joseph-de-la-Rive June-Sept daily 6:30am–11:30pm every hour. Rest of the year daily 7am–11pm frequently. ♿ Société des traversiers du Québec ☎418-438-2743, toll-free 1-877-787-7483. www.traversiers.gouv.qc.ca

Named by Jacques Cartier in 1535 for its abundant hazel trees (coudriers), this enchanting island occupies a spectacular offshore **site**.

A tour of the island (21km/13mi) by car or bicycle offers views of the north and south shores of the St. Lawrence. The **Musée les voitures d'eau**★ (Schooner Museum) presents the region's maritime history (🅿⏱Open mid-Jun–mid-Sept daily 10am–5pm, mid-May–mid-June & early Sept–early Oct weekends 10am–5pm. ⬅$3.50. ☎418-438-2208, toll-free 1-800-463-2118.). **Les Moulins de l'Isle-aux-Coudres**★ (Île-aux-Coudres Mills) provide a rare opportunity to compare the mechanisms of a windmill and a water mill (🅿⏱Open Jun 24–mid-Aug daily 9am–6:30pm. Late May–Jun 23 & mid-Aug–mid-Oct daily 10am–5pm. ⬅$2.75. ☎418-438-2184. www.tourismeisleauxcoudres.com.

La Malbaie-Pointe-au-Pic★

26km/16mi northeast of Île aux Coudres.
Occupying a beautiful **site**, this resort community was named "Malle Baye" (bad bay) by Samuel de Champlain in 1608, when his anchored ships ran aground. Later, Scottish soldiers renamed it Murray Bay in honour of the colony's chief administrator. The picturesque **Manoir Richelieu** (*in Pointe-au-Pic*) is a grand reminder of the resort hotels that sprung up during the 19C.

Baie-Sainte-Catherine★

74km/46mi northeast of La Malbaie.
Whale-watching cruises★★ have become a popular attraction, just as in Tadoussac across the fjord. Overlooking the mouth of the Saguenay in the **Saguenay-St. Lawrence Marine Park**, a lookout tower provides occasional glimpses of the large mammals frolicking in the water below (*182 rue de l'Église, PO Box 220 Tadoussac QC, G0T 2A0. Interpretation Centre, Pointe Noire* ♿🅿🕒*Open mid-Jun–Labour Day daily 9am–6pm. Rest of Sept–mid-Oct Fri–Sun 9am–5pm.* ☞*$5.45.*☎*418-235-4703. www.pc.gc.ca & www.parcmarin.qc.cq*).

CÔTE-NORD ★

Long known as an untamed wilderness of forests with occasional fishing villages, Côte-Nord underwent gradual industrialization with the development of **pulp mills** in the 1920s and 30s and, later, with the discovery of rich **iron-ore** deposits. In the 1960s the region's enormous hydroelectric potential was harnessed, prompting another surge of economic growth.

- 🗊 **Information:** Association touristique régionale de Manicouagan, 337, boul. LaSalle, bureau 304, Baie-Comeau QC, G4Z 2Z1. ☎418-294-2876, toll-free 1-888-463-5319. www.tourismecote-nord.com
- ▶ **Orient Yourself:** The Côte-Nord, or North Shore, of the St. Lawrence River extends from the mouth of the Saguenay River north to the Labrador border.
- ⊛ **Don't Miss:** A drive along Route 138 leads through desolate stretches of pristine, rocky landscape, interrupted by developing towns and hydroelectric plants.
- 🕒 **Organizing Your Time:** The northernmost part, between Havre St-Pierre and Blanc-Sablon, is accessible only by boat or plane.
- ⚑ **Also See:** LE BAS SAINT-LAURENT, LES ILES DE LA MADELEINE, ÎLE D'ANTICOSTI

Sights

Complexe Manic-Outardes

Manic-5 is located 210km/130mi north of Baie-Comeau (422km/262mi northeast of Quebec City) on Rte. 389.
Begun in 1959, the harnessing of the Manicouagan and Outardes rivers took 20 years to complete. The first power plant of the complex to produce electricity was **Manic-2**★ (🅿 ◷*visit by 1hr 30min guided tour only, Jun 24–Labour Day daily at 9am, 11am, 1:30pm & 3:30pm.* ☎*866-526-2642. www.hydro-quebec.com.* The spectacular **Daniel Johnson Dam**★★ of **Manic-5**★★ is the largest arch-and-buttress dam in the world (*same conditions as for Manic-2. 1hr45min*).

Sept-Îles★

640km/397mi northeast of Quebec City by Rte. 138. Occupying a superb **site**★★ Sept-Îles' deepwater port enables ocean-bound vessels to transship coal and iron ore throughout the year. The old wharf gives views of the magnificent bays and the seven islands.
Le Vieux-Poste (Old Trading Post) pays tribute to the region's first inhabitants, the Montagnais (*500, boul. Laure, Sept-Îles QC, G4R 1X7.* 🅿🕒*Open Jun 24–Labour*

Day daily 9am–5pm. Rest of year Tue–Fri 10am–noon & 1pm–5pm, Sat–Sun 1pm–5pm. ☞$5. ☎418-968-2070. www.mrcn. qc.ca). Offshore, the **Parc régional de l'Archipel des Sept-Îles**★ (Sept-Îles Regional Park) offers an introduction to the Côte-Nord.

The community of **Havre-Saint-Pierre** marks the end of Route 138. The fer- ries for Anticosti Island and the **Mingan Archipelago**★★, a national park reserve, depart from the wharf. Havre-Saint-Pierre is also the departure point for the boat trip (*3 days*) to Blanc-Sablon, situated 1.5km/1mi from the Labrador border. *☝ For more information, consult the Michelin GREEN GUIDE Quebec.*

CANTONS DE L'EST★★

MAP PP 312-313

The **Eastern Townships** (sometimes called *Estrie*) is an area of lush rolling hills east of Montreal. After the American Revolution, Loyalists settled here. Their towns and villages reflect their New England heritage. Today the population is predominantly Francophone.

- 🛈 **Information:** Tourism Cantons-de-l'est, 20 rue Don-Bosco Sud, Sherbrooke QC, J1L 1W4. ☎819-820-2020, toll-free 1-800-335-5755. www.cantonsdelest.com
- ▶ **Orient Yourself:** The Eastern townships are in the southwest corner of the province, along the US border.
- 🚢 **Don't Miss:** A cruise on Lake Memphrémagog.
- 🕐 **Organizing Your Time:** There are lots of lovely inns and restaurants, beaches and art galleries.
- **Kids** **Especially for Kids:** The Granby Zoo is popular with all ages.
- 🕯 **Also See:** VALLÉE DU RICHELIEU

Topography

This area of deep valleys, tree-covered hills rising nearly 1,000m/3,280ft, and beautiful lakes such as Brome, Memphrémagog, Magog and Massawipi is a popular retreat for Montrealers. The northeastern section, in particular the towns of **Asbestos** and **Thetford Mines**, is known for its asbestos production. To the east, the flat fertile farmland referred to as the **Beauce**★ contains the greatest concentration of maple groves in Quebec. In spring, sugaring-off parties are a popular pastime.

Sylvain Majeau/Tourisme Cantons-de-l'Est

Abbaye de St-Benoît-du-Lac

Sights

Sherbrooke★
150km/93mi east of Montreal by Rtes. 10 and 112.

At the confluence of the Saint-François and Magog rivers, this is the principal city of the townships. The **Musée des Beaux-Arts** (Museum of Fine Arts) exhibits a fine collection of Quebec art. *(241, rue Dufferin, Sherbrooke QC, J1H 4M3. 🕭 🅿 🕐Open Jun 24–Labour Day Tue–Sun 10am–5pm. Rest of the year Tue–Sun 11am–5pm. 🕐Closed Dec*

24–26 & Dec 31–Jan 2. ⊚ $7.50. ☎819-821-2115. www.mbas.qc.ca). Standing atop the Marquette Plateau, is the imposing Gothic Revival **cathedral**★, from which the **view**★ encompasses the entire city.

Magog★

124km/74mi east of Montreal by Rte. 10.
This popular resort community enjoys a splendid **setting** on the shores of Lake Memphrémagog, which stretches over 50km/31mi, crossing the border into Vermont. **Scenic cruises**★ afford splendid views of Mt. Orford, Sugar Loaf and Owl's Head (✕ 🅿 ⏱*Depart from Quai Magog Jun 24–Labour Day daily 9am–4pm, mid-May–Jun 23 & rest of Sept–mid-Oct weekends noon–2pm. Round-trip 1hr 45min ⊚$15. 7hr-cruise ⊚ $55. Rervations required. Croisières Memphrémagog Inc. ☎819-843-8068.www. croisiere-memphremagog.com).*

Abbaye de Saint-Benoît-du-Lac★ (Saint-Benoît-du-Lac Abbey)

20km/12mi south of Magog by Rte. 112 west; follow signs. ⏱Open year-round daily 8am–5pm. 🅿 ☎819-843-4080. www.st-benoit-du-lac.com.
The pleasant drive to this Benedictine monastery offers lovely glimpses of the sparkling lake waters. The monks are famous for their Gregorian chants and for their cheese (L'Ermite and Mont-Saint-Benoît).

Parc du Mont-Orford★ (Mount Orford Park)

116km/72mi east of Montreal by Rte. 10 (Exit 115) and Rte. 141. Park ⏱Open daily year-round. Le Cerisier Interpretation Centre ✕ 🅿 ⏱Open year-round daily 8am–4:30pm. ⊚$3.50 adult. Camping. ☎819-843-9855. www.sepaq.com.
This provincial park is dominated by Mt. Orford (881m/2,890ft), a well-known ski centre. Follow a short path around the television tower at the summit for a sweeping **panorama**★★.

Centre d'Arts Orford (Orford Arts Centre)

3165, ch. du Parc, Orford QC, J1X7A2.

✕ 🅿 ⏱*Open year-round daily 9am–9pm. ☎819-843-9871, toll-free 1-800-567-6155. www.arts-orford.org.*
The centre is renowned for its annual summer music festival (Festival Orford).

Compton

172km/107mi east of Montreal by Rtes. 10, 143 and 147.
This is the birthplace of **Louis-Stephen Saint-Laurent** (1882-1973), Canada's 12th prime minister. He fought to establish a distinct Canadian identity during his years in office (1948-57).

Lieu historique national du Canada Louis-S.-St-Laurent★ (Louis-S.-St.-Laurent National Historic Site of Canada)

Rue Principale. ⏱Open mid-May–late Aug. daily 10am–5pm. Sept 10am–noon, 1–5pm. ⊚$4. ☎819-835-5448, toll-free 1-888-773-8888. www.pc.gc.ca.
The clapboard house has been restored to represent various periods of the prime minister's life. A **multimedia biography** (*20min*) presents the highlights of Saint-Laurent's life and career.

Granby

80km/50mi southeast of Montreal by Rte. 10 (Exit 68) and Rtes. 139 and 112.
Set on the banks of the Yamaska River, Granby is especially known for its **zoo**★ Kids one of the largest in Canada (*Blvd. Bouchard. ✕ 🅿 ⏱Open late Jun–Aug daily 10am–7pm, early Jun10am–5pm, Sept–early-Oct weekends only 10am–5pm. ⊚ $27. ☎450-372-9113, toll-free 1-877-472-6299. www.zoodegranby.com).*

Valcourt

130km/81mi east of Montreal by Rte. 10 (Exit 90) and Rtes. 243 and 222.
Joseph-Armand Bombardier (1907-64) developed the **Ski-Doo**, which went on to transform life in the north.

Musée J.-Armand Bombardier★ (J.-Armand Bombardier Museum)

Kids *1001 Ave J.-A. Bombardier, Valcourt QC, J0E 2L0. 🅿 ⏱Open May–Labour Day daily 10am–5pm. Rest of the year Tue–Sun 10am–5pm. ⏱Closed Jan 1–2,*

Dec 24–26 & Dec 31. 🎫*$7.* ☎*450-532-5300. www.museebombardier.com.*
This fascinating museum highlights the life and work of Valcourt's native son.

Drummondville
110km/68mi east of Montreal by Rte. 20 (Exit 177). Founded as a military outpost after the War of 1812, this community is today an important industrial centre for the garment industry.

Village québécois d'antan★ (Québécois Village of Olden Times)
Kids *125 Rue Montplaisir, Drummondville OC, J2V 7T5. Exit 181 off Rte. 20.* 🍴 P ⏰*Open Jun–Labour Day daily 10am–5:30pm. Sept Fri–Sun 10am–5pm.* 🎫 *$19 adult.* ☎*819-478-1441, toll-free 1-877-710-0267. www.villagequebecois.com.*
About 70 authentic buildings were relocated to this pleasant site to re-create life in the region during the 19C. Costumed interpreters explain the daily life of the former occupants. (*English limited*).

GASPÉSIE★★★

This peninsula extends along the southern shore of the St. Lawrence, advancing into the gulf. The interior is largely an impenetrable wilderness, dominated by the **Chic-Choc** mountains. Tiny fishing villages dot the rocky northern coast of the peninsula, culminating in the breathtaking beauty of Forillon and Percé. The region offers excellent cuisine and some of the best salmon fishing in Quebec.

🛈 **Information:** Quebec Maritime, 84 rue Saint-Germain Est, Rimouski QC, G5L 1A6. ☎418-742-7889. www.quebecmaritime.ca
▶ **Orient Yourself:** Percé Rock marks the eastern tip of the peninsula and is the most common destination.
🚳 **Don't Miss:** The drive along the coast; Percé Rock.
🕐 **Organizing Your Time:** From Matane, allow at least 5 hours to reach Percé.
Kids Kids: At the fish ladder in Matane, you can see Atlantic salmon make their way through the counting station. Fossil enthusiasts will like Miguasha Park.

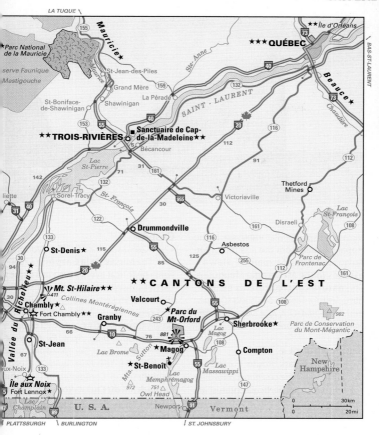

The North Coast

Jardins de Métis★★ (Métis Gardens)

200, Rte 132, Grand-Métis QC, G0J 1Z0. 350km/217mi southeast of Quebec City. ✕ &. 🅿 ⏱ *Open Jul–Aug daily 8:30am–8pm (last entrance 6pm). Jun & Sept–mid-Oct daily 8:30am–6pm (last entrance 5pm).* ✆ *$16 adult.* ☎ *418-775-2222. www.refordgardens.com.*

In 1918 Elsie Stephen Reford inherited this tract of land from her uncle, Sir George Stephen, president of the Canadian Pacific Railway Co. She created magnificent gardens, now owned by the government of Quebec.

In the centre of the gardens stands the **Villa Reford**. The first floor houses dining facilities and a craft shop.

Matane

55km/34mi east of Métis Gardens. This small industrial centre is known for its salmon fishing and shrimp production. In the town centre, a **fish ladder**★ (*passe migratoire*) enables salmon to travel upstream from mid-June to October.

Parc de la Gaspésie★ (Gaspésie Park)

1981, Rte du Parc, Saint-Anne-des-Monts QC, G4V 2E4. 103km/64mi east of Matane. ✕ &. 🅿 ⏱ *Open daily year-round. Hiking, fishing, camping, canoeing, cross-country skiing.* ✆ *$3.50.* ☎ *418-763-7494. www.sepaq.com.*

The **Mont Albert Sector** reflects vegetation characteristic of the northern tundra. In the **Lake Cascapédia Sector**, the ridges of the Chic-Choc Moun-

Rocher Percé

tains offer spectacular **views**★★ of the Appalachians. From the summit of Mt. Jacques Cartier an expansive **view**★★ extends to the McGerrigle Mountains. The **nature centre** presents exhibits, films, lectures and slide shows (*Open mid-May–mid-Oct, late Dec–early Apr. Hours vary, call park.*

Scenic Route★★

Past Gaspésie Park, Route 132 follows the contours of the coastline, affording splendid views. Of particular interest are the impressive shale cliffs around **Mont-Saint-Pierre** and the expansive views of the gulf from the bustling fishing village of **Rivière-au-Renard**.

Parc national Forillon★★ (Forillon National Park)

122 Gaspé Bvd, Gaspé QC, G4X 1A9. 217km/135mi east of Gaspésie Park. Open daily year-round. Visitor centres open daily Jun–early fall (closing varies). $7 adult. 418-368-5505, toll-free 1-888-773-8888. www.pc.gc.ca.
Located on the eastern tip of the peninsula, this 245sq km/95sq mi park includes limestone cliffs towering over the sea; forested mountains; wildflower meadows; and sandy beaches in hidden coves. A road leads to **Cape Bon Ami**, providing magnificent **views**★★ of the sea and the limestone cliffs. At **Cape Gaspé**★, a pleasant walk affords **views**★ of the Bay of Gaspé and Île Bonaventure. Nearby in the former fishing village of **Grande-Grave**★, several historic buildings have been restored.

Gaspé★

42km/26mi south of Forillon National Park. The **Musée de la Gaspésie**★ highlights historical events such as Jacques Cartier's discovery of the peninsula in 1534, the Mi'kmaq Indian population and regional geography (*80, boul de Gaspé, Gaspé QC, G4X 1A9. Open Jun–Oct daily 9am–5pm. Rest of year Mon–Fri 9am–5pm, Sar 1pm-5pm. $7 adult. 418-368-1534. www.museedelagaspesie.ca*). Completed in 1969, the **Cathédrale du Christ-Roi**★ (Cathedral of Christ the King) is distinguished by its cedar exterior that blends harmoniously with the environment.

The South Coast

Percé★★★

76km/47mi south of Gaspé. This bustling tourist town was named for the massive offshore rock pierced (*percé*) by the sea. The landscape is marked by reddish-gold limestone and shale, folded into a variety of cliffs, bays and hills.

Rocher Percé★★

(Percé Rock) This mammoth rock wall is 438m/1,437ft long and 88m/289ft high, connected to **Mont Joli**★★ by a sandbar, accessible at low tide.

The Coast★★★

The shoreline along Route 132 offers spectacular **views**★★ of the area. **Cape Barré** affords a view to the west of the cliffs known as Trois-Sœurs ("Three Sis-

Address Book

For dollar sign categories, see the Legend on the cover flap.

WHERE TO STAY

$$ Au Pirate, L'Auberge à Percé – *169 Rte. 132 Ouest, Percé QC, G0C 2L0 .* ☎418-782-5055. *7 rooms. Reservations advised.* ✕▣ Wonderfully comfortable rooms and beautiful views of Percé Rock await you at the Pirate's House. The **dining room ($$)** attracts visitors from around the country with an imaginative menu featuring local seafood.

$$ Auberge du Centre d'art Marcel Gagnon – *564 Route de la Mer, Sainte-Flavie QC, G0J 2L0.* ☎418-775-2829 *toll-free 1-866-775-2829. 10 rooms.* ✕▣. Simple, clean, comfortable rooms are located on the upper floor of this art centre. At the restaurant **($$)** on the ground floor, the main attraction is Marcel Gagnon's composite sculpture *Le grand rassemblement (The Great Gathering)*.

$$$ Gîte du Mont-Albert – *Route du Parc, Sainte-Anne-des-Monts. G4E 2V4.* ☎418-763-2288, *toll-free 866-727-2427. www.sepaq.com. 60 rooms, 25 cabins.* ✕&▣. Located within the Parc de la Gaspésie, this charming inn provides a comfortable base for enjoying the park's seasonal activities. Efficient service and clean, cozy rooms—all with views of Mont-Albert.

$$$ Hôtel la Normandie – *221 Rte. 132 Ouest, Percé QC,.* ☎418-782-2112, *toll-free 1-800-463-0820. www.normandieperce. com. 45 rooms.* ✕▣. A waterfront hotel in the most traditional sense, the Normandie offers tastefully decorated rooms, most with views of the ocean and Percé Rock. The **dining room ($$).** offers a *table d'hôte* (fixed-price) menu, with an ample choice of seafood, meat or poultry, all in the style of modern French *fine cuisine*. Extensive wine list.

WHERE TO EAT

$$ Chez Pierre – *96 Boul. Perron Ouest, Sainte-Anne-des-Monts QC, G4V 3C3 (Tourelle).* ☎418-763-7446. & **Seafood**. To appreciate the bounty of the St. Lawrence River, take time for a meal at Chez Pierre. Order from the menu or try the *Dégustation poissons* (fish sampler). Reasonable prices, efficient service, and a nice view of the water.

$$ La Maison du Pêcheur – *155 Place du Quai, Percé QC, G0C 2L0.* ☎418-782-5331. *www.maisondupecheur.restoquebec.com.* **Québécois.** Located next to the public pier, the Fisherman's House serves breakfast, lunch and dinner. For dinner, there is a table d'hote featuring pizza, well-prepared seafood or a steak. Locals favour the seaweed soup (*potage aux algues marines*).

ters"). South of Percé, **Côte Surprise** offers another superb view.
Rising 320m/1,050ft above Percé, **Mont Sainte-Anne** features extraordinary red-rock formations. Lookouts provide increasingly expansive **views**★★★ of Percé rock, the village and the surrounding area. Along the sheer cliff on the west side of Mt. Sainte-Anne, another trail provides views of the **Great Crevasse**, a deep fissure in the rock.

Parc de l'Île-Bonaventure-et-du-Rocher-Percé★

(Île Bonaventure and Percé Rock Park) – ✕▣ ⏲ *Open Jun–mid-Oct daily 9am–5pm.* ☞*$3.50.* ☎*418-782-2240. www.sepaq.com.*

In summer this flat-topped island is home to North America's largest **gannet** colony, with some 60,000 birds. A pleasant **boat trip** leads past Percé Rock and then around the island, affording superb views (&▣⏲*Depart from Percé wharf mid-May–mid-Oct daily 9am–5pm. Round-trip 1hr 15min. Reservations required.* ☞*$20 adult. Les Bateliers de Percé Inc.* ☎*418-782-2974. www. infogaspesie.com*).

Bonaventure

131km/81mi southwest of Percé. Founded The **Musée acadien du Québec** illustrates the influence of these people on Quebec's culture (*95, av. Port-Royal, Bonaventure QC, G0C 1E0.* ✕&▣⏲*Open Jun 24–Labour Day daily 9am–6pm. Rest of* *the year Mon–Fri 9am–noon, 1pm–4.30pm, Sun 1pm–4:30pm. ☜$7. ☎418-534-4000.www.museeacadien.com).*

Carleton

63km/39mi west of Bonaventure. From the summit of **Mont Saint-Joseph**, rising to 558m/1,830ft, the **panorama**★★ encompasses Chaleur Bay from Bonaventure to the Miguasha Peninsula and south to New Brunswick.

Parc de Miguasha★

231, Rte Miguasha Ouest, PO Box 183 Nouvelle QC, G0C 2E0. 24km/15mi west of Carleton. ✕ ☍ ☐ ◷ *Open Jun–Aug daily 9am–6pm. Sept–early Oct daily 9am–5pm. Rest of year Mon–Fri 8:30am–noon & 1pm–430pm. ◷Closed statutory holidays and Christmas period. ☜$11.50 adult. ☎418-794-2475, toll-free 1-800-665-6527. www.sepaq.com.*

This park lies on an escarpment jutting out into Chaleur Bay, which contains fossils from the Devonian Period (400 million years ago). The interpretation centre offers several programs.

Lieu historique national du Canada Bataille-de-la-Ristigouche (Battle of the Ristigouche National Historic Site of Canada)

44km/27mi from Miguasha Park. ☍ ☐ ◷*Open Jun–early Oct daily 9am–5pm. ☜$4 adult. ☎418-788-5676. www.pc.gc.ca.*

France's last attempt to save its North American colony from British domination during the Seven Years' War was thwarted in the estuary of the Ristigouche River in 1760. A **visitor centre** displays the hull and anchor of the French warship *Le Machault*.

GATINEAU★

POPULATION 242 124

Gatineau functions primarily as an annex to Canada's federal capital. The downtown area has witnessed a great deal of change, including the construction of two large federal government complexes and the creation of a new campus for the University of Quebec.

- 🛈 **Information:** www.tourismoutaouais.com
- ▶ **Orient Yourself:** Gatineau is on the Québec side of the Ottawa River. Roads on the Gatineau side are narrow and winding.
- 🅿 **Parking:** Meters on downtown streets operate from 8am–5pm, 25 cents/10 min. You can purchase a smart card ($20, $100) at the Maison du Citoyen, 25 rue Laurier.
- 🜚 **Also See:** OTTAWA, UPPER CANADA VILLAGE, LAURENTIDES

Sights

Musée canadien des Civilisations★★★

(Canadian Museum of Civilization) *100 Rue Laurier, Gatineau QC, K1A 0M8.* ✕ ☍ ☐ ◷*Open Ju1–Labour Day daily 9am–6pm (Thu–Fri 9pm). May–Jun & rest of Sept–mid-Oct daily 9am–6pm (Thu 9pm). Rest of the year Tue–Sun 9am–5pm (Thu 9pm). ☜ $10 (supplements for IMAX theatre, Canadian War Museum and special exhibits). ☎819-776-7000, toll-free 1-800-555-5621. www.civilization.ca.*

The sweeping curves of the two large buildings designed by **Douglas Cardinal** evoke the emergence of the North American continent and its subsequent molding by wind, water and glaciers. The **Canadian Shield Wing** houses administrative offices and conservation laboratories, while the **Glacier Wing** provides 16,500sq m/177,600sq ft of exhibit halls.

In the **Canada Hall** artifacts and reconstructed buildings re-create 1,000 years of Canadian heritage. The delightful **children's museum** 🄺🄸🄳🅂 encourages

Canadian Museum of Civilization

young people to explore the world, from a Mexican village to a Pakistani street.

Parc de la Gatineau★★ (Gatineau Park)

✕ & 🅿 🕒 *Park open daily year-round. Parkways* 🕒 *closed from first snowfall until early May. Visitor centre* 🕒 *Open daily 9am–5pm.* 🕒 *Closed Christmas morning.* ⌨ *$9/car.* ☎*819-827-2020, toll-free 1-800-465-1867. www.capcan.ca.* Covering 356sq km/137sq mi, this park nestles between the valleys of the Ottawa and Gatineau rivers. **Champlain Lookout** offers a magnificent **panorama**★★ of the Ottawa Valley.

Domaine Mackenzie-King★

(Mackenzie King Estate) ✕ & 🅿 🕒*Open mid-May–mid-Oct Mon–Fri 11am–5pm, weekends & holidays 11am–6pm.* ⌨*$8/car.* ☎*819-827-2020.www.capcan.ca* **Moorside,** the residence of **William Lyon Mackenzie-King** (1874-1950), Canada's tenth prime minister, features exhibits and a tea room.

Address Book

WHERE TO EAT

$ Le Twist Café Resto Bar – *88 Rue Montcalm, Gatineau QC, J8X 2L7.* ☎*819-777-8886.* Operating within a funky converted old house, Le Twist makes a good spot for informal lunch or dinner.

$$$ Restaurant Le Sans-Pareil –*71 Blvd. Saint-Raymond, Hull QC, J8Y 1S3.* ☎*819-771-1471. www.lesanspareil.com.* This Belgian outpost offers the inevitable moules-frites, but also a classic seasonal menu with Canadian touches (cranberries) to *fine cuisine Belge.*

LAURENTIDES★★

MAP P 312

Stretching along the north shore of the St. Lawrence, this range of low, rounded mountains rises to an altitude of 968m/3,175ft at **Mont Tremblant.** Part of the Canadian Shield, the Laurentians (*Laurentides* in French), formed more than a billion years ago in the Precambrian era, are among the oldest mountains in the world. The area north of Montreal between Saint-Jérôme and Mt. Tremblant is especially noted for its string of resort towns that offer an attractive blend of recreational activities and fine cuisine. Several renowned summer theatres open their doors to visitors.

- **Information:** Tourisme Laurentides, 14-142, rue de la Chapelle, Mirabel QC, J7J 2C8. 450-436-8532. www.laurentides.com or www.hautes-laurentides.com
- ▶ **Orient Yourself:** Hwy. 15 (The Laurentian Autoroute) takes you north from Montreal to Ste-Agathe. The area resorts are a short drive from the highway.
- **Don't Miss:** In any season, take the ski lift to the top of Mont-Tremblant for spectacular views, particular in the fall when leaves change colour.
- **Organizing Your Time:** It is a two-hour drive from downtown Montreal to Mont-Tremblant, over Hwy. 15 to Ste-Agathe, then Hwy. 117 north.
- **Especially for Kids:** A sugar shack for the experience of eggs poached in maple syrup.
- **Also See:** GATINEAU, MONTREAL

Sights

Sainte-Adèle★

68km/42mi north of Montreal by Rtes. 15 and 117.

Occupying a lovely **site** on the small Lake Sainte-Adèle, this town is dominated by the luxurious **Hôtel Chantecler** *(1474, chemin Chantecler, Ste-Adèle, QC, J8B 1A2. ☎450-229-3555, toll-free 1-888-916-1616 (US/Canada). www.lechan*

tecler.com), which has its own ski hill. Frequented by artists and writers, the village features numerous restaurants and charming country inns.

Sainte-Agathe-des-Monts★

18km/11mi north of Sainte-Adèle by Rte. 117.

Set on the shores of **Sables Lake★★**, this town is the capital of the Laurentians region. A **scenic cruise** reveals

Parc du Mont-Tremblant Village

Address Book

For dollar sign categories, see the Legend on the cover flap.

WHERE TO STAY

$$$$ Fairmont Tremblant – *3045 Chemin de la Chapelle, Mont-Tremblant QC, J8E 1E1.* ☎819-681-7000, toll-free 1-800-441-1414. www.fairmont.ca. *314 rooms.* ✗ 🅿 💪 🈂 Reigning above Mont-Tremblant Village, this resort hotel remains in character with the re-created 18C atmosphere of its surroundings. Despite its austere exterior, the hotel exudes rustic comfort inside. Employees in 17C Nouvelle France outfits show guests to charming rooms with pine furnishings and plaid drapes and bedspreads. You can watch skiers from the heated outdoor pool.

WHERE TO EAT

$$$$ Restaurant La Forge – *4031, ch. de la Chapelle, Mont-Tremblant Resort, J8E 1B1.* ☎819-681-4900. **Regional Canadian.** This inviting octagonal, two-level restaurant, with a bistro on the main floor, is located right at the base of the ski lifts. The open kitchen prepares regional dishes grilled over wood, like Boileau deer tournedos with morello cherries and peppercorns, or rack of Quebec piglet served with Oka cider and golden Sainte-Julie honey.

$$ Restaurant aux Tourterelles – *1141 Chemin Chantecler, Sainte-Adèle QC, J8B 2Y3.* ☎450-229-8160. **French.** This cozy restaurant near the lake has a stone fireplace and walls tinted in plum and sunset orange. The three-course table d'hôte (fixed-price) of modern French cuisine varies often, but the *carré d'agneau* (lamb) is a mainstay.

$ Cabane à sucre Millette – *1357 Rue St-Faustin, Saint-Faustin–Lac Carré QC, J0T 1J3.* ☎ 819-688-2101, toll-free 877-688-2101. www.tremblant-sugar-shack.com. 🚻**Quebecois.** For a truly authentic Québécois experience, don't miss a meal at the Millette family's "sugar shack." After touring the syrup-making facilities, enjoy folk music while you savour copious servings of *soupe aux pois* (pea soup); *jambon fumé au sirop d'érable* (maple-syrup smoked ham); and *saucisses dans le sirop d'érable* (sausages in maple syrup); or the notorious *oreilles de Criss* (possibly fried pork fat). Finish it all off with *crêpes au sucre à la crème chaude* (crêpes topped with warm maple cream). Be prepared to wait, and to sit elbow-to-elbow with total strangers.

PARC LINÉAIRE LE P'TIT TRAIN DU NORD

Access by Rte. 15 and/or Rte. 117 from St-Jérôme or any of the 23 towns and villages that lie along the park. 🕐*Open Dec–Apr for cross-country skiing and snowmobiling, May–Oct for hiking and bicycling.* 🚲 *biking $5/daily or $15/season, skiing $7/daily $45/season.* ☎ 450-224-7007, toll-free 1- 800-561-6673 (US/Canada). www.laurentides.com. For over 70 years before it closed, the railway line the P'Tit Train du Nord brought nature lovers to the Laurentians. Today, hikers, cyclists, cross-country skiers and even snowmobilers cherish the "linear park" for its 200km/124mi of maintained pathways. Val-David and Mont-Tremblant are the most popular of the 23 village access points. Former train stations now operate as trail service centres.

SNOWSHOES AND SAUNAS

Opportunities for exercise don't wane much in winter either. **La Source Aquaclub** (☎819-681-5668. www.tremblant.ca) is a fitness center that features an indoor pool with waterfalls. Diversions include **snowshoe** excursions or **dogsledding** (☎ 819-681-4848. www.tremblantactivities.com.com) at a neighbouring forest trail. For muscle-bruised skiers, the nearby **Le Scandinave** (☎819-425-5524. www.scandinave.com) offers a spa experience in a woodsy outdoor setting along Rivière du Diable. The idea is to slowly raise your body temperature in a cycle of heat, cold and rest while working up the nerve to jump into the hole cut in the frozen river! The Finnish sauna, Jacuzzi and Norwegian steam baths are joined by outdoor heated sidewalks. Compared to the river—which fewer than a quarter of visitors brave—the bracing Nordic waterfall seems tame. Swedish massages are offered here too.

the lake and homes lining its shores (&⊞🕐*Depart from dock at foot of Rue Principale June–late Oct daily 10:30am, 11:30am, 1:30pm, 2:30pm & 3:30pm. Additional departures Jun 25–late Aug 5pm & 7pm. Round-trip 50min. ⌚$12 adult. Les Croisières Alouette. ☎819-326-3656. www.croisierealouette.com).*

Parc du Mont Tremblant★

(Mt. Tremblant Park) *About 140km/87mi north of Montreal. Park ✗&⊞🕐Open daily mid-May–Sept 7am–9pm. Oct–April daily 9am–4pm. Sections of the park's roads are closed during winter. ⌚$3.50. ☎877-688-2289. www.sepaq.com.* Dominating the long, narrow Lake Tremblant, Quebec's oldest provincial park abounds in lakes and hiking trails.

Laurentides

62km/38mi north of Montreal by Rte. 15, then east on Rte. 158. This town is known as the birthplace of **Sir Wilfrid Laurier** (1841-1919), the first French-Canadian prime minister of Canada (1896-1911). The **Lieu historique national de Sir-Wilfrid-Laurier** (National Historic Site) stands on the place of Laurier's presumed birthplace *945 12th Ave., St-Lin QC,J5M 2W4. &⊞➤Visit by 1hr guided tour only. Mid-Mid-June–Labour Day daily 9am–5pm, May–mid-Jun Mon–Fri 9am–5pm. ⌚$4. ☎450-439-3702, toll-free 1-888-773-8888. www.pc.gc.ca).*

ÎLES DE LA MADELEINE★★

Located in the Gulf of St. Lawrence, these eight islands plus islets are connected by sand spits that form a hook-shaped mass about 72km/45mi long. In 1755, they became a refuge for **Acadians** deported from Nova Scotia, ancestors of today's Madelinots. Supplemented by agriculture, logging and tourism, fishing remains the primary economic activity of the archipelago.

🛈 **Information:** Tourist Office, 128, ch. Principal, Cap-aux-Meules, QC, G4T 1C5. ☎418-986-2245, 877-624-4437 or www.tourismeilesdelamadeleine.com

▶ **Orient Yourself:** The islands are near Cape Breton Island and Prince Edward Island.

🕐 **Organizing Your Time:** The islands are on Atlantic time.

👶 **Also See:** PRINCE EDWARD ISLAND, NOVA SCOTIA, NEW BRUNSWICK

Île du Cap-Aux-Meules

Access

Ferry *from Souris, PEI, to Cap-aux-Meules (5hrs): Apr–Jun & Sept–Oct Tue-Sun, from Cap-aux-Meules (8am) and from Souris (2pm). Daily service Jul–Aug. Limited service Nov–Jan. One-way �$43.25/adult, additional �$80.50/car. Reservations required. Cruises from Montreal, with stops en route.* ✗♿️🅿️ *CTMA Traversier Ltd. Cap-aux-Meules ☎418-986-3278, 888-986-3278 (US/Canada) or Souris ☎902-687-2181. www.ilesdelamadeleine. com/ctma.* **Flights** *between Montreal and Havre aux Maisons Island on Air Canada Jazz (☎ 888-247-2262. www.aircanada. com) and Pascan Aviation Inc. (☎ 450-443-0500, toll-free 1-888-313-8777. www. pascan.com).*

Sights

Île du Cap-Aux-Meules★★ (Cap aux Meules Island)

Cap-aux-Meules' highest point, **Butte du Vent**, affords **views**★★ of the entire chain of islands. The western coast features dramatic **rock formations**.

Île du Havre Aubert (Havre Aubert Island)

The **Musée de la Mer**★ (Maritime Museum) acquaints visitors with the maritime history and culture of the Magdalen Islands *(1023, Rte 199, Havre-Aubert QC, G4T 9C8.* ♿️🅿️🕐*Open Jun 24– Labour Day Mon–Fri 9am–6pm, weekends 10am–6pm. Rest of the year variable hours. Call to confirm.* �$6. *☎418-937-5711. www.ilesdelamadeleine.com).* The historic site of **La Grave**★ has stores, ironworks, *chaufauds* (sheds where cod was dried) and warehouses.

Île du Havre aux Maisons★ (Havre aux Maisons Island)

Examples of local architecture include the **baraque**, designed to shelter hay. At **Dune du Sud**★ a beach and rock formations attract visitors.

On **Île de la Grande Entrée**★ (Grande Entrée Island), coastal hiking trails afford **views**★★★ of jagged cliffs, tidal pools and twisted trees. The **Grande Échouerie Beach**★★ to the northeast is considered the archipelago's loveliest.

MONTREAL★★★

METRO POPULATION 3,635,571

Canada's second-largest metropolis after Toronto is located on a large island in the St. Lawrence River, some 1,000 miles from the Atlantic. This cosmopolitan city has emerged as a leading industrial, commercial and financial centre. Home to the world's largest Francophone population outside Paris, Montreal offers visitors a wealth of cultural attractions and a diversity of urban settings.

Information: Tourisme Montreal, 1001 Square Dorchester. ☎514-873-2015, toll-free 1- 877-266-5687. www.tourisme-montreal.org

▶ **Orient Yourself:** The main downtown area sits at the foot of the southeast slopes of Mont-Royal. The Montreal Métro system can move you quickly and safely around the city. Signage is in French, but pictographs are often used.

P Parking: Downtown parking meters are computerized; you note the number of your meter, pay at a nearby automatic kiosk, and keep your coupon. Later, you can "feed" your meter from any kiosk.

Don't Miss: Old Montreal's cobblestone streets, especially around Place Jacques-Cartier; the Olympic Park area, with the Biodôme and Jardin Botanique.

Organizing Your Time: In the evening, return to the city centre to take in the night life in Old Montreal and on Crescent and St. Denis streets.

Kids Especially for Kids: The Biodôme and Insectarium in the Olympic Park are perfect for kids. In the Old Port area, don't miss iSci, with its interactive exhibits

Also See: LES LAURENTIDES, LA VALLÉE DU RICHELIEU, LES CANTONS DE L'EST

A Bit of History

Early Exploration – While searching for a route to the Orient in 1535, Jacques Cartier visited the Mohawk village of **Hochelaga** on the island of Montreal. In 1611, Samuel de Champlain, founder of Quebec City, sailed upriver and set foot on the island of St. Helen. However, European settlement of the area did not occur until the arrival, in 1642, of Paul de Chomedey, **Sieur de Maisonneuve** (1612-76), who is considered the founder of Montreal.

Under the French Regime – In the 17C the Sulpician order in France chose de Maisonneuve to sail across the Atlantic and establish the mission of **Ville-Marie** (City of Mary), present-day Montreal. Amid fighting between Iroquois Indians and the French settlers, Ville-Marie developed into a commercial centre and was renamed Montreal in the early 18C. French fur-trading forays across the Great Lakes brought wealth and when Montreal surrendered to the British in 1760, it was a thriving community. Most of the French nobility returned to France, while a large number of Scots, attracted to the fur trade, and an influx of Loyalists from the US swelled the Anglophone population.

From Rebellion to Confederation Montreal was the centre of one of the **Rebellions of 1837,** a political uprising which, in Quebec, contested the power held by the Crown-appointed governor and his council. Led by Louis-Joseph Papineau, George-Étienne Cartier and other French Canadians, the **Patriots** engaged British troops several times. Although the insurgents were defeated, the British government granted Quebec a representative government.

By the time of Confederation in 1867, Montreal stood at the forefront of railway development and claimed the world's largest grain port. Financial institutions along Rue Saint-Jacques supported Montreal's dominance of Canada's financial sector until the 1970s.

Montreal Today – Following a period of slow growth after the Great Depression, Montreal emerged in the 1960s as an international centre of commerce and culture. In addition to hosting the 1967 World Fair (**Expo '67**), the **1976 Olympic Games** and the **1980 International Floralies**, the city has launched annual international festivals in jazz, film and comedy, attracting thousands of visitors. Montreal's premier cultural complex, **Place des Arts**★★, is home to the Montreal Symphony Orchestra, the Grands Ballets Canadiens and the Montreal Opera.

The city remains a major centre of Francophone culture, with numerous cafes and restaurants, especially along Rue Saint-Denis and Rue Crescent, and a lively night-life as well as fashionable shops and boutiques.

The ⏾ symbol indicates a subway station.

Vieux-Montréal★★★ (Old Montreal)

⏾ *Place d'Armes.*

Bounded by the Old Port, Saint-Jacques, Rue Berri and Rue McGill, Montreal's historic core was originally enclosed within imposing stone walls erected in the early 1700s. As Montrealers moved outside the fortifications, the area fell into decline. Interest in Old Montreal was revived in the 1960s: the surviving 18C homes were renovated, warehouses were transformed into apartment buildings and condominiums, and restaurants and shops opened.

▶ *Horse-drawn carriages (calèches) depart from Rue Notre-Dame, Place d'Armes, Rue de la Commune and Place Jacques-Cartier.*

Place d'Armes★

Designed in the 17C by the Sulpician Dollier de Casson, this square long served as military drill grounds. A **monument**★ **(1)** (Louis-Philippe Hébert) in the centre honours the founder of Montreal, Sieur de Maisonneuve, who, according to legend, killed the local Indian chief on this site during a 1644 battle. The west side of this charming space is dominated by the **Banque de Montréal**★ (1847), a fine example of the Neoclassical style.

The financial heart of Canada until the 1970s, **Rue Saint-Jacques**★, extending south, is lined with elegant 19C and 20C edifices. Note in particular the Canadian Imperial Bank of Commerce *(no. 265)*, with its facade of fluted Corinthian columns, and the **Banque Royale du Canada**★ (Royal Bank of Canada) *(no. 360)*, whose tower is a distinct feature of the city's skyline.

The **Le Centre de Commerce mondial de Montréal** (World Trade Centre Montreal), opened in 1992 at 380 Rue St-Antoine Ouest, fuses the façades of 11 historic buildings and whose glass atrium incorporates a remnant of the former wall, Ruelle des Fortifications.

Basilique Notre-Dame★ (Notre Dame Basilica)

Rue Notre-Dame Ouest. ⏾*Place d'Armes.* ♿⏾*Open year-round Mon–Fri 8am–4:30pm, Sat 8am–4pm, Sun noon–4pm.* 🎫*$4. Sound and light show 5pm.* ☎*514-842-2925, toll-free 1-866-842-2925. www.basiliquenddm.org.*

This 1829 Gothic Revival basilica is renowned for its magnificent **interior**. As visitors enter, eyes are drawn to the imposing **reredos** that stands out against the background's soft blue hues. The massive black walnut **pulpit** is the work of Louis-Philippe Hébert.

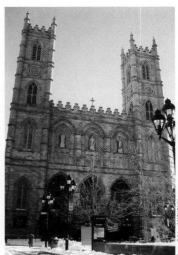

Notre-Dame Basilica

Pierre Ethier/MICHELIN

Address Book

GETTING AROUND

BY PUBLIC TRANSPORTATION

Local metro and bus service are provided by the Société de transport de Montréal (STM) (☎514-786-4636. *www.stm.info*). The metro system operates from 5:30am–1am *(lines 1, 2 & 4)* or 12.15am *(line 5)*. Each metro line is designated by a number and a color. The bus service has 169 and 20 night-time routes, as well as commuter trains to the far suburbs. Starting in 2008, rechargeable "smart cards" for paying fares are being gradually introduced. Passengers may also buy disposable cards charged with six fares *($11.75)* or pay a single fare *($2.75)* in cash in a bus (exact fare only) or in a metro station. Cards are on sale in metro stations and at many conveniences stores. Tourist passes *(cartes touristiques)* are also available *($9/day or $17/3 days)*. Lost and found: ☎514-786-4636+8+4+2.

BY CAR

Rental agencies include Avis ☎514-866-2847. Budget ☎514-866-7675. Discount ☎514-849-2277. Hertz ☎514-842-8537. National-Tilden ☎514-481-1166.

BY TAXI

Atlas ☎514-485-8585. Champlain ☎514-273-2435. Co-Op ☎514-725-9885. Diamond ☎514-273-6331. La Salle ☎514-277-2552

GENERAL INFORMATION

ACCOMMODATIONS AND VISITOR INFORMATION

Infotourist Office: 1001 Square Dorchester, Montreal QC, H3B 4V4. (corner Peel and Ste-Catherine) 🕙Peel or 174 Notre-Dame E. in Old Montreal 🕙 Champ-de-Mars. *(🕙Open late Jun–Labour Day daily 8:30am–7:30pm. Rest of the year daily 9am–6pm.* ☎514-873-2015 or 877-266-5687. *www. tourisme-montreal.org)*.

🕙 The **Montreal Museums Pass** gives free access to 30 museums over 3 days for $35. For another $10, you get public transit as well. The pass can be purchased at any participating museum. *www.museesmontreal.org*

LOCAL PRESS

Daily newspapers: English – the *Gazette*. French– *Le Journal de Montréal, Le Devoir, La Presse.*

ENTERTAINMENT

For current schedules and for addresses of principal theatres and concert halls, consult the free tourist publications *Mirror (www.montrealmirror.com)* and *Hour (www.hour.ca)* (English), *Le guide Montréal (www.guideroyal. com)*(bilingual) and *Voir* (www.voir. ca)(French) or the weekend arts and entertainment supplements in local newspapers. **Tickets** may be purchased from Admission ☎514-790-1245, *toll-free 1-800-361-4595.www.admission.com.* Telspec ☎514-790-1111, *toll-free 1-800-848-1594. www.tel-spec.com.* Arrière Scene Inc. ☎514-935-9999, *toll-free 1-800-684-8994. www.billets.ca.* Place des Arts ☎514-842-2112. *www.pda.qc.ca.*

SPORTS

Montreal Canadiens (National Hockey League) season from Oct–Apr at the Bell Centre (🕙Lucien-L'Allier) ☎514-932-2582.*www.canadiens.nhl. com.* **Montreal Alouettes** (Canadian Football League), season Jun-Nov at Percival Molson Stadium (🕙McGill or Square Victoria, shuttle service to stadium 2hrs before games). ☎514-790-1245 or toll-free 1-800-361-4595. *www.montrealalouettes.com.* **Montreal Impact** (United Soccer League) season May-Sept at Saputo Stadium, corner Sherbrook and Viau 🕙Viau. ☎514-328-3668. *www.montrealimpact.com.* Every August, Montreal hosts the **Roger's Cup Canadian Open**, a Tier 1 tennis tournament that draws the world's best players. Montreal and Toronto (Rexall Centre) alternate hosting the men's and women's events. Uniprix Stadium 🕙de Castelnau ☎514-273-1515, *toll-free 1-866-338-2685. www. tenniscanada.ca.*

USEFUL NUMBERS ☎

AREA CODES 514 AND 450

Dial all 10 digits (area code plus the phone number) for local calls.
* **Police–Ambulance–Fire**: 911 (Emergencies only)

◆ **Police:** 514-280-2222 (non-emergencies)

◆ **Sûreté du Québec** (provincial police): 514-310-4141

◆ **Tourisme Montréal:** 514-873-2015. *www.tourisme-montreal.org*

◆ **Tourisme Quebec:** 514-873-2015. *www.bonjourquebec.com.*

◆ **Central Train Station (Bonaventure Station)** (VIA Rail): *895 Rue de la Gauchetière Ouest, H3B 4G1,* 514-989-2626 1-888-842-7245. *www.viarail.ca*

◆ **Orléans Express** (bus service within Quebec)**:** 514-842-2281 or 1-888-999-3977. *www.orleansexpress.com*

◆ **Vermont Transit** (bus service to New England and New York): 1-800-552-8737. *www.vermonttransit.com*

◆ **Greyhound** (bus service Canada and US): 514-287-1580. *www.greyhound.com.*

◆ **Station Centrale d'Autobus:** *1717 rue Berri, H2L 4E9.* 514-843-4231.*www.stationcentrale.com,*

◆ **Montréal-Trudeau International Airport:** 514-394-7377. *www.admtl.com*

◆ **Canadian Automobile Assn.:** *1180 Drummond St.,H3G 2R7.* 514-861-7575

◆ **Jean Coutu Drugstore** (open 8am–midnight): *1675 Ste-Catherine, H3H 1L9.* (✪Guy) 514-933-4221

◆ **Pharmaprix Drugstore** (open 24hrs) *5122 Côte des Neiges, H3T 1X8* (✪Côte des Neiges) 514-738-8464

◆ **Weather** (24hr): 514-283-4006

✎ *For dollar sign categories, see the Legend on the cover flap..*

WHERE TO STAY

$ L'Auberge de Jeunesse – *1030 Rue Mackay, H3G 2H1.* ☎514-843-3317, toll-free 1-866-843-3317. *www.hostellingmontreal.com. 243 beds.* ✕.
This Hosteling International affiliate in downtown Montreal offers a non-smoking environment, kitchen services, a television room, wireless Internet service, a laundromat and washrooms with each room. Private and group rooms available.

$$ Hôtel de l'Institut – *3535 Rue St-Denis, H2X 3P1.* ☎514-282-5120, toll-free 1-800-361-5111. *www.ithq.qc.ca. 42 rooms.* ✕⚐🅿. Occupying the top floors of the bunker-like structure that houses the Institut de Tourisme et d'Hôtellerie du Québec, this hotel offers modern rooms and the impeccable service you would expect from students of the art of hospitality. Standard amenities including wireless Internet. Close by lie the Plateau Mont-Royal and the Quartier Latin.

$$$ Auberge de la Fontaine – *1301 Rue Rachel Est, H2J 2K1.* ☎514-597-0166, toll-free 1-800-597-0597. *www.aubergedelafontaine.com. 21 rooms.* ♿🅿⌑. This 19C Victorian mansion sits in the trendy Plateau Mont-Royal district facing beautiful La Fontaine Park. Colourful contemporary rooms, wireless Internet, access to the kitchen for snacks and beverages, and a generous breakfast buffet served in the sunny dining room make for a restful stay.

$$$ Château Versailles – *1659 Rue Sherbrooke West, H3H 1E3.* ☎514-933-8111, toll-free 1-888-933-8111. *www.versailleshotels.com. 173 rooms.* ♿🅿⌑. Composed of four interconnected 19C Victorian town houses and a modern tower annex (Le Meridien) across the street, this hotel offers excellent service and convenient location at the western edge of downtown. Amenities include dataports and wireless Internet. Breakfast is served in the restaurant,
Le Brontë ($$$) in the Meridian tower.

$$$ Fairmont La Reine Elizabeth – *900 Blvd. René-Lévesque Ouest, H3B 4A5.* ☎514-861-3511, toll-free 1- 800-441-1414. *www.fairmont.ca. 1,039 rooms.* ✕♿🅿 Spa ⌑. The cavernous Queen Elizabeth enjoys a convenient location above Montreal's underground city and the railway station. Spacious rooms have been renewed with wallpaper and chintz bedspreads. Besides a large health club, a beauty salon and a shopping arcade, the hotel boasts the **Beaver Club ($$$$),** known for its fine French cuisine.

$$$$ Hostellerie Pierre du Calvet – *405 Rue Bonsecours, H2Y 3C3.* ☎514-282-1725, toll-free 1-866-544-1725. *www.pierreducalvet.ca. 10 rooms.* ✕🅿⌑. This 1725 merchant's home sits on a cobblestone street in Old Montreal. The decoration is opulent, with Victorian antiques and Oriental rugs. Rooms have original stone walls, fireplaces and canopy beds and all the amenities. American-style breakfast is served in

Dining in Montreal

the **Filles du Roy** restaurant **($$$)** on the ground floor.

$$$$ Hôtel Place d'Armes – *701 Côte de la Place d'Armes. H2Y 3X2.* ☎514-842-1887, *toll-free 1-888-450-1887. www. hotelplacedarmes.com. 135 rooms.* ✗ ♿ P Spa. This charming boutique hotel is located on Place d'Armes in the centre of Old Montreal. Rich mahogany furnishings and amenities including bathrobes, down comforters, data port and Internet access. Large windows afford splendid views of Chinatown, downtown Montreal and the Notre-Dame basilica. The restaurant, **Au Cuisine du Terroir ($$$)** offers a very up-market take on Quebec cuisine.

$$$$$ Hôtel Le Germain – *2050 Rue Mansfield., H3A 1Y9.* ☎514-849-2050, *toll-free 1-877-333-2050. www.hotel germain.com. 101 rooms.* ✗ ♿ P ⛾. This office-building cum boutique hotel offers Asian minimalist design in the light-filled rooms, with dark wood furnishings handcrafted by local artisans. Sumptuous bedding and amenities including wireless Internet, CD players and the morning newspaper.

WHERE TO EAT

$ Beauty's – *93 Ave. Mont-Royal Ouest, H2T 2S5.* ☎514-849-8883. **American**. If you want breakfast any time of day, come wait in line at this popular 1950's-style diner. Bagels, smoked salmon, and blueberry pancakes are the main

attractions, but you can also order a good lunch salad or sandwich.

$ Le Duc de Lorraine, *5002 Chemin de la Côte-des-Neiges.H3V 1G6.* ☎514-731-4128. *www.ducdelorraine.com.* Renowned for its breads, pastries, cheeses and meats, this windowed tea room is also a fine spot to sample croissants or enjoy a light meal.

$$ Restaurant Daou – *519 Rue Faillon Est, H2R 1L6.* ☎514-276-8310. **Lebanese**. Located in the Villeray area, this spot, occasionally enlivened with belly dancers in the evenings, offers Middle Eastern specialties such as tabbouleh, kibbeh, shish kebab and hummus. The decor is ordinary, but expect good food for a good price.

$$ Le Piton de la Fournaise – *835 Rue Duluth Est. H2L 1B2. Dinner only. Closed Mon.* ☎514-526-3936. ♿ **Réunion/**

BYOW

Bring your own wine. Restaurants that don't have a liquor license can allow patrons to bring in their own favorite vintages. Most BYOW *(apportez votre vin)* eateries are located in the Plateau Mont-Royal district and the Quartier Latin.

Table d'hôte

These fixed-price meals typically include a three-course menu consisting of a starter, main dish and dessert.

◆ **Police:** 514-280-2222
(non-emergencies)
◆ **Sûreté du Québec** (provincial
police): 514-310-4141
◆ **Tourisme Montréal**: 514-873-2015.
www.tourisme-montreal.org
◆ **Tourisme Quebec:** 514-873-2015.
www.bonjourquebec.com.
◆ **Central Train Station (Bonaven-
ture Station)** (VIA Rail): *895 Rue de la
Gauchetière Ouest, H3B 4G1, 514-989-
2626 1-888-842-7245. www.viarail.ca*
◆ **Orléans Express** (bus service within
Quebec)**:** 514-842-2281 or 1-888-999-
3977. *www.orleansexpress.com*
◆ **Vermont Transit** (bus service to
New England and New York): 1-800-
552-8737. *www.vermonttransit.com*
◆ **Greyhound** (bus service Canada and
US): 514-287-1580. *www.greyhound.
com.*
◆ **Station Centrale d'Autobus**: *1717
rue Berri, H2L 4E9. 514-843-4231.www.
stationcentrale.com,*
◆ **Montréal-Trudeau International
Airport:** 514-394-7377. *www.admtl.com*
◆ **Canadian Automobile Assn.:** *1180
Drummond St.,H3G 2R7.* 514-861-7575
◆ **Jean Coutu Drugstore** (open
8am–midnight)*: 1675 Ste-Catherine, H3H
1L9.* (🚇Guy) 514-933-4221
◆ **Pharmaprix Drugstore** (open
24hrs) *5122 Côte des Neiges, H3T 1X8*
(🚇Côte des Neiges) 514-738-8464
◆ **Weather** (24hr): 514-283-4006
🕯 *For dollar sign categories, see the
Legend on the cover flap..*

WHERE TO STAY

$ L'Auberge de Jeunesse – *1030
Rue Mackay, H3G 2H1.* ☎*514-843-
3317, toll-free 1-866-843-3317. www.
hostellingmontreal.com. 243 beds.* ✕.
This Hosteling International affiliate in
downtown Montreal offers a non-smoking environment, kitchen services,
a television room, wireless Internet
service, a laundromat and washrooms
with each room. Private and group
rooms available.

$$ Hôtel de l'Institut – *3535 Rue
St-Denis, H2X 3P1.* ☎*514-282-5120,
toll-free 1-800-361-5111. www.ithq.
qc.ca. 42 rooms.* ✕♿🅿. Occupying the
top floors of the bunker-like structure
that houses the Institut de Tourisme et
d'Hôtellerie du Québec, this hotel offers

modern rooms and the impeccable
service you would expect from students
of the art of hospitality. Standard
amenities including wireless Internet.
Close by lie the Plateau Mont-Royal and
the Quartier Latin.
$$$ Auberge de la Fontaine – *1301
Rue Rachel Est, H2J 2K1.* ☎*514-597-
0166, toll-free 1-800-597-0597. www.
aubergedelafontaine.com. 21 rooms.*
♿🅿☟. This 19C Victorian mansion
sits in the trendy Plateau Mont-Royal
district facing beautiful La Fontaine
Park. Colourful contemporary rooms,
wireless Internet, access to the kitchen
for snacks and beverages, and a generous breakfast buffet served in the sunny
dining room make for a restful stay.
$$$ Château Versailles – *1659 Rue
Sherbrooke West, H3H 1E3.* ☎*514-933-
8111, toll-free 1-888-933-8111. www.ver-
sailleshotels.com. 173 rooms.* ✕♿🅿☟.
Composed of four interconnected 19C
Victorian town houses and a modern
tower annex (Le Meridien) across the
street, this hotel offers excellent service
and convenient location at the western
edge of downtown. Amenities include
dataports and wireless Internet. Break-
fast is served in the restaurant,
Le Brontë ($$$) in the Meridian tower.
$$$ Fairmont La Reine Elizabeth
– *900 Blvd. René-Lévesque Ouest, H3B
4A5.* ☎*514-861-3511, toll-free 1- 800-
441-1414. www.fairmont.ca. 1,039 rooms.*
✕♿🅿 Spa☟. The cavernous Queen
Elizabeth enjoys a convenient location
above Montreal's underground city and
the railway station. Spacious rooms
have been renewed with wallpaper
and chintz bedspreads. Besides a
large health club, a beauty salon and a
shopping arcade, the hotel boasts the
Beaver Club ($$$$), known for its fine
French cuisine.
$$$$ Hostellerie Pierre du Calvet
– *405 Rue Bonsecours, H2Y 3C3.* ☎*514-
282-1725, toll-free 1-866-544-1725. www.
pierreducalvet.ca. 10 rooms.* ✕🅿☟.
This 1725 merchant's home sits on a
cobblestone street in Old Montreal. The
decoration is opulent, with Victorian
antiques and Oriental rugs. Rooms
have original stone walls, fireplaces
and canopy beds and all the amenities.
American-style breakfast is served in

Dining in Montreal

the **Filles du Roy** restaurant **($$$)** on the ground floor.

$$$$ Hôtel Place d'Armes – *701 Côte de la Place d'Armes. H2Y 3X2.* ☎*514-842-1887, toll-free 1-888-450-1887. www.hotelplacedarmes.com. 135 rooms.* ✕&ⓅSpa. This charming boutique hotel is located on Place d'Armes in the centre of Old Montreal. Rich mahogany furnishings and amenities including bathrobes, down comforters, data port and Internet access. Large windows afford splendid views of Chinatown, downtown Montreal and the Notre-Dame basilica. The restaurant, **Au Cuisine du Terroir ($$$)** offers a very up-market take on Quebec cuisine.

$$$$$ Hôtel Le Germain – *2050 Rue Mansfield., H3A 1Y9.* ☎*514-849-2050, toll-free 1-877-333-2050. www.hotel germain.com. 101 rooms.* ✕&Ⓟ⬜. This office-building cum boutique hotel offers Asian minimalist design in the light-filled rooms, with dark wood furnishings handcrafted by local artisans. Sumptuous bedding and amenities including wireless Internet, CD players and the morning newspaper.

WHERE TO EAT

$ Beauty's – *93 Ave. Mont-Royal Ouest, H2T 2S5.* ☎*514-849-8883.* **American**. If you want breakfast any time of day, come wait in line at this popular 1950's-style diner. Bagels, smoked salmon, and blueberry pancakes are the main

attractions, but you can also order a good lunch salad or sandwich.

$ Le Duc de Lorraine, *5002 Chemin de la Côte-des-Neiges.H3V 1G6.* ☎*514-731-4128. www.ducdelorraine.com.* Renowned for its breads, pastries, cheeses and meats, this windowed tea room is also a fine spot to sample croissants or enjoy a light meal.

$$ Restaurant Daou – *519 Rue Faillon Est, H2R 1L6.* ☎*514-276-8310.* **Lebanese**. Located in the Villeray area, this spot, occasionally enlivened with belly dancers in the evenings, offers Middle Eastern specialties such as tabbouleh, kibbeh, shish kebab and hummus. The decor is ordinary, but expect good food for a good price.

$$ Le Piton de la Fournaise – *835 Rue Duluth Est. H2L 1B2. Dinner only. Closed Mon.* ☎*514-526-3936.* &**Réunion/**

BYOW

Bring your own wine. Restaurants that don't have a liquor license can allow patrons to bring in their own favorite vintages. Most BYOW *(apportez votre vin)* eateries are located in the Plateau Mont-Royal district and the Quartier Latin.

Table d'hôte

These fixed-price meals typically include a three-course menu consisting of a starter, main dish and dessert.

Creole. This vibrant restaurant offers cuisine of Île de la Réunion in the Indian Ocean, blending Indian, African and French influences. Just listening to the staff speak Creole is a treat. BYOW—and make reservations well in advance.

$$ Stash Café, *200 Rue Saint-Paul Ouest. H2Y 1Z9. ☎514-845-6611. www. stashcafe.com.* **Polish.** Patrons at this atmospheric Polish restaurant near Place d'Armes share polished old tables and enjoy savoury Polish dishes such as bigos (sauerkraut with sausages and mushrooms) or plaki (potato pancakes with apple and sour cream).

$$$ Hélène de Champlain – *200 Tour de l'Île, Île Ste-Hélène, H3C 4G8. ☎514-395-2424. www.helenedechamplain.com.* **Contemporary.** Five minutes from downtown and the Casino de Montréal, this Québécois-style building sits in a beautiful park on Île Ste-Hélène. The food is standard, but the dining rooms with their fireplaces and views of the city and rose garden make for a delightful dining experience.

$$$ La Marée – *404 Place Jacques-Cartier, H2Y 3B2. ☎514-861-8126.* **Seafood**. This charming restaurant in an 1808 building never ceases to delight with classic seafood dishes such as *escalope de saumon au ragoût de pineau des charentes* (grilled salmon in a sauce flavored with pineau des charentes liquour).

$$$ Moishes – *3961 Blvd. St-Laurent, H2W 1Y4 ☎514-845-3509. www.moishes-steakhouse.com.* ⎙**Steak house**. Since 1938, this Montreal institution has been justifiably renowned for its house-aged, charcoal-grilled steaks, which are even better when paired with a selection from Moishes' fine wine list.

$$$$ Toqué! - *900, Place Jean-Paul Riopelle, H2Z 2B2. Dinner only. Closed Sun & Mon. ☎514-499-2084. www. restaurant-toque.com.* ⎙**French**. This post-Modern restaurant in the Plateau Mont-Royal district is one of the finest in the city. Chef Normand Laprise's contemporary French cuisine, artfully presented using the freshest local produce is the reason why. The menu follows the season and the market.

AROUND TOWN

Les Deux Pierrots–*104 Rue Saint-Paul Est, H2Y 1G6.☎514-861-1270. www.lespierrots.com. Open Fri–Sat and evenings before holidays 8pm–3am.* A veritable Montreal institution, this nightclub is the perfect place to expose your ears to traditional Quebec music in most convivial setting.

Le Delta Centre Ville – *777 Rue Université, H3C 3Z7. ☎514-879-1370. www. deltahotels.com.* For a great view of Montreal, ride the elevator to the 28th floor to the city's only revolving dining room (*Open 5:30-11:pm and for Sunday brunch 10:30am–3:30pm*), a great place for an evening cocktail and dinner.

Formule 1 Emporium –*2070-B Rue Crescent, ☎514-284-3799. www.f1emporium.ca).* Here, in this small shop, race team memorabilia and clothing share space with a selection of small-scale, die-cast replicas of notable competition and passenger cars. Ferrari merchandise is a specialty.

Vieux Séminaire de Saint-Sulpice★ (Old Sulpician Seminary), the oldest structure in the city, stands beside the basilica. Note the facade **clock,** installed in 1701, believed to be the oldest public timepiece in North America.

Place Jacques-Cartier★★

Lined with outdoor cafes and flower parterres, this charming cobblestone square is especially lively in the summer. Marking the north end of the plaza, a **statue (2)** of Horatio Nelson (1809) commemorates the British general's victory at Trafalgar. Montreal's **Hôtel de Ville**★ (City Hall), an imposing Second Empire building, stands at 275 Rue Notre-Dame ♦*Champs de Mars. (*⎙*visit by 1hr guided tour only, June-Labour Day Mon–Fri 8:30am–4:30pm.* ◷ *Closed major holidays. 872-0077 ☎514-872-3355.www.old.montreal.qc.ca).* Charles de Gaulle delivered his famous "Vive le Québec libre" speech in 1967 from the balcony overlooking the main entrance. The south end of the square leads to **Rue Saint-Paul**★★, lined with 19C buildings housing shops and artists' studios.

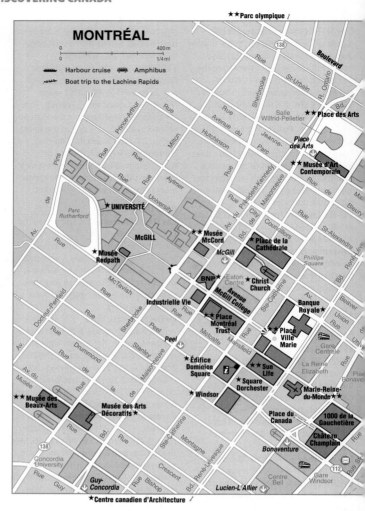

MONTRÉAL

Harbour cruise · Amphibus
Boat trip to the Lachine Rapids

★★ Parc olympique /

★★ Place des Arts

Salle Wilfrid-Pelletier

Place des Arts

★★ Musée d'Art Contemporain

★ UNIVERSITÉ

Parc Rutherford

McGILL

★★ Musée McCord

★ Musée Redpath

McGill

★★ Place de la Cathédrale

BNP ★

Eaton Centre

★ Christ Church

Industrielle Vie

Avenue McGill College

Banque Royale ★

★★ Place Montréal Trust

★ Place Ville Marie

Gare Centrale

La Reine Elizabeth

★ Édifice Dominion Square

★★ Sun Life

★ Square Dorchester

Marie-Reine-du-Monde ★★

★★ Musée des Beaux-Arts

Musée des Arts Décoratifs ★

★ Windsor

Place du Canada

1000 de la Gauchetière

Château Champlain

Concordia University

Bonaventure

Centre Bell

Gare Windsor

Guy-Concordia

Lucien-L'Allier

★ Centre canadien d'Architecture /

| Monument de Maisonneuve | 1 | Colonne Nelson | 2 | Obélisque | 3 |

Vieux-Port★ (Old Port)

Stretching along the St. Lawrence River, at the foot of Place Jacques-Cartier, the former port has been transformed into a pleasant waterfront park with bike and walking paths; a skating rink; exhibition spaces; **iSci**★, the Montreal Science Centre, ⟲*Champs de Mars.* (✕♿🅿⟲*Open year-round Mon–Fri 9am–4pm, Sat–Sat 10am–5pm. ⬡$12 adult ($13.50 with IMAX). ☎514-496-4724, toll-free 1-877-496-4724. www.isci.ca)*; and an IMAX cinema ($12). Stroll along the wide boardwalk or take a **harbour cruise**★

to enjoy scenic **views**★ of the city and the majestic river (✕♿🅿*Departs from King Edward Pier May–Oct daily 11:30am, 2pm & 4pm. Round-trip 1hr30min. ⬡$26 adult. Croisières AML ☎514-842-3871, toll-free 1-800-563-4643. www.croisieres aml.com*

Expéditions dans les rapides de Lachine (Jet Boat Trips on the Lachine Rapids)

Depart from Quai de l'Horloge May–Oct daily 10am–6pm, every 2hrs. Round-trip 1hr. Reservations required. ⬡$60 adult.

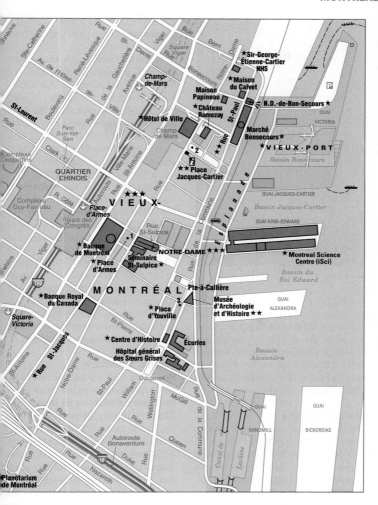

 📶 ($12) *Lachine Rapids Tours/Saute-Moutons.* 🕐*Champ de Mars.* ☎514-284-9607. www.jetboatingmontreal.com.
Passengers on this wet and exciting voyage are whisked upriver through the ferocious Lachine Rapids. The **views**★★ of Montreal and the surrounding areas are spectacular.

Château Ramezay★
280 Rue Notre Dame Est, Montreal QC, H2Y 1C5🕐*Champs de Mars.* ✕♿🕐*Open Jun–early Oct daily 10am–6pm. Rest of the year Tue–Sun 10am–4:30pm.* 🕐*Closed Jan 1–2 & Dec 25–26.* 🎟*$8 adult.* ☎514-861-3708.
www.chateauramezay.qc.ca.

This squat, fieldstone residence (1705) was constructed for Claude de Ramezay, 11th governor of Montreal during the French regime. It served as the British gubernatorial residence until 1849.
The highlight of the **museum** inside is the exquisite, hand-carved 1725 mahogany **panelling** from Nantes, France.

Lieu historique national du Canada de Sir George-Étienne Cartier★ (Sir George-Étienne Cartier National Historic Site of Canada)
458 Rue Notre-Dame, Montreal QC, H2Y 1C8.. ♿🕐*Open Jun–Labour Day daily 10am–6pm. Apr–May & Sept–late Dec Wed–Sun 10am–noon & 1pm–5pm.* 🎟*$4.*

Place Jacques-Cartier

☎514-283-2282, toll-free 1-877-773-8888. *www.pc.gc.ca.*
This mansard-roofed structure, composed of two adjoining houses, was the home of **George-Étienne Cartier** (1814-73), one of the Fathers of Confederation. Period rooms illustrate the lifestyle of 19C middle-class society.

Rue Bonsecours★

This attractive street leads from Rue Notre-Dame to Rue Saint-Paul. At no. 440 stands the **Maison Papineau** (Papineau House), topped by a steeply pitched roof pierced by two rows of dormer windows. It was home to six generations of the Papineau family, including Louis-Joseph, leader of the Patriots during the 1837 Rebellions. The **Maison du Calvet★** (Calvet House) (1798), at the corner of Rue Saint-Paul, is a traditional 18C urban residence.

Chapelle Notre-Dame-de-Bon-Secours★ (Chapel of Our Lady of Perpetual Help)

400 Rue Saint-Paul Est, Montreal QC, H2Y 1H4. ◔*Champs de Mars*
This small church, topped by a copper steeple, with a statue of the Virgin facing the port, stands on the site of a wooden edifice commissioned by Marguerite Bourgeoys in 1657 and destroyed by fire in 1754. Climb the observatory,

accessible from the tower, to enjoy a **panorama★** of the river, Old Montreal and the Old Port.
Located in the basement, the **Musée Marguerite Bourgeoys** (&◔*Open May–Oct Tue–Sun 10am–5:30pm; Mar–Apr & Nov–mid-Jan Tue–Sun 11am–3:30pm.* ◔*Closed mid-Jan–Feb.* ✇*$6 adult.* ☎514-282-8670. *www.marguerite-bourgeoys.com*) depicts the life of Bourgeoys (1620-1700), who came to Montreal with Maisonneuve in 1653 to found the Congregation Notre-Dame. She was canonized in 1982.
Near the church, on Rue Saint-Paul, stands the **Marché Bonsecours★** *350 Rue St Paul St. Est, Montreal QC, H2Y 1H2.* ✗&🅿◔*Open June 24–Labour Day 10am–9pm, Apr–Jun & Labour Day–Dec Sun–Wed & Sat 10am–6pm, Thu–Fri 10am–9pm, Jan–Mar 10am–6pm..* ☎*514-872-7730.www.marchebonsecours.qc.ca*), a large Neoclassical stone structure crowned by a lofty dome. It served as the city hall from 1852 to 1878, and today is leased for office space, temporary exhibits and other purposes.

Place d'Youville★

Housed in a brick structure reflecting the Dutch Baroque architectural style, the **Centre d'Histoire de Montréal★** (Montreal History Centre) presents the city's rich past. (*335 Place d'Youville, Montreal QC, H2Y 3T1* ◔*Square Victoria.* &◔*Open mid-Jan–mid-Dec Tue–Sun 10am–5pm.* ◔*Closed mid-Dec–mid-Jan.* ✇*$4.50 adult.* ☎514-872-3207. *www.ville.montreal.qc.ca/chm*). To the east of the square stand the **Écuries d'Youville** (Stables), an ensemble of grey stone structures (1828) enclosing a lovely garden courtyard. Spanning the block between Saint-Pierre and Normand Streets, the **Hôpital général des Soeurs Grises** (Grey Nuns Convent) was erected in 1694 and extended in 1753 by Marie d'Youville, founder of the Grey Nuns order.

Pointe-à-Callière (Callière Point)

A 10m/33ft **obelisk (3)** commemorates the occasion of de Maisonneuve's landing in May 1642. Opened in 1992, the **Musée d'Archéologie et d'Histoire de Montréal★★** (Montreal Museum of Archaeology and History) presents Montreal's fascinating history (*350 Place Royal, Montreal QC, H2Y 3Y5* ⏺*Place d'Armes.* ✕&⏰*Open 23 Jun–Aug Mon–Fri 10am–6pm, Sat–Sun 11am–6pm. Rest of the year until 5pm.* ⏺*Closed Thanksgiving, Dec 25, Jan 1 & Easter Monday.* ⬭*$13 adult.* ☏*514-872-9150. www.pacmusee. qc.ca).*

Downtown★★

⏺*Rue Peel.*
The city's commercial heart lies to the west of Old Montreal. A walk along Sherbrooke, one of the most prestigious arteries in the city, reveals a lively retail sector alongside choice residences. Rue Sainte-Catherine is home to major department stores (Ogilvy, Simons, Les Ailes, La Baie) and commercial centres, while Avenue McGill College is lined with 20C skyscrapers.

Dorchester Square★

Long considered the centre of the city, the square (formerly Dominion Square) is surrounded by a group of remarkable buildings, including the imposing Renaissance Revival **Dominion Square Building**★ (1929) and **The Windsor**★, formerly an elegant hotel, now restored as an office building, with its mansard roof pierced by dormer and œil-de-bœuf windows. The **Sun Life Building**★★, an imposing Beaux-Arts edifice erected in 1913, dominates the north side of the square. Facing Dorchester Square is **Place du Canada,** a small green plaza bordered by the **Hôtel Marriott Château-Champlain** (1967), marked by convex, half-moon windows, and **1000 de la Gauchetière** (1992), Montreal's tallest skyscraper.

Basilique-Cathédrale Marie-Reine-du-Monde★★ (Mary Queen of the World Basilica-Cathedral)

Main entrance on Blvd. René-Lévesque. 1085 Rue de la Cathédrale, Montreal QC, H3B 2V4. ⏺*Bonaventure.* &⏰*Open year-round daily 9am–5pm.* ☏*514-866-1661.www.cathedralecatholiquede montreal.org*

Consecrated in 1894, the cathedral is modelled after St. Peter's in Rome. Inside is the gold-leaf **baldachin** (1900), a replica of the 16C ornamental canopy created by Bernini for St. Peter's Basilica. On the left side of the nave, a **mortuary chapel** (1933) contains the tombs of several archbishops and bishops.

Place Ville-Marie★★

Dominating the complex is I.M. Pei's 42-storey **Banque Royale Tower**★ (1962), a cruciform structure sheathed in aluminum. A concrete esplanade affords an unparalleled **vista**★ west to McGill University and Mt. Royal.

Extending from Place Ville-Marie to McGill University, **Avenue McGill College** is a showplace for the city's post-Modern architecture. Completed in 1989, the enormous **Place Montréal Trust**★★ *(no. 1500)* features a pastel blue glass cylinder encased in a square base of rose marble and glass. Across the street *(no. 1981)* rise the sprawling, metallic-blue twin towers of the **Tours de la Banque Nationale de Paris/Banque Laurentienne**★ (National Bank of Paris/Laurentian Bank Towers). The granite-clad **Tour l'Industrielle Vie** (Industrial Life Tower) *(no. 2000)* presents an elegant exterior enlivened by a post-Modern fanlight window.

Christ Church Cathedral★

Entrance from Rue Sainte-Catherine between Rue University and Ave. Union. 1444 Av. Union, Montreal QC,H3A 2B8. ⏺*McGill.* &⏰*Open year-round daily 8am–6pm.* ☏*514-843-6577. www.montreal.anglican.org/cathedral.*
This handsome edifice (1859) exemplifies the Gothic Revival style. The graceful interior has magnificent stained-glass windows and a beautifully carved stone **reredos.**
Rising behind the church is the **Place de la Cathédrale**★, a modern office tower.

Musée McCord d'histoire canadienne★★ (McCord Museum of Canadian History)

690 Rue Sherbrooke Ouest, Montreal QC, H3A 1E9. ⏺*McGill.* ✕&⏰*Open year-round Tue–Fri 10am–6pm, weekends*

10am–5pm (Jul–Sept Mon 10am–5pm). $12 adult. ☎514-398-7100. www.mccord-museum.qc.ca.

One of Canada's foremost historical museums, the McCord's holdings provide a fascinating insight into Canadian history, including an outstanding compilation of over 750,000 photos.

McGill University★

End of Ave. McGill College. McGill. Set on the slopes of Mt. Royal, Canada's oldest university (1821) today claims an enrolment of some 32,000 students. Housed in a large structure designed in the style of an antique temple, the **Musée d'histoire naturelle Redpath**★ (Redpath Museum of Natural History) displays vertebrate and invertebrate fossils, minerals, zoological artifacts, African art objects and Egyptian antiquities (*Open Mon–Fri 9am–5pm, Sun 1pm–5pm (June 24–Labour Day closed Thu). Closed major holidays.* ☎514-398-4086. www.mcgill.ca/redpath).

Musée des Beaux-Arts de Montréal★★ (Montreal Museum of Fine Arts)

1380 and 1379 Rue Sherbrooke Ouest, PO Box 3000, Succursale H, Montreal QC, H3G 2T9 Peel. Open year-round Tue 11am–5pm, Wed–Fri 11am–9pm, Sat–Sun 10am–5pm). Closed Jan 1 & Dec 25. $15 (half price Wed after 5pm. Permanent collection no charge). ☎514-285-2000, toll-free 1-800-899-6873. www.mbam.qc.ca.

The Beaux-Arts main edifice (1912), presents Canadian art, decorative arts and antiquities, while the new pavillion, created by **Moshe Safdie** (1991), displays temporary exhibits as well as international art. The buildings are linked by underground galleries that exhibit Ancient and Oceanic art. The Musée has acquired the 1894 Romanesque Revival Erskine and American Church, at 1339 Sherbrooke, and will build $40 million wing that will display Canadian art.

Musée des Arts décoratifs de Montréal★ (Montreal Museum of Decorative Arts)

2200 Rue Crescent. Admission included in entrance fee to Montreal Museum of Fine Arts; same hours).

Formerly located at Château Dufresne, the international design collections were moved in 1997 to exhibit space next to the Museum of Fine Arts: a passageway connects the two museums.

Centre canadien d'Architecture★ (Canadian Centre for Architecture)

1920 Rue Baile, Montreal QC, H3H 2S6. Guy-Concordia. Open year-round Wed–Sun 10am–5pm (Thu 9pm). Closed Jan 1 & Dec 25. $10. ☎514-939-7026. www.cca.qc.ca.

Montreal Museum of Fine Arts

Designed by Peter Rose and Phyllis Lambert, the CCA (1989) is an acclaimed museum and research facility as well as an example of post-Modern architecture. Forming the core of the building is **Shaughnessy House,** a Second Empire mansion built in 1874.

Also open to the public are the Shaughnessy House reception rooms and the delightful **conservatory** and **tea room**.

Across Boulevard René-Lévesque is an **architectural garden** by Melvin Charney.

Musée d'art contemporarin de Montréal★★ (Museum of Contemporary Art of Montreal)

185 Rue Sainte-Catherine Ouest, Montreal QC, H2X 3X5. ◐*Place-des-Arts.* ◑*Open year-round Tue–Sun 11am–6pm (Wed 9pm).* ♿ 🅿 ☚ *Guided tour.* ✆*$8 adult (no charge Wed evening).* ☎*514-847-6226. www.macm.org.*

Housed in the Place des Arts complex, this museum presents selections from the permanent collection, 60 percent of which is Quebec art.

Planétarium de Montréal (Montreal Planetarium)

1000 Rue Saint-Jacques, Montreal QC, H3C 1G7. ◐*Bonaventure.* ♿ 🅿 ◑*Open 23 Jun–Labour Day Mon 12:30pm–5pm, Tue–Thu 9:30am–5pm, Fri 9:30am–4:30pm & 7pm–9:30pm, weekends 12:30pm–4:30pm & 7pm–9:30pm. Rest of the year Tue–Thu 9:30am–5pm, Fri–Sun 10am–5pm, 6:45–9:30pm . Call for show times.* ✆*$8 adult.* ☎*514-872-4530. www. planetarium.montreal.qc.ca.*

Superb multimedia shows *(50min)* are shown in the planetarium's 385-seat theatre. Temporary and permanent exhibits showcase recent astronomical events.

Grande Bibliothèque de Montréal (Montreal Public Library)

475 bl. de Maisonneuve Est, H2L 5C4. ☎*514-873-1100, toll-free 1-800-363-9028. www. banq.qc.ca.* ◐*Berri-Uquam.* ♿◑*Open daily Tue–Fri 10am–10pm, weekends 10–5pm.*

The 5-storey, $91 million Montreal central library opened in 2005 and houses some 4 million items. The unusual façade sports green-glass panels on vertical copper supports. Despite recurring problems with the glass panels (they keep shattering), the interior has plenty of reading space. On the whole, the library has been a great success with the public.

Mont-Royal and Surroundings★★

Rising abruptly from the otherwise flat plain, the 233m/764ft Mont-Royal forms part of the Monteregian Hills, a series of eight peaks located between the St.

Ice Hockey

A winter preoccupation for more than 100 years, hockey is truly Canada's national game. And the enthusiasm isn't limited to televised games of the major leagues either: more than 580,000 young Canadians in some 25,000 teams participate in organized minor hockey tournaments. Community rinks are ubiquitous.

Derived from the French *hoquet* ("shepherd's crook") for the shape of the stick, hockey originated from variations of stick and ball games brought to Canada by English soldiers in the 1850s. In 1875 Montreal student J.G. Creighton formalized rules and replaced the ball for a flat disk (puck) to give better control on ice.

The fast and often rough play made the sport appealing to spectators. The game spread quickly as rivalry among college amateur teams intensified. Professional teams soon followed. Formed in 1917, the National Hockey League has added US teams over the years and now consists of 30 teams, with only six in Canada. A trophy donated by Governor General Lord Stanley in 1893 is still awarded to the league's winning team in the Stanley Cup championships held each June. The original silver cup is on display in Toronto's Hockey Hall of Fame.

Lawrence and the Appalachians. The hills are actually igneous plugs of solidified lava. To the west of Mt. Royal lies the town of **Westmount**, once largely Anglophone and still one of the city's choicest residential areas. On the hill's eastern flank is the borough of **Outremont,** home to Montreal's Francophone bourgeoisie.

Parc du Mont-Royal★★ (Mt. Royal Park)

Drive up Voie Camillien-Houde or Chemin Remembrance to the parking areas or climb on foot from Rue Peel at Ave. des Pins. Ⓜ*Mont-Royal.* ✕♿🅿Ⓞ *Open year-round daily 6am–midnight.* ☎*514-843-8240. www.lemontroyal.qc.ca.*

Opened in 1876, the park was designed by American landscape architect **Frederick Law Olmsted**, creator of New York City's Central Park.

Viewpoints

The terrace fronting the **Belvédère du Chalet** (Chalet Lookout) affords a splendid **view**★★★ of the bustling downtown and the Monteregian Hills. The walk around the summit leads to the **cross**, a 36.6m/120ft metal structure, illuminated at night, that commemorates a wooden cross placed here by de Maisonneuve. From the popular **Belvédère Camillien-Houde** (accessible by vehicle on the Voie Camillien-Houde), the superb **view**★★ of eastern Montreal is dominated by the Olympic Stadium.

Oratoire Saint-Joseph★★ (St. Joseph's Oratory)

Entrance on Chemin Queen Mary. Ⓜ*Côte-des-Neiges.* ✕♿🅿Ⓞ *Open year-round daily 7am–10pm.* ☎*514-733-8211. www.saint-joseph.org.*

The oratory's origin was a small chapel erected in 1904 by Alfred Bessette, known as Brother André, who gained a reputation as a healer. Today, the shrine, with its colossal dimensions and octagonal, copper-clad dome, draws a million pilgrims annually.

From the wide terrace is an excellent **view** of northern Montreal and the Laurentian Mountains. Within the complex are the **Musée du Frère André** (*same*

hours as the oratory*) and the **chapelle du Frère André**. The **Stations of the Cross**★ are in a hillside garden.

Boulevard Saint-Laurent

Established in 1672, the artery long formed Montreal's principal passageway, hence its nickname "the Main." During the 19C Chinese settled in the southern section, giving rise to a lively **Quartier chinois**★ (Chinatown) *(at Rue de la Gauchetière)*. Succeeding waves of immigrants have given the area its reputation for vibrant commercial activity.

Musée des Hospitalières de l'Hôtel-Dieu de Montréal (Hospitallers Museum)

201 Ave. des Pins Ouest, Montreal QC, H2W 1R5. Ⓜ*Sherbrooke. Entrance at Rue Saint-Urbain and Ave. du Parc.* ♿Ⓞ*Open mid-Jun–mid-Oct Tue–Fri 10am–5pm, weekends 1pm–5pm. Rest of the year Wed–Sun 1pm–5pm.* Ⓞ*Closed Good Friday, Easter Monday & Dec 25–Jan 1.* ⊜*$6.* ☎*514-849-2919. www.museedeshospitalieres.qc.ca*

This museum traces the history of the Hospitallers of St. Joseph (a religious order devoted to caring for the sick) and their presence in Montreal.

Olympic Park Area★★★

Parc Olympique★★ (Olympic Park)

Ⓜ*Viau, or by car (entrance to the parking lot* 🅿 *from 3200 Rue Viau). Information desk and ticket office at base of tower. Shuttle service (free; no service in winter) to and from the park, the botanical garden and the Biodôme.*

Constructed to accommodate the 1976 Olympic Games, this gigantic sports complex includes a stadium and tower, a sports centre with six swimming pools, and a velodrome, which now houses the Biodôme. The **Olympic Village**—two 19-storey towers which lodged 11,000 athletes during the Games—now contains a residential and commercial complex.

Begun in 1973, the stadium wasn't completed until 1987 and was tremendously expensive ($1.2 billion). It is known locally as "The Big Owe."

Stadium

✗♿🅿︎🚌 *Visit by guided tour (30min) only, June–Labour Day daily. English tours 12:40pm & 3:40pm. French tours 11am & 2pm. Rest of the year 5 bilingual tours daily 11am–3:30pm. ☞$8 adult. ☎514-252-4737, toll-free 1-877-997-0919. www.rio.gouv.qc.ca.*

Conceived by French architect Roger Taillibert, this immense concrete structure consists of 34 cantilevered ribs crowned by a structural ring and dominated by the world's tallest inclined tower, originally designed to be covered by a retractable roof. Hovering at a 45° angle above the stadium, the 175m/574ft **tower** can be ascended by a funicular elevator *(✗♿🅿︎($12) ◷Open mid-Jun–labour Day daily 9am–7pm. Rest of the year 9am–5pm. ☞$14 adult.* From the observation deck, the **panorama**★★★ extends as far as 80km/50mi, weather permitting.

Biodôme

✗♿🅿︎*($8) ◷Open late June–Labour Day daily 9am–6pm. Rest of the year 9am–5pm. Oct–Feb closed 2nd week of month. ☎514-868-3000. www.biodome.qc.ca.*

Shuttle service (free; no service in winter) between the Biôdome, the botanical garden and Olympic Park.☞$16 adult.

Opened in 1992, this museum occupies a **velodrome** constructed as an Olympic cycling venue. Re-created habitats support plants and animals indigenous to a tropical forest, the Laurentian forest, the St. Lawrence basin and the polar region.

Jardin botanique de Montréal★★ (Montreal Botanical Garden)

Kids *4101 Rue Sherbrooke Est, Montreal QC, H1X 2B2. ◐Pie-IX. ✗♿🅿︎ ($8) ◷Open mid-May–early Sept daily 9am–6pm, Sept–Oct 9am–9pm. Rest of the year Tue–Sun 9am–5pm. ☞ Mid-May–Oct $16. Rest of the year $13.75. ☎514-872-1400. www.ville.montreal.qc.ca/jardin. Shuttle service (free) to and from the Biôdome, Olympic Park and the Botanical Garden.*

Founded in 1931, this garden is one of the world's finest horticultural facilities.

The Chinese Greenhouse, called the "Jardin céleste," displays the superb **Wu Collection** of *penjing*, or "landscape in a pot." Opened in 1991, the **Jardin de Chine** (Chinese Garden) is a replica of a typical Ming dynasty (14-17C) garden from southern China. The 2.5ha/6.2 acre **Jardin japonais** (Japanese Garden), and

Montreal Botanical Garden

©iStockphoto.com/Vladone

the **Japanese pavilion** include a Zen garden, a tea garden and a collection of **bonsais** *(on view seasonally)*.

Other sections not to be missed include the **Rose Garden,** the **Marsh and Bog Garden,** a re-created **monastic garden**, an Alpine garden and an enclosure of toxic plants. The **Arboretum** features over 10,000 tree specimens.

Near the Rose Garden is the **Insectarium de Montréal** (Montreal Insectarium), built in the shape of a giant bug.*Hours same as Botanical Garden.*

Château Dufresne★

2929 av. Jeanne-d'Arc, Montreal QC, H1W 3W2 ✪Pie-IX. South corner of Rue Sherbrooke and Blvd. Pie-IX. ♿🕐 Open year-round Thu–Sun 10am–5pm. ⌖$7 adult. ☎514-259-9201. www.chateaudufresne. qc.ca.

Completed in 1918, this sumptuous 44-room Beaux-Arts mansion evokes the lifestyle of Montreal's moneyed class in the 1920s and 30s.

Other Areas of Interest

Île Sainte-Hélène★

Access by car on Jacques-Cartier or Concorde Bridge; ✪ Jean-Drapeau.

Located east of Montreal, this small island, which Samuel de Champlain named for his wife, Hélène Boulé, is a pleasant park.

Vieux-Fort

(Old Fort) ✕🅿🕐 *Open late-May–early-Oct daily 10am–5pm. Rest of the year Wed–Mon 10am–5pm. ⌖$10 adult. ☎514-861-6701. www.stewart-museum. org.*

Located in the Old Fort, the **Musée David M. Stewart**★ (David M. Stewart Museum) presents the history of European settlement in Quebec.

A geodesic dome designed by Buckminster Fuller, the **Biosphère**★ 🄺🄸🄳🅂, constructed to house the US pavilion at the 1967 World Fair, now contains Canada's first Eco-Watch Centre (*160 Chemin Tour de l'Île, Montreal QC, H3C 4G8. ✕♿🅿🕐Open Jun–Oct daily 10am–6pm. Rest of the year Tue–Fri noon–6pm*

(open 10am weekends). 🕐*Closed Jan 1, Dec 25–26.* ⌖*$9.50 adults.* ☎*514-283-5000. www.biosphere.ec.gc.ca.).*

La Ronde 🄺🄸🄳🅂 , Montreal's major amusement park, occupies a pleasant site on the north end of the island *(*✕♿🅿🕐 *open mid-May–early Jun weekends 10am–8pm; early Jun–late Jun daily 10am–8pm; late Jun–early Sept daily 10am–10:30pm;* ⌖*$37 above 1.37m/4ft6in;* ☎*514-872-4537; www. laronde.com).*

The road skirting the island's western edge provides **views**★ of Old Montreal, the port installations, and the **Cité du Havre** peninsula, which links the city to St. Helen's Island via the Concorde Bridge. **Habitat**★ (Moshe Safdie), a modular apartment complex built for Expo '67, dominates the peninsula.

Île Notre-Dame★ (Notre Dame Island)

Access by car on Concordia Bridge or by free bus service from Jean-Drapeau metro station on Île Sainte-Hélène.

This artificial island, created in 1959 and enlarged in 1967, contains a Formula One racetrack, a pleasant lake and beach, and a **floral garden** designed for the International Floralies of 1980 and 2000 *(*✕♿🅿🕐 *open year-round daily 6:30am–midnight;* ☎*514-872-6120; www.parcjeandrapeau.com).* The Expo '67 French pavilion houses the **Casino de Montréal** (Montreal Casino).

Cosmodôme★★

Located in Laval, 12km/7mi northwest of Montreal, at 2150 Autoroute des Laurentides, Laval QC, H7T 2T8. From Montreal, take Rte. 15 (Exit 9) and follow signs. Space Science Centre ✕♿🅿🕐*Open Jun 24– Labour Day daily 10am–6pm. Rest of the year Tue–Sun 10am–5pm.* 🕐*Closed Jan 1 & Dec 25.* ⌖*$11.* ☎*450-978-3600. www. cosmodome.org.*

In the **Space Science Centre,** interactive exhibits, replicas and models, as well as mural panels and videos, introduce visitors to the history and exploration of space. **Space Camp Canada** offers space-oriented educational activities for children and adults *(some programs necessitate overnight stays).*

Sault-au-Récollet

Located 12km/7mi north of Montreal (by Rte. 138) between Christophe-Colombe and Papineau avenues. Gouin Blvd. is a one-way street heading east.

Set on the rapids beside the Praiiries River, Sault-au-Récollet is best known for its **Église de la Visitation-de-la-Bienheureuse-Vierge-Marie**★ (Church of the Visitation of the Blessed Virgin Mary), the oldest religious structure on the island (the front section is more recent). The edifice boasts an elaborate **interior**★★. Of particular interest are the turquoise and gold vault and the **pulpit,** a beautiful piece of liturgical furniture.

The neighborhood itself is charming. Boulevard Gouin is lined with many lovely old houses.

NUNAVIK★★

Officially recognized in 1988, after creation in 1986 by referendum, as the homeland of Quebec's Inuit population, the province's northernmost region offers the adventurous visitor a unique travel experience. Located on the Ungava Peninsula, this vast territory also encompasses numerous offshore islands and part of the James Bay region to the west. The lack of vegetation is characteristic of regions with harsh climates. In fact, most of the peninsula is under permafrost, reaching 275m/902ft in depth in Nunavik's northernmost areas.

🅘 **Information:** Nunavik Information Centre, 1204 Cours du Général Montcalm, Quebec City, Quebec, G1R 3G4. ☎418-522-2224. www.nunavik.ca.

▶ **Orient Yourself:** Nunavik lies north of the 55th parallel, with Hudson Bay to the west, Ungava Bay and the Hudson Strait to the north and Labrador to the east.

🐾 **Don't Miss:** Some 50 species of birds nest high on the Ungava Penninsula. There are also polar bears, musk oxen, seals, walruses, whales and great herds of caribou.

🕐 **Organizing Your Time:** The season in which you visit will determine what you can see.

A Bit of History

The region's first inhabitants were hunters from Asia who are believed to have crossed the Bering Strait some 4,000 years ago. Today the majority of the Inuit population of 10,000 inhabits 14 coastal villages and has access to schooling and professional training.

Visit

The largest among the 14 villages, **Kuujjuaq**★ is the seat of regional government offices. Located to the west, **Inukjuak** serves as headquarters for the Avataq Cultural Institute, a nonprofit organization devoted to the preservation and development of the Inuit herit-

---

PRACTICAL INFORMATION

GETTING THERE

The 14 villages lining Nunavik's eastern and western shores are accessible by airplane only. Contact First Air *(☎1-800-267-1247. www.firstair.ca),* Air Inuit *(☎514-636-9445 or 1-800-361-2965. www.airinuit.com)* or Air Creebec *(☎1-800-567-6567. www.aircreebec.ca)* for schedules and flight information.

ACCOMMODATIONS AND VISITOR INFORMATION

For information on outfitters, accommodations and events, contact: **Nunavik Tourism Association,** *P.O. Box 779, Kuujjuaq, QC J0M 1C0.* ☎819-964-2876, toll-free 1-888-594-3424. *www.nunavik-tourism.com.*

age in Nunavik. The northeasternmost villages of **Kangiqsujuaq** and **Salluit** are especially remarkable for their spectacular **sites**★★, surrounded by rugged mountains and jagged cliffs. Located on the western shore, **Puvirnituq** has gained recognition as a centre for Inuit sculpture. Situated just north of James Bay, **Kuujjuarapik** is home to a sizable number of Cree Indians and to most of Nunavik's nonnative population.

QUÉBEC★★★
QUEBEC CITY
METRO POPULATION 717,600

Built atop the Cape Diamant promontory jutting into the St. Lawrence River, Quebec's capital has delighted visitors for centuries with its multitude of historic and religious monuments, fortifications and narrow cobblestone alleys. The distinctive French flavour is enhanced by fine restaurants, outdoor cafes and a lively nightlife. In 1985 the city became the first urban centre in North America to be inscribed on UNESCO's World Heritage list.

- ⛴ **Information:** Quebec City Tourism, 399 Rue Saint-Joseph Est, ☎418-641-6654, toll-free 1-877-783-1608. www.quebecregion.com
- ▶ **Orient Yourself:** Québec City is 255km/158mi from Montreal, on the north bank of the St Lawrence River. It is divided into an Upper Town and Lower Town. The city of Lévis is on the opposite bank, linked by two bridges as well as ferries.
- 🅿 **Parking:** Municipal lots and street parking throughout the city. In winter, respect snow clearing times: cars will be towed if in the way of snow clearing.
- 😎 **Don't Miss:** Fairmont Château Frontenac, "the castle on the cliff" overlooking the St. Lawrence River, is Quebec City's iconic landmark.
- 🕐 **Organizing Your Time:** Plan to walk within and below the walls of the city—but be aware 😎 that you'll be climbing or descending stairs frequently.
- 🧒 **Especially for Kids:** Fortifications of the Citadel; Montmorency Falls (just east of the city); the Musée du Fort, with its lively show.
- 👣 **Also See:** COTE DE CHARLEVOIX, FIJORD DU SAGUENAY

A Bit of History

Birthplace of New France – Long before Jacques Cartier's arrival in 1535, Indian hunters and fishermen inhabited the area of the village of Stadacona. In 1608, **Samuel de Champlain** constructed a rudimentary wooden fortress, known as the **Habitation.**

The first settlers arrived in Quebec during the 17C. Primarily craftsmen and merchants attracted to the profitable fur trade, they erected houses in the Lower Town, which became the centre of commercial activity. Religious institutions and the colonial administration settled in the Upper Town, within fortifications.

18C and 19C – Quebec City's location atop the 98m/321ft-high Cape Diamant promontory provided the colony with a naturally fortified area. Nevertheless, the French city was repeatedly attacked—first by the Iroquois, then by the British. The Battle of the Plains of Abraham precipitated the British Conquest of 1759.

Following the Treaty of Paris in 1763, Quebec City became capital of the new British dominion. Owing mainly to its busy port activities, the city maintained a competitive position with Montreal until the mid-19C.

Quebec City Today – Since the turn of this century, most jobs have been related to public administration, defence

Doug Rogers/MICHELIN

Upper Town

and the service sector. The growth of the provincial government in the past 25 years has provided the capital city with renewed vitality. Anglophones have steadily moved away over the past century, giving the city a distinctly Francophone character. The main metropolitan event is the famous winter **Carnival** in February, which attracts thousands of visitors.

Vieux-Québec★★★

Haute-Ville★★★ (Upper Town)

The site of Samuel de Champlain's Fort Saint-Louis (1620), Upper Town retained its administrative and religious vocation for over two centuries.

It was only during the 19C that elegant residential neighbourhoods evolved along the Rues Saint-Louis, Sainte-Ursule and d'Auteuil, and Avenues Sainte-Geneviève and Saint-Denis. Today Upper Town still functions as the city's administrative centre.

Place d'Armes and Vicinity★★★

Bordered by prestigious buildings and restaurants, this pleasant square, once used for military drills and parades, forms the heart of Old Quebec. It is dominated by the city's most prominent

landmark, the **Château Frontenac**★★. Erected in 1893 by the Canadian Pacific Railway in its distinctive Chateau style, this renowned hotel stands on the site of the former governor's residence. (*Guided tours May–mid Oct daily. Rest of the year weekends 1–5pm.* ☎418-691-2166. www.tourschateau.ca) Next to the chateau, the Governors' Garden features the **Wolfe-Montcalm Monument (1)** (1827), a joint memorial to the two enemies who died in combat.

Located behind the chateau, **Terrasse Dufferin**★★★, a wide wooden boardwalk, is perched 671m/2,200ft above the majestic St. Lawrence, offering breathtaking **views**★★ of Lower Town and the river. A **monument (2)** to Samuel de Champlain marks the northern end of the terrace. At the southern end, a flight of steps ascends to the **Promenade des Gouverneurs**★★ (Governors' Walk) (*closed in winter*) precariously suspended along the steep cliff that leads from the terrace to National Battlefields Park.

In the narrow **Rue du Trésor**, a quaint pedestrian street off Place d'Armes, artists exhibit sketches of city scenes.

Musée du Fort (Fort Museum) (M¹)

Kids *10 rue Sainte-Anne, CP 833, Québec QC, G1R 4S7. ⏱Open Apr–Oct daily 10am–5pm. Rest of the year Thu–Sun 11am–4pm. (Dec 26–1st Sun after Jan*

Address Book

 For dollar sign categories, see the Legend on the cover flap.

WHERE TO STAY

$ Centre international de Séjour de Québec – *19 Rue Ste-Ursule G1R 4E1. ☎418-694-0755, toll-free 1-888-694-0950. www.cisq.org. 240 beds.* ✕&. Located within the walls of the Old City, this youth hostel is a member of Hostelling International. Open year-round, it offers rooms accommodating from two to 12 people, some with private bathrooms. The Café Bistro and a kitchen are available on site.

$$ Hôtel Particulier Belley – *249 Rue St-Paul G1K 3W5. ☎418-692-1694. 8 rooms.* ✕&P. Brick walls and exposed beams, coupled with a great location in the Vieux Port, make for a comfortable and reasonably priced stay. Downstairs is **The Tavern Belley ($)**, which serves salads and sandwiches. The hotel also rents apartments across the street for longer stays.

$$$ Château Bonne Entente – *3400 Chemin Ste-Foy G1X 1S6. ☎418-653-5221 or 800-463-4390. www.chateaubonneentente.com. 150 rooms.* ✕&P Spa. Occupying a wooded site convenient to both Old Quebec and the airport, the Bonne Entente offers the charm of a country inn with the amenities of a modern hotel. Pamper yourself at the Amérispa Health Centre, then settle in front of the fireplace in the Tea Room, for tea and petit-fours. Family suites feature bunk beds and toys for the kids

$$$ L'Hôtel Dominion 1912 – *126 Rue St-Pierre G1K 4A8. ☎418-692-2224, toll-free 1-888-833-5253. www.hoteldominion.com. 60 rooms.* &P⌐. Located in a nine-storey commercial building constructed in 1912 for Dominion Fish and Fruit, Ltd., this boutique hotel sits in the heart of the Old Port district. Stained glass and ironwork highlight the exquisitely decorated lobby and reading room. Natural light floods the spacious, ultra-modern guest rooms, and goose-down duvets and pillows wrap guests in comfort. Rate includes continental breakfast.

$$$ L'Hôtel du Vieux Québec – *1190 Rue St-Jean G1R 1S6. ☎418-692-1850,* toll-free 1- 800-361-7787. www.hvq.com. 44 rooms. ✕&P⌐. A good bet for families and student groups, this carefully restored century-old brick hotel in the Latin Quarter has recently renovated rooms with sofas, private baths and mini-refrigerators; some have kitchenettes. Rates include continental breakfast and, in summer, an orientation session (1hr) on Old Quebec.

$$$$ Auberge Saint-Antoine – *8 Rue St-Antoine G1K 4C9. ☎418-692-2211, toll-free 1-888-692-2211. www.saint-antoine.com. 94 rooms.* &P. A renovated 1822 warehouse and an adjoining 1720's English merchant's house now compose one of the city's finest hotels. Many rooms and suites have the original stone walls and hand-hewn beams, along with amenities such as wireless Internet.

$$$$ Fairmont Le Château Frontenac – *1 Rue des Carrières G1R 4P5. ☎418-692-3861, toll-free 1- 800-441-1414. www.fairmont.ca. 618 rooms.* ✕& ⌿ P Spa. Completed in 1893, the regal copper-roofed château towers above Old Québec as an enduring symbol of the city; it has hosted Queen Elizabeth and Winston Churchill among many notables. The bustling lobby lined with elaborate wood paneling reflects 19C opulence. Well-appointed rooms vary in size, shape and view; amenities include a large gym, as well as baby-sitting, limousine service and in-house dogs you can walk. **Le Champlain ($$$$)** serves French/Quebecois dishes that celebrate produce from the terroir (region).

$$$$ Ice Hotel Quebec – *143 Rue Duchesnay, Pavillion l'Aigle, St-Catherine-de-la-Jacques-Cartier G0A 3M0.* ◷*Open early Jan–late Mar, weather permitting as ice hotel melts.* ☀*Tours (30min) from 10:30 am–4:30pm (English on the hour, French on the half-hour).* ☜*$15.* ☎*418-875-4522, toll-free 1- 877-505-0423. www.icehotel-canada.com. 36 rooms.* ✕⌐. Fashioned from 10,000 tons of snow and 350 tons of ice, the ice hotel features two art galleries and a movie theatre. Cozy sleeping bags nestled on deer pelts keep off the chill and, yes, the bathrooms are heated. One-night accommodations include a vodka cocktail, a dinner at the Auberge Duchesnay and a buffet breakfast.

WHERE TO EAT

$$ Aux Anciens Canadiens, *34 Rue Saint-Louis G1R 4P3.* ☎418-692-1627. *www.auxancienscanadiens.qc.ca.* **Québécois.** Situated in a historic white house with red trim (1675), this venerable restaurant offers a delicious introduction to la *cuisine québécoise.* Traditional favourites include pea soup and *tourtière* (meat pie), *ragoût de boulettes* (meatballs in gravy) as well as game and seafood. For dessert, try maple-syrup pie drizzled with cream.

$$ Le Café du Monde – *57 Rue Dalhousie G1K 4B2.* ☎418-692-4455. *www. cafedumonde.com.* **French.** Typical Parisian bistro fare of *steak frites* (steak and French fries), *magret de canard* (breast of duck) and *moules* (mussels), a cozy atmosphere and gregarious waiters in white aprons make for a pleasant dining experience.

$$ Café-Restaurant du Musée du Québec, *In the National Battlefields Park.* ☎418-644-6780. *www.museeduquebec.org.* **Contemporary.** Located in the Quebec Museum, this restaurant offers imaginative lunches, *pauses-café* and Sunday brunch, carefully prepared and served with flair. Natural light floods the vast dining room, where immense windows offer a superb view of the Plains of Abraham. In summer, take a table on the terrace to admire the surrounding countryside.

$$ Les Épices du Szechwan – *215 Rue St-Jean G1R 1N8.* ☎418-648-6440. ♿**Chinese.** Located in an old house in the St-Jean-Baptiste district of Old Quebec, Les Épices offers good Chinese fare, which emphasizes the fiery spices typical of the Szechwan region in south-central China.

$$ La Playa – *780 Rue St-Jean G1R 1P9.* ☎418-522-3989. **International.** Latin, Cajun and Thai flavours pepper La Playa's shrimp, fish and poultry specialties. Try one of the 60 exotic martinis. In summer ask for a table on the terrace.

$$ 47e Parallèle – *24 Rue Ste-Anne* ☎418-692-4747. *G1R 5G2. www.le47.com.* **International.** This vibrant restaurant, popular for business lunches, serves basically French cuisine, with exotic

touches inspired by Vietnam, Mexico etc. Selections on the changing menu may include grilled medallions of venison or Morroccan lamb couscous.

$$ Portofino Bistro Italiano – *54 Rue Couillard G1R 3T3.* ☎418-692-8888.*www. portfino.qc.ca.* 🅿**Italian.** In this 1760 stone home, you can choose from more than 20 varieties of homemade pasta and 30 different wood-fired pizzas, complimented by a good Italian wine. Or sample specialties such as veal scallopini and rack of Quebec lamb. The atmosphere is exuberant, and a musician entertains diners nightly. **$$$**

L'Astral, *1225 Cours du Général- De Montcalm G1R 4W6, in Loews Le Concorde Hotel.* ☎418-647-2222. *www.loewshotels.com.* **Contemporary.** The 28th floor of Loews Le Concorde Hotel offers a panorama of the city. Quebec's only revolving restaurant affords views of the St-Lawrence, Old City, Île d'Orléans and the Charlevoix Coast. Watch the sun set to live piano music *(Tue–Sun evenings),* enjoy a nightcap or discover the popular Sunday brunch.

$$$ Le Continental – *26 Rue St-Louis G1R 3Y9.* ☎418-694-9995. *www.restaurantlecontinental.com.* ♿**Contemporary.** One of the oldest restaurants in the city, this local favorite near Château Frontenac serves classic specialties such as rack of lamb and duckling *à l'orange* as well as seafood and steak. Dark blue walls and wood paneling impart a simple elegance to the dining room.

$$$$ Le Saint-Amour – *48 Rue Sainte-Ursule G1R 4E2.* ☎418-694-0667. *www. saint-amour.com.* **Québécois.** Dine in casual elegance in the tile-floored Winter Garden, the Saint-Amour's cheery atrium. *Foie gras de canard du Québec* (Quebec duck foie gras), *saisie de caribou des Inuits aux baies de genièvre* (caribou steak with juniper berries) and *crème brûlée à la mure* (blackberry crème brûlée) typify the traditional cuisine crafted with a nouvelle twist by chef Jean-Luc Boulay. Treat yourself to the nine-course *menu découverte,* with accompanying wines.

SHOPPING

Lambert & Co. – *1 Rue des Carrières G1R 5J5.* ☎418-694-2151. This diminutive boutique just opposite Le Château Frontenac sells cold-weather necessities. In addition to woolen stockings, you'll find handcrafted soaps, maple products, and smoked-salmon pâté prepared by the hotel's chef.

La Boutique de Noël de Québec *–47 Rue Buade G1R 4A2.* ☎*418-692-2457*. In any season, this boutique entrances young and old with its brightly lit trees and myriad decorations, including intriguing strands of lights and an enormous variety of Christmas-tree ornaments.

Boutique des Métiers d'Art – *29 Rue Notre-Dame G1K 4E9.* ☎*418-694-0267*. Specializing in the work of Quebec artisans, this little boutique features a broad selection of art objects incorporating an enormous variety of materials. At the rear of the gallery you'll find lovely glass sculptures, ceramics, and leaded-glass windows in vibrant colours.

1 open daily.) ⌖*$7.50.* ☎*418-692-2175.* *www.museedufort.com*
This museum features a sound and light presentation *(30min)* that traces the city's military and civil history.

Basilique-cathédrale Notre-Dame-de-Québec★ (Basilica-Cathedral of Our Lady of Quebec) (B)

16 Rue Baude Québec QC, G1R 4A1. ♿ 🕐 *Open daily 8:30am–4pm.* ⌖ *Guided tours May–Nov daily. Rest of the year Sat.*⌖*$1.* ☎*418-694-0665. www. museucapitale.qc.ca.*
The original 1674 cathedral was destroyed during the battles of 1759. It was reconstructed between 1768 and 1771 by Quebec's distinguished family of architects, Jean and François Baillargé and, in the next generation, Thomas, who designed the 1843 façade.

Destroyed by fire in 1922, the church was rebuilt in its original appearance.
The majestic **Hôtel de ville de Québec** (Quebec City Hall) dominates the Place de l'Hôtel de ville across from the basilica. In the square stands a **monument (3)** to Elzéar Alexandre Taschereau, the first Canadian cardinal.
North of the basilica, the **Quartier Latin**★ (Latin Quarter) is the oldest residential district in Upper Town.

Séminaire de Québec★★ (Quebec Seminary)

2 Côte de la Fabrique. ♿ 🅿 *($11/day)* ⌖ *Guided tours of the seminary available in summer.* ⌖*$6 (includes admission to the Museum of French America).* ☎*418-692-2843.www.mcg.org.*
Founded in 1663 by Msgr. François de Laval to train priests, this institute of higher learning is the oldest in Canada.

Château Frontenac and Terrasse Dufferin

In 1852 the seminary was granted a university, Université Laval, which moved to the Sainte-Foy campus in 1950.

The seminary comprises three sections arranged around an inner court. Note the sundial on the facade of the **Procure Wing**, completed in 1681. The highlights of the guided tour include the **Msgr. Olivier Briand Chapel**, noteworthy for the fine wood panelling adorning its walls, and the **Congregational Chapel**, featuring a statue of the Virgin Mary crafted by Thomas Baillairgé.

Operated since 1995 as part of the Museum of Civilization, the **Musée de l'Amérique Française**★ (Museum of French America) **(M²)** presents France's historic, cultural and social heritage in North America *(2 Côte de la Fabrique, PO Box 460 Haute Ville, Quebec QC, G1R 4R7. Open Jun 24–Labour Day daily 9:30am–5pm Rest of the year Tue–Sun 10am–5pm. $6. 418-692-2843. www. mcq.org).*

Musée des Augustines de l'Hôtel-Dieu de Québec★ (Augustine Monastery)

32 Rue Charlevoix, Québec QC, G1R 5C4.
Founded by Augustinian nuns in the 1640s, this monastery is best known for its hospital, the Hôtel-Dieu, which still operates today. The **church** *(same hours as museum, below)*, designed by Pierre Émond in 1800, features a Neoclassical facade adorned with a sculpted Ionic portal.

The **Musée des Augustines de l'Hôtel-Dieu de Québec (M³)** (Augustine Museum) traces the Augustinian Nuns' history and heritage *(Open year-round Tue–Sat 9am–noon, 1:30–5pm, Sun 1:30pm–5pm. www.quebecregion. com. $5. 418-692-2492).* The museum includes one of the foremost collections of **paintings**★ dating back to the time of New France.

Rue Saint-Louis

The **Maison Maillou**★ **(C)** (Maillou House) (1736), located next to the Château Frontenac, now houses the Quebec City Chamber of Commerce. The offices of the Consulate General of France occupy the adjacent house, the **Maison Kent (D)** (Kent House), dating from the 1830s. Standing at the corner of Rue des Jardins, is the 1674 **Maison Jacquet★ (E)** (Jacquet House). Reputedly the oldest house in Quebec City, it is occupied today by a restaurant specializing in Quebec cuisine.

Monastère des Ursulines★★ (Ursuline Monastery)

12 Rue Donnacona, CP 760,
Québec QC, G1R 4T1.
Founded in 1639 by Madame de la Peltrie and Marie Guyart (Mère Marie-de-l'Incarnation), the monastery is the oldest educational institution for young women in North America and is still in operation. The **chapel** (1902) is particularly remarkable for its **interior decoration** *(Open May–Oct Tue–Sat 10am–noon, 1–5pm. Sun 1–5pm. 418-694-0413.*

The **Musée des Ursulines (M⁴)** (Ursuline Museum) occupies the site of the house belonging to Madame de la Peltrie, the order's benefactress, in the 17C *(Open May–Sept Tue–Sat 10am–noon, 1–5pm, Sun 1–5pm. Rest of the year Tue–Sun 1–4:30pm. $5 adult. 418-694-0694. www.museocapitale. qc.ca.com).* Reflecting the occupations of the Ursuline nuns, the collection features documents, furnishings, paintings, sculptures and numerous **embroideries**★ of rare beauty.

Price Building★

65 Rue Sainte-Anne, Québec QC,
G1R 3X5
This 16-storey 1930 Art Deco edifice, Quebec City's first skyscraper, was the head office of Price Brothers, who introduced the pulp and paper industry to the Saguenay region.

Cathédrale anglicane de la Sainte-Trinité★ (Holy Trinity Anglican Cathedral) (F)

31 Rue des Jardins, Québec OC, G1R 4L6
Modelled after London's Church of St. Martin in the Fields, this edifice (1804) was the first Anglican cathedral built outside the British Isles. King George III provided the funding and sent English oak from the royal forests of Windsor for the pews. In summer, the courtyard is a gathering place for artists.

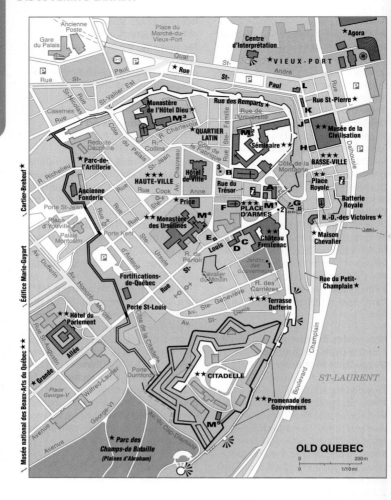

Basse-Ville★★★ (Lower Town)

From Dufferin Terrace, take the steep Frontenac stairway to Lower Town. Follow Côte de la Montagne down the hill to the Casse-Cou stairway on the right descending to Rue du Petit-Champlain. A funicular (cable car) also connects Dufferin Terrace to the Lower Town (◐In service year-round. June 20–Labour day 7:30am–midnight, late Oct–Mar 7:30am–11pm. Rest of the year 7:30am–11.30pm. ⦿$1.75. ☎418-692-1132. www.funiculaire-quebec.com).

This narrow stretch of land dominated by Upper Town was the site of Champlain's "Habitation." As port activities declined in the 1860s, the neighbour-

hood fell into decay. In 1970 the Quebec government began restoring the area. Lined with shops and art galleries, the pedestrian **Rue du Petit-Champlain**★ reflects the quarter's 18C appearance.

Maison Chevalier★ (Chevalier House)

60, rue du Marché-Champlain, Québec QC, G1K 8R1 (corner Blvd. Champlain). ◐Open Jun 24–Labour Day daily 9:30am–5pm. May– June 23 & Sept–mid-Oct Tue–Sun 10am–5pm. Rest of the year weekends 10am–5pm. ☎418-646-3167. www.mcq. org.

This imposing stone structure is composed of three separate buildings. The west wing was built in 1752 for a wealthy merchant, Jean-Baptiste Chevalier. The house now serves as part of the Museum of Civilization and exhibits traditional Quebec architecture and furniture.

Batterie Royale (Royal Battery)

At the end of Rue Sous-le-Fort and Rue Saint-Pierre. ♿🕑 *Open daily year-round.* ☎*418-646-3167.*

Constructed in 1691, this thick, four-sided earthen rampart was destroyed during French-British fighting in 1759 and gradually buried. Archaeologists unearthed it in 1972. It has been reconstructed and replicas of 18C cannon are positioned in the 11 embrasures.

Verrerie la mailloche★ (Economuseum of Glass) (G)

58, rue Sous-le-Fort at Rue du Petit-Champlain, Québec QC, G1K 4G8. 🕑*Open mid-Jun–Oct daily 9am–9pm, Nov–May daily 9am–5pm, (Thu–Fri 9pm).* ☎*418-694-0445. www.lamailloche.com.*

Examples of richly coloured glass are on view in the studio. Glass blowers can be seen at work and visitors can ask them questions about the process.

Place Royale★★

This charming cobblestone square was the hub of the city's economic activity until the mid-19C. Bordered by typical 18C stone houses, the square features a bronze bust of King Louis XIV as its centrepiece. The **interpretation centre** offers guided tours of the area *(29, rue Nôtre Dame, Québec QC, G1K 8R5.* 🐾🕑 *Open 24 June–Labour Day daily 9:30am–5pm. Rest of the year Tues–Sun 10–5.* 💳 *$5 adult.* ☎*418-646-3167. www.mcq.org).*

Église Nôtre -Dame-des-Victoires★ (Church of Our Lady of the Victories)

32, rue Sous-le-Fort, Place Royale, Québec QC, G1K 4G7. 🕑*Open May–mid-Oct daily 9:30am–5pm. Rest of the year Mon–Sat 10am–6pm.* 🕑*Closed to public when weddings, baptisms or funerals in process.* ☎*418-692-1650.*

Completed in 1723, this stone edifice topped by a single spire stands on the site of Champlain's "Habitation." Inside, the magnificent **retable** represents the fortified city.

Musée de la Civilisation★★ (Museum of Civilization)

85 Rue Dalhousie, CP 155, Succursale B, Québec OC, G1K 7A6. ✗♿🅿🕑*Open Jun 24–Labour Day daily 9:30am–6:30pm. Rest of the year Tue–Sun 10am–5pm.* 💳*$10 adults.* ☎ *418-643-2158. www.mcq.org.*

Designed by Moshe Safdie, the museum is housed in two angular buildings crowned by copper roofs and a glass campanile. A monumental staircase

Place Royale

links them and leads to a terrace over-looking an inner court and the 1752 **Maison Estèbe** (Estèbe House).

Among the permanent exhibits, **Mémoires** (Memories) describes more than four centuries of Quebec history and culture. **Nous, les premières nations** (Encounter with the First Nations) documents the history and culture of the eleven First Nations that inhabit Quebec.

Rue Saint-Pierre★

Among the noteworthy commercial buildings still lining the street are the **National Bank (H)** (no. 71); the former **Molson Bank (J)** (no. 105), now occupied by the post office; and the **Imperial Bank of Canada (K)** (nos. 113-115). Dominating the corner of Rues Saint-Paul and Saint-Pierre, the **Canadian Bank of Commerce (L)** exemplifies the Beaux-Arts style.

Rue Saint-Paul★ is renowned for its antique shops and art galleries.

Vieux-Port★ (Old Port)

Created by the federal government in the 1980s, the **Agora**★ complex includes an amphitheatre, a wide boardwalk on the river and a marina. The Old Port of Quebec **interpretation centre** is devoted to the port city's prominence during the 19C (*100 Rue Saint-André. ☛The centre is closed and will re-open*

TASTES OF LOWER TOWN

After a day of sightseeing, relax in one of the Lower Town's inviting restaurants. **L'Ardoise Resto Bistro ($$)** *(71 Rue Saint-Paul.G1K 3V8. ☎418-694-0213)* will win you over instantly with its cheerful combination of dark woods, wicker chairs and rustic stone. The service is friendly and the food is delicious: try one of the excellent fish dishes. Or, stop in for breakfast. Located near the Museum of Civilization, **L'Échaudé ($$)** *(73 Rue Sault-au-Matelot, G1K 3Y9. ☎418-692-1299. www.echaude. com)* serves a tempting variety of beautifully prepared and presented meat, fish and poultry dishes as well as salads. The service is always attentive, even when there's a crowd.

---

in 2009. ☎418-648-3300. www.pc.gc.ca). The glassed-in terrace on the top floor serves as a fine **viewpoint** for Lower Town and the modern port.

Fortifications★★

Much of the charm of Quebec City stems from its city walls. **Lord Dufferin**, governor general of Canada between 1872 and 1878, refurbished the fortified enceinte, rebuilt the gates to the city and cleared the ramparts.

Citadelle★★ (Citadel)

Entrance at end of Côte de la Citadelle. ♿🅿️☕☎ Visit by guided tour (1hr) only. Jul–Labour Day 9am–6pm. Sept 9am–4pm. Oct 10am–3pm. Nov-Apr bilingual tour 1:30 pm daily.Apr 10am–4pm. Changing of the guard June 13–Labour Day daily 10am. ∞$10 adult. ☎418-694-2815. www.lacitadelle.qc.ca.

Some areas of the Citadel are off-limits, as it is still a military base for the Royal 22nd Regiment. Erected between 1820 and 1832, this massive fortress is typical of star-shaped fortifications. Occupying the old powder magazine, the **musée du Royal 22e Régiment (M⁵)** contains a collection of military objects dating from the 17C to the present.

Lieu historique national des Fortifications-de-Québec (Quebec Fortifications National Historic Site)

100, rue Saint-Louis, CP 10, succursale B, Québec QC, G1K 7A1. ♿🕐Open early May–early Oct daily 10am–5pm. Rest of the year by reservation. ∞$4. ☎418-648-7016, toll-free 1-888-773-8888. www. pc.gc.ca.

The **interpretation centre** presents the history of Quebec's defence systems. Visitors can stroll south along the ramparts over the **Porte Saint-Louis** (St. Louis Gate) and the Kent and St-Jean gates to Artillery Park.

Lieu historique national du Parc-de-l'Artillerie★ (Artillery Park National Historic Site)

The main entrance at 2 Rue d'Auteuil is located near St-Jean gate. Visitor centre

Open Apr–early Oct daily 10am–5pm. Rest of year by reservation. $4. 418-648-4205, toll-free 1-888-773-8888. www.pc.gc.ca.

This huge site includes barracks, a redoubt and an old foundry commemorates three centuries of military, social and industrial life in Quebec City. Housed in the **old foundry,** the visitor centre contains a remarkable **scale model**★★ of Quebec City, produced between 1806 and 1808 by British engineers.

Rue des Remparts★

A pleasant stroll down the street allows visitors to recapture the atmosphere of the old fortified city.

Outside the Walls

Grande Allée★

Departing from the St. Louis Gate and extending southward from Old Quebec, this wide avenue is lined with restaurants, bars, outdoor cafes, boutiques and offices.

Hôtel du Parlement★★ (Parliament Building)

Visit by guided tour (30min) only, Jun 24–Labour Day Mon–Fri 9am–4:30pm, weekends & holidays 10am–4:30pm. Rest of the year Mon–Fri 9am–4:30pm. Visitors enter via Door No. 3 (corner Grande-Allée and Honoré-Mercier Ave). 418-643-7239. www.assnat.qc.ca.

Overlooking the Old City, this majestic edifice is the finest example of Second Empire architecture in Quebec City. Note the imposing **facade,** which presents a historic tableau commemorating the great names of Quebec history.

Parc des Champs-de-Bataille★ (National Battlefields Park)

Open mid-Jun–mid-Oct daily 9am–5:30pm. Rest of the year daily 9am–5pm. 418-648-4071. www.ccbn-nbc.gc.ca.

A large section of the park occupies the former **Plains of Abraham,** where the French and British armies fought a major battle (1759) that sealed the fate of the French colony. Don't miss the **Discovery Pavilion of the Plains of Abraham**, which presents the history of the Plains of Abraham through multi-media displays *(835 Av. Wilfred-Laurier, Quebec QC. Open Jun–Labour Day daily 8:30am–5:30pm. Rest of the year Mon–Fri 8:30am–5pm, Sat 9am–5pm; Sun 10am–5pm. $10 adult (Includes Martello Tower, Odyssey exhibit, Abraham's bus tour of grounds). 418-648-4071. www.ccbn-nbc.gc.ca).*

Musée national des Beaux-Arts du Québec★★ (Quebec Museum of Fine Art)

Parc des Champs de Bataille, Quebec QC, G1R 5H3. In the National Battlefields

Parliament Building

Park. ✕ & 🅿 🕓*Open Jun–Labour Day 10am–6pm (Wed 9pm). Rest of year Tue–Sun 10am–5pm (Wed 9pm).* 🎟*$15 adult.* ☎*418-643-2150, toll-free 1-866-220-2150. www.museeduquebec.org.*

This remarkable three-building complex provides an overview of Quebec art from the 18C to the present.

Observatoire de la Capitale (Édifice Marie-Guyart/ Observatory of the Capital, in the Marie Guyart Building)

1037 Rue de la Chevrotière, 31st floor, Quebec QC, G1R 5E9. & 🕓*Open June 24–mid-Oct daily 10am–5pm. Rest of the year Tue–Sun 10am–5pm.* 🎟*$5 adult.* ☎*418-644-9841, toll-free 1-888-497-4322. www.observatoirecapitale.org.*

The observatory occupying the 31st floor of this administrative building provides a splendid **view**★★ of Old Quebec.

Lieu historique national du Cartier-Brébeuf★ (Cartier-Brébeuf National Historic Site)

75 Rue de l'Espinay, CP 10, Succursale B, Quebec QC, G1K 7A1. 3km/2mi from St. John Gate by Côte d'Abraham, Rue de la Couronne, Drouin Bridge and 1 re Ave. & 🅿 🕓*Open May–Labour Day daily 10am–5pm, 1st 3 weeks Sept 1–4pm.* 🎟*$4.* ☎*418-648-4038. www.pc.gc.ca.*

This park commemorates Jacques Cartier, who wintered on this spot in 1535-36, and Jean de Brébeuf, a Jesuit missionary killed by the Iroquois.

Excursions

Côte de Beaupré★★ (Beaupré Coast)

Bordering the St. Lawrence, this narrow stretch of land extends from Quebec City to Cape Tourmente. A pleasant drive along Route 360 leads through a string of charming communities dating from the French Regime.

Parc de la Chute-Montmorency★★ (Montmorency Falls Park)

10km/6mi east of Quebec City. 🄺🄸🄳🄼 & 🅿 🕓*Open year-round daily.* ☎*418-663-3330. www.sepaq.com. (Click on resorts)*

The Montmorency River cascades over a cliff in spectacular falls 83m/272ft high (30m/98ft higher than Niagara Falls). In winter, the spray creates a great cone of ice that sometimes exceeds 30m/98ft in height. Elegant **Montmorency Manor** (1780) houses a restaurant and a **visitor centre**, which presents the area's heritage *(*✕ & 🅿 🕓*Open daily Thu–Sat 9am–5pm.* ☎*418-663-3330).* From the **upper lookout**, visitors can fully appreciate the height and force of the falls. At the **lower lookout** visitors can approach the base of the falls (rain gear is advised). An **aerial tram** returns visitors to the upper level (🕓 *Late Apr–late Oct daily 8:30am, closing hours vary. Dec 26–Jan 7 10am–4pm. Rest of the year, call for hours.* 🎟*$8.25 round trip.* ☎*418-663-3330).*

Sainte-Anne-de-Beaupré Shrine★★

Sainte-Anne-de-Beaupré QC, G0A 3C0. 35km/22mi east of Quebec City. & 🅿 🕓*Open mid-Jun–mid-Sept daily 6:30am–9:30pm. Rest of the year daily 7am–4:30pm. Museum open June–Labour Day 9am–5pm.* ☎*418-827-3781. www.ssadb.qc.ca.*

An imposing, Medieval-style basilica, consecrated in 1934, dominates the site. Divided into five naves separated by huge columns, the interior is lit by 240 **stained-glass windows**. Note also the glimmering **mosaics** adorning the barrel vault above the main nave.

Église Saint-Joachim★★ (St. Joachim Church)

172 Rue de l'Eglise, Saint-Joachim QC, G0A 3X0. 40km/25mi northeast of Quebec City. 🕓*Open mid-May–mid-Oct daily 9am–5pm.* ☎*418-827-8560.*

The small church (1779) is best known for its magnificent **interior,** fashioned between 1815 and 1825 by François and Thomas Baillairgé.

Île d'Orléans★★

10km/6mi northeast of Quebec City. Driving Route 368 along the 67km/41mi circumference of this island in the St. Lawrence, the visitor will discover splendid scenery and magnificent **views**★★ of the St. Lawrence shoreline.

The village of **Saint-Laurent**★claims the island's only marina. In **Saint-Jean**★, the **Manoir Mauvide-Genest**★, built in 1734, is considered the finest example of rural architecture under the French regime *(1451 Chemin Royal, St-Jean d'Orléans QC. G0A 3W0.* ♿🅿️🕐*June 24–Labour Day daily 10am–5pm. May–June & Sept–mid-Oct weekends only.* 🚶*$6 adult.* 🎧*With guided tour (45min) $8 adult.* ☎*418-829-2630. www.manoir-mauvidegenest.com).* The community of Sainte-Famille is best known for its tristeepled **church**★★ (1748), dating from the French Regime. This elaborate edifice contrasts with the **old church**★ in Saint-Pierre, remodelled in the 1830s by Thomas Baillairgé.

VALLÉE DU RICHELIEU★★

MAP P 313

Some 130km/81mi long, the majestic Richelieu River flows north from its source in Lake Champlain (New York) to join the St. Lawrence at Sorel. The region remains one of the richest agricultural areas in the province. A popular weekend retreat for Montrealers, the valley attracts thousands of tourists every summer.

- 🅸 **Information:** Quebec Tourism/Montérégie Region. ☎514-873-2015, toll-free 1-877-266-5687. www.bonjourquebec.com.
- ▶ **Orient Yourself:** The Richelieu Valley lies between Montreal and New York state. The towns of Acton-Vale, Chambly, Châteauguay, Contrecoeur, Lacolle, St-Jean-sur-Richelieu and Rougemont all have tourist offices.
- 👁 **Don't Miss:** In summer, colourful hot-air balloons often drift through the sky.
- 🕐 **Organizing Your Time:** In the autumn, the valley is famed for its apples and its icewine, made from grapes frozen on the vine.
- 🧒**Especially for Kids:** Go to Safari Park to see exotic animals up close.
- ♿ **Also See:** CANTONS DE L'EST, MONTREAL

A Bit of History

Samuel de Champlain discovered the waterway in 1609; it was named later for **Cardinal Richelieu,** chief minister of Louis XIII. The river served as an invasion route and was heavily fortified during the French regime. The forts at Chambly, Saint-Jean-sur-Richelieu, Lennox and Lacolle were built initially to protect Montreal against attacks by Iroquois, and later by British and American troops. To facilitate transportation between the US and Quebec, an extensive canal system was built along the Richelieu in the mid-19C.

Sights

Chambly★
30km/19mi from Montreal by Rte. 10.
A pleasant walk along the river in this residential suburb of Montreal leads past the canal and Fort Chambly to **Rue Richelieu**★, lined with sumptuous 19C residences.

Lieu historique national du Fort-Chambly★★ (Fort Chambly National Historic Site)
2 Rue de Richelieu, Chambly QC, J3L 2B9. Beside the river. ♿🅿️🕐 *Open mid-May – Labour Day daily 10am–5pm (June 23–Labour Day 6pm).Sept–Oct & Apr–mid-May Wed–Sun 10am–5pm.* 🚶*$6.* ☎*450-658-1585, toll-free 1-888-773-8888. www.pc.gc.ca.*
Located in a magnificent park on the Chambly Basin, this fort, erected

between 1709 and 1711, is the only remaining fortified complex in Quebec dating back to the French Regime.

The fort is laid out in a square with bastions at each corner. A **visitor centre** explains the history of the fort and the restoration project. Located near the fort, the **Guard House** (Corps de Garde) (1814) exemplifies the Palladian style adopted by the military throughout the British colonies. Built in 1820, the small fieldstone **St. Stephen's Church** served as the garrison's place of worship.

Centre de la nature du mont Saint-Hilaire★★ (Mt. Saint-Hilaire Nature Centre)

23km/14mi north of Chambly. 422 Chemin des Moulins, Mont-Saint-Hilaire QC, J3G 4S6. ✕ ♿ ⊙*Open year-round daily 8am–1hr before dusk.* ✆*$5.* ☎*450-467-1755. www.centrenature.qc.ca*

Rising abruptly above the valley, Mt. Saint-Hilaire (411m/1,348ft) is the most imposing of the Monteregian Hills. Several trails (hiking, snowshoeing and cross-country skiing) crisscross the lush forests and lead to the summit, which affords sweeping **views**★★ of the Richelieu Valley. The **Visitor Centre** explains the topography of the region (⊙*Open daily 9am–5pm*).

Saint-Denis-sur-Richelieu★

33km/20mi north of nature centre.

This agricultural community was the site of a Patriot victory in 1837. At the **Maison Nationale des Patriotes**★ (Patriots' National House) displays and an audio-visual presentation *(23min)* explain *(in French only)* the background of the uprising. *610 Chemin des Patriotes, St-Denis-sur-Richelieu QC, J0H 1K0.* ♿ 🅿 ⊙*Open May–Sept Tue–Sun 10am–noon, 1–5pm, Oct Sun 10am–noon, 1–5pm, Nov Tue–Fri 10am–noon, 1–4pm, April weekends 1–1–5pm.* ✆*$6 adult.* ☎*450-787-3623. www.mndp.qc.ca).*

Saint-Jean-sur-Richelieu

40km/25mi southeast of Montreal by Rtes. 10 and 35.

Known today for its Hot Air Balloon Festival and as a manufacturing centre

for pottery and ceramics, this city once formed part of the chain of fortifications erected by the French along the Richelieu River. The **Musée du Fort Saint-Jean** (Fort Saint-Jean Museum) contains a collection of weapons, uniforms and other military artifacts *15 Rue Jacques-Cartier Nord, St-Jean-sur-Richelieu QC, J3B 8R8.* ♿⊙*Open late May–Labour Day Wed–Sun 10am–5pm.* ✆*$4 adult.* ☎*450-358-6500, ext. 5769. www.museedufort-saintjean.ca*

Île aux Noix

48km/30mi south of Montreal by Rtes. 10, 35 and 223.

This 85ha/210 acre island was fortified by the French in 1759 and captured by the British the following year. The island is now preserved as a National Historic Site.

Lieu historique national du Fort-Lennox★ (Fort Lennox National Historic Site)

1 Av. 61, St-Paul-de-l'Île-aux-Noix QC, J0J 1G0. ✕ ♿ 🅿 ⊙*Open mid-May–Labour Day 10am–6pm, Sept 4-Oct 7 weekends and Thanksgiving 10am–6pm.* ✆*$7.25(ferry & visit of fort).* ☎*450-291-5700, toll-free 1-888-773-8888. www.pc.gc.ca.*

Erected in the 1820s, this bastion-type fortress occupies a pleasant **site** overlooking the Richelieu River. The Neoclassical stone buildings have been restored to re-create life on a British army base in the mid-19C.

Parc Safari★★

(Safari Park) 🚸 *63km/39mi south of Montreal by Rtes. 15 and 202.* ✕ ♿ 🅿 ⊙ *Open mid-May– June 10am–4pm, July–Aug 9:30am–7pm, Sept–mid-Oct 10am–4pm.* ✆*$35 adult.* ☎*450-247-2727, www.parcsafari.com.*

This zoological park is renowned for its animals that roam freely in large enclosures. Required to remain in their vehicles, visitors can follow the **Car Safari** *(4km/2.5mi)* along which they can take photographs. Highlights include the **Enchanted Forest,** a jungle walk, a theatre and a circus.

FJORD DU SAGUENAY★★★

MAP PP 306-307

Located at the southern tip of the Saguenay region, the immense, saucer-shaped Lake Saint-Jean empties into the Saguenay River. Measuring 155km/96mi in length, this river flows into the southernmost fjord in the world, the majestic Saguenay Fjord, which discharges its waters into the St. Lawrence. The region is famous for the landlocked salmon known as **ouananiche**; the wild **blueberries**, or bleuets, found on the north shore of the lake; and the famous nine-day **International Swim Marathon** held in July. The spectacular, natural **Parc du Saguenay**★★ (Saguenay Park) has been created to preserve part of the shoreline (*91 Notre-Dame, Rivière-Éternité QC, G0V 1P0.* ✕🅿🕒*Open daily year-round.* ☜ *$3.50.* ☎*418-272-1556, toll-free 1-800-665-6527. www.sepaq.com).*

🛈 Information: Regional Tourism Association, 412 Boul. Saguenay Est, Bureau 100, Chicoutimi QC, G7H 7Y8. ☎418-543-9778, toll-free 1-877-253-8387. www.saguenaylacsaintjean.net

▶ Orient Yourself: The Saguenay extends from Lac Saint-Jean past Alma, Jonquière, and Chicoutimi, to enter the St Lawrence at Tadoussac/Baie Ste-Catherine at the north edge of the Charlevoix region.

⊘ Don't Miss: The fjords of the Saguenay and whales of the St. Lawrence at Tadoussac are best seen by cruises. There are several operators in the Tadoussac area.

🕒 Organizing Your Time: The best wildlife viewing time is dusk or dawn.

🄺🄸🄳🅂 Especially for Kids: Whale watching; the zoo at St. Felicien.

⚲ Also See: CÔTE DE CHARLEVOIX, BAS ST-LAURENT

A Bit of History

The Lake Saint-Jean area remained unsettled until the mid-19C, when the first sawmills were built and the rivers were harnessed for electricity. Hydro-electric power plants, pulp mills and aluminum smelters still line the shores of the lake and the Upper Saguenay. Beyond Saint-Fulgence, the deep river channel was gouged in Precambrian rock by glaciers during the last Ice Age. Lined by rocky cliffs, the channel is 1,500m/4,920ft wide in places, having an average depth of 240m/787ft. Most

Anse Tabatiere, Fjord du Saguenay

visitors choose to take a scenic river cruise, but the fiord can also be enjoyed by exploring the villages nestled along its shores.

Saguenay Fjord★★★

Tadoussac★★

220km/136mi northeast of Quebec City by Rtes. 40 and 138.

This tiny community occupies a magnificent **site** at the mouth of the Saguenay on the cliffs and dunes lining the St. Lawrence.

Settlers moved into the area in the mid-19C, and the community developed into a lovely vacation spot. Today Tadoussac's principal attractions are whales that swim up the St. Lawrence to the mouth of the Saguenay for a few months each year.

The village is dominated by the red roofs of the **Hotel Tadoussac,** dating from 1941. Facing the hotel, a boardwalk extends along the river. A short walk to the wharf affords fine views of the area.

Whale-watching Cruises★★

✗ ♿ 🅿 *Depart from the marina Jun–mid-Sept daily 10am, 1:15 pm (& 3:30pm summer). Rest of the year, call for hours. Round-trip 3hrs. Reservations required.* 👁*$57 adult. Croisières AML, 124 Rue St-Pierre, Québec QC, G1K 4A7.* ☎*418-692-2634, toll-free 1-800-563-4643. www.croisieresaml.com.*

✗ ♿ 🅿 *Depart marina May–Oct daily 9:30am, 1:30pm (& 4:45pm summer)* 👁*$57 adult. Croisières Dufour* ☎*888-222-3080. 1-800-463-5250. www.dufour.ca (Departures also from Baie Ste-Catherine, and excursions in Zodiac rubber rafts)*

At Tadoussac the St. Lawrence is more than 10km/6mi wide. Boats head for the centre of the river, where whales surface to breathe and to dive in search of food. The most common species sighted on cruises are the **fin, minke** and **beluga** (white whales). Occasionally, a fortunate visitor may glimpse a **humpback** or even the huge **blue whale.**

Scenic Cruises★★

✗ ♿ 🅿 *Depart from the pier Jun–Oct, to Baie-Éternité in the Saguenay fjord. Round-trip 6hrs leaves at 9:15am Tadoussac pier. Reservations suggested.* 👁*$79 adult.* 👁*See Croisières AML above.*

A boat trip is the most spectacular way to discover the Saguenay Fjord. Éternité Bay is a lovely cove dominated by twin cliffs, Cap Éternité and Cap Trinité. Rising some 518m/1,700ft over the fiord, **Cap Trinité**★★ is renowned for the impressive statue of the Virgin Mary standing on a ledge 180m/590ft above the water.

Sainte-Rose-du-Nord

94km/58mi inland from Tadoussac on north shore of Saguenay River.

Founded in 1838, this charming village occupies an exceptional **site**★★ in a cove nestled between two rocky escarpments. The small **nature museum** contains a fascinating collection of nature's oddities *(199 Rue de la Montagne, Sainte-Rose-du-Nord QC, G0V 1T0.* 🕐 *Open mid-Apr–mid-Sept 8:45–8pm. Rest of the year 8:45–6pm.* 👁*$5 adult.* ☎*418-675-2348, www.ste-rosedunord.qc.ca).*

Saguenay★

200km/124mi north of Quebec City by Rte 175.

The former town of Chicoutimi has, since 2002, been a borough of the town of Saguenay; the other boroughs are Jonquière and La Baie. Meaning "to the edge of deep waters" in the local Montagnais language, Chicoutimi has long been considered the point at where the river becomes a spectacular fiord.

Pulperie de Chicoutimi★ (Chicoutimi Pulp Mill)

300 Rue Dubuc, Saguenay QC, G7J 4M1. ♿ 🕐*Open Jun 24–early-Sept daily 9am–5pm. Rest of the year Wed–Sun 10am–4pm.* 👁*$10 adults.* ☎*418-698-3100, 877 998-3100. www.pulperie.com.*

This former pulp and paper mill (1896) was one of the most important industrial complexes in Quebec in the early 20C. The former workshop has been converted into an **interpretation centre** that features a fascinating audio-visual presentation on the mill and the lumber industry in general.

Maison Arthur-Villeneuve (Arthur Villeneuve House)

In Building 1921 of Pulp Mill. The home of painter Arthur Villeneuve (1905-90), who worked as a barber while painting in his spare time, was relocaed to this site. This simple dwelling is decorated with his colourful (and sometimes terrifying) murals.

Scenic Cruises★★

Depart from dock at bottom of Rue Salaberry Jun–Sept daily. Several cruises offered down river towards Sainte-Rose-du-Nord. Return by bus. Reservations required. ⊚Starting at $40. ✕ ▣ Croisières Marjolaine Inc. ☎418-543-7630, toll-free 1-800-363-7248, www.croisieremarjolaine.com. On the return trip, the views of Ha! Ha! Bay and of Chicoutimi itself are equally magnificent.

Lac Saint-Jean★★

Péribonka

270km/167mi north of Quebec City by Rtes. 175 and 169. After spending a few months in this community in 1912, the French author Louis Hémon (1880-1913) wrote his well-known novel *Maria Chapdelaine, récit du Canada français*. Informative exhibits at the **Musée Louis-Hémon**★ (Louis Hémon Museum) trace the life and work of the author (*700 Rte Maria-Chapdelaine, Péribonka QC, G0W 2G0*. ♿⏲Open Jun 24–Labour Day daily 9am–5pm. Rest of the year Mon–Fri 9am–4pm. ⊚$5.50. ☎ 418-374-2177. http//:museelh.destination.ca).

Saint-Félicien

67km/42mi west of Péribonka by Rte. 169. 2230 Boul du Jardin, Saint-Félicien QC, G8K 2P8. Located on the western shore of the lake, this agricultural community is best known for its **Zoo Sauvage**★★ Kids (*6km/4mi on Blvd. du Jardin*. ✕♿▣⏲Open Jun–Aug 9am–6pm (mid-Jul–mid-Aug to 8pm) May & Sept–Oct daily 9am–5pm.

⊚$29 adult. ☎418-679-0543, toll-free 1-800-667-5687. www.borealie.org). A train takes visitors through the park, allowing them to admire a variety of animals roaming in natural surroundings. Of particular interest is the **Nature Trails Park**★★, inhabited by some 950 animals native to Canada.

Roberval

25km/15mi south by Rte 169.
Located on the southwestern shore of Lake Saint-Jean, this community is today an important service centre for the area. It is also the finish point of the annual International Swim Marathon.

Musée Amérindien de Mashteuiatsh (Mashteuiatsh Amerindian Museum)

9km/6mi north of Roberval by Blvd. Saint-Joseph. 1787 Rue Amishk, Mashtieuiatsh (Pointe-Bleue), Lac Saint-Jean QC, G0W 2H0. ♿⏲Open mid-May–mid-Oct daily 10am–6pm. Rest of the year Mon–Thu 9am–noon, 1–4pm. ⊚$7 adult. ☎418-275-4842, toll-free 1-888-875-4842. www.museeeilnu.ca. Located in Mashteuiatsh, an Indian reserve created in 1856, this museum traces the history of the Montagnais. A small shop offers handicrafts created in the area.

Val-Jalbert Historic Village★

9km/6mi south of Roberval by Rte. 169. The village can be visited on foot or by tram. ✕♿▣⏲Open June–early Oct daily 9am–5:30pm. May weekends only. ⊚$19 adult. ☎418-275-3132, toll-free-1-888-675-3132. www.sepaq.com.
Today a ghost town, Val-Jalbert was once the site of a thriving pulp mill built in 1902. By the late 1920s, stiff competition led to the mill's closing and the village gradually fell into ruins. Some older homes have been renovated and are available to visitors as rental units year-round. The **Vieux Moulin** (Old Mill), standing on the Ouiatchouan River, now contains an exhibit on the mill's operation. A steep stairway *(400 steps; cable car ascent ⊚ $4 adult)* leads to the top of an impressive waterfall on the Ouiatchouan River. From this vantage point, the **view**★★ encompasses Lake Saint-Jean and the surrounding area.

TROIS-RIVIÈRES★★

POPULATION 141 529 – MAP P 313

Capital of the Mauricie Region, this industrial centre is located on the north shore of the St. Lawrence River at the mouth of the Saint-Maurice. Just before joining the St. Lawrence, the Saint-Maurice branches around two islands, creating the three "rivers" for which the city is named.

Information: Office de Tourisme et des Congrès, 1457 Rue Notre-Dame Centre. ☎819-375-1222, toll-free 1-8800-313-1123. www.tourismetroisrivières.com

▶ **Orient Yourself:** Trois-Rivières lies about half-way between Montreal and Quebec City on Hwy 40. The town of Nicolet is on the south shore.

Parking: The city now has computerized parking meters (☺ see Montreal). The cost is $1/hr 9:30am–5pm Mon–Wed and to 9pm Thu-Fri. Weekends are free.

Don't Miss: The Quebec Museum of Popular Culture has fascinating and unexpected exhibits about the province's French and First Nations culture.

Organizing Your Time: A river cruise offers a look at both nature and the industrial development along the shores.

Especially for Kids: The Forges du Saint-Maurice Ironworks.

Also See: QUEBEC CITY, MONTREAL

A Bit of History

Sent by Champlain, **Sieur de Laviolette** established a fur-trading post here in 1634. Home to many great explorers, including Pierre Radisson, Sieur des Groseilliers and Sieur de la Vérendrye, the city flourished. In the 1850s a thriving pulp and paper industry took root in the area. By the 1930s Trois-Rivières was the world capital for the production of newsprint, a distinction it holds to this day. This bustling city is also the location of a University of Quebec campus.

Sights

Rue des Ursulines★

This charming street is lined with some of the oldest structures of the city, which survived a fire in 1908. Distinguished by a gracious dome and large wall sundial, the **Monastère des Ursulines** (Ursuline Monastery) is the jewel of Trois-Rivières' old quarter. Inside, the **museum** features fine collections of ceramics, silver, books and furniture (*734 Rue des Ursulines, Trois-Rivières, QC, G9A 5B5. ⊙Open May–Oct Tue–Sun 10am–5pm. Mar–Apr Wed–Sun 1–5pm.* ☺$3.50 adult. ☎819-375-7922. www.musee-ursulines. qc.ca.*). Other buildings of interest on

this street include St. James' Church, erected in 1742 by the Récollet Brothers, and the Gannes and Hertel de la Fresnière Houses.

Parc Portuaire★ (Waterfront Park)

This attractive terrace affords superb **views** of the river and Laviolette Bridge, erected in 1967. At the eastern end of the park, a monument commemorates the Sieur de la Vérendrye, first European to reach the Rockies. At the **Centre d'exposition sur l'industrie des pâtes et papiers** (Pulp and Paper Industry Exhibition Centre) displays provide a fascinating introduction to the dominant industry of Trois-Rivières (*800 Parc Portuaire, CP 368, Trois-Rivières QC, G9A 5H3.* ✕&⊙*Open June–Sept daily 10am–6pm.* ☺$4. ☎819-372-4633. www. ceipp.net*).

Scenic Cruise★

Departs from landing at the foot of Rue des Forges mid-Jun–Labour Day daily 3pm. Round-trip 2hrs. Reservations required. ☺$21. ✕P *Navire M/V Le Draveur Inc.* ☎819-375-3000, 800-567-3737. www.croisieres.qc.ca.* This cruise offers an unequalled view of the port at Trois-Rivières and the pulp and paper installations. The shrine at Cap-de-la-Madeleine (👣 below) is also visible.

Musée québécois de culture populaire★ (Quebec Museum of Popular Culture)

200 Rue Laviollette, Trois-Rivières QC, G9A 6L5. At the intersection with Rue Hart. ✖️♿🕐*Open Jun 24–Labour Day daily 10am–6pm. Rest of the year Tue–Sun 10am–5pm.* 🕐*Closed Jan 1-2 & Dec 24-26.* 💲*$8.* ☎*819-372-0406, 800-313-1123, www.culturepop.qc.ca.*

This museum offers an excellent look at Quebec culture. Exhibits display selections from a permanent ethnography collection of more than 80,000 objects and an archaeological collection of more than 20,000 artifacts of Amerindian and European cultures.

Adjoining the museum is the **Vieille Prison** (Old Trois-Rivières Prison), an imposing stone structure completed in 1822 and closed in 1986. The building houses an interpretation centre.

Excursions

Cap-de-la-Madeleine Shrine★★

5km/3mi east of Trois-Rivières by Rtes. 40 and 755 (Exit 10). 626 Rue Notre-Dame Est, Trois-Rivières QC, G8T 4G9. ♿🕐*Open May–mid-Oct daily 8am–9pm (mid-Aug 10pm). Rest of the year daily 8am–5pm.* ☎*819-374-2441. www.sanctuaire-ndc.ca.*

In the mid-19C Father Luc Désilets decided his growing congregation needed a new church to replace the one built on this site in 1717. When unusually mild weather prevented the St. Lawrence from freezing, Désilets could not transport stones across the river for the church's construction. The priest vowed to preserve the existing church in exchange for a miracle. In March 1879, ice appeared on the river, remaining just long enough for parishioners to take the stones across. On the night of the new church's consecration in 1888, another miracle is said to have occurred when the eyes of a statue of the Virgin reportedly opened before three witnesses. Begun in 1955 to accommodate an even larger congregation, the present basilica replaced Désilets' church and was completed in 1964.

The imposing octagonal basilica is adorned with magnificent **stained-glass windows** designed in the Medieval style by Dutch oblate father Jan Tillemans. Set in attractive grounds beside the basilica, the original stone church now serves as a votive chapel. The miraculous statue stands above the altar.

Mauricie Region★

Surrounding the valley of the Saint-Maurice River, this region is heavily industrialized. Forestry operations began in the 1850s, and hydroelectric plants were erected in the late 19C. Hugging the river, the drive along Route 155 affords fine **views**★ of the Saint-Maurice and the rocky cliffs lining its sides. Located northwest of Grand-Mère, the **Parc national de la Mauricie**★★ (Mauricie National Park) offers a glorious landscape of dense forests interspersed with numerous lakes and rivers (✖️♿🕐*Open year-round but only the southeast sector open in winter. Times vary considerably for camping, visitor centres, lodges (Wabenaki and Andrew Lodges): phone or check the website.* 💲*$7 for park entry.* ☎*819-538-3232. www.pc.gc.ca).*

Lieu historique national des Forges-du-Saint-Maurice★★ (Les Forges-du-Saint-Maurice Ironworks National Historic Site)

13km/8mi from Trois-Rivières by Blvd. des Forges. 1000 Boul des Forges, Trois-Rivières QC, G9C 1B1. ♿🅿🕐*Open mid-May–Labour Day daily 9:30am–5:30pm. Rest of Sept–mid-Oct daily 9:30am–4:30pm.* 💲*$4.* ☎*819-378-5116, toll-free 1-888-773-8888. www.pc.gc.ca.*

Established in 1729, these ironworks produced a variety of implements, including stoves, guns, ploughshares and dumb-bells until 1883, when the iron ore and wood of the region were depleted. At the **blast furnace** *(haut fourneau),* displays explain the smelting process. Beside the river a spring known as **Fontaine du Diable** (Devil's Fountain) is a source of natural gas.

ATLANTIC PROVINCES

Battered by the Atlantic Ocean on one side and washed by the calmer Gulf of St. Lawrence on the other, Canada's four Atlantic seacoast provinces (New Brunswick, Nova Scotia, Prince Edward Island, and Newfoundland and Labrador)—also known as Atlantic Canada—lie on the eastern side of the continent. They share the pervasive influence of the sea, which has molded, in great measure, their economic, political and cultural development.

🄸 **Information:** Each of the Atlantic provinces and major cities has a tourist office, whose contact information is given in the heading of the relevent section.

▶ **Orient Yourself:** New Brunswick, Prince Edward Island and Nova Scotia, collectively called the Maritime Provinces, are accessible by car, either by land or over bridges. The island of Newfoundland can be reached only by air or ferry.

🄳 **Don't Miss:** Whale-watching and bird-watching are superb in this region.

🄾 **Organizing Your Time:** Two weeks is barely enough to see the major sights.

🄺🄸🄳🅂 **Especially for Kids:** The sea at Prince Edward Island and New Brunswick is surprisingly warm for swimming.

🄰 **Also See:** LA GASPÉSIE AND LA CÔTE NORD IN QUEBEC

Geographical Notes

Landscape – Parts of the region, notably northern New Brunswick and Cape Breton Island, are hilly, lying near the end of the **Appalachian Mountain** chain. In the western part of Newfoundland, the **Long Range Mountains** (average height 610m/2,000ft) are part of this chain.

Barren and rocky by the sea while densely forested inland, the landmasses possess some fertile areas—the Saint John River Valley, the Annapolis Valley and Prince Edward Island. Their indented coastlines are studded with bays, inlets, cliffs and coves. The **Bay of Fundy** produces a phenomenal tidal bore. The highest recorded tide in the world

occurred at **Burncoat Head** on the Nova Scotia shore: a difference of 16.6m/54ft between high and low tides.

Climate – The sea largely determines the climate of this region. Moving south down the Atlantic coast, the cold **Labrador Current** enters the Gulf of St. Lawrence by the Strait of Belle Isle. Meeting warmer air currents moving in off the continent to the west, the cold waters of the current can cause fogs along Newfoundland's and Nova Scotia's coasts. Winters are stormy along the Atlantic but milder than inland. Summers are cooler and less humid than in Ontario and Quebec at the same latitude. The coast is cooler than inland.

In general, precipitation is evenly distributed throughout the year. Snow falls in all the provinces, but is heaviest in northwestern New Brunswick. Labrador experiences a more severe climate with more extreme temperatures but less precipitation.

Population – More than 2.3 million people live in the Atlantic provinces, with Nova Scotia the most populous (934,405), followed by New Brunswick (749,168). Prince Edward Island has

Peggy's Cove, Nova Scotia

©iStockphoto.com/John Archer

the lowest population (135,851). The most homogeneous of any province, Newfoundland and Labrador sustains a population of 505,469 with 98 percent declaring English as their mother tongue. The French-speaking minority (largely Acadians) is concentrated on Prince Edward Island (17 percent of the population) New Brunswick (33 percent). Nearly 30 percent of Nova Scotia's population is of Scottish origin. The Mi'kmaq are the most populous of the First Nations in Newfoundland, New Brunswick and Nova Scotia. Inuit and Montagnais-Naskapi Indians are found primarily in Northern Labrador. The African-Canadian population, less than 1 percent of the region's inhabitants, is concentrated primarily in the towns of Nova Scotia and New Brunswick.

A Bit of History

Native Cultures – Before the arrival of Europeans, the Atlantic provinces were inhabited by Indians of the **Eastern Woodlands** culture: **Mi'kmaq** in New Brunswick, Nova Scotia and Prince Edward Island lived by hunting and fishing; **Maliseets** cultivated the land in southern New Brunswick like their Iroquoian brothers in Ontario; and the **Beothuk** in Newfoundland also fished and hunted. The Beothuk's belief that all goods were held in common increased hostilities with the early European fishermen who frequently found their supplies missing. Mass murder and European diseases diminished these people greatly. The last known surviving Beothuk died in St. John's in 1829.

The First Europeans – Although he is credited as the first European arrival, **John Cabot** (1450-98)—an Italian navigator on a 1497 voyage of discovery for England's Henry VII—was not the first European to set foot in the region. Archaeological remains prove that the Norse settled on the Newfoundland coast about the year 1000. There is reason to believe the **Irish** reached the province's

shore in the 6C, and it is possible that **Basques** fished the North Atlantic as early as the 15C. At Red Bay in Labrador, archaeologists have discovered the presence of a large 16C Basque whaling port. Cabot's importance lies in his publicizing the region's rich fisheries. The Basques, English, French, Portuguese and Spanish came for the cod, especially abundant off Newfoundland's Grand Banks.

In 1583 Newfoundland was proclaimed the territory of Elizabeth I at St. John's. **Jacques Cartier** had claimed Prince Edward Island for France in 1534, renaming it Île-St.-Jean. Sieur de Monts and Samuel de Champlain established **Port Royal** in Nova Scotia in 1605.

"New Scotland" – In 1621 James I granted present-day Nova Scotia, Prince Edward Island and New Brunswick to **Sir William Alexander** to establish a "New Scotland" there (both men were Scots)—hence the Latin name *Nova Scotia* used on the original charter. In 1632 Charles I returned the region to the French.

"Acadie" – *Acadie* (Acadia) was what the French called a vague area covering much of Nova Scotia, Prince Edward Island, New Brunswick and Maine. The Acadians are descendants mainly of 17C French colonists.

British Regime – The English Crown granted a few charters in the 17C for colonies on Newfoundland, but authority for local law and order, granted in 1634 by Charles I, belonged largely to the **fishing admiral**—master of the first British ship to enter a harbour. French claims to the region ended in 1713 when, by the Treaty of Utrecht, France retained **Saint-Pierre** and **Miquelon**.

Nova Scotia Again – The Treaty of Utrecht gave Acadians the choice of leaving British territory or becoming British subjects. The Acadians stated they would take the oath with exemption from military service. Then, in 1747, nearly 100 New England soldiers billeted

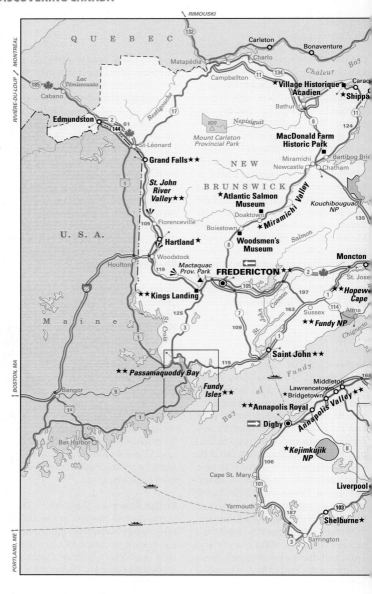

in the village of Grand Pré were killed, as they slept, in a surprise attack by a French force from Quebec. Treachery among the Acadian inhabitants was suspected.

Acadian Deportation – Fear of future attacks hardened the British toward the Acadians, especially after 1749 when Halifax was founded with 2,500 English settlers who could provision the army. In 1755 Gov. **Charles Lawrence** delivered his ultimatum—take an unqualified oath of allegiance or be removed from Nova Scotia. When the Acadians refused, Lawrence quickly issued the Deportation Order. Over the next eight years, 14,600 Acadians were forcibly deported. Unwelcome in the colonies, the Acadians were able to establish a new community

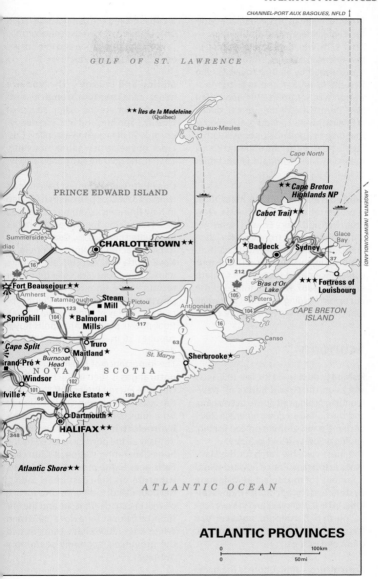

GULF OF ST. LAWRENCE

★★ Îles de la Madeleine
(Québec)

Cap-aux-Meules

PRINCE EDWARD ISLAND

Cape North

★★ Cape Breton
Highlands NP

Cabot Trail ★★

Summerside

Glace Bay

CHARLOTTETOWN ★★

★ Baddeck   ● Sydney

19

Fort Beausejour ★★
Amherst   Tatamagouche

212

Steam
Mill

Pictou

Bras d'Or
Lake

St. Peters

★★★ Fortress of
Louisbourg

123

105

CAPE BRETON
ISLAND

★ Springhill

104

Balmoral
Mills

117

Antigonish

104

Truro

7

16

Canso

Cape Split

215

Maitland ★

St. Marys

63

Sherbrooke ★

Grand-Pré ★   Burncoat
Head

99

N O V A   S C O T I A

Windsor

102

fville ★

101

Uniacke Estate ★

198

66

7

Dartmouth ★

348

HALIFAX ★★

Atlantic Shore ★★

ATLANTIC OCEAN

ARGENTIA (NEWFOUNDLAND)

37

ATLANTIC PROVINCES

0   100km
0   50mi

only in Louisiana and, as **Cajuns,** survive to this day. Some escaped to Saint-Pierre and Miquelon. Others fled to Île-St.-Jean until 1758, when the island was captured by a British expedition under **Lord Rolo,** and later annexed by Nova Scotia. Left untouched was a small settlement in the Malpeque area, the origins of Prince Edward Island's French-speaking population today. When peace was restored between England and France in 1763, most exiles returned to settle mainly in New Brunswick, where their descendants live to this day.

Scots, Loyalists and Other Settlers – After Deportation the British offered free land to anyone willing to settle in Nova Scotia. New Englanders from the south, groups from the British Isles and from the German Rhineland, and Scottish Highlanders accepted the offer. After 1776, when revolution erupted in the American colonies, Nova Scotia was transformed by 30,000 Loyalists who fled the new US. A separate administration was set up in 1784 and called New Brunswick for the German duchy of Braunschweig-Lüneburg, governed at that time by England's George III. Other Loyalists settled in Prince Edward Island, named in 1799 in honour of the father of Queen Victoria.

Confederation – In September 1864, representatives of Nova Scotia, New Brunswick and Prince Edward Island met with a delegation from Canada (then only Ontario and Quebec) to discuss British union in North America. This historic conference paved the way for Confederation in 1867. Newfoundland chose not to join, holding out until 1949, when it became Canada's 10th province.

Economy

Fishing Industry – In the late 1990s cod stocks on the **Grand Banks** off Newfoundland collapsed due to overfishing, and the Canadian government in 2003 declared a moratorium on cod fishing, ending a 500-year-old industry.

The most valuable catch for the Maritimes is **lobster**. Prince Edward Island is famous for **mussels** and Malpeque **oysters;** and Nova Scotia for Digby **scallops.** In New Brunswick and in Nova Scotia, north of Dartmouth, **aquaculture** focuses on the cultivation of mussels, clams and oysters.

Agriculture – Agriculture is the backbone of Prince Edward Island, most famous for its **potatoes.** Farms exist in Newfoundland on **Avalon Peninsula** and in **Codroy Valley,** but they supply local markets only.

Forest Products – New Brunswick's **pulp, paper** and **lumber** industries easily outdistance agriculture in domestic production. Newfoundland now includes mining and manufacture based on forest resources in its economic mix. Offshore oil production and tourism are among its leading industries.

Mining and Energy – The **iron ore** mines of the **Labrador Trough** in western Labrador are the major source of Canada's iron ore products. The discovery in 1993 of nickel in Voisey Bay, Labrador, opened a new source of wealth. Copper and gold are also mined in Newfoundland.

One of the world's largest base metals (zinc, lead and copper) mines is located in New Brunswick. Antimony is mined near Fredericton and two potash mines are situated near Sussex. **Coal** continues to be extracted at Minto-Chipman. In Nova Scotia coal, gypsum and salt are mined. New Brunswick's electric power resources are significant. A **nuclear power** station is located at Point Lepreau on the Bay of Fundy. Nova Scotia's tidal power plant at Annapolis Royal supplies 20 megawatts at peak production.

The importance of provincial **oil and natural gas** is seen in the huge Sable Offshore Energy Project off Nova Scotia, and in the Irving Oil Refinery at Saint John, Canada's largest. Labrador's **hydroelectric** potential is enormous. Virtually all the power produced by the huge generating station at **Churchill Falls** goes to the province of Quebec. **Hibernia** off the coast of St. John's, Newfoundland, is the most productive oil well in Canada. That site and the offshore oil fields at Terra Nova (2002) and White Rose (2005) have transformed the province's economy seemingly overnight.

Manufacturing – The food sector dominates Atlantic Canada's manufacturing. Some 300 companies engage in pharmaceutical and medical research, telecommunications and advanced technologies such as satellite remote sensing and ocean mapping. Music, film-making, and the plastic arts are also growing industries.

Recreation

For specific information on the activities below, contact the appropriate provincial tourism office: see NEW BRUNSWICK, NOVA SCOTIA, PRINCE EDWARD ISLAND, and NEWFOUNDLAND and LABRADOR.

Parks – All four provinces have excellent national and provincial parks with camping facilities and activities. Washed by the warm waters of the Gulf of St. Lawrence, Prince Edward Island National Park has lovely beaches. Miles of sand dunes are part of New Brunswick's **Kouchibouguac National Park**. Hiking trails abound in the province's Fundy National Park, Mactaquac Provincial Park and Mt. Carleton Provincial Park, as they do in Nova Scotia's National Park in Cape Breton's highlands and Newfoundland's national parks.

Water Sports – Water temperatures are surprisingly warm off Prince Edward Island's northern shores and New Brunswick's Northumberland Strait, in the vicinity of Shediac's Parlee Beach Provincial Park. On the beautiful Saint John River, where **houseboats** can be rented by the week. **Kejimkujik National Park** has several canoeing routes, and there are sailing and canoeing opportunities in Newfoundland's lakes and rivers. **Sea kayaking** is offered along Nova Scotia's eastern shore, off Cape Breton in particular. **Windsurfing** is practised on the bays and off the north shore beaches of Prince Edward Island (especially Stanhope Beach), in the Eel River Bar of New Brunswick's Restigouche region and off the Acadian Peninsula.

Fishing – Trout and salmon fishing in Newfoundland and Labrador are probably the best in eastern North America. A famous place to watch the salmon leap *(Aug)* is **Squires Memorial Park** near Deer Lake. Especially noted for its Atlantic **salmon** are the Margaree Valley in Nova Scotia and the Miramichi and Restigouche valleys of northern New Brunswick. **Fly fishing** is the only legal method for anglers to catch salmon in Nova Scotia. **Deep-sea fishing** is popular in the Maritimes, where boats can be chartered.

Whale Watching – Whales usually can be seen throughout the summer *(Aug and Sept, especially)* off the coasts of Newfoundland, New Brunswick and Nova Scotia. Cruises are available in Newfoundland in the vicinity of St. John's, Terra Nova National Park, Trinity and Twillingate. Deer Island, Grand Manan Island and St. Andrews are departure points for whale-watching voyages in New Brunswick. In Nova Scotia cruises depart from northern Cape Breton Island and from Digby Neck.

Bird Watching – The bird population of **Grand Manan Island** drew James Audubon to its shores to sketch its many species. In Nova Scotia, south of Liverpool, the **Seaside Adjunct** of Kejimkujik National Park protects a breeding grounds for piping plovers. Yarmouth harbors cormorants and black-backed gulls. The **Bird Islands** attract a variety of sea birds to their protected sanctuaries and McNab's Island in Halifax Harbour provides a nesting site for osprey. At its three famous sea-bird colonies— **Cape St. Mary's, Witless Bay** and **Funk Island**—gannets, murres, kittiwake gulls, razor-billed auks, puffins, guillemots and dovekies can be observed. Bald eagles, and even occasionally a golden eagle, are sighted along the south coast.

Other Activities – **Adventure tours** on foot, by riverboat, dogsled or **snowmobiles** are offered in Newfoundland. Operating mainly from Halifax, wilderness expeditions include backpacking and cross-country skiing.March trips to see baby harp seals on ice floes in the Gulf of St Lawrence, are organized by Natural Habitat Adventures, *(2945 Center Green Court, Boulder, CO 80301 USA. ☎303-449-3711 or 800-543-8917 (Canada/US. www.naturalhabitat adventures.com).*

NEW BRUNSWICK

POPULATION 749,168 – MAP PP 358-359

Bounded by the US on the west and Quebec to the north, New Brunswick is the Atlantic provinces' connection to the continental mainland. The province is linked to Nova Scotia by the Isthmus of Chignecto. Although the Northumberland Strait separates New Brunswick from Prince Edward Island, since 1997 the two provinces have been connected by the 13km/8mi-long Confederation Bridge.

- **Information:** Tourism and Parks, Campbellton. ☎1-800-561-0123. www.tourismnewbrunswick.ca.
- **Organizing Your Time:** For the Bay of Fundy tidal bore at Moncton, check www. waterlevels.gc.ca for the tides, which can be predicted a year in advance.
- **Especially for Kids:** The beaches along the Acadian coast are among the warmest north of Virginia.

Geographical Notes

An extensive coastline faces Chaleur Bay in the north, the Gulf of St. Lawrence to the east and the Bay of Fundy in the south. Extending into the bay are the three **Fundy islands** of Deer, Campobello and Grand Manan. The interior consists of mountainous uplands, central highlands, the Saint John River Valley, and a plain east to Chaleur Bay. This 673km/418mi Saint John River flows northeast from northern Maine along the US/New Brunswick border to empty into the Bay of Fundy.

Turbulent at Grand Falls gorge, the river cascades over 25m/76ft cataracts and 18m/59ft at Beechwood—both sites of hydroelectric dams. After the provincial capital of **Fredericton,** it gradually broadens, traversing picturesque farmland. At its mouth, the river is thrown back by the mighty Fundy tides in a gorge called **Reversing Falls.** Fredericton and the major port city of **Saint John** are situated on the river's banks.

A Bit of History

Era of Wooden Ships – Saint John became one of the world's great shipbuilding centres by the mid-19C. Skilled craftsmen perfected clipper ships, schooners, brigs and barques.

By Confederation in 1867, New Brunswick was wealthy, and in the late 19C, the province was the most prosperous in Canada. However, by 1900 steam had replaced sail power and steel hulls superseded wooden ones; the age of prominence was over.

Cultural Heritage – The social fabric of New Brunswick was woven by a diverse population of Mi'kmaq and Maliseet Indians, New England Loyalists, Acadians, Scots, Irish, Germans, Danes and Dutch. The richness of place names, such as Kouchibouguac, Memramcook, Shediac and Richibucto, stems from original Indian designations. The Acadians' yearly "Blessing of the Fleet," Canada's largest Irish festival, an annual folk music celebration and a Francophone festival illustrate the cultural variety of the province.

©iStockphoto.com/Edzard de Rantz

Whale-watching in the Atlantic provinces

Practical Information

GETTING THERE

BY AIR
Air Canada and its affiliates provide direct air service to Saint John and Fredericton (☎902-429-7111, toll-free 1-888-247-2262 Canada/US. www.aircanada.com).

BY TRAIN
VIA Rail services Moncton via Montreal, with connecting bus service to Saint John (☎506-842-7245, toll-free 1-888-842-7245. www.viarail.ca). Service between Montreal and New Brunswick daily except Tuesday.

BY BOAT
Government-operated ferries *(free)* provide service in the lower Saint John River area and to islands in the Bay of Fundy. Ferries *(toll)* connect the province with Nova Scotia and Quebec. For information, contact New Brunswick Tourism (👆*see below*).

GENERAL INFORMATION

ACCOMMODATIONS AND VISITOR INFORMATION
The official tourist office publishes an annual travel guide giving information on history, attractions and scheduled events, which you can order or download from the Net. Government-inspected hotels and motels, bed-and-breakfast lodgings and country inns, farm vacations and campgrounds are also listed. Contact **New Brunswick Tourism,** *Tourism and Parks, PO Box 12345, Campbellton, NB, E3N 3T6.* ☎1-800-561-0123. *www.tourism newbrunswick.ca*

LANGUAGE
New Brunswick is officially bilingual; approximately 35 percent of the population speaks French. All road signs are in English and French.

ROAD REGULATIONS
The province has good paved roads. Speed limits, unless otherwise posted, are 80km/h (50mph) on provincial highways and 50km/h (30mph) in cities. **Seat belt** use is mandatory. **Canadian Automobile Assn. (CAA)** *378 Westmorland Rd, Saint John NB, E2J 2G4.* ☎506-634-1400, toll-free 1-800-561-8807 www.caa.maritimes.ca

TIME ZONE
New Brunswick is on Atlantic Standard Time. Entering from the US or Quebec, set your watch ahead 1hr. Daylight Saving Time is observed from the 2nd Sunday in March to the first Sunday in November.

TAXES
In New Brunswick, the national GST has been combined with the provincial sales tax to form a Harmonized Sales Tax (HST). The HST for New Brunswick is levied at a single rate of 13% (some items are exempt). Nonresidents may be entitled to a rebate on certain goods taken out of the country within 60 days of purchase.

LIQUOR LAWS
The legal drinking age is 19. Liquor is sold in government stores. Some privately owned stores sell liquor as agencies for the provincial liquor corporation.

PROVINCIAL HOLIDAY
New Brunswick Day: 1st Monday in August

RECREATION
👆*See individual provinces for specific information.*

PRINCIPAL FESTIVALS

Jul	**Loyalist Days Festival**: *Saint John*
	Lobster Festival: *Shediac*
	Irish Festival: *Miramichi*
Jul–Aug	**Foire Brayonne**: *Edmundston*
	Bon Ami Festival Get Together: *Dalhousie*
Aug	**Festival Acadien**: *Caraquet*
Sept	**Harvest Jazz and Blues Festival**: *Fredericton*

Fort Beauséjour★★

MAP P 359

Overlooking the Cumberland Basin (an arm of Chignecto Bay), the Missiguash River Valley and the Tantramar Marshes, this former French fort is exceptional for its impressive **panorama**★★ of the surrounding country *(fog or rain may hamper visibility)*.

▣ **Information:** Fort Beauséjour-Fort Cumberland National Historic Site, 111 Fort Beauséjour Road, Aulac NB, E4L 2W5. ☎506-364-5080. www.pc.gc.ca

▶ **Orient Yourself:** The fort is situated in Aulac near Nova Scotia border, just off Trans-Can Hwy., Exit 550A. It stands on the Chignecto Isthmus, a narrow strip of land joining New Brunswick and Nova Scotia, southeast of Moncton.

⟳ **Also See:** MONCTON, FUNDY NATIONAL PARK, PASSAMAQUODDY BAY

A Bit of History

In 1672 the Acadians first settled in this area, which they called Beaubassin, reclaiming it from the sea by an extensive system of dikes. After the Treaty of Utrecht ceded mainland Nova Scotia to Britain in 1713, they found themselves in the middle of a border conflict. The British built Fort Lawrence on their side of the isthmus; the French built Fort Beauséjour on their side. Captured in 1755 by a British force under Col. Robert Monckton, Fort Beauséjour was renamed Fort Cumberland. The Acadians were removed under the Deportation Order of that same year. Strengthened by the British, the fort withstood an attack in 1776 by New England settlers sympathetic to the American Revolution. In 1926 the fort, rechristened Fort Beauséjour, was designated a National Historic Site.

Visit

♿⊙*Open Jun–mid-Oct daily 9am–5pm.* ◉*$4.* ☎*506-364-5080. www.pc.gc.ca.* The **visitor centre** houses displays on the site. Three restored underground casemates can be visited, and the earthworks are in good repair.

Fredericton★★

POPULATION 50,535 – MAP P 358

Set on a bend in the Saint John River, this quiet city is the capital of New Brunswick. Largely due to the munificence of **Lord Beaverbrook (1879-1964)**, Fredericton is the cultural centre of the province.

▣ **Information:** Fredericton Tourism, 11 Carleton St., ☎506-460-2041, 1-888-888-4768 or www.tourismfredericton.ca.

🅿 **Parking:** Visit the Tourism Centre at City Hall at 397 Queen St. for a free three-day visitors' parking pass. ☎506-460-2019.

⊙ **Organizing Your Time:** Use Fredericton as a base for visiting other sights.

A Bit of History

Fredericton's true beginning came, like Saint John's, with the arrival of the Loyalists in 1783. Upon the formation of the province in 1784, the settlement they founded, complete with a college that is now the **University of New Brunswick,** was chosen as the capital and named Fredericton after the second son of George III.

By the 20C most of the population worked for the provincial government or the university. The 21C, however, has seen more diversification, with rapid growth in the information technology industry in particular.

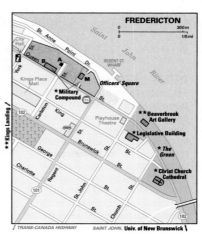

Sights

Stretching along the southern bank of the Saint John River is a strip of parkland known as **The Green**★.

Beaverbrook Art Gallery★★

703 Queen St., Fredericton, NB, E3B 5A6 &⃝ *Open July–Sept daily 9am–5:30pm (Thu 9pm). Rest of the year Mon–Sat 9am–5:30pm, Sun noon–5.30pm.* ⃝ *Closed Jan 1, Dec 25.* ⃝*$8.* ☎*506-458-8545. www.beaverbrookartgallery.org.*
The gallery features Lord Beaverbrook's collection of British, European and Canadian art. The collection of **British art** is the most comprehensive in Canada. The **Canadian Collection** features works by most of the country's best-known artists, including Cornelius Krieghoff.

Legislative Building★

&⃝*1st Mon in June–mid-Aug daily 9am–5pm. Rest of the year Mon–Fri 9am–4pm.*

Lord Beaverbrook

Born William Maxwell Aitken in Ontario, and reared in Newcastle, New Brunswick, Lord Beaverbrook (1879-1964) was a successful businessman in Canada before leaving for England in 1910. After entering politics he was elevated to the peerage in 1917, adopting his title from a small New Brunswick town. Having established Beaverbrook Newspapers, he built a vast empire on London's Fleet Street. Influential in the government of **Winston Churchill,** he held several key cabinet posts during World War II. Although absent from the province most of his life, Beaverbrook never forgot New Brunswick. In addition to gifts to Newcastle, he financed, in whole or in part, an art gallery, a theatre and several university buildings in Fredericton.

⃝*Closed major holidays.* ☎*506-453-2527. www.gov.nb.ca.*
Opposite the art gallery stands the stately 1880 Georgian seat of provincial government, with its classical dome.

Christ Church Cathedral★

168 Church St., Fredericton NB, E3B 4C9. pen ⃝*Open year-round Mon–Fri 9am–noon & 1pm–3:30pm, and Sun for services.* ☎*506-450-8500. www.christchurchcathedral.com.*
Completed in 1853 the stone church is an example of decorated Gothic Revival architecture. The interior has a hammer-beam wooden pointed **ceiling**.

Military Compound★

Changing of the guard Jul–Aug Tue–Sat, weather permitting.
Now a pleasant park known as **Officers' Square,** the old parade ground is

Changing of the Guards, Military Compound

Address Book

⌖For dollar sign categories, see the Legend on the cover flap.

WHERE TO STAY

$$ Lord Beaverbrook Hotel – *659 Queen St., E3B 5A6. ☎506-455-3371, toll-free 1-888-561-7666. www.cpfredericton. com. 168 rooms.* ✕&🅿🛁. Newly renovated and now part of the Crowne Plaza group, the 1947 Lord Beaverbrook has an unbeatable location in the downtown core (the Beaverbrook Art Gallery is right next door). The spacious, if austere, guestrooms have all the modern amenities. Three on-site restaurants range in offerings from bar/snack food to upscale cuisine.

$$ The Colonel's Inn – *843 Union St., E3A 3P6. ☎506-452-2802, toll-free 1-877-455-3003. www.bbcanada.com/1749. html. 3 rooms.* 🅿🛁. Impeccably maintained, this 1902 residence is just across the river from downtown Fredericton, accessible by shuttle boat or a pleasant walking trail. Each of the three air-conditioned bedrooms has a private bath, phone and TV/VCR. Breakfast included.

$$ On the Pond – *20 Rte. 616, Mactaquac. ☎506-363-3420 or 800-984-2555. www.onthepond.com. 8 rooms.* 🅿Spa. Just 20 minutes east of Fredericton, this waterside retreat offers recreation and relaxation. Guest quarters in the English-cottage-style lodge are decorated in a woodland theme. Downstairs you'll find a cozy great room with stone fireplace. Spa packages include massages, whirlpool access and more.

$$ Very Best Victorian B&B – *806 George St., E3B 1K7. ☎506-451-1499. www.bbcanada.com/2330.html. 5 rooms.* 🛁🛋. This handsome 19C house is located in a quiet residential neighbourhood within walking distance of downtown. All the antique-filled bedrooms have modern amenities. Features include an outdoor pool, a cedar sauna and a pool table. Breakfast is served in the dining room or in the gazebo near the pool.

WHERE TO EAT

$$ Brewbakers – *546 King St. ☎506-459-0067. www.brewbakers.ca.* **International**. This well-frequented eatery contains dining rooms on several levels. The place still has enough nooks and hideaways to afford privacy and quiet to couples. The menu roams from pizza and pasta to sesame chicken.

$$ Piper's Palate – *466 Street St., E3B 1B6. ☎506-450-7911. www.thepalate. com.* **International.** This casual bistro boasts an open kitchen, local art on the walls, background jazz and menus leaning toward the eclectic such as Mexican-inspired pork, Thai chicken or lamb ossobucco. Enjoy your selections inside, or on the umbrella-shaded front patio.

$ El Burrito Loco – *304 King St. E3B 1E3. ☎506-459-5626.* &**Mexican.** Though housed in a former fast-food joint on a busy downtown intersection, this restaurant is renowned for its authentic Mexican fare. Once a restaurateur in Puerto Vallarta, the owner has transported his recipes northward to the delight of many customers.

$ Schade's Restaurant – *536 Queen St.E3B 1B9. ☎506-450-3340.* **German.** Despite heavy wood furnishings, a light-hearted atmosphere prevails at this family dining spot opposite Officers' Square. Daily specials include a variety of schnitzels, and groups of four or more can call ahead to order regional specialties such as Schweinehaxe or Sauerbraten.

the site of the former British **officers' quarters,** constructed in 1839 with additions in 1851. A few blocks to the west, the **Guard House (A)**, built in 1827, stands adjacent to the **soldiers' barracks (B)**. Both have been restored and furnished.

York-Sunbury Historical Society Museum (M)

571 Queen St.,E3B 5C88. In officers' quarters. ⏱*Open late Jun–Labour Day daily 10am–5pm. Apr–May & Sept–Dec Tue–Sat 1pm–4pm.* ✎*$3. ☎506-455-6041.*
This museum provides a portrait of the area from its settlement by the Native American population to the present.

Fundy National Park★★

MAP P 358

Extending 13km/8mi along the Bay of Fundy's steep cliffs, this rolling parkland is interrupted by deep-cut rivers and streams in deep valleys. Created by 9m/29ft or higher tides, the vast tidal flats, explorable at low tide, contain a wealth of marine life.

🛈 **Information:** ☎506-887-6000. www.pc.gc.ca

▶ **Orient Yourself:** The park is located near Alma, on Rte.114, which follows the coast south of Moncton. This is not the spot for the famed Fundy tidal bore. That can be seen from Bore Park in Moncton.

Kids **Especially for Kids:** This park has plenty of recreational facilities for all seasons.

☾ **Also See:** MONCTON, FORT BEAUSÉJOUR

Visit

✕♿⏲*Open year-round. Camping, golf, fishing, boat rental, swimming pool, playgrounds, tennis, mountain biking, hiking, cross-country skiing, snowshoeing.* ⏲*Visitor centre (east entrance) open mid-Jun–Labour Day daily 8am–10pm. Mid-May–mid-Jun & Labour Day–early-Oct daily 8am–4:30pm.* ⊜*$7 entry fee.* ☎*506-887-6000. www.pc.gc.ca. Note: views described may be obscured by fog.*

Eastern Park Entrance

From the park gate there is a fine **view**★ of the tranquil Upper Salmon River, the hills to the north, the small fishing village of Alma, Owl's Head and the bay. To appreciate the contrast, visit at both low and high tides.

Herring Cove

11km/7mi from entrance. At the end of the road, there is a good **view**★ of the cove from above and a display on the tides. A path leads down to a cove that has tidal pools brimming with limpets, barnacles, sea anemones and other life at low tide.

Point Wolfe★★

10km/6mi from entrance.
The road crosses Point Wolfe River by a covered wooden bridge, below which is a small gorge forming the river's entry into Wolfe Cove. To collect logs floated downstream, a dam was constructed. Schooners loaded the sawed wood at wharves built in the coves. Today only the bridge and dam remain.

At the end of the road, a path leads to the cove, providing good **views**★★ on the descent. At low tide the sand and rock pools are alive with sea creatures.

Miramichi Valley★

MAP P 358

The name Miramichi has long been associated with fine salmon fishing. A major spawning ground for Atlantic salmon, the river has two branches (the Southwest Miramichi and the Little Southwest Miramichi), which together traverse the province. The area is also lumber country; Miramichi, (formerly Newcastle and Chatham) near the river's mouth, is known for its shipbuilding past. Joseph Cunard, founder of the famous shipping line, was born in Chatham.

🛈 **Information:** ☎800-561-0123. www.tourismnewbrunswick.ca

▶ **Orient Yourself:** The valley is found in east central New Brunswick. Drive north from Fredericton on Hwy 8.

- 🕭 **Don't Miss:** The towns of Carqaquet and Shippagan are pleasant stops.
- 🕐 **Organizing Your Time:** Allow 2 days to see the major sights.
- 📷 **Especially for Kids:** The Aquarium and Marine Centre at Shippagan; the Village historique acadien.

Sights

Atlantic Salmon Museum★

263 Main St., Doaktown NB, E9C 1A9. 94km/58mi northeast of Fredericton by Rte. 8. ♿🕐*Open Jun–mid-Oct, daily 9am–5pm, mid-Apr–May Mon–Fri 9am–5pm.* ⬭*$5 adult.* ☎*506-365-7787, toll-free 1-866-725-6662. www.atlanticsalmon-museum.com.*

Overlooking a series of pools on the Miramichi River, this museum is devoted to the area's famed Atlantic salmon.

Central New Brunswick Woodmen's Museum

6342 Rte 8, Boiestown NB, E6A 1Z5. 68km/42mi north of Fredericton by Rte. 8 in Boiestown. 🕐*Open mid-May–mid-Oct daily 9:30am–5pm.* ⬭*$5 adult.* ☎*506-369-7214. www.woodsmenmuseum.com.*

This museum presents life in a lumber camp. On display is a sawmill with its original equipment and a range of tools from axes to chain saws. The re-created bunkhouse and cookhouse evoke the flavour of camp life. A small **train** *($2)* runs continuous tours around the site.

MacDonald Farm Provincial Historic Site

600 Rte 11, Bartibog Bridge NB, 13km/8mi east of Miramichi on Rte. 11. 🕐*Open mid-Jun–Labour Day daily 9:30am–4:30pm,* *late May–mid-June Mon–Fri 9:30am–4:30pm.* ⬭*$2.50 adult.* ☎*506-453-2324.*

Overlooking the Miramichi estuary, this old stone farmhouse (1820) has been restored to the period when Alexander MacDonald and his family lived in it. Visitors can participate in domestic farm chores and learn traditional crafts.

Excursions

Shippagan★

104km/65mi northeast of Bartibog Bridge.

This town on the Acadian peninsula has commercial fishing and peat-moss processing plants. From Lameque Island a bridge crosses to Miscou Island, which has fine beaches on the Gulf of St. Lawrence.

Aquarium and Marine Centre★

📷*100 Aquarium Dr., Shippagan NB, E8S 1H9.* ✕♿🕐*Open mid-May–Sept daily 10am–6pm.* ⬭*$8.* ☎*506-336-3013. www.tourismnewbrunswick.ca.*

In a series of aquariums, outdoor seal pool and touch tank, fish native the St. Lawrence River and New Brunswick's lakes and rivers are on view. Visitors can enter the cabin of a reconstructed trawler.

Caraquet

Just east of Village Historique Acadien lies the town of Caraquet (11km/7mi), home of the 1891 **Hôtel Paulin ($$$)** *(143 Blvd. Saint-Pierre West, Caraquet NB, E1W 1B6.* ☎*506-727-9981, toll-free 1-866-727-9981. www.hotelpaulin.com).* Located on the second and third floors, the guest rooms have a country look with patterned quilts and rustic furniture. Downstairs features an open sitting area and a public **dining room ($$),** where the focus is on seafood and upscale Acadian-style cuisine. Overnight guests can help themselves to a continental breakfast in the morning.

You'll want to visit Caraquet in August, when the town hosts its annual Acadian festival, opened by a blessing of the fleet, symbolic of Christ's benediction to the fishermen of Galilee.

Village Historique Acadien★

📷 *14311 Rte 11, Caraquet NB, E1W 1B7. 47km/29mi west of Shippagan on Rte. 11.* ✕⚪◷ *Open Jun–mid-Sept daily 10am–6pm. Mid-Sept–mid-Oct daily 10am–5pm.* ⊙*$15 adult.* ☎*506-726-2600, toll-free 877-721-2200. www.villagehistoriqueacadien.com.*

This reconstructed village depicts the life of the Acadians from 1780 to 1890, after their return from Deportation. Staffed by Acadians wearing traditional costumes, the village extends along a road nearly 1.6km/1mi long.

Moncton

POPULATION 64,128 – MAP P 358

Set on a bend of the Petitcodiac River, Moncton is famous for its tidal bore, which rushes up the river from the Bay of Fundy. The first settlers in the area were German families from Pennsylvania, but they were joined by Acadians returning to British territory after Deportation. Today one-third of the population is French-speaking.

- 🛈 **Information:** Tourism Moncton, City Hall, 655 Main St. ☎506-853-3590, 1-800-363-4558. www.gomoncton.com
- ▶ **Orient Yourself:** Moncton is at the southeastern edge of the province.
- 🅿 **Parking:** Moncton has electronic meters, fed by coin or by a card purchased at city hall. Finding a space is not generally a problem.
- 🕐 **Organizing Your Time:** From Moncton, you are only an hour from Prince Edward Island or Nova Scotia, via bridges.
- 📷 **Especially for Kids:** The Hopewell Rocks are fun.
- ♿ **Also See:** FUNDY NATIONAL PARK, FORT BEAUSÉJOUR

Sight

Tidal Bore★

In certain V-shaped bays or inlets, the tide enters the broad end and literally piles up as it moves up the bay. This buildup occurs in the Bay of Fundy, 77km/48mi wide at its mouth, narrowing and becoming shallower along its 233km/145mi length. Thus, the tide is squeezed as it travels the bay, a ripple increasing to a "bore" as it enters the rivers emptying into the bay. At Moncton the bore varies from a few inches to nearly two feet. The highest bores occur when the earth, moon and sun are aligned.

Bore Park

♿*Off Main St. at the corner of King St. Bore schedules available from the tourist office at city hall or from the website. Arrive 20min prior to view lowest level and return 1hr later to see high tide.* ♿☎*506-853-3590. www.gomoncton.com.*

The tidal bore and changing levels of the Petitcodiac River are best viewed from the park. At high tide the river widens to 1.6km/1mi and the water level increases by up to 7m/23ft.

Excursions

Monument Lefebvre National Historic Site★

480 Rue Centrale, Memramcook NB, E4? 3S6. 20km/12.5mi southeast by Rte. 106 in St.-Joseph. ♿◷*Open Jun–mid-Oct daily 9am–5pm.* ⊙*$4 adult.* ☎*506-758-9808 (summer). www.pc.gc.ca.*

Located in the Lefebvre Building of the **College St.-Joseph,** the first Acadian institution of higher learning, the site chronicles the history of this French-speaking culture.

Founded by Rev. Camille Lefebvre in 1864, the college is now part of the Université de Moncton.

Hopewell Rocks

Hopewell Cape★★

35km/22mi south of Moncton by Rte. 114. Directional signs en route. ☺ *Be sure to climb stairs at the posted time to avoid the 10m/32ft tides.*

Near this little village overlooking Shepody Bay is an interesting phenomenon known as **The Rocks.** Tiny tree-covered islands at high tide, these shapes become "giant flowerpots" at low tide, their narrow bases widening to support balsam fir and dwarf black spruce at the top. Visitors can walk around them when the tide is out.

Passamaquoddy Bay/ Fundy Isles★★

MAP P 358

This inlet of the Bay of Fundy between Maine and New Brunswick is dotted with islands and indented with harbours, and includes the estuary of the **St. Croix River.** A popular resort, the area is also famous for its lobster and an edible seaweed known as **dulse,** a regional delicacy that is served in a variety of ways.

- 🛈 **Information:** ☎1-800-561-0123. www.tourismnewbrunswick.ca, or www.standrewsnb.ca
- ▶ **Orient Yourself:** St Stephen, the biggest town on the Canadian side, is about 90 mInutes west of Saint John. St Andrews sits on a small penninsula just south.
- ☺ **Don't Miss:** Campobello, home of Franklin D. Roosevelt.
- 🕓 **Organizing Your Time:** Plan your itinerary around ferry times.
- 🄺ids **Especially for Kids:** The HMSC Aquarium-Museum.
- 🕯 **Also See:** SAINT JOHN

A Bit of History

In 1604 Samuel de Champlain chose the bay as the site of his first settlement and wintered on St. Croix Island (today in Maine). Loyalists, arriving in 1783, settled the communities of St. Stephen, St. Andrews and St. George, and of Deer and

Campobello islands. *Fog and cold weather occur even in summer, particularly on the islands.*

Sights

St. Andrews★

Founded by Loyalists, St. Andrews became a prosperous mercantile and fishing town. In 1842 some of its century-old houses were floated intact across the estuary when the Webster-Ashburton Treaty declared the Canadian/US border to be the St. Croix River—and some Loyalists discovered they were on the "wrong" side of it.

The town's quaint main thoroughfare, **Water Street**, mixes boutiques and cafes. *For more information about the town: ☎506-529-5120. www.townofstandrews.ca or www.standrewsnb.ca*

HMSC Aquarium-Museum★

Kids *Huntsman Marine Science Centre, St. Andrews NB, E5B 2L7. At Brandy Cove. ◷Open mid-May–Labour Day daily 10am–5pm, Sept Thu–Sun 10am–5pm. ◷Closed Sep–mid-May. ☏$7.50 adult. ☎506-529-1202. www.huntsman marine.ca.*

This interesting little aquarium has fish tanks and displays on the marine ecosystems of the Bay of Fundy and neighbouring Atlantic waters. A family of harbour seals performs for visitors. Films are shown regularly in the theatre.

St. Andrews Blockhouse

454 Whipple St., Saint John NB, E2M 2R3. On Joe's Point Rd. ◷Open Jun–Aug daily 10am–6pm. ☏$1 adult. ☎506-529-4270. www.pc.gc.ca.

Built to protect New Brunswick's western frontier from American invasion during the War of 1812, this is the only blockhouse remaining of the original 14 erected.

Deer Island★

Car ferry departs from Letete year-round daily 6:30am–

10:30pm. ☏No charge. ☎506-466-7340, toll-free 1-888-747-7006. www.tourism-newbrunswick.ca. From Eastport, Maine (www.eastcoastferries.nb.ca.) Jul–Aug daily 9:30am–6:30pm, Jun & Sept daily 9:30am–5:30pm. Hourly. ☏$3 per person, $17/vehicle maximum. 🅿 ☎506-747-2159. Note: ferries operate on first-come, first-served basis. Lines form on weekends and at peak times.

This Fundy island is inhabited primarily by fishermen. The world's largest lobster pound is located on its western side. A pleasant **trip**★ is the ferry ride to the island from Letete, among the smaller islands covered with birds. In the narrow inlet of **Northern Harbour,** a corral for lobsters has been built with nets and fences. At the southern end of the island, a large whirlpool forms when the Fundy tides are running strong. Called **"Old Sow"** for the noise it makes, this vortex is visible from Deer Island Point or from the ferry to Campobello Island.

Campobello Island★★

Car ferry departs from Deer Island Deer Island– Campobello Island late Jun–mid Sept 8:30am–6:30pm, Jun & Sept 8:30am– 5:30pm. ☏$3/person, $22/vehicle maximum. 🅿 ☎506-747-2159. www.eastcoastferries.nb.ca. Accessible by bridge from Lubec, Maine. Non-Americans

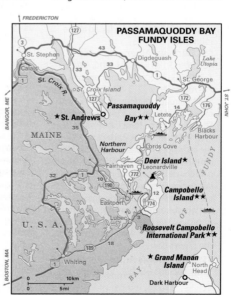

PASSAMAQUODDY BAY FUNDY ISLES

need valid passport. ⓖ *See also Michelin's* THE GREEN GUIDE *New England.*

Known as the "beloved island" of US President **Franklin D. Roosevelt** (1882-1945), the site is a summer resort. First settled in the 1770s, Campobello was named for **William Campbell,** the governor of Nova Scotia, and for its beauty *(campo bello means "beautiful pasture" in Italian).* By the end of the 19C, it had become a retreat for wealthy Americans. FDR spent summers on Campobello with his parents and later with his wife, Eleanor. In 1921, FDR contracted polio and left the island for 12 years. In 1964 the Canadian and American governments jointly established the park to commemorate him.

Roosevelt Campobello International Park★★

459 Rte 774, Welshpool NB, E5E 1A4. ⓖⓞ*Grounds open year-round. Visitor centre open late May–Oct daily 10am–6pm (Last 2 weeks Oct to 5pm).* ⓐ*No charge.* ☏*506-752-2922. www.fdr.net.*

Address Book

ⓖ *For dollar sign categories, see the Legend on the cover flap.*

WHERE TO STAY

$$ Windsor House – *132 Water St.,St. Andrews NB, E5B 1A6.* ☏*506-529-3330, toll-free 1- 888-890-9463. www.insite. com. 6 rooms.* ⓖⓧ⌷. This two-storey wood building, dating to 1798, is brightly painted and embellished with dormers and porch railings. It contains a parlour bar, billiards room and a **dining room ($$$)** that serves superb continental cooking with a contemporary twist. Spacious guest rooms have fireplaces, armoires or secretary desks, loveseats or settees and marble-tiled bathrooms. Fancy but not fussy, Windsor House will make you feel right at home. Breakfast is included in the room rate.

$$$ Fairmont Algonquin – *184 Adolphus St.* ☏*506-863-6310, toll-free 1-800-663-7575. www.fairmont.com. 234 rooms.* ⓧⓖⓟ⌷ⓢ. This sprawling 1889 railroad hotel rises from a carpet of lawn and trees on a bluff overlooking St. Andrews. The long lobby and adjoining front porch are perfect for idling; the cozy library is filled with volumes; and spa facilities, a beauty salon and a golf course with sweeping bay views encourage indulgence. Rooms are appointed with handsome fabrics and period reproduction or contemporary furniture. The **Passamaquoddy Dining Room ($$$),** open May–Oct, is one of the town's best.

$$$$$ Kingsbrae Arms – *219 King St.,St. Andrews NB, E5B 1Y1.* ☏*506-529-1897. www.kingsbrae.com. 8 rooms.* ⓧⓟ⌷. A rambling 1897 shingled manor house, this upscale inn, furnished with fine art and antiques, is the only Relais & Chateaux property in the Maritimes. Bathrooms feature whirlpool or cast-iron tubs and touch-control showers. After evening cocktails, guests dine around a massive table *(restaurant open to guests only).* Guests may also enjoy Kingsbrae's parlour, library and lovely gardens

WHERE TO EAT

$$ Niger Reef Teahouse – *1 Joe's Point Rd.,E5B 2J7.* ☏*506-529-8007. Closed after Christmas to May.* **Contemporary.** This waterwide restaurant is near the St. Andrews Blockhouse. The 1927 shingle and log structure retains its original Asian-style murals depicting New Brunswick's coastline. While best known for teas and creative sandwiches at lunch, Niger Reef offers a dinner menu featuring local seafood as well as steak kebabs and daily specials. On pleasant evenings, take a table on the rustic deck for great views of the bay.

$$ Rossmount Inn – *4599 Rte. 127, E5B 2Z3.* ☏*506-529-3351. www.rossmountinn.com.* **Canadian.** *(Dinner only).* This shingled Victorian pile is found 10 minutes from St. Andrews' waterfront. The cheery dining room permits distant views of the northern bay. The menu changes daily, featuring seafood and fresh vegetables from the restaurant's garden. With most main dishes under $20, the restaurant remains one of St. Andrews' better dining values.

The southern part of the island is natural parkland crisscrossed by several lovely **drives.** Note the view of Passamaquoddy Bay from Friar's Head (*turn right at picnic area sign just south of visitor centre*), and of Herring Cove from Con Robinson's Point (*follow Glensevern Rd. East*). Built in the Dutch Colonial style, the red-shingled, green-roofed **cottage** (*same hours as visitor centre*) with 34 rooms belonged to FDR. Films on the life of Roosevelt are shown in the **visitor centre.** North of the visitor centre, **East Quoddy Head Lighthouse** (*12km/7mi by Wilson's Beach and gravel road to the Point*) overlooks Head Harbour Island.

Cottage at Roosevelt Campobello International Park

Grand Manan Island★

✕♿🕐*Car ferry departs Blacks Harbour Jun 27–mid-Sept daily 7:30am, 9:30am, 11:30am, 1:30pm, 3:30pm, 5:30pm & 9pm (no departure Sun 7:30am). Rest of the year approximately 4 crossings daily. 1hr 30min.* ⊜*$31.40/car, $10.50/adult.* ☎*506-642-0520. www.coastaltransport.ca.*

The largest of the Fundy islands, Grand Manan is noted for its rugged scenery, picturesque harbours and sizable bird population. On the island's rocky west coast, **Dark Harbour** is a processing centre for **dulse**, which grows on submerged rocks in the Bay of Fundy. Collected at low tide and dried in the sun, dulse can be added to soups and stews and eaten raw or toasted.

Saint John★★

POPULATION 68,043 – MAP P 358

The province's largest city, this industrial centre and major port is fondly called "fog city" because of the dense sea mists that roll in off the Bay of Fundy. Its rocky, hilly site at the mouth of the Saint John River at the junction with the bay has resulted in a city with few straight roads and many culs-de-sac.

- **Information:** ☎506-658-2855, 1-866-463-8639. www.tourismsaintjohn.com
- **Orient Yourself:** Saint John lies opposite Annapolis Royal in Nova Scotia; a ferry crosses the bay.
- **Parking:** Parking is ample downtown: metered, in city lots and garages.
- **Don't Miss:** Reversing Falls is so famous you have to see it.
- **Especially for Kids:** The New Brunswick Museum.

A Bit of History

Part of Acadie – In 1604 Samuel de Champlain and the Sieur de Monts landed briefly at the mouth of the river. Another Frenchman, **Charles de La Tour,** built a trading fort in 1630 on the site of present-day Saint John, which a compatriot burned down. The trade rivalry among the French in Acadia was compounded by the Anglo-French struggles. The area was ceded by the 1763 Treaty of Paris to the English.

The Loyalists Arrive – In 1783 some 14,000 Loyalists disembarked at the mouth of the river. They possessed few pioneering skills, but they created a prosperous city of shipyards. Thriving on trade and shipbuilding, Saint John was known as the "Liverpool of America" during the 19C.

Address Book

WHERE TO STAY

$$ Homeport Historic B&B – *80 Douglas Ave. E2K 1E4. 10 rooms.* 🅿 ⛉. ☎*506-672-7255, toll-free 888-678-7678. www. homeport.nb.ca.* Set on a rocky ridge that offers views across downtown to the bay, the Italianate manor dates to 1858. Opened as a bed-and-breakfast inn in 1997, it has 10 sizable guest rooms, furnished with Victorian-era antiques gleaned from local shops and auctions. Breakfasts include a hot dish, fresh fruit and homemade granola.

$$ Shadow Lawn Inn – *3180 Rothesay Rd., Rothesay NB, E2E 5V7.* 🅿 ⛉. ☎*506-847-7539, toll-free 1-800-561-4166. www. shadowlawninn.com. 9 rooms.* Located in the outlying village of Rothesay, the inn is well worth the 10min drive from downtown Saint John. The elaborate house was built in 1870 as the summer home for a local department store magnate. Rooms are furnished with a mix of antiques and period reproductions. Continental breakfasts are included in the rate. The inn's restaurant serves Canadian fare in an upscale setting.

WHERE TO EAT

$ Taco Pico – *96 Germain St., E2L 2E7.* ☎*506-633-8492.* **Mexican.** Guatemalan immigrants opened this restaurant in 1994 and serves traditional black bean soup, soft tacos, fajitas and other Mexican staples as well as scallops, shrimp, and mussels in green sauce or *pepian* (a spicy Guatemalan-style beef stew).

$$ Billy's Seafood – *49-51 Charlotte St., E2L 2H7.* ☎*506-672-3474.* **Seafood.** This attractive emporium serves as a fish shop by day and a classy, informal restaurant by night. Less pricey than the tourist-oriented eateries on the waterfront, Billy's specializes in seafood. You can order plain boiled lobster or pan-seared scallops, or something more complex, like the house bouillabaisse. Whatever you choose, it won't disappoint.

Decline and Renewal – From 1860 to 1880, however, Saint John began to decline: demand for wooden ships was decreasing; an international depression had set in by early 1874; and in 1877 more than half the city was destroyed by a great fire. After a century of decline, the city began to revive in the 1960s. Today, high tech, oil and plastics industries are bringing prosperity. A new sports and entertainment venue, Harbour Station, has been constructed and the Imperial Theatre has been revived.

Every July the city recalls its founding with a celebration known as **Loyalist Days.** Inhabitants dress in 18C costumes and re-enact the landing of 1783.

Downtown★★

Saint John's downtown has been revitalized, making it a pleasant area for visitors to explore on foot *(contact tourist office for designated walks).*

Market Square Area★★

The square contains an attractive shopping mall with a central atrium and several levels, a hotel, convention centre and the New Brunswick Museum.
A row of late-19C warehouses fronts a pleasant plaza around the **market slip** where Loyalists landed in 1783. In summer there are outdoor cafes and concerts in the plaza.
On the plaza's south side stands an 1867 clapboard structure with gingerbread decoration, **Barbour's General Store (A)**, a museum stocked with merchandise of the period (🅿 🕑 *Open mid-Jun–*

Market Square Area

New Brunswick Tourism

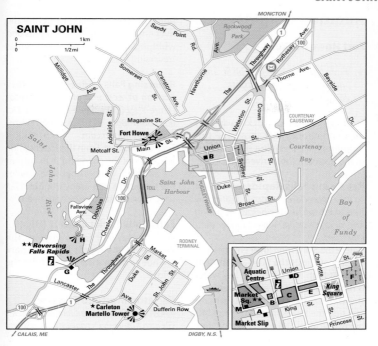

SAINT JOHN

CALAIS, ME

DIGBY, N.S.

mid-Sept daily 10am–6pm. ᨋ*No charge.* ᨙ*506-658-2939. www.tourismsaintjohn. com).* Over St. Patrick Street a pedestrian bridge links the square with the Canada Games **Aquatic Centre** (*www.aquatics.nb.ca*) and **City Hall (B)**. **Brunswick Square (C)** is a complex of shops, offices and a hotel.

New Brunswick Museum★ (M)

Market Square, Saint John NB, E2L 4Z6. ♿ᨎ*Open daily Mon–Fri 9am–5pm (Thur 9pm), Sat 10am–5pm, Sun noon–5pm.* ᨎ*Closed Mondays Nov 7–May 15 & statutory holidays.* ᨋ*$6 adult.* ᨙ*506-643-2300. www.nbm-mnb.ca.* The museum has excellent examples of Indian birchbark, quill- and beadwork. The gallery of natural science features displays of the province's animal life and geological specimens.

Loyalist House (D)

120 Union St., Saint John NB, ᨎ*Open July–Aug daily 10am–5pm. June Mon–Fri 10am–5pm.* ᨋ*$3.* ᨙ*506-652-3590. www. loyalisthouse.com*

One of the oldest structures in the city, this house was built in 1817 by David Merritt, a Loyalist who fled New York state in 1783. One of the few buildings to escape the fire of 1877, the house has a shingled exterior on two sides and clapboard on the other. The plain exterior belies the elegant and spacious Georgian interior.

King Square Area

Generally considered the centre of Saint John, this square has trees, flowerbeds arranged in the form of the Union flag and a two-storey bandstand. In one corner stands the old **city market (E)**, where a variety of New Brunswick produce can be bought, including dulse. On the other side of the square, the **Loyalist burial ground (F)** can be seen.

Martello Towers

Not one of the Martello towers constructed in British North America between 1796 and 1848 was ever attacked. Of the total 16 (Halifax 5, Kingston 6, Quebec City 4 and Saint John 1), 11 remain to this day.

Additional Sights

Fort Howe Lookout

▶ *From Main St., take Metcalf St., then make a sharp right turn onto Magazine St.*

From this wooden blockhouse (not open) on a rocky cliff above the surrounding hills, there is a **panorama**★ of the docks, harbour, river and city.

Reversing Falls Rapids★★

To fully appreciate the rapids, visit at low tide, slack tide (👍 see below) and high tide. or check online www.tourismsaint-john.com.

Where the Saint John River empties into the Bay of Fundy the tides are 8m/28ft high. At high tide when the bay water is more than 4m/14ft above river level, the water flows swiftly upstream. At low tide the bay is more than 4m/14ft below the level of the river, so the river rushes into it. As the tide rises, the rush of river water is gradually halted and the river becomes as calm (slack tide) before gradually being reversed in direc-

tion. The narrow bend just before the river enters the bay creates rapids and whirlpools, a phenomenon known as "reversing falls rapids."

Reversing Falls Bridge Lookout (G)

Parking at west end of bridge. Visitor centre ✕ ℗ ⊙Open mid-May–early-Oct daily 8am–8pm. ☎506-658-2937. www.tourismsaintjohn.com.
Take steps to roof. From this lookout fine **views**★★ of the changing river current are afforded. Visitors unable to stay for the tidal cycle may enjoy the **film** *($2)*, which condenses the 24-hour event.

Falls View Park Lookout (H)

Parking at end of Falls View Ave. The **views**★ *of the rapids from the park are not as dramatic as those from the bridge.*

Carleton Martello Tower★

454 Whipple St. West, Saint John NB, E2M 2R3. ⊙Open Jun–early Oct daily 10am–5:30pm. ☜$4. ☎506-636-4011. www.pc.gc.ca.
Today a National Historic Site, this Martello tower was built in 1813 as a defence for the city.

Saint John River Valley★★

MAP P 358

Communities sprang up throughout the valley when some 4,000 of the Loyalists who arrived in 1783 settled here. In the 19C numerous steamboats moved among these communities.

- **ℹ Information:** Department of Tourism, PO Box 12345, Campbellton NB, E3N 3T6, ☎1-800-561-0123.ww.tourismnewbrunswick.ca
- ▶ **Orient Yourself:** The Trans-Canada Highway parallels the river valley for much of its length.
- **Don't Miss:** Grand Falls is a notable New Brunswick sight.
- **Organizing Your Time:** From Grand Falls, you can turn east across the interior wilderness towards the Miramichi Valley and the east coast.
- **Especially for Kids:** Kings Landing offers a look at old-fashioned life.

From Fredericton to Edmundston

285km/177mi

Fredericton★★

👍 *See FREDERICTON.*

▶ *Leave Fredericton on the Trans-Can Hwy. (Rte. 2).*

The highway follows the river upstream to the Mactaquac Dam, New Brunswick's largest power project.

New Brunswick Tourism

Kings Landing Historical Settlement

On the north bank of the head pond lies **Mactaquac Provincial Park**, a haven for sports enthusiasts. The Trans-Canada Highway travels the south side of the pond with fine **views**★ as the country becomes increasingly rural.

Kings Landing Historical Settlement★★

Kids *20 Kings Landing Road, Kings Landing NB, E6K 3W3. 37km/23mi.* ✕🕐*Open Jun–earlyOct daily 10am–5pm.* 🕐*$15 adult.* ☎*506-363-4999. www.kingslanding.nb.ca.*

This restored village, which provides a glimpse of life from 1783 to 1900, has a beautiful **site** on the sloping banks of the Saint John.

About 100 costumed interpreters explain aspects of 19C rural life.

Beside the millstream is an operating water-powered **sawmill.** An example of a roadhouse of the period, the **Kings Head Inn** serves refreshments.

Moored at the wharf (the "landing"), is a half-size replica of a 19C **wood boat.** Between Kings Landing and Woodstock, there are excellent **views**★★ of the Saint John River traversing lovely rolling country of farms and forests.

▶ *After Woodstock, leave Trans-Can Hwy. and take Rte. 103 to Hartland.*

Hartland★

Settled by Loyalists, this town is known for the longest **covered bridge** in the world. Completed in 1901 and rebuilt in 1920, the 391m/1,282ft bridge crosses the Saint John River in seven spans, linking Routes 103 and 105.

Descending the hill on Route 103, note the good **view**★ of the bridge. The woodwork construction can be appreciated only from the interior *(cars can be driven through; no trucks).*

Take Rte. 105 on the east bank to Florenceville and Trans-Can Hwy. to Grand Falls.

There are fine **views**★ from the highway of the river and farms north of Florenceville. The Saint John gradually approaches the Maine border and enters the mountainous country of the north.

▶ *Leave Trans-Can Hwy. and enter Grand Falls.*

Fiddleheads

Harvested from the riverbanks of the Saint John in spring, edible fiddlehead ferns, boiled and topped with butter and lemon, are a New Brunswick delicacy.

Canadian Canines

Of the 143 dog breeds officially recognized by the Canadian Kennel Club (CKC), five are unique to Canada: the **Tahltan Bear Dog**, the **Canadian Eskimo Dog**, the **Nova Scotia Duck Tolling Retriever**, the **Labrador Retriever** and the **Newfoundland**. Now extinct, the Tahltan Bear Dog was a small dog in the Spitz line developed by the Tahltan Indians of northwestern British Columbia to hunt bear and lynx. The Canadian Eskimo Dog, similar in appearance to the Siberian Husky, was bred to pull sleds in the Arctic. The foxlike Nova Scotia Duck Tolling Retriever is trained to play along the shoreline, thus enticing curious ducks to swim within gunshot range—a behavior known as tolling.

The most popular among these five breeds are the Newfoundland and the Labrador Retriever. Vikings who came to Newfoundland as early as AD 1000 as well as Basque fishermen wrote accounts of large, long-haired dogs working beside native fishermen. Equipped with webbed feet and a dense, oily outer coat, the Newfoundland is able to swim for hours in icy water. Adult males average 28 inches high at the shoulder and 150 pounds— powerful Newfs are often used for water rescue, and anecdotes of their bravery abound.

Also originating in Newfoundland, the versatile Labrador Retriever helped fishermen retrieve drifting nets and haul carts of fish to market. Fishermen brought the retriever to England around 1800, where the British nobility developed the animal as a hunting dog. To this day, the Lab's short, water-repellant coat, "soft" mouth and thick otterlike tail (which makes a great rudder while swimming) serve it well in retrieving waterfowl for hunters.

Grand Falls★★
Falls and Gorge Commission ☎506-475-7769, toll-free 1-877-475-7769. www.grandfalls.com. The previously wide and tranquil river plunges over falls and, for about 1.6km/1mi, churns through a deep and narrow gorge. A power plant has diverted much of the water of the falls, but there are two good vantage points from which to see the gorge.

Falls Park
Accessible from Malabeam information centre on Madawaska Rd. ✕♿⏱Open Jun–early Aug daily 9am–9pm. Mid-May–late May & mid-Aug–mid-Oct daily 9am–6pm. ☎506-475-7788.
This park offers a good **view**★ of the gorge and the falls.

La Rochelle Centre★
In Centennial Park. Accessible from Malabeam reception centre on Madawaska Rd. ⏱Open daily mid-May–Labour Day. ✎$3. ☎506-475-7766.

Stairs descend into the gorge, which has walls as high as 70m/230ft in places. At the bottom, there are some deep holes in the rock called wells, but it is the **gorge**★★ that is impressive.

▶ *Continue north on Rte. 144.*

After Grand Falls the Saint John becomes wide and placid again, marking the Canadian/US border. The towns and villages seen across it are in Maine.

Edmundston
Situated at the junction of the Madawaska and Saint John rivers, this industrial city is dominated by the twin-spired **Cathedral of the Immaculate Conception**. The city's inhabitants are mainly French-speaking. The **Madawaska Museum** *(195 Herbert Blvd., Edmundston NB, E3V 2S8. At Trans-Can Hwy. ♿⏱Open daily 9am–8pm. ✎$3.50.☎506-737-5282)* presents the history of this region.

NOVA SCOTIA

POPULATION 934,405 – MAP PP 358-359

Surrounded by the Gulf of St. Lawrence, Atlantic Ocean, Northumberland Strait and Bay of Fundy, Nova Scotia has 7,460km/4,625mi of serrated coastline. Proximity to the sea and natural harbours have defined its historical role as largely strategic. The provincial capital, Halifax, has long served as a military stronghold.

- **Information: Tourism Nova Scotia**, ☎902-425-5781, toll-free 1-8800-565-0000. www.nova scotia.com.
- **Don't Miss:** Cape Breton island and the Cabot Trail are spectacular.
- **Organizing Your Time:** Halifax is a good base for seeing most sights, but Cape Breton Island requires a move north.
- **Especially for Kids:** Louisbourg offers costumed soldiers and lots of running space.

Geographical Notes

The Peninsula – The mainland is largely flat terrain, except for a rocky, indented eastern shore and a forested interior **South Mountain** forms the northern border of this upland interior. Stretching from Cape Blomidon to the tip of Digby Neck, the **North Mountain** range parallels South Mountain for 190km/118mi along the Bay of Fundy shore. Sheltered between them is the fertile Annapolis and Cornwallis river valleys. The cropped 300m/984ft **Cobequid Mountain** extends 120km/74mi over Cumberland County, which borders the Isthmus of Chignecto.

The Island – Northern Cape Breton Island is mostly a wooded plateau. At the northern end is **Cape Breton Highlands National Park**. A vast inland sea 930sq km/359sq mi wide, **Bras d'Or Lake** nearly bisects the island.

Practical Information

GETTING THERE

BY AIR

Air Canada and its affiliates offer daily flights from the US and from Toronto and Montreal to Halifax, and connections within Atlantic Canada. ☎ 514-393-3333, 902-429-7111, toll-free 1-888-247-2262 (Canada/US). www.aircanada.ca.
Robert L. Stanfield International Airport Halifax ☎902-873-4422. www.hiaa.ca
Sydney Airport ☎902-564-7720. www.sydneyairport.ca
Yarmouth Airport ☎902-742-6484.

BY BUS AND TRAIN

Bus travel within the province is provided by **Acadian Lines** (SMT-Eastern) (☎ 902-453-8912, toll-free 1-800-567-5151. www.smtbus.com). **VIA Rail** connects Nova Scotia through Toronto and Montreal (☎1-888-842-7245 Canada/US. www.viarail.ca).

BY BOAT

Passenger and car ferry service connects **Bar Harbor** (3hrs) and **Portland** (5hrs 30min), Maine, with **Yarmouth** NS (*Departure times June –1st week Oct are 8am and 4pm, but service alternates between Bar Harbour and Portland. Check schedules. No service 3rd week Oct–May. Reservations required. US$10 port and security fee each way. US$63/adult Bar Harbor, US$89/adult Portland. US$105/vehicle Bar Harbor, US$149/vehicle Portland. Fuel surcharge US$25/vehicle. ☎ 1-877-359-3760 (Canada/US). www.catferry.com*)
Saint John NB with **Digby NS** (*departs daily year-round. One-way 2hrs 45min. Reservations required. $80/vehicle, $40/adult passenger plus $20 fuel surcharge*). For ferry schedules & reservations

contact **Bay Ferries** (☎1-800-249-7245 (Canada/US). www.bayferries.com).

GENERAL INFORMATION

ACCOMMODATIONS AND VISITOR INFORMATION

For a free copy of a tourist guide and a map, contact **Tourism Nova Scotia.** (PO Box 456, Halifax, NS, B3J 2R5. ☎902-425-5781, toll-free 1-800-565-0000 (Canada/US). www.noviascotia.com).

CHECK-IN NOVA SCOTIA

Check-in Nova Scotia arranges hotel and campground reservations, car rentals and offers tourist information. ☎1-800-565-0000.

ROAD REGULATIONS

Nova Scotia has good paved roads; some interior roads are loose-surface. Speed limits, unless otherwise posted, are 100km/h (62mph) on the Trans-Canada Highway, 80km/h (50mph) on highways and 50km/h (30mph) in cities and towns. **Seat belt** use is mandatory. **Canadian Automobile Assn. (CAA)**, (Halifax ☎ 902-443-5530; www.caa.ca).

TIME ZONE

Nova Scotia is on Atlantic Standard Time. Daylight Saving Time is observed from the 2nd Sunday in March to 1st Sunday in November.

TAXES

In Nova Scotia, the national GST has been combined with the provincial sales tax to form the Harmonized Sales Tax (HST). The HST for Nova Scotia is levied at a single rate of 14% (some items are exempt). There is no longer a federal or provincial rebate program for foreign visitors.

LIQUOR LAWS

The legal drinking age is 19. Liquor is sold in government stores and in some retail outlets, and is served in licenced bars and restaurants. Licenced vineyards may also serve wine.

PRINCIPAL FESTIVALS

May–Jun	**Apple Blossom Festival:** *Annapolis Valley*
Jul	**Nova Scotia International Tattoo:** *Halifax*
	Metropolitan Scottish Festival and Highland Games: *Halifax*
	Antigonish Highland Games: *Antigonish*
	Gathering of the Clans and Fishermen's Regatta: *Pugwash*
	Acadian Days: *Grand-Pré*
Aug	**Natal Day:** *Province-wide*
	Nova Scotia Gaelic Mod: *St. Ann'*
	International Buskerfest: *Halifax*
Sept	**Nova Scotia Fisheries Exhibition & Fishermen's Reunion:** *Lunenburg*
	Kentville Pumpkin People: *Kentville*
Oct	**Octoberfest:** *Lunenburg*
	Celtic Colours Festival: *Cape Breton*

A Bit of History

Seafaring Nation – One great industry established by the Loyalists was **ship-building**, especially during the Napoleonic Wars (1803-15) when Britain needed wooden ships and ship parts. Sailors on Nova Scotia's renowned schooners were called **Bluenoses,** an American term of derision for people who could survive the region's cold climate. By 1900 shipbuilding waned; today wooden vessels are still crafted in the Lunenburg area.

Preserving the Past – Nova Scotia boasts more historic sites than any province in Canada except Quebec. More than 20 historic sites are open to the public.

Genealogy is popular here: local museums, schools and universities, genealogical societies and churches have archival facilities for tracing one's roots. The province's food promotion, "**Taste of Nova Scotia**," is offered by over 45 dining establishments. The **Gathering of the Clans** recalls the province's Scottish beginnings. Rug-hooking guilds, craft cooperatives and quilting groups are common across Nova Scotia.

Annapolis Royal★★
POPULATION 444 – MAP P 358

One of Canada's oldest settlements, Annapolis Royal has a pleasant **site** overlooking the great basin of the Annapolis River. Acadians reclaimed the marshland by building a dam across the river with floodgates to control the water level. Twice a day the Bay of Fundy tides rush in, reversing the river's flow. This gracious town was the site of French-English battles and Acadian struggles.

- **Information:** Town Hall, 285 St. George St., ☏902-532-5769, toll-free 1- 877-522-1110. www.annapolisroyal.com
- ▶ **Orient Yourself:** Annapolis Royal lies opposite Saint John NB, from which a ferry runs to nearby Digby.
- Ⓟ **Parking:** There are no parking meters, and three municipal lots. Overnight parking on the street is tolerated.
- ⊘ **Don't Miss:** The tidal generating station is one of very few in the world.
- Ⓞ **Organizing Your Time:** Lovely Kejimkujik National Park is only 48km/30mi from town.
- Kids **Especially for Kids:** The Port Royal "habitation" is nicely sinister.
- Ⓐ **Also See:** ANNAPOLIS VALLEY, SAINT JOHN

A Bit of History

The earliest settlement was a French colony at **Port Royal** under nobleman **Pierre du Gua, Sieur de Monts**, destroyed in 1613 by a force from Virginia. By 1635 the French governor **Charles de Menou d'Aulnay** had rebuilt the town. Over the next century the French settlement grew, forming the region called Acadia. In 1710 the fort fell to a New England expedition under Col. Francis Nicholson.

Renamed Annapolis Royal after England's **Queen Anne**, the town became the capital when the mainland was ceded to the British by the Treaty of Utrecht in 1713. However, it was subject to frequent French attack and in 1749 the capital was relocated to Halifax.

Much of the area's history is evident today: de Monts' habitation has been reconstructed near Port Royal, Fort Anne has been partially re-created and the older buildings along **Lower Saint George Street** have been renovated.

Habitation at Port Royal National Historic Site

Gwen Cannon/MICHELIN

Sights

Fort Anne National Historic Site★

Grounds ⏰ open year-round. Visitor centre ♿ 🅿 ⏰ open July–Aug daily 9am–6pm. Mid-May–June and Sept–mid-Oct 9am–5:30pm. 💰$4. ☎902-532-2397. www.pc.gc.ca.

This fort was once the most fought-over place in Canada, suffering 14 sieges during the Anglo-French wars. In 1917 Fort Anne became the first National Historic Park (now Site) in Canada.

In one of the bastions stands a stone **powder magazine** of the French period. From the earthworks there is a **view**★ of the Annapolis Basin.

Officers' Quarters★

Built in 1797 by order of Prince Edward, the quarters, now restored, house a **museum,** which includes a display on the fort's military history.

Historic Gardens★

On Upper Saint George St. (Rte. 8) just south of Fort Anne. ♿ ⏰ Open Jul–Aug daily 8am–dusk. May–Jun & Sept–Oct daily 9am–5pm. 💰$8.50. ☎902-532-7018. www.historicgardens.com.

Overlooking Allain's River, a tributary of the Annapolis, this series of theme gardens exemplifies the horticultural diversity of the region's past as well as recent gardening technology.

The **Acadian Garden** has a traditional cottage and a replica of the dike system. The **Governor's Garden** is characteristic of formal 18C gardens. The **Victorian Garden** reveals a more natural setting. The **Rose Garden** traces the development of this ever-popular species.

Annapolis Tidal Generating Station★

On the Causeway (Rte. 1). Visitor centre ♿ 🅿 ⏰ open mid-May–mid-Oct daily 10am–6pm. ☎902-532-5454. www.nspower.ca.

North America's first tidal power project, this station harnesses the enormous energy of the Bay of Fundy tides to produce electricity. The exhibit area explains the project and its construction. A causeway over the dam affords views of tidal activity and of the generating station.

Excursions

North Hills Museum★

5065 Granville Rd. in Granville Ferry (on road to Port Royal). ♿ ⏰ Open Jun–mid-Oct Mon–Sat 9:30am–5:30pm, Sun 1pm–5:30pm. 💰$3. ☎902-532-7754. http://museum.gov.ns.ca.

Despite a series of modifications, this small wood-framed 18C house has retained a pioneer look. It provides a fitting setting for the predominantly 18C antique collection of a retired Toronto banker.

Port-Royal National Historic Site★★

10km/6mi from Annapolis Royal Causeway. This habitation (French word for "dwelling") is a replica of Canada's first European settlement of any permanence. The collection of dark, weathered, fortified buildings joined around a central courtyard was designed in a style reminiscent of 16C French farms by **Samuel de Champlain** (1567-1635), captain and navigator of the expedition of Sieur de Monts.

Destroyed in 1613 by English forces, the buildings were reconstructed in 1938 by the Canadian government, using Champlain's sketch and writings as guides.

Visit

🅿 ⏰ Open July–Aug daily 9am–6pm. Mid-May–Jun & Sept–mid Oct 9am–5:30pm. 💰$4. ☎902-532-2898. www.pc.gc.ca.

Over the gateway entry hangs the **coat of arms** of France and Navarre, ruled by King Henry IV. A **well** with a shingled roof stands in the middle of the courtyard. Around it are the residences of the governor, priest and artisans. The kitchen, blacksmith's shop, community room where the Order met, and the chapel can be visited, as can the storerooms, wine cellar and trading room where Indians brought their furs. All furnishings are meticulous reproductions of early-17C styles.

A building technique known as **colombage,** the term used in France for log-filled, wooden frame construction, was employed to form the walls. No nails or spikes join the timbers: they are mortised and tenoned and pinned together.

Kejimkujik National Park★

PO Box 236, Maitland Bridge, Annapolis Country NS, B0T 1B0. Rte. 8. From Annapolis Royal 48km/30mi to park entrance, near Maitland Bridge. &○Open mid-Jun–Labour Day daily 8:30am–9pm. Rest of the year daily 8:30am–4:30pm. ○Closed Dec 25. $5.50. Visitor centre same hours except may be closed weekends in late fall (call for hours). Hiking, camping, cycling, swimming, canoeing, cross-country skiing. Canoe & bicycle rental at Jakes Landing. ☎902-682-2772. www.pc.gc.ca.

For centuries the park's waterways served the Mi'kmaq Indians as canoe routes and still afford peaceful passage through largely untouched wilderness, with many accessible lakes.

The **Mill Falls** hiking trail leads through fern-filled woods along the amber **Mersey River** to its foamy rapids. The viewing tower (*on main park road, 10km/6mi from park entrance*) permits an elevated **view**★ of lovely Kejimkujik Lake.

Annapolis Valley★★

MAPS PP 358-359

Some of the earliest French colonists settled in this region, only to be deported by the British in 1755. The Acadians built dikes to reclaim the marshland for agricultural production. In addition, the valley is sheltered on both sides from heavy wind and fog by the North and South mountains, a feature that has nurtured the valley's famed **apple orchards.**

- **Information:** ☎902-425-5781, toll-free 1-800-565-0000. www.novascotia.com.
- **Orient Yourself:** Flowing to the sea, the **Annapolis River** widens into the **Annapolis Basin,** a tidal lake connected to the Bay of Fundy by a narrow outlet known as Digby Gut. The Annapolis Valley extends from Digby to Windsor on the Minas Basin.
- **Don't Miss:** The old homes in Windsor are very authentic.
- **Organizing Your Time:** Windsor, at the end of the valley, connects to Halifax on the Atlantic side via Hwy 101.
- **Also See:** ANNAPOLIS ROYAL, HALIFAX

Driving Tour: From Digby to Windsor

213km/132mi

Digby

From this waterfront town ferries cross to New Brunswick. The harbour is often busy with fishing fleets. Local restaurants feature **Digby scallops** prepared in a variety of ways.

- *Take Hwy. 101 and then Rte. 1.*

Highway 101 follows the shore of the Annapolis Basin with pleasant views until it turns inland at Deep Brook, where Route 1 continues along the shoreline.

Annapolis Royal★★

See ANNAPOLIS ROYAL.

Remains of the old French dike system can be seen from the road. Route 1 crosses the river; wide meadows line the riverbanks. At **Bridgetown**★ elm-shaded streets contain fine houses, many built by Loyalists. **Lawrencetown** and **Middleton** are similarly graced with trees. Apple orchards line the hills, particularly between Kingston and Water-

Address Book

DIGBY DEGUSTATION

When you're in Digby, you should make an effort to sample the town's famous scallops, which are quite large. A number of restaurants along Water Street prepare these sizable mollusks grilled, fried, stuffed, boiled, broiled, or rolled in cornmeal and sautéed in butter. While dining, watch the town's inshore scallop fleet from the vantage point of **The Fundy Restaurant ($)** (34 Water St. ☎902-245-4950), the **Shoreline Restaurant ($)** (78 Water St. ☎902-245-6667. Closed Nov-Apr. www.shorelinecomplex.ca) or **Captain's Cabin ($)** (2 Birch St. ☎902-245-4868. www.captainscabin.ns.ca).

THE BLOMIDON INN

195 Main St., Wolfville NS, B0V 1C3. ☎902-542-2291, toll-free 1-800-565-2291. www.blomidon.ns.ca. This elegant 19C sea captain's mansion occupies four acres of grounds and Victorian gardens near Acadia University. Dine (**$$**) in one of two warm, wood-panelled rooms, or sit outside on the terrace in summer. The seasonally changing menu here emphasizes fresh local ingredients, such as Maritime lobster tails, Digby scallops, Maritime beef and caribou. Pastas are homemade.
The Inn also has 29 guest rooms (**$$**), decorated with period antiques and modern amenities; many have Jacuzzi tubs and four-poster beds.

---

ville, where fruit stands and "U-pick" farms are common.

▸ *Continue 57km/35mi on Rte. 1 to junction with Rte. 358.*

Excursion to Cape Split★★
28km/17mi north by Rte. 358.

Prescott House Museum★
1633 Starr's Point Rd. in Starr's Point, off Rte. 358, about 5km/3mi north of Rte. 1. ⏱*Open Jun–mid-Oct Mon–Sat 9:30am–5:30pm, Sun 1pm–5:30pm.* ⚲*$3.* ♿☎*902-542-3984. http://museum.gov.ns.ca.*
This attractive whitewashed brick house, set amid lovely grounds, was built in the early 19C by **Charles Prescott**, legislator, merchant and acclaimed horticulturalist. On this estate Prescott experimented with new strains of wheat and of fruit. He is partly responsible for the development of the apple industry in this area.
The interior is attractively furnished with some original pieces. A pleasant **sun room** was added by Prescott's great-granddaughter. The **garden** is also worth visiting.

▸ *Return to Rte. 358 and continue north.*

The Lookoff★★
Approximately 14km/9mi north of Starr's Point. Follow the signs on Rte. 358. Watch for paved pull-off with steel barricade. Although there is no official marker for this site, one cannot pass by without stopping. The **view**★★ of Annapolis Valley is magnificent. At least four counties are visible from this popular vantage point, some 200m/600ft above the valley floor.
About 8km/5mi north of The Lookoff, as Route 358 descends into the tiny community of Scots Bay, there is a lovely **view**★ of this bay, the Minas Channel and the Parrsboro Shore.

Cape Split
Rte. 358 ends. Hiking trail 13km/8mi through woods to tip of cape.
This hook of forested land juts into the Bay of Fundy, edged by magnificent cliffs. From road's end there are **views** of the wide bay, the shoreline of the cape and the Parrsboro Shore.

▸ *Return via Rte. 358. After about 9km/6mi, take the unpaved road on the left (Stewart Mountain Rd.). At junction turn left. Road terminates at provincial park. Follow signs. Hiking trails for Cape Blomidon are shown on the panel in the visitor parking lot.*

Beach at Cape Blomidon

Gwen Cannon/MICHELIN

Blomidon★

As the road leaves the woods and descends into flatlands, the first **view**★ of the Minas Basin is grand. Bright red barns and two-storey farmhouses dot the landscape, dominated by the red cliffs of Cape Blomidon. From the end of the picnic area, the **views**★★ in both directions of the wide red beach (at low tide), and the stratified pink cliffs, contrasted with the blue waters of the basin, are breathtaking.

▶ *At Blomidon junction, continue south via Pereau and Delhaven to Rte. 221.*

About 2km/1.2mi south of the junction, there is a **view**★ from Pereaux Small Crafts Harbour of the hole in a rock formation known locally as **Paddys Island,** fully visible at low tide.

▶ *At the junction with Rte. 221, turn right to Canning for Rte. 358 back to Rte. 1.*

Wolfville★

This charming town is home to Acadia University, founded in 1838. Several mansions have been converted into wayside inns.

Grand-Pré National Historic Site★

Just north of Rte. 1, 4km/2.5mi east of Wolfville.

Before Deportation, Grand-Pré was the most important Acadian settlement in Nova Scotia, with about 200 farms along the edge of the Minas Basin. Residents who had moved here from Port Royal constructed a system of **dikes** to keep the sea out, while marsh water was

Sam Slick

Thomas Chandler Haliburton became famous as the creator of the character Sam Slick, a fictitious Yankee peddler. His stories about Sam—22 in all—were first published in installments in the newspaper the *Novascotian*. In 1836 the newspaper's owner, Joseph Howe, published them as a book under the title *The Clockmaker; or, The Sayings and Doings of Samuel Slick of Slickville*. It was so popular, an estimated 80 editions were printed during the 19C. The book is basically a series of moral essays, made palatable by Haliburton's humor. A caricature of the proverbially dishonest 19C Connecticut salesmen who roamed rural areas, Slick travels all over Nova Scotia, making fun of its unenterprising inhabitants. Many of the epigrams he coined are still in use today: "six of one and half a dozen of the other," "an ounce of prevention is worth a pound of cure," "facts are stranger than fiction," "the early bird gets the worm," "as quick as a wink," and "jack of all trades and master of none" are among the most familiar.

allowed to escape through floodgates. The cultivated land soon supported crops, livestock and orchards. After Deportation, the farmlands were given to planters from New England, and later to Loyalists.

The American poet **Henry Wadsworth Longfellow** chose Grand-Pré as the setting for his poem *Evangeline*. Published in 1847, the work describes a young couple's separation during Deportation.

Visit

PO Box 150, Grand-Pré NS, B0P 1M0. 🚶♿️🅿️🕐 Open mid-May–mid-Oct daily 9am–6pm. 🎫$8 adult. ☎902-542-1952, toll-free 1-866-542-3631. www.grand-pre. com.

On the site of the first church of Grand-Pré stands a small **chapel** (1930) constructed of local stone in a style reminiscent of churches in France. Inside, there are **displays** illustrating Acadian settlement, the British takeover and the final Deportation. A bronze **statue** of Evangeline by **Louis-Philippe Hébert** stands on the grounds.

Windsor

Famous as the home of Thomas Haliburton, one of the most prominent Nova Scotians of his day, the town is set at the confluence of the Avon and St. Croix rivers. The Avon is sealed off from the Bay of Fundy by a causeway. The community was once the 18C Acadian settlement of Piziquid, which was taken over by New Englanders after Deportation and renamed Windsor.

Haliburton House Museum★

1414 Clifton Ave, Windsor NS, B0N 2T0. Follow signs from causeway. 🕐Open Jun–mid-Oct Mon–Sat 9:30am–5:30pm, Sun 1pm–5:30pm. 🎫$3.25. ☎902-798-2915. http://museum.gov.ns.ca.

At the end of a long, impressive drive stands this house, built in 1836 on the tree-covered estate of **Thomas Chandler Haliburton** (1796-1865), judge, legislator and author. A lawyer and a justice on the provincial Supreme Court, he was the first Canadian author to achieve international renown with the publication of *The Clockmaker; or, The Sayings and Doings of Samuel Slick of Slickville.*

Shand House Museum

389 Avon St., Windsor NS, B0N 2T0. (Street parking prohibited.) Upon entrance to Windsor, watch for signs to separate parking area. 🚶Uphill walk to the house. 🕐Open Jun–mid-Oct Mon–Sat 9:30am–5:30pm, Sun 1pm–5:30pm. 🎫$3.25. ☎902-798-8213. www.shand. museum.gov.ns.ca.

The most imposing of the houses atop Ferry Hill overlooking the Avon River, this Victorian dwelling was completed in 1891. Furnishings are those of the original and only owners. Visitors can ascend the square tower.

Fort Edward National Historic Site

Off King St. near causeway. 🅿️🕐Grounds open year-round. Fort open Jul–Aug Tue–Sat 10am–6pm. 🎫No charge. ☎902-532-2321.www.pc.gc.ca.

Built in 1750 as a British stronghold in Acadian territory, the blockhouse was later a point of departure for Acadians assembled for Deportation.

From the grassy fortification, there are **views** of the tidal river, the causeway and Lake Pesaquid in the distance. Made of squared timbers, the dark wooden **blockhouse** is the only remaining building of the fort. Inside, there are displays on the blockhouse defence system and the fort's history.

Atlantic Shore★★

MAP PP 358-359

Nova Scotia's eastern shore is known for its rugged coastline, granite coves, sandy beaches, pretty fishing villages and attractive tree-lined towns with elegant houses built from shipbuilding or privateering fortunes. The greatest concentration of quaint seaside communities is found south of Halifax.

- **Information:** Dept of Tourism, PO Box 456, Halifax NS, B3J 2R5. ☎902-425-5781, toll-free 1-800-565-0000. www.novascotia.ca
- **Orient Yourself:** The route lies between Halifax and Liverpool to the south.
- **Don't Miss:** A cruise on the Bluenose II, if only for the bragging rights.
- **Organizing Your Time:** This excursion requires about two days.
- **Especially for Kids:** The Ross Farm Museum offers demonstrations of farm activities
- **Also See:** HALIFAX

Driving Tour: From Halifax to Liverpool

348km/216mi.

Halifax★★
See HALIFAX.

▸ *Leave Halifax by Rte. 3. Turn left on Rte. 333.*

As the coast is approached, the landscape becomes wild, almost desolate. Huge boulders left by retreating glaciers, and stunted vegetation give the area a lunar appearance. *Fog is least common mid-July to October but can occur anytime.*

Peggy's Cove★★
Immortalized by artists and photographers across Canada, this tiny village is set on a treeless outcropping of massive, deeply lined boulders. Its tranquil harbour, with colourful boats and fishing shacks built on stilts over the water, is indeed picturesque. The **lighthouse** stands alone on a huge granite slab pounded by the Atlantic Ocean. *Sudden high waves and slippery boulders have resulted in tragedy. Use extreme caution when walking in this area.*

Peggy's Cove

Nova Scotia Tourism, Culture and Heritage

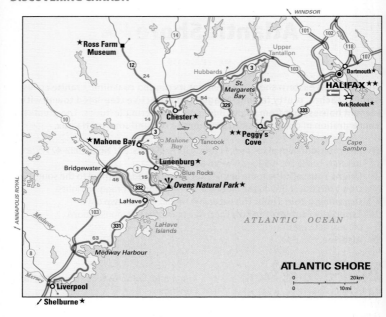

ATLANTIC SHORE

Note the **carvings** of village residents done in the granite rock by William deGarthe (1907-83).

A dramatic **memorial** to Swissair Flight 111, which crashed offshore on Sept 2, 1998, killing 229 passengers and crew, is located at The Whalesback, 1km/.5mi northwest of Peggy's Cove.

The road follows the coast with views of the villages on **St. Margarets Bay.**

▶ *Rte. 333 joins Rte. 3 at Upper Tantallon; follow Rte. 3 until Rte. 329 turns off after Hubbards. Tour the peninsula and rejoin Rte. 3 just before Chester.*

Chester★

Perched on cliffs rising out of Mahone Bay, this charming town, founded by New Englanders in 1759, is a popular summer residence of Americans and retirement spot for Canadians.

▶ *Take Rte. 12 North, 7km/4mi after Chester.*

Ross Farm Museum★

Kids *RR#2, New Ross NS, B0J 2M0. 24km/15mi one way.* ◷*Open May–Oct daily 9:30am–5:30pm. Rest of the year Wed–Sun 9:30am–4:30pm.* ⊠*$6 adult.*

☎*902-689-2210, toll-free 1-877-689-2210. http://rossfarm.museum.gov.ns.ca.*

Cleared from wilderness in 1816 by William Ross, this farm belonged to five generations of his family before acquisition by the Nova Scotia Museum Complex. Maintained as a living museum, the farm features coopering, candle making, forging, sheep shearing and other demonstrations that vary with the season.

▶ *Return to Rte. 3.*

Mahone Bay★

Between 1756 and 1815 hundreds of small ships sailed from Nova Scotia ports to harass French, Spanish, Dutch and American vessels. After obtaining a license, a privateer could attack only enemy ships. All prizes had to be taken to Halifax, where the Court of Vice Admiralty decided their legality. Profits were enormous and coastal communities prospered.

Upon approaching the town, there is a lovely **view**★ of the town's three neighboring churches reflected in the water.

▶ *Follow Rte. 3 South 10km/6mi.*

Lunenburg★

Situated on a hilly peninsula with "front" and "back" harbours, picturesque Lunenburg is named for the northern German hometown (Lüneburg) of the first settlers who arrived in 1753. Colourful historic houses grace the streets. Lunenburg was inscribed as a World Heritage Site in 1995.

Once a pirates' haven, the town was sacked by American privateers in 1782. The **Bluenose**, constructed here, was undefeated champion of the North American fishing fleet and winner of four international schooner races from 1921 to 1938. The *Bluenose II*, a replica of the original, was also constructed here in 1963 and offers seasonal cruises when in port *(Departs from Fisheries Museum. Contact Lunenburg Marine Museum Society for sailing reservations. ☎902-634-4794. ☜$35. ♿🅿Bluenose II Preservation Trust, 121 Bluenose Drive, PO Box 1963, Lunenburg NS, B0J 2C0. ☎902-634-1963, toll-free 1-800-763-1963 Canada/US. www.bluenose2.ns.ca)*.

Every August the popular **Fisheries Exhibition and Fishermen's Reunion** is celebrated in Lunenburg.

Fisheries Museum of the Atlantic★★

Kids 68 Bluenose Drive, PO Box1363, LunenburgNS, B0J 2C0. Lunenburg harbour. ✕♿🅿🕒*Open July–Aug Tue–Sat 9:30am–7pm, Sun–Mon 9:30am–5pm. May–June & Sept–Oct daily 9:30am–*

5:30pm. Rest of the year Mon–Fri 9:30am– 4pm. ☜$9 adult. ☎902-634-4794, toll-free 1-866-579-4909. www.fisheries. museum.gov.ns.ca.

This centre features exhibits ranging from the history of the *Bluenose* and the illicit "rum-running" trade during Prohibition to the banks fishery.

Moored at the wharf, the **Theresa E. Connor,** one of the last saltbank schooners to fish the Grand Banks, can be boarded. The steel-hulled side trawler **Cape Sable** can also be boarded.

▷ *Follow Rte. 3 and turn left on Rte. 332 for 15km/9mi. Turn left at Feltzen South and right on Ovens Rd.*

Ovens Natural Park★

PO Box 38, Riverport NS, B0J 2W0. ✕🅿🕒*Open mid-May–mid-Oct daily 8:30am–9pm. Rest of the year, call for hours. ☜$8. ☎902-766-4621. www. ovenspark.com.*

This private park has a lovely site, which offers **views**★ across Lunenburg Bay to Blue Rocks. Several sets of stairs lead to the ovenlike caves, cut into the cliffs by the action of the sea.

▷ *Continue on Rte. 332 and then left on Rte. 3.*

The road follows the wide and tranquil estuary of LaHave River, lined with frame houses and trees. The river is crossed at **Bridgewater,** a large, industrial town.

▷ *Turn left on Rte. 331.*

The road passes the town of **LaHave**, where Isaac de Razilly, lieutenant-governor of Acadie, built a fort in 1632. The road continues with many pleasant views, especially in the vicinity of **Medway Harbour.**

Liverpool

Founded in 1760 by New Englanders, Liverpool, like its great English namesake, is on the Mersey River.

Perkins House Museum★

105 Main St.,PO Box 1708,Liverpool NS, B0T 1K0. 🅿🕒*Open Jun–mid-Oct Mon– Sat 9:30am–5:30pm, Sun 1pm–5:30pm.*

The schooner Theresa E. Connor

Gwen Cannon/MICHELIN

🐚 *$2 adult.* ☎ *902-354-4058. http:// museum.gov.ns.ca.*

This New England frame house was built in 1767 for Col. Simeon Perkins, a merchant and ship owner from Cape Cod. On display next door in the Queens County Museum is a copy of the colonel's diary, which captures life in a colonial town from 1766 to 1812.

Excursion

Shelburne★

64km/38mi south by Hwy. 103 to Exit 25. Tourist bureau on Dock St. ☎ *902-875-4547.*

Founded by Loyalists in 1783, this small waterfront town was briefly one of the largest cities in North America.

Work continues at the barrel factory and in the **Dory Shop Museum** *(PO Box 39, Shelburne NS, B0T, 1W0.* 🅿 🕐*Open Jun–Sept daily 9:30am–5:30pm.* 🐚*$3 adult.* ☎*902-875-3219. http://museum.gov.ns.ca).*

Ross-Thomson House and Store Museum★

Charlotte Lane, PO Box 39, Shelburne NS, B0T 1W0. 🕐*Open Jun–mid-Oct daily 9:30am–5:30pm.* 🐚*$3 adult.* 🅿 ☎*902-875-3219. http://museum.gov.ns.ca.*

This two-storey structure was in use by 1785 as a combination house, store and warehouse. Seasonal flower and herb gardens grace the front entrance.

Balmoral Mills★

MAP P 359

Standing beside a stream in a pleasant valley, this fully operational gristmill was built in 1874.

ℹ️ **Information:** Balmoral Grist Mill, RR#4, Tatamagouche, NS, B0K 1V0. ☎902-657-3016. http://museum.gov.ns.ca

▶ **Orient Yourself:** Tatamagouche is between Amherst and New Glasgow along Hwy 6 on the north coast.

🕐 **Organizing Your Time:** The Tatamagouche Provincial Park is nearby.

👣 **Also See:** TRURO, SPRINGHILL, FORT BEAUSEJOUR

Visit

Balmoral Grist Museum, 600 Matheson Brook Rd, Balmoral Mills, NS. 10km/6mi southeast of Tatamagouche by Rte. 311. 🕐*Grounds open year-round. Gristmill museum open Jun–mid-Oct Mon–Sat 9:30am–5:30pm, Sun 1pm–5:30pm.* 🐚*$3.25.* ☎*902-657-3016. http://gristmill. museum.gov.ns.ca.*

When in operation *(a few hours daily)*, the mill is a hive of activity. Weighing over a tonne, the original millstones grind barley, oats, wheat and buckwheat into flour and meal *(for sale)*. Various milling processes are explained. Below the mill the revolving waterwheel can be seen.

Excursion

Sutherland Steam Mill Museum

3169 Denmark, NS. 10km/6mi northeast by Rte. 311, minor road and Rte. 326. ◷*Open Jun–mid-Oct Mon–Sat 9:30am–5:30pm, Sun 1pm–5:30pm.* ☞*$3.25.* ☎*902-657-3016. http://steammill.museum.gov.ns.ca.*

Alexander Sutherland built this sawmill in 1894. All machinery is in working order, and the mill "steams up" once a month *(phone ahead for schedule).*

Cabot Trail★★

MAP P 393

Named for explorer John Cabot, who is reputed to have landed at the northern tip of Cape Breton Island in 1497, this route is one of the most beautiful drives in eastern North America. Opened in 1936, the paved, two-lane highway makes a circle tour of the northern part of the island.

- 🗎 **Information:** Destination Cape Breton Association. ☎902-563-4636. www.cbisland.com
- ▶ **Orient Yourself:** Cape Breton, an island off the north end of Nova Scotia, is connected to the mainland by the Canso Causeway.
- 🅿 **Parking:** There are places to pull over along the road; do not stop on the shoulder because traffic may not be able to avoid you.
- ◉ **Don't Miss:** The trail can be driven in either direction, but visitors may prefer clockwise travel for the security of hugging the mountainside during steep, curvy stretches.
- ◷ **Organizing Your Time:** You can make the circuit in a day.
- 🄺🄸🄳🅂 **Especially for Kids:** The coal mining museum at Glace Bay offers tours of an actual mine.
- ৬ **Also See:** FORTRESS OF LOUISBOURG

Driving Tour

Round-trip of 301km/187mi from Baddeck.

Baddeck★

Overlooking Baddeck Bay, this charming village is the starting point of the Cabot Trail. The popular resort town has a lovely **site★★** on the north shore of **Bras d'Or Lake.** This immense inland sea's resemblance to a Scottish loch has attracted many settlers of Scottish origin. Among them was **Alexander Graham Bell** (1847-1922), humanitarian, researcher and prolific inventor.

Alexander Graham Bell National Historic Site★★

On Hwy. 205 in Baddeck. Bell's favourite shape, the tetrahedron, is used extensively in the design of this fascinating museum.

In 1885 Bell first visited Baddeck, where he was to conduct much of his aeronautical work. Eventually he chose the location for his summer residence, naming his home *Beinn Bhreagh,* "beautiful mountain" in Gaelic. The discovery of the telephone in 1874 had brought him fame and the capital to continue other research. In 1907, with other pioneer aviators, he founded the Aerial Experiment Assn. and sponsored the first manned flight in Canada when the **Silver Dart** flew across Baddeck Bay in 1909. His hydrofoil craft reach the incredible speed (for 1919) of 114kmh/70mph on Bras d'Or Lake.

Visit

PO Box 159, Baddeck NS, B0E 1B0. ৬🅿◷*Open Jul–mid-Oct 8:30am–6pm, June 9am–6pm, May & late Oct 9am–*

Cabot Trail at dawn

5pm. $7.15 adult. 902-295-2069. www.pc.gc.ca.

There are models of the telephone, as well as many other ingenious devices. A highlight is the superb **photograph collection,** recording Bell's life and work. One wing of the museum is devoted to his hydrofoil, the HD-4. From the museum's rooftop garden, there is a **view** of the wooded headland across Baddeck Bay. Beinn Bhreagh (*not open to the public*), can be seen among the trees.

From Baddeck to Chéticamp★

88km/55mi.

The Cabot Trail follows the valley of the Middle River, passes the Lakes O'Law and joins the Margaree River's verdant **valley**★.

North East Margaree

This tiny rural community has a museum of note.

Address Book

WHERE TO EAT

$ Restaurant Acadien - *At the Acadian Museum, Chéticamp.* 902-224-3207. *www.co-opartisanale.com.* Prepare to enjoy an authentic Acadian meal served by women in gingham skirts and lace caps at this popular roadside restaurant. Chicken Fricot (chicken and potatoes cooked in chicken stock), meat pie and fish chowder share the menu with more standard fare (fish & chips, pork chops, hamburgers). Dessert pies are hard to resist. Breakfast, lunch and dinner are served seven days a week, beginning at 7am.

WHERE TO STAY

$$ Normaway Inn - *691 Egypt Rd., PO Box 100, Margaree Valley NS, B0E 2C0. (3km/2mi off Cabot Trail).* 902-248-2987, *toll-free 1-800-565-9463. www. normaway.com.* Nestled within acres of forest and meadows, this sequestered resort lodge appeals to nature lovers with its mountain biking and hiking, and proximity to trout and salmon fishing and canoeing waters. Guest accomodations include lodge rooms as well as cabins with Jacuzzis and woodstoves. Nightly dining (**$$**) *(open to the public)* typically features fresh produce from the inn's own garden, Atlantic salmon, and locally raised lamb from the Margaree Valley. In summer and fall, live music is offered on some evenings.

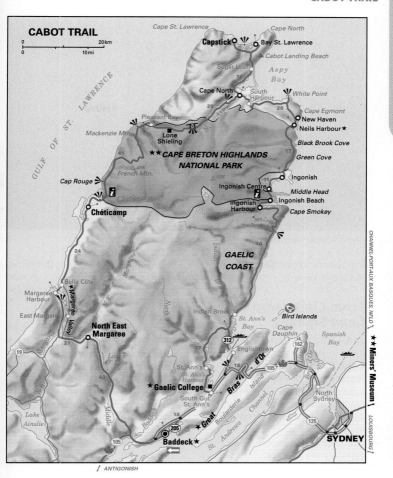

CABOT TRAIL

CHANNEL-PORT-AUX BASQUES, NFLD \ ★★★Miners' Museum \ LOUISBOURG \

/ ANTIGONISH

Margaree Salmon Museum★

♿🕐 *Open mid-Jun–mid-Oct daily 9am–5pm.* 👓*$1.* ☎*902-248-2848. http://fortress.uccb.ns.ca*

This pleasant little museum features a large collection of colourful fishing flies and rods. The life cycle of the Atlantic salmon is illustrated.

The Cabot Trail parallels the Margaree River northward, affording pastoral **views**★. As the road descends, the **view**★ of Margaree Harbour is lovely. The trail crosses the estuary of the Margaree River and heads north along the Acadian coast, with views of the Gulf of St. Lawrence.

Chéticamp

An enclave of Acadian culture, this fishing community lies opposite Chéticamp Island. A stone church dedicated to St. Peter distinguishes the town. Hand-hooked rugs are Chéticamp's claim to fame.

Acadian Museum

PO Box 98 Chéticamp NS, B0E1H0. 🍴♿🅿🕐 *Open May–Oct Mon–Fri 8am–9pm, weekends 9am–5pm. Rest of the year Tue & Fri 1pm–3pm.* ☎*902-224-2170. www.co-opartisanale.com.*

Operated by a cooperative of Acadian women, the museum and gift shop feature hooked mats, rugs and other crafted items. There are demonstrations of hooking, spinning, carding and weav-

Capstick houses and the St. Lawrence

ing. The on-site **restaurant** specializes in Acadian cooking.

From Chéticamp to Cape Smokey

124km/77mi.

Cape Breton Highlands National Park★★

Spanning coast to coast across northern Cape Breton, this 950sq km/367sq mi wilderness park combines seashore and mountains.

The west coast borders the relatively calm waters of the Gulf of St. Lawrence. On the eastern side the Atlantic Ocean pounds the bare rocks with great force, yet there are several fine beaches throughout this preserve. Whales, and even bald eagles, can be found on either shore.

Visit

Ingonish Beach NS, B0C 1L0. ♿🅿🕐*Open year-round.* 🚗*$6 entry fee. Information centres* 🕐*open late Jun–late Aug daily 8am–8pm. Late Aug–late Sept 8am–6pm. Early-May–late-Jun & rest of Sept–mid-Oct daily 9am–5pm) at park entrances north of Chéticamp (*☎ *902-224-3814) and at Ingonish Beach (*☎*902-224-2306). www.pc.gc.ca.*
From the park entrance at the Chéticamp River, Cabot Trail winds up Chéticamp Canyon to emerge on the coast, parallel to the sea, affording fine **views**★★.

From **Cap Rouge** lookout, there is an especially lovely **view**★★. The road gradually climbs French Mountain and heads inland across the plateau.
The road descends to Mackenzie Mountain. Then, by a series of switchbacks, it reaches Pleasant Bay with outstanding **views**★★ on the descent. The **Lone Shieling** *(about 6.5km/4mi from Pleasant Bay, then short walk)* is a replica of a Scottish crofter's cottage. The road climbs North Mountain, descends steeply, affording pretty **views**★, and then enters the valley of the North Aspy River, which it follows to the village of **Cape North.**

Bay St. Lawrence★★

38km/24mi round-trip from Cape North.
 This scenic drive rounds Aspy Bay, affording views of its long sandbar, and then heads inland to St. Lawrence Bay at the north end of Cape Breton Island.
At the end of the road is the tiny fishing village of **Bay St. Lawrence**. Near the approach to the village, a large white clapboard church (St. Margaret's) is prominent. From its grounds the **view**★ of the bay community is picturesque.

▶ *Upon leaving Bay St. Lawrence, turn right and continue 3km/1.8mi to Capstick.*

Capstick

This hillside settlement consists of a few isolated houses above the seacliffs. The dramatic **views**★ of the inlets through the scraggy pines are enhanced by the beauty of the water's color.

▶ *Return to Cabot Trail. After South Harbour, take coast road.*

After fine **views**★ of Aspy Bay, its sandbar and the long Cape North peninsula, the road turns south after White Point through the charming fishing villages of **New Haven** and **Neils Harbour**★.

▶ *Rejoin Cabot Trail.*

This section of the trail is an especially splendid drive along the coast, particularly after **Black Brook Cove.** Worn pink boulders stretch into the sea, while green forests cover the inlands. **Green Cove** is a lovely spot. From Lakie's Head lookout the narrow peninsula of **Middle Head** and towering Cape Smokey can be identified.

The Ingonishs

Ingonish Centre, Ingonish Beach, Ingonish Harbour and other Ingonish designations are popular resort spots. The bay itself is cut into two parts by Middle Head, the dramatic setting of the **Keltic Lodge,** one of Canada's best-known resort hotels. To the south **Cape Smokey** rises out of the sea.

The Gaelic Coast: Cape Smokey to Baddeck

89km/55mi.
The trail climbs over Cape Smokey and then drops again, permitting several good **views**★.
Offshore are the **Bird Islands**, a sanctuary where vast numbers of seabirds nest in summer. The trail rounds St. Ann's Harbour, offering lovely views at South Gut St. Ann's.

Gaelic College★

In St. Ann's. Founded in 1938 by Rev. A.W.R. MacKenzie, this school is the only one on the continent to teach the Gaelic language and Highland arts and crafts. During July and August, the college hosts a *ceilidh* (KAY-lee) featuring local performers *(Wed evening).*

Great Hall of the Clans

51779 Cabot Trail Rd., on campus. ♿🅿🕐*Open early-Jun–Aug daily 9am–5pm. Sept Mon–Fri 9am–5pm.* ✆*$5 adult.* ☎*902-295-3411. www.gaeliccollege.edu.*
Inside the large meeting hall, wall **exhibits,** some interactive, illustrate clan history and life. At one end of the hall stands a statue of Angus MacAskill (1825-63), the 236cm/7ft 9in-tall, 193kg/425-pound "Cape Breton giant" who toured the US with the midget Tom Thumb.

Alternative Route★

22km/14mi by Rte. 312 and Trans-Canada Hwy.
This road enters St. Ann's Bay via a narrow spit of land that divides the bay from St. Ann's Harbour. At the end of the spit, there is a ferry across the outlet (24hrs daily, every 10min. Feb–Apr no crossing if ice. ♿☎*902-861-1911. www.gov.ns.ca).*

Excursions

Great Bras d'Or★

18km/11mi northeast along Trans-Can Hwy. from South Gut St. Ann's.
The road ascends Kelly's Mountain with a fine **view**★ from the lookout of the harbour, the spit of land and the ferry. Crossing Cape Dauphin peninsula, it descends to the Great Bras d'Or. There are good **views**★ of this stretch of water, of the bridge that spans it and, in the distance, of **Sydney,** Cape Breton's principal city.

Miners' Museum★★

42 Birkley St., PO Box 310, Glace Bay NS, B1A 5T8. 19km/12mi northeast of Sydney. Follow museum signs from town to Quarry Point.
Overlooking the vast Atlantic Ocean, this low-lying, geometric museum stands as a monument to Cape Breton's coal-mining history, which ended in 1984.

Visit

✕♿🅿🕐*Open Jun–Aug daily 10am–6pm (Tue 7pm). Sept–Oct Mon–Sun 9am-4pm. Rest of the year Mon–Fri 9am–4pm. Res-*

taurant May–Oct noon–8pm. ⬅$5 adult (🚶‍guided mine tour an additional $5. Protective clothing provided). ✆902-849-4522. *www.minersmuseum.com.*

Retired miners conduct **mine tours** *(30min)*, interspersing commentary with tales from personal experience. *Note: low mine ceilings may necessitate stooping for periods of time.*

Beside the museum building, a **miners' village** has been reconstructed. In addition to a store, a miner's house of the period 1850-1900 has been re-created.The restaurant *(hours vary)* serves home-cooked specialties such as "coal dust pie."

Halifax★★

POPULATION 359,183 – MAP P 359

The capital of Nova Scotia overlooks one of the finest harbours in the world. The deep outer inlet of the Atlantic Ocean narrows into a protected inner harbour called the **Bedford Basin**. The foot-shaped peninsula upon which the city was built is dominated by a hill, topped with a star-shaped citadel. These two factors—a natural harbour and a man-made fortress—were the basis of the city's founding.

🛈 **Information:** Scotia Square Visitors' Centre, 5251 Duke St., ✆902-490-5963. www.halifaxinfo.com

▶ **Orient Yourself:** Halifax lies on the east coast of Nova Scotia, at about the mainland's mid-point, facing the Atlantic Ocean.

🅿 **Parking:** Downtown Halifax is quite congested and parking is difficult. Meters are colour-coded to indicate the maximum time you can park. Red means 30min, grey 1hr, green 2hrs and yellow 5hrs. The rate is $1 an hour. There are also public and private lots.

🚲 **Don't Miss:** The citadel is historic and has lovely views; a cruise on Bluenose II, if possible.

🕐 **Organizing Your Time:** You will need at least two days to see Halifax; it is a good base from which to tour the area.

🧒 **Especially for Kids:** The Museum of the Atlantic has actual ships berthed alongside, including Bluenose II, and the Museum of Natural History has exhibits for children. The Pier 21 immigration shed has exhibits for children.

🖐 **Also See:** ATLANTIC SHORE, ANAPOLIS VALLEY

Harbourfront, Halifax

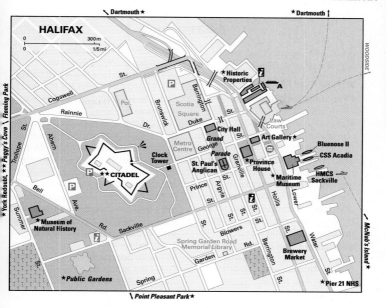

HALIFAX

A Bit of History

Early History – Halifax came into being because of the existence of Louisbourg. New Englanders had successfully captured the French fortress in 1745, only to see it later returned to France. Responding to their anger, in 1749 the governor of Nova Scotia, Col. **Edward Cornwallis,** and about 2,500 English settlers constructed a fortified settlement on the site of the present-day city.

From its inception Halifax was shaped by shaped the military—from the social gatherings of the nobility (officers in both services) to the presence of brothels along the wharves. Even law was martial; citizens had no power for nearly 100 years, until Halifax achieved city status.

The Royal Princes – Forbidden by their father to remain in England, two scapegrace sons of **George III** made Halifax their home. The future **William IV** spent his 21st birthday in wild revels off the port. His brother **Edward,** Duke of Kent, and later the father of Queen

The Halifax Explosion

During both world wars, Halifax's Bedford Basin was used as a convoy assembly point so ships could cross the Atlantic in the safety of numbers if German submarines were encountered. In December 1917 a French munitions ship, the **Mont Blanc,** was carrying a lethal combination of picric acid, guncotton, TNT and benzola. It collided in the harbor with a Belgian relief ship, the **Imo.** Until the atom bomb was dropped on Hiroshima in 1945, the resulting explosion was the largest man-made cataclysm in world history. The entire north end of the city was leveled. Windows were shattered as far as Truro, 100km/60mi away. The explosion was heard over 160km/100mi away. Only the *Mont Blanc's* cannon (found in Albro Lake behind Dartmouth) and an anchor shaft (which landed more than 3km/2mi away) were left. Miraculously, the crews survived, having abandoned ship in time. However, 1,400 people were killed outright, an estimated 600 died later, 199 were blinded and another 9,000 were injured. There are people in Halifax today who, injured for life as children, are still receiving compensation.

Address Book

For dollar sign categories, see the Legend on the cover flap.

WHERE TO STAY

$ Fountainview Guest House – *2138 Robie St., B3K 4M5.* ☎*902-422-4169, toll-free 1-800-565-4877. www. angelfire.com/id/fountainview. 8 rooms.* 🅿️.Situated across from Halifax Commons and a short walk from Citadel Hill, this guest house lies close to restaurants and commercial services. Fountainview offers variously sized clean rooms with shared bathrooms. For an extra charge, a light breakfast can be served in your room.

$ Fresh Start B&B – *2720 Gottingen St., B3K 3C7.* ☎*902-453-6616, toll-free 1-888-453-6616. www.bbcanada. com/2262.html. 8 rooms.* 🅿️🛏️.
This restored Victorian house is located near Macdonald Bridge, about a mile from Citadel Hill. Clean, comfortable rooms come with private or shared bathroom. Breakfast features fresh-baked pastries and fruit salad with eggs Benedict, ham and cheese casserole or hot egg salad on an English muffin.

$$ Citadel Halifax Hotel – *1960 Brunswick St., B3J 2G7.* ☎*902-422-1391, toll-free 1- 800-565-7162. www.citadel-halifax.com. 267 rooms.* ✕🅿️🛏️. Located on the edge of the central downtown core, this modern hotel sits on a hillside, within easy walking distance of the Halifax Citadel, and offers an economical alternative to the large downtown chain hotels. Recently renovated guest rooms offer modern amenities, while the restaurant, botaniCa, **($$)** offers a menu of Canadian fare.

$$ Halliburton House Inn – *5184 Morris St., B3J 1B3.* ☎*902-420-0658, toll-free 1-888-512-3344. www.halliburton.ns.ca. 29 rooms.* ✕🅿️🛏️. Housed in three contiguous early 19C town houses, this downtown hostelry has the charm of a country inn. A tasteful sitting room with wing chairs, oil portraits and a fireplace greets arriving guests. Rates include a light breakfast. **Stories ($$$)**, (☎*902-444-4400*) the hotel restaurant, is renowned for its inventive fusion-style entrées (caribou ravioli, ahi tuna

with Asian tomato vinaigrette). Enjoy the garden courtyard in summer.

$$ The Lord Nelson Hotel and Suites – *1515 South Park St., B3J 2L2.* ☎*902-423-6331 or 800-565-2020. www.lordnelson-hotel.com. 260 rooms.* ✕♿🅿️. Recently overhauled, this 1928 landmark, built by the Canadian Pacific Railway, preserves its Edwardian ambience while offering 21C amenities. The spacious lobby has warm walnut panelling and a coffered ceiling. Renovated rooms are handsomely decorated in soothing colors; many overlook the neighbouring Public Gardens. The English pub-style **Victory Arms** restaurant **($)** serves breakfast, lunch and dinner.

$$ Prince George Hotel – *1725 Market St. B3J 3N9.* ☎*902-425-1986, toll-free 1-800-565-1567. www.princegeorgehotel. com. 203 rooms.* ✕♿🅿️. Situated in the heart of downtown near the Metro Centre (a hockey and entertainment venue) and six blocks from the waterfront, the Prince George features a fitness centre with state-of-the-art exercise equipment and a heated indoor pool. The **Gio** restaurant **($$$)** offers a sophisticated menu with local products, such as sablefish with herb risotto, or lamb with roasted beets and blue potatoes. (☎*902-425-1987*). For excursions, the hotel will pack a lunch for you.

$$ Waverley Inn – *1266 Barrington St., B3J 1Y5.* ☎*902-423-9346, toll-free 1-800-565-9346. www.waverleyinn.com. 34 rooms.* ♿🅿️🛏️. Guest rooms in this historic 1870s inn are richly furnished with Victorian antiques, massive wooden beds and modern amenities. Deluxe rooms feature feather duvets and whirlpool baths. A hospitality suite provides round-the-clock snacks as well as a complimentary breakfast.

WHERE TO EAT

$ Cellar Bar & Grill – *5677 Breton Pl. off South Park St.* ☎*902-492-4412.* **Mediterranean**. This two-room establishment caters chiefly to a loyal clientele with its wood-burning fireplaces and knowledgeable staff. A variety of gourmet pizzas (smoked salmon and chèvre) and pastas (topped with sausage and peppers; spinach and prosciutto; or curried chicken and shrimp) are offered along with entrées such as haddock, salmon, and jambalaya with grilled cornbread.

$ Economy Shoe Shop Café – *1661-1663 Argyle St.* ☎*902-423-7463. www.economyshoeshop.ca.* **Canadian.** A neon sign from an old cobbler's shop inspired this odd name. The place is several businesses in one. The **Shoe Shop** is a bar frequented by artistic types. The **Backstage** restaurant caters to the after-theatre crowd; a fake tree stands in the middle. The **Diamond** is a musician's bar with juke-box music where smoking is permitted. The **Belgian Bar** serves beer amidst a lot of green foliage, for some reason.

$ Tomasino's Pizzeria and Cellar Ristorante – *5173 South St. B3J 1A2.* ☎*902-422-9757.* **Italian.** Located at Hollis Street, across from the Westin, this subterranean trattoria with brick walls and flickering candles features gourmet pizzas and pastas. Chicken fusilli (chicken breast in pesto, tomatoes and cream) is popular. In summer patrons can dine on the sidewalk patio.

$ Bluenose II Restaurant – *1824 Hollis St., B3J 1W4.* ☎*902-425-5092.* **Greek.** For over 25 years the Bluenose has been serving home-style food at wallet-pleasing prices at the corner of Duke and Hollis, near Historic Properties. Famous for milk shakes, clams and chips, and Greek staples like souvlaki and moussaka, the restaurant recently added vegetarian selections such as spinach lasagna, fettuccine Alfredo, veggie burgers.

Bud the Spud, *Spring Garden Rd. near Memorial Public Library.* A familiar sight in warm weather, this red and white "chip wagon" has had a seasonally reserved parking space in front of the city's main library for years. Visitors and local residents, ensnared by the scent of vinegar and ketchup, gather on park benches or rest on the stone wall along Spring Garden Road to munch Bud's spuds by the trayful. Most Haligonians consider these french-fried potatoes unrivalled anywhere and best eaten with bare fingers. So get in line and grab a stack of paper napkins. Bud's fries are greasy, but good!

$$ Il Mercato Ristorante – *5650 Spring Garden Rd.B3J 3M7.* ♿☎*902-422-2866. www.il-mercato.ca.* **Italian.** Situated on a bustling shopping street, this lively restaurant offers creative pasta, pizza and focaccia sandwiches as well as well-prepared main courses. Favourites include ravioli stuffed with roasted chicken and linguine with seafood medley.

$$$ Da Maurizio Dining Room – *1496 Lower Water St.B3J 1R7. Dinner only. Closed Sun.* ☎*902-423-0859. www.damaurizio.ca.* ♿**Italian.** Haligonians consider this restaurant, located in the historic Alexander Keith brewery, one of the finest in the city. Chef Maurizio Bertossi's offers a menu that is refined, imaginative and authentically Italian. Signature dishes include *agnello scotta-dito* (roasted rack of lamb with roasted garlic, lamb stock and red wine reduction), and *scallopini de vitello all'astice* (veal scallopini sautéed with Atlantic lobster in an herbed cream).

ENTERTAINMENT

Neptune Theatre - *1593 Argyle St., B3J 2B2.* ☎*902-429-7070, toll-free 1-800-565-7345. www.neptunetheatre.com.* For 45 years, this theatre has delighted thousands of patrons with professionally staged musicals, dramas and comedies. A showcase of Maritime talent, the Neptune balances fresh compositions by new artists with traditional favourites. Many productions have been written by regional playwrights and performed by local actors and dancers as well as international stars. Operating season-ally *(Sept–May, sometimes to Jul)*, the Neptune allots most shows a month-and-a-half run, although the first regional production of the popular *Les Miserables* extended well beyond that. Initially built as a vaudeville house and later used as a cinema, the structure was converted in 1963 to a playhouse. In 1997 a multimillion-dollar transformation resulted in virtually a new complex with improved seating, air-conditioning, an expanded backstage area and intimate studio space.

Victoria, served as commander in chief in Halifax from 1794 to 1800. Spending a fortune on defences, he made Halifax a member of the famous quadrilateral of British defences, which included Gibraltar and Bermuda. He installed the first telegraph system in North America by which he could relay orders to his men from Annapolis Royal or from Bedford Basin, where his mistress lived.

The City Today – Halifax is the largest city in the Atlantic provinces and the region's commercial and financial heart as well as a major seaport and as the Atlantic base of the **Canadian Navy.** Halifax's hilly streets are stacked with colourful wooden houses. During the summer months, seaside restaurants and cafes bustle, boats from nearby yacht clubs fill the harbour and large cruise ships linger in port.

Sights

Halifax Citadel National Historic Site★★

The present star-shaped citadel is the fourth fort since 1749 to crown the hill over looking Halifax. Begun in 1828 at the order of the Duke of Wellington, the fort was completed in 1856. Although never attacked, it was occupied by the military until after World War II.

The citadel's site offers **views**★ of the city, harbour, Dartmouth, George's Island and the Angus McDonald suspension bridge. Note the attractive **clock tower,** the symbol of Halifax; the 1803 original was ordered by Prince Edward.

The fortification contains a large central parade ground where soldiers attired in 19C uniforms perform military drills *(mid-Jun–Labour Day daily)*.

Visit

✕🅿️🕐*Grounds open year-round. Citadel open Jul–Aug daily 9am–6pm; May–Jun and Sept–Oct 9am–5pm. Rest of the year grounds open without services.* 🕐*Closed Dec. 25.* 🎫*$11 ($7.15 off-season).* ☎902-426-5080. www.pc.gc.ca.

Visitors can walk on the ramparts and visit the outer ditches and ravelins. An audiovisual presentation *(50min)*, **Tides of History,** covers the history of Halifax and its defences. Precisely at midday every day, the **noon gun** is fired.

Historic Properties and the Harbour★

Off Upper Water Street, the pedestrian area between Duke Street and the Cogswell interchange is called the Historic Properties. Several 19C stone ware-

CSS Acadia, Maritime Museum of the Atlantic

houses and wooden buildings house shops, studios, restaurants and pubs. From Historic Properties visitors can walk west through a series of restored buildings to the Granville Street Mall and Scotia Square. A **boardwalk** follows the harbourfront north around the Sheraton Hotel and south past the Law Courts and the terminus of the passenger ferry to Dartmouth to the **brewery market.** A former brewery, the complex now houses several restaurants, shops and a farmers' market (*Sat 7am–1pm*).

Harbour Cruise★★ (A)

Departs from the Cable Wharf mid-May– mid-Oct daily 10am & 2pm (also 6:30pm Mon–Wed in peak season). Round-trip 2hrs. $22 adult. 1hr tour at 4:30pm $18 adult. Murphy's on the Water Tours 902-420-1015. www.murphysonthewater.com.

The Haligonian III cruise provides a view of the installations around Halifax harbour. The cruise rounds Point Pleasant and enters the **North West Arm,** a lovely stretch of water extending along the peninsula's west side and bordered by expensive homes and yacht clubs.

Maritime Museum of the Atlantic★

1675 Lower Water St., Halifax NS, B3J 1S3. Open May–Oct daily 9:30am– 5:30pm (Tue 8pm; Sun opens 1pm May & Oct). Rest of the year Tue–Sat 9:30am– 5pm (Tue 8pm), Sun 1–5pm. Closed Jan 1, Good Friday, Dec 25–26. $8.50 adult ($4 Nov–Apr). 902-424-7490. http:// maritime.museum.gov.ns.ca.

Note the restored ship's **chandlery,** housed in an old warehouse. Other highlights include an extensive display on the *Titanic* and a recounting of the Halifax explosion.

Outside, moored at the museum's wharf, The **CSS Acadia,** a steamship built in 1913 for the Canadian Hydrographic Service, can be boarded (*May to mid-Oct*).

In summer the **Bluenose II,** a replica of the schooner that held the International Fishermen's trophy for 17 years, offers **cruises** in Halifax Harbour when not visiting other ports (*Departs from museum's wharf Jun–Sept. Call Lunenburg Marine*

FISHERMAN'S COVE

200 Government Wharf Rd., Eastern Passage NS, B3G 1M7. (to end of Rte. 111 South from either harbour bridge, then Rte. 322 South). Visitor Information Centre, Bldg 24. 902-465-8009. www.fishermanscove.ns.ca.

Situated on the Atlantic Ocean side of Dartmouth, this little cove is accessible by car or Taxsea from Halifax's Cable Wharf. Fishing boats bob in the water along the wharf and colourfully painted huts resemble fishermen's quarters. Crafts sold include fine Nova Scotian artwork and regionally published books. Fresh seafood and sky-high lemon meringue pie are popular dishes at **Boondock's Dining Room** (*200 Government Wharf Rd., Blg #6, 902-465-3474. www.boondocksdining.ca*). A raised boardwalk leads through the sea grass near the water's edge.

Museum for schedule and reservations 902-634-634-4794. Bluenose II Preservation Trust 902-634-1963 or 866-579-4909 Canada & US. www.bluenose2.ns.ca).

The restored **HMCS Sackville,** a World War II corvette that served in the Battle of the Atlantic, can also be boarded (*Jun–Oct. $2. 902-429-2132*).

Province House★

1726 Hollis St., Halifax NS, B3J 2Y3. Open Jul–Aug Mon–Fri 9am–5pm, weekends & holidays 10am–4pm. Rest of the year Mon–Fri 9am–4pm. To book a tour 902-424-4661. www.gov. ns.ca/legislature. Visitors must secure a pass from the front desk.

This Georgian 1819 sandstone structure houses the Legislative Assembly of Nova Scotia, which has existed since 1758. Visitors can see the **Red Chamber,** where the Legislative Council used to meet, and observe debates in the **assembly chamber**. Once housing the provincial Supreme Court, the **legislative library** was the site, in 1835, of the self-defence of journalist **Joseph Howe** against a charge of criminal libel. His acquittal marked the beginning of a free press in Nova Scotia.

SHUBENACADIE PARK

Locks Rd., Dartmouth (Rte. 111 South from either harbour bridge, take the Waverley Rd. exit, watch for signs). ☎902-462-1826. Over a century ago, the historic Shubenacadie Canal linked Halifax Harbour with the Bay of Fundy through a series of connected lakes and rivers. Today part of the canal route cuts through a park with scenic walking and biking trails that edge two lakes. Restored canal locks lie along the trails, and there is an historical exhibit at the Fairbanks Centre. The park includes a campground, playground, swimming area and boat rentals (canoes, kayaks, paddleboats).

Art Gallery of Nova Scotia★

1723 Hollis St., Halifax NS, B3J 3C8. ✕ ♿ ◷*Open daily 10am–5pm, Thur 9pm.*◷*Closed Dec 24-26 & Jan 1.* ⊜*$12 adult.* ☜*Tours daily 2:30 pm, Thu also 7pm.* ☎902-424-7542. *www.agns.gov. ns.ca.*

Housed in the stately Dominion Building and the adjacent Provincial Building, this modern museum exhibits Canadian art, including paintings of the **Group of Seven,** as well as international art. Regional **folk art**—painting, sculptures, paper and textiles—is a highlight. The museum possesses a small but excellent collection of **Inuit art.** Since 2006, a satellite branch is located in Yarmouth.

Grand Parade

Bordered by **City Hall** at one end and **St. Paul's Anglican Church** at the other, this pleasant square has been the centre of Halifax since its founding. The small, timber-framed church is the oldest Protestant church in Canada (1750).

Museum of Natural History★

Kids *1747 Summer St., Halifax NS, B3H 3A6.* ♿ 🅿 ◷*Open Jun–mid-Oct Mon– Sat 9:30am–5:30pm (Wed 8pm), Sun 1pm–5:30pm. Rest of the year Tue–Sat 9:30am–5pm (Wed 8pm), Sun 1pm–5pm.* ⊜*$5.50 summer, $3.50 winter adult. No charge Wed after 5pm.* ☎902-424-7353. *www.nature.museum.gov.ns.ca.*

Mi'kmaq exhibits and archaeological displays, natural-history dioramas and marine life, especially whales and sharks, can be viewed. Kids especially will enjoy the saltwater touch tank and re-created beehive, and, at the **nature centre,** snakes, frogs and Gus the turtle.

Public Gardens★

Main entrance at corner of Spring Garden Rd. and South Park St. ♿ ◷*Open mid-Apr–mid-Nov daily 8am–dusk.* ☎902-490-4894. *www.halifaxpublicgardens. ca.*

Opened to the public in 1867, this 7ha/17-acre park is a fine example of a Victorian garden, with weeping trees, ponds, fountains, statues, formal plantings and an ornate bandstand. Note the massive wrought-iron entrance gate.

Point Pleasant Park★

◷*Closed to traffic; parking on Point Pleasant Dr. at Tower Rd. and near container terminal.* ◷*Open year-round daily dawn–dusk.* ☎902-490-4894. *www. pointpleasantpark.ca.*

Situated at the southernmost point of the peninsula, this lovely 75ha/186-acre park has excellent **views★★** of the harbour and the North West Arm. In 2003, an almost direct hit by Hurricane Juan destroyed more than 75,000 trees in the park. An extensive two-year series of public consultations led to a long-term plan to renew the park.

Prince of Wales Tower

◷*Grounds open year-round. Tower open Jul–Labour Day daily 10am–6pm.* ☎902-426-5080. *www.pc.gc.ca.*

The prototype of what came to be called a **Martello tower,** this circular stone structure was the first of its kind in North America. Prince Edward ordered its construction in 1796, naming the tower for his brother—the future George IV.

Pier 21★

Kids *1055 Marginal Rd., Halifax NS, B3H 4P6.* ♿ 🅿 ◷*Open May–Nov daily 9:30am– 5:30pm. Dec–Mar Tue–Sat 10am–5pm. April Mon–Sat 10am–5pm.*◷*Closed Dec 45–35.* ⊜*$8.50.* ☎902-425-7770. *www. pier21.ca.*

Over a million refugees, immigrants and war brides passed through this immigration shed from 1928 until 1971. The pier was also the departure point for World War II troops on their way to Europe. Displays recount the compelling story of the largely European influx. Children especially will enjoy the hands-on activities and the period railway car.

Excursions

McNab's Island★

Access by ferry from Halifax waterfront. For schedules contact the tourist office in Halifax: ☎902-490-5946.

Located in Halifax Harbour, east of Point Pleasant Park, the island has thick forests, colourful wildflowers and large pond. Old roads serve as walking and cycling trails that lead to the remains of Fort McNab *(at the south end)*, sand beaches and good views, especially from the lighthouse.

Sir Sandford Fleming Park

5.5km/3mi by Cogswell St., Quinpool Rd. and Purcell's Cove Rd. (Rte. 253). ◷Open year-round daily 8am–dusk. Walking trails, swimming, boating, picnic area. ♿ℙ☎902-490-4000.

This park is a tribute to **Sir Sandford Fleming** (1827-1915), a Scottish engineer who helped build Canada's continental railway system, designed the nation's first postage stamp and urged the adoption of international standard time.
The long stretch of North West Arm can be seen in its entirety from **Dingle Tower** (◷*Open May–Oct daily 8am–5pm*).

York Redoubt★

11km/7mi by Cogswell St., Quinpool Rd. and Purcell's Cove Rd. (Rte. 253). ℙ◷Grounds open year-round. ☎902-426-5080. www.pc.gc.ca.

First constructed in 1793, the defences were strengthened by Prince Edward, who named the redoubt for his brother, the Duke of York. During World War II, helped defend against German attack. At the south end, the **command post** contains displays on the defences, and

from it *(weather permitting)* there are good **views**★ of the harbour.

Dartmouth★

Site of a large naval dockyard and research centre, Halifax's twin city on the other side of the inlet has a pleasant waterfront with several shop-lined streets descending to it. A small waterside park, a venue for summer concerts, features the World Peace Pavilion. Connected to Halifax by two bridges, Dartmouth is serviced by **ferry,** from which the views of both cities are expansive (♿ℙ◷*Departs from Lower Water St. in Halifax daily. ◷No service Jan 1, Good Friday, Easter Sunday & Dec 25. 12min.⊜$2. ☎902-490-4000. www.region.halifax. ns.ca/metrotransit*).

The Quaker House

57 Ochterloney St., Dartmouth NS, B2Y 1C3✎Visit by guided tour only. ◷Early Jun–Labour Day Tue–Sun 10am–1pm, 2pm–5pm.☎902-464-2253. www.dartmouthheritagemuseum.ns.ca.

A short stroll from the ferry terminal, this heritage house is the sole survivor of 22 dwellings built for a group of Quaker whalers who moved to the province from New England in 1785.

Black Cultural Centre for Nova Scotia

1149 Main St., Dartmouth NS, B2Z 1A8 ♿ℙ◷Open Jun–Sept Mon–Fri 9am–5pm, Sat 10am–3pm. Rest of the year Mon–Fri 9am–5pm. ⊜$6 adult. ☎902-434-6223, toll-free 1-800-465-0767 (US/Canada). www.bccns.com.

This sizable museum, library and meeting hall foster the province's black history and culture. There is a memorial to naval hero **William Hall** (1827-1904), the first Nova Scotian and first black to be awarded the Victoria Cross, the Commonwealth's military medal for exceptional courage.

Uniacke Estate Museum Park★

758 Main Rd., in Mt. Uniacke, 40km/25mi northwest by Rtes. 7 and 1. Grounds ℙ◷Open year-round daily dawn–dusk. House open Jun–mid-Oct Mon–Sat 9:30am–5:30pm, Sun 11am–5:30pm.

$3.25 adult. ☎902-866-0032. http://museum.gov.ns.ca.

This fine example of plantation-style Colonial architecture, completed in 1815, was the country home of Richard Uniacke, attorney general of Nova Scotia from 1797 to 1830.

The interior looks today as it did in 1815, including several mahogany pieces crafted by George Adams of London.

Peggy's Cove★★

43km/27mi. ♿See description under ATLANTIC SHORE.

Fortress of Louisbourg★★★

MAP P 359

Guarding the entrance of the St. Lawrence River, the approach to Quebec, Louisbourg was once the great 18C fortress of New France, manned by the largest garrison in North America. The $25 million restoration of this National Historic Site is the most expensive preservation project ever undertaken by the Canadian government.

- **Information:** Fortress of Louisbourg National Historic Site, PO Box 160, Louisbourg NS, B0A 1M0. ☎902-733-2280. www.louisbourg.ca. Also pc.gc.ca
- ▶ **Orient Yourself:** Cross the Canso Causeway to Cape Breton Island and follow Route 4 or 105 to Sydney, then southwest on Route 22 to Louisbourg.
- **Parking:** Free parking at the visitor centre; 7–10 minute bus ride to the fortress.
- **Don't Miss:** A meal in one of the three period restaurants, served on earthenware and pewter by costumed staff.
- **Organizing Your Time:** Bring what you'll need for the visit: returning to your car is time-consuming.
- **Especially for Kids:** There is a Children's Interpretive Centre at the Rodrigue House in July–August.
- **Also See:** CABOT TRAIL

A Bit of History

A Bleak Beginning – When the French lost the mainland of Nova Scotia in 1713, they decided to construct a fortified town on the eastern peninsula of Île Royale (now Cape Breton); work began in 1719.

The massive undertaking was riddled with problems: a harsh climate, a boggy site, scarce building materials and a few corrupt French officials. Difficult living conditions and lack of discipline among the common soldiers contributed to a mutiny in 1744.

A Not-So-Impregnable Fortress – In 1745, prior to completion, 4,000 New Englanders attacked the "impregnable" fortress. Less than two months later the French surrendered. In 1748 the British agreed to return the fort to the island colony of King **Louis XV,** founding Halifax as a counter-fortress. Ten years later Louisbourg surrendered again, this time to British regulars. **James Wolfe,** the second in command, went on to capture Quebec City in 1759. To prevent further threat, the British destroyed Louisbourg in 1760.

Since 1961 one-quarter of the fortress has been rebuilt according to the original plans and historical records.

Access

37km/23mi south of Sydney by Rte. 22, southwest of town of Louisbourg.

Visit

✕♿🅿️🕐Open Jul–Aug daily 9am–5pm. May–Jun & Sept–Oct daily 9:30am–5pm. May & Oct 16–31, no costumed interpre-

Streetscape, Fortress of Louisbourg

Gwen Cannon/MICHELIN

tors or services; tours led by Parks Canada guide. ◐*Closed Nov–Apr.* ﹩*$13.50 adult Jun–Sept, $5.50 adult May & Oct.*. ☎*902-733-2280. www.louisbourg.ca. Also pc.gc. ca. Note: Be prepared for cool temperatures, rain and fog. Comfortable walking shoes recommended.*

Models of the fortress and displays on the history of Louisbourg provide orientation in the **visitor centre** *(departure point for bus to fortress)*. Visitors enter the walled town through the elaborate **Dauphine Gate,** manned by a sentry. Over 50 buildings *(most open to the public)* are constructed of wood or roughcast masonry, some furnished to their 1740s appearance, others containing themed exhibits. In the summer season, costumed staff portray 18C French society's leisure, propertied and working classes. Popular attractions include a **bakery,** where bread similar to the kind King Louis' troops lined up for in

1744 can be purchased. Along the quay stands the high wooden **Frédéric Gate,** the entrance through which important visitors to this once-bustling port were ushered from the harbour. The rich furnishings on the ground floor of the **ordonnateur's residence** include a harpsichord of the period. Archaeological artifacts recovered during reconstruction are on display at various locations.

King's Bastion★★

Quarters for the garrison provide insight into the lives of the privileged and impoverished in Old World society. The **governor's apartments** consist of 10 elegant rooms, lavishly furnished. Not as comfortable but well accommodated are the **officers' quarters.** The **soldiers' barracks** are drafty and spartan. The **prison** and a **chapel** can also be visited.

Maitland

MAP P 359

Maitland was once an important shipbuilding centre best known as the site of the construction of the largest wooden ship built in Canada, the **William D. Lawrence.** Today Maitland's fine houses attest to the wealth created by the former industry.

- **Information:** Lawrence House Museum, 8660 Hwy. 215, RR#1, Maitland NS, B0N 1T0. ☎902-261-2628., toll-free 1-888-743-7845 (US/Canada) http://museum.gov.ns.ca.
- ▶ **Orient Yourself:** Maitland overlooks Cobequid Bay in the Minas Basin, directly east of Saint John.
- **Parking:** There is parking near the museum.
- **Don't Miss:** You can look through binoculars from the housetop to appreciate William Lawrence's view of his shipyard.
- **Organizing Your Time:** The Maitland-Truro area is an easy excursion from Halifax.
- **Especially for Kids:** There is an outdoor educational display about shipbuilding.
- **Also See:** TRURO, BALMORAL MILLS

Sight

Lawrence House Museum★

Open Jun–mid-Oct Mon–Sat 9:30am–5:30pm, Sun 1pm–5:30pm. $3.50. ☎902-261-2628. http://museum. gov.ns.ca.

Surrounded by elm trees, this two-and-a-half-storey house is a splendid example of the grand residences of Nova Scotia's shipbuilders and sea captains. William Dawson Lawrence built this house (c.1870) to overlook his shipyard on the Shubenacadie River at the point where it joins Cobequid Bay. Believing he could double a ship's size without doubling its operating costs, Lawrence constructed an 80m/262ft ship that weighed 2,459 tonnes and had three masts, the highest being over 60m/200ft. Launched in 1874, the ship sailed all over the world.

The house contains most of its original furnishings, including shipbuilding artifacts, pictures of 19C ships and a 2m/7ft model of the *William D. Lawrence.*

A lookout area across the road from the house affords visitors a good **view**★ of the tidal flats.

Sherbrooke★

MAP P 359

Once the location of a French fort (1655), the settlement was abandoned after capture by the English in 1669 until people were attracted by the rich timberlands in 1800. During the early 19C, sawmills sprang up and wooden ships were built. Gold was discovered in 1861, and for about 20 years the town flourished. Today it is a centre for sports fishing and tourism.

- **Information:** Sherbrooke Village, PO Box 209, Sherbrooke NS, B0J 3C0. ☎902-522-2400. http://museum.gov.ns.ca
- **Orient Yourself:** Sherbrooke lies on the St. Mary's River, on the northeast coast of the mainland.
- **Parking:** There is parking near the village.
- **Don't Miss:** A photograph in 19C costume will make you grateful for modern fashion.
- **Organizing Your Time:** From Sherbrook, you can continue on Hwy 7 towards the Canso Causeway and Cape Breton Island.
- **Especially for Kids:** Unusually for a restored village, Sherbrooke is a real town, so children may find it particularly lively, especially the jail.
- **Also See:** HALIFAX, CABOT TRAIL

Sherbrooke Village★★

This historic village is actually an extension of the town of Sherbrooke. Streets have been closed to traffic.

Visit

🄺🆇🅰🅿🕐*Open Jun–mid-Oct daily 9:30am–5:30pm. ☜$9. ☎902-522-2400, toll-free 1-888-743-7845 (US/Canada). http://museum.gov.ns.ca.*
Built in 1862 with separate downstairs and upstairs cells for men and women, the **jail** occupied half the jailer's house.

Of particular interest is the **boatbuilding shop** where wooden boats are still constructed. Above Cumminger Brothers' general store, visitors can don 19C costumes and be photographed in the ambrotype **photography studio.** The hotel serves 1880s fare such as cottage pudding and gingerbread.
Removed from the village is **McDonald Brothers' Mill** *(.4km/.3mi)*, an operational water-powered sawmill. A short walk away, a reconstructed **lumber camp** of the 19C shows the living conditions of loggers.

Springhill★★

POPULATION 3,941 – MAP P 359

This town is famous for its coal-mine disasters. In 1891 an enormous blast in one of the mines followed by a flame killed 125 men. Then, in 1916, a subterranean fire caused much damage, though no deaths. An explosion and fire in 1956 caused 39 deaths. The next year a fire razed the business district of the town. Finally, in 1958, an underground upheaval, or "bump," killed 76 men. The mines closed in 1962.

- **Information:** Tourist Information Booth at Community Centre, 6 Main St., Springhill NS, ☎902-597-3000. http://town.springhill.ns.ca
- **Orient Yourself:** Springhill is located inland on the "arm" of the peninsula, east of the Isthmus of Chignecto, just off the Trans-Canada Highway.
- **Also See:** FORT BEAUSÉJOUR, BALMORAL MILLS

Sight

Miners' Museum★★

On Black River Rd. Follow signs along Rte. 2 (Parrsboro direction). Open Jun–mid-Oct daily 9am–5pm. $4.50. 902-597-3449. http://town.springhill.ns.ca.
This museum commemorates the disasters and the bravery of the rescuers through displays such as newspaper clippings and mining equipment. The interesting **mine tour** is conducted by retired miners. Equipped with hard hats, rubber coats and boots, visitors descend about 270m/900ft into the old Syndicate Mine via a tunnel of regular height, rather than those along which the miners had to crawl. Both old and new mining methods are demonstrated.

Truro

POPULATION 11,765 – MAP P 359

Set on the Salmon River near its mouth, this city experiences the high tides of the Bay of Fundy and the tidal bore. Site of a thriving Acadian community called Cobequid before the Deportation, Truro was later settled by people from Northern Ireland and New Hampshire. Today this manufacturing centre is home to the Nova Scotia Agricultural College.

- **Information:** Welcome Centre, Victoria Square. ☎902-893-2922 (May–Oct). www.town.truro.ns.ca
- **Orient Yourself:** Truro lies at the very end of Cobequid Bay, a long finger of the Bay of Fundy.
- **Parking:** Parking area beside Palliser restaurant.
- **Organizing Your Time:** Contact the Welcome Centre for time of next bore.
- **Also See:** SPRINGHILL, MAITLAND, BALMORAL MILLS

Sight

Tidal Bore★

- *Viewpoint: leave Hwy. 102 at Exit 14 and take Tidal Bore Rd. (left on Robie and left again on Tidal Bore Rd., if coming from Halifax).*

Twice a day the tide rushes up the Salmon River from the Bay of Fundy, causing a wave that may vary from a ripple to several feet in height. What is more interesting than this tidal wave is the tremendous inrush of water and the rapid rise in water level immediately following it. In fact, high tide is reached just over an hour after the arrival of the bore.

PRINCE EDWARD ISLAND

POPULATION 135,851 – MAP P 414

The birthplace of Canadian Confederation, and Canada's smallest province, this crescent-shaped island is only 225km/140mi long. Iron oxides give the soil its characteristic brick red color; and on summer days the landscape presents a kaleidoscope of green fields, blue sea and sky, red soil and puffy white clouds.

🅘 **Information:** Tourist Office, 6 Prince Street, Charlottetown PE, C1A 4P5.
☎902-368-4444 or 888-734-7529 or www.gentleisland.com
▶ **Orient Yourself:** Separated from Newfoundland by the Gulf of St. Lawrence, the island is just 14km/9mi from New Brunswick and 22km/14mi from Nova Scotia across the Northumberland Strait.
🕓 **Organizing Your Time:** You can tour the island from a base in Charlottetown.
♿ **Also See:** NOVA SCOTIA, NEW BRUNSWICK, NEWFOUNDLAND

A Bit of History

Île-St.-Jean and the Acadian Deportation – Jacques Cartier claimed the island for France in 1534, naming it Île-St.-Jean. In the 18C, French settlers founded **Port la Joye,** near the present site of Charlottetown. When in 1758 England removed the Acadians under the Deportation Order, about 30 families went into hiding.

Prince Edward and Confederation – In 1799 the colony was named Prince Edward Island in honour of a son of King George III of England.

The island was the site of the historic **Charlottetown Conference** in September 1864, the first of several meetings that led to Canadian Confederation in 1867.

The Island Today – Principal industries today are agriculture (especially **potatoes**), tourism and fishing. Annually over 700,000 visitors are drawn to the unhurried pace of life; **farm vacations** are popular, and **lobster suppers**, held during the summer in church and community halls, provide a sampling of fresh regional seafood and abundant garden produce.

©Benoit Desjardins

Confederation Bridge

Practical Information

GETTING THERE

BY AIR

Air Canada and **Air Canada Jazz** provide direct flights from Toronto, Montreal and Halifax (☎902-429-7111 or 888-247-2262). www.aircanada.ca. **WestJet** (☎1-800-538-5696, www.westjet.com) and **Sunwing Airlines** (☎1-800-761-1711. www.sunwing.ca)offers flights from Toronto and Montreal, **Northwest Airlines** (☎1-800-225-2525. www.nwa.com)from Detroit and **Delta** (☎1-888-750-3284. www.delta.com) from Boston.
Charlottetown Airport is less than 5km/3mi from downtown. ☎902-566-7997. www.flypei.com. Taxis and major car rental agencies are at the airport.

BY CAR

Opened in 1997, the 13km/8mi two-lane **Confederation Bridge** links Borden/Carleton, Prince Edward Island (PEI), with Cape Jourimain, NB and takes approximately 12min to cross. A toll is collected at Borden/Carleton upon exiting the island (☜$40.75/vehicle. Cash, debit card and major credit cards accepted. ☎1-888-437-6565. www.confederationbridge.com).

BY BOAT

Northumberland Ferries connects the eastern part of the island at Wood Islands with Caribou, NS (departs PEI May–mid-Nov daily 6:30am–7:30pm, Late-Nov–late Dec hours vary. Departs NS May–mid-Nov daily 8am–9pm. Late Nov–lat Dec hours vary. No service late Dec–Apr. One way 1hr 15min. ☜$14/adult passenger, $59/car round trip. ✕☜☎902-566-3838, toll-free 1-888-249-7245. www.nfl-bay.com). From Souris a ferry crosses to the Magdalen Islands, Quebec. (☎1-888-986-3278. www.ctma.com)

GENERAL INFORMATION

ACCOMMODATIONS AND VISITOR INFORMATION

The official tourist office publishes an annual **Visitors Guide** and map you can order or download from the Web.. Tourism Prince Edward Island, (PO Box 2000, Charlottetown PE, C1A 7N8. ☎1-800-463-4734 (Canada/US). www.gov.

pe.ca/visitorsguide). **Road Regulations** – Main roads are paved, particularly along the coasts; some roads have either dirt or gravel surface. Speed limits, unless otherwise posted, are 90km/h (55mph) or 80km/h (50mph) on highways and 50km/h (30mph) in urban districts. **Seat belt** use is mandatory. **Canadian Automobile Assn. (CAA)**, Charlottetown ☎902-892-1612.

TIME ZONE

PEI is on Atlantic Standard Time. Daylight Saving Time is observed from the 2nd Sunday in March to the 1st Sunday in November.

TAXES

The national GST of 5% and a provincial sales tax of 10% are levied. There is no provincial sales tax on clothing or footwear purchases.

LIQUOR LAWS

The legal drinking age is 19. Liquor is sold in government stores.

WHERE TO STAY

$ Heart's Content – *236 Sydney St. (at Weymouth), Charlottetown PE, C1A 1H1.. ☎902-566-1799. www.stayincharlottetown.com. ☲. 4 rooms.* A downtown location within walking distance of waterfront and city attractions makes this B&B a good value for the money. The 2 bathrooms are shared. Tidy rooms, storage for bicycles and a continental breakfast.

$$ Warn House – *330 Central St., Summerside PE, C1N 3N1. ☎902-436-5242, toll-free 1-888-436-7512. www.warnhouse.com. 4 rooms.* ▣☲. This immaculately clean, centrally located bed and breakfast is tastefully furnished with Canadian art, antiques and modern fixtures. The friendly hosts, preapre a hearty breakfast served in the handsomely decorated dining room.

$$$ Inns on Great George – *58 Great George St., Charlottetown PE, C1A 4K3. ☎902-892-0606, toll-free 1- 800-361-1118. www.innsongreatgeorge.com. 42 rooms.* ♿▣☲. Located near Province House in the heart of downtown, this inn is a cluster of 13 heritage buildings. Guests can choose from loft bedrooms and efficiency units, two-storey suites, and two-bedroom flats equipped with laundry facilities and kitchen. An exercise room and breakfast served in the cozy Pavilion lobby round out the amenities.

$$$ Briarwood Inn – 253 *Matthew's Lane, Alberton PE, C0B 1B0.* ○*Open mid-June–mid Sept.* ☎*902-853-2518, toll-free 1-888-272-2246. www.briarwood.pe.ca. 22 rooms.* ♿🅿➰. Located on the banks of the Dock River near Cascumpec Bay, this compound containing cottages, a lodge and a three-storey inn makes a heavenly hideaway for longer-stay vacations. Briarwood's river cruise is a highlight.

$$$$ Dalvay-by-the-Sea – *PO Box 8, Dalvay PE, C0A 1C0. North shore, near the east entrance to PEI National Park.* ○*Open Jun–early Oct.* ☎*902-672-2048, toll-free 1-888-366-2955 (US/Canada). www.dalvaybythesea.com. 26 rooms, 8 cottages.* ✕♿🅿➰. Former residence of oil magnate Alexander MacDonald, this gabled Queen Anne-style mansion now houses a prestigious resort. Breakfast and dinner are included in the rates. Dalvay's formal **MacMillan Dining Room ($$$)** provides delicious continental cuisine featuring local seafood and farm products. Tennis, biking, croquet and lake boating are some of the many available activities.

$$$$ Fairholm Inn – *230 Prince St. (corner Fitzroy), Charlottetown PE, C1A 4S1.* ☎*902-892-5022, toll-free 1-888-573-5022. www.fairholm.pe.ca. 7 rooms.* 🅿➰. This stately two-storey mansion (1839) with its double-bay facade has spacious high-ceilinged rooms equipped with marble fireplaces, while bathrooms feature clawfoot tubs and Jacuzzis. Catch up on your reading in the ornate sitting room, or relax in the cheerful sun room and enjoy garden views. Breakfast is served in the formal dining room. The downtown core is only a short walk away.

$$$$ Inn at Spry Point – *Souris RR#4, PE, C0A 2B0. On Rte. 310 (Spry Point Rd.) just off Rte. 2, Souris.* ○*Open mid-Jun–late Sept.* ☎*902-583-2400, toll-free 1-888-687-3745. www.innatsprypoint.com. 15 rooms.* ✕🅿. A remote promontory above Northumberland Strait provides the setting for this large, airy inn. Trails cross the forests near the inn's grounds, and waves crash on the nearby sandy beach. All of the large rooms have private balconies or terraces that afford lovely views. Overlooking the ocean, the **dining room ($$$)** offers local produce, fresh fish and Island meats; the table d'hôte menu changes daily.

WHERE TO EAT

$$$ Inn at Bay Fortune – *Rte. 310, just off Rte. 2, Bay Fortune PE, C0A 2B0.* ○*Open late May–mid-Oct. Dinner only.* ☎*902-687-3745. www.innatbayfortune. com.* **Regional Canadian**. This upscale inn is fast gaining a reputation for its Maritime cuisine. Served in an airy glass-enclosed veranda, the menu focuses on the bounty of the island's forests (venison, wild mushrooms), fields (wild watercress, spearmint) and waters (Island blue mussels, Colville Bay oysters). Produce from the inn's gardens (✏*guided tasting tours 10:30am daily*) forms the basis of the daily Kitchen Gardens Menu. Reserve the Chef's Table in the kitchen and watch Bay Fortune's talented team tailor a memorable meal to your tastes.

$$ Lobster on the Wharf – *Prince St. Wharf, PO Box 2367, Charlottetown PE, C1A 8C1.* ☎*902-894-9311 toll-free 1-877-919-9311. www.lobsteronthewharf.com.* **Seafood**. ♿For a wide array of fresh seafood, head for this casual waterside eatery, where families can indulge indoors or out at checkered-cloth-covered tables. Lobster, snow crab, clams, scallops, shrimp, oysters, haddock and salmon are all on the menu, along with island lobster roll and fish-and-chips. Most plates include potato or rice and vegetables. Children's menu.

$$ Trailside Inn and Café, *109 North Main Street St., Mount Stewart.* ♿. ☎*902-676-3130; www.trailside.ca.* **Seafood**. Don't let the exterior of this renovated country store scare you away. Trailside's varied menu concentrates on seafood. Be sure to try the signature tarragon-scented seafood stew or the salmon pie, and enjoy an ambitious program of live music throughout the summer. On Sundays regulars frequent the gospel brunch. The inn offers rooms for overnight stays, and Trailside Adventures rents bicycles and canoes.

Charlottetown★★

POPULATION 32,245 – MAP P 414

This gracious provincial capital is also a thriving commercial centre, its port serving as a funnel for the region's agricultural bounty. Named for the wife of King George III, the city was founded in 1768.

🖸 **Information:** Visitor Information Centre, 6 Prince St., C1A 4P5. ☎902-368-4444, toll-free 1-800-463-4734. www.walkandseacharlottetown.ca

▶ **Orient Yourself:** Charlottetown is located near the confluence of the West, North and Hillsborough rivers at Northumberland Strait.

🅿 **Parking:** Parking is metered, and often hard to find downtown; spaces are often the "nose-in" variety. Meters cost $0.50/an hour, rigourously enforced.

Sights

Attractively situated along the water's edge, **Victoria Park** is home to the regal, Neoclassical **Government House,** designed by Isaac Smith as the lieutenant-governor's official residence (☛*not open to the public*). From the shore, expansive **views**★ extend across the harbour to the site of Fort Amherst.

Province House National Historic Site★★

At the top of Great George St. ♿🕒*Open Jul–Aug daily 8:30am–6pm. Jun & Sept–mid-Oct daily 8:30am–5pm. Rest of the year 9am–5pm.* ☎*902-566-7626. www. pc.gc.ca.*

A native of Yorkshire, England, Isaac Smith designed this three-storey sandstone building (1847) in the Georgian style with Neoclassical details. The **Confederation Chamber,** site of the Charlottetown Conference, is restored to its 19C appearance. The provincial legislature still meets here.

Confederation Centre of the Arts★

145 Richmond St., Charlottetown PE, C1A 1J1. Ajacent to Province House. ✗♿🕒*Open Jun–Sept Mon–Sat 9am– 9pm. Rest of the year Mon–Sat noon–5pm.* ☎*902-628-1864, toll-free 1-800-565-0278. www.confederationcentre.com.*

Commemorating the centennial of the 1864 Charlottetown Conference, this national memorial arts centre (1964) houses theatres, the provincial archives, display areas and a restaurant. The **art gallery** features works by Canadian artists, and the main theatre hosts the annual **Charlottetown Festival** musical production *Anne of Green Gables.*

St. Dunstan's Basilica

45 Great George St., Charlottetown PE, C1A 4K1. ♿🕒*Open year-round Mon–Fri 8:30am–4pm.* ☎ *902-894-3486. www. stdunstans.pe.ca.*

The twin 61m/200ft spires of this Gothic edifice (1917) gracefully punctuate Charlottetown's skyline. Interior features include fan vaulting, streaked marble and a stunning rose window from Munich, Germany. The contemporary stained-glass windows were designed by island native Henry Purdy.

NIGHT LIFE

42nd Street Lounge, *125 Sydney St. C1A 1G5.* ☎*902-566-4620.* This lounge above **Off Broadway Restaurant** (known for its steaks and fresh mussels) is a place to relax. Soft lighting, comfortable wing chairs and antique tables encourage conversation and conviviality. In addition to wines and spirits, the lounge offers appetizers and desserts. It's a great place for after-dinner drinks or post-theatre snacking.

Blue Heron Drive ★★

MAP P 414

This scenic drive encompasses the stunning white beaches of the north coast; charming Acadian fishing villages; sights related to *Anne of Green Gables;* and the red cliffs of the southern coast, bordered by Northumberland Strait.

🅸 **Information:** Information Centre, 6 Prince Street, Charlottetown, C1A 4P5. ☎902-368-4444. www.gentleisland.com.

▸ **Orient Yourself:** This popular drive circles most of Queens County and central Prince Edward Island.

👁 **Don't Miss:** The beaches of the Prince Edward Island National Park spread out under pink sandstone cliffs.

🕓 **Organizing Your Time:** The tour takes a leisurely day.

🄺 **Especially for Kids:** The Anne of Green Gables House; the miniatures of famous buildings at Woodleigh.

Driving Tour

190km/118mi circuit indicated by blue and white signs depicting a blue heron. Visitor centre in Charlottetown.

Prince Edward Island National Park★

In Cavendish, 24km/15mi northwest of Charlottetown. 🚶🅿🕓*Open year-round.* 🎫*$6 entry fee. Cavendish visitor centre open mid-Jun–mid Aug 8am–9pm, mid-Aug–mid-Oct 9am–various closing times.* ☎ *902-672-6350. www.pc.gc.ca. To preserve the dunes, please use boardwalks and designated footpaths.*

One of Canada's smallest but most popular national parks stretches for about 40km/25mi along the north shore of the island, fringing the Gulf of St. Lawrence. Interspersed with boardwalks and paths to the water's edge, the **Gulf Shore Parkway** offers lovely **beaches,** sand dunes, sandstone cliffs, salt marshes and freshwater ponds.

Green Gables House★

🄺*In Cavendish on Rte. 6 west of Rte. 13, in PEI National Park.* 🍴🚶🅿🕓*Open late June–late Aug daily 9am–6pm. May–late Jun & late Aug–Oct 9am–5pm. Nov–Dec & Apr Sun–Thu 10am–4pm, Jan 7–Mar Thu–Sun noon–4pm.* 🕓*Closed Jan 1–6, Dec 24–26 & 31.* 🎫*$7.15 adult.* ☎*902-963-7874. www.pc.gc.ca.*

Parks Canada PEI/John Sylvester

Green Gables House

ART GALLERY-CAFE

The Dunes Gallery –*RR#9, Brackley BeachPE, C1E 1Z3.* ☎902-672-2586. *www.dunesgallery.com.* This dramatic cedar and glass structure houses the studio of artist Peter Jansons, an art gallery, a gift shop and a cafe. Canadian-made pottery, paintings, jewellery, blown glass, baskets and other crafts are for sale along with imports. The cafe serves creative cuisine on the gallery's attractive pottery. At lunchtime, try the Lebanese chicken sandwich on pita. For dinner, try the Dunes Duet (seared scallops and jumbo shrimp in a red pepper cream sauce and topped with peach salsa). Floral arrangements of huge dahlias, daisies, gladiolas, zinnias and other flowers grown on the premises add an artistic flair. Be sure to visit the tranquil garden, the deckside lily pond *(3rd floor)* and the top-floor lookout, accessible via a striking spiral wooden staircase.

This small green and white farmhouse belonged to relatives of **Lucy Maud Montgomery**, author of *Anne of Green Gables*. She used the house as a setting for the novel, which tells the story of an irrepressible orphan girl adopted by a strict but kindly brother and sister living at Green Gables farm.

Anne of Green Gables Museum at Silverbush

In Park Corner on Rte. 20. &⬛🅿🕒*Open Jun–Sept daily 9am–4pm (Jul–Aug to 5pm). May & Oct daily 11am–4pm* 🎫*$2.75.* ☎902-886-2884, 1-800-665-2663. *www.annesociety.org.*
Throughout her life, author Lucy Maud Montgomery visited relatives at this spacious house; her 1911 wedding was held in the drawing room. The dwelling and its surroundings appear in the *Anne of Green Gables* series.

Woodleigh★

🄺🄸🄳🅂*Burlington, RR#2, Kensington PE, C0N 1M0. On Rte. 234 northeast of Kensington.* ✕🕒*Open Jul–Aug daily 9am–7pm. Jun & Sept daily 9am–5pm.* 🎫*$8.50.* ☎902-836-3401. *www.woodleighreplicas.com.*
Scattered about a pleasant, tree-shaded site are some 17 large-scale replicas of historic British structures such as York Minster Cathedral, complete with 145 glass windows and St. Paul's Cathedral in London.

Victoria

Overlooking Northumberland Strait, this tiny seaside community is undoubtedly the island's most picturesque hamlet, complete with an active wharf and a provincial park. Dominating the end of Main Street, the colourful **Orient**

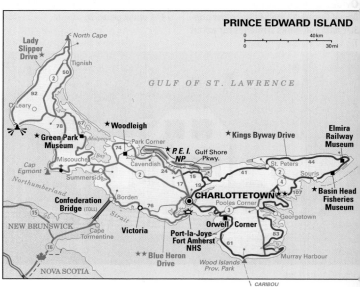

Hotel ($$) (☎902-658-2503, toll-free 1-800-565-6743. www.theorienthotel.com) welcomes overnight guests and patrons of **Mrs. Proffit's Tea Room.**

Port la Joye–Fort Amherst National Historic Site

In Rocky Point, on Blockhouse Point Rd. off Rte. 19. ✕◷*Grounds open daily mid–June–late Aug.* ☞*No charge.* ☎902-566-7626. www.pc.gc.ca.

The British, who captured the area from the French in 1758, erected Fort Amherst and occupied the post until 1768. Today only the earthworks remain—rolling, grass-covered mounds from which sweeping **views**★★ of Charlottetown harbour extend.

Kings Byway Drive★

MAP OPPOSITE

Side roads lead through lush forests past small communities with names such as Cardigan, Greenfield and Glenmartin that hearken back to the province's British heritage.

▪ **Information:** Information Centre, 6 Prince Street, Charlottetown, C1A 4P5. ☎902-368-4444. www.gentleisland.com.

▶ **Orient Yourself:** The drive follows the deeply indented bays and harbours of the island's eastern coast.

◷ **Organizing Your Time:** This drive takes most of a day.

Kids **Especially for Kids:** The Orwell Corner village is diverting.

Driving Tour

375km/233mi circuit indicated by purple and white signs depicting a royal crown. Visitor centre at junction of Rtes. 3 and 4 in Pooles Corner.

Orwell Corner Historic Village

Kids *Vernon RR#2, PE, C0A 2E0 In Orwell, 30km/19mi east of Charlottetown on the Trans-Can Hwy.* ✕▣◷*Open Jul–Labour Day daily 9:30am–5:30pm. June Mon–Fri 9am–5pm. Labour Day–mid-Oct Sun–Thur 9am–5pm.* ◷*Closed mid-Oct–May.* ☞*$7.50.* ☎902-651-8510. www.orwell-corner.isn.net.*

This superbly restored crossroads village, settled in the early 19C by pioneers from Scotland and Ireland, retains the atmosphere and flavour of the island's agricultural origins. Fiddle music and step dancing are features of the tradi-

Lobster Suppers

An island tradition, lobster suppers began more than 40 years ago as a fund-raiser for the Junior Farmers Organization; the first meal cost $1.50. The summertime (mid-June–late Sept) suppers have since been commercialized to cater to huge crowds. **St. Ann's Church** (☎902-621-0635. www.lobstersuppers.com) in Hope River offers daily afternoon and evening sittings (except Sunday) in its large basement. **St. Margarets Lobster Suppers** (☎902-687-3105) serves lobster and ham dinners in its licensed dining room, and **New Glasgow Lobster Suppers** (☎902-964-2870. www.peilobstersuppers.com) operates in a two-level, 500-capacity hall, with lobster pounds on-site.

Paying a set price as they enter, patrons are seated at long wooden tables. The meal starts with fish chowder, followed by salads (potato, coleslaw and green). Steamed mussels follow. Next comes the lobster itself (1, 1-1/2 or 2 pounds, based on what you paid), served in the shell. Cake or pie with ice cream is often served as dessert. Ham or fish are often offered for those who don't like lobster.

tional *ceilidh* (KAY-lee) *(Jun–Sept every Wed 8pm).*

Basin Head Fisheries Museum★

In Basin Head, 10km/6mi east of Souris on Rte. 16. ✕🅿🕓*Open mid-Jun–Labour Day daily 10am–6pm, Sept 9am–5pm.* ☎*$4.* ☎ *902-357-7233. www.gentle island.com*

Boats, nets, hooks, photographs and dioramas illustrate the life and work of an inshore fisherman. Outside, small wooden buildings house a small boats exhibit.

Elmira Railway Museum

In Elmira, 16km/10mi east of Souris on Rte. 16A. ♿🅿🕓*Open June–Sept daily 10am–6pm.* ☎*$3.* ☎*902-357-7234. www. elmirastation.com*

Formerly the eastern terminus of a railway system linking the island with the continent, this charming station has been transformed into a museum that recounts the railway's 19C–early-20C development.

Lady Slipper Drive★

MAP P 414

Named for the province's official flower, this scenic circuit introduces the visitor to shipbuilding at Green Park; the Malpeque Bay, famed for its fine oysters; and fox farming, a major island industry from 1890 to 1939.

🛈 **Information: Information:** Information Centre, 6 Prince Street, Charlottetown, C1A 4P5. ☎902-368-4444 or www.gentleisland.com.

▶ **Orient Yourself:** The picturesque landscape of western Prince Edward Island is fringed with capes and beaches.

🕓 **Organizing Your Time:** The time needed depends on the museums you visit.

🧒 **Especially for Kids:** The lighthouse is fun.

Driving Tour

288km/179mi circuit indicated by red and white signs depicting a lady-slipper blossom. Visitor centre on Rte. 1A in Wilmot, 2km/1mi east of Summerside.

Acadian Museum of Prince Edward Island

c/o Mme Cécile Gallant, PO Box 159, Miscouche PE, C0B 1T0, 8km/5mi west of Summerside, on Rte. 2. ♿🕓*Open late Jun–Labour Day daily 9:30am–5pm (Jul–Aug 7pm). Rest of the year Mon–Fri 9:30am–5pm, Sun 1pm–4pm.* ☎*$3. ☎902-432-2880. www.teleco.org/musee-acadien.*

Erected in 1991, this modern facility for the preservation of Acadian heritage combines a historical museum with a documentation centre for genealogical research.

Green Park Shipbuilding Museum★

In Port Hill, 34km/21mi northwest of Summerside on Rte. 12. 🕓*Open Jun–late Sept daily 10am–5:30pm.* ☎*$5. ☎902-831-7947. www.peimuseum.com.*

Formerly the grounds of an active shipyard, Green Park is today a provincial heritage site.

Yeo House (1865) is a large, steeply gabled Victorian structure restored to reflect the lifestyle of a prominent family of the period. Maps, photographs and tools on display in the **visitor centre** present the industry's 19C heyday.

West Point Lighthouse

PO Box 429, O'Leary PE, C0B 1V0. Cedar Dunes Provincial Park on Rte. 14. ✕🅿🕓*Open mid-May–Sept daily 9am–9pm.* ☎*$2.50. ☎ 902-859-3605 or 800-764-6854. www.westpointlight house.com.*

West Point Lighthouse

This distinctive 30m/85ft striped lighthouse (1875) was automated by electricity in 1963. The tower contains numerous examples of lighthouse lenses and lanterns. From the observation platform at the summit, **views** stretch across the shoreline's dark red dunes. The lighthouse also serves as an inn, with a restaurant open to the public.

Potato Museum

PO Box 602, O'Leary PE C0B 1V0. Off Rte. 142 at 1 Heritage Lane in O'Leary, west of Rte. 2. ✕ ♿ 🅿 🕐 *Open mid-May–mid-Oct Mon–Sat 9am–5pm, Sun 1pm–5pm.* 💲$6. ☎ *902-859-2039. www.peipotatomuseum.com.*

Here, visitors can learn how Sir Walter Raleigh, Sir Francis Drake and even Thomas Jefferson promoted the versatile tuber, first cultivated in Peru perhaps as early as 10,000 years ago. At the canteen, sample potato maple-butter tarts, potato fudge or even a potato dog.

Our Lady of Mont-Carmel Acadian Church

In Mont-Carmel, on Rte. 11, east of Rte. 124. ♿ 🅿 🕐 *Open Jun–Sept daily 8am–8pm. Rest of the year Sun 9am–5pm.* ☎ *902-854-2789.*

Overlooking Northumberland Strait just east of Cap-Egmont, this twin-steepled brick church (1896) replaces two earlier wooden structures The symmetrical facade and rounded interior vaults are reminiscent of religious architecture in France's Poitou region, original home of most of the island's first Acadian settlers.

ADDRESS BOOK

At the **PEI Preserve Co.** *(2841 New Glasgow Rd, PO Box 5501, Hunter River PE, C0A 1N0. Off Rte. 13 near Cavendish at junction of Rtes. 224 and 258.* ☎*902-367-1888, toll-free 1-800-565-5267. www.preservecompany.com),* you can sample dozens of preserves and several mustards and chutneys, as well as the tea of the day. The cheery, on-site **Café on the Clyde** *(*☎*902-964-4301)* serves breakfast, lunch and casual evening fare complemented by views of the river view and a bit of the adjacent **New Glasgow Country Gardens**, *(*☎*902-964-4300)* which have 2km/1.5mi of walking trails and Sunday concerts. (The company has a location in Charlottetown, too.) The **River Theatre** on the grounds offers late-morning ceilidhs (Gaelic music) in Jul–Aug and country music ensembles in the evenings *(for information* ☎*1-800-424-9155).*

NEWFOUNDLAND AND LABRADOR

POPULATION 505 469 – MAP P 421

The largest of the Atlantic provinces, Newfoundland and Labrador consists of the rocky island named Newfoundland and the mountainous mainland of Labrador, with a combined landmass of 405,720sq km/156,648sq mi. The remote shores and wilderness interior of Canada's easternmost province appeal particularly to nature lovers in search of adventure.

Information: Newfoundland and Labrador Tourism, PO Box 8700, St. John's NL, A1B 4J6. ☎709-729-2830, toll-free 1-800-563-6353. www.newfoundlandlabrador.com

Orient Yourself: The island of Newfoundland lies at the eastern end of the Gulf of St. Lawrence. It is separated from Quebec and Labrador by the Strait of Belle Isle, and from Nova Scotia by the Cabot Strait. Laborador, on the mainland, abuts Quebec and reaches north nearly to the Arctic.

Geological Notes

The Island – Called "The Rock" for its craggy profile, the island of the province has a beautiful, deeply indented 9,650km/6,000mi-long coastline, studded with bays, coves and islands. In the north and west, the coast is grandiose with towering cliffs and deep fiords. From the heights of the **Long Range Mountains** in the west, a continuation of the Appalachians, the land slopes east and northeast. Parts of the interior are heavily forested; others are expanses of rocky barrens and boggy peat lands, a legacy of glaciers, as are the multitude of lakes and rivers.

Labrador – A rugged land of high mountains (Cirque Mountain, in the **Torngats** of the north, reaches 1,676m/5,500ft), Unlike the island, Labrador forms part of the Canadian Shield. Its 29,000 people reside primarily along the coast and around the mines in its rich iron-ore belt.

Collapse of the fishery – The "Banks" are vast areas of shallow water that lie in the Atlantic to the south and east of the province. For 500 years these waters have attracted fishermen to the fish-breeding grounds. The largest and richest of the grounds is the **Grand Banks,** where the cold Labrador Current meets

Woody Point near Gros Morne National Park

Oral Traditions

Visitors to Newfoundland are captivated by the wealth of unusual idioms and wonderful accents of its inhabitants. Centuries of isolation have chiselled a character that is independent, individualistic and humorous. Where else are there settlements named **Stinking Cove,** Useless Bay, **Jerry's Nose,** Cuckold Cove, **Come by Chance** and Happy Adventure, or local terms like *tickle* (a narrow waterway)?

English is the first language of 98 percent of the islanders, but remarkably varied dialects enrich the provincial tongue. Some have definite Irish overtones; others are reminiscent of England's West Country (Dorset, Devon, Cornwall). Local expressions such as "to have a noggin to scrape" (a very hard task), "to be all mops and brooms" (to have untidy hair) and "long may your big jib draw" (good luck for the future) add color and humor to everyday conversations.

the warmer Gulf Stream. Sinking below the warmer one, the cold current stirs up plankton on the seabed. The plankton rises to the surface, attracting great schools of fish.

In 1992, however, it became evident that cod stocks had collapsed due to overfishing and the Canadian government placed a moratorium on commercial cod fishing; some 40,000 people lost their jobs. Ten years later, stocks had shown no signs of recovery and on April 24, 2003, the fisheries minister announced the closing of the Candian commercial cod fishery. The social and economic consequences might have been devastating but for the emergence of a new and far more profitable industry: mineral extraction, particularly oil and gas.

Newfoundland Today

Offshore Oil – Completed in 1997, the **Hibernia oil platform**, secured to its drill site some 315km/200mi out in the Grand Banks, weighs over 1.2 million tonnes/1.3 million tons, heavy enough, it is projected, to withstand collision with the giant icebergs common in these waters. Production began in 1997; output from one well is currently about 150,000 barrels of oil a day, and new wells are being developed.

In 2002 production began from the **Terra Nova** site, and in 2005 from the **White Rose** site, both some 350km/219mi off the coast. The two sites operate from innovative "floating production storage and off-loading" vessels that can be moved in case of inclement conditions.

Boats along Frenchman's Cove

Practical Information

GETTING THERE

BY AIR

– St John's International Airport
(☎709-758-8500. www.stjohnsairport.com)
Air Canada provides direct flights from Calgary, Toronto, Montreal and Halifax (☎1-88-247-2262.www.aircanada.com).
West Jet (☎1-800-538-5696. www.westjet.com) flies directly from Calgary, Toronto and Halifax. **Continental** (☎1-800-231-0856. www.continental.com) flies from Newark, NJ, and **Lufthansa** (1-800-563-5954. www.lufthansa.com.) from Toronto and Halifax.
– Air Canada Jazz (☎1-888-247-2262. www.aircanada.com) flies into **Gander International Airport** (☎709-256-6668. www.ganderairport.com) in Labrador.
Air Labrador (☎709-753-5593,toll-free 1-800-563-0342. www.airlabrador.com) and **Provincial Airlines** (☎709-576-1666, toll-free 1-800-563-2800. www.provincialairlines.ca) provide regular connections within the province.

BY BOAT

Passenger & car ferry service is available from North Sydney, NS, to Channel-Port aux Basques (*Departs year-round daily.6hrs 30min, 5hrs in summer. Connecting bus service to inland destinations* **DRL Coachlines** ☎709-263-2163*)* and to Argentia (*June 15–1st week Sept Mon, Wed 7:30am, Fri 3:30pm. Rest of Sept Mon 6am. 14hrs*). For schedules & reservations contact **Marine Atlantic**, North Sydney, NS (☎1-800-341-7981 (Canada/US). www.marine-atlantic.ca).
Provincial Ferry Services (☎709-729-2300. www.tw.gov.nl.ca) serves seacoast towns in Newfoundland and eastern Laborador. **Relais Nordic** (☎1-800-463-0680. www.relaisnordic.com) links Quebec's lower north shore and Labrador.
Note: Advance reservations are suggested for all ferry services. Fuel tanks must be no more than three-quarters full. *For ferry service to* **Saint-Pierre and Miquelon** *see SAINT-PIERRE AND MIQUELON.*

GENERAL INFORMATION

ACCOMMODATIONS AND VISITOR INFORMATION

Travel guides, hunting & fishing guides and road maps are available free of charge from **Newfoundland and Labrador Tourism**, *PO Box 8700, St. John's NL, A1B 4J6.* ☎709-729-2830, toll-free 1-800-563-6353. www.newfoundland-labrador.com

ROAD REGULATIONS

The Trans-Canada Highway Rte. 1 *(910km/565mi)*, which traverses Newfoundland from Channel-Port aux Basques to St. John's, and most secondary highways are paved. The condition of gravel roads varies according to traffic and weather. Main roads are passable during winter, but it is advisable to check with local authorities before departure (☎709-729-2381, Dec–Mar or check Tourism website above). **Seat belt** use is compulsory. Speed limits, unless otherwise posted, are 100km/h (60mph) on four-lane divided highways, 80km/h (50mph) on secondary highways and 50km/h (30mph) on gravel roads..

TIME ZONES

Most of Labrador observes Atlantic Standard Time. Newfoundland Standard Time is 30min ahead of Atlantic Standard Time and 1hr 30min ahead of Eastern Standard Time. Daylight Saving Time is observed from the 2nd Sunday in March to the 1st Sunday in November.

TAXES

In Newfoundland and Labrador a Harmonized Sales Tax (HST) is levied at a single rate of 14%. Nonresidents may be entitled to a rebate on certain goods taken out of the country within 60 days of purchase and may request a rebate.

LIQUOR LAWS

Liquor and wine are available only from government stores except in remote areas where local stores are licensed. Beer is available in most convenience stores. The legal drinking age is 19.

PROVINCIAL HOLIDAY

The Queen's Birthday (Victoria Day):
Monday nearest May 24

PRINCIPAL FESTIVALS

mid-Feb	**Corner Brook Winter Carnival:** *Corner Brook*
Jul–early Aug	**Stephenville Festival:** *Stephenville*
Aug	**Royal St. John's Regatta:** *St. John's*

	Annual Newfoundland and Labrador Folk Festival: *St. John's*
mid-Aug	**Labrador Straits Bakeapple Folk Festival :** *Point Amour*

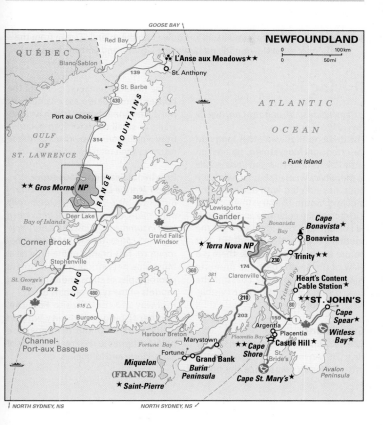

In addition, the Voisey's Bay Nickel Company is investing $3bn to mine and process nickel from a site discovered in 1993 in Labrador. Thus, despite the disaster in the cod fishery, the outlook for the province is one of guarded euphoria.

Lifestyle and Food – About one-quarter of the island's population resides in the capital city of St. John's; the remainder lives mainly in coastal fishing villages known as **outports,** tiny coastal settlements In some outports a small "museum" preserves each community's past.

With the traditional cod largely removed from the menu, arctic char, lobster, salmon, snow crab and halibut are favourite dinners, and **squid burgers** are an island peculiarity. Game includes caribou steaks and even moose. Fruits of the region include blueberries, partridgeberries and yellow **bakeapples,** raspberry-like in appearance, but with a rich, distinctive taste.

Burin Peninsula

MAP P 421

This is the doorstep to the once- vast offshore fishing industry in the **Grand Banks.** Just off the "toe" are the island remnants of France's once-great empire in North America: Saint-Pierre and Miquelon.

🛈 **Information:** Newfoundland and Labrador Tourism, PO Box 8700, St. John's NL, A1B 4J6. ☎709-729-2830, toll-free 1-800-563-6353. www.newfoundlandlabrador.com

▶ **Orient Yourself:** The penninsula juts down into the Atlantic Ocean from the southern coast of Newfoundland between Placentia and Fortune bays.

Driving Tour

203km/126mi south of Trans-Can Hwy. by Hwy. 210 to Fortune.
The drive on Highway 210 is long and deserted until **Marystown,** situated on Little Bay. Its huge shipyard *(inaccessible to the public)*, where fishing trawlers are built, has suffered with decline of the industry. South of Marystown, Route 210 crosses the peninsula and descends to Fortune Bay, providing views of the southern coast of Newfoundland. Just before entering Grand Bank, there is a view of the south coast and Brunette Island. To the west the coast of the French island of Miquelon is just visible, weather permitting.

Grand Bank

199km/123mi south of Trans-Can Hwy. by Hwy. 210. An important fishing centre, this community was once the home of the famous "bankers." Some of the houses from that era are examples of the Queen Anne style with their widow's walks or small open rooftop galleries from which women could watch for the return of their men from the sea.

Provincial Seamen's Museum★

Kids *54 Marine Dr., PO Box 1109, Grand Banks NF, A0E 1W0.* ♿🕐*Open daily May–mid-Oct 9am–4:45pm (may open later in summer).* 🕐*Closed statutory holidays.* 🎟*$2.50* ☎*709-832-1484. www.therooms.ca.* This branch of the Provincial Museums network features displays photographs of ships and fishing, and **models** of the types of ships used.
Highway 210 continues to **Fortune**, another fishing community with an artificial harbour and the departure point for ferries to the French islands of Saint-Pierre and Miquelon.

The Cape Shore ★★

MAP P 421

Newfoundland's most dramatic coastline, extending from Placentia to St. Bride's, delights visitors with its natural wonders and historic sites as well as magnificent ocean views and remnants of Europe's territorial struggles.

🛈 **Information:** Newfoundland and Labrador Tourism, ☎709-729-2830, toll-free 1-800-563-6353. www.newfoundlandandlabrador.com.

▶ **Orient Yourself:** The Cape Shore lies on the southwest arm of the Avalon Penninsula, which extends off the east coast of the island.

🖰 **Don't Miss:** The drive along the Cape Shore provides spectacular views.

🕐 **Organizing Your Time:** Start early and check the weather before starting.

Kids **Especially for Kids:** At the St. Mary's bird sanctuary, you can get near the birds.

Sights

Castle Hill★

PO Box Box 10, Jerseyside, Placentia Bay NF, A0B 2G0. In Placentia, 44km/27mi south of Trans-Can Hwy. by Rte. 100. About 8km/5mi from Argentia ferry. ♿⏱*Grounds open year-round. Visitor centre open May 15–Oct 15 10am–6pm.* ✆*$4.* ☎*709-227-2401. www.pc.gc.ca.*

This park contains the remains of France's early 17C Fort Royal, rebuilt and renamed Castle Hill by the British. Overlooking the small town of **Placentia**, the site affords a **panorama**★★ of the city itself, Placentia Bay and **The Gut**—a small channel that separates the bay from two long, deep inlets.

During World War II, a large American base was built at at nearby **Argentia,** the site of the famous 1941 offshore meeting between Churchill and Roosevelt that produced the **Atlantic Charter,** a statement of peace goals adopted in 1942 by the United Nations.

An interesting **visitor centre** describes the French and English presence in the area. A pleasant pathway through evergreen forests leads to **Le Gaillardin,** a redoubt built by the French in 1692.

Cape Shore Drive★★

46km/29mi from Placentia to St. Bride's on Rte. 100. Fuel and food available infrequently. Fog may hamper visibility.

Traversing a rugged, hilly coast, Route 100 provides spectacular **views**. Sparsely populated communities such as picturesque **Gooseberry Cove** *(25km/16mi south of Placentia)* dot the wide inlets. Colourful flat-topped houses, woolly sheep and an occasional fishing boat anchored offshore are common scenes until the road turns inland at St. Bride's. The landscape then changes to isolated flatlands and pale green hillocks extending to the horizon.

Cape St. Mary's
Ecological Reserve★

About 14km/9mi east of St. Bride's. Leave St. Bride's via Rte 100. Turn right on paved road (turnoff for reserve is clearly marked) and continue 14km/8mi. ⏱*Open year-round. Mid-May–mid-Aug is best season to view birds.*

Located at the southwest end of the cape, this sanctuary for seabirds is one of the largest nesting grounds in North America for **gannets,** relatives of the pelican family. Atop a dramatic shoreline alive with the sights and sounds of over 70,000 birds, its pastoral **setting** is unique.

Visitors can get within several feet of the birds. Providing spectacular **views**★ of the rugged coast, a trail from the lighthouse and visitor centre over short-grass hills often covered with grazing sheep leads to **Bird Rock,** the precarious domain of hundreds of gannets. Surrounding cliffs attract throngs of noisy black-legged kittiwakes, common murres and razorbills.

Gros Morne National Park★★

MAP P 425

This vast, pristine park, designated a UNESCO World Heritage Site in 1987, includes some of the most spectacular scenery in eastern Canada. Consisting of rock more than a billion years old, the flat-topped **Long Range Mountains** are the northernmost part of the Appalachians. Between them and the coast lies a poorly drained plain, sometimes high above the sea, with a variety of cliffs, sandy shores and little fishing communities.

▤ **Information:** Parks Canada, Rocky Harbour. ☎709-458-2417. www.pc.gc.ca

▸ **Orient Yourself:** The park covers 1,805sq km/697sq mi along the west coast of Newfoundland's Great Northern Peninsula.

◉ **Don't Miss:** A guided boat tour gives perspective to the mountains.

◑ **Organizing Your Time:** For information on accommodation, contact Newfoundland and Labrador Tourism (♿*see Introduction*). For information on travel during the off-season, contact Gros Morne Gatherings at ☎709-458-3605, toll-free-866-732-2759. www.grosmornetravel.com.

Kids **Especially for Kids:** The park recreation complex, open daily late June to Labour Day, includes a 25m/69ft indoor swimming pool.

Access

44km/27mi northwest of Deer Lake. Take Rte. 430 from Deer Lake to Wiltondale, then Rte. 431 to park, 13km/8mi.

Visit

⏱*Open year-round.* 💲*$9 entry fee adult (May–Oct). Hiking, camping, cross-country skiing, fishing kayaking, swimming . Contact visitor centre near Rocky Harbour for guided boat tours and trail information (♿⏱Open mid-May–mid-Oct daily 9am, closing hours vary. 1st 2 weeks May & late Oct Mon–Fri 9am–4pm. ⏱Closed Nov–Apr.)* ☎709-458-2417. www.pc.gc.ca.

Bonne Bay Area★★

Take Rte. 431 from Wiltondale 50km/31mi to Trout River (food, fuel).

This is a beautiful drive along a deep fiord surrounded by the squat peaks of the Long Range Mountains. The road travels westward along the **South Arm** from Glenburnie, offering gorgeous **views★★** of the bay.

From Woody Point, as Route 431 ascends to the west, the red-brown rubble of a desertlike area known as the **Tablelands** is abruptly visible. These mountains consist of rock that was once part of the earth's mantle—a magnesium and iron layer surrounding the planet's core—and are evidence of **plate tectonics,** the shifting of the plates within the earth's crust. For a closer look at the Tablelands, stop at the turnoff *(4.5km/2.8 mi from Woody Point),* where a **panel display** describes this unique natural feature. This vantage point offers a striking **view** of the barren expanse. A footpath leads from the parking area into the heart of the Tablelands (💬*for information on guided hikes, contact the visitor centre).* Beyond the little fishing village of Trout River is the long finger lake called **Trout River Pond** (♿⏱*Tour boats depart Jul–Aug daily 10am, 1pm, 4pm. Jun& Sept 1pm.round-trip 2hrs 30min. Reservations required.* 💲*$25. For reservations* ☎*709-451-7500, toll-free 1-866-751-7500).*

Dominating the return drive to Woody Point is the vast bulk of **Gros Morne Mountain** (806m/2,644ft) to the north,

Trout River Pond

the park's highest point. Stop at Parks Canada's new **Discovery Centre** (⏰*Open late Jun–Labour Day 9am–6pm (Wed & Sun to 9pm), mid-May–late Jun and early Sept–early Oct 9am–5pm.*)on the south side of Bonne Bay for a look at the geology and ecology of the area.

Water taxi service (no vehicles) from Woody Point to Norris Point may be available. Otherwise, motorists must retrace the route to Wiltondale. From Wiltondale Route 430 travels northeast along **East Arm,** a vantage point for lovely **views**★★ of Bonne Bay, and along Deer Arm.

From Rocky Harbour to St. Pauls

40km/25mi by Rte. 430. Fuel and food available in communities along the way. Overlooking a wide inlet of Bonne Bay, the small coastal community of **Rocky Harbour** functions as a service centre for park visitors.

On a promontory just north of Rocky Harbour, **Lobster Cove Head Lighthouse** (⏰*open daily in summer*) provides expansive **views**★★ of the town, Gros Morne Mountain, the mouth of the bay and the Gulf of St. Lawrence. Built on a narrow plain between the sea and the Long Range Mountains, the road affords a pretty drive up the coast past Sally's Cove, a little fishing communities. Before the turnoff to Western Brook Pond's trailhead, the rusty remains of the **SS Ethie** shipwreck can be seen on the beach. A small panel describes the fate of the ship's 1919 voyage.

Western Brook Pond★★

29km/18mi from Rocky Harbour. Western Brook runs through a gorge (which, in typical Newfoundland understatement, is called a "pond") in the Long Range Mountains before it crosses the narrow coastal plain

and reaches the sea. The pond is flanked by almost vertical cliffs where snow remains even in August.

A trail leads across the boggy coastal plain *(boardwalks over marshy areas)* to the edge of the pond *(3km/2mi walk to boat dock).* The only way to see the interior of Western Brook Pond is to take the **boat trip** *(Departs Jul–Aug daily 10am, 1pm & 4pm. Jun & Sept daily 1pm. Round-trip 2hrs. ✆$39 adult. 🅿3km/1.8 mi walk from parking lot. Park pass required. Warm jacket recommended entire season. Bon Tours. ☎709-458-2016, toll-free 1-888-458-2016. www.bontours.ca). .*

After Western Brook Pond, the road follows along the coast with views of the mountains. The road continues to **St. Pauls,** a small fishing settlement at the mouth of a deep fiord.

Designated "The Viking Trail," Route 430 exits the park above Shallow Bay and continues north along the coast for another 300km/200mi to L'Anse aux Meadow. Several native burial grounds are located at the archaeological site in **Port au Choix National Historic Site** *(135km/84mi north of St. Pauls).*

Port au Choix NHS / *L'ANSE AUX MEADOWS*

DEER LAKE

Heart's Content Cable Station ★

MAP P 421

Founded about 1650, Heart's Content is the site of the first successful landing, in 1866, of the **transatlantic telegraph cable.** The landing was the result of years of work by the New York, Newfoundland and London Telegraph Co., led by American financier Cyrus W. Field. After failed attempts in 1858 and 1865, Field in 1866 successfully used the ocean liner *Great Eastern* to lay the cable between Valencia, Ireland, and Heart's Content, where it joined a cable to New York. Messages initially cost $5 a word, and the station handled 3,000 messages a day. The station closed in 1965.

- **Information:** Newfoundland and Laborador Tourism ⏃ see Introduction.
- ▶ **Orient Yourself:** Heart's Content is located on Trinity Bay, which separates the Avalon Penninsula from the main part of the island.
- ⏃ **Also See:** ST. JOHN'S, THE CAPE SHORE

Visit

58km/36mi north of Trans-Can Hwy. by Rte. 80, Avalon Peninsula. ⏱*Open mid–May–Sept daily 10am–5:30pm.* 🎟*$3.* ☎*709-583-2160 (during season) or 709-729-0592 (year-round). www.tcr.gov. nl.ca/tcr/historicsites.*

There is a **film** *(20min)* and special section on the laying of the transatlantic cables. Costumed guides are on site for tours of the replica of the first cable office (1866) and operating room.

L'Anse aux Meadows ★★

MAP P 421

On a grassy ledge facing Epaves Bay, the remains of the oldest authenticated European settlement in North America are preserved for posterity. This remote site, a National Historic Site of Canada, has been included on UNESCO's World Heritage list as a property of universal value.

- **Information:** Parks Canada. ☎709-623-2608.www.pc.gc.ca
- ▶ **Orient Yourself:** L'Anse aux Meadows is located on the Great Northern Peninsula, at the farthest northern tip of Newfoundland, opposite Labrador.
- 🕐 **Organizing Your Time:** Highway 430, the Viking Trail, leads here from Gros Morne. Services and accommodation are available in nearby St. Anthony.

A Bit of History

In 1960, **Helge Ingstad**, a Norwegian explorer and writer, and his archaeologist wife, **Anne Stine**, began a systematic search of the coast from New England northward. Led to a group of overgrown mounds near L'Anse aux Meadows by a local resident, they excavated them from 1961 to 1968. Foundations of eight sod buildings of the type the Norse built

in Iceland were uncovered and several artifacts undeniably Norse in origin were found. Evidence of iron working—an art unknown to the North American Indians—was unearthed. Samples of bone, turf and charcoal were carbon-dated to around AD 1000.

Experts believe L'Anse aux Meadows was a base for further exploration in search of timber and trading goods. Occupied by about 100 men and women, the camp

Vinland

By AD 900 the Vikings (also known as the Norse) from present-day Scandinavia had settled in Iceland, and from there explored Greenland, Baffin Island and beyond. The account of a land sighting by a Greenland-destined ship blown off course inspired **Leif Ericsson,** then residing in Greenland, to go exploring. About AD 1000 Ericsson landed at a fertile spot and built a settlement for the winter. He named the location "Vinland" for the wild grapes his crew is said to have found there. This story is preserved in two Norse tales: the *Saga of the Greenlanders* and the *Saga of Eric the Red,* which were communicated by word of mouth for hundreds of years before being recorded.

Though many scholars have tried to find Vinland, its location is unknown. Once generally thought to be on the southeastern coast of the US because of the grapes, this location was determined to be too far for ships to have sailed in the time suggested by the sagas.

was probably deserted after five or ten years. Newfoundland's harsh conditions, coupled with the growing accessibility of southern European markets, most likely led to its abandonment.

Access

453km/281mi north of Trans-Can Hwy. by Rtes. 430 and 436.

Visit

 ⟐ *Open Jun–early Oct daily 9am–6pm.* ⟐*$9.* ⟐*709-623-2608. www.pc. gc.ca.*
In the **visitor centre** displays depict what a Norse settlement might have looked like, but the highlight is the collection of artifacts found on-site. A stir-ring **film** *(28min)* on the Ingstads' search introduces the visit.

Completely excavated, the site has been preserved as grassy borders that outline the foundations of the original structures. The layout of the dwellings, work buildings and a smithy can be clearly distinguished. Nearby, three **sod buildings**—a long house, a building and a work shed—have been reconstructed. Inside, wooden platforms that served as beds line the walls. Fire pits are placed at intervals in the middle of the earthen floors. Costumed staff demonstrate Viking skills.

At the end of "The Viking Trail," **St. Anthony**, a large service centre, is the nearest city *(food, accommodations and air service)* to L'Anse aux Meadows. At the turn of the 19C, a British doctor, **Sir**

L'Anse aux Meadows

Len Klingen

WHERE TO STAY

$ Tickle Inn - *RR#1. At Cape Onion via Raleigh.* ☎*709-452-4321 (Jun–Sept).* ☎*709-739-5503 off season, toll-free year-round 1-866-814-8567. www. tickleinn.net. 4 rooms.* 🅿 ☲.
This refurbished two-storey 1890s is aretreat for travellers to this remote peninsula. Guests gather in the dining room for a meal of island favourites such as Newfoundland shrimp and scallops or poached Atlantic salmon, concluding with Northern berry flan. Rates include a deluxe continental breakfast.

Wilfred Grenfell (1865-1940), began his medical missionary work in the area, including Labrador. St. Anthony preserves his memory through the hospital he established, a cooperative craft shop and the house local residents built for him, now the **Grenfell House Museum** *(PO Box 93, St. Anthony NL, A0K 4S0.* ♿🕑*Open Mon–Sun 9am–8pm.*☎*$6.* ☎*709-454-4010. www.grenfell-properties.com).*

St. John's★★

POPULATION 100,646 – MAP P 431

One of the oldest cities in North America, this historic seaport owes its founding to a fine natural harbour that now services an international shipping trade.

- 🛈 **Information:** Tourist Office, Gentara Building, 348 Water St. ☎709-576-8106 or www.stjohns.ca.
- 🅿 **Parking:** Parking meters are in effect 8am–6pm Mon–Fri. Cost is $0.25 for 15min, up to a maximum of 2hrs. Extended time meters on Harbour Drive permit parking for up to 8hrs. Check signs for snow-clearance and street-cleaning hours.
- 🧒 **Especially for Kids:** Signal Hill has a military tattoo.
- ☼ **Also See:** THE CAPE SHORE, HEART'S CONTENT

A Bit of History

Early Years – According to tradition, **John Cabot** entered the harbour on Saint John's day in 1497. Throughout the 16C, ships from European countries used the harbour as a fishing base. Under charter from Elizabeth I of England, **Sir Humphrey Gilbert** (c.1537-83) arrived in St. John's harbour in 1583 and declared Her Majesty's sovereignty. He thus is credited with giving England its first possession in the New World. Determined to maintain their fishing monopolies, England's West Country merchants opposed settlement of Newfoundland; from 1675 to 1677 a formal ban on settlement was in effect.

The Anglo-French Wars – Fear of French expansion changed the attitude of the British government toward permanent settlement. The French had established fortifications at Placentia in 1662 and attacked British harbours, especially St. John's. The city fell three times to the French, with the final battle in 1762 at the end of the Seven Years' War.

Devastating Fires – In the 19C the capital suffered five fires that virtually wiped out the entire community each time, the most extensive of all in 1892. Each time, the city was rebuilt, primarily in prevailing architectural styles such as Gothic Revival and, after the 1892 fire, Second Empire.

Confederation and Beyond – St. John's was a wealthy city in the early 20C and during World War II when it served as a base for North American convoys. After the war the Dominion of Newfoundland's decision to enter Confederation resulted in a decline in

St. John's seen from Cabot Tower

the city's economy, despite a substantial infusion of federal funds. Due to changes in the industry, St. John's importance as a fish-exporting centre declined. Finally, the 1992 collapse of the commercial cod fishery dealt a blow to fish-processing plants.

In the 21st century, however, the city has found prosperity underpinned by the province's vast mineral wealth. The huge nickel mine at Voisey's Bay, Labrador, began production in 2005, three offshore oil fields are producing and mining companies invested $160 million in exploration in 2007.

Harbour and Old City★★

The city's **site** borders a harbour almost landlocked except for a slim passage to the ocean known as **The Narrows,** which is flanked by cliffs rising on the north side to form Signal Hill. Gradually the harbour widens to nearly 800m/.5mi, surrounded by the steep slopes on which the city is built. Parallel to the water, **Harbour Drive** skirts the busy dock where ships from around the world are often berthed. The main thoroughfares of the old city, **Water** and **Duckworth streets,** contain restaurants, shops and banks. Colourful, **George Street** is home to pubs and eateries.

The Rooms (what compounds of fisheries buildings were once called) houses the Provincial Museum, the Provincial Archives, and the Art Gallery of Newfoundland and Labrador. The basement features an ongoing archaeological dig of a 1775 fort.

The Rooms Provincial Museum★ (M)

9 Bonaventure Ave. ✕ ◷*Open Jun–mid-Oct Mon–Sat 10am–5pm (Wed–Thu 9pm). Sun & holidays noon–5pm. Rest of the year closed Monday.* ◷*Closed Jan 1, Good Friday, Remembrance Day, Dec 25-26.* ⊛*$5.* ☏*709-757-8000. www.therooms.ca.*
This small museum is devoted to Newfoundland's history and prehistory. Displays on native cultures, notably those of the Beothuk Indians and Labrador

---

Regatta Day

Each year **Quidi Vidi** (KID-dy VID-dy) **Lake** is the site of St. John's Regatta, the oldest continuously held sporting event in North America (since 1826). Held on the first Wednesday in August (or the first fine day thereafter), the regatta is probably the only civic holiday decided that morning. The local population waits for the cry, "The races are on!" and then crowds the lakeshore to watch competitors row the 2.6km/1.6mi course, the major event of the all-day carnival.

Duckworth Street

Inuit; and exhibits about the lives of fishing families.

Commissariat House★

King's Bridge Rd. ◷*Open mid-Jun–mid-Oct daily 10am–5:30pm.* ⌷*$2.50.* ☎*709-729-6730. Off-season 709-729-0592.*
Dating from 1820, this clapboard house was one of the few buildings to escape the 19C fires. It was used for many years by the commissariat, which provisioned the military post of St. John's. After 1871 it became the rectory for adjacent **Church of St. Thomas (A)**. A **coach house** lodges an exhibit on the commissariat's function.

Within walking distance *(Military Rd.)* stand the residence of the lieutenant-governor, **Government House,** *(only the grounds can be visited without appointment. For tours ☎709-729-4494. www.mun.ca/govhouse)* and the former seat of the provincial assembly, the **Colonial Building** *(*▣◷*Open year-round Mon–Fri 9am–4:15pm.* ☎*709-729-3065),* which now houses the provincial archives.

Basilica Cathedral of St. John the Baptist (B)

200 Military Rd, St. John's NL, A1C 2E8. Corner of Harvey Rd., Military Rd. and Bonaventure Ave. ♿▣◷*Open year-round Mon–Fri 8am–4:45pm, Sat 8am–6pm, Sun 8:30am–12:30pm.* ◷*Closed major*

holidays except for mass. ☎*709-754-2170. www.thebasilica.ca*
This twin-towered 1850 Roman Catholic church is a landmark visible from the harbour and Signal Hill. The interior is ornate with statuary and altar carving.

Anglican Cathedral of St. John the Baptist (C)

9 Cathedral St, St. John's NL, A1C 3Y4. ◷*Open early Jun–30 Sept. Mon–Fri 9am–5pm, weekend hours vary.* ☞*Tours daily.* ☎*709-726-5677. www.infonet.st-johns.nl.ca/cathedral*
This Gothic Revival stone structure was designed in 1843 by British architect Sir **George Gilbert Scott** (1811–78). Destroyed by fire in 1892, the church was reconstructed in the 20C .The interior has wooden vaulted ceilings and **reredos,** an ornamental stone or wooden partition behind an altar. The **Cathedral Crypt Tearoom** serves a traditional afternoon tea. (◷*Jul–Aug Mon– Fri , 2:30–4:30pm (Wed 2pm)*

Signal Hill★★

Topped by Cabot Tower, Signal Hill rises steeply at the mouth of the harbour, permitting splendid views of the city.
In 1901 **Guglielmo Marconi** chose the site for an experiment to prove that radio signals could be transmitted long distances by electromagnetic waves. When he reputedly received the letter "S" in Morse code from Poldhu

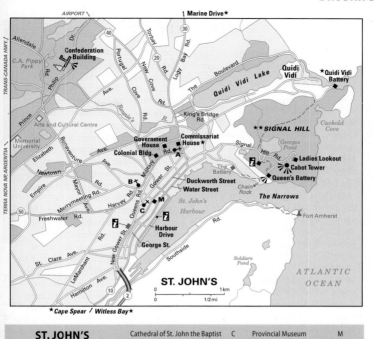

AIRPORT ⟍ ⟍ Marine Drive★

Confederation Building

TRANS-CANADA HWY.

Allendale

C.A. Pippy Park

Portugal Cove Rd.

New Cove Rd.

Torbay Rd.

Logy Bay Rd.

Boulevard

The

Quidi Vidi Lake

Quidi Vidi

★Quidi Vidi Battery

Cuckold Cove

King's Bridge Rd.

Prince

Arts and Cultural Centre

Memorial University

Elizabeth

Bonaventure Ave.

Newtown

Empire

Mayor Ave.

Merrymeeting Rd.

Harvey Rd.

Freshwater Rd.

Queens Rd.

New Gower St.

St. Clare Ave.

LeMarchant Rd.

Hamilton Ave.

Government House
Colonial Bldg.

Military Rd.

Gower St.

Commissariat House★

Signal Hill Rd.

★★SIGNAL HILL

Georges Pond

Signal Hill

Ladies Lookout
Cabot Tower
Queen's Battery

The Battery

Chain Rock

The Narrows

Fort Amherst

Duckworth Street
Water Street

St. John's Harbour

Harbour Drive

George St.

Southside

Soldiers Pond

ST. JOHN'S

ATLANTIC OCEAN

0   1km
0   1/2mi

★Cape Spear / Witless Bay★

| ST. JOHN'S | Cathedral of St. John the Baptist | C | Provincial Museum | M |
| | Basilica of St. John the Baptist | B | St. Thomas | A |

in Cornwall, England—a distance of 2,700km/1,700mi—he made history.

Visit

P **⊙**Grounds open year-round daily. Visitor centre open mid-May–mid-Oct daily 10am–6pm. Rest of the year Mon–Fri 8:30am–4:30pm. ⊙Closed Jan 1, Dec 25-26) ∞$4. ☎709-772-5367. www.pc.gc.ca. Completed in 1898, **Cabot Tower** (⊙Jun–Labour Day 8:30am–9pm, Apr–May & Sept–mid-Jan 9am–5pm. ⊙Closed mid-Jan–Mar 31) affords a **panorama★★★** of the city.

A path leads to **Ladies Lookout,** the crown of the hill (160m/525ft). From **Queen's Battery** (1833) there is a good **view★** of the harbour. On the other side of the Narrows stand the remains of Fort Amherst (1763), now housing a lighthouse.

In the summer, students in the 19C uniforms of the Royal Newfoundland Regiment perform a **military tattoo** (Jul–mid-Aug Wed, Thu & weekends 3pm & 7pm, weather permitting. ∞$2.50) consisting of fife-and-drum corps and military drills near the visitor centre.

Additional Sights

Quidi Vidi Battery★

▸ Take King's Bridge Rd. Turn right on Forest Rd. When road becomes Quidi Vidi Village Rd., drive 2km/1.2mi to Cuckhold's Cove Rd. Turn right.

⊙Open Jul–mid-Oct daily 10am–5:30pm. ∞$2.50. ☎709-729-2977. Built by the French during their occupation of St. John's in 1762, this emplacement was strengthened by the British in the early 19C. The house re-creates the living quarters of soldiers stationed there. Below is the tiny fishing community of **Quidi Vidi,** which has a narrow channel connecting to the larger Quidi Vidi Lake, site of the annual St. John's Regatta.

Confederation Building

Prince Philip Dr. ✕&**P** ⊙Open year-round Mon–Fri 8:30am–4pm. ⊙Closed major holidays. Information office on 10th floor. ☎709-729-2300.

Newfoundland's Parliament and some provincial government offices are

Address Book

For dollar sign categories, see the Legend on the cover flap.

WHERE TO STAY

$ Roses B&B – *9 Military Rd, A1C 2C3.* ☎709-726-3336, toll-free 1-877-767-3722. *www.therosesbandb.com. 6 rooms.* ⬛. Located in the same neighbourhood as the Fairmont Newfoundland, this bed-and-breakfast is within walking distance of downtown and Signal Hill. The best choice for budget accommodations, The Roses consists of four adjacent row houses that have been spruced up nicely for guests. The rooms are bright and pleasantly furnished, some with antiques and original woodwork. Suites are spacious and have kitchens, perfect for families.

$$ McCoubrey Manor – *6-8 Ordnance St. A1C 3K7.* ☎709-722-7577, toll-free 1-888-753-7577. *www.mccoubrey.com. 6 rooms.* ⬛. Situated just across the street from the Fairmont Newfoundland, this pair of 1904 Queen Ann Revival town houses offers good value. Architectural details—such as the double oak mantel in the living room and plaster rosettes on the ceilings—lend an historic air. The innkeepers offer wine and cheese in the afternoons, guest laundry facilities, and all modern amenities. Included in the room rate is a hearty breakfast. Four housekeeping apartments are in nearby buildings.

$$ Winterholme – *79 Rennies Mill Rd. A1C 3R1.* ☎709-739-7979 or 800-599-7829. *www.winterholme.com. 11 rooms.* ⬛⬛⬛. Occupying a 1905 Queen Anne Revival house on leafy grounds, Winterholme sits in St. John's Heritage District 15 minutes from downtown. Inside, the magnificent oak woodwork commands your attention; the downstairs parlours are architectural marvels. Varying in size and appointments, guest rooms range in decor from simply furnished (third floor) to mildly decadent (the former billiards room). Breakfast is served in the attractive dining room.

$$$ Murray Premises – *5 Becks Cove, A1C 6H1.* ☎709-738-7773, toll-free 1-866-738-7773. *www.murraypremises hotel.com. 28 rooms.* ⬛⬛⬛. This downtown boutique hotel, which opened in 2001, occupies the third and fourth floors of a converted trading house (called "premises" throughout the province). While many of the beams and timbers are old, and some rooms are still tucked under eaves, the space has a modern gloss. Luxurious touches abound, such as whirlpool tubs and heated towel racks in guest bathrooms. The lively music scene on George Street is entertaining, but boisterous weekends might take a toll on your sleep. Continental breakfast included.

$$$ Fairmont Newfoundland – PO Box 5637, 115 *Cavendish Sq. A1C 5W8.* ☎709-726-4980, toll-free 800-441-1414. *www.fairmont.com. 301 rooms.* ⬛⬛⬛⬛⬛. This modern hotel, part of the upscale Fairmont chain, sits on a knoll over the harbour, giving great views of The Narrows. What the hotel lacks in down-home charm, it makes up in top-flight service and attention to detail. Rooms decorated in a contemporary style feature dataports and cordless phones with voicemail. The **Cabot Club ($$$$)** ranks as one of the city's best dining rooms, noted for its seafood dishes and tableside flambés. Less formal fare is available at the Bonavista Café and The Narrows Lounge.

WHERE TO EAT

$$$ The Cellar – *152 Water St., Fourth Floor.* ☎709-579-8900. **Contemporary**. Popular with local residents, this fine dining restaurant occupies the spacious fourth floor of an office building. Favourites include blackened scallops with lemon cream, sautéed pork tenderloin with apricots and fruit brandy, and traditional pan-fried cod with pork scruncions. A distinctive selection of single-malt scotches helps take the chill off a foggy night.

$$$ Stonehouse Renaissance – *8 Kennas Hill. A1A 1H9.* ☎709-753-2425. **Canadian**. Housed in an historic stone building near Quidi Vidi Lake, Stonehouse offers creative, exquisitely prepared fare. The dining rooms are intimate and the menu is ambitious. The emphasis is on fresh local seafood and wild game. A table d'hôte menu is offered nightly.

$$ Aqua – *310 Water St. A1C 1B8.* ☎*709-576-2782. www.aquarestaurant.ca.* **Thai.** Aqua boasts the spare decor and urban sensibility of a SoHo restaurant. A favourite on the Thai-influenced menu is the blue mussels in basil pomodora sauce; the spring rolls are also popular. The cumin-crusted lamb with a fig glaze is widely admired.

$$ Duck Street Bistro – *252 Duckworth St. Dinner only.* ☎*709-753-0400.* **International.** International without putting on airs, this homey bistro has the casual feel of a 70s hippie pad—albeit decorated by someone with impeccable style. When in season, local mushrooms add zest to dishes, and there's a good selection of curries and international dishes. Desserts are outstanding: try the warm gingerbread with hot rum sauce, or the fresh fruit crisp.

$ Zachary's – *71 Duckworth St. A1C 1E6.* ☎*709-579-8050.* **Canadian.** Simple, tasty home-style fare with a regional bias served in relaxed surroundings rules the day here. Expect great value for your dollar. Breakfast, served all day, is the best option, but lunch and dinner are also served. Fish is cooked just perfectly, vegetables are served while still crunchy, and Zachary's partridgeberry cheesecake for dessert leaves patrons smiling.

housed in this building. Constructed in 1960 and expanded in 1985, the edifice provides a good **view** from its front entrance of the harbour and Signal Hill. When in session the **legislative assembly** can be observed *(sessions Feb–May Mon–Fri, third-floor visitors' gallery).*

Excursions

Cape Spear National Historic Site★

About 11km/7mi south; follow Water St. to Leslie St. Turn left at Leslie St. Go over bridge, continue straight after stop sign, following the road (Hwy. 11). ◷*Grounds open year-round. Visitor centre open mid-*

©City of St. John's

View from Queen's Battery

WALK ON THE WILD SIDE

One of Newfoundland's marvels is the utter lack of development along much of the wild and rugged coast—early settlers migrated to the more placid coves and inlets, leaving the headlands to the terns and gulls. On the 🥾 **East Coast Trail**, an intrepid hiker can trek southward from downtown St. John's along the edge of the crashing surf for a total of some 450km/281mi. The trail is well suited for day hikes, with parking at access points along the route, and superb options for walks among wildflowers and memorable vistas. Guidebooks and maps are available for purchase in many shops around the city. (*East Coast Trail Assn. 50 Pippy Pl., PO Box 8034, St. John's NL, A1B 3M7. ☎709-738-4453. www.eastcoasttrail.com*).

May–mid-Oct daily 10am–6pm. 🎟$4. *☎709-722-5367. www.pc.gc.ca.* 🕭*Wear warm clothing. It is colder here than in St. John's.*

At longitude 52°37'24", Cape Spear is North America's most easterly point. On clear days there are **views**★ of the coast. Whales can usually be seen in the waters off the cape seasonally (*May–Sept*). The restored square **1836 lighthouse** (🕐*Open mid-May–mid-Oct daily 10am–6pm.* 🎟*$2.50*) is the province's oldest. The return trip to St. John's (*30km/19mi*) can be made via the fishing villages of Maddox Cove and **Petty Harbour**.

Witless Bay Ecological Reserve★

Embarkation from town of Bay Bulls, 30km/19mi south of St. John's via Rte. 10. Then watch for directional signs of your chosen boat tour company to the dock. ✗🕭▣🕐*Departures May–Sept daily. Round-trip 2hrs 30min. Reservations required.* 🎟*$55 adult. For sched-*

ule, contact **O'Brien's Whale & Bird Tours** *☎709-753-4850, toll-free 1-877-639-4253. www.obriensboattours.com. Departures May–Oct daily. Round-trip 1hr 30min.* 🎟*$47. For schedule, contact* **Gatherall's Puffin and Whale Watch**. *☎709-334-2887, toll-free 1-800-419-4253. www.gatheralls.com*

The fish-filled waters and shore islands of Witless Bay (*disembarkation on the islands is not permitted*) attract thousands of sea birds annually. The **Atlantic puffin** colony here is reputedly the largest on the east coast of North America. An additional highlight of the cruise is **whale watching**★★ (*late spring and summer*).

Marine Drive★

12km/8mi north on Hwys. 30 and 20. Leave St. John's on Logy Bay Rd. (Rte. 30). After 5.5km/3mi, turn right to Marine Dr. The **view**★ from **Outer Cove** is especially lovely. At **Middle Cove** there is an accessible beach, good for strolling along the shore.

ONE-STOP NOSHING

Looking for a snack or a picnic lunch? **Auntie Crae's Food Shop** located in a former hardware emporium, is the place to go in downtown St. John's. Open daily 8am–7pm, Auntie Crae's offers goodies such as sandwiches, fresh-baked cookies and soothing teas. You can eat in the Fishhook Neyle's Common Room next door, or order take-out for a hike. The shop is also a great spot for buying inexpensive souvenirs: Auntie Crae's homemade partridgeberry jam is always welcome. On Tuesday noons, Auntie Crae's House Band plays traditional music. (*272 Water St., A1C 1B7. ☎709-754-0661. www.auntiecraes.com*).

555

Saint-Pierre and Miquelon★
(FRANCE)
POPULATION 6,125– MAP P 421

These French islands, ceded to France by the 1763 Treaty of Paris, have a decidedly continental lifestyle. The two principal islands are Saint-Pierre and the larger Miquelon, connected by a long sandbar to what was once a third island, Langlade. Today, the only industries are tourism and fishing.

- **Information:** Comité Général du Tourisme, Place du Général de Gaulle. ☎011-508-41-02 00. www.st-pierre-et-miquelon.info
- **Orient Yourself:** These tiny islands are 48km/30mi by boat from Newfoundland.
- **Organizing Your Time:** The islands' time zone is 30min ahead of St. John's and 1hr ahead of Halifax.
- **Also See:** BURIN PENINSULA

Visit

Saint-Pierre★
At the entrance to the harbour sits at **Ile-aux-Marins**★ *(accessible from Saint-Pierre, in front of the tourist office, by 10min ferry ride)*, once a community of over 800 inhabitants. Centered in the old schoolhouse, the **museum** contains a presentation of isle history *(Place du Général de Gaule, St-Pierre 97500. Open May–Oct Tue–Sat 10am–noon, 2pm–4pm, Sun 2–5pm. 3 €. ☎011-508-41-58-88)*. The treeless terrain permits

---

Practical Information

GETTING THERE
BY BOAT
Passenger ferry from Fortune to Saint-Pierre island: Jul –Labour Day departs from Fortune daily 2:45pm; departs from Saint-Pierre daily 1:30pm. Jun & Sept–mid-Oct departs from Fortune Fri & Sun 2:45pm; departs from Saint-Pierre 1:30pm. 1hr–1hr 35min. Schedule may vary: call to confirm. Winter service varies. One-month advance reservations required. Round-trip ⚓$93.50 adult. 🅿($10/night) SPM Tours and Lake Travel. ☎709-832-2006, toll-free 1-800-563-2006 (Canada/US), ☎011-508-41-24-26 in Saint-Pierre. www.spmexpress.net ⚠*Warning: the sea crossing can be rough.*

BY AIR
Air service from St.John's NL, Sydney and Halifax NS, and Montreal QC, provided by Air Saint-Pierre. *For information & reservations, contact Air Saint-Pierre 1-877-277-7765 (Canada1US) ☎011-508-41-00-00 in Saint-Pierre, or access www.airsaintpierre.com.*

CUSTOMS
European and USA citizens must carry a valid passport, which is necessary to transit Canada. Canadian cizens must provide an official ID card with picture and proof of citizenship (birth certificate). Other nationalities must have valid passport and in some cases a visa., which can be obtained from the nearest French embassy or consulate.

LANGUAGE
English is not commonly spoken on the islands. Telephone operators and tourist office staffs are bilingual, however.

ACCOMMODATIONS AND INFORMATION
Contact in advance the Comité Régional du Tourisme, Place du Général De Gaulle, BP 4274, 97500 St-Pierre-et-Miquelon. ☎011-508-41-02 00. www.st-pierre-et-miquelon.info (click "en" button in upper right-hand corner for English version)

views of Saint-Pierre and the remains of one of the more than 600 shipwrecks in the archipelago.

Miquelon and Langlade

Boat departures to Miquelon and Langlade available from Saint-Pierre. In summer, daily ferry to Langlade. Transportation by shuttle van to the village of Miquelon is available in summer or may be arranged off-season (✆contact Cmité de Tourisme above). Except for the small working town of the same name, the northern island of Miquelon is untouched moorland. Seals might be seen lying on the sands of **Grand Barachois**. The road crosses the isthmus known as the Dune of Langlade, a sandbar formed in part by debris from shipwrecks. Situated at the southern end is the uninhabited "island" of Langlade. Along the east side of the dune, a wide beach stretches out in the vicinity of Anse du Gouvernement.

Terra Nova National Park★

MAP P 421

Scarred by glaciers of the past, this 396sq km/153sq mi area is a combination of rolling country and indented coastline. Deep fiords, or "sounds," reach inland, and in early summer these coastal waters are dotted with icebergs that float down with the Labrador Current.

- 🛈 **Information:** ☎709-533-2801. www.pc.gc.ca
- ▶ **Orient Yourself:** Tera Nova Park lies on the west side of Bonavista Bay. It is crossed by Trans-Canada Hwy 1.
- 🕐 **Organizing Your Time:** Ask at the visitor centre about boat tours of Newman Sound.
- ✆ **Also See:** TRINITY

Access

On Trans-Can Hwy. 58km/36mi from Gander, or 210km/130mi from St. John's.

Visit

✗♿🕐*Open year-round.* 🎫*$5.50/day use fee. Visitor centre open mid-Jun–Labour Day daily 9am–7pm; mid-May–early Jun & Sept–early Oct daily 10am–5pm. Rest of the year Thur–Mon 11am–3pm.* 🕐*Closed Dec–early Jan.* ☎*709-533-2801. www.pc.gc.ca.*

Bluehill Pond Lookout★★

7km/5mi from park's north entrance.

- ▶ *Turn onto gravel road and continue approximately 2km/1mi to the observatory platform.*

From the lookout platform there is a **panorama★★** of the whole park. To the south is Newman Sound and the ocean, scattered with icebergs (in season).

Newman Sound★

12km/8mi from park's north entrance.

- ▶ *Take road to the visitor centre and Newman Sound. About 1.5km/1mi to the trail.*

This deep inlet with a sandy beach can be appreciated by walking the trail along its wooded shore. Seasonal wildflowers and tiny seashells complement the setting.

Ochre Lookout

18km/11mi from park's north entrance.

- ▶ *Take gravel road to the tower, about 3km/2mi. Observation deck.*

From this lookout tower, another **panorama★** allows visitors to comprehend the vastness of the park. At this height, Clode and Newman sounds are clearly visible, weather permitting.

Trinity★★

This seaside community has a lovely **setting** and the small protected harbour. In 1615, the town became the site of the first Admiralty Court in Canada's history. Trinity's standing receded in in the 1850s when St. John's became the provincial capital. Today it is a popular area for **whale watching** (*Departures Jun–Labour Day weather permitting. 4hrs, including orientation, gear supplied. ⌕$75. Ocean Contact Ltd., PO Box 10, Trinity NL, A0C 2S0. ☎709-464-3269.www.oceancontact.com*).

ⓘ Information: Campbell House B&B, 49 High St., ☎709-464-3377, toll-free 1-877-464-7700. www.trinityvacations.com

Kids Especially for Kids: The whale-watching boats are 9m/29ft rubber dinghies, much like Zodiacs. This is an adventure only for older children.

Ⓒ Also See: TERRA NOVA NATIONAL PARK

Access

74km/46mi northeast of Trans-Can Hwy. by Rte. 230. Turn off Rte. 230 for 5km/3mi.

Visit

Located in a restored house overlooking the harbour, the **interpretation centre** presents the community's history (*ⒸOpen mid-May–Sept daily 10am–5:30pm. ☎709-464-2042, toll-free 1-800-563-6353. www.tcr.gov.nl.ca/historicsites*). Housed in a seven-room "salt box" dating to the 1880s, the **Trinity Historical Society Museum** contains artifacts and historical documents (*ⒸOpen Jun–Sept daily 10am–1pm & 2pm–5:30pm. ⌕$2. ☎709-464-3599. www.trinityhistoricalsociety.com*).

WHERE TO STAY

$$ The Village Inn - *Taverner's Path (Rte. 239-10). ☎709-464-3269. www.oceancontact.com. 9 rooms.* This early 1900s two-storey wooden structure offers rooms with wooden floors and brass beds. The sitting area features a fireplace and two dining rooms that serve home-cooked meals **($)**. Newfoundland cod, salmon, halibut, shrimp, shepherd's pie, and rice and nut roast. Breakfast, lunch and dinner are served. There's even an on-site pub. (The inn serves as the headquarters for Ocean Contact whale-watching cruises.)

The 1881 **Hiscock House** has been restored to its early-1900s appearance and contains some original furnishings (*ⒸOpen mid-May–Sept daily 10am–5:30pm .⌕$2.50. ☎709-464-2042, toll-free 1-800-563-6353*).

St. Paul's Anglican Church (1892) stands as a village landmark. The 31m/102ft clock spire of this large wooden house of worship towers above the town. The **Holy Trinity Roman Catholic Church** has been In use for over 150 years.

Excursion to Cape Bonavista

From Trinity, Route 230 northbound continues inland and returns to the sea at Port Union and Catalina, two fishing communities set along the shore. At Catalina, Route 237 crosses the peninsula, ending at Amherst Cove, where Route 235 continues northward to the cape town of Bonavista (*52km/31mi north of Trinity*).

W. Sturge/Government of Newfoundland

Cape Bonavista Lighthouse

NORTHWEST TERRITORIES

A vast region composing more than a tenth of Canada's size, the Northwest Territories embrace a varied landscape: mountains and forests, lakes and rivers, tundra and swamps. Two UNESCO World Heritage Sites, **Wood Buffalo National Park** and **Nahanni National Park Reserve**, lie partly or wholly within its boundaries. Except for the capital city of Yellowknife, few large settlements exist in this frontier wilderness. Although the size of the Northwest Territories was more than halved when Nunavut separated into an autonomous region in 1999, the Territories remains a diverse area suited for lovers of adventure, wilderness, wildlife and indigenous cultures.

- **Information:** Northwest Territories Tourism, PO Box 610, Yellowknife NT, X1A 2N5. ☎867-873-5007, toll-free 1-800-661-0788, international inquiries 867-873-7200. www.explorenwt.com
- ▶ **Orient Yourself:** Comprising lands above the 60th parallel, the Territories stretch from the broken-lands tundra above Saskatchewan to the Yukon. They include the extreme western parts of the Arctic Archipelago between the mainland and the North Pole.
- **Don't Miss:** Outfitters can ensure a pleasant adventure no matter what your level of experience.
- 🕐 **Organizing Your Time:** The drive from Edmonton to Yellowknife takes one very long day, or two shorter days.
- **Kids Especially for Kids:** They are sure to see a great deal of wildlife.
- **Also See:** NUNAVUT, YUKON TERRITORY

Topography

Landscape – Two distinct landscapes border this vast region. In the east lies the giant plain between Hudson Bay and the Beaufort Sea. In the west rise the Mackenzie, Selwyn and Richardson mountain ranges. East of the Mackenzie Mountains is a broad river valley through which run the great Mackenzie River and its tributaries: the Slave and the Liard. East of the Mackenzie Lowlands lies the

Hiking in Nahanni country

Aurora Borealis

Also known as the Northern Lights, this amazing phenomenon can usually be viewed in fall and winter. The sky "dissolves" into folded curtains of elusive, dancing lights, sometimes many coloured, other times black and white. They seem to occur when electrically charged particles, emitted by the sun, collide with atoms and molecules in the earth's outer atmosphere, causing the latter to emit radiation, sometimes in the form of visible light. Research on these displays has been conducted at Churchill, Manitoba.

Aurora Borealis

NWT/T. Parker

Canadian Shield, pitted with lakes, rivers and muskeg swaps left by glaciers that retreated 10,000 years ago.

Permafrost – Permafrost, where the ground remains at or below 0°C/32°F, generally starts about 0.3m/1ft or more below the surface. To prevent roadbeds and foundations from sinking, builders must avoid melting the frozen soil during construction work.

Vegetation – The tree line crosses the Territories diagonally northwest to southeast from the Mackenzie Delta to Hudson Bay at the Manitoba border. South and west of this line extends the **boreal forest** of spruce, poplar, tamarack (mascot tree of the Territories) and jack pine. To the north and east is the **tundra,** sometimes called "the barren lands" for its bleak look in winter and lack of trees. In summer dwarf shrubs, tiny flowers of all hues and lichens thrive in the surface ground above the permafrost. Known as **muskeg,** this surface ground is sometimes very boggy because it cannot drain.

Climate – Annual precipitation over much of the Territories is so low (Yellowknife 254mm/10in, Inuvik 276mm/11in) that a great part of the region would be desert if the permafrost did not cradle what moisture there is on the surface. Generally the winters are long, cold and dark and the summers surprisingly warm and sunny, with long hours of daylight (and no real darkness in midsummer). The southern region has 20 hours of daylight, while north, in the Arctic Circle, daylight is continuous. The mean daily maximum temperatures for July are 21°C/70°F in Yellowknife and 19°C/66°F in Inuvik.

A Bit of History

Earliest Settlement – People who arrived from Asia some 15,000–20,000 years ago, across the land bridge now covered by the Bering Strait, settled south of the ice cap that covered the continent. Later, about 4,000 years ago, the ancestors of the Inuit crossed from Sibera into Alaska, eventually moving east. Today there are two distinct indigenous groups, the Dene and the Inuit, the latter of whom compose the majority of Nunavut's population.

The Dene – Of the 41,464 inhabitants in the Northwest Territories, slightly less than half claim aboriginal origin. Of these, the majority are Dene, who make up roughly a quarter of the population. The Inuit (Inuvialuit) account for about 10 percent. The rest are Métis and nonaboriginal residents.
The Athapaskan-speaking peoples of the subarctic hunted caribou and fished, constantly on the move to find food. Today some of these people have preserved a fairly traditional lifestyle, but many live on the fringe of contemporary society. Dene settlements have benefited economically from mineral exploration. Dene peoples are known for their intricate beadwork.

Fur Traders – **Samuel Hearne** of the Hudson's Bay Company traversed much of the region, especially during his famous 1770-72 trip from Churchill to Great Slave Lake, seeking furs. Not long afterward, in 1789, **Alexander Mackenzie** of the rival North West Company travelled the river that bears his name. Some of the trading posts established after the two fur companies joined in 1821 remain to this day.

20C Development – In the late 19C and early 20C, the Geological Survey of Canada mounted expeditions under such men as **Joseph Burr Tyrrell,** Sir **William Logan** (after whom Mt. Logan is named), **George Mercer Dawson** (of Dawson City fame) and **Vilhjalmar Stefansson** to explore and map the Territories. By this time both Anglican and Roman Catholic missionaries were established in the region. In the 1930s major mineral finds (ⓒ *see below*) encouraged more outsiders to come to the Territories.

Partitioning of the Territories – In 1992 the residents of the Northwest Territories voted to divide their land to create a new territory in the central and eastern portions. Named **Nunavut** (meaning "our land" in the native language, Inuktitut), this new territory became autonomous in 1999.

Resources and Industries

Mining – Since the 1930s the basis of the economy has been mining. Fur trapping, forestry, fishing, tourism and the sale of native arts and crafts also contribute, but to a much lesser extent. Deposits of pitchblende—a source of uranium—and silver were discovered on the shores of the Great Bear Lake in 1930. Subsequent gold discoveries at Yellowknife underpinned the economy for more than 50 years; the Con mine in Yellowknife closed in 2003, but other minerals are coming to the fore.
Diamonds were discovered in 1991 in the Lac de Gras area northeast of Yellowknife. One mine entered production in the late 1990s and two more were producing by 2003. A third will open at Snap Lake northeast of Yellowknife. Canada is now the world's third-largest diamond producer by value, after Russia and Botswana.

Oil and Gas – Near Fort Liard, the largest natural gas well in Canada began production in 2000, and producing oil wells and a refinery at Norman Wells on the Mackenzie represent long-established fields. Two potentially rich areas for oil and gas are the Mackenzie Delta–Beaufort Sea region, and the high Arctic islands. Hearings are underway about building a 1220-km/763-mi supply pipeline southward, the Mackenzie Gas Project, to tie into the extensive pipeline grid in Northern Alberta.

Practical Information

Getting There

BY AIR

Most flights to the Northwest Territories connect through Edmonton or Calgary, Alberta, to airports in Yellowknife and Innuvik. You can also connect through the Nunavut capital, Iquluit. Within the Northwest Territories, scheduled and chartered flights are provided by **Canadian North** (☎867-873-4484. 1-800-661-1505 (Canada/US). www. canadiannorth.com) and **First Air**, an Air Canada affiliate (☎1-800-267-1247. www.firstair.ca). **Northwestern Air Lease** (☎867-872-2216. www.nwal.ca.) Air Canada connects Yellowknife and Edmonton.(☎1-888-247-2262 (Canada/US). www.aircanada.com)

GENERAL INFORMATION

ACCOMMODATIONS AND VISITOR INFORMATION

Every year Northwest Territories publishes the Explorers' Guide, which lists hotels, motels, lodges, camps and outfitters. There are also a guides for campgrounds, hunting, fishing and for viewing the aurora borealis. Contact **NWT Tourism**, (Box 610, Yellowknife, NT, X1A 2N5. ☎ 867-873-5007, toll-free 1-800-661-0788 (Canada/US). www. explorenwt.com). You can download the guides from the website. Yellowknife, the provincial capital, has an extensive group of hotels, motels and bed-and-breakfast inns.

DRIVING IN THE NORTH

While the Mackenzie Highway is paved all 1500km/938mi from Edmonton to Yellowknife, other highways are generally hard-packed gravel. Motorists are cautioned to pass other vehicles slowly to prevent flying rocks or skidding, and to pull to the right. Unless otherwise posted, the speed limit is 90km/h (55mph). **Seat belt** use is mandatory. Most communities along highways have service stations, but it is advisable to fill up frequently; it is not necessary to carry extra fuel. Full windshield-washer fluid reserves are essential. Drivers should be alert for **moose**, bison and other large animals along roadways; collisions with wildlife can be disastrous.

It is recommended that motorists carry at least one spare tire, jack, water, insect repellent, first-aid kit, emergency flares and, in winter, snow shovel, sand or cat litter for traction, candles, matches, high-calorie snacks, gloves, parka, warm clothes, and a sleeping bag for each person in the vehicle. For highway conditions ☎1-800-661-0750 (Canada). www.dot.gov.nt.ca

Government ferry service (free) is provided along the Mackenzie, Dempster and Liard highways (for information ☎1-800-661-0750 (Canada). www. dot.gov.nt.ca). To access Yellowknife, Highway 3 crosses the river at Fort Providence. The **Dempster Highway** crosses the Mackenzie River at Arctic Red River (Tsiigehtchic) and the Peel River, near Fort McPherson, to reach Inuvik. Near Fort Simpson the **Mackenzie Highway** crosses the Liard River. There are ice bridges across these rivers in winter. During the three- to six-week freeze-up and thaw periods (Nov & May), the rivers cannot be crossed. The many cross-country winter roads and ice roads in the Northwest Territories are not advisable for use by passenger cars, and some privately published maps show roads that are not suitable for two-wheel-drive vehicles (4-wheel drive vehicles are recommended).

TIME ZONES

The Northwest Territories is in the Mountain Standard time zone. Daylight Saving Time is observed from the 2nd Sunday in March to 1st Sunday in November.

TAXES

There is no provincial sales tax, but the 5% GST applies.

LIQUOR LAWS

The legal drinking age is 19. Liquor, wine and beer are sold in government liquor stores in the larger communities. Some communities have voted for restrictions on liquor, including prohibition of possession.

TERRITORIAL HOLIDAY

National Aboriginal Day: Jun 21

RECREATION

OUTDOOR ACTIVITIES

The Northwest Territories is a wonderland for outdoor enthusiasts. Charter planes transport hikers, hunters, fishermen and **canoeists** (with their canoes) to remote regions. Outfitters organize and equip wilderness travel year-round. One of the world's great canoe trips is down the **South Nahanni River**, but other routes of varying degrees of difficulty are available. There are also opportunities for hiking and mountain biking, including an arduous and memorable trek along the **Canol Heritage Trail** through the Mackenzie Mountains from Norman Wells to the Yukon. All wilderness travellers (including boaters, canoeists, cyclists and hikers) are asked to register with the Royal Canadian Mounted Police detachment nearest their point of departure, and to notify the police when their trip is completed. Substantial wilderness equipment, including warm clothing, a sleeping bag, a stove, fuel and a GPS system should be carried. Bear safety precautions are essential, and travellers lacking wilderness experience are strongly advised to hire local outfitters. Wilderness lodges are scattered on remote lakes and coasts from the Mackenzie Mountains to the Arctic coast, where **fishing** is superb (Arctic char, Arctic grayling, northern pike and lake trout, among others). Licenses are required, and all nonresident hunters of big game (wolf, moose, caribou, Dall sheep, grizzly, black bears and polar bears) must be accompanied by a licensed outfitter. Details regarding seasons, package tours, accommodations, outfitters, wilderness excursions as well as hunting and fishing regulations are available from Northwest Territories Tourism (see above).

Handicrafts – Delicate carvings are fashioned from caribou antlers or, more exotically, mammoth tusks uncovered from beneath the tundra. Clothing suited to this climate, particularly Dene mukluks (waterproof boots, often made of sealskin) decorated with beautiful beadwork, has become popular farther south. Fort Liard and Fort Simpson are good places to shop for beaded apparel.

MACKENZIE DELTA★★

The 100km/70mi-wide delta—one of the world's largest—is the estuary of the vast and fast-moving Mackenzie River. Abundant with wildlife, the delta supports innumerable muskrats, beavers, mink, marten, foxes, bears, moose, caribou and smaller mammals. Its channels and lakes abound with fish. Beluga whales calve in the warm waters, and migratory birds congregate here in the spring. Many delta communities depend on trapping, hunting and fishing. However, huge reserves of oil and gas recently discovered under the Beaufort Sea have impacted the area.

- **Information:** NWT Tourism. ☎867-873-7200, toll-free 1-800-661-0788. www.explorenwt.com
- ▶ **Orient Yourself:** The Mackenzie River Delta consists of a labyrinth of channels among thousands of lakes, 160km/100mi from the Beaufort Sea, at the northwest edge of the Territories' mainland.
- **Don't Miss:** Try to fly over the Mackenzie Delta to appreciate its complexity.
- **Organizing Your Time:** Tuktoyaktuk, although remote, does offer accommodation and services.

Access

Dempster Highway from the Yukon (Dawson City to Inuvik 798km/496mi), 🕒*open year-round except during freeze-up and thaw periods. Few services on road. Motorists should be outfitted for emergencies. Also accessible by air from Edmonton via Yellowknife, and from Whitehorse, Yukon. The best way to appreciate the delta is to fly over it; charters can be arranged in Inuvik. For information contact NWT Tourism, Yellowknife, NT ☎867-873-7200, toll-free 1-800-661-0788 (Canada/US). www.explorenwt.com.*

Visit

The Delta

Viewed from the air, the tangle of muddy arteries belonging to the Mackenzie and the Peel rivers, which join at this point, can be distinguished from the lakes by their color. The western edge is clearly marked by the frequently snowcapped **Richardson Mountains**, the eastern edge by the low, humped **Caribou Hills**. Heading north, the land gives way as the areas of water become greater, until the vast Beaufort Sea is reached.

Except for areas of tundra along the coast, the land is covered with low scrubs (dwarf willow and juniper) that turn bright yellow with the first frost (usually late August). The tundra itself is full of lakes, and many colourful, multihued mosses, lichens and flowers bloom in the short but light (24 hours of daylight) Arctic summer.

Inuvik

On Dempster Hwy.; airport; accommodations. Meaning "place of man" in Inuktitut, this outpost lies on a large stretch of flat land beside the east channel of the Mackenzie. Inuvik is an administrative centre of the territorial government.

Houses are constructed on pilings, steamed into the permafrost before construction, so that heat from the house does not melt the permafrost underneath, causing the house to sink. Water, sewage and heating ducts are housed together in above-ground **utilidors**, or covered corridors, to keep them from freezing.

The **Roman Catholic Church**, built in the shape of an igloo, features an **interior**★ with paintings of the Stations of the Cross done in 1960 by Mona Thrasher, then a young Inuit girl.

Tuktoyaktuk★

Daily flights from Inuvik; ice road in winter; accommodations. This pleasant little community on the shores of the Beaufort Sea is known simply as "Tuk" to northerners. It is best known for one of nature's most curious phenomena: **pingos**, or huge moss- and turf-covered mounds of solid ice pushed out of the otherwise flat tundra by permafrost action. From the air, they resemble giant boils.

At the **Fur Garment Shop**, visitors can observe Inuit women making parkas and other items of clothing.

View of the Makenzie Delta

NAHANNI NATIONAL PARK RESERVE★★★

A wild, remote and staggeringly beautiful place, this reserve in the southwest corner of the Northwest Territories was designated by UNESCO as a World Heritage Site in 1978.

Early in the 20C, tales of placer gold lured prospectors to the valley of the South Nahanni. In 1908 the headless bodies of two adventurers were found. Other men disappeared without a trace. Stories of fierce native inhabitants and of mythical mountain men were spread abroad, and the South Nahanni became known as a place to avoid.

The mystery remains and the legends are recalled by names in the park such as Deadmen Valley, Headless Range, Broken Skull River and Funeral Range. The park's very inaccessibility is part of its beauty. Unlike other national parks, it will probably never have roads and tourist facilities. But for those willing to make the effort, one of the world's great natural glories awaits.

- **Information:** NWT Tourism, PO Box 610, Yellowknife NT, X1A 2N5. ☎867-873-7200, toll-free 1-800 661-0788.www.explorenwt.com or Parks Canada, Nahanni National Park, PO Box 348, Fort Simpson NT, X0E 0N0. ☎867-695-3151. www.pc.gc.ca.
- ▶ **Orient Yourself:** This park covers a large section of the South Nahanni River, which flows through the Selwyn, Mackenzie and Franklin mountains before joining the Liard River, a tributary of the mighty Mackenzie.
- **Don't Miss:** A canoe trip down the South Nahanni River is one of the world's great wilderness trips.
- **Organizing Your Time:** A river trip takes 7–21 days, depending on where you start and end. This destination is popular, but access is limited, so book well in advance. Peak times are July and August.
- **Especially for** Kids: This park would not be suitable for younger children.
- **Also See:** THE ALASKA HIGHWAY, YELLOWKNIFE

Access by Road and Air

Overland routes are demanding. From British Columbia: take Alaska Highway to Fort Nelson, then Liard Highway to Fort Liard. From the Yukon: take Alaska Highway to Watson Lake (the road onward to Tungsten is frequently impassable). In the Northwest Territories: take Mackenzie Highway to Fort Simpson, or Liard Highway to Fort Liard.

The vast majority of visitors arrive by chartered float plane. The only designated landing sites are Virginia Falls and Rabitkettle Lake. Charter air transportation is available from several locations including Yellowknife, Fort Simpson, Fort Liard, Fort Nelson, Watson Lake, and Munco Lake. For chartered air companies, contact NWT Tourism or Parks Canada (see above).

Access by Water

Outfitters offer trips descending the river by rubber raft or canoe (equipment is flown in first). Intermediate white-water specialists can descend the river in their own canoes; reservations must be made with the park first. Parks Canada has licensed only three outfitters to operate in the park; all guided trips must by led by one of these outfitters (see the Parks Canada, above).

Visit

Open year-round.All visitors planning to spend the night in the park must register at the Parks Canada office in Fort Simpson, and must de-register upon their return. Office hours are June 15–Sept 15

Virginia Falls

daily 8am–noon, 1–5 pm. Rest of the year Mon–Fri 8:30am–noon, 1–5pm. ⊜ *$25/ day-use fee ($149 annual).*

South Nahanni River

For more than 320km/198mi, this magnificent, serpentine waterway coils through the park, entering majestic canyons, cascading over a precipice twice the height of Niagara and passing a series of hot mineral springs that nourish vegetation unusual at this latitude (61°–62°N). Each year the river attracts countless canoeists and raft-riders to its adventurous waters and wilderness beauty.

The following describes highlights of a descent of the river. The 200km/125mi excursion downriver from Virginia Falls to Nahanni Butte is one of the world's great wilderness trips. Over this distance the river drops more than 120m/400ft (which is why canoeists generally prefer to descend it, rather than canoe up).

The jewel of the park and one of the North's most spectacular sights is **Virginia Falls.** Parted by a central pointed rock at the precipice, volumes of water plunge 90m/294ft to the gorge below. The Albert Faille Portage can be followed around the falls *(1.6km/1mi).* From it, a trail leads to the brink of the cataract where the river can be seen in spectacular rapids just before it cascades over the rocks. Fourth Canyon is the first of four awesome canyons with immense cliffs and depths as great as 1,200m/3,900ft. Then come the surging waves of Figure of Eight Rapids. The river makes a 90-degree turn known as The Gate, guarded by mighty Pulpit Rock. Third Canyon is followed by the 34km/21mi stretch of Second Canyon. **Deadman Valley,** where headless bodies were found, separates Second Canyon from First Canyon, a twisting 27km/17mi channel. The river passes close to a hot spring where pools of water, at nearly 37°C/98°F, have caused ferns, chokecherries, rose bushes and flowering parsnip plants to proliferate. Before reaching Nahanni Butte, the river divides into a series of channels known as the **Splits.**

WOOD BUFFALO NATIONAL PARK★★

NORTHWEST TERRITORIES, ALBERTA

Designated a UNESCO World Heritage Site in 1983, Wood Buffalo is one of North America's most valuable wildlife preserves, containing two important features that are unique: one of the largest free-roaming **bison herds** on earth—2,400 strong; and the last natural nesting grounds for the endangered **whooping crane**.

Accessible by car along all-weather gravel roads, the park offers visitors a subtle, tantalizing beauty that exemplifies the northern boreal plain, as well as an opportunity to view wild animals seldom seen elsewhere. (Much of the park, however, is remote, explorable only by boat or plane.) The Peace/Athabasca Delta at the west end of Lake Athabasca is one of the largest inland deltas in the world and a vitally important wetland. Owing to four North American flyways that pass through the park, the delta is well known for its abundance of geese, duck and other species. The surrounding plains are the northernmost fringe of the Great Plains that extend all the way to Mexico.

- **Information:** NWT Tourism, PO Box 610, Yellowknife NT, X1A 2N5. ☎867-873-7200, toll-free 1-800 661-0788.www.explorenwt.com or Parks Canada, Wood Buffalo National Park, Box 750, Fort Smit NT, X0E 0P0. ☎867-872-7900. www.pc.gc.ca.
- **Orient Yourself:** Canada's largest national park (44,807sq km/17,300sq mi) straddles the border dividing the province of Alberta from the Northwest Territories. About two-thirds of the parkland lies within Alberta, but park headquarters and principal access are located at Fort Smith in the Northwest Territories.
- **Don't Miss:** The road between Fort Smith and Pine Lake is lovely; you can stop for short hikes.
- **Organizing Your Time:** Although there is road access to the park, it is a long way from anywhere: 748km/468mi from Yellowknife, 1310km/819mi from Edmonton. You may consider flying in and renting a car in Fort Smith.
- **Especially for Kids:** The park offers hikes and canoe routes that are not strenuous for older children.
- **Also See:** YELLOWKNIFE

Access by road

748km/464mi south of Yellowknife via Rte. 3, Mackenzie Hwy. and Rte. 5 (near Hay River) to the park entrance (Rte. 5 continues through the park to Fort Smith). From Fort Smith, an all-weather gravel road leads into Wood Buffalo's interior as far as Peace Point Reserve (119km/74mi). There is no all-weather road to Fort Chipewyan, although, for three months in the winter, a road is sometimes open linking Fort Smith, Fort Chipewyan and Fort McMurray.

Access by air

Northwestern Air Lease *operates scheduled flights from Edmonton and Yellowknife. ☎867-872-2216. Charter flights to Fort Smith and Fort Chipewyan available. For information, contact NWT Tourism (see above). Car rentals available in Fort Smith.*

Visit

Open year-round. Hiking, camping, boating, fishing. Accommodations in Fort Smith. Park map and list of licensed guides and outfitters available at the two park visitor centres: Fort Smith (126 McDougal Rd. at Portage Ave. Open 3rd weekend in May–Labour Day Mon–Fri 9am–noon &

Wood Buffalo National Park

NWT/T. Parker

1pm–5pm, weekends 1–5pm. Rest of the year closed weekends. ☎867-872-7960) and Fort Chipewyan (MacKenzie Ave. Open year-round Mon–Fri 8:30am–noon & 1pm–5pm. In summer, open most weekends 1–5pm. ☎780-697-3662). ◇No entry or gate fees. Park administration ☎ 867-872-7900. www.pc.gc.ca.

Route 5

The approach to the park from the vicinity of Hay River is a pretty **drive** through boreal spruce and aspen forest. Bison can often be seen grazing by the roadside closer to Fort Smith. At the Angus Fire Tower, a large **sinkhole** typifies the region's *karst* (limestone) topography. A short side road *(30km/19mi west of Fort Smith)* leads to the Salt River Plains **overlook★**, which provides an intriguing vista of a salt flat. This broad plain of the Salt River shimmers white in the summer sun, the river winding sinuously through scattered patches of forest and meadow, as well as beds of salt.

Fort Smith★

Once the major town in the Territories, Fort Smith is yet another of the historic fur-trading sites that dot Canada's North. At the park visitor centre *(for hours ♿ see above)*, a multimedia **presentation** *(18min)* offers an excellent grounding in the national park's history and ecology. Just a few blocks away, **Northern Life Museum** *(McDougal Rd. and King St. Call for hours. ☎867-872-2859)* and **Fort Smith Mission Historic Park★** offer insight into the area's history *(Breynat St. & Mercredi Ave. ◷Open daily. ☎867-874-6702)*. The city's Slave River boardwalk *(end of Simpson St.)* affords a view of the **rapids,** where a party of early explorers perished. *For accommodations, contact Visitor Infocentre, PO Box 147 Fort Smith X0E 0P0. ☎867-872-3065 www.fortsmithtourism.ca.*

Carver Extraordinaire

Fort Smith carver **Sonny MacDonald** is a self-taught native artist who began whittling toy boats and slingshots at age seven. Today his works, crafted from northern wood and bone, depict fish, wildlife and other denizens of the subarctic world. In addition to caribou and moose antlers, animal claws and teeth, the materials from which he fashions his creations include narwhal, and even fossilized mammoth, tusks. His pieces range from small amulets and earrings to large garden sculptures. Sonny was born in Fort Chipewyan, where he grew up; he now resides in Fort Smith and maintains a studio there. *To visit MacDonald's studio, contact him directly ☎867-872-5935.*

Wilderness by Water

Exploring Wood Buffalo National Park by its waterways offers a peaceful encounter with nature, reminiscent of the way aboriginal inhabitants travelled centuries ago. Wilderness **canoe trips** along the park's two major rivers, the Peace and the Slave, require back-country experience, considerable planning and a park permit. Canoe trips along smaller rivers into the park's backcountry are also possible (*rentals available in Fort Smith*). Guided canoe tours into the park are offered by several local outfitters (*contact the park visitor centre*). Boating on Pine Lake is confined to its northern section. Motorboats are allowed on major rivers. *Contact park authorities regarding natural hazards within the park's river systems. Use of personal watercraft is not permitted in the park.*

Fort Smith to Pine Lake★★

The all-weather gravel road into the heart of the park affords access to several notable sights and the opportunity to see bison anywhere along the road. The Salt River day-use area (*25km/15.5mi south of Fort Smith*) provides a short hiking path, the **Karstland Trail**, through the park's unusual broken topography. At 31km/19mi the South Loop trailhead initiates a pleasant (*4km/2.5mi*) hike through beautiful boreal forest down to **Grosbeak Lake**, an otherworldly salt flat dotted with boulders dropped by retreating glaciers. **Pine Lake Campground,** at 60km/37mi, is an attractive facility overlooking a turquoise lake with a sandy beach, a spot long used by natives as a summer retreat. The lake is a particularly good place for swimming.

Fort Chipewyan

Access by air or water only. Situated on the shores of Lake Athabasca, "Fort Chip" is the gateway for boat or canoe trips into the Peace-Athabasca Delta and the site of the park's second visitor centre.

YELLOWKNIFE★

POPULATION 19,429

The administrative and economic capital of the Northwest Territories lies on a pretty site, set on pink, glacier-scarred granite topped by small trees and almost completely surrounded by the water of Great Slave Lake. A pleasant "old town" (c.1934) coexists with a modern "new town," where most of the population lives, shops and works.

- **Information:** Northern Frontier Visitors Association. #4−4807-49th St., Yellowknife NT, X1A 3T5. ☎867-873-4262, toll-free 1-877-881-4262 or www.northernfrontier.com
- ▶ **Orient Yourself:** Yellowknife lies beside Yellowknife Bay on the northern shore of the Great Slave Lake.
- **Parking:** Only the downtown core has metered parking ($0.25/15min), Mon–Fri 9am–6pm. There is one public lot, in Centre Square Mall.
- **Don't Miss:** The Old Town is less scruffy than it used to be, but still fun.
- **Organizing Your Time:** During spring and fall, Yellowknife is accessible only by air.
- **Especially for Kids:** Several trails around the city are easy, and you can rent canoes or kayaks for short excursions.
- **Also See:** THELON WILDLIFE SANCTUARY, WOOD BUFFALO NATIONAL PARK.

NWT/T. Parker

Yellowknife's waterfront

A Bit of History

Foundation of Gold – Named not for the color of the gold underneath it, but for the copper knives traded by local Indians, Yellowknife was visited by Samuel Hearne in 1771, Alexander Mackenzie on his epic journey to the mouth of the river that bears his name, and John Franklin, none of whom noticed the gold. Prospectors en route for the Klondike at the end of the 19C did record some sightings, but without pursuit. Not until the discovery of pitchblende in 1930 on the shores of the Great Bear Lake was there interest in the rest of the region. In 1934 exposed gold was found beside the bay and a boomtown sprang up only to collapse until the next gold discoveries after 1945. Yellowknife became territorial capital in 1967 and is now a well-established community. The last gold mine closed in 2004, but a new find north of the city—diamonds—has fuelled continued growth.

The Diamond Boom – The first confirmed find of diamonds in 1991 kicked off the greatest mineral exploration rush since the Klondike gold stampede. Production began in 1998 at the **Ekati** diamond mine about 322km/200mi northeast of Yellowknife; two other mines (**Diavik** and the **De Beers' Snap**

Lake mine) in the same Lac de Gras area have followed and another is projected. The **Diavik Mines Visitors' Centre** at 5007-50th Ave. has a self-guided display about the mine. (*Open Mon–Fri 8:30am–5pm.* 867-669-6500. www.diavek.ca.)

Midnight Twilight – The city lies just north of latitude 62° and thus, in summer, experiences nearly 24 hours of daylight. Every year a golf tournament is held on the weekend closest to June 21, with tee-off at midnight.
Yellowknife is a major centre for boating, canoeing, fishing and camping. Its stores carry a fine selection of Dene and Inuit art and handicrafts. Its float plane base in Old Town is the departure point for numerous wilderness lodges and camps elsewhere in the Territories. The city itself has a thriving community of bed-and-breakfast inns as well as business hotels *(for accommodations, contact Northern Frontier Visitors Assn. see Intro).*

Access

The route from Edmonton, comprising Mackenzie Hwy (Hwy 1) and the Yellowknife Hwy (Hwy 3), is paved for all 1500km/938mi. To access the city, take the Mackenzie River ferry (free) in summer; an "ice road" bridges the river in

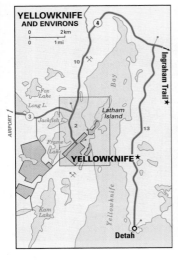

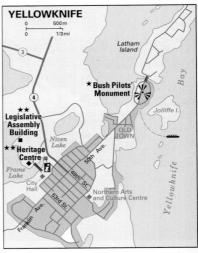

winter. No road access during freeze-up and thaw periods. Also accessible by scheduled flights via **Canadian North** (from Calgary, Edmonton and Ottawa. ☎867-669-4000, toll-free 1-800-665-1505. www.canadiannorth.com), **First Air** (from Edmonton. ☎1-800-267-1247. www.firstair.ca) and **Air Canada Jazz** (from Calgary and Edmonton. ☎1-888-247-2262. www.flyjazz.ca)

Sights

Prince of Wales Northern Heritage Centre★★

4750-48th St., PO Box 1320, Yellowknife NT, X1A 2L9. ✕♿🕐*Open Jun–Aug daily 10:30am–5:30pm. Rest of the year Mon–Fri 10:30am–5pm, weekends noon–5pm.* 🕐*Closed statutory holidays.* 🚌*Contribution suggested.* ☎867-873-7551. *www.pwnhc.ca.*

Overlooking Frame Lake, this attractive museum houses displays on the history of settlement of the Territories and a fine collection of Inuit sculpture. The ways of life of Dene and Inuit peoples are described, as are the reasons European settlers came to the North. One room is devoted to bush pilot operations, and a small display explains the gold and diamond mining industries.

Legislative Assembly Building★★

Entrance off Ingraham Trail, in the capital park. PO Box 1320, Yellowknife NT, X1A 2L9. 🚶*Tours Jun–Aug Mon–Fri 10:30am, 1:30pm, 3:30pm and Sun 1:30pm. Rest of the year Mon–Fri 10:30am. Confirm hours at* ☎867-669-2230, *toll-free 1-800-661-0784. www.assembly.gov.nt.ca.*

This striking, dome-topped building (1993), sheathed in weather-hardy zinc panels, is designed to make maximum use of available light. Highlights include the **Great Hall,** with overhead banners depicting the subarctic seasons. Crafted by regional artists, the assembly's ceremonial **mace** is made of silver and bronze, with gold and diamond embellishments. A gallery accessible during tours contains a remarkable **quilt** created by residents of the Deline community.

Bush Pilots' Monument★

Steps from Ingraham Trail in Old Town. From this spot there is a splendid **panorama**★ of the city, the surrounding waters and the rocky site. The red-topped tower of the former Cominco gold mine dominates the skyline. The bay ripples with numerous float planes arriving from the mining camps or departing with supplies for exploration teams.

Below the monument, Old Town holds amazingly diverse houses stretching along famed Ragged Ass Road, whose street signs became such popular theft items they are now offered for sale.

From Old Town, a causeway crosses to **Latham Island**, where houses perch on rocks and stilts. Here, a Dogrib Indian settlement and views of the former Giant and Con gold mines can be seen.

Boat Trips

Cruises (7-9days) on the Mackenzie River to Inuvik depart from Hay River on the west arm of the Great Slave Lake late Jun–Jul: contact M.S. Norweta ☎866-667-9382, www.norweta.com. For other excursions, contact Northern Frontier Visitors Assn. Ꮭsee Introduction.

These cruises enable visitors to see portions of this enormous lake (28,930sq km/11,170sq mi), which is part of the Mackenzie River system and an important fishing area.

Excursions

Detah and the Ingraham Trail

These excursions by vehicle in the vicinity of the capital allow the visitor to see the landscape in this transitional area of the Canadian Shield between boreal forest and tundra. The drive to Detah provides views of Yellowknife and its bay.

Detah

25km/16mi. This Dogrib Indian settlement has a fine **site**★ on flat rocks overlooking the Great Slave Lake.

Ingraham Trail★

64km/40mi to Reid Lake. This all-weather road northwest of Yellowknife skirts five lakes—a paradise for campers and canoeists. Prelude Lake Territorial Park has a sandy beach and extensive campgrounds. Numerous other points along the trail offer access to more remote wilderness lakes and rivers. For canoe and kayak outfitting and area wilderness expertise, contact Narwal Adventures (*☎867-873-6443. www.ssimicro. com/~narwal*).

NUNAVUT

Contrary to the misconception that the Canadian North is a frozen wilderness, this spectacular continental rooftop abounds in varied landscape, transformed by the light of the midnight sun. The Territory's diverse wildlife is the principal attraction for most visitors. In the **Baffin** region, floe-edge tours offer opportunities to see polar bears, bowhead whales, and narwhals. In the **Kivalliq** region, travellers come to view belugas, polar bears, snowy owls, gyrfalcons and other northern birds. Farther west, in the region of **Kitikmeot,** human encounters with shaggy musk-oxen and caribou are real possibilities.

- ℹ **Information:** Nunavut Tourism, ☎1-866-686-2888. www.nunavut.com
- ▶ **Orient Yourself:** Stretching some 2,000,000sq km/772,000sq mi nearly to Greenland from the Manitoba border, Nunavut is, by far, Canada's biggest province or territory, making up one-fifth of the country's total landmass.
- 😊 **Don't Miss:** Inuit art and crafts are widely available today, but the next generation may not acquire the skills; now is the time to acquire a few heirlooms.
- 🕐 **Organizing Your Time:** Arrangements must be make well ahead of time.
- 🧒 **Especially for Kids:** There are few kid-specific activities. Children and adults will share the same experiences.
- 👁 **Also See:** NORTHWEST TERRITORIES

Geographical Notes

Landscape – Located north of the 60th parallel, Nunavut lies west of Denmark's Greenland, across the Davis Strait. Its southern border in the west vaguely follows the tree line (northern limit of growth), then runs straight south to Manitoba's northern boundary and across Hudson Bay, wrapping around the southern end of Baffin Island. Nunavut includes most of the Arctic archipelago between the mainland and the geographic North Pole, and the Hudson and James Bay islands south of the parallel, as well as Arctic mainland and major channels, straits and sounds. Of Canada's 26 largest islands, more than half are in Nunavut. The biggest—**Baffin Island**—is the size of Spain.

Rocky, treeless **tundra**, snow-covered most of the year, describes Nunavut's landscape. **Permafrost** can reach depths of 370m/1,220ft, as at Resolute on Cornwallis Island. Yet, from one end to the other there is diversity. While gulls and jaegers soar overhead, mosses and lichens carpet the land in the short spring and summer season. Hardy shrubs and flowers brighten the lowlands around Hudson Bay, and rolling hills elsewhere, with fluffy tufts of Arctic cotton, the tiny, fragile blossoms of white mountain avens or berries of purple and red. Glacial debris—huge boulders, piles of moraine, **eskers** (narrow ridges of sand and gravel) and **drumlins** (elliptical-shaped hills inclining in the direction of the glacier's retreat)—bear witness to the region's geological history. Sand eskers, basically leftover glacial river sediment, snake across the land like huge worm casts, some hundreds of kilometres long. These eskers provide perfect dens for wolves and foxes, and raised, windy "highways" for migrating caribou. Other phenomena common in the North are **polynyas** (open water in sea ice) and **shore leads** (channels of water through a field of ice).

Lofty mountains with glacier-filled valleys, including 2,616m/8,633ft **Mount Barbeau,** Nunavut's highest peak, rise all along the eastern coasts of Baffin, Devon and Ellesmere islands.

Dogsledding near Resolute

Climate – Annual precipitation in Nunavut is sparse (Baker Lake 208mm/8in, Iqaluit 409mm/16in), less than half what a city in southern Canada receives. Generally winters are long, cold and dark, and summers (July and August) are surprisingly warm and sunny, with long hours of daylight. Towns near the coast or in the Baffin region are colder. In summer, the southern part of Nunavut has 20 hours of daylight, while farther north of the Arctic Circle, it never gets dark. The mean daily maximum temperatures for July are 15°C/59°F in Baker Lake and 12°C/53°F in Iqaluit.

A Bit of History

Early Settlement – Paleoeskimo people inhabited Canada's Arctic coasts and islands about 4,000 years ago. Though archaeologists disagree as to their origins, Paleoeskimos are believed to have crossed from Siberia over the Bering Strait into Alaska shortly before that time. They eventually moved eastward into the Canadian Arctic, where they lived in skin tents, travelled by foot or kayak and evolved into the **Dorset** culture (500 BC-AD 1500). New waves of migration brought families of **Thule** people (AD 1000-1600) into Nunavut and into contact with the Dorset. Over the next few hundred years, the Dorset were eventually driven off, or wiped out,

by the Thule. Thule were different from the Dorset people—they travelled faster and farther on *qamutiit* (dogsleds) and in large *umiak* boats. Ancestors of today's Inuit, the Thule moved south into the interior to hunt caribou and along the Arctic coast and archipelago to find whales and other sea animals.

Although European explorers, traders and whalers journeyed to this area in the late 1500s (Norse explorers some 500 years earlier), their effect was minimal until the early 1800s, when whalers from both Europe and the Americas started coming to the Baffin region to hunt bowhead whale.

The Inuit – Nunavut is four times the size of France, yet is one of the least densely populated areas in the world: about one person per 100sq km/39 sq mi. Of the 27,000 Nunavummiut (inhabitants of Nunavut), 85 percent are Inuit. The rest, including people of the Dene Nation, is non-Inuit. Formerly known as Eskimo (now an unfavoured and obsolete Cree word), the Canadian Inuit (*Inuit* means "the people" in Inuktitut) make up part of a larger community of some 125,000 people in polar regions of Russia, Alaska and Greenland. In Canada, Inuit live in 53 northern communities (more than half of which are in Nunavut), including those in Quebec's northern reaches and on Labrador's northern coast. A sizable number of Inuit inhabit

In Person

A trip to Nunavut is a discovery of another world, and of insights into Inuit ways. Heading out on the ocean in sturdy Lake Winnipeg boats, visitors find themselves enjoying the bobbing harp seals one minute, then wrapped up in the excitement of a hunting tradition that has fed and clothed these aboriginal people for thousands of years. Next may come a chance meeting with a carver, sawing stone in his backyard and complaining that prices have dropped. Or with a brilliant Inuit woman, working, taking a multiyear course, and destined for upper management; on weekends, she hunts seal with her husband and two sons. Or an encounter on the airplane with an Inuit singer, who, in this roadless land, flies five times more than the average Canadian, belittling the sissy pilot hesitant to land in a thick fog, then launching into some indescribable throat singing for the benefit of her seatmate.

their Quebec homeland of **Nunavik,** a sociocultural region recognized by the provincial government in 1988.

The life of the people of the Arctic Coast revolved largely around hunting sea mammals—especially seal and whale—as a source of food; blubber for heat and light; skins for clothing, shelter and boats; and bone or ivory for the blades of their harpoons or other tools. They hunted from one-man **kayaks**, while women, traditionally, paddled cargo and passengers in larger **umiaks**, which held up to 12 people. The occasional excursion south was made by **dogsled** to hunt caribou, the skins of which were used for clothing or bedding. The hunters built stone markers, or rock cairns, called **inuksuks** in the shape of human figures to serve as landmarks or guides for hunting caribou; inuksuks can still be seen in Nunavut today.

The Inuit were seasonally nomadic— several families living and moving together. In winter they constructed an **igloo** (iglu), a dome-shaped snow house made of blocks of ice, and entered by a tunnel; for insulation, the interior was lined with skins. In summer they lived in tents made of skins. Time not spent hunting or making clothes was devoted to carving bone and stone, a craft for which they are famous.

The Inuit of Nunavut still hunt and fish for caribou, seal and char; however, many now work in tourism, government, transportation, and related supply and service companies.

The Northwest Passage – A sea route between the Atlantic and Pacific oceans around the north of the American continent was the quest of explorers for centuries. British sailor **Martin Frobisher**

Two Inuit girls

Practical Information

ART IN THE NORTH

For centuries, the nomadic Inuit carved only small pieces they could carry with them. Today, they have transferred age-old artisic sensibilities to larger art-forms, notably **sculpture**. The best-known forms are rounded human and animal shapes, created from black, grey or green stone. Bone (including ancient whale-bone), antlers or tusks are carved as sculpture or jewellery. Tapestries, stone-cut prints, and metalwork are popular, too, while some communities specialize in ceramics or miniature dolls. Below are selected shops in Rankin Inlet, Iqaluit and Pangnirtung that offer the arts and crafts of the North. You can also order items on-line from the **Arctic Nunavut Online Store** (www.ndcorp. nu.ca) Many artists sell from their homes, and keen shoppers should ask around town how to see their wares. Few places in Nunavut have addresses. Instead, visitors must use town maps or ask locals to point them in the right direction.

RANKIN INLET

Ivalu Ltd. (down the alley from Royal Bank in Keewatin Meat and Fish building. ☎867-645-3400. www.ndcorp.nu.ca) is a retail outlet for arts and crafts from across Nunavut. **Matchbox Gallery** (call for directions. ☎867-645-2674. www.matchboxgallery.com) sells carvings, castings, drawings, paintings and prints as well as a unique form of ceramics: terra-cotta creations reflecting the "literacy of touch" of an Inuit artist working with a soft medium, instead of the more familiar stone.

IQALUIT

Across from the airport, at **Iqaluit Fine Arts Studio** (Coman Bldg 1127, Box 760, Iqaluit NU, X0A 0H0. ☎867-979-5578), owners Thomas and Helen Webster display prints, watercolours, tapestries and sculpture. This is a gallery, not a gift shop, so prices generally range from a few hundred dollars to several thousand. **DJ Sensations** (Tumiit Bldg. across from the post office. ☎867-979-0650, toll-free 1-888-979-0650) is a gift and stationery store featuring a big selection of ivory jewellery and at least 200 mostly hand-size stone carvings. At the display room (Building 723, near Northern Stores) of **Northern Country Arts** (☎819-979-0067, toll-free 1-888-979-0067. www.nunanet.com) you'll find Inuit carvings from Baffin Island. You can also order directly frrom the website. In a huge building on Ring Road, **Arctic Ventures** (Building 192. ☎867-979-5992), a grocery and department store, has an excellent selection of books on the Arctic. In her house studio (phone ahead for directions. ☎867-979-6420), long-time resident **Janet Ripley Armstrong** produces accomplished watercolours that capture the feel of the North.

At **Iqaluit airport**, look at the excellent arts and crafts displays featuring more than a dozen communities, such as the tapestries of Pangnirtung or the stone-cut prints or stone sculptures of **Cape Dorset,** a major centre for Inuit art. For that last-minute purchase, stop at **Coman Arctic Galleries** (Building 1127 ☎867-979-6300), right outside the airport doors. Coman features large corporate pieces, but small, less costly items are also on hand.

PANGNIRTUNG

For a wide array of native works, and to order on-line, visit **Uqqurmiut Centre for Arts and Crafts (**PO Box 453, Pangnirtung NU, X0A 0R0. ☎867-473-8870. www.uqqurmiut.com).

For more information on art in Nunavut, contact the **Nunavut Arts and Crafts Association** (☎867-979-7808. www. nacaarts.org). To see a virtual museum of Inuit art, visit the Web site: www. virtualmuseum.ca.

GETTING THERE

BY AIR

Flights are virtually the only way to access Nunavut; no roads enter Nunavut from the south and no roads connect the communities. The access cities from the south are Calgary, Edmonton, Winnipeg, Ottawa and Montreal, from which flights reach gateway cities in Nunavut: Cambridge Bay is the gateway city for the Kitikmeot region (via Yellowknife); Rankin Inlet for Kivalliq (Keewatin); and Iqaluit for Baffin. Airlines providing these connections, as well as scheduled service within Nunavut, are **Canadian North** (☎1-800-661-1505. www.canadiannorth.com), **First Air** (☎1-800-267-1247/Canada only. www.firstair.ca) and **Calm Air** (☎1-800-839-2256. www.calmair.com). Within Nunavut, scheduled and chartered service is provided by **Unaalik Aviation** (☎867-979-0040. www.unaakik.com), **Air Nunavut** (☎867-979-4018. airnunavut@northwestel.net) **Kenn Borek Air Ltd**. (☎403-291-3300. www.borekair.com) and **Air Inuit** (Based in Quebec.☎1-800-361-2965. www.airinuit.com)

GETTING AROUND

Although all-terrain vehicles (called bikes by the locals) and full-size cars and trucks are seen within communities, no roads connect the towns. Chartered float planes and scheduled commercial flights are the only means of transportation between communities, except for watercraft or snowmobiles. Most settlements are small enough to cover on foot, but snowmobiles, ATVs or bicycles can sometimes be rented. Taxis service is available in some communities. Dogsleds are used mostly for tourist excursions.

GENERAL INFORMATION

ACCOMMODATIONS AND VISITOR INFORMATION

The free *Nunavut Travel Planner,* as well as guides for hunting, fishing, bird watching, whale watching and iceberg-viewing can be ordered on-line or downloaded from www.nunavuttourism.com. *The Nunavut Handbook* ($40 plus shipping), published by Nortext, can be ordered from www.arctic-travel.com. Iqaluit has nine overnight accommodations, but most communities have only one or two places to stay. Homestays and overnighting in an iglu may be arranged with local guides. Rankin Inlet and Pangnirtung each have only one hotel; in bad weather, guests may have to share a room with strangers.

LANGUAGE

The official languages of Nunavut are Inuktitut, the native tongue of the Inuit, which is spoken by 85 percent of the population, English and French. In major communities such as Iqaluit and Ranklin Inlet, many Inuit speak English and Inuktitut. Tourist information is generally available in English, and most signs are in English and Inuktitut. French is spoken in some communities, particularly in Iqaluit.

TIME ZONES

Nunavut uses three time zones and observes Daylight Saving Time: the Baffin Region is on Eastern Standard Time, the Kivalliq Region (Southampton Island excepted) uses Central Standard Time and Keewatin observes Mountain Standard Time.

TAXES

There is no territorial sales tax, but the 5% GST applies.

LIQUOR LAWS

Determined by local vote, restrictions vary by community. Towns are designated dry, restricted or unrestricted. In dry communities, alcohol is not allowed to be brought in. In restricted communities, an approval form is required to bring liquor in. In **Rankin Inlet,** guests at the hotel may order a drink in the lounge when it opens in the evening. In **Iqaluit,** restaurants and hotels are licensed, but there is no liquor store in town. In unrestricted communities, limits are set for the amount of alcohol that may be brought in. Contact the RCMP or the Liquor Commission (☎867-874-2100) for current regulations in each community. Trading alchohol for anything is illegal. Do not leave unused alchohol behind.

TERRITORIAL HOLIDAY

Nunavut Day: July 9

TOURS AND EXCURSIONS

OUTFITTER TOURS

Tourism in Nunavut continues to develop, yet it is destination with few specific sights and attractions. The joy of travelling here comes from spending time out on the land or water and from spontaneous cultural experiences—chatting with a hunter along the beach or dropping in at a local square dance. Because of the need for safe, comfortable travel in this remote and often harsh land, many visitors book ahead with experienced outfitters. Most excursions operate from June to August. **Dogsledding** or ski trips run from April to June. The Nunavut Tourism website (*www.nunavuttourism. com*) provides excellent information on outfitters. For example, **Arctic Odysseys** (*☎206-325-1977, toll-free 1-800-574-3021. www.arcticodysseys.com*) organizes adventure trips in the high arctic. **Frontiers North** (*☎204-949-2050, toll-free 1-800-663-9832. www. frontiersnorth.com*) sponsors wildlife-watching tours. The Canadian Tourism Commission (*www.travelcanada.ca*) is another source of information.

SPECIAL EXCURSIONS

In the northern corner of **Ellesmere Island,** accessible from Resolute Bay, lies **Quttinirpaaq National Park** (formerly Ellesmere Island National Park Reserve). This is the world's northernmost park (latitude 82°N) covering nearly 40,000sq km/15,000sq mi of mountains, glaciers, valleys and fiords. It also has 4,000-year-old archeological remains. (*PO Box 278, Iqaluit , X0A 0H0. ☎867-975-4673. www.pc.gc.ca*).

Hiking in the Arctic Circle

Nunavut Tourism

made the first attempt in 1576. His voyages were followed by those of **John Davis, Henry Hudson** and **William Baffin,** all of whom have left their names on the map. Their reports of ice-filled seas somewhat dampened enthusiasm for the passage. Except for exploration at the western end, no more attempts were made until the early 19C.

Naval Explorers – The 1789 voyage of Alexander Mackenzie on the river that bears his name sparked new interest in a northwest passage. **John Franklin** made two overland trips to the western end, sailing a third time, in 1845. Years passed with no word from him. A series of expeditions, 38 in all, were sent to discover his fate. It was established that he and his entire crew had perished after being marooned in the frozen waters. One effect of this tragedy was the exploration by his would-be rescuers of a large part of the North. A passable route of the passage between the Canadian mainland and the Arctic islands was successfully navigated by Norwegian **Roald Amundsen** between 1903 and 1906. Since then many ships have followed the hazardous route which, with global warning, will likely become a major shipping route.

Nunavut Today – As with the Northwest Territories, mineral as well as oil exploration continue to attract investment. In 1964 vast zinc and lead deposits were found at Pine Point on Great Slave Lake, in the Northwest Territories; these minerals are being mined at Nanisivik near Arctic Bay in the north of Baffin Island and on Little Cornwallis Island. The high Arctic islands are potentially rich areas for oil and gas extraction.

Nunavut's tourism is rapidly developing—so far, without damaging consequences. The Territory has many territorial parks, heritage rivers, bird sanctuaries, game preserves and proposed ecological sites, as well as polar bears, whales and more than five major caribou herds. Some of the best places to access the landscape are the three national parks: Auyuittuq and Sirmilik national parks near Baffin Island's south and north ends, respectively, and Quttinirpaaq National Park, farther north, on Ellesmere Island.

BAFFIN REGION★★

Nunavut's largest, most inhabited area, **Baffin Island**★★ receives the greatest number of visitors. Mountains rise to 2,100m/7,000ft with numerous glaciers, and coastlines are deeply indented with fiords. About two-thirds of Baffin Island lies north of the Arctic Circle (66.5°N); **Quttinirpaaq National Park**, on Ellesmere Island, is above 80°N. But it is the majestic and relatively accessible **Auyuittuq National Park** where visitors can best experience the high mountains of the Arctic ranges. Here, in the continuous daylight of summer, the tundra blooms with an infinite variety of tiny, colourful flowers, such as broad-leafed willow herb and Arctic poppies.

- ℹ **Information:** Nunavut Tourism. ☎1-866-686-2888. www.nunavuttourism.com
- ▶ **Orient Yourself:** The Baffin region includes Ellesmere and Baffin islands, part of the Melville Peninsula, and the High Arctic islands of Cornwallis, Axel Heiberg and others.
- 👓 **Don't Miss:** The boat trip to Auyuittuq National Park, organized through the Angmarlik Visitor Centre
- 🕐 **Organizing Your Time:** Parks Canada warns that you should take no risks with the weather; always leave time in your itinerary to wait out a bad stretch .
- 🧒 **Especially for Kids:** Children will enjoy exploring Iqaluit and taking the less rigorous boat trips, but don't overestimate their endurance.
- 🕯 **Also See:** KITIKMEOT REGION, KIVALLIQ (KEEWATIN) REGION

A Bit of History

Although English seamen **William Baffin** and **Robert Bylot** mapped the south shore of Baffin's namesake island in 1616, others came before. Seeking the Northwest Passage, Sir **Martin Frobisher** discovered the island in a 1576 expedition. In 1585 **John Davis** explored Cumberland Sound. **Henry**

Hudson followed what is now called Hudson Strait into Hudson Bay in 1610. For 200 years after Baffin's voyage, there was little outside interest in exploring the region. Then, in a resurgence of the quest for the Northwest Passage, and coinciding with the onset of *qallunaat* (white people) whaling, came explorers John Ross (1818), William Edward Parry (1819), and Sir **John Franklin** (1845) on

Pangnirtung

his famous, fateful expedition. Searches for the Franklin party ensued over 12 years, the accounts of which prompted Charles Francis Hall to travel the terrain (1860-1862) using Inuit travel methods and native guides Tookoolito and Ebierbing.

By the early 1900s whaling had ended; trading and scientific exploration were on the increase; and missionaries, the Hudson's Bay Company and Royal Canadian Mounted Police (RCMP) were essentially "taking charge" of the Inuit. In the 1950s the presence of a Distant Early Warning (DEW) line meant **Iqaluit** (eh-CALL-oo-it)—formerly called Frobisher Bay—would become a regional supply centre. It is now the capital of Nunavut and its largest town. The 1960s introduced federal schools and housing, marking the end of traditional Inuit camp life.

Today most inhabitants of the region live either in Iqaluit or in a dozen small settlements along the coast of Baffin and Ellesmere islands. Inuit stone carvings, prints and lithographs, especially those from **Cape Dorset,** on Baffin Island's west coast, are internationally renowned.

Pangnirtung★★

300km/186mi north of Iqaluit on Baffin Island's Pangnirtung Fiord, a northern finger of Cumberland Sound.

Dominated by the snowcapped mountains surrounding the **Penny Ice Cap** in Auyuittuq National Park—in particular, the steep face of **Mount Duval** to the southeast—this hamlet occupies a spectacular **site** on Pangnirtung fiord. Situated just south of the Arctic Circle, Pangnirtung is an ideal spot for viewing the midnight "light" in summer (there is no sun at midnight, but it never gets dark). It is also a good place to study the tundra landscape and wildlife (small mammals, and some large sea mammals in Cumberland Sound) and to purchase locally woven goods and soapstone carvings at the Inuit cooperative.

Although the Hudson's Bay Company established a trading post here in 1921, families did not begin to move off the land into Pangnirtung to any great extent until the early 1960s. Today dominant livelihoods include marine mammal harvesting, sculpture and handicrafts, and tourism.

Most visitors come here to hike the glacier-strewn landscape of Auyuittuq National Park *(accessible by boat, ♿ see below).*

Angmarlik Interpretation Centre

PO Box 227, Pangnirtung NU, X0A 0R0. ♿🕐Open mid-Jun–mid-Sept Mon–Sat 9am–9pm, Sun 1pm–9pm. Rest of the year Mon–Fri 8:30am–5pm. ☎867-473-8737.

Displays and artifacts tell the story of the Inuit of Cumberland Bay. Trips to Kekerten Territorial Historic Park, a whaling station in the late-19C, or boat rides to Mt. Overlord warden station (Auyuittuq park entrance) can be arranged here. From inside the centre is a **view**★★ of the steep, blue-layered fiord, where frigid water surges in some of the highest tides in the world.

Uqqurmiut Centre for Arts and Crafts★

PO Box 453, Pangnirtung NU, X0A 0R0. ♿🕐Open mid-Jun–mid-Sept Mon–Fri 9am–9pm, weekends 1pm–5pm. Rest of the year Mon–Fri 9am–5pm and by appointment. ☎867-473-8870. www. uqqurmiut.com.

Housed in three distinctive circular buildings joined by boardwalks and designed to resemble a cluster of Inuit tents, this complex has an international reputation for its woven blankets, prints and tapestries.

Ikuvik and Ukama Trails★

🚶Two splendid hiking trails that begin in town are well worth taking. Even with the brochure map provided by the Angmarlik Visitor Centre, the 13km/8mi Ikuvik Trail, which begins across from the campground and climbs the shoulder of 671m/2,214ft Mt. Duval, is difficult to follow. Nonetheless, a hike partway up the mountain presents a bird's-eye **view** of town and a clear **view**★★ down the fiord. Far more trodden, the 6km/4mi Ukama Trail begins at the road past the arena and follows boulder-strewn Duval River along a steep slope, past pools and waterfalls, to a large boulder at a fork in the river. From here, an unmarked trail continues about 8km/5mi to a campsite and a group of small lakes.

Boat Trip★

Departs Jul–Sept. One-way 1hr 20min. ₪more than $100. Warm clothing essential. For information & reservations, contact Angmarlik Interpretive Centre. ☎867-473-8737.

Even if a visit to Auyuittuq National Park is not planned, the trip down the fiord to the park entrance by boat or by snowmobile is impressive. Small wooden boats (some with interior cabins for warmth) ply the waters through the high mountains of Pullosi Canyon to Mt. Overlord. From there, visitors may hike in for two or three hours to get a hint of the park's grandeur.

Auyuittuq National Park★★

Open year-round. ₪$25 day-use fee. Accessible by boat trip (above) or snowmobile. Parks Canada interpretation centre located in Pangnirtung will provide a list of operators; park visitors must register there in advance (open year-round Mon–Fri 8:30am–noon & 1pm–5pm). ☎867-473-2500. www.pc.ca.

This remote, yet most accessible, Arctic park on the southeastern edge of Baffin Island is a stark landscape of perpetual ice, jagged peaks of 2,100m/7,000ft and glacier-scarred valleys that become deep fiords along a coast of sheer cliffs (up to 900m/3,000ft high). *Auyuittuq* (ow-you-EE-took) means "land that never melts" in Inuktitut. Fully one quarter of its 21,470sq km/8,290sq mi is covered by the Penny Ice Cap.

The park draws climbers from all over the world to scale its rugged peaks, including Mt. Thor, the highest uninterrupted cliff face in the world, and Mt. Asgard. The most visited region is **Akshayuk (formerly Pangnirtung) Pass**, a huge U-shaped trench that stretches almost 100km/60mi across the peninsula and rises to 390m/1,280ft.

Iqaluit★

300km/186mi south of Pangnirtung, on Baffin Island

Set on the slightly pitched bank of lovely Koojesse Inlet on Frobisher Bay, Iqaluit is a community of brightly colored houses, apartment units and newly erected government buildings. The capital of Nunavut, Iqaluit is the "bright lights, big city" of the Territory, even with an estimated population of only 6,200.

While residents here hunt, fish and carve, they work in transportation, communications and other industries in the region as well. Tourism and government work resulting from Nunavut's birth in

Auyuittuq National Park

Hiking the Pass

Backpackers come to Akshayuk Pass for the challenge of hiking in this remote, yet breathtakingly grand landscape. Properly equipped and experienced hikers prepared to ford icy streams of glacial meltwater can hike the pass north to south in about 10 days. Most hikers, however, hire a boat from Pangnirtung to the Mt. Overlord warden station, then traverse 20km/12mi to the height of land along the pass at Summit Lake before returning to Pangnirtung. In addition to the cold-water crossings (*pack neoprene socks*), the trail offers plenty of moraine climbing, day scrambles, an Arctic Circle crossing and, always, stunning views of glaciers creeping down a valley flanked by peaks 1,200m/3,960ft and higher in five hues of blue. By early July the pass is usually free of snow and ice at the south entrance of Pangnirtung Fiord, and by late July, at North Pangnirtung Fiord. There is constant wind, little shelter, and much of the route is over glacial moraine (ridges of boulders). However, this is a spectacular trip for those willing to make the effort on their own, or with an organized tour.

1999 are on the increase. More than 40 percent of the residents here are non-Inuit and of those, 400 speak French as a first language.

For tourists, Iqaluit is a jumping-off point for destinations farther north, or for the **Itijjagiaq Trail**, which traverses the Meta Incognita Peninsula to Kimmirut, a 10-day hike. Yet, plenty of one-to three-day trips can be arranged here, including boat cruises, snowmobile or ski trips to Kimmirut, and floe-edge wildlife tours. The town itself also warrants a visit of at least two days. A drive from the centre of town climbs up the bank through suburbs, each higher—and newer—than the previous one and offering more spectacular **views**★★ over the ruddy rock coastline. Tours of Iqaluit are available from Polynya Adventure and Coordination Ltd. (☎867-979-6260, toll-free 866-366-6784; www.polynya.ca).

Unikkaarvik Centre★

&♿⏰*Open Jul–Aug Mon–Fri 10am–8pm, weekends 10am–5pm. Rest of the year Mon–Fri 9am–6pm, Sat 1–4pm.* ☎867-979-4636.

Inside this helpful, friendly complex, among other things, is a list of things to do in town. The central theme of the exhibits is "Man on the Land", focusing on all three regions of Nunavut, the life of the Inuit, and dioramas of wildlife. The centre also houses the offices of Nunavut Tourism (☎866-686-2888. www.nunavuttourism.com), which distributes a list of licensed tour operators. To the

right is the Iqaluit Centennial Library, where the **Thomas Mann Collection**★ of northern books can be handled with gloves *(provided)*.

Nunatta Sunakkutaangit Museum★

Next to Unikkaarvik Centre. ⏰*Open Jun–Sept daily 1pm–5pm. Rest of the year Tue–Sun 1pm–5pm.* ☎867-979-5537.

This small museum is housed in a renovated Hudson's Bay Company warehouse. Displays include Inuit clothing, tools, toys and carvings, pottery, sculptures and a changing collection of prints.

Qaummaarviit Historic Park★★

12km/7mi west of Iqaluit across Peterhead Inlet. To visit the park by dog team, snowmobile, or boat ride (30min) in summer, contact Unikkaarvik Centre: ☎867-979-4636. *For information: Nunavuk Parks.* ☎867-975-7700. www.nunavutparks.com

Archaeologists believe the **Thule** (TWO-lee) people lived on this tiny but beautiful island until about 200 years ago, drawn by whale, seal and caribou.

Some 3,000 artifacts, such as ingenious antler bows and ivory harpoons, and 20,000 animal bones have been found among 10 subterranean sod houses (thought to be used as a winter camp). Guides anchor their freighter canoes and Lake Winnipeg boats at one end of the island so visitors can follow a boardwalked trail past the sod houses to the island's other end, where meat caches (2ft-high circular rock fences) and graves with human ribs and skulls testify to the harsh environment. On an evening trip, ask the guide to stop the boat's motor so harp seals in the inlet can be heard breathing, barking and even growling as they feed in groups of a dozen or more.

KITIKMEOT REGION

The biggest centres in this region are Cambridge Bay (also known as Iqaluktuuttiaq) on the southeast end of Victoria Island, and Kugluktuk on the Coppermine River. More than 300km/186mi to the east of Kugluktuk lies the community of Bathurst Inlet, also known as Kitikmeot (population 20-25), on an inlet of the same name.

- 🛈 **Information:** Nunavut Tourism. ☎1-866-686-2888. www.nunavuttourism.com
- ▶ **Orient Yourself:** This region comprises the central Arctic, including a swath covering almost the entire northern coastline of mainland Canada up to the Gulf of Boothia, as well as King William Island, the southern section of Prince of Wales Island, and the eastern and southern parts of Victoria Island.
- 😊 **Don't Miss:** A trip out onto the land, hiking or skiing. For bird-watchers, the Queen Maud Migratory Bird Sanctuary.
- 🕐 **Organizing Your Time:** Recourse to outfitters is the best way to ensure your time is well – and safely – spent.
- **Kids Especially for Kids:** These strenuous tours are for older children only.

👣 **Also See:** BAFFIN REGION, KIVALLIQ (KEEWATIN) REGION

Bathurst Inlet

48km/30mi north of the Arctic Circle
This area of Nunavut is an especially good place to experience a mid-Arctic blend of wildlife and traditional culture plus the thrills of fishing, rafting and canoeing on Arctic rivers. For more than a quarter century, the people at naturalist hostelry **Bathurst Inlet Lodge** have been devoted to interpreting the Arctic world for outdoor enthusiasts. In spring and summer knowledgeable staff provide guided hikes and natural history interpretations of the barrens and river gorges of this part of the mainland. Outpost camps for fishing or wildlife watching are also available, and activities from cross-country skiing to dogsledding can be arranged. Seven-day packages include air transportation from Yellowknife, accommodations, meals and guided excursions. *For information, access and reservations, contact Bathurst Inlet Lodge and Bathurst Arctic Services: Box 820, Yellowknife, NT X1A 2N6. ☎867-873-2595. www.bathurstinletlodge.com.*

Cambridge Bay

On the southeast coast of Victoria Island Canada's second-biggest island (after Baffin) is **Victoria Island**, located across the Queen Maud Gulf from the Arctic mainland. Kitikmeot's regional centre, Cambridge Bay is also its most populous community. The 1,300 or so residents still hunt caribou and fish for char, but now many also work for the new Nunavut government, for mineral extraction companies, the co-op fishery or themselves. Cambridge Bay is situated along the Northwest Passage; in fact, Roald Amundsen's ship, which sank after it was acquired by the Hudson's Bay Company, is still visible in the bay. At the **Arctic Coast Visitor Centre,** across from the Elders' Centre, visitors can learn about Amundsen and other explorers who, for centuries, risked their lives searching for an easier route between Europe and Asia. The staff will help arrange a local tour and provide a guidebook and information for Ovayok (Mount Pelly) Territorial Park. Char fishing and muskox viewing are also popular activities here. The Intuit name for Cambridge Bay, Iqaluktuuttiaq, means "good place with lots of fish."

KIVALLIQ (KEEWATIN) REGION★

The community of **Rankin Inlet**, one of the string-of-pearl hamlets along the northwest coast of Hudson Bay, serves as the main regional transportation and communications centre. Miles offshore, lovely **Marble Island** sits, surrounded by the waters of the bay. To the northwest, the town of Baker Lake occupies a fine site on its namesake body of water, the departure point for Sila Lodge, a popular spot for wildlife viewing on **Wager Bay**. (🕐*Open July–Aug. Contact Sila Lodge Ltd, PO Box 40063, Naim RPO, Winnipeg MN, R2L 2G2. ☎204-949-2050, toll-free 1-800-663-9832.)*

📶 **Information:** Nunavut Tourism. ☎1-866-686-2888. www.nunavuttourism. com; Kivalliq Regional Visitor Center, located at the airport. ☎1-866-686-2888 (Canada/US), or toll-free from outside North America 1-800-0491-7910

▶ **Orient Yourself:** This region includes the west coast of Hudson Bay and the mainland west to the border of the Northwest Territories near Dubawnt Lake and the Thelon Wildlife Sanctuary, as well as Southampton Island and Coats Island.

😊 **Don't Miss:** Marble Island, for its wildlife, scenery and poignant historical remains.

🕐 **Organizing Your Time:** Rankin Inlet, a major transport hub, will be your headquarters for excursions.

Kids **Especially for Kids:** A teenager, might appreciate the adventure.

👓 **Also See:** THELON WILDLIFE SANCTUARY, KITIKMEOT REGION, BAFFIN REGION

Visit

Rankin Inlet★ (Kangiqtiniq)

1,560km/975mi north of Winnipeg and about midway between Yellowknife and Iqaluit, Rankin Inlet sits on the west coast of Hudson Bay, on the north side of an inlet that extends some 27km/16m inland.

The centre of transporation and com- munications for the region, Rankin Inlet (population 2,200) is also a major hub for commercial airline flights. In sum- mer, purple fireweed adds color to an otherwise rocky, dusty place.

The community was established when the North Rankin Nickel Mine opened in the 1950s. Although the mine closed in 1962, the federal government set up a school and housing. Eventually, people found work in construction, transpor- tawith the Inuit, and eventually died of scurvy and starvation. In the 1800s the island, with its protected lagoon, was a popular wintering spot for whalers.

A walk on Deadman Island (part of Mar- ble) reveals a dozen or so rock graves, some with crosses and whalebones, as well as spectacular **views** past the low cliffs of Marble Island and the bay.

Iqalugaarjuup Nunanga Territorial Park★

On east side of Iqalugaarjuk (Meliadine) River, 10km northeast of Rankin Inlet via road by arena, the only road out of town. To hire a guide, contact the Kival- liq Regional Visitors' Centre at the airport ☎867-686-2888.

While locals come to picnic on the windy esker, fish or collect water from the river or to stroll at Siksik Lake farther up the road, the attraction for visitors is a major archaeological site here, Qumaviniqtak, ("place of old sod houses"). A foot-wide circular interpretive **trail** (*about 1km; to access, turn right at the fork to a parking lot with outhouse*) set in the flat, tree- less but beautiful valley, leads past more than two dozen 15C and 16C tent rings—circles of stones used to hold the skins down in the wind. Another 100 are located on the other side of the Iqalugaarjuk River, where the Thule people channelled Arctic char into stone weirs in order to spear them in shallow water. Food caches, burial cairns and other indicators of a Thule hunting and fishing camp can be seen. Five sunken areas near the riverbank are Thule winter houses—once large and subterra-nean, covered with skin and sod—that these people lived in as far back as 800 years ago.

Local elders have constructed a sod house at the site, and cultural per-formances are often held here, with drum-dancing, throat-singing, games and story-telling. The park guidebook (*download from www.nunavutparks. com site, or pick up at the airport visi-tors' centre*) provides a key for numbers printed on the rocks, to explain various structures.

THELON WILDLIFE SANCTUARY★★

NUNAVUT, NORTHWEST TERRITORIES

The Thelon is a remote, Denmark-size refuge of rolling, rocky tundra, threaded with meandering **sand eskers** so large, pilots navigate by them (eskers are ridges composed of the sedimentary remains of glacial rivers). The 1,000km/620mi-long **Thelon River,** designated a heritage waterway for its forest oasis along one stretch and for its rich Inuit history, flows through the sanctuary from its headwaters in Whitefish Lake to Baker Lake, west of Hudson Bay. In 1927 the game preserve was formally established by the government to protect resident herds of musk-oxen. Today the Thelon expanse falls under the jurisdiction of Nunavut.

- 🛈 **Information:** Nunavut Parks, PO Box 1000, Station 1340, Iqaluit NU, X0A 0H0. ☎867-975-7700. www.nunavutparks.com
- ▶ **Orient Yourself:** This colossal game preserve—Canada's largest—straddles both Nunavut and the Northwest Territories.
- 🕐 **Organizing Your Time:** An expedition here must be organized months ahead.

Access by Air
Access by chartered aircraft from Baker Lake, Fort Smith or Yellowknife, or by canoe via lakes and the Thelon River. Nunavut Parks (🕐See above) offers a list of licensed outfitters who can organize trips and provide guides. The jumping-off point for canoe trips is Baker Lake.

Visit
The contrast of high spruce groves in a sinuous oasis among the treeless, see-forever tundra is stunning. The sanctuary and the land for miles around it attract white tundra wolves, hairy muskoxen, barren-land grizzly, caribou and raptors. A 30m/99ft-high esker skirts Whitefish Lake. Though not within the borders of the sanctuary, the esker falls along the migratory path of the Beverly herd of caribou, one of Canada's biggest, esti-mated at 275,000. The Qamanirjuaq herd estimate is half a million. These are two of four major herds of **barren-ground caribou** in Canada's North.

The Beverly herd moves as far as 700km/434mi south from the calving grounds at Deep Rose Lake and Sam Lake to the tree line in the Northwest Territories and northern Saskatchewan for the winter. The caribou often use the eskers as highways. Wolves, bears and foxes may den in the eskers and often prey on the herd's young.

The following describes highlights of a guided outfitters' tour:

The Great Summer Caribou Migration tour is conducted in July with departures from Yellowknife. For details on it and other wildlife photo tours, contact Great Canadian Ecoventures in Yellowknife, NT. ☎715-254-9318, toll-free 1-800-667-9453 (Canada/US). www.thelon.com. Three-months' advance reservations and deposit required.

©Catherine Senecal

Caribou herd

10m/30ft from a Caribou Herd

Near the headwaters of the Thelon River, I held my arms over my head like antlers, moving from one scrub spruce to the next, inching to within 10m/30ft of 10,000-plus snorting, bleating, grunting caribou. Spotted from the air minutes earlier, the herd was so massive it made the ground shake. Yet this conclave composed a mere fraction of the entire Beverly herd. We had come to see the annual caribou migration that occurs each summer after the flooding of the calving grounds. The thrill of watching wildlife at close range out in the wilds is an experience like no other. (Staying at an isolated fly-in camp in relative luxury elevates the experience even more!) During the remainder of the 14-day wildlife photo tour at Whitefish Lake's north camp, I stalked a solitary musk-ox to within 6m/20ft, watched an abandoned wolf pup wail plaintively to the pack, and enjoyed the escapades of the camp *siksik* (Arctic ground squirrel) as it foraged around the cookhouse.

Set up to afford close access to the 100km/62ft Boomerang esker, our comfortable camp, complete with GPS (Global Positioning System) receiver, satellite phone, airplanes, motorboats, canoes, first-aid kits, pepper spray (bear repellent), great cooks, skilled pilots and top-notch wilderness guides, was *the* place to enjoy a fascinating wilderness experience. We slept in individual expedition tents with wooden floors, foam-cushioned beds, heaters and easy-to-use propane lanterns. A hot-shower hut and pit toilets stood nearby. The cookhouse was a cozy space with a well-stocked pantry, two propane stoves, an oil heater and a common room/library for guests.

One day, while heading out on Whitefish Lake for trout fishing, we were buzzed by one of the airplanes. Upon landing, the lead guide poked his head out the door, "We have a musk-ox—let's go." Back at camp, we grabbed our cameras and jumped into the float planes, flying to the site where the lone ox had been spotted. So far, our ox was oblivious to us and our whirring cameras. But, it was a hot, buggy day for this 400-pound beast—a perfect day to be aggravated. We crept closer until he started grazing toward us. At about 6m/20ft, he looked up, with body language that said "Whoa, where'd you come from?" Directly facing our small group (with me in the back because I'm a mom), he started swaying his head and pawing the ground. This was not a good sign. Musk-oxen do not like water, so I had my escape plan figured out. We glanced at our guide (who appeared unfazed), then back at the ox, then at our guide—it was like watching a tennis match—waiting for a signal. Tell us to run, back up, anything! Suddenly, the musk-ox simply turned and walked away in a huff, his shiny black skirt swaying in the wake.

A

Acadians 358
Accessibility 19
Accommodations
   Bed and Breakfasts 25
   Colleges 25
   Country inns 25
   Farm 26
   Fishing Camps 27
   Fly-in Lodges 27
   Guest Ranches 26, 82
   Hostels 25
   Houseboats 28
   Igloos 28
   Motels 24
   Ranches 26
   Teepees 28
   Universities 25
   Wilderness Camps 27
Act of Union 47, 49
African Lion Safari 231
Airlines
   Air Canada 20
Airports
   Calgary International Airport 20
   Edmonton International Airport 20
   Lester B. Pearson International
      Airport (Toronto) 21
   Ottawa International Airport 21
   Pierre Elliott Trudeau International
      Airport (Montreal) 21
   St. John's International Airport 21
   Vancouver International Airport 20
   Winnipeg International Airport 20
Air Travel 20
Aitken, William Maxwell 365
Alaska Highway 77, 164
Alberta Badlands 171
Annapolis Royal 381
Annapolis Tidal Generating Station 382
Annapolis Valley 383
Arctic Ranges 42
Art 52
Art Gallery of Ontario 286
Art Gallery of Windsor 299
Artillery Park National Historic Site 346
Arts and Crafts 31
Assembly of First Nations 48
Athabasca Glacier 118
Atlantic Provinces 356
Atlantic Salmon Museum 368
Atlantic Shore 387
Atlin 80
Augustine Monastery 343
Aurora Borealis 439
Austin 174
Auyuittuq National Park 460

B

Baddeck 391
Baffin Region 458
Baie-Saint-Paul 308
Baie-Sainte-Catherine 309
Balmoral Mills 390
Banff 106
Banff National Park 106
Banks 35
Barkerville 82, 83
Bar U Ranch 182
Bas-Saint-Laurent 305, 307
Basic Information 35
Basilique-Cathédrale Marie-
    Reine-du-Monde 331
Basilique-Cathédrale Notre-
    Dame-de Québec 342
Basilique Notre-Dame 323
Bata Shoe Museum 291
Batoche National Historic Site 203
Battlefords 174
Bay St. Lawrence 394
BC Forest Discovery Centre 155
Beaverbrook, Lord 365
Beaverbrook Art Gallery 365
Bed and Breakfasts 25
Bell, Alexander Graham 221
Bellevue House 234
Bell Homestead National Historic Site 221
Beringia Interpretive Centre 160
Bethune Memorial House
    National Historic Site 228
Billings Estate Museum 258
Biosphère 336
Black Creek Pioneer Village 295
Blomidon 385
Blue Heron Drive 413
Bluehill Pond Lookout 436
Bonanza Creek 87
Bondar, Roberta 264
Bonne Bay Area 424
Books 33
Border Information Service 19
Brantford 221
British Columbia 70
   Climate 71
   Economy 73
   Geography 70
   History 72
   Recreation 75
   Road Regulations 74
   Visitor Information 74
British North America Act 47
Broken Islands Group 147
Buffalo Paddock 157
Bus 20

INDEX

Bush Pilots' Monument 450
Butchart Gardens 154

C

Cabot, John 49
Cabot Trail 391
Cajuns 359
Calendar of Events 30
Calgary 176
Calgary Tower. 177
Calgary Zoo 177
Cameron, James 61
Cameron Lake 145
Campbell House 286
Campgrounds. 26
Camping. 26
Campobello Island 371
Canada Agriculture Museum. 258
Canada Aviation Museum 256
Canada Border Services Agency 19
Canada Science and Technology Museum . 256
Canadian Automobile Association 22
Canadian Automotive Museum 247
Canadian Centre for Architecture 332
Canadian Centre for Firearms 19
Canadian Confederation. 47
Canadian Food Inspection Agency 19
Canadian Museum of Nature. 256
Canadian Pacific Railway 47
Canadian Shield. 41
Canadian War Museum 256
Cantons de l'Est 310, 311
Canyon Sainte-Anne 308
Cap-de-la-Madeleine Shrine. 355
Cape Breton Highlands National Park 394
Cape Merry National Historic Site 185
Cape Shore 422
Cape Shore Drive. 423
Cape St. Mary 423
Cardston. 182
Cariboo, The 81
Cartier, Jacques 49
Cartier-Brébeuf National Historic Site 348
Car Travel 22
Casa Loma 292
Cassiar Mountains. 79
Cathedral Grove. 146
Central New Brunswick
    Woodmen's Museum. 368
Centre de la nature du mont Saint-Hilaire . 350
Centre d'Histoire de Montréal. 330
Chambly. 349
Champlain, Samuel de. 45, 49
Chapelle Notre-Dame-de-Bon-Secours . . . 330
Château Dufresne 336
Château Frontenac 339

Château Ramezay 329
Chemainus. 155
Chester 388
Chicoutimi (see Saguenay). 352
Children 30
Churchill. 183
Cinema 61
City Centre. 231
Clearwater Lake. 83
Climate 17, 44
CN Tower 277
Coach Travel 21
Constitution Act 49,50
Consulates 18
Cordillera Indians 45
Cosmodôme 336
Côte-Nord 309
Côte de Beaupré 348
Côte de Charlevoix 308
Country Inns 25
Credit Cards. 35
Currency Exchange. 36
Currency Museum. 256
Customs 19
Cypress Hills 185

D

Dance 59
Dartmouth. 403
Davidson, Reg. 53
Davidson, Robert. 53
Dawson City 84
Dawson Creek. 77
Deer Island 371
Detah. 451
Dieppe Gardens. 299
Dinosaur Provincial Park. 172
Dinosaur Trail 171
Discounts. 33
Discovery Harbour 224
Dominion Lands Act. 50
Dresden 222
Driving 22
Driving Tours
    British Columbia 10
    Maritime Provinces. 15
    Newfoundland. 16
    Northern British Columbia. 11
    Northern Ontario 13
    Prairies 12
    Quebec. 14
    Rockies 10
    Southern Ontario 14
    Yukon 11
Drumheller 171
Dundurn Castle 231
Dynamic Earth 268

E

Eagle Pass 95
Easter Seals Canada 19
Economy 62
Edmonton 187
Edmundston 378
Electricity 35
Elgin and Winter Garden Theatre Centre . . 285
Elk Island National Park 191
Embassies 18
Emergencies 35
Emergency Numbers 37
Emergency road service 22
Englishman River Falls 144
Erickson, Arthur 131
Esquimalt 149

F

Farmers' Markets 31
Farm vacations 26
Films 34
Fisheries Museum of the Atlantic 389
Fisherman's Cove 401
Fishing Camps 27
Fjord Du Saguenay 351
Fly-in Lodges 27
Food 67
Foreign Affairs Canada 18
Fort Anne National Historic Site 382
Fort Battleford 175
Fort Chambly National Historic Site 349
Fort Edmonton Park 190
Fort Henry 234
Fort Langley National Historic Site 143
Fort Lennox National Historic Site 350
Fort Macleod 192
Fort Malden 299
Fort Nelson 77, 78
Fort Smith 447
Fort St. James 88
Fort St. John 77
Fort Steele Heritage Town 93
Fort Walsh National Historic Site 186
Fort William Historical Park 269
Fraser Canyon 89
Fraser Canyon Country 89
French Words 34
Fundy Isles 370, 371
Fundy National Park 367
Fur Exchange 31

G

Gardiner Museum of Ceramic Art 288
Gasoline 22
Gaspé 314
Gaspésie 312, 313
Gatineau 316, 317

Gatineau Park (Quebec) 260
Geography 42
Georgian Bay 223
Getting There & Getting Around 20
Glenbow Museum 176
Goderich 226
Golden 97
Government 65
Graham Island 102
Grand-Pré National Historic Site 385
Grand Falls 378
Grand Manan Island 373
Gravenhurst 228
Great Bras'Or 395
Gretzky, Wayne 221
Greyhound 21
Gros Morne National Park 423
Gross Domestic Product 64
Guest Ranches 26, 82
Gwaii Haanas National Park Reserve 104

H

Haida 102
Haliburton House Museum 386
Halifax 387, 396
Halifax Citadel National Historic Site 400
Hamilton 229
Harbourfront Centre 279
Hartland 377
Hat Creek Ranch 91
Head-Smashed-In Buffalo Jump 193
Health 19
Hearts Content 426
Hell's Gate 89
HMSC Aquarium-Museum 371
Hockey Hall of Fame 282
Holidays 36
Hope 89
Hopewell Cape 370
Horne, William Van 48
Horseshoe Bay 141
Hostels 25
Hostelling International Canada 25
Hôtel de Ville 327
Hotels 24, 29
Hotels (*also see "Where to Stay"*)
  Calgary
    Big Springs Estate B&B 178
    Fairmont Palliser 178
    Inglewood B&B 178
    Kensington Riverside Inn 178
    Lord Nelson Inn 178
    Westways B&B 178
  Halifax
    Citadel Halifax Hotel 398
    Halliburton House Inn 398
    Lord Nelson Hotel and Suites 398

INDEX

Prince George Hotel 398
Waverley Inn 398
Montreal
   Château Versailles 325
   Fairmont La Reine Elizabeth 325
   Hostellerie Pierre du Calvet 325
   Hôtel de l'Institut 325
   Hôtel Le Germain 325
   L'Auberge de Jeunesse 325
New Brunswick
   Colonel's Inn 366
   Homeport Historic B&B 374
   Hôtel Paulin 368
   Kingsbrae Arms 372
   Lord Beaverbrook Hotel 366
   On the Pond 366
   Very Best Victorian B&B 366
Nova Scotia
   Cooper's Inn 390
   Normaway Inn 392
Ontario
   Blue Bay Motel 225
   Elora Mill Inn 237
   Grandview Motel 225
   Harborside Motel 225
   Hotel Belvedere 233
   The Little Inn of Bayfield 227
   Rosemount Inn 233
   Upper Canada Guest House 298
Ottawa
   A Rose on Colonel By B&B 249
   Auberge McGee's Inn 249
   Auberge The King Edward 249
   Fairmont Château Laurier 249
   Gasthaus Switzerland Inn 249
   Hostelling International Ottawa:
      Ottawa Jail 249
   Lord Elgin Hotel 249
Prince Edward Island
   Dalvay-by-the-Sea 411
   Fairholm Inn 411
   Inn at Spry Point 411
Quebec
   Centre d'art Marcel Gagnon 315
   Fairmont Tremblant 319
   Gîte du Mont-Albert 315
   Hôtel la Normandie 315
Quebec City
   Auberge Saint-Antoine 340
   Centre international de
      Séjour de Québec 340
   Château Bonne Entente 340
   Fairmont Le Château Frontenac 340
   Hôtel Particulier Belley 340
   Ice Hotel Quebec 340
   L'Astral 341

   L'Hôtel Dominion 1912 340
   L'Hôtel du Vieux Québec 340
   Reservations Services 25
Toronto
   Fairmont Royal York 275
   Hotel Victoria 274
   Le Royal Meridien King Edward 275
   Metropolitan 274
   Residence College Hotel 274
   Strathcona Hotel 274
   Sutton Place 274
   Windsor Arms 275
Whitehorse
   Tincup Wilderness Lodge 158
Winnipeg
   Beechmount B&B 207
   Charter House Hotel 207
   Delta Winnipeg 207
   The Fairmont Winnipeg 207
   Fort Garry Hotel 207
   Hostel International Downtowner 207
   Maison Grosvenor B&B 207
Howe Sound 142
Hudson's Bay Company 47, 49
Hudson, Henry 49
Hunting Fossils 173

I

Icefields Parkway 116
Ice Hockey 333
Île aux Coudres 308
Île aux Noix 350
Île d'Anticosti 304
Île d'Orléans 348
Île du Cap-Aux-Meules 321
Île du Havre aux Maisons 321
Île Notre-Dame 336
Île Sainte-Hélène 336
Îles de la Madeleine 320, 321
Ingraham Trail 451
Inside Passage 92
Insurance - Yellow card 22
International Visitors 18
Inuit 45
Inuit Art 53
Inuvik 443
Iqaluit 460

J

Janvier, Alex 53
Jardin botanique de Montréal 335
Jardins de Métis 313
Jasper 119
Jean, Michaëlle 51
Juan de Fuca Trail 145

K

Kakabeka Falls 269
Kamloops................................ 91
Kamloops Lake.......................... 91
Kaslo 94
Keewatin 463
Kejimkujik 383
Kelowna 100
Kennedy Lake........................... 146
Kimberley 94
Kings Byway Drive 415
Kings Landing Historical Settlement 377
Kingston............................... 232
Kingston and The Thousand Islands....... 232
Kitchener-Waterloo 236
Kitikmeot Region 462
Kivalliq 463
Kluane Lake............................ 164
Kluane National Park Reserve............ 165
Know Before You Go..................... 18
Kootenay National Park................. 121
Kootenays 93

L

Lac Saint-Jean......................... 353
Lady Slipper Drive..................... 416
Lake Louise 114, 115
Lake Superior Drive 264
La Malbaie-Pointe-au-Pic............... 309
L'Anse aux Meadows 426
La Pocatière........................... 306
Laurentides......................318, 319
Laurier House 258
Les Forges-du-Saint-Maurice
    Ironworks National Historic Site....... 355
Lethbridge............................. 194
Lévis.................................. 305
Liard River Hot Springs Park 78
Lieu historique national des
    Forges-du-Saint-Maurice.............. 355
Lieu historique national des
    Fortifications-de-Québec............. 346
Lieu historique national du Canada
    Bataille-de-la-Ristigouche........... 316
Lieu historique national du Canada de la
    Grosse-Île-et-le-Mémorial-des-Irlandais
    (Grosse-Île and the Irish Memorial
    National Historic Site of Canada) 305
Lieu historique national du Canada des
    Forts-de-Lévis (Lévis Forts National
    Historic Site of Canada 305
Lieu historique national du
    Canada Louis-S.-St-Laurent........... 311
Lieu historique national du
    Cartier-Brébeuf 348
Lieu historique national du Fort-Chambly . 349
Lieu historique national du Fort-Lennox... 350

Lieu historique national du
    Parc-de-lArtillerie 346
Literature............................. 57
Little Qualicum Falls.................. 145
London................................ 238
Long Beach 147
Lower Fort Garry National Historic Site ... 212
Lunenburg............................. 389
Lytton 90

M

MacDonald Farm Provincial Historic Site .. 368
Mackenzie Delta 442
Mackenzie House 285
Mactaquac Provincial Park.............. 377
Magog................................. 311
Mahone Bay 388
Maid of the Mist....................... 242
Mail 35
Maison du Calvet....................... 330
Maitland.............................. 406
Malahat Drive.......................... 155
Maligne Canyon......................... 120
Maligne Lake 121
Manitoba Agricultural Museum........... 174
Manitoba Museum 206
Manning Provincial Park................ 89
Manulife Financial..................... 19
Marché Bonsecours 330
Maritime Museum of British Columbia 153
Marsh Lake 80
Martello Tower......................... 376
Mauricie Region 355
McGill University...................... 332
McMichael Canadian Art Collection 295
McNabs Island 403
Medicine Lake 121
Meech Lake Accord...................48, 50
Mennonites.........................212, 237
Midland 223
Midnight Dome 87
Miette Hot Springs 121
Miner, Billy........................... 94
Miner, Jack............................ 299
Miquelon 435
Miramichi Valley 367
Monastère de lHôtel-Dieu de Québec 343
Monastère des Ursulines 343
Money................................. 35
Montreal............................... 322
Moose Jaw............................. 195
Moraine Lake 115
Moresby Island......................... 104
Morrisseau, Norval 53
Motels................................ 24
Mount Revelstoke Summit Parkway........ 95
Mount Robson Provincial Park 121

INDEX

Mt. McKay 268
Muncho Lake 78
Muncho Lake Provincial Park 78
Murtle Lake 83
Musée Amérindien de Mashteuiatsh 353
Musée canadien des Civilisations 316
Musée d'archéologie et
    d'histoire de Montréal 330
Musée d'art contemporarin de Montréal .. 333
Musée David M. Stewart 336
Musée de la Civilisation 345
Musée des Arts décoratifs de Montréal ... 332
Musée des Beaux-Arts de Montréal 332
Musée des Hospitalières de
    l'Hôtel-Dieu de Montréal 334
Musée du Québec 347
Musée J.-Armand Bombardier 311
Musée McCord d'histoire canadienne 331
Musée québécois de culture populaire 355
Museum of Civilization 345
Music 59

N

Nahanni National Park Reserve 444
National Gallery of Canada 255
National Ukrainian Festival 201
Nature 40
Nelson 94
New Brunswick 362
New Brunswick Museum 375
Newfoundland and Labrador 418
New France 46
Newsprint 62
Niagara-on-the-Lake 243
Niagara Falls 240
Niagara Parkway (North) 242
Nipigon Bay 270
Nisga'a Treaty 49
North American Free Trade
    Agreement (NAFTA) 50, 66
North Bay 245
North Shore Lake Superior 269
North West Company 47
Northwest Territories 438
Nunatta Sunakkutaangit Museum 461
Nunavik 337
Nunavut 452

O

108 Mile Ranch 82
Odjig, Daphne 53
Okanagan Valley 98
Olympics 127
Ontario 214
Ontario Parliament 288
Ontario Place 281
Ontario Science Centre 293

Oratoire Saint-Joseph 334
Orillia 246
Osgoode Hall 285
Oshawa 246
Ottawa 247
Ottawa River Parkway 260
Ouimet Canyon 270
Outdoor Fun 29
Ovens Natural Park 389

P

Pacific Rim National Park Reserve 146
Pacific Salmon 90
Painting 54
Pangnirtung 459
Parc de la Chute-Montmorency 348
Parc de la Gaspésie 313
Parc de l'Île-Bonaventure-et-
    du-Rocher-Percé 315
Parc de Miguasha 316
Parc des Champs-de-Bataille 347
Parc du Bic (Bic Park) 306
Parc du Mont-Orford 311
Parc du Mont-Royal 334
Parc du Mont Tremblant 320
Parc du Saguenay 351
Parc national de la Mauricie 355
Parc national Forillon
    (Forillon National Park) 314
Parc Olympique 334
Parc Safari 350
Parkwood Estate 246
Parliament Hill 251
Passamaquoddy Bay 370, 371
Passports 19
Peggy's Cove 387
Penetanguishene 224
Percé 314
Péribonka 353
Perkins House Museum 389
Peterborough 260
Plains Indians 45
Planning Your Trip 9
Point Pelee National Park 261
Point Wolfe 367
Polar Bears 184
Population 66
Port-Royal National Historic Site 382
Port Alberni 146
Prairie Provinces 166, 169
Prescott 262
Prescott House Museum 384
Prince Albert National Park 196
Prince Edward Island 409
Prince Edward Island National Park 413
Prince of Wales Northern Heritage Centre . 450
Prince Rupert 124

Q

Qaummaarviit Historic Park 461
Qu'Appelle Valley 199
Québec 338
Quebec 300
Quebec City 338
Queen Charlotte Islands 102
Queens Park 287
Quw'utsun Cultural and Conference Centre . 155

R

Radar Hill 148
Rail Service
    Amtrak 20
    Via Rail 20, 21
Ranch Vacations 26
Rankin Inlet 463
Ray, Carl 53
Regina 197
Reid, Bill 53
Rental Cars 23
Restaurants 24, 28
Restaurants (also see "Where to Eat")
  Calgary
    Buzzards Cowboy Cuisine 179
    Deane House 178
    The Ranche 178
    River Café 179
    Thai Sa-On 178
  Edmonton
    Hardware Grill 189
    Jack's Grill 189
  Halifax
    Bluenose II Restaurant 399
    Boondock's Dining Room 401
    Cellar Bar & Grill 398
    Da Maurizio Dining Room 399
    Economy Shoe Shop Café 399
    Il Mercato Ristorante 399
    Tomasino's Pizzeria and
      Cellar Ristorante 399
    Victory Arms 398
  Montreal
    Beauty's 326
    Beaver Club 325
    Hélène de Champlain 327
    La Marée 327
    Le Piton de la Fournaise 326
    Moishes 327
    Restaurant Daou 326
    Toqué! 327
  New Brunswick
    Billy's Seafood 374
    Brewbakers 366
    El Burrito Loco 366
    Piper's Palate 366
    Schade's Restaurant 366

    Shadow Lawn Inn 374
    Taco Pico 374
  Nova Scotia
    Blomidon Inn 384
    Captain's Cabin 384
    Fundy Restaurant 384
    Restaurant Acadien 392
    Shoreline Restaurant 384
  Ontario
    Alexandria's 267
    Ancaster Old Mill Inn 230
    Apollo 267
    Desert Rose Café 237
    E.J.'s 237
    Elora Mill Inn 237
    Kennedy's Restaurant & Pub 237
    Le Chien Noir Bistro 233
    Leeside Restaurant 225
    Michael's on the Thames 238
    Olde Heidelberg Restaurant
      and Brew Pub 237
    Olde School Restaurant 222
    Pasta è Vino 267
    The Riverview Restaurant 238
    The Gardens' Café 230
    Villa Cornelia 238
    White House on the Hill 226
    Willard's 298
  Ottawa
    Blue Cactus 249
    Canal Ritz 250
    The Elgin Café 249
    Empire Grill 250
    Le Café 250
    Le Jardin 250
    Papagus Taverna 250
    Roses Café 250
    Trattoria Zingaro 250
    Wilfrid's 249
    Yang Sheng 250
  Prince Edward Island
    Inn at Bay Fortune 411
    Lobster on the Wharf 411
    MacMillan Dining Room 411
    Trailside Inn and Café 411
  Quebec
    Cabane à sucre Millette 319
    Chez Pierre 315
    La Maison du Pêcheur 315
    Restaurant aux Tourterelles 319
    Restaurant La Forge 319
    Restaurant Le Sans-Pareil 317
  Quebec City
    Aux Anciens Canadiens 341
    L'Ardoise Resto Bistro 346
    L'Échaudé 346
    La Playa 341

INDEX

Le Café du Monde 341
Le Champlain 340
Le Continental 341
Le Saint-Amour 341
Portofino Bistro Italiano 341
Tavern Belley 340
Toronto
Brasserie Aix 287
Café Victoria 275
Cawthra Square 274
Courtyard Café 275
Fred's Not Here 275
Lai Wah Heen 275
Le Papillon 276
Myth 276, 279
Pappas Grill 279
Red Tomato 275
Rodney's Oyster House 275
Romancing the Home 279
Shopsy's Deli 275
Southern Accent 276
Splendido 276
Spring Rolls 275
Suckers 279
Taste of the Danforth 279
Xacutti 287
Winnipeg
Amici 207
Bombolini 208
Broadway Room 207
Café La Scala 207
Chutneys 208
Civita 208
The Livery Barn Restaurant 212
Pasta La Vista 208
Restaurant Dubrovnik 208
Rib Room Restaurant 207
Tavern in the Park 208
Revelstoke 95
Reversing Falls Rapids 376
Rideau Canal 253
Rideau Canal Driveways 259
Rideau Falls 258
Riding Mountain National Park 200
Riel, Louis 199
Rimouski 306
Rivière-du-Loup 306
Road Regulations 22
Roberval 353
Rocher Percé (Percé Rock) 314
Rockies 70, 76
Rocky Mountain House
National Historic Site 182
Rocky Mountain Parks 105
Rogers Centre 278
Rogers Pass 96
Roosevelt Campobello International Park . 372

Ross-Thomson House and Store Museum . 390
Ross Farm Museum 388
Royal British Columbia Museum 151
Royal Ontario Museum 288
Royal Saskatchewan Museum 198
Royal Tyrrell Museum 171
Roy Thomson Hall 283
RV Parks 26

S

Saguenay 352
 Saguenay Fjord 352
Saint-Boniface 210
Saint-Denis-sur-Richelieu 350
Saint-Félicien 353
Saint-Jean-sur-Richelieu 350
Sainte-Adèle 318
Sainte-Agathe-des-Monts 318
Sainte-Marie among the Hurons 223
Sainte-Rose-du-Nord 352
Saint John 373
Saint John River Valley 376
Saskatoon 201
Sault-au-Récollet 337
Sault Ste. Marie 263
Sault Ste. Marie Canal
National Historic Site 263
Science North 266
Sculpture 54, 55
Seasons 17
Sea to Sky Highway 141
Secwepemc Museum and
Native Heritage Park 91
Senior Citizens 33
Sept-Îles 309
Seven Years' War 49
Shelburne 390
Sherbrooke 310, 407
Sherbrooke Village 407
Shippagan 368
Ship Travel 21
Shopping 30
Shubenacadie Park 402
Shuswap Lake 91
Sightseeing 32
Six Nations Iroquois Confederacy 49
Skagway 161
Skeena Valley 123
Smoking 36
SnoCoach Tours on the Glacier 118
Spadina Museum 293
Spas 30
Springhill 408
SS Klondike 158
St. Andrews 371
St. Johns 428
St. Lawrence Seaway 50

Stanley Park 127
Statute of Westminster 48, 50
Stewart-Cassiar Highway 79
Stowe, Harriet Beecher 222
Stratford................................. 265
Sturgeon Falls............................ 245
Sudbury 266
Sussex Drive and Rockcliffe Parkway 258
Swan Lake Christmas Hill Nature Sanctuary 154

T

Tadoussac 352
Tagish Lake 80
Taxes 36
Taylor..................................... 77
Teepee Camping 193
Telephones 36
Telus World of Science Edmonton 191
Teslin Lake................................ 80
Thelon Wildlife Sanctuary 464
Thompson Canyon 90
Thousand Islands, The.............. 232, 234
Thunder Bay 268
Tidal Bore................................. 369
Time....................................... 37
Tips....................................... 37
Tobermory................................. 225
Tofino 148
Top of the World Highway 164
Toronto................................... 271
Toronto-Dominion Centre 282
Toronto Islands 279
Toronto Reference Library 292
Toronto Shopping.......................... 276
Totem Poles................... 53, 102, 125
Tourist Offices............................ 18
Tours 17
Train Travel 21
Trans-Canada Highway 153
Transcontinental Railway 47
Treaty of Paris....................... 47, 49
Treaty of Utrecht 46
Trinity 437
Trois-Rivières 354
Truro 408
Tuktoyaktuk 443

U

Ukrainian Cultural and Educational Centre 209
Uncle Tom's Cabin Historic Site 222
Unikkaarvik Centre........................ 461
Upper Canada Village 297
Uqqurmiut Centre for Arts and Crafts 459

V

Val-Jalbert Historic Village............... 353
Vallée du Richelieu 349
Vancouver 126
Vancouver Island.......................... 144
Vernon 100
Verrerie La Mailloche 345
VIA Rail
   CANRAILPASS........................... 21
Via Rail 20
Victoria 149
Village Québécois Dantan 312

W

Wasaga Beach 224
Waterton Lakes National Park............. 156
Watson Lake 79
Websites.................................. 18
Welland Canal 244
Wells 83
Wells Gray Park........................... 83
West Coast Trail 146
Western Brook Pond 425
Western Cordillera 42
Western Development Museum 175, 213
Whale Watching 147
What to See and Do 29
When and Where to Go.................... 17
Where to Eat 28
Where to Stay 24
Whistler 142
Whitehorse 78, 157
White Pass and Yukon Route Railroad 161
Wilderness Camps 27
Wildlife 30, 43
Williams Lake 81
Windsor 299
Wineries 31
WINNIPEG 205
Witless Bay Ecological Reserve........... 434
Wolfville.................................. 385
Wood Buffalo National Park.............. 446

Y

Yellowhead Highway 121
Yellowknife 448
Yoho National Park....................... 115
Yorkton................................... 213
Yorkville 291
Yukon 70, 77
Yukon Circuit............................. 162

INDEX

WHERE TO EAT

Also see "Restaurants"

British Columbia
Monashees and Selkirks
  Eagle's Eye Restaurant............... 97
Skeena Valley
  Cow Bay Café 125

Manitoba
Winnipeg
  Livery Barn Restaurant 212

New Brunswick
Caraquet
  Hôtel Paulin 368
St. Andrews
  Niger Reef Teahouse 372
  Passamaquoddy Dining Room...... 372
  Rossmount Inn..................... 372
  Windsor House Dining Room 372

Newfoundland
St. John's
  Aqua 433
  Cabot Club......................... 432
  Duck Street Bistro 433
  Stonehouse Renaissance 432
  The Cellar.......................... 432
  Zachary's 433

Ontario
Brantford
  John Peel Steak and Seafood 222
Georgian Bay
  SiSi on Main....................... 226
  Sterios Steak & Seafood 226
  White House on the Hill 226
Kingston
  Chez Piggy......................... 233
  Hotel Belvedere.................... 233
Kitchener-Waterloo
  Kennedy's Restaurant 237
London
  Café Milagro 238
  Miestro........................... 238
North Bay
  Churchills.......................... 245
Stratford
  Church Restaurant 265
  The Belfry.......................... 265
  The Old Prune...................... 265
Sudbury
  Alexandria's 267
The Thousand Islands
  Gananoque Inn and Spa 235
Toronto
  Canoe 276
  Sassafraz 276

Prince Edward Island
Café on the Clyde 417
Off Broadway Restaurant............. 412

Quebec
Gatineau
  Le Twist Café Resto Bar 317
Montreal
  Au Cuisine du Terroir 326
  Filles du Roy 326
  Le Brontë 325
  Stash Café 327
Quebec City
  47e Parallèle 341
  Café-Restaurant du
    Musée du Québec............ 341
  Il Teatro........................... 347
  Le Saint-Amour 341
  Les Épices du Szechwan 341

Rockies
Baker Creek Bistro.................... 109
Banffshire Club....................... 110
Becker's Gourmet Restaurant 111
Buffalo Mountain Lodge dining room . 110
Edith Cavell Room.................... 111
Maple Leaf.......................... 111
Post Hotel dining room.............. 111
The Pines 111

The Yukon
Whitehorse
  The Chocolate Claim 158

Vancouver
Bacchus 134
Bishop's 135
Blue Water Cafe 135
Buddhist Vegetarian Restaurant 135
C Restaurant 135
Diva 134
Fleuri 134
Gerard's 134
Hiwus Feasthouse.................... 142
Imperial Chinese Seafood Restaurant . 136
LaRua 135
Lumiere 135
Pink Pearl Chinese Restaurant 136
Sawasdee............................ 135
Stepho's Souvlakia 135
Sun Sui Wah Seafood Restaurant...... 136
The Wildflower....................... 134

Vancouver Island
Common Loaf Bake Shop 148
Sooke Harbour House 145

Victoria
Aerie dining room.................... 150
Cafe Brio............................ 151
Da Tandoor 150
Paprika Bistro 151
Spinnaker's 151

WHERE TO STAY

Also see "Hotels"

British Columbia
  Alaska Highway
    Northern Rockies Lodge.............. 79
    Trapper Ray's Liard River Lodge...... 79
  BC Guest Ranches...................... 82
  The Cariboo
    Big Bar Ranch........................ 82
    Douglas Lake Ranch.................. 82
    Echo Valley Ranch................... 82
    Flying U Ranch...................... 82
    Hills Health Ranch.................. 82
    Sundance Guest Ranch.............. 82
    Helmcken Falls Lodge............... 82
    Wells Gray Ranch.................... 82
  Fraser Canyon
    Quaaout Lodge..................... 91
  Inside Passage
    King Pacific Lodge.................. 92
  Monashees and Selkirks
    Alpine Meadows Lodge............. 97
  Okanagan Valley
    Cathedral Lakes Lodge............. 98
New Brunswick
  St. Andrews
    Fairmont Algonquin................ 372
    Kingsbrae Arms.................... 372
    Windsor House 372
Newfoundland
  L'Anse aux Meadows
    Tickle Inn.......................... 428
  St. John's
    Fairmont Newfoundland.......... 432
    McCoubrey Manor 432
    Murray Premises 432
    Roses B&B 432
    Winterholme 432
Nova Scotia
  Halifax
    Fountainview Guest House 398
    Fresh Start B&B 398
Ontario
  The Thousand Islands
    Gananoque Inn and Spa........... 235
    Trinity House Inn.................. 235
  Toronto
    Sutton Place 275
Prince Edward Island
  Heart's Content 410
  Inns on Great George............... 410
  Warn House......................... 410

Quebec
  Montreal
    Auberge de la Fontaine............. 325
    Hôtel Le Germain 326
    Hôtel Place d' Armes 326
  Percé
    Au Pirate, L'Auberge à Percé 315
Rockies
  Baker Creek Chalets 109
  Blue Mountain Lodge 109
  Brewster's Mountain Lodge.......... 109
  Buffalo Mountain Lodge............. 111
  Emerald Lake Lodge................. 110
  Fairmont Banff Springs 110
  Fairmont Chateau Lake Louise 110
  Fairmont Jasper Park Lodge 110
  HI-Lake Louise Alpine Centre 109, 111
  Lake O'Hara Lodge 111
  Num-Ti-Jah Lodge 109
  Paradise Lodge and Bungalows....... 109
  Post Hotel 111
  Spruce Grove Inn................... 110
  Station Restaurant at Lake Louise..... 111
  Tekarra Lodge...................... 110
The Yukon
  Dawson City
    Bombay Peggy's 87
  Whitehorse
    Tincup Wilderness Lodge.......... 158
Vancouver
  Edgewater Lodge 133
  The Fairmont Chateau Whistler 134
  The Fairmont Hotel Vancouver....... 134
  The Fairmont Waterfront 134
  Hostelling International Vancouver ... 133
  Hotel Georgia...................... 133
  Listel Vancouver 134
  Metropolitan Hotel................. 134
  Residences on Georgia 133
  Sutton Place Hotel Vancouver 134
  Sylvia Hotel........................ 133
  Thistledown House 133
  Wedgewood........................ 134
Vancouver Island
  Clayoquot Wilderness Resort 145
  Eagle Nook Ocean Wilderness Resort . 145
  Wickaninnish Inn.................... 148
Victoria
  The Aerie 150
  Bedford Regency.................... 150
  English Inn and Resort.............. 154
  Fairholme Manor.................... 150
  The Fairmont Empress............... 150
  Haterleigh Heritage Inn 150
  Laurel Point Resort................. 150

MAPS AND PLANS

LIST OF MAPS

THEMATIC MAPS

Map of Principal Sights . . . . Inside Covers
Regional Driving Tours 10
Time Zones 37
Natural Regions 41
Native Cultures 46
Early Exploration 46

BRITISH COLUMBIA/ ROCKIES/YUKON

Major Relief Features 71
Monashee and Selkirk Mountains, BC 96
Southern British Columbia 101
Queen Charlotte Islands, BC 103
Banff Townsite and Area 112
Lake Louise and Area 114
Rocky Mountain Parks, AB/BC 118-119
Jasper Area 120
Skeena Valley, BC 124
Downtown Vancouver, BC 128-129
Vancouver Area 138-139
Sea to Sky Highway, BC 143
Vancouver Island, BC 146-147
Victoria, BC 152
Excursion to Skagway, Alaska 160
Yukon Circuit from Whitehorse, YT 163

PRAIRIE PROVINCES

Alberta Badlands, AB 172
Downtown Calgary, AB 180
Downtown Edmonton, AB 188
Urban Edmonton 191
Downtown Regina, SK 198
Downtown Saskatoon, SK 202
Downtown Winnipeg, MB 210
Urban Winnipeg 211

ONTARIO

Overview of Ontario Province 216-217
Hamilton 230
Kingston 234
Downtown Niagara Falls 241
Niagara Falls Region 242
Niagara Falls Excursions 243
Downtown Ottawa 251
Urban Ottawa 257
Ottawa and Environs 259
Sault Ste. Marie 264
Thunder Bay Excursions 270
Urban Toronto 280
Downtown Toronto 284
Metropolitan Toronto 292

QUEBEC

Bas-Saint-Laurent and Saguenay 306-307
Laurentides and Cantons de l' Est 312-313
Downtown Montreal 328-329
Quebec City (The Old City) 344

ATLANTIC PROVINCES

New Brunswick, Nova Scotia,
    Prince Edward Island 359
Fredericton, NB 365
Passamaquoddy Bay and the Fundy Isles . 371
Saint John, NB 375
Atlantic Shore, NS 388
Cabot Trail, Cape Breton Island, NS 393
Downtown Halifax, NS 397
Prince Edward Island 414
Newfoundland 421
Gros Morne National Park, NF 425
St. John's, NF 431

NORTHWEST TERRITORIES

Yellowknife 450

MICHELIN COMPANION PUBLICATIONS

NORTH AMERICA ROAD ATLAS

* A geographically organized atlas with extensive detailed coverage of the USA, Canada and Mexico. Includes 246 city maps, distance chart, state and provincial driving requirements and a climate chart
* Comprehensive city and town index
* Easy to follow "Go-to" pointers

MAP 585 WESTERN USA AND WESTERN CANADA

* Large-format map providing detailed road systems; includes driving distances, interstate rest stops, border crossings and interchanges.
* Comprehensive city and town index
* Scale 1:2,400,000
  (1 inch = approx. 38 miles)

MAP 583 NORTHEASTERN USA AND EASTERN CANADA

* Large-format map providing detailed road systems; includes driving distances, interstate rest stops, border crossings and interchanges
* Comprehensive city and town index
* Scale 1:2,400,000
  (1 inch = approx. 38 miles)

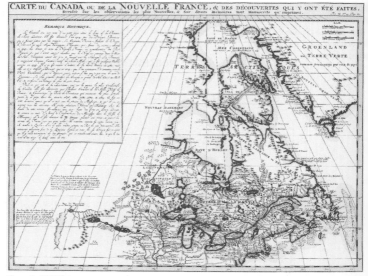

Canada (1719)

LEGEND

★★★   **Highly recommended**
★★   **Recommended**
★   **Interesting**

Sight symbols

Recommended itineraries with departure point

Church, chapel – Synagogue	Building described
Town described	Other building
AZ B Map co-ordinates locating sights	Small building, statue
Other points of interest	Fountain – Ruins
Mine – Cave	Visitor information
Windmill – Lighthouse	Ship – Shipwreck
Fort – Mission	Panorama – View

Other symbols

Interstate highway (USA)	US highway	Other route
Trans-Canada highway	Canadian highway	Mexican federal highway

Highway, bridge	Major city thoroughfare
Toll highway, interchange	City street with median
Divided highway	One-way street
Major, minor route	Pedestrian Street
15 (21) Distance in miles (kilometers)	Tunnel
2149/655 Pass, elevation *(feet/meters)*	Steps – Gate
△6288(1917) Mtn. peak, elevation *(feet/meters)*	Drawbridge - Water tower
Airport – Airfield	Parking – Main post office
Ferry: Cars and passengers	University – Hospital
Ferry: Passengers only	Train station – Bus station
Waterfall – Lock – Dam	Subway station
International boundary	Digressions – Observatory
State boundary, provincial boundary	Cemetery – Swamp
Winery	Long lines

Recreation

Gondola, chairlift	Stadium – Golf course
Tourist or steam railway	Park, garden
Harbor, lake cruise – Marina	Wildlife reserve
Surfing – Windsurfing	Wildlife/Safari park, zoo
Diving – Kayaking	Walking path, trail
Ski area – Cross-country skiing	Hiking trail
Sight of special interest for children	

Abbreviations and special symbols

MP Marine Park	NP National Park	NF National Forest
NHS National Historic Site		PP Provincial Park

Visitor centre :   Local - 🅡   Provincial - 🅡

16 Yellowhead Highway   Ⓜ Subway station (Montreal)

All maps are oriented north, unless otherwise indicated by a directional arrow

Michelin Apa Publications Ltd

A joint venture between Michelin and Langenscheidt

Suite 6, Tulip House, 70 Borough High Street, London SE1 1XF, United Kingdom

No part of this publication may be reproduced in any form
without the prior permission of the publisher.

© 2007 Michelin Apa Publications Ltd
ISBN 978-1-906261-24-5
Printed: November 2007
Printed and bound in Germany

Although the information in this guide was believed by the authors and publisher to be accurate
and current at the time of publication, they cannot accept responsibility for any inconvenience,
loss, or injury sustained by any person relying on information or advice contained in this guide.
Things change over time and travellers should take steps to verify and confirm information,
especially time-sensitive information related to prices, hours of operation, and availability.